The State of African Cities 2010

Governance, Inequality and Urban Land Markets

Nairobi, November 2010

UN-HABITAT

Foreword by UN-HABITAT

Events in the early years of the 21st century have all but done away with the widespread belief in linear development, the start of worldwide accumulative growth, and broad access to a global consumer society. The free-market ideology has facilitated a number of serious world-wide mistakes in governance, environmental management, banking practices and food and energy pricing which in recent years have rocked the world to its foundations. The message of these systemic shocks is that we can no longer afford to continue with 'business as usual'. There is need for a significantly higher level of global political determination to make deep changes, if humankind is to survive on this planet.

The world's wealthiest governments have shown that rapid adaptation and reform are possible. Despite the predominance of a free-market ideology opposed to government interference, when faced with a deep financial crisis that imperilled the world's global banking system the governments of the more advanced economies were capable of generating, almost overnight, the political will to put on the table the billions of dollars required to bail out the world's largest financial institutions. These funds did not seem available when they were requested for the global eradication of poverty.

It should be noted, however, that the African banking sector was not as severely hit by the financial crisis as its counterparts in more advanced economies. African banks had behaved with significantly more responsibility and therefore had little exposure to toxic assets and the inevitable consequences of dangerous financial derivatives. Nevertheless, Africa has become exposed to the impacts of the global recession through lower demand for commodities, declining income from tourism and subsequent loss of income and jobs.

However, on the whole, the news from Africa remains good. In 2007 and 2008, the continent's growth rates were on par with China's and India's, while forecasts for 2010 and 2011 suggested a 4.8 per cent pace. Much of this growth is driven by virtually unprecedented political stability and burgeoning domestic demand from Africa's rapidly emerging middle classes. African entrepreneurship has also increased, powered in part by a reversal of the 'brain drain' into a 'brain gain'.

Just as the Asian powerhouses, Africa stands to benefit from the rapid expansion of its cities. Urbanization is jump-starting industrialization and the 40 percent of Africa's population that now lives in cities produces 80 percent of its GDP. However, the continent remains hampered by the difficulties and costs of doing business there. Nevertheless, foreign direct investment is at an all-time high and global business is beginning to outsource manufacturing to Africa.

On the reverse side, as the urbanization of African poverty makes further progress, the prospect of a dignified and productive life continues to elude the poorest among Africans. More and more Africans are forced into informality, whether as a sheer survival strategy or because their living environments are defined by unregulated, non-serviced urban settlements and slums.

Whereas the number of urban slum dwellers has been significantly reduced in Northern Africa over the past two decades, much remains to be done in this respect in sub-Saharan nations. The key to success lies in closing widespread governance gaps by learning from the pragmatism of African civil society. However, the embarrassingly unequal share of the resources, opportunities and benefits of urban life that are reaped by politically and economically privileged elites, on the one hand, and the exclusion of millions upon millions of disenfranchised and deprived urban dwellers, on the other, *must* be addressed if African cities are to continue to play a meaningful role in achieving the targets of the Millennium Development Goals and in providing productive lives for the rapidly growing numbers of urban dwellers.

Joan Clos
Under-Secretary General, United Nations
Executive Director
UN-HABITAT

Foreword by UNEP

Poor planning has remained the Achilles heel of many towns, impeding both sustainable growth and healthy living environments for an increasing population of urban dwellers across Africa.

As the world reviews its performance to date on the Millennium Development Goals, and with less than five years to run, evidence shows that effective urban planning and sustainable cities can make a critical contribution.

There is no doubt that decisions made now will have long-term consequences and can lock a city and its dwellers into patterns that may positively or negatively affect urban sustainability and quality of life for generations to come. Inappropriate location of residences and work can generate significant but unnecessary mobility demand, private car dependence, air pollution and traffic congestion. Any future reversal of erroneous spatial decisions in cities can be extremely expensive and difficult.

We know the issues and challenges. Burgeoning city populations with increasing consumption and production patterns overtax limited natural resources and the effects are usually first felt by the ill-equipped urban poor. Urban poverty, in turn, is often accompanied by health and environmental problems related to lack of access to clean water and adequate sanitation.

However, the converse is also true. Effective urban environmental management will provide for and benefit all city dwellers by promoting efficient use of energy in urban mobility options, creating less-polluting fuels, encouraging the uptake of more energy-efficient household appliances and producing less waste.

We cannot separate human lives and livelihoods from both our impact and reliance on the environment. Prudent planning will take this into account.

Climate change is expected to create short- to long-term impacts on urban areas, with increasing frequency and severity of extreme weather events such as hurricanes, storm surges and heat waves, as well as semi-permanent or permanent effects such as sea level rise, falling groundwater tables or increased desertification. Climate change will also likely exacerbate urban problems through voluntary or involuntary eco-migration to Africa's large and intermediate cities away from flood-prone localities. Many African city assets such as ports, arterial railways, road infrastructure and industrial zones may also be under threat. In some cases, important agricultural zones supplying the urban food market may suffer a similar fate.

Around half the world's population is already living in cities and the number look set to rise. The economic and health imperative to plan for and generate sustainable cities is not a luxury, but a necessity of increasing urgency if the 21st century is to provide a secure and sustainable way of life for a world population that over the next four decades will increase in size by a third.

Cities are central in bringing about tomorrow's 'green' economic benefits and welfare, the provision of decent jobs and human well-being within an environment liberated from the risks and threats of climate change, pollution, resource depletion and ecosystem degradation. The quest for sustainability will be increasingly won or lost in our urban areas. With foresight, political will and intelligent planning, cities can be the blueprint and map to a sustainable future.

Achim Steiner
Under-Secretary General, United Nations
Executive Director
UNEP

Acknowledgements

In an effort to review in detail the conditions and trends prevailing across the African continent, this report has drawn on the knowledge of a wide range of specialists. This included a peer review process of the consolidated draft by an editorial board meeting of experts, held from 5 to 7 July 2010 at the UN-HABITAT Headquarters in Nairobi.

The report was designed and coordinated by Jos Maseland and Lusungu Kayani, of UN-HABITAT's Regional Office for Africa and the Arab States (ROAAS).

Chapter One was drafted by David Simon and UN-HABITAT staff. The regional chapter on Northern Africa was prepared by Mona Serageldin. Cheikh Gueye, Ousmane Thiam, Babatunde Agbola and Alain Durant-Lasserve drafted the Western Africa chapter. The Eastern Africa chapter was prepared by Alfred Omenya, Paul Syagga and ROAAS staff. The Central Africa chapter was written by Guillaume Iyenda, Alain Durant-Lasserve and ROAAS staff, while Beacon Mbiba and Resetselemang Leduka provided the draft for the Southern Africa chapter. The report's Statistical Annex is based on that of the *State of the World's Cities 2010* report, updated with data from *World Urbanization Prospects: The 2009 Revision*, by UN-HABITAT's Global Urban Observatory.

The following also contributed to the report: Johanna Drach, Lisa Junghans and Katharina Rochell.

Thierry Naudin edited the English version of the report and, together with Martin Ebele-Tobbo, translated it into French.
UN-HABITAT is grateful for the generous financial support provided by the Government of Norway and the United Nations Environment Programme (UNEP).

Contents

“ We shall work to expand the supply of affordable housing by enabling markets to perform efficiently and in a socially and environmentally responsible manner, enhancing access to land and credit and assisting those who are unable to participate in housing markets. ”

PARAGRAPH 9,
THE ISTANBUL DECLARATION ON HUMAN SETTLEMENTS, ENDORSED ON 14 JUNE 1996 BY ALL UNITED NATIONS MEMBER STATES AT THE HABITAT II CONFERENCE, ISTANBUL.

Women carrying cargo in the port of Mopti, Mali.
©Hector Conesa /Shutterstock

Introduction

The State of African Cities 2010: Governance, Inequality and Urban Land Markets report is the second in a series of regional, Africa-focused reports produced by UN-HABITAT. It should preferably be read in conjunction with UN-HABITAT's globally-focused *State of the World's Cities 2010/11* report.

The current report elaborates in greater detail on particular urban processes and themes relevant to Africa, illustrating them with recent data and relevant examples. While much of the scope does focus on cities, no specific settlement size threshold is used and this report addresses urbanization and urban areas in general.

A synthesis of the findings and key messages appears as a separate section after this introduction.

The report is divided into seven chapters. The first chapter introduces key ideas and messages grouped under seven sub-stantive areas: Urban geography, economic growth and human development; Urban inequality; Government or governance?; Public and private urban financing; Local government finance; 10 years of MDGs in Africa; and Africa's largest cities.

The first chapter highlights the importance of understanding cities as human creations, designed to meet human needs and aspirations, rather than just as representing physical concentrations of urban hardware like buildings and infrastructures. Importantly, too, cities operate as parts of wider economic, social and political systems that are more and more tightly integrated across space and political boundaries - nationally, regionally and globally. This provides many new opportunities for human development in the broadest sense, but also unparalleled challenges in terms of sharp inequalities and new vulnerabilities and risks.

Chapters two to six address urban trends and current conditions in Africa, as divided into five broad geographical regions: Northern, Western, Central, Eastern and Southern Africa, respectively. This approach provides more nuanced coverage, highlighting commonalities and differences within and between these African regions. Each of the regional chapters has an identical structure, assessing social geographies, economic geographies, urban land markets, geographies of climate change, and emerging issues. The authorial team has consulted and exchanged successive drafts to maximize compatibility while attempting to avoid the false impression that the somewhat arbitrary regional divisions somehow have unique or inherent meanings.

For ease of reference, city names have been emphasized with bold italics. Throughout this report, shortened popular country names have been used, i.e. 'Tanzania' rather than 'United Republic of Tanzania'. The exception is South Africa, which is referred to by its long name 'The Republic of Southern Africa' to avoid confusion with 'Southern Africa' which refers to the region.

This report uses the most recent data from the United Nations, Department of Economic and Social Affairs, Population Division (2010) as contained in its publication *World Urbanization Prospects: The 2009 Revision*, CD-ROM Edition - Data in digital form (United Nations, 2009). The shortened form 'WUP 2009' indicates this source throughout the document. However, these statistical data have introduced, by necessity, some discrepancies between regional statistics and the regional country distribution applied for the substantive discussion in this report. Whereas Mozambique, Zambia and Zimbabwe are, for statistical purposes, designated as constituting Eastern African nations in *World Urbanization Prospects: The 2009 Revision*, the current report has grouped these three nations in the Southern African region as they are for the purposes of political and economic grouping more closely associated with the nations of the Southern African than the Eastern African region. Likewise, Angola has been discussed in both the Southern African and Central Africa chapters for the same reasons, whereas for statistical purposes Angola is part of the DESA Central Africa group. It is anticipated that in subsequent versions of this Africa-focused report these discrepancies between regional statistics and substantive groupings will be overcome.

The term 'geography' as used in this report refers not to the academic discipline as such but to spatially evident processes and the resulting patterns or relations. In other words, it includes both static and dynamic elements. Social, economic, political, environmental, developmental and urban relations can be expressed spatially, e.g social, economic, political geography, etc., while such patterns and processes in turn feed back into the dynamics of these relations.

Executive Summary and Policy Recommendations

Overall Summary

Population and Urbanisation

In 2009 Africa's total population for the first time exceeded one billion, of which 395 million (or almost 40 per cent) lived in urban areas. Whereas it took 27 years for the continent to double from 500 million to one billion people, the next 500 million will only take 17 years. Around 2027, Africa's demographic growth will start to slow down and it will take 24 years to add the next 500 million, reaching the two billion mark around 2050, of which about 60 per cent living in cities. Africa should prepare for a total population increase of about 60 per cent between 2010 and 2050, with the urban population tripling to 1.23 billion during this period.

Strong demographic growth in a city is neither good nor bad on its own. Experience shows that across the world, urbanisation has been associated with improved human development, rising incomes and better living standards. However, these benefits do not come automatically; they require well-devised public policies that can steer demographic growth, turn urban accumulation of activities and resources into healthy economies, and ensure equitable distribution of wealth. When public policies are of benefit only for small political or economic elites, urbanisation will almost inevitably result in instability, as cities become unliveable for rich and poor alike.

Around 2030, Africa's collective population will become 50 per cent urban. The majority of political constituencies will then live in cities, demanding means of subsistence, shelter and services. African governments should take early action to position themselves for predominantly urban populations. In the early 2040s, African cities will collectively be home to one billion, equivalent to the continent's total population in 2009. Since cities are the future habitat for the majority of Africans, *now* is the time for spending on basic infrastructure, social services (health and education) and affordable housing, in the process stimulating urban economies and generating much-needed jobs. Deferring these investments to the 2040s simply will not do. Not a single African government can afford to ignore the ongoing rapid urban transition. Cities *must* become priority areas for public policies, with investment to build adequate governance capacities, equitable services delivery, affordable housing provision and better wealth distribution. If cities are to meet these needs, municipal finance must be strengthened with more fiscal freedom and own-source funding.

Regional Urban Configurations

City regions, urban development corridors and mega urban regions continue to emerge or become increasingly visible across Africa. Their spatial and functional features demand

GRAPH 1: **AFRICAN URBAN POPULATION TREND 1950-2050**

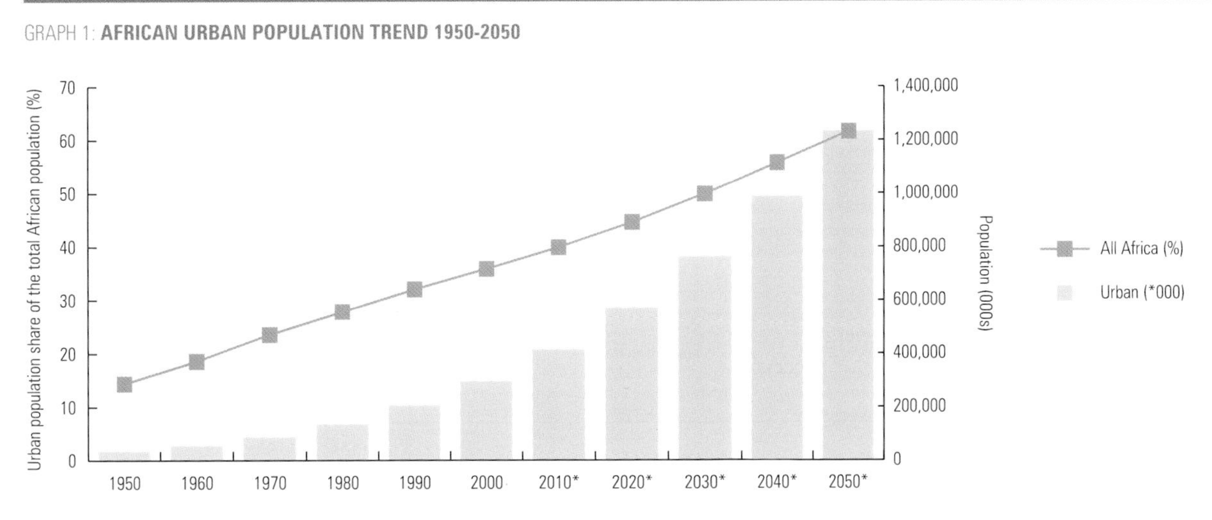

* Projections
Source: WUP 2009

new urban management methods to ensure consistent area-wide governance. Sweeping reform is also critical for effective delivery of affordable housing, services and urban infrastructures commensurate with the magnitudes of these rapidly expanding urban concentrations. Different political traditions, economic circumstances and location-specific features make every African nation and city unique. Therefore, effective reform and adaptation must be location-specific. Still, a few broad concepts for holistic area-wide urban management have emerged from comparable situations around the world and African governments should not ignore them, as outlined in Section 1.3, *Government or Governance?*

Urban Poverty and Slums

In recent years, Africa as a whole has shown that informal settlements can be reduced effectively as 24 million African slum dwellers saw their living conditions improved during the 2000/10 decade. Progress has been uneven across the continent, though. Northern Africa collectively managed to reduce from 20 to 13 per cent the share of slum dwellers in its urban population. Egypt, Morocco and Tunisia have been the most successful countries in this respect. Tunisia in particular, as it has successfully eradicated the slum phenomenon within its national boundaries. However, south of the Sahara the number of slum dwellers decreased by only five per cent (or 17 million), with Ghana, Senegal and Uganda at the forefront as they managed to reduce the proportion of slum dwellers in their urban populations by more than 20 per cent. Much remains to be done with regard to urban poverty and slum incidence, particularly in view of the rapid demographic growth of African cities, most of which results in the proliferation of informal settlements south of the Sahara. Urban slums are one of the major threats to African urban stability and, by extension, to overall political stability.

Urban Land Markets

Formal urban markets, by their very operations and rules, prevent access to land by the majority of city dwellers all over Africa. As a result, informal markets fill this exclusion gap and this is where the overwhelming majority of African urban land transactions take place nowadays. This report concludes that governments should seek the most effective entry points for an overhaul of the often abysmal failures of their formal urban land administration systems, with their unresponsive institutions, excessive delays, cumbersome land transaction administration and the associated corruption. Stigmatising informal urban land markets as inappropriate, illegal, illegitimate or undesirable negates the realities on the ground. There is much that formal land markets can learn from their informal counterparts. Any assessments and subsequent policies should put formal markets in a position gradually to embrace some informal practices in order to relieve overburdened public land administration. Governments should also rationalize fee structures, improve registration systems, and gradually phase out the debilitating legal and procedural dual systems in urban land markets, as explained in individual regional chapters of this report.

Africa-wide Recommended Intervention Areas

- Polarization and confrontation have increased in African cities due to *laisser-faire* attitudes to rapid urbanisation. The unfolding pattern is one of disjointed, dysfunctional and unsustainable urban geographies of inequality and human suffering, with oceans of poverty containing islands of wealth. Socio-economic conditions in African cities are now the most unequal in the world. This situation threatens systemic stability, affecting not only the continuity of cities as socio-political human eco-systems but also entire nations.
- Africa's urbanisation must not necessarily be seen as problematic. The challenge of urban sustainability calls for a focus on cities as people-centred concentrations of opportunity. Harnessing rather than alienating human energies is essential to maintaining urban dynamism, which cannot be fostered or maintained with rising urban inequality. The urban poor should not be punished for their poverty. Instead, urban planning and building regulations should reflect a country's degree of national development and its institutional capacities while keeping costs at affordable levels for all. Construction standards should be set more realistically in order to facilitate rather than restrict the creation of housing and livelihoods.
- Increasingly well-defined urban regions and urban development corridors introduce complex and highly fluid spatial, regulatory and political realities. As urban systems and inter-urban flows of people, goods, communications and funds extend across national borders, policies must follow suit if they are to have any realistic prospect of influencing the outcomes. The management tools of the traditional mono-centric city are not appropriate for today's multi-nuclear urban configurations. The need for governance reform to introduce holistic area-wide planning and urban management simply cannot be over-emphasized.
- The geographic extension of existing urban administrative territories should be considered. Complex as the enlargement of municipal territory may be, the benefits of extended municipal boundaries are sure to outweigh any inconveniences. This would allow for improved management of further urban growth, while land values can be captured through sales and taxation, in the process adding to municipal own-source revenues.
- African governments should also consider the relocation to their secondary cities of all government departments and agencies that have no overriding reasons to be located in the capital. With today's information and communication technologies, the physical presence of many government departments in highly congested capitals has become unnecessary. Relocation would better spread economic activity, reduce traffic congestion, and relieve the pressures on urban land and housing markets in capital cities.
- The scarcity of data on urban Africa continues to remain a challenge. Short of timely, objective and accurate city-specific data, urban managers will keep on operating in a knowledge vacuum, resulting in uninformed policy- or

decision-making, or the wrong scale or focus. This leads to predatory politics that hollow out good governance, while imposing additional burdens on the majority of urban residents that goes largely overlooked in the process. Good governance can only emerge with reliable and accurate data to inform policy and strategy decisions.

- The manner in which cities are developed today will affect future options for resilience in the face of climate change. Today's planning decisions can cause inefficiencies and ecologically unfriendly urban configurations further down the road. Spatial separation of related urban functions is evident among most metropolitan areas and increases transportation needs. Urban mobility must become a key factor in spatial decisions, and improved mass transit systems can significantly reduce private vehicle use. Cities are in a unique position to contribute to global and local climate change adaptation, mitigation and protection, and they must take advantage of it. However, forward-looking spatial planning decisions alone are not enough. In order to prevent any policy gaps, it is important to link national, regional and local environmental adaptation and mitigation policies through vertical and horizontal cooperation across *all* tiers of government as well as all relevant stakeholders.
- Many African municipalities are financially weak because their revenue- and finance-generating structures are inadequate and inefficient. Decentralising responsibilities without fiscal decentralisation contributes to urban decay, poor services and the proliferation of slums. *Fiscal* must match *political* decentralisation in order to create more revenue-generating options and decision-making power for local authorities. An appropriate municipal tax regime can boost cities' own revenue sources. Property tax is currently the major revenue source for municipal authorities although, at times, it can place an inequitable burden on property owners. Alternatives are available, as explained in Sections 1.4 and 1.5.
- Slums are, in a large part, the outcome of lack of access to urban land and housing finance. Land plots under informal tenure expose those occupying them to eviction, and they cannot be used as collateral to back up bank loans. These two factors do not encourage slum dwellers to improve their homes. This situation must be changed to encourage the urban poor to undertake improvements through self-help.
- Many urban managers deeply underestimate the risks associated with urban food and water insecurity. African governments should heed the warning bells of 2008 and seriously consider the potential effects of urban food and water shortages. Significant amounts of African land and water resources are purchased or long-term leased by foreign governments and foreign food processing corporations. Some even bring agricultural workers into Africa. Importing agricultural labour and exporting food are the two kinds of trade flows which increasingly urban and periodically undernourished African populations can ill afford. Africa is well-placed to make strategic, forward-looking decisions on the wise use of its rich water and agricultural resources. However, governments must bargain harder for better and more transparent deals, so that foreign investment can contribute to Africa's future food and water security, with benefits spread out among local communities in terms of additional business, cash payments and employment opportunities.

Northern Africa Summary

Population and Urbanisation

The demographic and economic dominance of Northern African cities was well established by the beginning of this century. With the exception of Sudan, whose urban population is still increasing at over 4.3 per cent per annum, the subregion's rate of urban demographic growth has noticeably slowed down.

The peri-urban sprawl and overcrowding of lower-income districts that characterized Northern African cities in the post-independence period have been the targets of vigourous public policies over the past 20 years. This was particularly the case in Egypt, Libya, Morocco and Tunisia, which have reduced their collective number of slum dwellers from 20.8 million in 1990 to an estimated 11.8 million in 2010. Tunisia has managed to eradicate slums altogether; a feat for which it should be commended. Today, nine out of 10 urban slum households in Northern Africa suffer from only one shelter deprivation, mainly lack of improved sanitation (Egypt) and insufficient living area (Morocco).

Starting in Tunisia in the 1990s urban rehabilitation and housing strategies have gradually shifted away from direct government intervention and towards public-private partnerships with a proven ability to deliver both low-income and market-rate housing units. These interventions have been a welcome evolution away from largely ineffective top-down housing authorities which proved unable to meet the needs of the region's rapidly growing urban populations. Despite significant progress in Northern Africa over the last decade, redress of past urbanisation trends must come hand in hand with adequate housing for new households.

Urban Economies and Governance

With fiscal support from governments, Northern Africa has experienced a steady shift to urban-based economies and a better balance between agriculture, manufacturing and diversified services and industries. Consequently, the subregion has seen a significant reduction in poverty, with Sudan the only exception. Still, urban unemployment remains a problem, particularly for youths, underscoring the persistent missing link between the education system, skills and development of a vigorous private sector.

Urban management institutions and structures remain less than adequate in Northern Africa. Local authorities are relatively weak and lack decision-making autonomy and financial resources, as these are still centralised at the national level. Collection of local taxes is difficult due to the inability of cadastral systems to keep up with developments, particularly in the informal housing and land sector.

▲
Marrakech, Morocco. ©**Narvikk/iStockphoto**

The desirability of stronger capacities and financial resources for local authorities is now under debate in the subregion. The need to consult city dwellers is also gaining recognition, particularly in Egypt, Morocco and Tunisia. The challenges posed by the probable effects of climate change in the subregion can also best be met through fully participatory dialogue addressing issues such as diminishing water resources and rising sea levels.

Urban Land Markets

The urbanisation rate in Northern Africa doubled between the 1970s and the 1980s after constraints on urban land ownership were lifted and when, consequently, it became possible to convert agricultural land to urban uses. The result was a chaotic proliferation of unplanned subdivisions and the rapid emergence of densely populated peri-urban informal settlements which, over the past 30 years, have accommodated most of the demographic expansion of Northern African cities. Where agricultural land has been converted to urban uses without any authorisation, land and property rights have been transferred through private notarial acts without the title registration demanded by property registration procedures. This has established two *de facto*, parallel property transaction systems.

In Northern Africa, new towns have developed to absorb demographic growth and meet the concomitant increase in demand for urban housing. These new areas are transforming the larger cities into structured city regions, changing the spatial distribution of urban land and raising its values. Urban land prices have doubled every three years since 1970 in the established urban areas. In urban extension zones, new development areas and new towns, prices have doubled every year or every other year. High land values effectively bar low-income households from access to formal land markets, pushing them into informality.

Public authorities in the subregion are beginning to grasp the potential of land as a revenue source and are learning how to use their assets and regulatory powers to bring about and capture higher land values through sales and taxation. This brings much-needed new land into urban development while paying for infrastructures in under-serviced areas.

Emerging Issues: Transnational Urban Systems

Two major transnational urban systems are currently emerging in Northern Africa:

1 The incipient Southern Mediterranean Coastal Region corridor is to consolidate with a combination of tourism and manufacturing. However, the area is rife with conflicts over land uses, and national plans must be supplemented by transnational agreements that take holistic views of the Southern Mediterranean coast.
2 The Nile Valley Corridor has traditionally acted as a link and a bond between the countries in the watershed. The major issue today relates to the use of the Nile waters. While individual country shares are governed by international agreements, the allocation of shares among cities within each country and the rationalization of water use are both high priorities, particularly in Egypt. A complicating factor

▲
Cairo, Egypt. ©**Guido Potters**

is the forthcoming referendum in Southern Sudan, which may very well lead to the formation of a new riparian Nile state and the attendant need for international renegotiation of national shares in Nile waters.

Recommended Intervention Areas in Northern Africa

- Whereas commendable inroads have been made in slum reduction in Northern Africa, more remains to be done to redress the outcomes of past urbanisation trends - especially sprawling, densely populated, informal settlements in peri-urban areas.
- Over the next decade, availability of serviced land and enforcement of development regulations will continue to pose significant challenges. Demand for affordable housing, both rental and ownership, will require significant improvements in land management, including a redefinition of the roles of local authorities and the private sector.
- Governments are urged to facilitate fiscal decentralisation, allowing for effective local tax-raising powers. Likewise, governments should consider phasing out parallel hierarchies of appointed executives and elected councils at the provincial and municipal levels, in order to allow for greater self-determination.
- Property registration must be made simpler and more affordable, with the following five benefits: promotion of adherence to the procedure, enhanced security of tenure, better development controls, improved land taxation and rent collection, and enhanced municipal own-source income from land transactions and land ownership.
- Climate change-induced sea level rise is bound to affect coastal settlements and threaten ecologically important areas. In areas at risk, urbanisation should be prohibited and any proliferation of settlements or marinas contained through land management. Coastal municipalities should work closely with central government departments in favour of holistic coastal management plans that regulate urbanisation, tourism development and industrial uses, in order to safeguard the natural environment. In-depth research should help establish subregion-wide guidelines and regulations to protect the marine ecology, including beach flora and fauna.

Western Africa Summary

Population and Urbanisation

In West Africa, too, urban populations are expanding rapidly. During the 2010/20 decade, cities in the subregion will become hosts to an additional 58 million, and another 69 million during the 2020/30 decade. Even by then, urban demographic growth will not subside because, despite a projected decline in urbanisation growth rates after 2030, West African cities will still have to accommodate an additional 79 million until 2040, and another 84 million between 2040 and 2050. This demographic expansion is neither good nor bad in itself. Outcomes can be positive or negative, depending on how it is spatially distributed and how the benefits of urban agglomeration are shared.

Urban Economies and Governance

Concentrations of business and populations in cities generate efficiency and economic gains in some areas and urban centres, while some others are left behind. In those cities and areas that are found lagging, as in the lower-income urban areas of the economically stronger nations, stark spatial disparities and socio-economic polarization are becoming increasingly visible as urban inequality increases. As the pace of urbanisation and urban growth speeds up, the capacity of most West African nations to manage the consequences of undesirable urban trends is decreasing, due to inadequate spending on human and institutional capacities, services delivery, adequate and affordable housing and job opportunities. The social, economic and environmental effects of these failures fall heavily on the poor, who are excluded from the benefits of urban prosperity.

Over-urbanisation, whereby populations grow much faster than urban economies, is becoming visible across the subregion. Symptoms include major social and economic challenges like high unemployment rates, slum proliferation, social polarization and crime, which all result from systemic governance failure and unequal distribution of urban or national wealth. Rapidly growing cities can be major assets for political, social and economic development of a nation or region, provided that this growth is properly steered, managed and sustained with fair distribution of public funding in social and basic infrastructures, social development and employment generation for broader-based well-being.

Poverty can only weaken any society's capacity to tackle organized crime, human trafficking, armed conflict, terrorism, social unrest and the spread of diseases. These, in turn, can have severe security and other implications not only for the countries where they are rife, but also for neighbouring states and the global community. In a global age, the outcomes associated with high poverty can no longer be contained within national boundaries; they imply linkages between alleviating poverty and maintaining regional and global stability.

Urban Land Markets

The structure of the urban land market in Western Africa has predominantly been influenced by colonial traditions rooted in both English and French law. Governments are in control of land allocation and title distribution. With the exception of Burkina Faso, most governments have been reluctant to release land on the required scale. Due to rapid urbanisation, demand for secure urban tenure and freehold titles by investors and rising middle class has been sustained in Western African cities. This demand has contributed to the development of the formal private land market. New land laws and codes are being adopted across the region in order to facilitate appropriation or restriction of private land allocation. Though these reforms have introduced some form of private land ownership, they do not guarantee full protection or security of tenure.

While the management of land has been increasingly decentralised from central government to local entities, in many West African countries the responsibility for land allocation and title registration remains in the hands of central government. Despite government resistance, popular demand for upgrading and regularisation policies is rising sharply. Securing and safeguarding formal tenure for informal settlers remains the greatest challenge and housing development projects still fail to reach out to the urban poor. Land markets and prices are the main drivers of urban spatial expansion and geographic social patterns. Urban land prices are steadily increasing while most city-dwellers' incomes are not, and as a result communities living close to urban centres are increasingly faced with eviction. Overly cumbersome and time-consuming tenure regularisation procedures are linked with corruption and vested interests, turning land management and administration into a challenge.

Emerging Issues: National and Transnational Development Corridors

The geographic and economic conditions underlying the emergence of urban development corridors in Western Africa are nothing new, as they rediscover age-old trade routes. Novel dimensions, however, include the nature of the forces at play, the emergence of West-East corridors and the growth of formerly stagnant urban nodes.

Western Africa's regional urban configurations, city regions and urban 'ribbon' developments are the outcomes of dynamic urbanisation driven mainly by larger cities. Regional city and urban corridor patterns are the results of shifts in metropolitan spatial organisation and associated functional specialization. While metropolitan central business districts and immediate surroundings increasingly host top-level political, economic and commercial urban functions, the peri-urban and adjacent rural areas are left to cope with rising demand for housing and commercial functions that have been forced out from more central urban areas by rising land prices. In view of the major role cities play in regional development, regional urban clusters and their interlinking through urban corridors deserve special attention, especially where they are the result of spontaneous urbanisation processes.

Regional urban patterns are often conducive to national economic and social development, but they become of regional importance when they cross national borders and link with similar configurations in neighbouring countries. For this reason, urban development corridors are considered as positive for spatial integration, socio-economic systems and the economy on a regional scale. They are not without drawbacks, though. Unless well-steered and managed, regional urban configurations can produce severe economic and spatial imbalances in areas outside the corridors. This can, and will, result in spatial and functional gaps, particularly affecting the transit towns that are incapable of leveraging the opportunities created by the larger cities along the corridor. Moreover, regional agreements on the free movement of people, goods, finance and communications are an important pre-condition if the beneficial outcomes of regional development and trade are to be maximised.

▲
Street Life, Île de Gorée, Dakar, Senegal. ©**Guido Potters**

Prominent domestic development corridors have emerged in Western Africa, including the ***Dakar-Touba*** corridor in Senegal; ***Bouaké-Abidjan*** in Côte d'Ivoire; and between ***Ouagadougou*** and ***Bobo-Dioulasso*** in Burkina Faso. As these domestic corridors grow, they connect with similar corridors in neighbouring countries. This creates new impulses for economic and political integration in the subregion. A good example of the trans-national expansion of domestic corridors is the emerging ***Maradi-Katsina-Kano*** corridor, linking Niger and Nigeria, with ***Katsina*** a major transit city. A trans-national corridor is also consolidating between land-locked Burkina Faso and Côte d'Ivoire (i.e., the Gulf of Guinea) with cities like ***Bobo-Dioulasso, Korogho, Banfora*** and ***Ferkessédougou*** as the intermediate nodes.

In the future, these corridors are expected to strengthen their significant social, economic and political roles. In Western Africa, distance and isolation remain major determinants of spatial relations, even though the policies and technologies designed to mitigate them are becoming more and more effective. Since regional interconnectivity lags the expansion of those corridors, emerging transnational urban configurations call for proper planning, otherwise they stand to lose much of their significance.

Recommended Intervention Areas in Western Africa

- Sweeping governance reforms focused on improved urban management are needed in Western Africa. Significant new spending on basic services, infrastructure, affordable housing and urban mobility (transportation) is in order in the decades to come. This spending is urgently needed because the longer it is postponed, the higher the financial, social and political costs will be.
- 'Permits to occupy' and administrative permits do not provide sufficient security of tenure and this is why they must be converted to secure land titles. In order to facilitate this process, interim land titles should be formalized. On the other hand, some existing mechanisms should be eliminated. This includes lifting restrictions on conversion

of residential property titles, such as *'mise en valeur'* (the obligation to develop a plot before a title can be formalised) and, in a similar vein, the cancellation of usage rights on properties that have not been developed within a specific timeframe.

- The capacities of central and local administrations are inadequate, particularly with regard to land registration and property identification. This causes a major operational bottleneck in the delivery of property titles and implementation of large-scale property identification and registration. This situation calls for stronger capacities for the land registration system.
- Since most land tenure is of a customary nature in Western Africa, governments must acknowledge this traditional land occupation practice. Such integration in the land markets must happen gradually for the sake of proper links between customary and statutory systems. The first step in this process involves identification of the major land systems operating in a country, based on an inventory of habits and customs. The basic rationale for public policies is to ensure market fluidity through the smooth mainstreaming of customary into formal land markets. This effective disappearance of customary property must be accompanied by fair compensation schemes for customary holders.
- Governments in the region have so far been in control of land allocation and title distribution. Therefore, it is incumbent on them to release more public land in order to relieve demand pressure (especially in urban and peri-urban areas, on land with strong agricultural potential, or located close to agricultural land or trunk roads). The broad objective for policies should be to encourage pluralistic land markets that are able to respond to different social, economic and environmental policy needs and the needs of different segments of the population, the priority being enhanced tenure security.
- The public sector should establish and maintain a 'level playing field' where various suppliers of land, credit and building services can compete on equal terms. Procedures for land allocation, transfers and registration should be streamlined in order to reduce corruption and nepotism.
- In the absence of capital market funding, alternative sources (like the Housing Bank in Burkina Faso, created in 2005) should be made available, including micro-credit.

Eastern Africa Summary

Population and Urbanisation

With only an estimated 23.5 per cent of the population living in urban areas, Eastern Africa remains the least urbanised subregion on the continent. Nevertheless, it is rapidly catching up. Between the year 2000 and 2005, the populations of ***Nairobi*** and ***Dar-es Salaam*** experienced annual average growth rates of four per cent. Rather than rural migration, these increases largely reflect natural demographic growth, with the balance resulting from displacement induced by local conflicts. For instance, prolonged civil war in Mogadishu has pushed many people to Somalia's smaller, secondary towns.

Accommodating rapidly growing urban populations is clearly a challenge in Eastern Africa. Urban areas are plagued by seemingly ever-increasing unemployment rates, spontaneous, uncontrolled expansion of urban slums and informal settlements, residential overcrowding, deterioration of already overstretched infrastructures and services, environmental degradation and acute housing shortages.

Eastern Africa's future is unquestionably urban, although it is to take another 40 years before a majority of the population lives in towns and cities. In view of the already challenging conditions summarised above and the sustained pace of prospective demographic growth, it is imperative for governments to take their responsibilities seriously with regard to good governance, housing, infrastructure and employment in the subregion's urban areas.

Urban Poverty and Slums

As urbanisation proceeds apace, good governance and urban management will become both more necessary and more complex, as will the social issues associated with poverty. The ongoing urbanisation of poverty in Eastern Africa calls for strong and effective policies, including an end to exclusion of the poor by political and business elites.

Although most Eastern African economies have continued to grow over the past few years, income inequalities remain high. Eastern Africans largely depend on the informal sector for jobs and housing. Informality is a problem, not a solution. Urban poverty fuels crime, violence and social unrest. Inequality and inadequate housing combine with lack of labour and social policies to fuel violent, urban-based politico-religious militias that contribute to further insecurity. This phenomenon has its root-causes in deep-seated frustration, especially among the young, in the face of high unemployment and poor socio-economic conditions.

Urban Land Markets

In Eastern African cities, low-income residents have little if any access to formal land or housing markets. Therefore, they acquire land informally and develop it outside formal systems. Governments in the subregion are now overwhelmed by the needs of the ever-expanding numbers they have failed to accommodate since independence. Informality has taken on such proportions that it has become the norm. Consequently, simply declaring informality 'illegal' is no longer an option. Acknowledging the conditions now prevailing is a first step in the way forward. Governments must open up outdated formal systems and embrace some of the informal procedures that make land and housing accessible to the low-income majorities of urban populations.

Emerging Issues

As new economic and urban development corridors develop in Eastern Africa, larger cities must consider expanding their municipal boundaries to accommodate future demographic growth. Municipal authorities must also expand own-source

▲
Nairobi, Kenya. ©**Guido Potters**

revenues through land sales at market prices while creating space for urban planning. Expanding municipal boundaries is a complex exercise but the longer-term benefits will outweigh the short-term difficulties. The need for holistic regional planning and economic decentralisation is inevitable.

Eastern Africa's primate capital cities should also consider the relocation to secondary cities of all government departments, agencies and functions that do not necessarily need to be located in the capital. This would relieve traffic, housing, office space and population pressures on capital cities while stimulating growth and economic opportunities in the remainder of the country. This may be a complex and expensive exercise, but again, the longer-term benefits will easily outweigh short-term inconveniences.

Recommended Intervention Areas in Eastern Africa

The inability of Eastern African governments to supply affordable land to low-income city dwellers is the result of bureaucratic inertia, expensive administrative procedures, allocation inefficiencies and inappropriate use of public office. Most of these deficiencies can be addressed with relatively little effort, which suggests that the underlying issue is lack of political will. The inadequacies and outright failures which plague formal land and housing markets impose significant costs on society at large, and make the majority of city residents vulnerable and landless. Over the past several decades, experience has amply demonstrated that any inadequacies or failings among government institutions are inexorably compensated for by non-state operators deploying legal, semi-legal or illegal means. Although specific vested interests may have a stake in the *status quo* of imperfect or failing urban housing and land markets, the price will be paid by the urban poor majorities in the short run, and society at large in the longer term. In order to address current, highly inequitable urban land access conditions, national and urban decision-makers would be well-advised to consider and acknowledge that:

- Urban planning must become more efficient and forward-looking, in order to enhance urban densities and reduce transportation needs, cut per-unit land costs, provide more efficient and affordable basic services as well as improved living environments for all citizens. This will require a better grip by public authorities on urban land use and land allocation. This, in turn, calls for legislative amendments that allow for more pragmatic urban land administration and management approaches.
- As in most other regions of the world, urbanisation in Eastern Africa comes with special challenges requiring systematic local planning, provision of infrastructure and shelter as well as delivery of urban services as needed to

improve general welfare, particularly for the poor. These policy responses have critical roles to play not only within metropolitan boundaries, but also in peri-urban areas where the more significant unplanned changes take place, often on high-potential agricultural land that is required to feed the city.

- In order better to meet these challenges, early harmonization of the dual systems of customary 'user rights' tenure and 'ownership' is in order, the rationale being to discard the prevailing notion that customary or informal systems are merely there for 'survival'. Both systems come with their specific benefits and shortcomings; whether any phasing out over time of the customary system is desirable and feasible must be determined in view of local or national conditions and circumstances. Where it appears that both systems should be maintained, the interface between them should be clarified and made workable.
- Since more extensive municipal boundaries are needed to add to public holdings of vacant land, state-owned land should be converted to municipal land. This would enable municipalities to use land as a revenue source, provided it is sold at market rates, and better control the peri-urban developments which today lie beyond their administrative control.
- The spatial, institutional and social impacts of migration to urban areas and urban demographic growth must be better managed. While it is not possible to interfere with demographic patterns, urban managers must seek ways better to integrate new arrivals into the formal system. Therefore, they must develop realistic land-use plans and infrastructure standards. Special attention should be paid to easing the procedures and lowering the costs of land subdivision, particularly in rapidly growing peri-urban areas.

Central Africa Summary

Population and Urbanisation

The urban population of Central Africa has more than doubled from 23.7 million in 1990 to an estimated 55.6 million in 2010. The 100-million mark should be reached around 2022, with further growth to 112.7 million by 2030 and 185.9 million by 2050. Inter-decade urban growth rates will start a steady declining trend between 2020 and 2030. However, since these declining growth rates apply to ever-larger numbers, the region's urban population will continue to expand significantly in absolute terms: from 19.1 million over the past decade, additions to Central African urban populations are expected to grow to 25.9 million in 2020/30, 31.2 million in 2020/30, 35.4 million in 2030/40 and 37.8 million 2040 and 2050.

In 2010, the subregion's three most urbanised countries were Gabon (86 per cent), São Tomé e Príncipe (62.2 per cent) and Congo (62.1 per cent). Least urbanised were Chad (27.6 per cent), the DRC (35.2 per cent) and Equatorial Guinea (39.7 per cent), who all remained below the Africa-wide urbanisation average of 39.9 per cent. The CAR, the DRC and Equatorial Guinea are not projected to become predominantly urban until after 2030, while Chad is likely to do so only around 2042.

During the 2000/10 decade, Angola and Cameroon were the region's most rapidly urbanising countries with decade rate increases of 9.5 and 8.5 per cent respectively. Over the 2010/20 decade, the growth of Central African urban populations is likely to be highest in Chad (22.8 per cent), compared with 12.8 per cent in Angola, 12.1 per cent in Cameroon and 3.1 per cent in Gabon, suggesting a convergent trend over time, although at different paces.

Urban Economies and Governance

Many Central African countries are richly endowed with natural resources that make their economies fairly privileged on the continent. This results in good growth rates, though not necessarily in good socio-economic development. Indeed, many countries experience stagnating or declining incomes per head, as well as rapid spread of extreme poverty and rising income inequality in urban areas. The overall deterioration in urban living standards for increasing numbers has become acute. This comes largely as the result of highly unequal distribution of national wealth, poor governance and rampant corruption. The latter is especially the case in the primary sector (oil, minerals and forestry).

Because national income and wealth are poorly shared, large sections of the Central African population are deprived of basic needs satisfaction. Oil-rich Angola stands out as the most unequal country in the region in almost every aspect of life. These disparities are reflected in the distribution of income, access to adequate housing, urban land, basic infrastructure and social services (water, sanitation, electric power, education, and healthcare). Angola's major problem clearly has to do with wealth distribution. Cities and their populations cannot develop or perform optimally if only a small group has access to most of the resources and economic opportunities. Given the region's mineral wealth, significantly higher spending is required for the sake of broad access to affordable urban land and housing as well as social and basic infrastructures. Particular attention should be paid to improved energy security in support of enhanced productivity, employment generation and poverty reduction in cities.

Urban Poverty and Slums

The failure of Central African countries to address inequality and the resultant urban poverty has led to a proliferation of urban slums. In the process, large shares of the urban population have been deprived of decent living conditions that are clearly within reach, if only the right policies were deployed. Besides severe inequality and socio-economic exclusion, many urban slum dwellers in Central Africa also experience malnutrition. Today, widespread incidence of low-calorie intakes and even hunger are entirely preventable, and yet many poor, including urban, households face periodic malnourishment.

▲
Butembo, DRC. ©**Guido Potters**

Data on Central African cities shows that the informal economy (on which the majority of urban dwellers relies) has limitations, and therefore efforts to promote access to formal employment must be stepped up. History has amply shown that industrialisation and urban productivity will progress faster where government takes a pro-active, enabling role. Europe, North America, Japan and, more recently, East Asia, have all shown that successful socio-economic development follows proactive government assistance to urban-based industrial development, especially through enhanced transportation systems.

Today, with ongoing economic liberalisation, income and consumption inequality is rising in Central Africa. If they are to take advantage of their rich resources to improve the living conditions of the majority of their populations, Central African countries must reform urban governance, enhance the transparency of public sector management and improve the distribution of national riches while addressing corruption and impunity in a far more pro-active way.

In the region's urban slums, women are major contributors to households' financial and material conditions. This puts them in a position to act as major agents of change within these communities. But then as many as 95 per cent of female slum dwellers need various forms of support, including short- and medium-term credit. Their needs, abilities and capabilities must be better reflected in the design of any development programmes that affect their lives. Financial assistance to female-owned small businesses would go a long way towards strengthening their contributions to the fight against poverty, in the process promoting alternative household survival strategies and improving the welfare of the most deprived segments of the urban population.

Urban Land Markets

In Central Africa, too, urban land is neither well managed nor well allocated or distributed. Some central governments or local authorities in the subregion have started to improve urban land policies, but much more effort is needed to meet the needs of the majority of urban populations. It is incumbent on local authorities to update their land administration and management practices, taking lessons from the hands-on, needs-based approaches that are the defining features of informal markets, that provide for the vast majority of urban land transactions. Formal recognition of this plain fact of urban life is long overdue. Rather than stigmatising informality, public authorities should review the arrangements and mechanisms prevailing in informal urban land markets. Formal markets have much to learn from the sheer cost effectiveness and expediency that informal urban land transactions offer.

New and affordable technologies are now available for urban land management and administration. If combined with greater transparency and better understanding of the links between land distribution, population growth, climate change and development, they have a crucial role to play in improved welfare for all and the protection of the urban environment.

Against a background of relentless demand and price rises, capturing land values has a more critical role to play than ever in the funding of urban infrastructures. The problem in Central African cities is that amid an ever-more intense scramble for urban land, the sale of public (municipal and state) land is increasingly shrouded in secretive allocation procedures and abuse of office. Where governance is weak and corrupt, public urban land is often captured by privileged individuals and sold or illegally transferred for private gain. Unless illegitimate transfer and sale of this non-renewable municipal resource is curbed, the outcome can only be the perpetuation of significant foregone municipal own-source funding. Urban land has already ceased to be a key source of revenue for municipalities in many Central African cities. Corruption has become so commonplace that it has now started to affect urban development mechanisms. A rigorous debate on the use of land revenues and land administration and management is needed to explore alternatives, in order to enable urban land once more play its crucial role in the funding of municipal policies.

Emerging Issues

Regional Mobility

Migration is encouraged by the Economic Community of Central African Countries (ECCAC), but some Central African nations remain hostile to free movement of people, goods and financial flows. Cross-border migration can bring benefits such as enhanced welfare on both sides of national boundaries. Authorities at local, city and national levels should more objectively analyze the impacts of cross-border migration. Most migrants are highly motivated people and act as vectors of economic, technological and cultural exchange. They bring different knowledge and cultures that can complement local ones. Well-administered and well-governed cities that are open to new ideas, cultures and technologies can act as a host country's best catalyst of economic growth and human development.

Regional Urban Development Corridors

Major cross-border development areas are emerging in Central Africa as they do elsewhere on the continent. One is the ***Luanda-N'Djamena*** development corridor, and another links ***Brazzaville*** and ***Kinshasa*** into a mega urban region, and there are many others. The ***Brazzaville-Kinshasa*** link involves populations in excess of 10 million and already stands out as the world's most populous and fastest-growing cross-border metropolitan area. This mega urban region features high concentrations of the economic, industrial, social, health and political activities of both Congo and the DRC, providing employment opportunities to large numbers of people on both sides of the river Congo. If the current degrees of political, economic and spatial cooperation can be sustained and improved, the ***Kinshasa-Brazzaville*** mega urban region could very well become one of the most dynamic in Africa.

However, public authorities in both countries must be aware that this high-potential dynamism remains hostage to a number of problems. Both capital cities experience rapid demographic growth against backgrounds of substandard urban governance and management. Basic and social infrastructures are poorly maintained and in need of serious upgrading; this is particularly the case with roads, because rapidly increasing numbers of vehicles cause traffic congestion and countless road accidents. Other problems include poor energy supply and substandard waste management. Most other urban problems also remain unaddressed and both ***Kinshasa*** and ***Brazzaville*** urgently must boost their respective productive potentials through improved management performance.

The emerging 2,000 km long ***Luanda-N'Djamena*** corridor between Angola and Chad is one of the most important new spatial developments in Central Africa. The subregion as a whole is still deeply underdeveloped in terms of road, rail and waterway connections, severely hampering mobility of people, goods and services between the larger cities and poses a significant obstacle to regional economic cooperation, integration and development.

The Member States of the Economic Community of Central African States (CEEAC) have adopted a plan to develop a reliable and competitive regional transportation network in a bid to stimulate effective and affordable regional movements and integration. Since 80 per cent of goods and 90 per cent of people in the subregion move by road, priority was accorded to the development of road connections, supported by a pledge of US $6.4 billion to develop or improve trunks roads between the region's capital cities by 2010. However, progress is slow and it became clear that the objective would not be met by 2010.

The fact remains that early construction of this regional road network should be a matter of the highest regional priority, as it would connect an estimated 20 million city dwellers in the major cities and also unlock an estimated additional five million people in secondary towns, villages and rural areas along its path. Many of the larger conurbations are major port cities and the interconnection of these urban economic hubs could greatly enhance logistics, trade and labour flows, including the prospect of elevating some of the domestic ports to regional prominence.

Unhampered cross-border flows of people, goods and services as well as well-adapted intra-regional regulation are critical to better productivity, poverty alleviation and food and energy security in Central African cities. However, strengthening transnational and regional logistic corridors and major new road networks will not be enough. Governments of the ECCAC states must do far more to simultaneously stimulate the economic and social development of their cities as the engines of national and regional growth.

Recommended Intervention Areas in Central Africa

- National and urban governance practice must improve in the face of very rapid, increasingly problematic urban demographic growth. Efforts must, in particular, focus on enhancing local capacities for urban management in order to maintain cities' role as national and regional engines of growth and development.
- Central Africa's wealth of oil resources, hydro-electric potential and employment opportunities are significant, but the benefits must be shared more equitably if current symptoms of over-urbanisation are to be eradicated. When *demographic* outpaces *economic* momentum, poverty and slums proliferate. Upgraded and expanded infrastructures would improve the productivity of cities, create jobs and improve the living conditions of the poor, who represent the vast majority of Central Africa's urban populations. Substituting 'clean' and cheap energy sources for fuel wood would reduce health and safety hazards among the urban poor and slow down deforestation.
- Municipal authorities in Central Africa must pay more attention to urban services in an effort to improve the urban environment and adapt to climate change. Inadequate waste collection and excess-water drainage systems are a case in point, being major causes of urban flooding, as is informal urban expansion in hazardous locations.
- Faced with the challenge of climate change, national and urban authorities should seek support from development partners in order to enhance public awareness of the effects of climate change on cities. Once properly informed, all citizens can and must act on local causes of climate variability and prepare for climate change-induced hazard mitigation. More than just an additional environmental concern, public authorities should acknowledge climate change as a serious threat to cities and sustainable development.
- Migrants are agents of change and development. Given the high degree of mobility that characterizes the subregion, governments should take early steps to facilitate freedom of movement of people, goods and services within and among countries in order to facilitate trade, cultural and political exchange.
- Even though they are already twinned, both geographically and symbolically, ***Brazzaville*** and ***Kinshasa*** should strengthen political cooperation between them in order to improve infrastructures and provide holistic urban management and administration. This includes well-adapted regulation and facilitation of migratory flows between them for the sake of their economic and social development.
- Public authorities must also focus on employment generation in urban areas. At the moment, the mismatch between demographic growth and economic opportunities is filled in by the informal economy and self-employment, but these short-term palliatives only fuel poverty and socio-economic insecurity across generations. Informality is a problem; not a solution. In this critical area, too, governments must anticipate on future problems and stimulate urban-based industrial and manufacturing activities. Urban unemployment and inequality must rank among Central African governments' prime concerns.
- Corruption, mismanagement of public funds and inappropriate use of public office are major factors behind the unequal distribution of incomes and rising urban poverty. The illegitimate control of power, wealth and resources by a minority, or, in other words, corruption, is obviously part and parcel of the larger process of underdevelopment.

▲
Cape Town, South Africa. ©**Don Bayley/iStockphoto**

- Central African governments are urged to pay attention to the management and guidance of emerging domestic urban corridors and the regional interlinking of domestic corridors. This should go hand in hand with regional agreements on free movement of people, goods, services and finance in order to optimize the economic, social and political benefits of these novel urban configurations.

Southern Africa Summary

Population and Urbanisation

With a projected 61.7 per cent of its population living in urban areas, Southern Africa remains the most urbanised subregion on the continent, and this proportion is expected to swell to two-thirds by 2020. With the exception of Botswana, Lesotho and Namibia, demographic growth is now steadily slowing down, from a 9 per cent rate in 2000/10 to 5.7 per cent 2040/50 decade. Contrary to other subregions, rural to urban migration remains the dominant factor, with the balance due to natural increases.

Urban Economies and Governance

Deep-rooted inequalities inherited from the apartheid era have been perpetuated by the neoliberal economic policies that continue to rule urban development, even though the discriminatory pattern is based more and more on class than race. Uneven development has been felt mostly by youths, who make up the majority of the urban population. Governments have invested in education but employment creation falls well short of demand. City authorities in the region should better include young people in their service provision and governance strategies.

Widespread multiple deprivations persist in the low-income urban areas of Southern Africa. Deprived urban communities are the most vulnerable to disasters and disease, including HIV/AIDS, tuberculosis and cholera. Persistent spatial inequalities hark back to the conditions the Black majority experienced during the colonial and apartheid eras. Of all the continent's subregions, Southern Africa features the steepest degrees of socioeconomic inequality, with extreme poverty occurring along class and racial lines. Consumption of water, electricity and other urban utilities remains effectively segregated and very unequally distributed between wealthy and poor areas, although water is even more unequally distributed than income. Southern African income inequalities are growing in both rural and urban areas, except for the Republic of South Africa where marginal declines were observed between 2001 and 2005 due to redistributive policies.

As the result of neoliberal reform and deregulation of basic utilities, private firms now provide water, electricity, waste removal, education and health services in the South African Republic's cities. Commoditisation of services has shifted responsibility from local authorities to the private sector, which is not advantageous to the poorer sections of the population. The capacity to provide services and infrastructure as well as to plan, invest and create jobs has declined in Maputo, Harare, Luanda and Lusaka.

Urban Land Markets

As in other subregions, urban surface areas have expanded hand in hand with demographic growth, and formal urban land markets have only been able to serve the wealthy. Combining formal rules with social and customary practices, informal urban land markets provide access to land when the formal markets do not or cannot deliver. Poor land administration and unresponsive public institutions are increasingly failing to track formal and informal land transactions, which interferes with proper market mechanisms and taxation. A way forward would be for governments to recognize informal urban land governance in general, and informal urban land markets in particular, in order to improve the administration, management and supply of urban land. Municipal functions that could be devolved to the community and neighbourhood levels include the registration of occupancy, enforcement of basic land use regulations, dispute settlement and simple title registration by local chiefs. Transitory institutional structures should facilitate involvement by property development finance and undertake land management and planning at the neighbourhood level, with the ultimate aim of incorporating such structures into municipal operations.

Metropolitan Development and Mega Sporting Events

Metropolitan-wide initiatives embracing integrated development planning, infrastructure provision, rural-urban linkages and economic planning have dominated spatial developments in the region. A reasonably high degree of subregional integration has facilitated the sporting events of global and regional importance that have been the highlights of 2010 in Southern Africa: the African football cup in Angola, the world football cup in the Republic of South Africa, and the All Africa games in ***Maputo***. The FIFA World Cup showed how urban development can be influenced by spending on infrastructure. For example, post-2010 ***Durban*** is striving to become a successful port and sport city with stadiums and services that are able to host future Olympic, Commonwealth or Pan-African games. The major sporting events have sped up many urban development projects. For all their visible benefits, these events have also had negative impacts, including mass evictions and displacement of low-income residents.

Recommended Intervention Areas in Southern Africa

- As part of development policies, public authorities must mobilise urban young peoples' potentials and energies with proper training in entrepreneur skills and information/communication technologies, in order to enable them to set up and run their own businesses. Some urban authorities have tried to foster inclusive cities, but none have fully considered children and youth in their service provision and governance strategies. Cities should make more efforts to deliver broadband Internet to all urban neighbourhoods, rather than reinforcing existing inequalities in services delivery.
- Given its central position in the political economy, land should be treated as a matter for the national constitution, rather than just the statute book. National constitutions should provide guidance and clarification on critical land-related issues such as resolution of historical grievances, security and protection of rights irrespective of tenure, equitable land distribution and public land acquisition. Short of such clear constitutional guidance, land reform will fall short of existing needs and will be prone to legal challenges by vested interests.
- Land information is available, but *access* to information on procedures (land use plans, lease and purchase procedures, land taxes, population densities, infrastructure available etc.) must be improved. This could be done through government Websites as a minimum first step, with on-line applications made available at a subsequent stage. In the longer term, the expertise and capacities of land professionals (surveyors, town planners, valuers, architects, etc.) need improvement, too. Instead of relying on universities only, local authorities should come up with training programmes that include the sharing of expertise across various authorities and counties.
- Local authorities must enhance land-based revenues. They should consider a flat tax for all properties not yet on valuation rolls. This mechanism should remain in place until properties can be valued and formally added to rolls. New and additional taxation is broadly accepted if it is transparent and fair and if revenues are spent on tangible neighbourhood improvements. Before looking to broaden revenue bases, though, local authorities must exploit existing mandates to the full and improve fee collection, and in this regard ***Lusaka*** and ***Dar es Salaam*** show the way.
- On top of looking to reduce financial deficits, local authorities should renegotiate their mandates with central government. This opportunity is more readily available in countries in the process of constitutional change, such as Zimbabwe (and recently Kenya in Eastern Africa), which could set out explicit roles and financial mandates for local authorities, as has happened in Botswana.
- As any others in the world, Southern African urban authorities must become more familiar with climate change and its incipient or prospective effects on their respective areas. They can do so through networking and cooperation with research institutions, and as part of systematic efforts to deploy appropriate data and monitoring systems. Outside the South African Cities Network, these functions are rather weak at the moment. Indeed, most databases on urban conditions include limited (where any) city-specific local data.
- The Pretoria-Johannesbourg GauTrain - Africa's first high speed train - can reduce ***Johannesburg's*** notorious traffic jams and long commuting times. However, since the line bypasses the townships where the majority of the conurbation live, it misses an opportunity to break with the legacy of apartheid in the transportation sector.
- Cross-border economic corridors offer economic opportunities to the poor and investors alike. Economic and physical planners should take a well co-ordinated interest in the potential of these corridors. Any spatial development initiatives should be broadened to integrate urban components.
- Governance should encourage or reward energy conservation through retrofitting buildings, solar power and information to residents and industry, supported by appropriate technologies towards savings.

Chapter One

01

THE STATE OF AFRICAN CITIES

An eviction in Nairobi, Kenya.
©Julius Mwelu/IRIN

1.1
Urban Geography, Economic Growth and Human Development

People-centred Cities

One legacy of the domination of urban planning and management by engineers and town planners with strong physical planning traditions is that urbanisation and cities are often considered more in terms of their physical attributes than as living environments for those residing there. Similarly, academics concerned with commodity flows, globalization, institutional and governance challenges have all too easily lost sight of the very people who create, drive and are affected by these processes and institutions.

Cities are human artefacts, developed and modified over time according to perceived needs and values. Although cities are home to diverse populations, the dominant population groups are generally those whose values, interests and needs are reflected in the built environment, formal institutions and regulatory regimes. Over time, this predominance has effectively marginalised or excluded large groups within cities such as poor residents and new migrants, who face varying degrees of deprivation because they cannot afford to comply

▲
A market in Madagascar. **©Muriel Lasure/Shutterstock**

GRAPH 1.1: **HUMAN DEVELOPMENT INDEX**

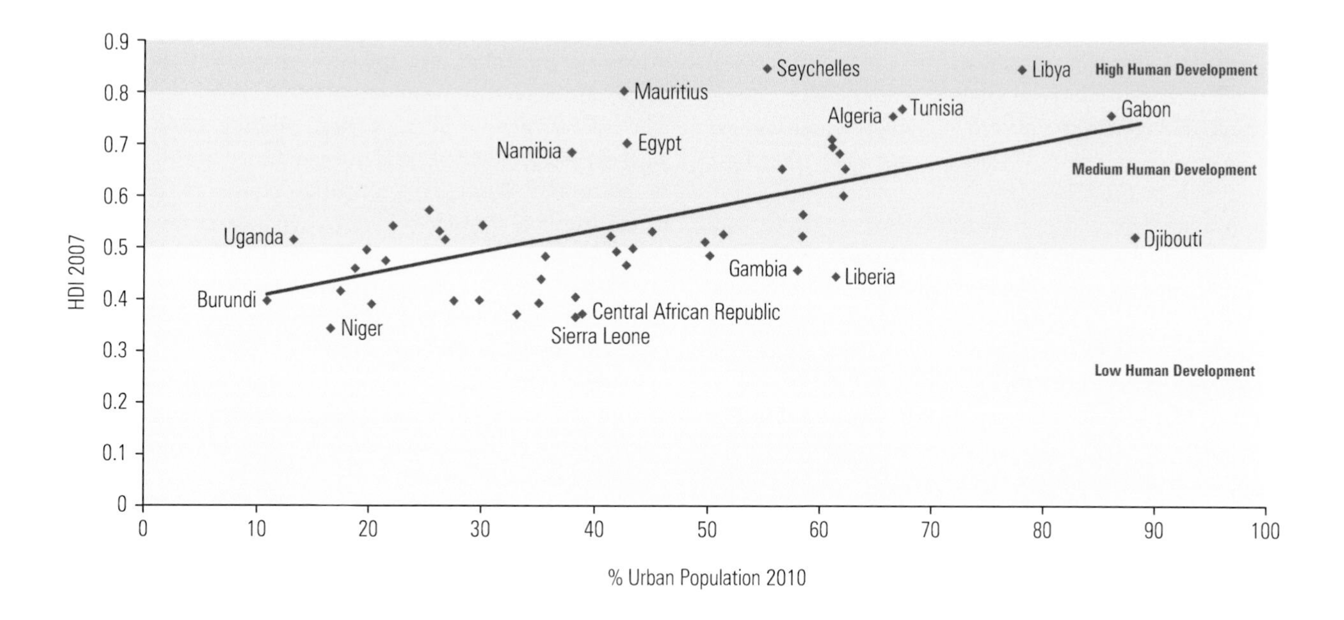

BOX 1.1: THE HUMAN DEVELOPMENT INDEX (HDI) AND URBANISATION RATES

One-off snapshots only have limited value and should therefore certainly not be confused with trends over time or causal relationships. Still, the statistical association between human development and the extent of urbanisation at the national level appears quite clearly. Graph 1.1 plots the Human Development Index (HDI) values for African countries and the estimated percentage of their respective national populations residing in areas classified as urban in 2010 (derived from data in UNDP *Human Development Report 2009*). The development index has been used instead of gross national product per head because, as a compound index comprising four social and economic variables, it can provide a better notion of people's access to resources and opportunities.

The trend line is quite clear, demonstrating a definite, albeit loose relationship between the development index and urbanisation. The looseness is the flip side of the comprehensive nature of the development index; given the diversity of the situations, different values for the constituent variables can yield identical scores, not to mention statistical 'outliers'. Countries towards the top and right of the graph exhibit relatively low urbanisation for high HDI scores (Egypt, Mauritius, Namibia and the Seychelles) or high urbanisation given their HDI score (Djibouti, Gambia, Liberia). On the left of the graph, Burundi lies close to the trend line with very low urbanisation and a low development index score, whereas Uganda finds itself in the reverse situation. Many of these extreme outliers feature particular circumstances, e.g., small island states or enclaves (Mauritius and the Seychelles, Djibouti) or oil-based economies (Gabon, Libya).

with systemic regulations that lie outside their reach in every possible way. Consequently, they are left with little option but to operate in the administrative or illegal margins. These excluded groups can only build informal shelter, often in hazardous locations shunned by the wealthier, while carving out livelihoods in ways that are often described as substandard, illegitimate or illegal. Because these groups constantly face the risk of eviction or prosecution, cities experience increased polarization, suspicion and open confrontations.

Uncontrolled 'self-help' urbanisation, especially by economically poor city dwellers, has come to be regarded as problematic by many spatial planners, urban managers and elites who fear a threat to their quality of life or their Western-derived urban aesthetics. However, given the prevalence of these popular forms of urbanisation and the sheer numbers involved, the efforts of the poor to meet their urban needs should be viewed more positively. Planning procedures should follow suit and become more flexible, except where objectively dangerous or inappropriate situations arise. Part of the sustainability challenge in our now predominantly urban world is to focus more on *cities as people-centred concentrations of opportunity*, not just problems. After all, it is in the world's urban areas that wealth, non-agricultural production, high-level social infrastructures and services as well as innovation are increasingly concentrated. The value of output in cities and urban regions, however measured, keeps exceeding by far that of rural regions.

A people-centred perspective highlights the need for more appropriate, realistic planning and building regulations that are affordable to the urban poor and that facilitate, rather than restrict, sustainable livelihoods. In other words, spatial planning and development control should focus less on impractical planning theory and imported notions of urban aesthetics or unattainable regulatory standards. Instead, they should embrace standards that reflect the needs of public authorities and the population, as well as current institutional capacities. Whereas efforts to adapt building codes, zoning regulations and review of outdated or restrictive policies have been undertaken in many African nations, so far they have met with only piecemeal success.

The management and planning problems associated with less-than-practical modalities of urban governance have often been exacerbated by rapid spatial expansion across municipal boundaries.

To date, uncontrolled demographic expansion has elicited three types of strategy from African public authorities.

During colonial rule and subsequently, public authorities have responded with bold initiatives to regain territorial integrity; they addressed spatial-administrative discrepancies with extensions of 'town lands' that brought the entire city and a surrounding green belt within a single jurisdiction. ***Harare***, Zimbabwe's capital is a case in point. Expanding the urban administrative territory is an option that should be considered by African governments and city managers, particularly in rapidly growing intermediate-size cities. Whereas this may be a complex challenge from legal and other perspectives, the longer-term political, financial, spatial and economic benefits are well worth the effort, as cities must accommodate current and expected demographic expansion over at least the span of a full generation, or longer.

More commonplace have been attempts to create metropolitan councils for area-wide, holistic and strategic planning, bringing together representatives of the constituent municipalities, as in ***Accra*** and ***Kumasi*** in Ghana. Such interventions may involve major political and institutional changes that are often fraught with difficulties, as section 1.3 of this report will outline. However, where such interventions have not taken place like, for instance, in metropolitan ***Dakar***, Senegal, the inevitable result is that no single authority serves as the apex body for multiple, distinct municipalities (more than 60 in the case of ***Dakar***), making any attempts at policy coordination virtually impossible.

The third option has proved to be the more popular one: fragmented urban governance based on inertia, inadequacy, inequity, lack of responsiveness, and corruption. Regardless of local circumstances, the outcome has been identical across Africa, namely, disjointed forms of spatial and functional governance that fall well short of the needs of the majority of city dwellers. This approach relies on a commoditisation of the city, with services and other urban benefits reserved for those who have the money or influence to access them. It involves deliberate urban partitioning into local political jurisdictions with different and highly inequitable access to public finance for public goods. Some argue that this is legitimate and appropriate, since services are distributed in proportion to taxes paid. Others contend that equity is enhanced if services instead are allocated in proportion to need.[1] However, through urban partitioning and spatial segregation, social distance and inequity are reinforced and, over time, frustration, disaffection and resistance are bound to increase.

In all these urban governance models, subsequent spatial expansion has frequently spilled over the new boundaries again under pressure from sustained demographic growth. The newer peripheral areas are typically controlled by adjacent local authorities and often classified as rural districts or customary land. This situation points to differences in institutional capacities, human and financial resources constraints, service levels and even political allegiances and orientations across administrative boundaries, that make it difficult on those living in ever-expanding urban fringes to claim better conditions or services. For example, waste collection, inadequate or sporadic as it may be, typically stops at formal metropolitan boundaries, as many rural districts do not provide this service, even for increasingly urbanised villages or overspill suburbs.[2]

A change of attitudes and practices is needed. If cities are to meet the challenges of economic, social and environmental sustainability, *all* residents must be taken seriously and given appropriate opportunities to share and participate equitably. Experience has shown over and again that authoritarian enforcement of governance through inappropriate planning or inequitable regulation will not succeed. Restrictive zoning regulations that inhibit people from living and working in close proximity, and inappropriate building standards that make compliance unaffordable to most urban dwellers, are but two examples of undesirable outcomes that will cause disaffection, resistance and alienation. Ultimately, this may lead to situations that undermine the very stability of our urban systems. Achieving people-centred, sustainable urban development requires major changes to more appropriately address the complex circumstances prevailing on the ground.

Equally important is the acknowledgement that people represent resources, not just problems. Harnessing rather than suppressing or alienating human energies is essential to maintaining urban dynamism and stability. It is also a prerequisite if human development needs are to be met in an effective, equitable way. However, fostering new cultures of urban citizenship and a sense of belonging among alienated and impoverished city residents will be no easy task. A first step should be an acknowledgement that many African cities are no longer geographical areas of wealth containing islands of poverty. The pattern currently unfolding is widespread: highly-disjointed, dysfunctional and unsustainable urban geographies of inequality and human suffering, with urban areas increasingly composed of small islands of well-being that are spatially and socially segregated from rapidly growing and increasingly impoverished masses - the 'urban divide'. Perpetuating and increasing the prevailing degrees of urban inequality is tantamount to cultivating the systemic instability of African cities. With urban areas the inevitable future home for the majority of Africans, the promotion of the social, economic and political failure of this increasingly important human habitat is simply not a viable option.

▲
The Nile riverfront in Cairo, Egypt. ©**Brian K/Shutterstock**

The Role of Cities in National and Global Economies

African cities have diverse historical origins, some of which going back many centuries. ***Cairo***, for instance, is one of the world's oldest continuously inhabited cities with a history of several thousand years involving successive dynasties and empires of regional and worldwide significance. ***Cairo*** remains an important political and cultural centre to this day and it is still Africa's most populous urban agglomeration. Others like ***Alexandria, Kumasi, Sofala*** and ***Timbuktu*** are today much diminished in economic and political importance, having once been the urban cores of regional empires with trade and diplomatic relations spanning much of the ***Maghreb*** and the ***Mashreq***, and reaching out to South Asia and even China. Many others, from ***Cape Town*** to ***Dakar*** and ***Nairobi*** have more recent origins, having been established by Europeans for mercantile, military/strategic, extractive or settlement purposes, as different parts of Africa were experiencing the early phases of economic, political and cultural globalization. Various hybrids and twin cities also emerged where colonial rulers built settlements adjacent to indigenous cities in order to maintain segregation, as in ***Rabat-Salé, Khartoum-Omdurman*** and ***Kampala-Mengo***. More recently, a number of post-independence capital cities have also emerged, often in ethnically or politically neutral territory, or as part of efforts to catalyse development in an impoverished region, like ***Abuja, Dodoma, Lilongwe*** and ***Yamoussoukro***. However, most of these new capital cities are struggling to emerge from the shadows of their longer-established predecessors.

Colonial conquest brought a profound reorientation of political and economic relations. It created a new outward and intercontinental focus as exploitation of natural resources gradually integrated the continent into different imperial patterns and, ultimately, the emerging modern world-system. Port cities became essential hubs in this system, with rail and road links to the resource-rich hinterlands.

In addition to political and military change, factors governing the ebb and flow of cities' fortunes have also included technology. The advent of the motor vehicle and eventually the aeroplane wrought successive changes on the spatial economies of many African cities and their hinterlands. Technological change within specific modes of transport sometimes had dramatic effects, such as the shift from loose to containerized cargo. The emergence of bulk carriers redefined port hierarchies as hub and feeder services were established. The air transport industry also had a significant impact on the fortunes of some African cities, as the shift from propeller to jet engines and long-haul autonomy– enabled longer, non-stop flights. An unintended consequence of this evolution was that many African airports that had thrived on refuelling or overnight stops *en route* lost out to the destination hubs.

Perhaps the most profound impact of technical progress arose from the rapid proliferation of information and communications technology (ICT). On top of reinforcing broad-based popular connectivity on the information highways, these technologies have also radically redefined spatial relations. This is true with respect to systems and networks among cities but also in terms of the relationships between cities, their peri-urban fringes and deeper rural hinterlands, as peasants and small commercial farmers, for instance, are now able to access market price information immediately, cutting out middlemen in the process. ICT is reshaping intra-urban relations, economic spaces and social networking in a similar manner, and the geographies of access to the Internet and educational resources are rapidly changing, redefining our traditional understandings of centrality and peripherality. This is further accentuated by the use of mobile phones and solar panels to sustain ICTs, enabling their use away from landlines and national electricity grids.

This is the general background against which Africa today sees the emergence of more and more clearly defined mega urban regions and urban development corridors straddling national boundaries and embracing tens of millions of people. Faced with these new challenges, traditional urban development policies are increasingly unable to address an unfolding set of complex and fluid spatial, regulatory and political realities. As interurban flows of commodities, people, communications, funds and physical urban patterns become more trans-national, governance and policy *must* follow suit if they are to be in any effective position to influence outcomes. More flexible and harmonized attitudes and policy will be needed along with innovative trans-boundary governance regimes, in order to bring some consistency and prevent investors from playing off cities and countries against each other.[3] This broad-ranging policy challenge is clearly illustrated with respect to global environmental and climate change, where the necessity for concerted international cooperation is now well accepted. The forthcoming 'post-Kyoto Protocol' regime must be mainstreamed into general urban policies beyond much-needed adaptation to, and mitigation of, the impacts of climate change.

Cities' Vulnerability to Systemic Shocks

Systemic shocks refer to strong impacts affecting substantial parts or all of an urban system (nationally or internationally), rather than having just isolated (e.g., sector-based or merely local) impacts. As such, these shocks have the potential to threaten the sustainability and survival of a system as a whole. Although these are no new phenomena, the rate and extent of technological change and globalization have significantly increased their likelihood, geographic scope and potential magnitudes. Some shocks may arise suddenly, like the global economic recession of 2008/09, while others have longer gestation periods, like demographic transition and climate change, the effects of which may be no less severe and will be much longer lasting.

Cyclical economic fluctuations naturally feature among the systemic shocks to which cities are now vulnerable, although this depends on their degree of integration in the international economy, including through information and telecommunication technologies. The recent global recession has demonstrated the speed and spatial extent of systemic financial vulnerability, leaving no country completely immune. Even though African banks largely kept away from the imprudent lending policies and high-leverage financial instruments that wreaked havoc in more advanced economies, the secondary effects of the global economic downturn has been felt in Africa under various forms, the more tangible of which were reduced tourism as well as reversals in both human development and progress towards the Millennium Development Goals, along with lower demand for commodities and reduced aid flows.

Since more and more of the world's population now lives in urban areas, the most dramatic effects on output and employment (and tax revenues) have been experienced in those urban areas providing services or commodities for the world market. Urban tourist hubs like ***Mombasa*** and ***Malindi*** in Kenya, ***Sharm al-Sheikh*** in Egypt or ***Victoria Falls*** in Zimbabwe (not to mention that country's internal political and economic crises) have experienced marked downturns, as have those towns across Africa that depend on agriculture for exports. In extreme cases, those towns and cities that had first been developed for a single purpose may even be abandoned, such as mining centres when the ore body is exhausted. ***Jos*** in Nigeria (tin), ***Kimberley*** in the Republic of South Africa and ***Lüderitz*** in Namibia (both diamonds) represent good examples of towns that first experienced booms but then went into severe long-term decline when their single-sourced *raison d'être* vanished.

These ever-changing economic geographies clearly illustrate how cities and their populations find themselves connected with each other within the wider framework of the global economy. Such integration can provide fresh opportunities for wealth creation and economic development as conditions change and competitiveness is enhanced. At the same time, integration can also make competitiveness more of a challenge, or force cities or countries to keep seeking new opportunities in the face of technical, economic or socio-political change that can wipe out former competitive or location specific advantages. Specialization can rapidly become a source of vulnerability. Because of scarce financial and entrepreneurial skills, African cities in particular have generally been poor at 'flexible specialization' in terms of the rapid adaptability which high-tech industries and production processes must achieve if they are to remain competitive under changing conditions.

As the rate of change accelerates in today's world, it becomes ever harder to keep up or to get ahead. Not every city can be a Geneva, a Singapore or a Dubai. Already, the latter's aspirations to become a global hub are facing tall challenges from the combination of world recession, mounting debt and competition from neighbouring Abu Dhabi (UAE) and Doha (Qatar). Global capitalism can be fickle and the price of failure can be very high, with a loss of dynamic residents through brain drain, a shrinking revenue base and resultant growing urban poverty, marginalization and social tensions. Under such circumstances, it becomes increasingly difficult to reinvent the city and address residents' needs in an equitable way.

Climate change is the second type of systemic shock threatening cities, with prospective unparalleled short- to long-term impacts. Climate change comprises two complementary elements: (a) the increasing frequency and severity of extreme weather events with short durations (e.g., hurricanes, storm surges or heat waves); and (b) slow-onset changes that are semi-permanent or permanent (e.g., sea level rise, falling groundwater tables or desertification). Although the continent contributes no more than 4 to 5 per cent of global greenhouse gas emissions, the Intergovernmental Panel on Climate Change's Fourth Assessment Report in 2007[4] said that Africa would experience some of the most severe effects of climate change. Since then, 2009 saw extreme events in various parts of Africa, e.g., flooding in the Namibian desert (parts of which had not seen rain for several years) and major drought-related famines in Eastern Africa. These may be linked to the *El Niño* phenomenon but more probably form part of a longer term trend consistent with climate change.

The particular combination of impacts will vary with latitude, region and among coastal and inland areas. Coastal areas are likely to experience storm surges, sea-level rises, increased flooding and (semi-) permanent inundation of low-lying areas. In many coastal cities, assets of strategic national economic value, such as ports, arterial railway/road infrastructure, industrial zones, leisure/recreation zones or residential areas, are under threat from climate change. In addition, coastal aquifers - on which these urban areas often depend for significant proportions of their fresh water supplies - stand to suffer as a result of saltwater intrusion through flooding or inundation. In some cases, significant agricultural areas supplying urban food markets will suffer a similar fate. Cities located on lagoons, estuaries, deltas or large river mouths - of which ***Alexandria, Cotonou, Dar es Salaam, Lagos, Maputo*** and ***Mombasa*** are good examples - are particularly vulnerable, as is the Cape Flats area of metropolitan ***Cape Town.***[5]

For inland cities, the main challenges are likely to include higher ambient temperatures and more frequent heat waves, leading to stronger heat island effects (with potential damage to infrastructure) and desiccating vegetation, shrinking water tables and associated urban water shortages, unless compensating supplies can be secured via engineered infrastructures. The more vulnerable cities will be those already experiencing heat stress and related problems during the summer season, as well as those in the Sahel on or close to the boundary between the desert and the bush, such as ***Kano*** and ***Ouagadougou.*** Several African inland cities have also become more vulnerable to flooding from sudden river surges following extreme weather events, such as ***Alexandra-Johannesburg, Brazzaville*** and several desert cities in Burkina

▲
The famous 'Tusks' in Kenya's port city of Mombasa. **©Sandro Senn**

Faso and Niger. Patterns of morbidity and mortality are also bound to change, with malaria and water-borne diseases becoming increasingly severe in inundated and more humid areas, while dehydration and other heat-related illnesses and deaths may increase - a pattern experienced during recent summer heat waves in Europe.

Climate change will certainly exacerbate the problems associated with voluntary or involuntary eco-migration to Africa's large and intermediate cities, away from flood-prone localities, as well as potentially large-scale internal and cross-border mobility away from agricultural zones undermined by changing climatic conditions or declining water availability. Coastal urban centres in Senegal, for instance, have already experienced ecology-related immigration from both the interior and adjacent countries. This has exacerbated urban poverty and unemployment, while contributing to the flows of migrants seeking to reach the Canary Islands, Southern Italy or Spain on board unseaworthy boats in a desperate hope of gaining access to the European Union.[6] City-specific examples of the challenges and early responses appear in Chapters 2-6.

Demographic shifts represent a third category of systemic shock for cities. These shifts are complex, with some like ageing occurring fairly slowly. However, those reflecting human behaviour patterns, such as mobility or the spread of HIV/AIDS or some forms of eco-migration, are often subject to rapid change and can be difficult to anticipate on account of spatial and socio-economic variations. While most African countries are hosts to predominantly young populations, average ages are increasing, as total fertility rates have been on the decline almost everywhere. The numbers of people surviving to old age are rising rapidly, although still representing relatively small proportions of total populations. This trend poses new challenges for social care where traditional extended family structures are dissolving, particularly in urban areas but also in rural areas where institutional care facilities still barely exist. Poverty, however, remains the key problem, often exacerbating the impact of pandemics and curable illnesses like measles, pneumonia and gastro-enteritis.

Cities for Human Development

It is important to retain a balanced perspective on the cross-relationships between urbanisation and development. Notwithstanding the various problems outlined above, African cities have been turning into centres of innovation, non-agricultural production and political and cultural life. The encouraging association between the human development index and urbanisation rates (see Box 1.1) suggest that urbanisation brings definite benefits. Indeed, as explained in Section 1.6, the prospects for achieving most of the Millennium Development Goals are intimately bound up with what happens in Africa's cities.

Under the conventional view that prevailed during the colonial period (and in the Republic of South Africa and Namibia during the apartheid era), Africa's urbanisation was culturally and socially inappropriate and would lead to an alienating 'detribalisation', since Africans had no tradition of urban life. This is demonstrably untrue, since highly sophisticated urban societies had previously existed or still exist in just about every part of the African continent. Rather, such prejudices served discriminatory policies in colonial settler societies, in a bid to preserve European political and economic dominance in urban areas, admitting Africans only under strictly controlled and exploitative conditions for the sole purposes of cheap urban labour.

Political independence in Africa led to the abandonment or relaxation of migration controls into urban areas. This resulted in very sudden and rapid demographic growth in cities and increasingly permanent urban residence for Africans. Initially, social and economic ties to rural extended families remained strong. These bonds are now gradually weakening. Nuclear African families are increasingly commonplace, especially among the middle classes and elites and in some countries also among low-income families, with a commensurate new and rising demand for urban housing units and associated services delivery. Elsewhere, circular or oscillating migration between one or more urban and one or more rural areas represents an important survival strategy, effectively spreading economic risk and providing access to services and livelihood opportunities in different localities. Misguided postcolonial policies that attempted to split the population into either urban wage earners or full-time rural farmers ignored these real-life factors, undermining legitimate livelihood or survival strategies and in the process exacerbating poverty.

Mobility and migration remain hugely important in Africa, as individuals and households nowadays rarely spend their entire lives in one and the same place. 'Multi-local' households are now widespread, with family members residing in different urban and rural locations for shorter or longer periods. Mobility patterns can shift very rapidly as conditions change and nowadays often span national or even continental boundaries. For instance, remittances from family members working in Europe, North America, the Middle East and Australasia now represent a vital resource for many households in all segments of society, as well as a major source of foreign exchange for African governments. Environmental changes due to climatic and other events are also displacing people within rural areas, from rural to urban areas and across national boundaries, as detailed in Chapter 3 on West Africa, for instance.

The sociology of urbanisation is complex and involves a variety of patterns. The ethnic segregation of the past has generally been replaced with socio-economic class segregation. Nevertheless, in poorer urban neighbourhoods, ethnic concentrations often remain significant, especially when reinforced by rural-urban migration. Whereas high-income urban areas may now feature higher degrees of diversity, social life often remains linked to ethnic or linguistic affiliations. Under conditions of duress and the implosion of formal government or social institutions, informality and innovative survival strategies emerge or are revived in hybrid forms.[7]

1.2 Urban Inequalities

Economic, social and environmental inequalities can be found at all spatial scales, including urban and intra-urban. Until very recently, accurate and reliable data has been scarce, and comparing the conditions that prevail among cities and within or among countries remained difficult. As data now becomes available, some generalisations can be made, notwithstanding considerable variations between neighbouring countries or those within particular sub-regions. Often these reflect specific historical circumstances and/or the impacts of particular policies. For instance, Northern African cities and those in low-income countries tend to feature lower degrees of inequality (as measured by Gini coefficients) than middle-income countries. Inequality is at its highest in Africa's former settler colonies, where statutory ethnic segregation and apartheid policies were enforced for extended periods. The inherited physical fabric of such cities keeps generating steep inequalities, even long after the abolition of discriminatory legislation.

▲
Soweto township. South Africa has the highest income-based inequality in Africa.

The diversity of urban patterns in Africa reflects different combinations of a number of factors: economic momentum, the extent and nature of a country's integration in the world economy and any attendant pressures, as well as the trends and patterns of urban demographic growth. It is surprising to find that at the two extremes of the urban spectrum - the more dynamic countries, and those wrecked by rural conflicts and poverty - capital and major cities have tended to grow faster than medium-size and smaller ones, and typically feature a much sharper 'urban divide'. Where urban demographic growth is slower, or redistributive policies are in place, capital cities will be as (un)equal as the country as a whole. Overall, though, cities tend to score higher than rural areas on most economic, social and environmental indicators, as they concentrate investment and opportunities, and this 'urban advantage' attracts rural migrants.

For the purposes of understanding the current state of African cities, the intra-urban scale is more useful as it can highlight the way conditions change from one area to another within a single city and how living standards are affected by geographical factors. However, the relevant data on intra-urban economic inequality remains scarce, and only a few selected examples can be discussed.

African cities on average exhibit the highest inequalities in the world, both individually (where city-specific data is available) and collectively (where Gini coefficients are available only for rural and urban areas). Many African cities can be found in the *very high* and *extremely high* inequality brackets. Whereas Latin American and Caribbean (LAC) cities were until recently the most unequal in the world, UN-HABITAT's *State of the World's Cities 2010/11* shows that they have been lagging African cities in recent years (income-based coefficients, urban areas: 0.529 on average in Africa, compared with 0.505. in LAC; average of available city-specific coefficients: Africa: 0.581; LAC: 0.528).

BOX 1.2: GINI COEFFICIENTS: MEASURING THE ECONOMIC DIVIDE

The Gini coefficient is a measure of statistical dispersion expressed in a figure between 0 and 1 that quantifies differences in welfare and compensation within a given population. A Gini coefficient of 1 represents total inequality, or a situation whereby one individual owns everything, while a coefficient of 0 means total equality of distribution and everyone owns the same. Sometimes the Gini coefficient is presented as an index, where the ratio is multiplied by 100 to range between 0 and 100.

The strength of the Gini coefficient is that it is based on ratio analysis. It compares income or consumption distributions across different segments of a given population. Gini coefficient time series indicate whether inequality is increasing or decreasing. If combined with gross domestic product, the Gini coefficient can also pinpoint other trends. For instance, if both the Gini coefficient and total output are rising, it means that increasing wealth is shared by fewer people and poverty may be on the rise for the majority of the population.

However, any Gini coefficient is only as good as the data used to calculate it. Since there are no international norms in this matter, the Gini coefficient can be manipulated either to decry extreme inequalities or to demonstrate that inequality is at a minimum. The Gini coefficient can further be misleading because societies with similar incomes and Gini coefficients can still feature different income and consumption distributions. However, when used in an objective manner and based on reliable statistics, the Gini coefficient can be a powerful indicator of inequality in wealth distribution and whether it is growing or declining in a particular community.

Before reviewing recent Gini coefficient evidence on urban inequalities, a few comments on definitions are in order. The data on income refer to money income only (both wages and social welfare payments from all sources), while those on consumption (household expenditures) include all categories, including non-monetary costs. While money income below appropriate thresholds is often an important indicator of poverty, the two are not synonymous since non-monetary sources of income, such as subsistence production, are excluded. This is one reason that consumption-based data may be more reliable in poor countries. However, consumption excludes the savings share of income and is therefore typically lower than actual income. The main exceptions are where savings are non-existent or very low, and where there is consumption of subsistence produce by household members (for example, from urban or peri-urban agriculture, or on rural land) or non-marketed services (such as reciprocal labour). These exceptions can be significant, especially in the informal sector. Decisions on whether to collect income or expenditure/consumption data are taken by national statistical authorities as a function of the expected accuracy of survey responses. In the Republic of South Africa, for instance, income prevails, while in Mozambique and Togo consumption data are collected.

The data on urban inequality used here have been prepared by UN-HABITAT's Global Urban Observatory (GUO) and reflect some of the difficulties referred to here. The bulk of the available data enable direct rural-urban comparisons at the national level; in some cases the largest city, and possibly one or more other centres, are identified separately.

Rural-Urban Economic Inequality

Regions, sub-regions and cities of the world feature substantial discrepancies in economic equality. UN-HABITAT's *State of the World's Cities Report 2010/11* identifies six distinct brackets based on Gini coefficients. As far as Africa is concerned, individual countries can be split in five brackets, from *'relatively low'* inequality (0.300–0.399, e.g., Algeria) to '*very high inequality*' (0.500-0.599, e.g., Ethiopia, Kenya, Nigeria, Botswana and Zimbabwe) and '*extremely high inequality*' (0.600 and more, e.g., Namibia, South Africa and Zambia). Coefficients above 0.400 are regarded as a source of concern.

Steep economic inequality is rife in most African cities. Topping the list is the Republic of South Africa, with a 0.76 income-based urban inequality coefficient in 2005, or the same magnitude as the ratios for individual major cities. In part, this reflects the legacy of more than a century of statutory racial segregation and then apartheid. While the legislative backbone of this segregation system could be abolished fairly rapidly, the embedded urban structures and the geographies of segregation will persist for far longer. Emerging trends reveal that ethnic segregation is increasingly replaced by class-based segmentation, as has occurred in other former settler colonies where similar systems of segregation once prevailed, e.g. Kenya, Namibia and Zimbabwe.

Africa's least unequal countries in terms of consumption coefficients include Togo (0.31 in 2006), Morocco (0.38 in 1998), Egypt (0.39 in 1997), Mauritania (0.39 in 2004) and Ethiopia (0.38 in 1999/2000). The lowest income coefficients were found in Algeria (0.35 in 1995), Cameroon (0.41 in 2001) and Uganda (0.43 in 2005/6). It should, however, be realised that a low Gini coefficient is not necessarily favourable as it is merely a relative indicator of equality. It may indicate - and in many cases it does - nationwide low levels of income, consumption and human development. The lowest coefficients are generally found in countries with a low human development index in sub-Saharan Africa and Islamic North African states, where poverty is widespread although settler discrimination was not so pronounced. This means that low Gini coefficients can in fact signal cities where all residents are 'equally poor'.

Moreover, trends can sometimes be complex even within one country, reflecting specific geographic or size-category dynamics. For instance, Botswana's income-based Gini coefficient declined from 0.56 in 1985 to 0.54 in 1993 and 0.51 in 2003. The national *urban* coefficient remained stable at 0.54 from 1985 to 1993, and then fell to 0.50 in 2003, while increasing from 0.45 to 0.52 in 'urban villages' over the same period (1993-2003). In ***Maputo***, the Gini coefficient is much higher than Mozambique's urban average. Similarly, in Côte d'Ivoire, the national urban Gini coefficient is 0.44, compared with 0.50 in ***Abidjan***. Conversely, in Burundi the national urban Gini coefficient for consumption stands at 0.49 compared with 0.47 in ***Bujumbura***, the capital. Therefore, disaggregation to the city level is important for any understanding of intra-urban patterns and dynamics.

City-level Economic Inequalities

City-level data on either a consumption or income basis are available for 39 African urban areas (Graph 1.2.a), while both measures are compiled for ***Addis Ababa***. No data for Northern African cities is available. As explained earlier, consumption-based coefficients of inequality are typically somewhat lower than those based on income. Even within these respective categories, direct comparisons are hindered by the different base years for the data, although in Graph 1.2.a the range is only seven years. By contrast, the range of 14 years in Graph 1.2.b means that the data for ***Accra, Maseru, Libreville/Port Gentil, Yaoundé*** and ***Douala*** should be treated cautiously for comparison purposes with data for the year 2000 and later. Nevertheless, none of the older data lie at the extremes of the range.

At 0.30, ***Lomé,*** Togo, features the lowest urban economic inequality coefficient, together with nine others in Africa that are below 0.399. Five more lie in the 0.4–0.49 range, with only two, ***Maputo*** and ***Addis Ababa***, above 0.50. Aside from any data deficiencies, this would appear to reflect that these urban areas are all located in some of the poorest African countries, all of which (except Uganda and Tanzania) with low rankings in the 2009 UNDP Human Development Index. This category now includes only 24 out of 182 countries in the

GRAPH 1.2.A: **AFRICAN URBAN ECONOMIC INEQUALITIES - CONSUMPTION-BASED COEFFICIENTS**

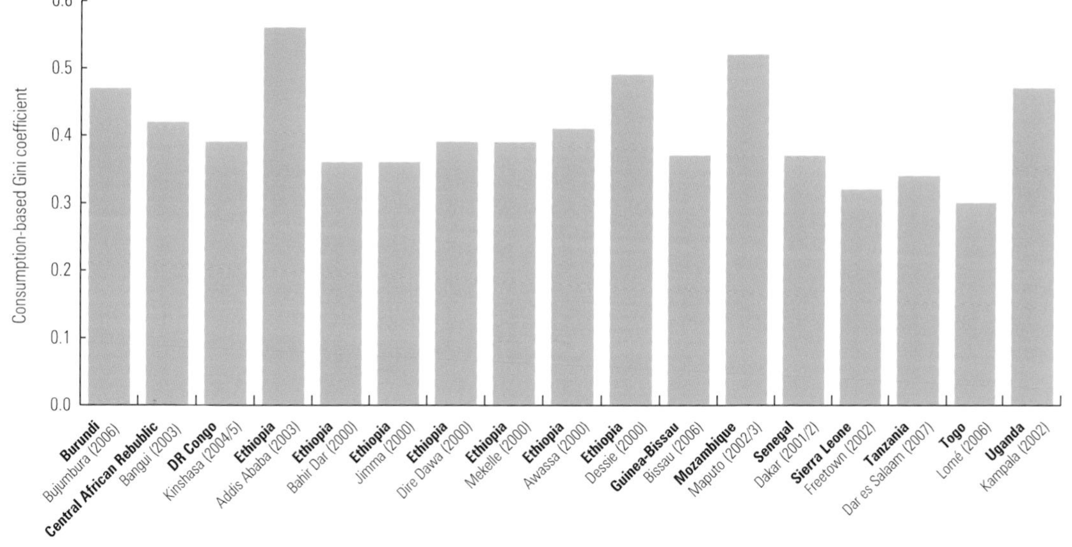

GRAPH 1.2.B: **AFRICAN URBAN ECONOMIC INEQUALITIES - INCOME-BASED COEFFICIENTS**

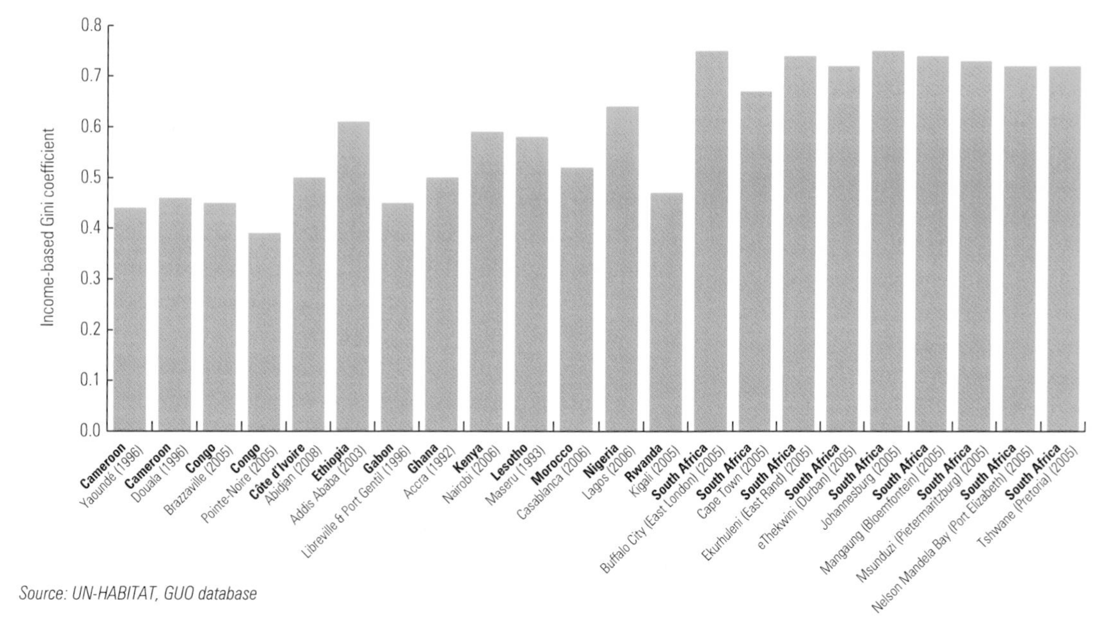

Source: UN-HABITAT, GUO database

▲
Addis Ababa, Ethiopia. ©**Manoocher Deghati/IRIN**

rankings, but Uganda and Tanzania lie close to the bottom of the *'medium'* human development category. Although some of these countries' economies have been growing in recent years, largely thanks to their capital cities - a potential factor behind increasing economic inequality - overall consumption-based inequalities tend to be less severe under conditions of relative poverty, notwithstanding the presence of small wealthy elites.

The data from Ethiopia are of particular interest since they enable direct comparison between ***Addis Ababa***, the primate city and capital, with six regional towns. With the exception of ***Dessie,*** the smaller centres all exhibit low degrees of consumption inequality, while Addis Ababa's is considerably higher at 0.56. This reflects urban primacy, a phenomenon that keeps drawing in ever more migrants and internally displaced people. Moreover, being the capital and home to various international organisations and most commerce and industry, Addis Ababa has been a focus for construction, infrastructural expansion and foreign investment since economic liberalisation in the early 1990s. Liberalisation itself has led to considerable price inflation, both for food and other everyday commodities, as well as for rented accommodation in a situation of excess housing demand. Indeed, comparative data show that ***Addis Ababa's*** consumption-based Gini coefficient increased by a full 24 per cent between the year 2000 and 2003, while ***Dessie*** and ***Dire Dawa*** experienced increases of 11 and eight per cent respectively. In contrast, ***Awassa, Bahir Dar*** and ***Jimma*** experienced significant declines in consumption inequality from 1994 to the year 2000, as the result of improved access to social and physical infrastructure and services.

In Mozambique, since the end of civil war in the early 1990s, a disproportionate share of economic momentum has been located in ***Maputo,*** where economic inequality rose 18 per cent between 1996 and 2003 (*SWCR 2010*).

The range of income-based Gini coefficients in Graph 1.2.b is far wider than the corresponding consumption data, from 0.39 (***Pointe-Noire***, Congo) to 0.75 in ***Buffalo City*** (East London) and ***Johannesburg*** in the Republic of South Africa. Indeed, all the South African cities in the list rank above 0.70, with the exception of ***Cape Town's*** 0.67. This reflects the legacy of racially-based disparities in incomes, welfare benefits and social investment during the apartheid era in the continent's most sophisticated economy. These inequalities are slightly lower than in the late 1990s due to redistributive policies by successive post-apartheid governments, including pensions and other welfare benefits, minimum wages and free basic water allowances. However, such steep degrees of inequality still pose substantial challenges to social and political stability. Indeed, grassroots pressure for accelerated redistribution is mounting, as the example of free water allowances in South Africa will explain in Chapter 6.

Nigeria's principal city ***Lagos*** is also characterised by sharp inequality, with widespread poverty amid substantial wealth and corruption in Africa's largest oil-producing country. At 0.61, the income-based Gini coefficient is higher than ***Addis Ababa's***. Income-based coefficients are subject to rapid change: ***Abidjan's*** Gini coefficient, for instance, increased by 21 per cent from 2002 to 2008, under the combined effects of civil conflict and the resultant economic disruption and displacement.[8]

TABLE 1.1: **URBAN SLUM POPULATIONS, SELECTED AFRICAN COUNTRIES, 1990 - 2010**

	1990	1995	2000	2005	2007	2010*	1990	1995	2000	2005	2007	2010*
	Urban population (000s)						Proportion of slum dwellers (%)					
Nigeria	33,325	42,372	53,048	65,270	70,539	78,845	77.3	73.5	69.6	65.8	64.2	61.9
South Africa	19,034	22,614	25,827	28,419	29,266	30,405	46.2	39.7	33.2	28.7	28.7	28.7
Egypt	23,972	25,966	28,364	31,062	32,193	34,041	50.2	39.2	28.1	17.1	17.1	17.1
Morocco	12,005	13,931	15,375	16,763	17,377	18,374	37.4	35.2	24.2	13.1	13.1	13.1

** Projections*
Source: UN-HABITAT, GUO (some of the data are interpolations)

The Dimensions of Multiple Urban Deprivations

Economic polarisation is closely associated with inequalities in basic needs satisfaction; most importantly, access to adequate shelter, safe drinking water and sanitation (including solid waste and sewage), health and education services and a safe living environment.

One key indicator of urban poverty and deprivation is the proportion of urban populations living in sub-standard housing (i.e., slums), because this typically signals that other basic needs are not satisfied either. In several African countries for which reasonably reliable figures are available in UN-HABITAT's GUO database, this proportion has been falling over the last two decades. The most dramatic declines in slum populations (as compared with total urban populations) were achieved in Egypt (from 50.2 to 17.1 per cent), Mali (from 94.2 to 65.9 per cent) and Senegal (from 70.6 to 38.1 per cent) between 1990 and 2005. In Ghana, the decline was from 68.7 per cent in 1990 to 38.1 per cent in 2010; in Madagascar, from 93.0 to 75.3 per cent; in the Republic of South Africa, from 46.2 to 28.7 per cent; and in Benin, from 79.3 to 69.3 per cent over the same period. In Kenya and Namibia, the figures remained almost constant, at just under 55 and 33-34 per cent respectively. Conversely, other countries have experienced deteriorations in the prevalence of sub-standard housing in cities, with increases of four to nine per cent over the past 20 years in Malawi (to 69.6 per cent), Mozambique (to 80.8. per cent) and the Central African Republic (to 96.4 per cent). These unfavourable trends suggest that the rates of rural-urban migration and natural urban population increases keep outstripping shelter regularisation as well as low-income housing construction and infrastructure upgrading programmes. In some cases, policy inconsistencies or reorientations (as in Namibia immediately after independence in 1990) and/or funding constraints have hindered progress. In Mozambique, the apparent relative increase in slum prevalence occurred despite strong positive economic growth following the end of its civil war in 1991. This is a clear indicator of the absence of substantive urban pro-poor programmes in the country. More generally, this situation also exemplifies the lack of clear relationships between economic growth and widespread improved living conditions in many African countries.

Even where the *proportions* of people in sub-standard urban housing have been significantly reduced, *absolute* numbers have often increased as a result of substantial urban demographic growth. As can be seen in Table 1.1, this applies to Nigeria and South Africa, though not to Egypt or Morocco. Indeed, Northern Africa is distinctive on the continent and among so-called developing regions for having achieved declines in both the proportions and absolute numbers of urban populations living in sub-standard shelter despite unabated demographic expansion.

One particular challenge to any sustained progress in shelter improvement is the high proportion of the urban poor living in areas most vulnerable to the effects of climate change and 'everyday' environmental risks. Increased flooding from more frequent severe storms and rising sea levels threaten mostly low-lying, marshy or flood-prone land in river valleys and adjacent floodplains, along estuary shores and in low-elevation coastal zones, while those urban poor living on steep slopes or adjacent to waste dumps may be vulnerable to landslides due to more frequent and heavier rainfall. Upgrading and regularising substandard shelter in such areas should receive priority, based on risk assessments that duly include the effects of climate change. In some cases, enhanced construction and infrastructural standards may be in order, too, e.g., raising foundations of buildings, strengthening roads and increasing storm water drainage capacity. In other instances, where higher frequency and severity of flooding or semi-permanent inundation as a result of sea level rise are anticipated, substantial flood defences or relocation of residents to safer localities may become necessary.

In all cases, sustainable shelter for the urban poor will require significantly higher amounts of capital investment and planned maintenance costs. The price of failure to do this would be far higher, though, in terms of more piecemeal capital expenditures over the years as disruption, dislocation, loss of livelihoods and potentially loss of life for the urban poor. Lack of action can only exacerbate poverty and deprivation. Failure to address climate change through mitigation and fundamental adaptive strategies is no longer an option or something that can be deferred to future generations. This is an immediate necessity, because the effects are already felt by many in African cities, both in low-elevation coastal zones, but also inland centres. Specific examples are provided in the following chapters.

1.3
Government or Governance?

Multi-level Governance

Under pressures from demographic growth, very large regional urban systems such as extended metropolitan regions, megacities and mega urban regions are now also emerging in Africa. All feature urban sprawl beyond formal administrative boundaries, in the process encroaching on adjacent rural areas and absorbing the smaller towns and villages that lie on their growth path.

A shared challenge among these new urban configurations is the provision of area-wide governance, planning and guidance to spatial developments, as well as holistic management of such regional urban systems. Traditional governance structures such as municipal government, provincial boards, federal district authorities, etc., have, without exception, proven inadequate because their legal and institutional structures have been designed for single-municipality, mono-centric cities, rather than multi-municipal, multi-nodal regional urban systems.

Many attempts have been made around the world to provide regional planning and holistic management for multiple-municipality urban systems through either cooperative or coordinating structures, but few have led to satisfactory results. Among the exceptions is the Delta Metropolis of the Netherlands, comprising the metropolitan regions of Amsterdam, Rotterdam, The Hague, Utrecht and a hierarchy of smaller settlements. However, this mega urban region has since 1945 been subject to continuous and consistent spatial and administrative interventions and updates by the Dutch central planning agency, in cooperation with provincial and municipal planning entities. In all other regional urban configurations around the world, it is becoming increasingly clear that governance as applied to traditional mono-municipal settlements is unable to meet the management demands of city regions. Attempts to bring about holistic governance have usually failed due to uncertainties in legal and spatial definition. The resulting autonomy overlaps and authority gaps have invariably undermined any clear articulation or allocation of public functions and authority. Friction in regional city governance is typically due to unresolved authority conflicts among or within three major groups of stakeholders: (a) central government; (b) local authorities; and (c) interest groups from civil society.

Since many city regions comprise the national capital, central government (directly or through ministerial departments) tends to interfere with urban governance at the expense of local autonomy. At the lower levels, provincial, municipal and neighbourhood councils often pursue conflicting agendas with overlapping jurisdictions and functions. The private sector and civil society also increasingly demand decision-making roles in urban policies and governance, adding to the general confusion. The sheer multiplicity of the parties at play, different institutional structures, divergent levels of power leveraging and their frequently antagonistic agendas combine to make the delivery of coordinated area-wide management, infrastructures and urban services in regional urban systems fraught with difficulties. As these stakeholders simultaneously seek to influence urban governance processes, there is a clear need for new approaches that provide unambiguous authority and management tasks for different governance levels within extensive urban configurations.

Although worldwide blanket governance and management models for regional urban configurations do not seem to be available, five basic steps appear to have applicability and a fairly general degree of practical relevance, as follows:

(1) A first step should be to create workable mechanisms for *region-wide urban planning coordination and development control.* The increasing complexity of city regions tends to shift important metropolitan issues and responsibilities either to the lower levels (municipality, neighbourhood and community) or the higher (national) level. But rather than simply (de)centralizing complex spatial problems, responsibility and authority should ideally be allocated to a range of cooperating macro-, intermediate and micro-levels to maintain supervision, integration and coordination at the regional scale and maximise political participation at the local level.

(2) Regional cities are typically in a constant state of spatial flux. Policies should therefore allow for *continuous adjustments to functional authority and administrative boundaries.* Such flexible arrangements may be difficult to put in place and operate, but they would provide the flexibility required to devise strategies that remain adaptable to on-going and newly emerging developments.

(3) *Centralized authority over a city region only tends to work for truly area-wide matters* such as overall road and traffic management, public transport planning, water and electricity provision, etc. Other functions should be organized under various forms of multi-level urban management which, for the sake of legitimacy, must be based on local control through decentralization, democracy and participation.

(4) While centralization of area-wide regulatory authority can lead to better coordination, *genuine grassroots participation can only happen through strengthened lower-tier decision-making powers.* In the face of ever-expanding, ever more complex metropolitan systems, and in view of dwindling municipal revenues, participation and community self-help can facilitate effective responses to local issues.

(5) It is essential to *re-assess centralized bureaucratic structures, where any, and make lower-tier decision-making more effective and responsive.* Local initiative and control enhance self-reliance and sustainability for many urban functions while steering the burden of micro-management away from higher governance levels. Well-guided local enablement also allows for more responsive mobilization of local private and community sectors.

In many African nations, metropolitan and regional urban systems face two major challenges: (a) matching political and fiscal decentralization to local needs while, at the same time, providing much-needed area-wide management of public works and services; and (b) addressing complex processes of socio-spatial segregation that cause substantial intra-metropolitan differences and inequality in service provision.[9]

Innovative metropolitan management reforms are under way around the world in the quest for practical approaches to area-wide urban governance. Drawing from different government traditions, constitutional frameworks, planning approaches, historical circumstances, socio-economic conditions and national political cultures, both advanced and developing countries have experimented with ideas on how to best plan and govern urban regions that encompass multiple municipalities. The experience over the past decades has yielded four broad types of area-wide governance structures: (1) autonomous local authorities; (2) confederate regional government; (3) mixed systems of regional governance; and (4) unified regional governance.[10]

(1) Autonomous Local Authorities

In some city regions, authority and power are embedded in local authorities that enjoy high degrees of autonomy, including spatial planning, policy development and legislation.

This type of area-wide governance is more suitable to countries with a tradition of strong local autonomy and municipal governance, but less so where central government is predominant. Experience has shown that this 'autonomous local authority' approach - the least invasive and easiest to deploy - tends to result in fragmented and uncoordinated regional outcomes; this is because there is little to prevent individual municipal authorities from pursuing their own agendas regardless of wider-ranging regional needs. Mitigating these shortcomings with monitoring and evaluation will be difficult, in the absence of a specific body to review individual municipal outcomes or to step in with mandatory course corrections.

(2) Confederate Regional Government

Under this configuration, local authorities enter into voluntary cooperation and agree on the regional-level functions to be carried out by a dedicated apex authority with clearly spelled out mandates and powers (such as a metropolitan development authority). This regional-level apex body comprises the chief executives of all local authorities in the city region, so that any decisions are informed by their views. The real power, however, remains with the local authorities.

The effectiveness of this governance arrangement clearly depends on the degree of effective power lodged in the regional authority. This approach can only succeed if all local authorities in the city-region participate in, and adhere to, the regional body's decisions. Because this 'confederate' approach allows for substantial control by the participating municipalities over the regional authority, consensus may at times be difficult to achieve. The regional authority may prove powerless and ineffective if the participating local authorities cannot reach consensus. A monitoring and evaluation system would have to be agreed upon, with peer pressure applied for corrective action.

(3) Mixed Systems of Regional Governance

Under mixed systems of regional governance, the higher tiers of government (national, state/provincial) share power with local authorities in the delivery of specific public functions. These are defined under a variety of flexible arrangements based on prevailing political conditions.

Clearly, the degree of success of this approach depends on specific local conditions, the nature of the agreements reached and the ultimate adherence by all to the decisions. One drawback of this approach is that local authorities must negotiate with a higher tier of government they are not part of, which implies that they hand over a degree of autonomy to that higher authority. Monitoring, evaluation and any corrective action are left to that higher government tier.

(4) Unified Regional Governance

Under this approach, one single government entity, typically a fully-fledged ministry is responsible for an entire city region. Planning, plan implementation, monitoring and evaluation are all lodged in this body.

Local authorities exercise power over a limited number of clearly spelled out lower-level assignments within an overall framework set by the higher authority. Given the significant reduction in the autonomy of individual local authorities within the city region, this type of area-wide governance is more suitable to countries with a tradition of strong, dominant central government rather than strong local autonomy and municipal governance. Unsurprisingly, region-wide outcomes under unified regional governance tend to have better overall coherence and coordination.

This review of existing practice suggests that the ultimate choice of best broad governance structure for city regions clearly depends on national and local political circumstances. The four alternatives outlined above all aim to overcome the negative impacts of fragmented urban governance. Past decades have clearly shown that market-driven urbanisation is generally unable to reconcile short-term economic interests with the reforms required for the sake of long-term social, political and environmental sustainability. It has also become clear that local communities, by themselves, cannot provide the corrective mechanisms required for large-scale or urban region-wide challenges, while central control cannot effectively micro-manage myriads of local needs. As African cities increasingly overrun administrative boundaries and turn into entirely new urban configurations, the need for fundamental change in the governance of these regional urban systems is beyond doubt.

African urbanisation calls for a radical review of the forces behind it, the resulting spatial and social forms and the new governance requirements for effective, responsive urban management. Consequently, it is for national and local authorities carefully to consider the options for reform of urban governance practice and institutions. The demands of newly emerging urban configurations are not just a matter of extending existing arrangements to larger cities or geographic areas: instead, a political, legal and institutional redesign of the very structure of urban governance is in order. The aim is to counter the urban fragmentation that almost inevitably results from attempts to govern multiple-entity urban configurations with obsolete and ineffective management mechanisms and practices, all the more so as these often have only been implemented in a partial, intermittent or opportunistic way.

Democracy and Participation

Since the early 1990s and under both internal and external pressure, Africa has experienced a wave of democratization, resulting in a transition to, or strengthening of, multi-party politics and elections across the continent.[11] As part of this process, landmark elections have recently taken place in Burundi, the Democratic Republic of the Congo, Liberia and Sierra Leone, while other African nations have gone through second, third or even fourth periodic rounds of national elections.[12]

Although recent political transition in Africa has generally been swift and relatively successful, it has also become clear that building truly sustainable democracies takes time. Genuine democracy cannot be imposed from above or outside. Rather, it should grow from within and be country-specific. Despite recent reforms, election processes and outcomes in Africa still lack transparency in some countries and many political parties remain poorly structured in terms of platforms and organisation for lack of resources, accountability or internal democratic procedures. Other challenges include inadequate or insufficient legislative progress toward transparent administrative procedures that promote the inclusion of all sectors of society in the political process.

▲
Listening to election results in Kano, Nigeria. **©Tugela Ridley/IRIN**

Current democratic deficiencies are clearly linked to Africa's colonial heritage. Upon independence, few African nations moved to alter the highly centralized systems of governance inherited from colonial rule. Strong patrimonial networks across all tiers of government have survived or even expanded to provide a selective and therefore exclusionary form of 'social security' that is often defined along ethnic or tribal lines. Soon after independence, centralized domestic politics became rife with corruption in many African nations, as patrimonial governments provided goods and services for those in power, rather than providing equitable, broad-based access to public services such as education, health care, sanitation, clean drinking water or effective legal systems as part of socio-economic policies in favour of productivity and human capital for broad-based development.[13] Instead of tackling these inequalities, recent democratization, liberalization and privatization processes in Africa have facilitated the widening of patronage networks from national power centres to provincial and local authorities.

In today's Africa, decentralization cannot remain blind to the politics of ethnic or regional tribal/clan conflicts and tensions. The persistence of ingrained traditional mores and customs is nothing new, and is now finding fresh forms of expression in African polities. The modern manifestations of traditional practice in statecraft and economic strategy in Africa should not be overlooked, because informality and network-driven challenges to conventional government can be exploited and exacerbated by poorly designed decentralization programmes focused on individualistic interests, such as those of the ruling elites.

Short of proper checks and balances (accountability and monitoring), decentralization can end up as little more than a shift of power and resources to the local level through decentralized 'institutions' or through 'central-local' linkages for the sole benefit of local elites, as witnessed in Kenya, Nigeria and Zimbabwe, where central authorities have maintained control through decentralized organs. That decentralization in these countries was largely unsuccessful cannot come as a surprise. For three decades in Nigeria, the military have been using local government to exercise power through 'local bosses' and agencies for patronage purposes. In Kenya and Zimbabwe, the central government is also focused on maintaining power at the local level as individual departments have been mostly de-concentrated to the lower levels. In Kenya, local members of Parliament have been working together with president-appointed district commissioners to make decisions at the local level regarding development and resources. In the end, decisions have been made around patronage systems and district authorities have been used by the centre to consolidate power at the local level. In Kenya, political coalitions have been the routine for some time. These coalitions are composed of ethnic groups who cannot garner enough votes on their own and need the support of other tribes to increase their constituency base. Smaller tribes, communities or clans have often managed to gain political ground by forming coalitions with others. But then the strength of tribal identity is such that many Kenyans are unclear what a 'nation' is about. Identities as defined by *'us* and *them'* are as solid as those based on blood and kinship. This is one of the major underlying factors that enable Kenyan political parties to seek definitions that are more embedded in tribal identity than in general values or principles.

An important post-independence political trend is the general move away from life-term African presidencies as,

▲
IDPs at Jamhuri ground, Nairobi, after the 2008 presidential poll. **©Allan Gichigi/IRIN**

BOX 1.3: **THE POLITICS OF DECENTRALISATION AND SUSTAINABLE CITIES**

Delegates arriving for the 22nd Session of the Governing Council of UN-HABITAT (GC 22). **©IISD Reporting Services (www.iisd.ca)**

As a follow-up to its landmark 1996 conference in Istanbul, UN-HABITAT has engaged key *Habitat Agenda* partners in dialogues on decentralization and improved delivery of basic services for the sake of sustainable urbanisation. In 1998/99, UN-HABITAT took the lead with a first draft of the *World Charter of Local Self-Government*, an international framework modeled on its European namesake setting out the rights and responsibilities of local authorities in connection with the *Habitat Agenda*.

Despite the 1996 call for more decentralized and participatory governance, no rapid consensus emerged as the draft *World Charter* was considered too ambitious or too inflexible for different national, socio-economic and historical backgrounds and conditions. In 2001, member states gave UN-HABITAT a mandate to reconcile antagonistic views. Some agreed that an international agreement would facilitate the implementation of the *Habitat Agenda,* but insisted on the need to adjust to different types of constitutional settings. Opponents felt that anything too formal was inappropriate and that any *World Charter* must be a mere declaration of principles in support of the ongoing 'Istanbul+5' process.

Many countries around the world continued the search for viable decentralization options to improve local democracy and delivery of basic urban services. Experience shows that it takes a lot more than just political will for decentralization to succeed. A range of actions are required at several levels, including improving public accountability and political management through promotion of democratic and participatory decision-making arrangements, as well as enhancing the legitimacy and effectiveness of sub-national tiers of government through legal and fiscal reforms and capacity development.

In 2002, UN-HABITAT commissioned a report on emerging decentralization trends, which was discussed with partners at the first World Urban Forum. Partners re-affirmed the potential for decentralization to strengthen local authorities and anchor democracy in developing and transition countries; they also argued that a determining factor for effective decentralization is the involvement of central government in the process. With local empowerment an essential building block of national and sub-national democracy, decentralization becomes a key element for democratic governance, economic growth and sustainable development at the local, national and international scales.

In 2003, the UN-HABITAT Governing Council endorsed a proposal to create an Advisory Group of Experts on Decentralization (AGRED) in order to (i) examine and review existing policies and decentralization legislation; (ii) develop principles and recommendations; and (iii) document best practice. In 2005, the Governing Council also requested UN-HABITAT to identify a number of underlying principles governing access to basic services for all and for the sake of sustainable human settlements, as they contribute to human dignity, quality of life and sustainable livelihoods. The task was given over to a separate working group of partners and experts, taking into account the discussions held at the second World Urban Forum in 2004 regarding "access to basic services for all: towards an international declaration on partnerships." Both processes were conducted in a parallel but complementary manner, as decentralization and strengthening local authority capacity has the potential to improve delivery of basic services, infrastructure and local development. With AGRED and Working Group support, UN-HABITAT developed two sets of principles derived from existing policies regulations and frameworks.

The *International Guidelines on Decentralization and Strengthening of Local Authorities* and the *International Guidelines on Access to Basic Services* were adopted by the Governing Council in 2007 and 2009, respectively. These guidelines are designed to assist policy reforms and legislation at the country level, and represent a significant milestone in UN-HABITAT efforts to mobilize and partner with the international community and member states. The guidelines can be accessed at http://www.unhabitat.org/pmss/pmss/electronic_books/2613_alt.pdf.

BOX 1.4: UN-HABITAT'S INTERNATIONAL GUIDELINES ON DECENTRALIZATION: AN OVERVIEW

▲
Delegates at the World Urban Forum in 2010. **©UN-HABITAT**

Decentralization complements democratic governance, and together they support sustainable development at all levels. UN-HABITAT emphasizes the need to strengthen local authorities and sub-national tiers of government, which are considered as the 'closest partners' of national governments in the implementation of the *Habitat Agenda*, the major outcome of the 1996 Habitat II Istanbul Conference.

At the end of a process involving normative work and consensus building at the global level, the UN-HABITAT Governing Council approved in 2007 a set of *International Guidelines on Decentralisation and Strengthening of Local Authorities* in order to promote good governance and strengthen local authorities.

The Guidelines include four main sections: (i) the principles of 'governance and democracy at the local level'; (ii) the 'powers and responsibilities of local authorities'; (iii) 'administrative relations between local authorities and other spheres of government"'; and (iv) the 'financial resources and capacities of local authorities'. They set out a number of basic rules underlying democratic governance, including representative and participatory democracy/decision-making, citizen empowerment and building the capacity of local government. The Guidelines also advise politicians and local authority officials to "discharge their tasks with a sense of responsibility and accountability. At all times, they should maintain a high degree of transparency."

The Guidelines highlight the principle of subsidiarity as the 'rationale underlying the process of decentralisation'. Subsidiarity promotes separation of powers and is closely related to the principle of 'proportionality'. While decision-making should be as close to the citizen as possible, decisions of public interest should be taken at the level where they can best be carried out; the Guidelines call for increases not just in local authority functions, but also in the capacity 'to exercise those functions.'

Local governments do not operate in isolation. They do so in a multi-level system of governance within which they should have autonomy while cooperating with other tiers of government. It is imperative for decentralized systems of governance to recognize the significant role played by local authorities at the sub-national level. This is why the Guidelines call for formal recognition of local authorities in national legislation (and, where possible, in the constitution) as autonomous sub-national entities with the potential to contribute to national planning and development. They further recommend that laws provide for clear and equitable sharing of powers and responsibilities, whereby the powers entrusted to sub-national tiers of government should be commensurate with the financial resources made available to facilitate the delivery of expected services. The Republic of Kenya is a case in point, with the 2010 Constitution introducing a new devolved government based on a bicameral Parliament including a National Assembly representing the interests of the people at the constituency level, and a Senate representing county authorities.

The Guidelines emphasize the importance of local autonomy, with a number of provisions enabling local authorities to fulfill their tasks and maintain their autonomy, even where grants are transferred from central government. This represents a major boost for local democracy, as this institutional framework is conducive to balanced national development. In a decentralized system of governance, it is important for the management of public finances to be based on principles of openness and accountability, including public participation, equitable distribution of national revenue and powers of taxation.

Following the adoption of the Guidelines by United Nations Member States, the next stage is to have them endorsed and implemented in individual countries, adapting them to the various local conditions with one single objective, i.e., improved urban policies and delivery of basic urban services. In this regard, UN-HABITAT makes three major recommendations (i) advocacy and partnerships at national level; (ii) capacity development; and (iii) monitoring and reporting on progress.

Source: Alain Kanyinda, UN-HABITAT.

▲
Dandora Municipal Dumping Site. ©**Julius Mwelu/IRIN**

since the early 1990s, several long-serving African leaders have been removed from office by dint of democratic polls. Significant structural governance and electoral reforms have also been achieved in many African nations and, today, despite the persistence of some volatile or even violent countries, politics in the region has generally become more pacified and institutionalized.[14] Political awareness is also improving, with far better grassroots recognition of the linkages between due political process, on the one hand, and, for instance, the price of public transport commutes or staple foods, on the other.

Grassroots support for democracy is generally high in Africa. An average 62 per cent of the population in 18 African countries now supports democratic regimes over other forms of government,[15] with support as high as 75 per cent in Ghana, Kenya and Senegal. In a related development, five in every six Africans now oppose traditional authoritarian rule. Nevertheless, it is important to acknowledge that elections *per se* do neither directly nor necessarily result in improved governance, socio-economic development, full political participation or peace and stability. Sometimes, democratic elections do not substitute for authoritarian rule and may also fail to lead to any change of power. As recently witnessed in Kenya and Zimbabwe, disputed election outcomes can lead to compromises, such as national union governments with the incumbent president remaining in power and the contending presidential candidate joining the government in a secondary power position. Moreover, massive election fraud, malpractice and other electoral irregularities are still rife in several African nations, and recent history has shown that these can easily result in protest, violence, displacement, bloodshed and loss of human life.

In the long run, however, democratic regimes are more likely to bring internal peace, even though the transition can be difficult, as seen in Burkina Faso, Mozambique and Nigeria where democratization came associated with widespread violence. Prevention of election-related conflict and violence requires well-established and widely accepted electoral structures and clear procedures that provide for impartial guidance and mediation in case of disputes over election outcomes. In Mozambique, for example, opposition parties have challenged the returns of three presidential and parliamentary polls with claims of fraud.[16] Dozens of protesters died in violent demonstrations triggered by official ballot returns in 1999. Likewise, following suspected fraud during a 2004 mayoral by-election, violence erupted once more in Mozambique.[17] In Kenya, the 2008 presidential poll led to widespread violence, deaths and displacement for hundreds of thousands due to alleged fraud and a disputed election result. The violence in Mozambique and Kenya could have been avoided if formal and objective redress procedures with legally binding enforcement mechanisms had been in place. However, these particular aspects of statehood building and constitutional definition had not yet been established, suggesting once more that establishing a genuine democracy takes more than just going to the polls.

In many other African countries, a variety of polls have been widely considered as transparent, free and fair, such as for instance in Ghana. That particular success was largely due to the establishment of an Electoral Commission that has strengthened democratic procedure through a code of conduct for political parties and investigation of complaints where they arise. While these institutions have provided effective checks and balances resulting in fair elections, they remain incomplete for lack of legal and binding enforcement mechanisms. Parliaments and civil society should generally be given a role in the appointment of electoral commissions, and widely accepted codes of conduct should ensure fair elections and lower degrees of related violence.[18]

Broad-based civil society, pro-governance and pro-democracy movements are increasingly prominent in Africa and help make governance more accountable. Many political organizations are now challenging undemocratic practices and/or human rights violations. They campaign for good governance, monitor government budgets, expose corruption and promote conflict resolution.[19] Civil society has been an important factor in improved urban governance and curbing corruption across Africa, including in Burkina Faso, Mali, the Republic of South Africa and Uganda.

Bamako provides a good example of positive civil society engagement in urban governance and poverty reduction. Prior to launch in the year 2000, the Malian capital made sure that all stakeholders were involved in the strategic planning for and preparation of the City Development Strategy. This was particularly the case with regard to the informal sector, which makes up a large part of the urban economy and whose needs for urban development had to be taken into account. Through a pro-poor approach, the municipality was able to define a shared vision and identify the main objectives of the implementation strategy.

The democratic inclusion of all stakeholders in decision-making is critical to the success of any decentralization reform.[20] In the Republic of South Africa, the constitution effectively makes participation mandatory as it spells out the duties and developmental responsibilities of local government in 'democracy, service delivery, economic and social development, environmental protection, community participation, poverty alleviation and integrated cooperation.'[21] Backed by this clear democratic mandate for pro-poor development,[22] South African local authorities have taken to extending service delivery and development to many previously marginalized communities. At the municipal level, access to water supply, for instance, soared from 59 per cent in 1994 to 86 per cent of the population in just over a decade, while access to sanitation increased by 30 per cent for all households. Over the same time period, access to electricity increased from 30 per cent in 1994 to 73 per cent in 2006/07.[23]

Decentralization can strengthen democracy with elements of good governance like participation, tolerance, political openness and respect for cultural, human and gender rights. Decentralization also has a major role to play in bringing government and governance closer to the people.

Decentralization

Decentralization is broadly defined as the transfer of responsibilities for planning, management and financing from the central to lower tiers of government and other subsidiary levels of authority. There are two aspects to decentralization: political and administrative.

Political decentralization grants citizens and elected officials increased decision-making capacities, particularly in policy development and implementation. The rationale behind political decentralization lies in proximity: locally elected officials are better positioned to respond to the needs of communities than national authorities, while communities have better access to elected representatives[24] that are responsible for local-level decisions. Decentralization typically allows for improved delivery of essential services such as safe water, sanitation and waste management, energy, transportation, health and education.

The most widespread forms of administrative decentralization are devolution, delegation and deconcentration (see Box 1.5 for World Bank definitions[25]).

In today's Africa, administrative decentralization often comes under hybrid forms, combining elements of both delegation and deconcentration, but practice varies widely across the continent.[26] Some countries are committed to political devolution, like Uganda, the Republic of South Africa and Zambia, while others emphasize deconcentration of administrative authority, like Côte d'Ivoire and Kenya. Yet others focus on both devolution and deconcentration, like Botswana, Ghana and Mozambique. In the latter cases, reform has been slow due to constant legislative change that has prevented full delegation of political power to subsidiary levels.

Decentralization and citizen participation are complementary and should happen together. Clearly defined

BOX 1.5: DECONCENTRATION, DELEGATION AND DEVOLUTION: HOW DIFFERENT ARE THEY?

Deconcentration is often considered the weakest form of decentralization and most frequently occurs in unitary states. It consists in a redistribution of decision-making, financial and management responsibilities among various tiers of national government. This process can (and often does) merely shift responsibilities from central government in the capital city to regions, states/provinces or districts. Alternatively, deconcentration can create field administration or local administrative capacity under the supervision of central government departments.

Delegation is a more extensive form of decentralization. Through delegation, responsibility for decision-making and administration of public functions is transferred by central government to semi-autonomous entities that are not under its full control but are ultimately accountable to it. Governments delegate responsibilities when they set up public enterprises or corporations, housing or transportation authorities, special service or semi-autonomous school districts, regional development corporations or special project implementation units. These organizations typically enjoy a great deal of discretionary decision-making. They may be exempt from regular civil service constraints and may be able to charge users directly for services delivered.

Devolution This refers to transfers of central government authority for decision-making, finance and management to quasi-autonomous local authorities with corporate status. Responsibilities for services are devolved to municipal authorities that elect their own mayors and councils, raise their own revenues, and can freely decide on capital expenditures. In a devolved system, local authorities are assigned clear and legally recognized geographical and functional boundaries over which they exercise authority and within which they perform public functions. This is the type of administrative pattern underlying most decentralized political structures today.

www1.worldbank.org/publicsector/decentralization/admin.htm

BOX 1.6: CITIES AND CONFLICT: A 'DECENTRALIZATION' OF SORTS

Throughout history, cities have played significant roles in conflicts, both as safe havens and bases for attack. In recent years, conflict trends have changed with notable declines in interstate and civil war incidence, but with a higher frequency of civic violence, since urban areas are increasingly where various forms of violence - including terrorist attacks - are emerging along the often hazy boundary between criminal activities and political positioning for control. Vying for control can be both the cause and the result of conflict; but the near-inevitable outcome in either case is that central government domination diminishes when local urban stakeholders take centre stage in the national or sub-national competition for political control and access to resources. Admittedly, this cannot be taken as a positive type of decentralization.

As they become more integrated in the world economy and their populations keep expanding, cities are increasingly drawn into important roles in the domestic economy and in governance. They become the primary localities where matters of control and exclusion are determined. With the growing importance of cities as national centres of political and economic power - hosting wealth and extreme poverty side by side - contests over political leverage and access to resources today tend to unfold in multi-layered, city-based civic conflicts.

Consequently, Africa almost always features a dynamic tension between cities and the state that can become particularly strong in conflict and post-conflict situations, when antagonistic claims for sovereignty and control tend to shape political and economic agendas at the national and local levels. The relationships between these various tiers of governance make these tensions palpable. Some African cities, for a host of historic and more recent political reasons, have become separate jurisdictional entities,[34] adding further complexities to the already overloaded urban development and governance agendas of African cities - whether in violent conflict or not. The outcome is that several African capitals (as well as some large non-capital cities) have become self-contained politico-economic concentrations that are divorced from the remainder of the nation. They operate in an environment of formal and informal economies, largely outside the regulatory purview of a state framework, and no longer serve as centres of national political activity. Prime examples of such isolated African cities are Kinshasa, Luanda, and Mogadishu.

urban management practices and institutions are a pre-condition for effective decentralization. Political and fiscal decentralization should always go hand in hand and come together, if municipal authorities are to be in a position to back up decisions with revenue-raising capabilities. Now, many countries are found lagging on fiscal decentralization. This is because they often saw administrative decentralization as an opportunity to hand over problems to lower tiers of authority, without disbursing the funds required to address them. This is why decentralization has been far from uniformly effective across Africa.

Democratic politics and state-of-the-art urban planning theory together posit that active citizenship has intrinsic value and better policies and implementation result when communities are involved. Increased participation in decision-making has indeed brought peace to previously tense environments. However, cultural, ethnic and historical factors have also influenced the ways in which countries have implemented reform. In much of sub-Saharan Africa, decision-making has been only consultative rather than genuinely participatory, with the attendant lack of effective impact. The fact of the matter is, a number of African countries have experienced increased tension or little significant change as outcome result of decentralization.

Conversely, Ghana, the Republic of South Africa and West Africa as a whole have claimed that decentralization had been a success as far as they were concerned. In Francophone West Africa, authorities resort to widely publicized public hearings to give people opportunities to object to or agree on draft master or sub-division plans. While enhancing awareness and participation, these hearings are often mere platforms for antagonistic organizational and individual interests to express their views, with public authorities left to take ultimate decisions.[27]

In the Republic of South Africa, the 1996 Constitution acknowledges the autonomy of local authorities, including their revenue-generating powers. The Government of South Africa[28] refers to this autonomous authority as 'developmental local government' that in practice is mandated to 'work with citizens and groups within the community to find sustainable ways to meet their social, economic and material needs and improve the quality of their lives.'[29] Citizens and community groups are now involved in the planning and delivery of basic urban services in South African cities. Likewise in Ghana, citizens' rights are fully protected under the constitution.[30] Institutions are strong and citizens are allowed to participate through parliament, district assemblies and civil society organizations.

Elsewhere in Western Africa, as governments withdrew from basic urban service provision in the wake of 'structural adjustment programmes', urban communities in Burkina Faso, Mali and Senegal took it upon themselves to become involved in urban management. A number of non-governmental and community-based organizations were created to meet the new challenges. Recently, Guinea, Mali and Senegal have prepared local participation planning guides to help better collaboration between communities and local authorities.

In a bid to determine the effect of decentralization on poverty reduction, a survey[31] has ranked them into the following four categories: 'positive', 'somewhat positive', 'negative', and 'somewhat negative'. Only South Africa and Ghana fell in the 'somewhat positive' and 'positive' categories. More than two-thirds of the countries surveyed fell in the 'negative' and 'somewhat negative' categories. In the negative categories, the following countries were reported to be worse off with decentralization: Burkina Faso, Egypt, Ethiopia, Guinea, Malawi, Mozambique and Uganda.[32] This is because in these countries, the process has been flawed as policies were chosen by default rather than design. The survey has identified three major factors for successful decentralization as: (a) adequate financial and human resources; (b) political will at national level; and (c) international/donor support. On the other hand, the survey pinpointed two major pitfalls: (a) non-transparent processes, where information flows between central and local government and civil society; and (b) limited popular participation, typically confined to elections only.

The results of the survey reiterate that decentralization should respond to the specific practical needs of a country, rather than replicate schemes that have taken place elsewhere. While decentralization should be generally encouraged for the sake of a healthy democracy, the particular approach a government goes for will largely determine how sustainable that healthy democracy is to be.

Decentralization has a significant role to play in the proper management of African cities, and can even help prevent conflict, as illustrated in Box 1.6. Africa has seen widespread urban governance reform, and it is important to realise that strong institutions should be complemented with both multi-party systems and a participating civil society. Communities should be empowered and the relationship between them and local government should be strengthened through legislation. UN-HABITAT has researched how decentralization reforms can lead to local economic development, promoting grassroots participation and improving service delivery. The findings reveal that so far, very little actual power has been decentralized to local communities and, in cases where the devolvement of power has been entrenched in newly drafted constitutions, any emphasis has been at the regional rather than the local level.[33]

BOX 1.7: **SMALL PLANNING DECISIONS, LARGE ENVIRONMENTAL EFFECTS**

▲
A roadside kiosk in Nairobi, Kenya. **©Sserwanga/MJS**

One example of a very frequent local intervention with unintended impacts is the clearance of roadside vending kiosks in African cities. These kiosks are often removed because they may be illegally occupying road reserves, be considered unsightly or otherwise be declared undesirable. This is ignoring that urban roadside kiosks provide numerous selling points for daily necessities like bread, milk, soap or washing powder. Their removal does not only deprive a low-income family of its livelihood, it also takes away from the neighbourhood a convenient small retail outlet. The alternative is to drive to down-town or peripheral shopping malls, which contributes to traffic congestion, air pollution and fossil fuel use. This goes to show that seemingly minor or inconsequential planning decisions can have direct impacts on environmental sustainability, and urban planners should become more aware of the true impacts of even minor decisions.

Cities and Climate Change[35]

Urban areas worldwide are facing a number of climate-related threats, varying from sea level rise and flood risks to future food and water insecurity. Climate change already causes significant numbers of disasters in cities since these are particularly vulnerable because of their high concentrations of population and productive assets.

Admittedly, the world's urban areas today consume a majority share of global resources while also generating the bulk of greenhouse gas emissions. This does not make cities the chief environmental culprits, though. Cities are indeed responsible for the lion's share of global consumption, greenhouse gases and waste production, but they do so because collectively they accommodate the majority of the world's population. Moreover, cities also fulfill a host of functions that go way beyond local geographic conditions. Cities are drivers of economic and social well-being for entire nations and many even play roles across national borders. It is precisely because cities are home to both inherently positive and negative externalities that they can make a unique contribution to global climate-change resilience, adaptation and protection. Local authorities hold mandates that are the key to cost-effective climate change responses, including land use planning, functional zoning, or water and waste management. The local level also provides the best locus to experiment with, and learn from, innovative governance on a relatively small scale. Cities are best placed to develop solutions that are adapted to often very specific local conditions and consistent with local priorities. At the same time, local success stories also have the potential to inform regional and national adaptation and mitigation approaches.

It is particularly important to understand that the manner in which cities are developed today will have impacts on future options for climate change resilience. For instance, depending on the nature of urban spatial planning decisions, demographic expansion can cause significant environmental inefficiencies and ecologically unfriendly spatial configurations. Spatial separation of related urban functions, such as residential areas, on the one hand, and work, schooling or shopping facilities, on the other, can dramatically increase urban transportation demand and contribute to carbon emissions from private vehicle use. Such a spatial structure is evident among many of the world's metropolitan areas, including in Africa. For instance, ***Cape Town*** in the Republic of South Africa has grown into a city region with a 100 km commuting radius. The resulting ecological footprint requires a land mass equal to the size of Greece to provide for the needs and process the wastes.[36] Similar patterns are found in ***Cairo, Dar es Salaam, Kinshasa, Lagos, Nairobi*** or just about any other large metropolitan area in Africa.

Urban planning involves large, long-term capital expenditure requirements in real estate, infrastructures and other public and private assets; therefore, a city will have to live with *any* urban planning decision for many years, whether or not it is conducive to long-term climate resilience. All the urban planning decisions made today will have an impact on the way infrastructure, economic activity, population and poverty are geographically distributed. These decisions may either exacerbate or restrict exposure and vulnerability to the growing threats of climate change. Consequently, there can be benefits in pro-active, forward-looking climate change-sensitive urban planning through spatial decisions and land-use management that take into account any and all likely future impacts, whether intended or unintended.

However, forward-looking and well-thought out climate change-sensitive spatial planning is not enough on its own. For effective adaptation strategies, it is also important to explore the linkages between national, regional and local policies to address climate change. Given the inherent limitations and strengths associated with each level of governance, multi-level approaches are invariably the most promising way forward, because they tend better to recognize opportunities for both vertical and horizontal cooperation, and can promote the involvement of a wide range of private-sector and non-governmental entities at the local level.

The vertical component of multi-level governance is especially important since national governments cannot effectively implement a national climate strategy without working closely with local authorities acting as their agents of change. Conversely, cities and local communities cannot be effective if they do not interact with all levels of government, as they often lack the authority, the resources or capacities to take action on their own. Nevertheless, cities and local communities are well-positioned to help develop policy and programmatic solutions that best meet specific local conditions. Active involvement of all interested public and private urban stakeholders will, therefore, be essential in the design and delivery of timely and cost-effective adaptation policies. Empowering local authorities would enable national policies to leverage existing local experiments, accelerate policy responses, mobilize more resources and engage local stakeholders.

Understanding climate change in the local context can highlight opportunities to maximize the crucial roles of local stakeholders and the benefits of mitigation and adaptation action, which in turn can facilitate political acceptance of often difficult decisions regarding climate change. Prior to that, it is essential, for experts and local stakeholders (including local government) to build a shared understanding about the way climate change may affect local development choices, and how those choices in turn can affect future climate patterns.

A priority for national governments is to encourage urban policy networks, and the engagement of regional and local non-governmental stakeholders in policy processes, in order to deepen knowledge as well as develop and implement strategies for mitigation and adaptation that resonate from the bottom up. This would put local authorities in a better position to shape social norms and review different possible urban forms and their interface with climate change. The aim is to allow for systemic changes in urban planning and development and cause behaviour change generate climate resilient, low-carbon economic growth.

Experience shows that climate change policies are modeled after three main institutional patterns, as follows:

(a) Government-led, top-down enabling frameworks: national policy steers local or regional authorities to take climate change into account at the local level. The frameworks deployed by central government can include national mandates that leave wide latitude for local authorities to shape policies on climate change in order to fit local conditions and circumstances.
(b) Locally-led, bottom-up action: learning and experience acquired through autonomous local initiatives inform and steer policymaking at higher levels of government.
(c) Hybrid models: central government provides enabling frameworks but gives local authorities enough discretion to tailor-make initiatives on the ground, and higher tiers of government can subsequently replicate best local practice on a broader scale.

Additionally, it is important to realise that - unlike municipal approaches to climate change mitigation and adaptation - regional approaches, due to their scale, are generally in a better position to bring about structural change, thanks to superior technical and financial capacities and environmental expertise. Regions can also develop strategies to link policies and programmes that would otherwise operate in isolation, e.g., connecting initiatives between urban and rural areas or across multiple adjacent municipal authorities.

Promoting participatory governance with regard to climate change across *all* levels of government and relevant stakeholders is crucial if policy gaps are to be prevented between local action plans and national policy frameworks (vertical integration) and if (horizontal) cross-scale learning between relevant departments or institutions in local and regional governments is to be encouraged. Vertical and horizontal integration brings two-way benefits: locally-led (or 'bottom-up'), where local initiatives influence national action; and nationally-led (or 'top-down'), where enabling frameworks empower local stakeholders. The most promising frameworks combine the two into hybrid models of policy dialogue, where any lessons learnt are brought to bear on enabling frameworks and are disseminated horizontally, in the process achieving more efficient local implementation of climate change strategies.

1.4 Public and Private Financing for Urban Housing and Infrastructure

Current finance for urban housing and infrastructure is inadequate both in terms of capital resources and of lending policies and conditions compared with the types of income and borrowing capacity of the large majority of Africa's urban populations. This inadequacy is only compounded by the rapid demographic expansion of cities in sub-Saharan Africa. This section reviews the current patterns of urban expansion, infrastructure and housing, as well as opportunities for future improvement.

Urban Growth Patterns

Although urban demographic growth is generally considered a positive force for economic development, very rapid urbanisation *can* pose great challenges for urban economies, particularly with regard to infrastructure and services. In no other region of the world today is urbanisation more sustained, but urban economic growth more sluggish, than in Africa. From 2010 to 2030, Africa's urban population is projected to grow about 45 per cent faster than the total for the region. By 2030, almost half of the African population will be living in areas classified as urban, and this share is projected to increase to well over 60 per cent by 2050 (See Table 1.2).

The Impact of Urban Growth on Housing and Infrastructure

Demographic expansion in African cities has created and will continue to create serious challenges in terms of affordable housing and water supply, transportation, waste collection and disposal, and controlling air and water pollution.[37]

For years, a number of troublesome forces have accompanied the process of rapid urbanisation in Africa. Municipalities have not been structured to cope with extremely fast-growing populations, and particularly migration to urban areas of large numbers of unskilled labour. Existing municipal revenue and finance-generating structures fall well short of the capital expenditures which upgrading or extension of infrastructure would require. Municipalities cannot afford investments in housing construction schemes, either; those central and local governments who tried this on an extensive scale in sub-Saharan Africa between 1970 and 1990 found that matching housing supply with population growth was the road to bankruptcy. Private sector investment in infrastructure is limited and typically focuses only on the largest economies, e.g. the Republic of South Africa. Any formal housing finance offered by local banks reaches only the top 15-20th income deciles of the population, partly because formal land titles and secure tenure are not available to the majority of urban populations. Informal housing finance is limited in size and cannot accommodate the vast potential demand. Finally, because much urban land use and investment in property is informal, municipalities lack a broad property tax base which could pay for urban infrastructure and neighbourhood improvement, a point to be discussed further in Section 1.5.

Municipal Investment in Infrastructure and Housing

Municipal investment in urban infrastructure has been uneven across Africa, but generally lags the needs of ever-growing urban populations. As discussed further in Section 1.5, municipal revenue collection is often inefficient, while

TABLE 1.2: **SUB-SAHARAN POPULATION GROWTH - 1990-2030**

Sub-Saharan Africa	2010*	2030*	2050*	% Growth 2010-2030*	% Growth 2030-2050*
Total population	866,948	1,308,461	1,760,724	150	135
Urban Population	323,525	630,351	1,064,736	195	169
Urban % of Total	37.3	48.2	60.5		

**Projections*
Source: World Urbanisation Prospects, The 2009 Revision, DESA, United Nations, New York, 2010

▲
Kibera, Nairobi. ©**Manoocher Deghati/IRIN**

TABLE 1.3: **PRIVATE SECTOR INVESTMENT IN PRIMARY INFRASTRUCTURE/SERVICES IN SUB-SAHARAN AFRICA (US$ MILLION)**

Investment Year	Energy	Telecom	Transport	Water and Sewerage	Total Investment
1990	40	0	0	0	40
1991	0	0	0	0	0
1992	0	20	0	0	20
1993	0	1	31	0	31
1994	76	553	18	0	647
1995	77	677	63	0	817
1996	744	961	28	20	1,753
1997	754	1,713	469	0	2,936
1998	716	1,150	336	0	2,201
1999	537	1,160	1,087	82	2,867
2000	463	1,460	183	31	2,137
2001	655	2,812	484	3	3,955
2002	484	2,751	101	0	3,335
2003	1,597	3,982	335	9	5,923
2004	240	3,563	187	0	3,990
2005	789	4,565	504	0	5,859
Grand Total	7,171	25,369	3,826	146	36,510

Source: Jerome, A., Private Sector Participation in Infrastructure in Africa, 2008

financial management is in many cases inappropriate. As a result, the financial condition of municipalities is generally weak, with most relying on central government disbursements to top up fiscal shortfalls. Added to this weak financial position is the increasing decentralization of service delivery functions to the local authority level, and continued high centralization of financial resources at the central government level.[38] This has resulted in rapidly increasing urban decay and the proliferation of slums, which accommodated 71.9 per cent of the urban population in sub-Saharan Africa in 2001.[39]

Private Sector Investment in Infrastructure

Sub-Saharan Africa attracted US $36.5 billion in private sector investments between 1990 and 2005. Half of these went to the Republic of South Africa and focused on infrastructure and services (See Table 1.3).

Private Sector Investment in Housing

Land and housing finance markets are rather underdeveloped in Africa's urban areas, with far-reaching impacts on overall urban conditions.

Access to Formal Urban Land

Access to formally surveyed and registered land is often scarce in African cities. Rapid expansion causes concomitant rises in land values in city centres and desirable new neighbourhoods, with scarcity boosting the price of formally registered land in particular. Most African households cannot afford formal urban land ownership, and south of the Sahara the only alternative for them is some form of informal settlement or slum. In addition, among the 28 per cent of the African urban population who do not live in slums, many stay in informal settlements, in non-permanent structures or without proper titles.

Access to Housing Finance

Due to lack of regular or predictable incomes for most city dwellers, and an absence of financial instruments that could adjust accordingly, only 15 per cent or so of Africa's urban population may be eligible for formal housing loans, effectively excluding the remaining 85 per cent.

Primary Loan Instruments: Formal housing finance includes mortgage and construction loans. These are typically offered by commercial banks and building societies, which demand a lien on land (i.e., the right to keep possession until the debt is discharged) or other pledge of property interest, as well as proof of income if a borrower is to be eligible. Savings societies, housing cooperatives and social housing funds also offer housing and home construction loans, typically through local membership schemes.

Secondary Finance for Housing and Construction: Their own funding constraints restrict the types and duration of lending services that banks and building societies can provide. The typical sources are deposits/savings, and borrowing, which can include bond issuance (either corporate or asset-backed, as in mortgage securitization), with the securities sold to pension funds, other banks and corporate institutional investors. In more advanced African economies, several secondary finance alternatives are available for housing and construction. In the Republic of South Africa, mortgage securitization started as early as the 1980s and the United Building Society securitized Rand250 million (or about US $36 million) mortgage loans in 1988.[40] The four major South African banks together hold over 85 per cent of all mortgage loans, accounting for Rand 167.1 billion (US $21.7 billion).[41] Where debt markets are not well developed, banks rely primarily on deposit funding to support housing and construction lending. In Zimbabwe, building societies provide 65 per cent of all mortgage loans, while the formal housing finance sector is very small. In 2007, the total amount disbursed in the formal housing sector in Zimbabwe was a mere US $1.15 million.[42]

Only the strongest financial institutions have access to foreign sources of funding and the ability to manage attendant exchange rate fluctuations. Even those institutions often lack access to long-term secondary financing sources, which restricts the maturities they can offer borrowers for construction or home loans. In addition, central banks or bank regulators typically restrict lending in the housing sector to formal mortgage finance, since it is secured by a formally registered lien on property.

Some African governments play a very important role in the financing of low-income housing. The Republic of South Africa, for instance, operates large-scale housing subsidy programmes for the lower-middle and low-income segments of the population. The broad-ranging subsidies are granted for individual ownership, rental and social housing subsidies, as well as for projects and institutions; the poorer receive full subsidies, while lower-middle income groups receive partial subsidies. Between 1994 and 2004 in South Africa, government-sponsored housing finance provided 2.4 million subsidies and facilitated access to ownership for more than seven million people.[43]

Informal Housing Finance

The vast majority of Africa's urban poor have no access to any formal financial instruments, and no alternative but to finance their houses through informal mechanisms. These include mainly personal savings, small loans from relatives, friends or microfinance institutions, or through incremental building. Short of access to these, renting is the only available alternative, often at highly inflated prices for poor quality shelter, which adds to the vicious spiral of poverty, unsanitary living conditions and lack of opportunity to climb the social ladder. The poor are denied access to formal housing finance due to lack of collateral resulting from the quality and/or legal status of their housing, limited incomes or uncertain employment status.

Prospects for Improvements

Potential improvements to Africa's current housing finance system include the following:

1. Reform of land regulations, property rights and land markets must allow private ownership, leasehold and transactions on open land markets;
2. Stronger tax bases for municipalities, putting them in a better position to borrow and access capital markets;
3. Encouraging greater private investment and finance in urban infrastructure and services, whether through guarantee schemes, creation of separate entities with service-fee revenue bases, or a combination of the above, including public-private partnerships with international financial institutions and private operators and/or investors;
4. Promotion of housing finance through microfinance institutions and housing cooperatives who know how to reach out to low-income urban communities and whose strong repayment record can attract private and donor funding;
5. Financial regulation *must* allow for a broader range of housing finance instruments, including those tailored to informal incomes;
6. Support for increased secondary finance for housing micro-loans and community projects;
7. More resources for well-designed government subsidy programmes (taking inspiration from foreign best practice (such as Chile's *Ahorro, bueno, credito* programmes, the Sofales experience in Mexico, current subsidy programmes for the urban poor in Indonesia, etc.); and
8. Promoting access by the poor to microfinance services, including loans for housing, construction materials, water and sanitation.

1.5
Local Authority Finance

Across the world, public finance for urban infrastructures and service delivery typically accrues from municipal tax revenues, user fees and government transfers. For many African municipalities, property tax is the major source. This is the case, for instance, in ***Nairobi***, where property tax provided 46.9 per cent of total municipal revenue in 1991-1992, compared with as much as 66 per cent in ***Mombasa*** (1975-1984) but only 21.5 per cent in ***Dar es Salaam*** (1996).[44]

Existing Municipal Revenue Sources

Municipal property tax revenues have been increasing in all nine major cities in the Republic of South Africa. They play important roles in ***Cape Town*** (25.5 per cent in 2007/08), ***Tshwane*** (more than 25 per cent in 2007/08) and ***eThekwini*** (30 per cent in 2007/08)[45] (see Graph 1.3).

In Somalia, the share of property tax in municipal revenues varies between 28 per cent in ***Hargeisa*** and barely 4 per cent in ***Berbera*** (see Graph 1.4).

In some African cities, user fees and service charges overtake property tax as major sources of municipal revenues. This is the case in all municipalities in the Republic of South Africa, where these revenues (2007-2008) were more than double those of property tax (Graph 1.3).[46] In ***Nairobi***, fees and service charges accounted for 46.7 per cent of total municipal revenue in 1996-1997.[47]

Transfers from higher government tiers are another important source of municipal resources. In the Republic of South Africa, these are the second largest contributor to municipal funding, accounting for 22.4 per cent of the total in 2007-2008, compared with 30 per cent in ***Nairobi.*** In contrast, the contribution of government transfers was 61 and 81 per cent in ***Accra*** and ***Cairo*** respectively (2008). However, in Somalia, inter-governmental transfers are almost negligible, reflecting the nation's almost complete lack of central government authority. Virtually all Somali municipal revenues are generated by the municipalities themselves, with commodity taxes and market fees the dominating sources of income.

▲
Cape Town City Hall. **©Squareplum/Shutterstock**

GRAPH 1.3: **SHARE OF PROPERTY TAX IN MUNICIPAL REVENUE, SOUTH AFRICAN CITIES (%)**

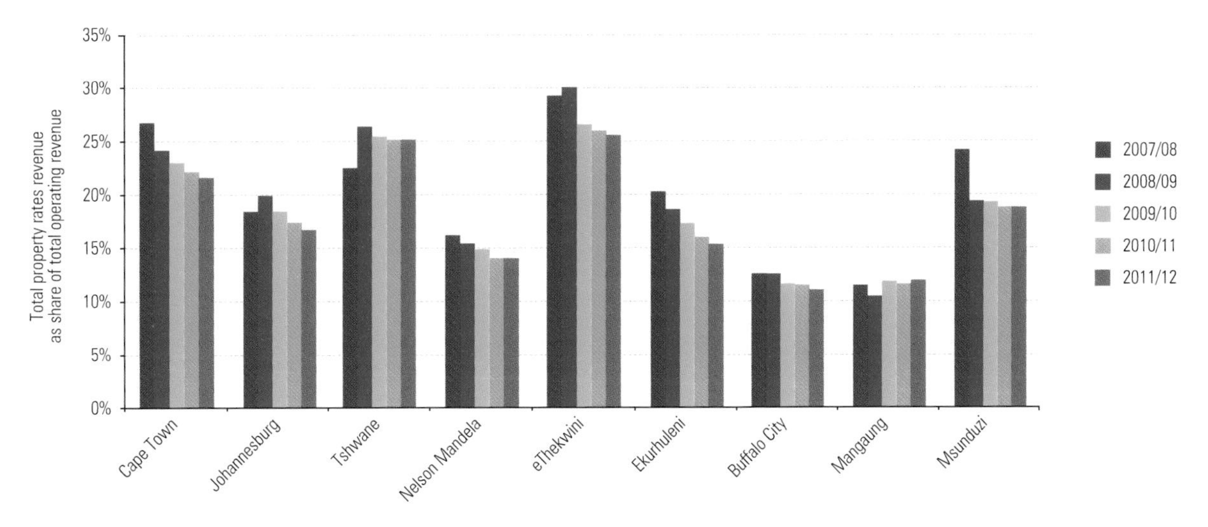

Source: PDG and Isandla Institute, 2009, Municipal Rates Policies and the Urban Poor, Johannesburg: South African Cities Network

GRAPH 1.4: **SOURCES OF MUNICIPAL REVENUE IN HARGEISA AND BERBERA, SOMALIA, 2009**

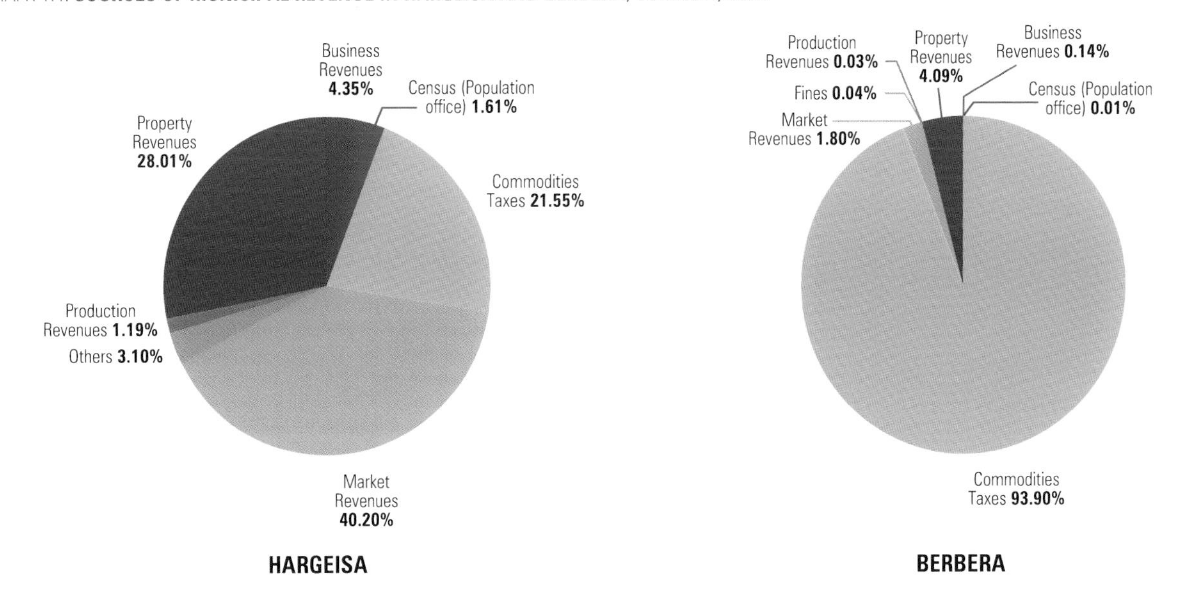

Source: UN-HABITAT Somalia Survey 2007

TABLE 1.4: **LOCAL GOVERNMENT REVENUE, TANZANIA, 2002-2005/06 (MILLION SHILLINGS)**

	2002	%	2003*	%	2004/05	%	2005/06	%
Transfers	247,027	81.0	313.873	86.5	386,768	89.9	452,831	89.9
Own-source revenues	57,740	18.9	48,344	13.0	42,871	10.0	49,291	9.8
Local borrowing	225	0.1	443	0.1	549	0.1	1,496	0.3
Total	304,993		362,659		430,188		503,618	

** Prior to 2004, revenue collections were reported based on calendar not fiscal years*
Source: Venkatachalam P (2009), Overview of Municipal Finance Systems in Dar es Salaam, Tanzania, London: LSE

GRAPH 1.5: **SERVICE CHARGE AND PROPERTY TAX REVENUES IN SOUTH AFRICAN CITIES, 2009-2010**

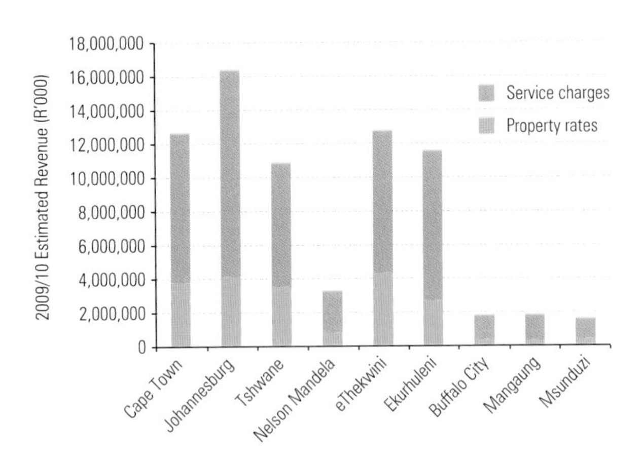

Source: PDG and Isandla Institute, 2009, Municipal Rates Policies and the Urban Poor, Johannesburg, SACN

GRAPH 1.6: **LOCAL AUTHORITY SPENDING IN SELECTED AFRICAN COUNTRIES (COMPARED WITH UK. 2003)**

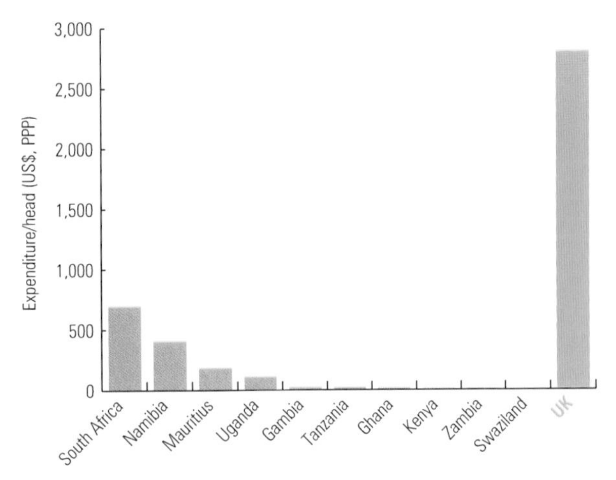

Source: Dirie, I, Municipal Finance, Coventry: Commonwealth Local Government Forum, 2005

Central Taxation and Decentralized Services: Funding local authority mandates

The wave of structural adjustment policies in the 1980s and 1990s resulted in widespread decentralization in Africa, where central government took to transferring some responsibilities to local authorities. The general idea behind decentralization was: (a) to enable local authorities to make decisions on public affairs within their jurisdictions; and (b) to improve the efficiency and effectiveness of service delivery and management to the local population.[48] However, effective decentralisation must also extend to financial allocations and powers, allowing local authorities to generate the revenues they need for increased service provision and management. In many cases, though, only the responsibility for service provision and management was decentralised, which led to significant 'vertical' fiscal imbalances. These fiscal imbalances have still not been remedied in many African countries, where decentralization remains largely ineffective as a result. African countries must improve local governments' financial capacities and enhance local resource mobilisation instruments.[49]

This situation does not preclude many municipalities from increasing their own revenue sources, even in the face (in some countries) of central government attempts to strengthen their own control over municipal authorities. For example, in Tanzania, government transfers increased from 81 per cent to 89.9 per cent of total municipal revenue between 2002 and 2005/06, with a concomitant relative decline in local revenue sources (from 18.9 per cent in 2002 to 9.8 per cent in 2005/06). Local authorities virtually have no borrowing powers as shown in Table 1.4). Due to central government control, local authorities often lack real power and in many cases can act only as mere implementation agents.

Those local authorities looking to be of better service to constituents must do what they can to increase their financial capacities. However, cities where property taxes are the main revenue source often unfairly place much of the burden of operational costs on real estate owners. On the other hand, those relying on business taxes may increase the burden on enterprises. Whatever the case, it is important to seek fair revenue generation means, and more diversified sources are a good way of achieving that.

How do Local Governments Cope?

Graph 1.6 highlights the huge expenditure gaps African cities would need to bridge if they were to achieve the standards prevailing in more advanced economies. In the UK in 2003, local authority expenditure per head was an equivalent US $2,798 (PPP). In Africa, the country with the highest local authority resources is the Republic of South Africa, amounting to only about 25 per cent of the UK's. In Swaziland, local governments only spent US $2.3 (PPP) per head in 2003, or less than 1/1,000th of UK spending. African cities such as ***Banjul, Harare*** and ***Windhoek***, to mention a few, receive no central government funding whatsoever, and therefore are left to their own devices. How do they and others cope? Clearly, innovative approaches are called for and some cities indeed are becoming extremely inventive when it comes to closing fiscal gaps.

Local infrastructure and services can be paid for in a number of innovative ways. In ***Harare,*** the main revenue sources are property taxation, business licenses and borrowing. Under its 2010 municipal expenditure plan (US $505 million), Zimbabwe's capital city raised US $230 million (or 45.5 per cent) from property tax, US $102 million (20.2 per cent) from water service charges, US $63 million (12.5 per cent) from water rates; US $25 million (5.0 per cent) from waste collection charges and the remaining 16.8 per cent from fees and charges on other types of services such as vehicle licences, market fees, health fees, etc.[50]

TABLE 1.5: **MAIN MUNICIPAL REVENUE SOURCES IN SOMALIA, 2007 (%)**

Municipality	Commodities Tax	Market Tax	Property Tax	Total
Hargeisa	21.6%	40.2%	28.0%	89.8%
Burao	39.1%	35.1%	19.6%	93.8%
Berbera	93.9%	1.9%	4.1%	99.9%
Borama	37.2%	28.3%	24.6%	90.1%
Erigavo	55.4%	14.1%	14.1%	83.6%
Lasanod	41.8%	8.0%	9.9%	59.7%
Average	48.2%	21.2%	16.7%	86.2%

Source: UN-HABITAT Somalia Survey 2007

Windhoek, the capital of Namibia, has more decentralized responsibilities than any other city in the country, but does not benefit from either VAT and/or central tax collection within its boundaries. Therefore, the city charges fees for all the services it provides. Its largest revenue sources in 2006 were electricity charges (398 million Namibian dollars (NAD), or US $52.7 million), general service charges (NAD 324.7 million, or US $42 million), and water charges (NAD 190 million, or US $25 million).[51] The city is, by necessity, very proactive with regard to land valuation and taxation. Properties are valued every five years for rating purposes and innovative methods include establishing additional revenue collection points and introducing new technology such as electronic payment terminals, while involving corporate partners in municipal bill collection.[52] This is the case[53] with electricity charges, under a partnership with First National Bank which enables consumers to pay bills through the bank's Automatic Teller Machines (ATMs). This makes payments easier for customers while saving significant labour costs for the power utility.

In Somalia, municipal revenue sources are very different from those in other African cities, with commodity, market and property taxes providing the lion's share of municipal revenues (see Table 1.5), which together contributed an average 86 per cent of municipal revenues in 2007, but 90 per cent and more in ***Hargeisa, Burao*** and ***Borama,*** and just short of 100 per cent in ***Berbera.***

Commodity tax stands out as the single most important source in these six Somali municipalities, contributing an average 48.2 per cent, which includes 93.9 per cent in ***Berbera,*** 55.4 per cent in ***Erigavo*** and 41.8 per cent in ***Lasanod.*** Market tax was the second-largest source of municipal revenues, with an average 21.2 per cent, which includes 35.1 per cent and 40.2 per cent respectively in ***Burbao*** and ***Hargeisa.*** Property tax comes third, averaging 16.7 per cent, with a maximum 28 per cent in ***Hargeisa*** and a minimum 4 per cent in ***Berbera.***

Treating Urban Land as a Revenue Source

With an appropriate regime, urban land can be turned into a major revenue source for municipalities through one of three types of taxes: (a) a tax based on annual or rental value of property; (b) a tax based on the capital value of land and any improvements; or (c) a tax based on the site or land value.[54] Property tax is now widespread in African cities and, as noted earlier, ranks among the most significant municipal revenue sources. But they still generate only a fraction of their potential. Africa's urban taxation problems are mainly due to poor property valuation and low collection rates. Municipal valuation rolls are often incomplete and out of date, as it the case, for example, in Kenya, Uganda and Zambia. In other localities, like for instance ***Berbera***, property assets are not well-recorded[55] and revenues are extremely low when compared with other Somali municipalities. Thanks to a UN-HABITAT property survey, ***Berbera*** in 2009 began to experience a significant increase in municipal tax revenues.[56]

▲
Kibera, Nairobi. **©Manoocher Deghati/IRIN**

BOX 1.8: MAKING LOCAL TAXATION AND REGULATIONS MORE BUSINESS-FRIENDLY

Apart from planning and services, municipal authorities shape local business environments through taxes, fees, utility and other charges, which contribute to their competitiveness, or otherwise. In other words, excessive local charges or complex compliance systems can severely dampen capital expenditure, business growth and job creation in any given city. Streamlined and transparent fee structures and regulations can reduce financial and compliance costs, while municipalities can fulfil their governance functions in a more effective way.

Depending on the degree of decentralization and in order to finance urban services, local authorities can draw on a combination of own-source revenues (tax and non-tax), intergovernmental transfers, borrowings and profits from public undertakings. With continuing decentralization in many African countries, local authorities face increasing pressures to find sustainable sources of revenue. This can lead to revenue maximization through a proliferation of fees that may not always be in their longer-term interests. If a better business environment and an enhanced, equitable tax base are to be brought about, municipal own sources need reform.

Local own-source revenues comprise: (1) taxes (compulsory payments that are not tied to specific goods or services delivery such as property, sales, income or excise taxes); (2) user charges (payments tied to delivery of goods or services like water, electricity or waste collection); (3) regulatory fees (permits, licenses and certification); and (4) other sources (interests, royalties, rents, fines and penalties).

Problems arise when local regulatory instruments are used for revenue-raising. In many cash-strapped African cities, regulatory fees have proliferated. In the interests of an improved business environment, reform should focus on four steps: (1) make a comprehensive inventory of all instruments involving payment by firms to local authorities; (2) abolish (or legalize) these instruments if not legally robust; (3) classify local financial instruments into the four types above; and (4) assess whether regulatory fees have a regulatory function or whether they are simply a revenue source.

When regulatory fees are found legitimate and set on a cost-recovery basis, collection must be streamlined. If no regulatory function is served or where revenue exceeds the costs of regulation, municipal authorities must (a) reduce or eliminate this quasi-tax and rely on other fiscal instruments, strengthening own-source revenues such as taxes and user charges to compensate for any revenue loss; and (b) collapse multiple fees into one single business levy in order to reduce administrative costs to firms and public authorities.

Local business taxes (corporate income, capital and non-residential property taxes, and other commercial levies) must also come under review. Popular as they may be with politicians and the public as they extract substantial revenues while reducing personal taxation, business taxes tend to influence companies' decisions to establish themselves in any given city. Therefore, in order to reduce these risks municipal authorities must set both a tax floor and a ceiling. On a discretionary assessment, business taxes should also be extended to small enterprises that do not keep formal accounts, with clear and transparent rules in order to prevent corrupt practices.

Integrated reform of the business environment is the next best thing to a panacea, as it has the potential to sustain long-term local economic development. Clear and predictable taxation regimes help build an environment where business can operate more efficiently, while widening the municipal tax base in a broader, more equitable way.

Source: Corthay, L., Local Taxes, Regulations, and the Business Environment, in Investment Climate in Practice, No. 5, April 2009, World Bank

Also important is *land value* tax (or site value tax), which is levied regardless of on-site buildings, improvements or personal property,[57] and is based on the value of the site at its best permitted (rather than current) use. On top of adding to municipal revenues, the land value tax dampens speculation and instead tends to bring unused or under-utilised sites into full use. This increases the supply of land for development and can be conducive to reduced land prices. Therefore, taxing land values and spending the revenues on infrastructure or public services can be instrumental in building a more sustainable and equitable urban community.

Timely expansion of municipal boundaries can also add to revenues through a broader tax base. Against a background of rapid demographic and spatial growth, anticipating on eventual urban encroachment on peripheral rural lands can create a significant additional source of municipal revenue. Boundary extensions will more often than not require central government intervention, but this can give municipal authorities a good opportunity to include significant amounts of government-owned land in their spatial and financial planning portfolios. An added benefit is that under these conditions, municipalities are in a position to pre-empt on speculators, as they stand to be the sole beneficiaries of the higher values which their long-term, forward-looking planning is going to bring to those boundary extensions. Not only is this wise governance in financial terms, it also gives the municipality, as the owner of the land, better control over future developments, including creation of green belts and access to land for future infrastructure planning.

By way of conclusion, if Africa's local and municipal authorities are better to match their financial resources with the increased responsibilities deriving from decentralization, public authorities should embark on the following three steps:

1. Promoting fiscal decentralisation, with more local revenue-raising power through local taxes and other financial instruments;
2. Promoting secondary borrowing by municipalities with strong balance sheets, whether from local banks or through national debt capital markets; and
3. Encouraging decentralized revenue-raising authority and public-private partnerships in order to stimulate greater private sector investment in revenue-generating municipal infrastructures.

1.6 Ten Years of the Millennium Development Goals

The eight Millennium Development Goals (MDGs) were adopted as part of a commitment by the world's governments to tackle poverty. Their significance is twofold: (1) collectively, they address some of the major dimensions of poverty, which is conceived far more broadly than merely money income; and (2) they are matched with 18 ambitious targets for 2015 against which progress and eventually outcomes can be measured on a set of 48 different indicators, and those responsible for implementation – mostly national and regional governments – can be held to account. Importantly too, the near-universal adoption of the Goals links both donor and recipient governments, with the former committing targeted official development assistance to help achieve them (see www.un.org/millenniumgoals for background information and details).

Critics argue that the Millennium Development Goals are too ambitious and somewhat arbitrary, with both discernible overlaps and gaps, or that they are little more than political sops that stand no more chance of being met than previous targets, such as that OECD members should give at least 0.7 per cent of gross domestic product in overseas development aid. While these claims have some validity, there can be no denying that sincere efforts are under way, with progress monitored and reported at regular intervals. It is, therefore, very likely that the Millennium Development Goals have already made a positive difference overall.

Most of the Goals and associated targets are for national, sector-based enforcement (e.g., providing universal primary education, eradicating extreme hunger and poverty, combating HIV/AIDS, malaria and other diseases), while some are explicitly gendered (e.g., improving maternal health). As with all such national indicators, they conceal often sharp differences at various sub-national scales and do not distinguish between urban and rural areas. Goal-oriented efforts must be made in a general sort of way but very few have any distinctive urban relevance. The most obvious exceptions are targets and indicators under MDG 7 (ensuring sustainable development), which address energy consumption per head, carbon dioxide emissions, and the proportion of populations with access to safe drinking water and improved sanitation, and – in particular – reducing the slum population as a percentage of the urban population. The *State of the World's Cities 2006/07* (UN-HABITAT 2006) outlines a qualitative urban balance sheet for each Millennium Goal, setting the positive factors of population densities, concentrations of educational and health facilities and personnel, greater awareness and physical accessibility against overcrowding and constrained capacity of services, widespread lack of affordability to the urban poor, and risky behaviour as the odd desperate effort to make ends meet.

It is now a full decade since the Millennium Development Goals were adopted and thus two-thirds of the time available to meet the targets has elapsed. Progress has been very uneven within and across countries and regions. Africa (especially south of the Sahara) is generally regarded as one of the weakest performers, with most countries unlikely to meet some, if any, of the targets. Indeed, only a minority of the targets are now likely to be met; others will take much longer or are very unlikely to be met at all. This was already apparent before the onset of the global financial crisis of 2008/09, but prospects around the world are now far poorer. The reduced ability of cash-strapped governments to sustain spending programmes in the face of falling export prices, coupled with reduced development aid by some OECD countries (notably not the UK which, despite the severity of its public sector deficit after bailing out the banks, has ring-fenced development aid), has had a negative impact, especially in the poorest countries. Furthermore, the purchasing power of many urban poor households has been eroded, even among those who have retained their jobs as factories shed labour. Emergency expenditure by governments facing extreme weather events or 'natural disasters', which have occurred in many areas, also divert funds and scarce human resources from longer-term development expenditure.

More positively, however, primary school enrolment in sub-Saharan Africa did increase by 15 percentage points between the year 2000 and 2007, while a combination of enhanced vaccination campaigns and accelerated distribution of insecticide-treated bed nets to combat malaria have reduced child mortality in recent years.

With respect to the more specifically urban Millennium Development Goals, progress has been more limited worldwide; indeed, "...slum improvements are barely keeping pace with the rapid growth of developing country cities"[58].

As reviewed by Satterthwaite, environmental health[59] problems highlight the current challenge of urban sustainability, which has to do with the dynamics of ongoing expansion in most regions of the world against a background that has changed to economic crisis and climate threats. For poorer regions, including much of Africa, this crisis will sharpen the perceived trade-offs between the apparently competing priorities of employment generation and meeting basic needs, on the one hand, and promoting longer-term environmental sustainability, on the other. In reality, however, as the 2006 Stern *Review on the Economics of Climate Change* demonstrated,[60] the ultimate costs of inaction in the face of climate change will exceed those of the 'green technologies' and sustainable resource uses that can mitigate the threat.

African countries will be able to address these dilemmas only with strong political leadership, backed by appropriate technology transfers and development assistance agreements. These efforts would come in support of the UN Framework Convention on Climate Change process as embodied in the Copenhagen Accord in December 2009 and the proposed legally binding agreement to be negotiated during 2010, as well as associated bilateral agreements. This ongoing process highlights the mismatch between Africa's small contribution to global warming and the fact that it stands to suffer heavily from climate change. While global carbon dioxide emissions increased from 21.9 to 28.7 billion metric tonnes between 1990 and 2006, the respective figures for Africa were only 0.7 and 1.0 billion tonnes (sub-Saharan Africa: 0.5 and 0.6 billion tonnes; North Africa: 0.2 and 0.4 billion tonnes), or 4.5 per cent of the total.[61] In Africa, these emissions have both urban and rural origins. In urban areas, the atmosphere is polluted by the consequences of economic momentum (industrial and motor vehicle emissions) and poverty (kerosene or biomass for lighting or cooking); in rural areas, greenhouse gas emissions have increased substantially with widespread forest clearance and burning.

The first target of Millennium Development Goal 7 (ensuring environmental sustainability) is to integrate the principles of sustainable development into country policies and programmes and to reverse the loss of environmental resources. Such commitments have indeed increasingly been incorporated into African national development plans and policy documents but are not yet widely implemented on the ground. Greater coordination is also required to ensure that rural-urban feedback and integration are adequately recognised. For example, ensuring adequate urban water supplies requires not only local supply augmentation and urban conservation measures (such as reducing leakage from outdated networks where any; reducing consumption per head among urban elites; and increasing water harvesting), but also rural environmental conservation in a bid to maximise water retention in soils and reduce soil erosion (and hence siltation in reservoirs), together with greater efficiency and effectiveness of agricultural irrigation. Several development Goals and targets can also be addressed simultaneously through appropriate interventions. For instance, reducing deforestation will not only improve rural and urban water availability, but also lower rural greenhouse gas emissions.

The target of halving the proportion of the population without sustainable access to safe drinking water and basic sanitation is unlikely to be met in many African countries, despite considerable progress, especially in urban areas. In 2006, some 242 million people had access to appropriate facilities in sub-Saharan Africa; however, in order to meet the target, this figure would have to increase by 370 million by the year 2015. This is a daunting challenge: in 2008, approximately 22 million urban and 199 million rural residents still practised open defecation – about 10 per cent of the worldwide total – with often considerable risks to public health.[62]

However, an even more challenging target for sub-Saharan Africa remains the "significant improvements in the lives of at least 100 million slum dwellers by 2020". This requires multiple interventions in the areas of sanitation and safe drinking water supply, as well as the upgrading of the physical fabric of buildings and other infrastructure and services. A significant decline in the proportion of sub-Saharan Africa's urban populations living with shelter deprivations occurred between 1990 and 2005, from 71 per cent in 1990 to 62 per cent in 2005; however, continuing demographic expansion has cancelled out that achievement, so that today many more people find themselves in those dire conditions.[63] Particular problems arise in countries where recent or ongoing armed conflicts have diverted public expenditure away from socio-economic development and/or where the urban fabric has been damaged or destroyed and people displaced on a large scale, as in Angola, Sierra Leone, Somalia and parts of Sudan. Such conflicts have exacerbated long-standing problems of urban underinvestment, lack of political will and widespread poverty. Rural conflicts can displace people to relatively secure urban areas, as is the case with ***Benguela, Lobito, Luanda,*** Angola and ***Freetown,*** Sierra Leone, whereas urban fighting and destruction can drive people out of cities, as in ***Mogadishu***, Somalia. In affected towns and cities, up to 80 per cent of urban dwellers live in substandard conditions. The proportion is the same in ***Addis Ababa***, although for different historical reasons. Across Africa, a variety of strategies will be required to facilitate any communal and household self-help efforts deployed to meet locally appropriate standards. Efforts in this direction would somewhat reduce the vulnerability of cities and poorer residents to systemic shocks (see Section 1.1).

It is worth pointing out that progress on Millennium Development Goals appears generally stronger in countries with strong political will and accountable forms of governance. This reflects a culture of responsiveness to the needs and demands 'from below' rather than just 'from above' in terms of donor conditions. Conversely, allocation of scarce capital to expensive prestige or lavish projects that detracts from anti-poverty investments tends to be more prominent in less responsive and accountable regimes, where the elite have more leeway to serve their own interests. Similarly, civil or cross-border conflicts and related instability cannot favour concerted poverty reduction interventions since they create fear and tension, divert government resources into unproductive military expenditure, and lead to direct

▲
Kroo Bay slum, Freetown, Sierra Leone. The MDG slum target is a challenge for sub-Saharan Africa. **©Ines Gesell/iStockphoto**

destruction of infrastructure and service breakdowns, while displacing or killing people. In other words, the nature of domestic governance has a direct bearing on the prospects of achieving the Millennium Development Goals.

Future prospects appear more uncertain at present than during the generally optimistic years of the decade preceding the current global economic crisis. As explained above, few countries in any region will achieve all the Millennium Goals; in Africa, more will be missed by more countries. Within individual countries, however, cities are more likely to achieve or at least come close to some Goals than most rural areas. Unless the data are disaggregated sub-nationally, regional or urban-peri-urban-rural differences will remain largely obscured.

This raises the question whether the Millennium Development Goals are likely to be achieved or not. Will the targets be scaled down to more achievable levels under prevailing conditions? Will the deadlines be extended instead, to buy more time and save face? Or, in order to steer clear of cynicism and 'MDG fatigue', will they be abandoned by the time the deadlines expire in favour of some new slogans and targets, in a bid to galvanise and justify ongoing development assistance and anti-poverty programmes? The answer is difficult to predict, since so many donor and recipient countries will hold elections before 2015. Nevertheless, much will depend on how close at least a set of key 'litmus test' countries in each region have come to the respective targets. If these results suggest only a modest boost or extension of deadlines, then these are likely. However, if many countries fall well short, the Millennium Development Goals might be abandoned in order to avoid embarrassment.

1.7
Africa's Largest Cities – 2005-2020

In 2010, the African continent was host to 47 cities with populations in excess of one million, or three more than forecast in the 2008 issue of this report. The combined population of these cities was 126.4 million or 11 million less than projected in 2008. Although their average size increased from 2.56 to 2.68 million, they did not reach the expected average of 3.11 million. Between 2005 and 2010 (projections), Africa's accumulated million-plus city population (as a share of total urban population) seems to have very slightly decreased (by 0.1 per cent) to 31.6 per cent, suggesting persistent demographic momentum in smaller cities.

At the top of the African city-size ranking, no change has occurred since 2005. ***Cairo***, with just over 11 million (2010 projections) remains Africa's largest urban agglomeration, followed by ***Lagos*** with 10.5 million and ***Kinshasa*** with 8.7 million. ***Luanda***, with a 2010 population of 4.7 million, has moved from sixth to fourth place in 2010, surpassing ***Alexandria*** (4.3 million) and ***Abidjan*** (4.1 million). It is projected that ***Luanda*** will keep its current position at least until 2025. It is further projected that by 2015, ***Cairo*** will be home to 11.6 million, only to be dwarfed by ***Lagos***, whose 14.1 million population will then make it Africa's largest conurbation. It is further projected that, by 2020, ***Kinshasa's***

▲
Cairo, Egypt. **©Jessica Morelli/iStockphoto**

TABLE 1.6: **AFRICA'S MILLION+ URBAN AGGLOMERATIONS 2005-2025 (000s)**

Rank (2010)	City	Country	2005	2010*	2015*	2020*	2025*
1	Cairo	Egypt	10,565	11,001	11,663	12,540	13,531
2	Lagos	Nigeria	8,767	10,578	12,427	14,162	15,810
3	Kinshasa	DRC	7,106	8,754	10,668	12,788	15,041
4	Luanda	Angola	3,533	4,772	6,013	7,080	8,077
5	Alexandria	Egypt	3,973	4,387	4,791	5,201	5,648
6	Abidjan	Côte d'Ivoire	3,564	4,125	4,788	5,500	6,321
7	Johannesburg	South Africa	3,263	3,670	3,867	3,996	4,127
8	Nairobi	Kenya	2,814	3,523	4,303	5,192	6,246
9	Cape Town	South Africa	3,091	3,405	3,579	3,701	3,824
10	Kano	Nigeria	2,993	3,395	3,922	4,495	5,060
11	Dar es Salaam	Tanzania	2,680	3,349	4,153	5,103	6,202
12	Casablanca	Morocco	3,138	3,284	3,537	3,816	4,065
13	Ekurhuleni	South Africa	2,824	3,202	3,380	3,497	3,614
14	Addis Ababa	Ethiopia	2,633	2,930	3,365	3,981	4,757
15	Durban	South Africa	2,638	2,879	3,026	3,133	3,241
16	Dakar	Senegal	2,434	2,863	3,308	3,796	4,338
17	Ibadan	Nigeria	2,509	2,837	3,276	3,760	4,237
18	Algiers	Algeria	2,512	2,800	3,099	3,371	3,595
19	Accra	Ghana	1,985	2,342	2,722	3,110	3,497
20	Douala	Cameroon	1,767	2,125	2,478	2,815	3,131
21	Abuja	Nigeria	1,315	1,995	2,563	2,977	3,361
22	Ouagadougou	Burkina Faso	1,328	1,909	2,643	3,457	4,332
23	Antananarivo	Madagascar	1,590	1,879	2,235	2,658	3,148
24	Kumasi	Ghana	1,519	1,834	2,139	2,448	2,757
25	Rabat	Morocco	1,647	1,802	1,973	2,139	2,288
26	Yaoundé	Cameroon	1,489	1,801	2,103	2,392	2,664
27	Bamako	Mali	1,368	1,699	2,086	2,514	2,971
28	Lomé	Togo	1,310	1,667	2,036	2,398	2,763
29	Maputo	Mozambique	1,341	1,655	1,994	2,350	2,722
30	Conakry	Guinea	1,411	1,653	2,004	2,427	2,906
31	Harare	Zimbabwe	1,513	1,632	1,856	2,170	2,467
32	Kampala	Uganda	1318	1,598	1,982	2,504	3,189
33	Kaduna	Nigeria	1,375	1,561	1,811	2,087	2,362
34	Lubumbashi	DRC	1,252	1,543	1,899	2,304	2,744
35	Mogadishu	Somalia	1,415	1,500	1,795	2,156	2,588
36	Mbuji-Mayi	DRC	1,190	1,488	1,838	2,232	2,658
37	Lusaka	Zambia	1,265	1,451	1,666	1,941	2,267
38	Pretoria	South Africa	1,274	1,429	1,514	1,575	1,637
39	Brazzaville	Congo	1,172	1,323	1,504	1,703	1,878
40	Benin City	Nigeria	1,124	1,302	1,523	1,758	1,992
41	Vereeniging	South Africa	1,029	1,143	1,211	1,262	1,313
42	Tripoli	Libya	1,059	1,108	1,192	1,286	1,364
43	Port Elizabeth	South Africa	1,002	1,068	1,126	1,173	1,222
44	Fes	Morocco	963	1,065	1,173	1,277	1,371
45	Niamey	Niger	848	1,048	1,302	1,643	2,105
46	Ogbomosho	Nigeria	904	1,032	1,201	1,389	1,576
47	Mombasa	Kenya	830	1,003	1,216	1,479	1,795

**Projections*

Source: World Urbanisation Prospects, The 2009 Revision, DESA, United Nations, New York, 2010

TABLE 1.7: **AFRICA'S TEN FASTEST GROWING LARGE CITIES (2005-2010)**

City	2005-10* Absolute Growth (000s)	City	2005-10* Proportional Growth (%)
Lagos	1,811	Abuja	51.7
Kinshasa	1,648	Ouagadougou	43.7
Luanda	1,239	Luanda	35.0
Nairobi	709	Lomé	27.2
Abuja	680	Nairobi	25.2
Dar es Salaam	669	Mbuji-Mayi	25.0
Ouagadougou	581	Dar es Salaam	24.9
Abidjan	561	Bamako	24.1
Dakar	429	Niamey	23.5
Alexandria	414	Maputo	23.4

*Projections
Source: World Urbanisation Prospects, The 2009 Revision, DESA, United Nations, New York, 2010

12.7 million exceed *Cairo's* projected 12.5 million, and push the Egyptian capital into third place.

As expected, the largest African cities have continued to grow rapidly during the five-year period 2005-10. The most rapidly growing cities in absolute and proportional terms are shown in Table 1.6.

Between 2005 and 2010 (projections), *Cairo* added 436,000 to its population, a 4.1 per cent increase. The next three largest African cities, however, each grew by more than one million: *Lagos* (by 1.8 million), *Kinshasa* (by 1.6 million) and *Luanda* (by 1.2 million), while *Nairobi* and *Abuja* were the fourth and fifth fastest growing with additions of 709,000 and 680,000 respectively. Despite the huge expansion in *Lagos* and *Kinshasa*, these were not the fastest growing large African cities in proportional terms, which instead included *Abuja* (+ 51.7 per cent), *Ouagadougou* (+ 43.7 per cent), *Luanda* (+ 35.0 per cent), *Lomé* (+ 27.2 per cent) and *Nairobi* (+ 25.2 per cent).

The combined population of Africa's million-plus cities increased 17.3 million between 2005 and 2010. Since the total urban population increased 63.8 million over the same period, it is clear that the largest cities are absorbing only a relatively small share (27.1 per cent) of Africa's urban transition. The bulk (72.9 per cent) of the increase occurred in cities with populations under one million, a continuation of the trend already highlighted in the previous (2008) issue of this report. Africa's largest cities are expected to absorb ever-lower shares of total urban population growth - 25.8 per cent over the 2010-2020 decade, on current projections. The policy implications should be clear: African governments should pursue further improvements in the management capacities of cities with populations under one million, where three-quarters of urban demographic growth are expected to occur.

This, however, does not imply that capacity-building, housing and urban services provision in Africa's largest cities can now be scaled back. Between 2010 and 2020, a projected 40.3 million will be added to those African cities with populations over one million. Although on the whole, they will be hosts to diminishing shares of total urban demographic growth, some will continue to grow, and even very fast.

During the 2010/20 decade, the 10 large African cities growing most rapidly in absolute terms will all add more than one million to their respective populations. *Kinshasa* is projected to grow fastest in absolute terms by no less than four million, a 46 per cent increase for its 2010 population of 8.7 million. *Lagos* is expected to be the second-fastest with a projected 3.5 million addition, or a 33.8 per cent increase on its 2010 population of 10.5 million. Likewise, *Luanda* can expect a 2.3 million addition, or a 48.3 per cent increase for its 2010 population of 4.7 million. *Dar es Salaam, Nairobi, Ouagadougou, Cairo, Abidjan, Kano* and *Addis Ababa* will all see their populations increase by more than one million over the next decade, as shown in Table 1.8.

Rapid demographic growth is neither good nor bad *per se* for any city: it all depends on whether it is properly accommodated (with infrastructures, amenities and services), and perceived as a factor that can strengthen local and national development objectives. Clearly, rapid demographic growth that merely results in massive urban slum proliferation, steep inequality and human misery is *not* good urban growth. When demographic expansion is harnessed in support of economic progress and development through job creation and higher productivity, this is 'good' urbanisation. Such progress and development is predicated on proper housing and basic services for all, among other dimensions of good urban governance.

TABLE 1.8: **AFRICA'S 10 FASTEST GROWING LARGE CITIES (2010-2020)**

City	2010-2020* Absolute Growth (000s)
Kinshasa	4,034
Lagos	3,584
Luanda	2,308
Dar es Salaam	1,754
Nairobi	1,669
Ouagadougou	1,548
Cairo	1,539
Abidjan	1,375
Kano	1,100
Addis Ababa	1,051

*Projections
Source: World Urbanisation Prospects, The 2009 Revision, DESA, United Nations, New York, 2010

TABLE 1.9: **AFRICA'S 10 FASTEST GROWING LARGE CITIES 2010-2020 (%)**

City	2010-20* Proportional Growth (%)
Ouagadougou	81.0
Niamey	56.7
Kampala	56.6
Dar es Salaam	52.3
Mbuji-Mayi	50.0
Lubumbashi	49.3
Abuja	49.2
Luanda	48.3
Bamako	47.9
Nairobi	47.3

**Projections*
Source: World Urbanisation Prospects, The 2009 Revision, DESA, United Nations, New York, 2010

▲
South Africa. **©MaxPhoto/Shutterstock**

This model is the reverse of the socio-economic conditions currently prevailing in African cities regardless of size, where demographic expansion is continuing against a background of significant and ever-growing shortfalls in housing, services and livelihood opportunities. These deficiencies can only worsen if African cities are allowed to mushroom under current *laisser-faire* modalities of urban expansion.

Urban demography is not only measured in absolute terms; it can also be expressed as proportional growth, i.e., demographic expansion as a share of current urban population figures. In the case of some African cities, projected *proportional* growth for the 2010-2020 period defies belief. With the exception of the largest cities in the Republic of South Africa and ***Brazzaville*** in Congo, the populations of all sub-Saharan million-plus cities are expected to expand by an average 32 per cent between 2010 and 2020. In that number, the average addition in the 10 proportionally fastest growing cities is more than 47 per cent. ***Abuja***, ***Bamako***, ***Luanda***, ***Lubumbashi*** and ***Nairobi*** are projected to grow at rates between 47.3 and 49.3 per cent over the current decade, while in ***Dar es Salaam***, ***Kampala***, ***Mbuji-Mayi*** and ***Niamey*** the range is projected between 50 and 56.7 per cent. Way ahead of this fast-expanding group will be ***Ouagadougou***, whose population is expected to soar by no less than 81 per cent, from 1.9 million in 2010 to 3.4 million in 2020 (see Table 1.9). Clearly, these 10 cities should, as a matter of priority, build their management capacities now if they are to cater to huge prospective demand for housing, services and livelihoods, not to mention the already existing backlogs. Failure to do so will ensure that many African cities will be heading for serious economic and social tension that may threaten local and national political stability.

The above figures refer to urban agglomerations only. City regions, mega urban regions and urban development corridors, as they have begun to emerge on the African continent, have not been taken into consideration as no accurate or verifiable population data is available for these new configurations. The size of the populations of huge regional urban concentrations like the North Delta Region in Egypt, the Greater Ibadan-Lagos-Accra (GILA) urban corridor along the Gulf of Guinea and the Gauteng mega urban region in South Africa can only be estimated.

These extraordinarily large multi-nodal urban configurations are comparatively new to Africa and will require urban management reforms that go well beyond the conventional 20th century mono-centric urban management pattern. Not only is serious reform required to deliver urban 'hardware' like housing, services and infrastructures commensurate with these expanding urban concentrations, but urgent attention should also be paid to their socio-political implications against a prevailing background of urban inequality, poverty and unemployment. On top of this, African governments must consider how they are to provide these huge urban populations with food and water security in the near future. As Box 1.9 argues, medium- and longer-term food and water security for Africa's rapidly growing urban populations is a matter of very serious concern.

BOX 1.9: **AGRICULTURAL POLICY AND FOOD AND WATER SECURITY FOR AFRICAN CITIES**

▲
Rice seedlings at a major commercial agricultural scheme in the Gambella region of Ethiopia. **©Ben Parker/IRIN**

Although Africa experienced waves of violent food riots during the 1980s, 1990s as well as in 2008, urban food and water insecurity hardly feature on the political agenda or on the list of potential causes of major social tension. In other regions, though, future food and water security is a mounting concern, prompting a number of potentially affected countries to look abroad to secure current and future supplies. Through state-owned entities or public-private partnerships, food-deficient countries have in recent years acquired an estimated 30 million ha of arable land in Africa. Large-scale international food suppliers and supermarket chains have also joined the scramble for food-producing acreage, sharply boosting the price of agricultural land in Africa. The terms of these acquisitions remain mostly cloaked in secrecy, but they typically allow for export of all produce, and come with generous tax exemptions and free access to freshwater resources in exchange for capital expenditure in rural development and infrastructure.

Throughout Africa, land politics is often linked to natural disasters, hunger or poor governance. Although every nation has its own unique dynamics in this respect, the argument that sales of vast tracts of land to foreigners is of any benefit to local populations through agricultural innovation and employment generation appears somewhat hollow. By the end of 2009, for instance, the estimated number of Chinese agricultural workers deployed in Africa on outsourced lands exceeded one million. Importing labour *into* Africa and exporting food *from* Africa are two types of flows that a rapidly urbanising, job-starved and food-insecure continent can ill afford.

With huge tracts held under customary tenure, African governments effectively own most of the land. But the acreage outsourced is in many cases already occupied by local subsistence farmers. These farming communities are compensated mostly for standing crops and land improvements, which therefore tends to disregard the real losses to the local population, who is rarely consulted. Although some instances of fair and equitable compensation for foreign land purchases can be found, the terms of most land deals are typically not in favour of local stakeholders. Subsistence farmers often become displaced and lose access to their land-based livelihoods. If countries like Ethiopia, Kenya or Sudan experience regular difficulties in feeding their current populations, foreign land purchases under the prevailing terms may not be the right course of action. Many such deals in Africa raise questions about the transparency of land and water-resource grabbing by the highest foreign bidder under what some now call 'agro-imperialism'.

For all their vast unexplored lands and fresh water resources, many sub-Saharan African countries are net food importers. Therefore, it is for African governments to make strategic and forward-looking decisions on the better utilization of precious food producing assets. Water shortages as repeatedly experienced in Eastern Africa, for instance, are a quite unnecessary result of poor governance and inappropriate water management. Increased investment in Eastern African road and water infrastructure can alleviate these shortages, make unexplored lands productive, increase the region's ability to feed its rural and urban populations and, possibly, also still allow for higher food export earnings. But then African governments must bargain harder for more beneficial and more transparent deals, so that foreign investment contributes to the continent's future food and water security, with genuine benefits for local communities under the form of additional business, fair cash payments and improved livelihood opportunities.

Today, an estimated 32 per cent of sub-Saharan Africans still experience chronic malnutrition. In Sudan, more than five million people rely on food aid, while Kenya has been struggling for years with drought-induced famines and its food insecurity is worsening sharply. Nevertheless, both countries are engaged in large international land outsourcing deals to provide food for other countries. Likewise, Ethiopia imports 150,000 tons of wheat every year and, in 2008, 11 million Ethiopians needed food aid. Still, the Ethiopian government has approved massive land outsourcing deals while it is unable to feed current, let alone future populations. In Zimbabwe, recent land reforms aimed at more equitable distribution of agricultural acreage have turned the country from a major food exporter into a food-deficient nation. This has not refrained the Zimbabwean government from entering into a land outsourcing agreement with China, allocating large tracts to new 'outsiders' in a most ironic turn of events.

Given the sharply rising demand for food and water by Africa's rapidly growing populations, the wisdom of selling off agricultural and fresh water resources to satisfy food security elsewhere in the world is a matter that may need careful re-consideration. Rather than simply turning precious food-producing assets into quick cash, vigorous stimulation of domestic agro-industries would be a much wiser strategy if current and future African food and water security is to be secured. This is particularly important for Africa's ever-expanding urban populations who, unlike their rural counterparts, cannot revert to subsistence farming as a food security strategy. Moreover, Africa's precious fresh water resources call for careful consideration. Balancing the water needs of thirsty cities with competing demands from agriculture and industry will be difficult enough without Africa feeding food-deficient nations on other continents.

ENDNOTES

1 Pacione, M. *Urban Geography: A Global perspective*, Glasgow 2005
2 Simon D, McGregor D, & Nsiah-Gyabaah K, "The changing urban-rural interface of African cities: definitional issues and an application to Kumasi, Ghana", *Environment and Urbanisation* 16(2) 2004 235-247; Simon D, McGregor D & Thompson D, "Contemporary perspectives on the peri-urban zones of cities in developing areas" in McGregor D, Simon D & Thompson D (eds) *The Peri-Urban Interface: Approaches to sustainable natural and human resource use*, London and Sterling, VA: Earthscan, 2006 1-17.
3 Parnell, S & Simon, D, 2010. "National urbanisation and urban policies: necessary but absent policy instruments in Africa", in: *Urbanisation imperatives for Africa: Transcending impasses*. Cape Town: African Centre for Cities, University of Cape Town, 38-47, http://africancentreforcities.net/papers/22/.
4 Intergovernmental Panel on Climate Change, *Fourth Assessment Report 2007*, Cambridge: Cambridge University Press, 2008 (4 volumes).
5 Simon D, "Cities and global environmental change: exploring the links", *Geographical Journal* 173(1) 2007 75-79; Simon D, "The challenges of global environmental change for urban Africa", *Urban Forum* 21(3) 2010 235-248; Awuor CB, Orindi VA, Adwera AO, "Climate change and coastal cities: the case of Mombasa, Kenya", *Environment and Urbanisation* 20(1) 2008 231-242; Dossou KMR & Gléhouenou-Dossou, B, "The vulnerability to climate change of Cotonou (Benin): the rise in sea level", *Environment and Urbanisation* 19(1)2007 65-79; Mukheibir P & Ziervogel G, "Developing a Municipal Action Plan (MAP) for climate change: the City of Cape Town", *Environment and Urbanisation* 19(1) 2007 143-158; Bicknell J, Dodman D & Satterthwaite D, eds *Adapting Cities to Climate Change: Urbanisation, poverty and environment in the 21st century*, London and Sterling, VA, Earthscan, 2009 (contains reprints of Mukheibir & Ziervogel, and Awuor *et al.*).
6 Guéye C, Fall AS, Tall SM, "Climatic perturbation and urbanisation in Senegal", *Geographical Journal* 173(1) 2007 88-92.
7 Potts D, "Urban lives: adopting new strategies and adapting rural links", in Rakodi C, ed, *The Urban Challenge in Africa: Growth and management of its large cities*, Tokyo and New York: United Nations University Press 1997 447-494; Tostensen, Al, Tvedten I & Vaa M, eds, *Associational Life in African Cities*, Uppsala: Nordiska Afrikainstitutet; Bryceson DF, "Fragile cities: Fundamentals of urban life in east and southern Africa", in Bryceson DF & Potts D, eds, *African Urban Economies: Viability, vitality or vitiation?* Basingstoke: Palgrave Macmillan, 2006 3-38; Simone AM & Abouhani, A, eds, *Urban Africa: Changing contours of survival in the city*, London, Pretoria, Dakar: Zed Books, UNISA Press, CODESRIA, 2005.
8 *SWC 2010*; section 2.2.
9 Brennan, E., *Policymakers' Needs*, Seminar on New Forms of Urbanisation: Conceptualising and Measuring Human Settlement in the 21st Century, Bellagio, Italy, March 11-15, 2002
10 Laquian, A., *The Governance of Mega-Urban Regions*, in *The Mega-Urban Regions of Southeast Asia*, Ed. T. McGeeand & I. Robinson, Vancouver 1995, pp. 215-241.
11 Hamdok, A. *Political Parties in Africa: Challenges for Democratic Governance*. "IDEA Framework Programme of Activity 2004-6: Stockholm, Sweden.
12 Global International IDEA Research Programme, web: http://www.idea.int/africa/index.cfm
13 Diamond, L., *Democratization in Africa: What Progress Towards Institutionalization?*, Conference Report. February 2008.
14 *Ibid.*
15 Bratton, M., 'Wide But Shallow: *Popular Support for Democracy in Africa: A comparative series of national public attitude surveys on democracy, markets and civil society in Africa*. Afrobarometer Paper no. 19, August 2002.
16 *Mozambique Democracy and Political Participation: A Discussion Paper*. Open Society Institute for Southern Africa, 2009.
17 *Ibid.*
18 *Ghana Democracy and Political Participation: A Discussion Paper*. Open Society Institute for West Africa, 2007.
19 Diamond, D. *Democratization in Africa.*
20 AMCHUD Background Paper: *Urban Governance in Africa: Experiences and Challenges. Incorporating the 5th Assembly of the African Population Commission Serving as the Expert Group Meeting for the Ministerial Segment.* 2005. Durban, South Africa.
21 *Constitution of the Republic of South Africa 1993*, ss 152 and 152)
22 Issue 2: January 2009. University of the Western Cape, South Africa.
23 Department of Provincial and Local Government, 2007:5
24 *Political Decentralization*: Decentralization and Sub-National Regional Economics Thematic Working Group. The World Bank Group, 2009.
25 World Bank Group, 2001 http://www1.worldbank.org/publicsector/decentralization/admin.htm
26 Lwendo, B. "Challenges for Decentralization and Local Government Reforms." AllAfrica.com, 6 Feb 2009. Website: http://allafrica.com/stories/200902060616.html
27 *Ibid.*
28 Visser, J. de, *Developmental Local Government in South Africa: Institutional Fault Lines.* Commonwealth Journal of Local Governance Issue 2: January 2009.
29 1998 White Paper on Local Government. Department of Constitutional Development, South Africa, 1998.
30 *Ghana Democracy and Political Participation: A Discussion Paper*. Open Society Institute for West Africa, 2007
31 Jütting, J. *et al. Decentralisation and Poverty in Developing Countries: Exploring the Impact.* OECD Development Centre Working Paper No. 236, August 2004. DEV/DOC(2004)05
32 *Ibid.*
33 AMCHUD Background Paper: *Urban Governance in Africa: Experiences and Challenges. Incorporating the 5th Assembly of the African Population Commission Serving as the Expert Group Meeting for the Ministerial Segment*. 2005. Durban, South Africa.
34 Putzel, J., *Phase 2 Research Framework 2006-2010*, www.crisisstates.com, downloaded 08/10/2009.
35 This section draws heavily on Corfee-Morlot, J. *et al.*, *Cities, Climate Change and Multilevel Governance,* OECD Environment Working Paper 14, 2009.
36 Corfee-Morlot, J. *et al.*, *Cities, Climate Change and Multilevel Governance,* OECD Environment Working Paper 14, 2009, p. 16.
37 UN-HABITAT, *Guide to Municipal Finance*, Nairobi, 2009
38 UN-HABITAT, *Enhancing Resource Allocation to Urban Development in Africa*, Nairobi, 2006.
39 UN-HABITAT, *Global Report on Human Settlements 2003: The Challenge of Slums*, Nairobi, 2003.
40 UN-HABITAT, *Housing Finance System in South Africa*, Nairobi, 2008.
41 *Ibid.*
42 *Ibid.*
43 *Ibid.*
44 UN-HABITAT, *Financing Cities for Sustainable Development*, Nairobi 1998.
45 PDG and Isandla Institute, *Municipal Rates Policies and the Urban Poor*, South African Cities Network, Johannesburg, 2009.
46 *Ibid.*
47 UN-HABITAT, *Financing Cities for Sustainable Development*, Nairobi, 1998.
48 Ribot, J. C., *African Decentralization*, United Nations Research Institute for Social Development, 2002.
49 www.cities-localgovernments.org/uclg/, accessed 4/12/2009
50 http://www.gta.gov.zw/ accessed 9/12/09
51 Office of Auditor-General, *Auditor's Report on Municipal of Windhoek, Windhoek*, Nambia, 2008.
52 *Speech by the Mayor of Windhoek, Mr. Matheus Shikongo* at the Launch of the New Payment Solutions, Windhoek, 11 April 2006
53 *Ibid.*
54 Grote, M., *Tax Aspects of Domestic Resource Mobilisation*, Rome, 2007
55 UN-HABITAT, *Enhancing Resouce Allocation to Urban Development in Africa*, Nairobi, 2006.
56 UN-HABITAT's property survey in Berbera, Somalia, 2009
57 http://en.wikipedia.org/wiki/Land_value_tax accessed 5/12/2009
58 UN MDGs Report 2009: 5
59 Satterthwaite D, "In pursuit of a healthy environment in low- and middle-income nations", in Marcotullio PJ & McGranahan G, eds, *Scaling Urban Environmental Challenges; From local to global and back*, London and Sterling, VA: Earthscan 2007 69-105.
60 Stern N, *The Economics of Climate Change; the Stern Review*, Cambridge: Cambridge University Press, 2007.
61 *UN MDGs Report 2009*: 40
62 *Ibid.* p.45
63 *UN MDGs Report 2009*: 47; Global Urban Observatory 2008; UN-HABITAT *State of the World's Cities 2010*, Parts 1.3 and 1.4

Chapter Two

02

THE STATE OF NORTHERN AFRICAN CITIES

Cairo, Egypt.
©Dudarev Mikhail/Shutterstock

2.1
The Social Geography of Urbanization

For the purposes of this report, Northern Africa includes seven countries: Algeria, Egypt, the Libyan Arab Jamahiriya, Morocco, Sudan, Tunisia and Western Sahara. The population of the subregion was an estimated 212.9 million in 2010. Most urban settlements are concentrated along the Nile River Valley and the north-western Mediterranean coast (see Map 2.2). As many as 40 per cent of the subregion's urban dwellers live in the Nile Valley and Delta region and 49 per cent live in the coastal areas.[1] More than one third (39.67 per cent) of the subregion's population, or 84.5 million, lives in Egypt. Between the year 2000 and 2005, the urban population in the region grew an average 2.4 per cent every year, and this rate is projected to remain steady through 2010.[2]

With the exception of Egypt and Sudan, the majority of the Northern African population now lives in urban areas. The high rates of rural-urban migration that prevailed in the 1980s and 1990s have largely abated in the last decade, with the exception of Sudan whose urban population is still increasing at over 4.3 per cent on an annual average basis as urbanisation seems to be 'catching up' after decades of civil strife. During 2005-2010, urban demographic growth was much slower in other Northern African countries: 1.56 per cent in Tunisia, 1.99 per cent in Egypt, 2.27 per cent in Morocco, 2.23 per cent in Libya and 2.48 per cent in Algeria.[3]

MAP 2.1: **NORTHERN AFRICAN COUNTRIES**

Currently, the proportion of the national population living in cities is 66.50 per cent in Algeria, 43.40 per cent in Egypt, 77.89 per cent in Libya, 58.24 per cent in Morocco, 40.10 per cent in Sudan, 67.28 per cent in Tunisia and 81.83 per cent in Western Sahara. By 2030, the region-wide proportion of the population living in cities is expected to increase to 60.53 per cent (see Table 2.1), while urbanisation rates are projected to grow further in all countries, reaching 82.88 per cent in Libya, 76.23 per cent in Algeria, 75.17 per cent in Tunisia and 69.18 per cent in Morocco. By 2030, Sudan's 54.54 per cent urbanisation rate will have overtaken Egypt's which by then will stand at 50.92 per cent (see Table 2.2).

All Northern African countries have progressed in economic terms between 2005 and 2008, with the highest increases in gross national income (GNI) per head recorded in Libya (97 per cent) and Sudan (92 per cent) and the smallest in Tunisia (15 per cent) and Morocco (29 per cent). While the economies of Algeria, Libya and Sudan still rely largely on mineral (mainly oil) resources, other countries in the subregion have made significant efforts to diversify away from agriculture and manufacturing to the service and high-technology sectors, with tourism taking advantage of historic, cultural and environmental assets. Significant disparities remain in the subregion as measured by the UN poverty index. Libya and Tunisia feature the lowest poverty rates and highest life expectancies, while the highest incidences of poverty are found in Algeria and Sudan (see Table 2.3).

Even though the agricultural sector still accounts for 42.7 per cent of overall employment in Northern Africa, cities have become the main engines of economic growth, with a steady shift to urban economic activities where output per job is on average five times higher than in agriculture (see Table 2.4).

In most Northern African countries, the major economic activities are concentrated in a small number of cities. Tourism, industry and real estate development are the main sectors

TABLE 2.1: **NORTHERN AFRICA - URBAN POPULATION 1950-2050**

Population	1950	1960	1970	1980	1990	2000	2010*	2020*	2030*	2040*	2050*
Urban (*000)	13,130	20,451	31,461	45,364	65,763	85,656	108,912	137,341	167,876	199,058	227,852
Urban (%)	24.78	30.29	36.22	40.15	44.50	47.71	51.15	55.48	60.53	65.88	70.96
All Africa (%)	14.40	18.64	23.59	27.91	32.13	35.95	39.98	44.59	49.95	55.73	61.59

** Projections*
Source: WUP 2009

GRAPH 2.1: **NORTHERN AFRICA - URBAN POPULATION 1950-2050**

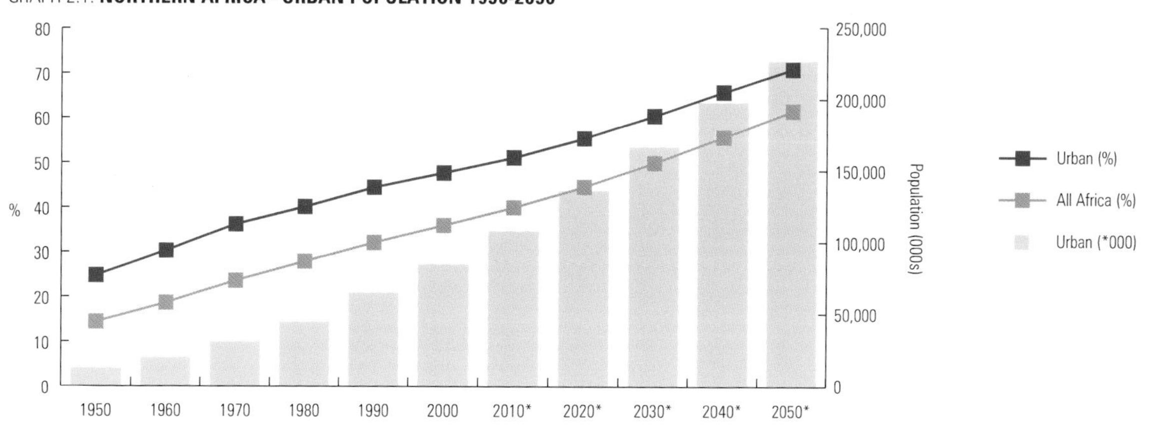

** Projections*
Source: WUP 2009

TABLE 2.2: **NORTHERN AFRICA URBANISATION RATES – 1950-2050 (%)**

Population	1950	1960	1970	1980	1990	2000	2010*	2020*	2030*	2040*	2050*
Algeria	22.21	30.51	39.50	43.54	52.09	59.81	66.50	71.85	76.23	80.12	83.50
Egypt	31.93	37.86	42.21	43.86	43.48	42.80	43.40	45.93	50.92	57.23	63.30
Libyan Arab Jamahiriya	19.55	27.32	49.67	70.09	75.72	76.37	77.89	80.29	82.88	85.19	87.23
Morocco	26.18	29.36	34.48	41.21	48.39	53.34	58.24	63.97	69.18	73.85	78.05
Sudan	6.82	10.75	16.52	19.96	26.62	33.41	40.10	47.42	54.54	61.32	67.69
Tunisia	32.29	37.51	43.48	50.57	57.95	63.43	67.28	71.23	75.17	78.80	82.03
Western Sahara	31.00	31.19	42.09	77.45	86.16	83.86	81.83	83.90	85.93	87.80	89.45

** Projections*
Source: WUP 2009

GRAPH 2.2: **NORTHERN AFRICA URBANISATION RATES – 1950-2050 (%)**

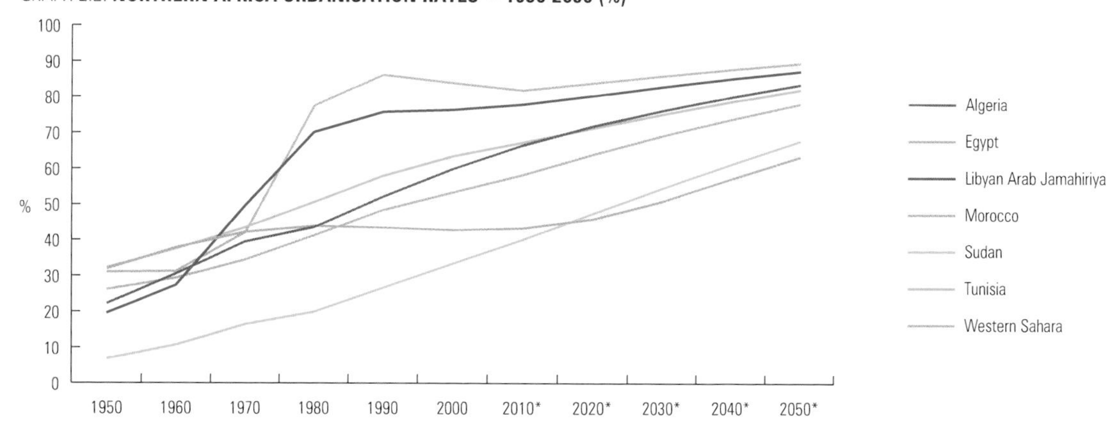

** Projections*
Source: WUP 2009

MAP 2.2: **POPULATION: URBAN SETTLEMENTS OVER 50,000 (YEAR 2000)**

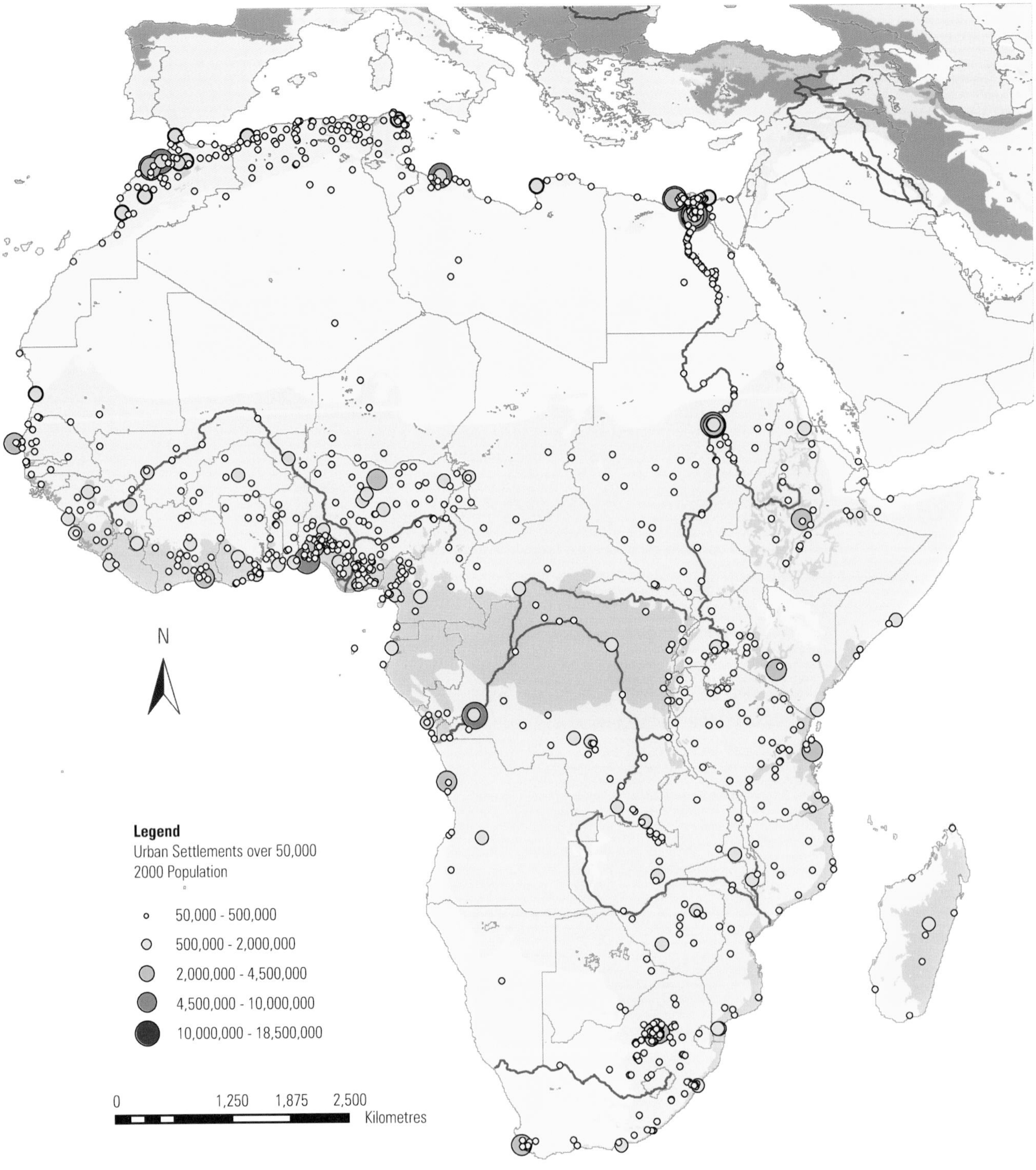

N

Legend

Urban Settlements over 50,000
2000 Population

- 50,000 - 500,000
- 500,000 - 2,000,000
- 2,000,000 - 4,500,000
- 4,500,000 - 10,000,000
- 10,000,000 - 18,500,000

0 1,250 1,875 2,500 Kilometres

Sources: Centre for International Earth Science Information Network (CIESIN), Columbia University; International Food Policy Research Institute (IPFRI), the World Bank; and Centro Internacional de Agricultura Tropical (CIAT), 2004

TABLE 2.3: **SELECTED HUMAN INDICATORS**

	GNI per head (current US $)		Population living on less than $1.25/ day (%)	Probability of not reaching age 40 (% of cohort)	Adult illiteracy rate (%)
	2005	2008			
Algeria	2,720	4,260	7.7	25.4	6.8
Egypt	1,200	1,800	7.5	28.6	< 2.0
Libya	5,870	11,590	4.6	13.8	..
Morocco	2,000	2,580	8.2	45.3	2.5
Sudan	590	1,130	26.1	39.1	..
Tunisia	2,870	3,290	4.6	23.1	2.6

Source: World Development Indicators Database - April 2009

attracting foreign domestic investment in Egypt, Morocco and Tunisia. This phenomenon reinforces the role of cities as the engines of national economies. Since these three major sectors have been affected by the 2008/09 financial crisis, governments are now looking to enhance their countries' global competitiveness. In Egypt, for instance, income taxes and custom duties have been significantly reduced. As a result, net flows of foreign domestic investment grew from US $2 billion in 2004 to US $13.1 billion in 2008. Nevertheless, Egypt's economy was unable to absorb the 700,000 new entrants in the labour force in 2008.[4]

Cairo and ***Alexandria*** are the main engines of Egypt's economy: 57 per cent of all manufacturing activities are located in Greater Cairo and another 22.5 in Alexandria, the country's main seaport.[5] In Morocco, ***Casablanca*** is host to 60 per cent of industrial workers and 55 per cent of the country's production units,[6] although the city accounts for only 10 per cent of the total population. In Sudan, three-quarters of industrial activities are concentrated in ***Khartoum***, the political and economic capital. However, 74 per cent of the labour force in urbanised areas was employed in the informal sector in 1996.[7]

Despite the steady rise in income per head, unemployment remains a problem and is increasingly concentrated in the larger Northern African cities. In Morocco, urban unemployment decreased only slightly, from 19.5 per cent in 2001 to 18.2 per cent in 2007.[8] As of 2007, 80 per cent of unemployed Moroccans lived in cities, as opposed to 50 per cent in 1990. Urban unemployment disproportionately affects the younger, more educated segment of the population. In 2004, the unemployment rate among urban workers with less than basic education was 11 per cent, compared with 32 per cent among those with secondary education degrees and 35 per cent among university graduates. Although women with higher education degrees represent only about 10 per cent of the labour force, they accounted for some 20 per cent of the unemployed.[9] These higher rates reflect parents' reluctance to let unmarried daughters accept jobs away from home, and of married women to commute for jobs far from home due to childrearing duties.

TABLE 2.4: **VALUE ADDED BY ECONOMIC SECTOR (% OF GDP)**

	Agriculture		Industry		Services	
	2000	2008	2000	2008	2000	2008
Algeria	9	9	59	69	33	23
Egypt	17	14	33	36	50	50
Libya	..	..	..	..	..	..
Morocco	15	16	29	20	56	64
Sudan	42	26	22	34	37	40
Tunisia	12	10	29	28	59	62

Source: World Development Indicators Database - April 2009

In Tunisia, unemployment has remained steady at 14.2 per cent of the active population.[10] In Algeria, the 2007 household survey arrived at an unemployment rate of 14.2 per cent for an urban labour force of nearly 6.2 million, and of 13.1 per cent for a rural labour force of 3.8 million. Young people accounted for the bulk of urban unemployment: 35 per cent of the active population under 20 years, 30 per cent of the 20-24 age group and 22 per cent of the 25-29 age group were looking for work in 2007. Taken together, those under 30 years of age account for 71 per cent of urban unemployment, with females accounting for 25.6 per cent.[11]

In Sudan, urban poverty has been on the rise as a result of internal displacement caused by war and natural disasters. Most of the urban poor live in the ***Khartoum*** Governorate, where many internally displaced citizens have found shelter in camps and informal settlements. The western and central Sudanese states also account for significant portions of the urban poor.[12]

In Northern Africa as a whole and despite significant progress over the past decade, disparities persist between urban and rural populations. In Algeria, Tunisia and Morocco, the proportions of the population living below national poverty lines are two to three times higher in rural than in urban areas. In 2004/05 in Egypt's urban governorates, average gross domestic product per head (10,457 Egyptian pounds (EGP),

TABLE 2.5: **SELECTED URBAN/RURAL INDICATORS**

	Under-5 mortality rate (/1,000)			Access to improved drinking water (%)	
	National	Rural	Urban	Rural	Urban
Algeria	39.0 (2005)	--	--	81% (2006)	87% (2006)
Egypt	40.0 (2005)	56.1 (2005)	39.1 (2005)	98% (2006)	99% (2006)
Libya	19.0 (2005)	--	--	68% (2000)	72% (2000)
Morocco	40.0 (2005)	69.4 (2004)	38.1 (2004)	58% (2006)	100% (2006)
Sudan	115.0 (2000)	144 (1990)	117 (1990)	64% (2006)	78% (2006)
Tunisia	24.0 (2005)	30.0	16.0	84% (2006)	99% (2006)

Source: WHO, 2009; World Bank Development Indicators Database, April 2009

or about US $1,800) was almost twice as high as in the rural governorates in the Delta (EGP 5,245, or about US $920) or Upper Egypt (EGP 5,197), or US $910). The percentage of the Egyptian population living below the poverty line was 5.7 per cent in metropolitan areas, and 39.1 per cent in the rural areas of Upper Egypt.[13]

Similar disparities can be found in most other countries in the subregion. In Morocco, about two-thirds of the population below the poverty line lives in rural areas with limited access to basic social services. Although the national poverty rate has declined from 19 per cent in 1999 to 15 per cent in 2009, most of the gains occurred in cities, as the rural poverty rate has stabilised at 22 per cent and about two-thirds of the poor live in rural areas.[14] In Sudan, education levels in rural areas are significantly lower than the national average. For instance, in 2001, only 30 per cent of males and 10 per cent of females in rural areas were literate, as compared with 60 per cent and 42 per cent respectively in the country as a whole.[15]

The concentration of health services in urban areas and a continuing, albeit diminishing, differential access to clean water sources are reflected in the infantile mortality gap between rural and urban areas. Most Northern African countries feature surfeits of doctors in urban areas and shortages of health care workers in rural and peri-urban areas.[16] In Sudan, nearly two-thirds of health expenditures go to 14 urban hospitals.[17] In addition, fees for health services hinder access for the rural population. In 2007, 25 per cent of the population in rural areas could not afford the fees, compared with five per cent in urban areas. Only one per cent of those who cannot afford the fees in rural areas have access to a social support system, compared with 62 per cent in urban areas.[18]

In Northern Africa, capital cities remain demographically and economically dominant, to the exception of Morocco whose principal city is ***Casablanca***, rather than the capital ***Rabat***. Recent urban demographic growth in Algeria, Egypt, Morocco and Tunisia has taken place in multiple, geographically dispersed, smaller cities, with a concomitant, steady decline in the primacy of the largest conurbations. Algeria's two largest cities, ***Algiers*** (2.8 million) and ***Oran*** (0.77

▲
Casablanca, Morocco. **©RJ Lerich/Shutterstock**

▲
View towards the medina and harbour in Tripoli, Libya. **©Danie Nel/Shutterstock**

million), are hosts to 10 per cent of the urban population but are now growing more slowly than the national urban average of 2.5 per cent. In Morocco, ***Casablanca*** (3.2 million), ***Rabat*** (1.8 million), ***Fes*** (one million) and ***Marrakech*** (0.9 million) collectively hold 22 per cent of the total and 38 per cent of the urban population. While ***Casablanca's*** population is growing at under one per cent per year, in other cities the rates are close to two per cent. In 2004, ***Tunis*** and ***Sfax***, the second largest city, had a combined population of 1.085 million[19], and accounted for approximately 16 per cent of the urban population. In Egypt, the degree of concentration in the largest cities is much greater, with ***Cairo*** accounting for 22 per cent and ***Alexandria*** for 13 per cent of the urban population as of the latest (2006) census.[20]

Both Egypt and Morocco have adopted ambitious policies to steer new urban populations to new areas. In Egypt, the strategy focuses on the need to stem losses of arable land to urban sprawl, redirecting demographic pressure away from Nile Valley conurbations and on to the adjacent desert plateau. As a result, new settlements are under development in the desert to the east and west of the Nile Valley. Concurrently, major land reclamation projects intended to bring desert land into agricultural use are under way to compensate for urban expansion on arable land in the delta region.

In Morocco, two "new towns" are under development by the dedicated central holding company, Al Omrane, as part of its mandate to eliminate substandard living conditions and focus on social housing; they are known as ***Tasmena,*** 15 km from ***Rabat,*** and ***Tamansourt,*** 7 km from ***Marrakech.***

Libya is Northern Africa's most urbanised country with 78 per cent of the 6.4 million population living in urban areas. It is also the wealthiest, with gross domestic product per head equivalent to US $13,100 (on a purchasing power parity basis). The country's two dominant cities, ***Tripoli*** (1.1 million)[21] and ***Benghazi*** (1.2 million)[22] account for 36 per cent of the urban population and are growing at 2 per cent and 2.7 per cent respectively. Libya's population is projected to be 80 per cent urban by 2020, with just over 55 per cent living in ***Tripoli*** and ***Benghazi.***

Sudan's total population has more than tripled since 1960 while its rate of urbanisation has quadrupled. Most of this growth has been concentrated in ***Khartoum*** (5.1 million), which currently houses 12 per cent of Sudan's total population and 29 per cent of its urban population. With 4.5 million in 2005, ***Khartoum's*** population is growing at an annual 2.7 per cent pace, adding some 130,000 every year. Demographic growth rates are projected to remain above two per cent into

2025, when the ***Khartoum*** population will reach about 8 million, accounting for 15 per cent of Sudan's total population. Smaller cities are located primarily along the Nile River. The few outliers include ***Port Sudan*** on the Red Sea coast (284,000 in 2008), and ***El Obeidid*** and ***Abu Zabad***, which are located along the major oil pipeline and railway line.

The Links Between Poverty, Inequality and Slums

Between 1990 and 2010, the numbers of urban slum dwellers in Northern Africa decreased from 20,794,000 to 11,836,000, or about 43 per cent.[23] The decline was significant between 1990 and 2005 in Morocco, Egypt and Tunisia, but remained around 12 per cent in Algeria. In , only 1.6 per cent of urban dwellings were classified as substandard in the 2004 census while 99 per cent had access to the municipal water supply system. In Morocco, most of the urban slums are located in the ***Casablanca-Fes-Tangier*** triangle, where economic activity is concentrated. About 30 per cent of the households in Morocco's informal settlements have access to safe drinking water.[24] In contrast in Sudan, the percentage of the urban population living in slums increased from 86 per cent in 1990 to 94.2 per cent in 2005[25] due to both rural to urban migration and internal strife.

Overall, health conditions in the Northern African slums are significantly worse than in non-slum urban areas, as evidenced in Egypt and Morocco, where post-neonatal mortality in informal settlements is twice that prevailing in non-slum areas.

Although they are often lumped together under the general term 'slum', a distinction must be drawn between older, dilapidated areas and informal settlements. Informal settlements include several forms of unplanned urbanisation that require different regularization or upgrading treatments because they amount to irregular subdivisions, illegal occupancy of publicly owned land, or unauthorized construction in environmentally hazardous areas. Older deteriorated neighbourhoods embedded in the urban fabric and former village cores engulfed in urbanisation are also referred to as slums and require special treatment.

Initially built in peri-urban locations, informal settlements are, for the most part, constructed of durable materials and have access to trunk infrastructure such as electricity, potable water supply and some form of sanitation. With high densities on agricultural land, they often lack adequate social infrastructure, including schools and government services, mostly due to lack of vacant sites where these could be provided.[26] The combination of accelerated urbanisation and rapid densification results in overloaded infrastructures and inadequate transportation networks.

In Egypt, the first enumeration of informal settlements was undertaken in 1993 and demonstrated the magnitude of the problem. A more accurate survey based on aerial photography showed that those settlements amounted to over 60 per cent of urbanised areas in 2008.[27] Although the percentage of the Egyptian urban population living in slums decreased from 58 per cent in 1990 to 17.1 per cent in 2005, absolute numbers remain high, with estimates varying between 16 and 21 million in 2008. Informal settlements have invariably grown around villages in peri-urban fringes, and therefore display mixes of rural and urban socio-economic characteristics. In ***Alexandria***, 30 informal settlements house about 1.4 million people, or almost 40 per cent of the city's population. One of these settlements, known as *Naga El Arab*, epitomizes the mix of rural and urban characteristics. In this area, 50 per cent of the streets are unpaved, densities are high, unemployment is running at 17 per cent, high illiteracy rates prevail (35 per cent of males while 62 per cent of females aged 30-65 years of age have never attended school), and access to sanitary, healthcare, education, and community facilities is inadequate. For all these deficiencies, though, most informal settlements in Egypt do not combine the four defining primary shelter deprivations set out by UN-HABITAT which involve access to safe water sources, sanitation, durable housing and sufficient living area. These settlements usually owe their 'slum' status to inadequate sanitation, as connections to municipal networks are often a function of the construction of new primary trunk and treatment systems.

▲
Naga El Arab, Alexandria, Egypt. **©Arndt Husar**

2.2 The Economic Geography of Cities

Economic Inequality

Gini coefficients generally provide good indicators of inequality based either on income or household consumption (except for any mention to the contrary, subsequent Gini coefficients are based on income). Most Northern African countries have maintained the low degrees of inequality associated with urban Gini coefficients ranging between 0.300 and 0.399, which are lower than the 0.46 (*'high inequality'*) average for Africa as a whole in 2008. However, Gini coefficients do not reflect the depth of poverty or such non-economic aspects of equality as access to services, education and health. Algeria is a case in point.

In Algeria, the Gini coefficient decreased from 0.39 to 0.35 between 1988 and 1995 in urban areas, reflecting an annual average 1.46 per cent narrowing of the urban divide[28], while gross domestic product per head *decreased* from US $2,447 to US $1,488 at current prices.[29] Inequality in rural areas was steeper than in cities. Since 1995, the situation has reversed, with economic development resulting in rising incomes and widening disparities within cities, as urban output per head kept rising every year, reaching an equivalent US $4,959 in 2008.

In Morocco, the nationwide Gini coefficient is higher than the urban one, signalling that cities are 'less unequal' than rural areas. In urban areas, the coefficient held steady at a *'relatively low'* 0.377[30] from 1990 to 1998 while output per head increased from US $1,163 to US $1,424 (at current prices).[31] However, at 0.52, the *'very high'* Gini coefficient for ***Casablanca*** in 2006 was significantly higher than that for the urban population as a whole, which goes to show that in the larger cities where business and finance are concentrated, the benefits of prosperity are not so broadly distributed.

In Egypt, Gini coefficients increased from 0.34 in 1990 to 0.39 in 1997 in urban areas, reflecting an annual average 1.78 per cent increase in inequality. During the same period output per head increased from US $682 to US $1,280 (at current prices). Between 2000 and 2005, the share in national income held by the lowest quintile remained stable at 9 per cent.[32]

Gini Coefficients: Measuring the Urban Divide

Named after an Italian statistician, the Gini coefficient is a broad measure of economic inequality, or what has become known as 'the urban divide' in connection with cities. The coefficient measures the distribution of either household income or consumption expenditure as a ratio of 0 to 1, where 0 indicates perfect equality (a proportional distribution of income/consumption), and 1 indicates perfect inequality (where one individual holds all of the income and no one else has any). In between, the coefficients denote the following degrees of inequality: below 0.299: low inequality; 0.3 to 0.399: relatively low; 0.4 to 0.449: relatively high; 0.45 to 0.499: high; 0.5 to 0.599: very high; and 0.6 and upwards: extremely high. The coefficients are generally available for individual countries as well as for rural and urban areas, and more infrequently for individual cities.

TABLE 2.6: **URBAN GINI COEFFICIENTS AND OUTPUT PER HEAD – SELECTED COUNTRIES**

	Algeria		Egypt		Morocco	
	1988	**1995**	**1990**	**1997**	**1990**	**1998**
Urban Gini coefficient	0.39	0.35	0.34	0.39	0.377	0.337
GDP per head (current US $)	2,447	1,488	682	1,280	1,163	1,424
GDP per head (PPP)	4,110	4,531	2,284	3,061	2,724	3,502

Sources: UN-Habitat, 2009; UN Statistics Division

In Tunisia's urban areas, the Gini coefficient worsened somewhat in the first half of the 1990s while remaining about stable in rural areas. In the second half of the 1990s, the situation was reversed as the Gini coefficient remained steady in cities, but increased slightly in rural areas.[33]

In Sudan, inequality has increased significantly. The urban Gini coefficient increased from a *'very high'* 0.56 in 1990 to an *'extremely high'* 0.72 in 1996,[34] creating a potential for social unrest. While urban inequalities have been higher than in rural areas, rural inequality has also been rising steeply, with the Gini coefficient soaring from 0.34 in 1967 to 0.65 in 1996.

How Slum Dwellers Survive

In spite of considerable progress over the last decade, Northern Africa's urban economies remain unable to provide jobs for significant segments of the labour force, as demonstrated by high rates of urban unemployment particularly among young people. Of special concern are the high proportions of individuals with secondary or higher education among the unemployed: 41 per cent in Algeria (2008), 44 per cent in Morocco (2007) and 46 per cent in Tunisia (2004). In addition, significant proportions of urban jobs are part-time or casual - for instance, 32 per cent in Algeria.

In all countries, middle-school graduates make up the largest proportions of the urban unemployed. In Morocco and Tunisia, unemployment is high among secondary school graduates. The superior benefits of higher education in the urban job market are only evident in Tunisia, where a combination of relative affluence, a solid middle class and a strong private business sector (tourism, manufacturing, services, etc.) is generating demand for qualified professional, managerial and technical occupations.

Morocco is the only country in Northern Africa where informal sector employment and production (including construction) have been surveyed (in 1984-85), followed by micro-enterprises in 1988. These surveys have not been updated and similar studies are not readily available. World Bank research shows that since the early 1990s, the unemployment rate in Morocco's informal and micro-enterprise sector has remained at an estimated 30 per cent.

Typical self-advancement strategies differ markedly between slums (as defined by the number of UN-HABITAT shelter deprivations), squatter areas (where lack of legal ownership rights hinders self-improvement strategies) and informal settlements. Squatters include poor families, widows, students and rural migrants who struggle to earn a livelihood. They lack security of both employment and occupancy, with unauthorized or outright illegal tenure. In contrast, residents in informal settlements enjoy secure occupancy rights and are generally upwardly mobile, median-income households seeking to improve their economic situation and social status through investment in asset-building and education.

Rural migrants seek low-skilled and menial jobs such as handling goods, removing construction debris and street-sweeping. They work as day labourers on informal construction sites and similar work, or earn a living peddling produce or rural artefacts. They typically settle in inner city slums, which are well embedded in the urban fabric, as these locations provide more opportunities for work. In older, deteriorating neighbourhoods, people tend to work as shopkeepers, restaurant owners, craftsmen, or in domestic or personal services.

Residents in urban informal settlements work in a variety of occupations that reflect their level of education, such as plant and machine operators, crafts, trades and service workers, clerical workers and technicians. In Egypt, nearly 76 per cent of household heads were employed (2004/05), and less than 25 per cent of the group fell into the following categories: unemployed, not in the labour force, and unpaid family worker.[35]

In informal settlements, residents chart self-improvement strategies based on individual household conditions. In those Northern African cities that are also sources of emigration, the typical pattern is as follows:

- Savings are mobilised to fund the migration of at least one family member. This includes travel and accommodation costs for those most likely to find work abroad. It often happens that the first remittances received go to fund the emigration of a younger sibling.
- Increasing shares of the remittances are saved in order to invest in asset building.
- Purchase of a land parcel. In Northern Africa, ownership of land or property is most lucrative and highly coveted, generating income and conferring

TABLE 2.7: **AGE STRUCTURE OF URBAN UNEMPLOYED**

	Algeria		Morocco		Tunisia*	
	2008		2007		2004	
< 24	453,000	44.8%	326,048	36.8%	158,088	37.0%
25 - 34	435,000	43.0%	393,384	44.4%	165,800	38.8%
35 - 44	90,000	8.9%	121,382	13.7%	64,487	15.1%
45 - +	34,000	3.4%	45,186	5.1%	39,031	9.1%

**Nationwide figures*

Sources: Algeria: Institut National de la Statistique; Morocco: Enquête nationale sur l'emploi, Direction de la Statistique; Tunisia: Institut National de la Statistique

▲
A cobbler in Fes, Morocco. **©Deiter Telemans/Panos Pictures**

TABLE 2.8: **URBAN UNEMPLOYMENT BY EDUCATION LEVEL**

	Morocco		Tunisia*		Egypt	
	2007		2004		2008	
No schooling	54,932	6.3%	52,405	12.1%	48,200	4.0%
Primary & Middle school	427,938	48.7%	179,613	41.6%	614,200	50.4%
Secondary school	207,324	23.6%	159,301	36.9%	104,100	8.5%
Higher education	188,718	21.5%	40,685	9.4%	453,100	37.2%

**Nationwide figures*
Sources: Morocco: Enquête nationale sur l'emploi, Direction de la Statistique; Tunisia: Institut National de la Statistique; Egypt: CAPMAS

social status. Purchasing a land plot is the first step in this process.

- The property is developed as fast as possible given the cumulative remittances and earnings that family members can generate.
- The value of real estate assets is enhanced with commercial and rental developments.
- The cumulative earnings can ensure a good education for the next generation.

In Northern African conurbations, informal settlements are predominantly hosts to medium- and lower-income households ranging from the 60th to the 20th percentile. Some of those with lower incomes can be found renting housing that has been built incrementally by households whose incomes are on either side of the median.

In Egypt, the residents of informal urban settlements represent a broad range of educational levels, incomes and occupations, including lower ranking civil servants.[36] As of 2005, the majority (52 per cent) had primary school education or more; 22 per cent were illiterate and 20 per cent could read and write. Approximately 25 per cent had an intermediate level of education and 16 per cent had a university degree. Fifty-five per cent of informal settlement dwellers were found to be regular wage earners, a proportion higher than the national average that reflects the need for low-income household members to cumulate incomes if they are to survive economically.[37] This multiplicity of wage earners and diversity of income sources is the cornerstone of household strategies for self-improvement.

In Northern Africa, informal settlements consist of multi-storey buildings on agricultural land held under legal though mostly unregistered titles. This category of settlements is referred to as *habitat spontané* in Morocco, Tunisia and Algeria. The typical settlement features only one shelter deprivation, and then only temporarily, i.e. water-borne sewerage, until the municipal network is extended to the area. These settlements are widely viewed as middle-class neighbourhoods. Household turnover is limited and follows the same pattern as in other middle-class areas. Despite the dense urban fabric, these settlements are attractive to a large segment of the population.

As settlements mature, they develop into dense urban neighbourhoods that are well integrated in the city's socio-economic fabric. They attract those families with above-median incomes whose wage earners are in professional or managerial occupations in the public or private sectors. Algeria, Egypt, Morocco, Sudan and Tunisia all run programmes for skills-based education (from vocational training to commercial schools, including computer training). However, and as in many developing countries, formal job creation has lagged behind the large numbers of new entrants into the labour force. If the creation of small and micro-enterprises is to be promoted, greater emphasis should be put on the development of entrepreneurial and managerial skills.

Addressing Inequality and Urban Fragmentation

The significant reduction in the overall number of slum dwellers (from 20,794,000 in 1990 to an estimated 11,836,000 in 2010) in Northern Africa is the result of vigorous and effective government programmes for slum upgrading and prevention, particularly in Egypt, Libya and Morocco. Between 1990 and 2010, Libya reduced its slum population by 71 per cent and Egypt and Morocco by 65.9 per cent and 65 per cent respectively.[38] In Morocco, 4.4 million people have moved out of slum conditions over the past 20 years, with the percentage of the urban population living in slums declining by about two thirds from 37.4 per cent in 1990 to an estimated 13 per cent in 2010. Egypt managed to reduce slum prevalence from 50 per cent in 1990 to an estimated 17.1 per cent in 2010, improving the living conditions of 11.2 million people. Tunisia has essentially eliminated all slums through a vigourous programme managed by *Agence de réhabilitation et de rénovation urbaine* (ARRU). Since the 1980s, the Tunisian government has been controlling urban sprawl, improving housing conditions in the older districts, regularizing substandard fringe settlements and providing the urban population with potable water, sanitation, schools and health facilities, especially in informal peri-urban areas. These achievements highlight one of the strengths of ARRU, i.e., its effective coordination with public authorities, and more specifically its ability to adapt to the greater role local authorities are playing as part of decentralization, and to build their inputs into its own policy schemes.

Today, thanks to the determined policies of a number of countries, nine out of 10 urban slum households in Northern Africa suffer from only *one* shelter deprivation, which typically involves improved sanitation in Egypt and adequate living areas in Morocco.

If it were to accommodate nationwide demographic growth (1.5 per cent on an annual average basis) and the associated 50 per cent proportion below 25 years of age, Egypt should build housing for 500,000 households annually. At the moment, government production is only about 85,000 units, which implies that 80 per cent of demand must be met by the private sector, both formal and informal. Government programmes offer a range of housing options: apartments (63 m^2) for low-income families; 30-40 m^2 units at nominal rents for families living below the poverty line; serviced plots (150 m^2) subject to a land or ground floor coverage ratio of 50 per cent and a maximum height of three floors; apartments on an ownership or rental basis (80^+ m^2) for medium-income families; and rural dwellings in new land reclamation areas. All these social housing programmes are heavily subsidized. The government contributes front-end subsidies and below-market interest rates on housing loans payable over 25 to 30 years. For serviced plots, loans are repaid over 10 years.[39]

In practice, though, these public sector programmes have all experienced delays. Deliveries have been running at 47 per cent of production targets, prompting the government to work in partnership with private developers to mobilise more resources and increase production. Still, this partnership programme is of particular interest since it has managed to attract private sector investment into social housing, with discounted land prices as an incentive. Tracts of land in new towns and urban expansion areas are allocated to developers at highly subsidized prices (EGP 70 (or US $12.00) per sq m for serviceable land, while the cost to the government is about EGP 400 (or US $70.00) per sq m for serviced land) on condition that developers fund on-site infrastructure and build housing for families with incomes below the national median (i.e., EGP 2,500 (or US $438.00) per month) on the land parcel. Under this type of partnership, 17,000 units were built in 2009, and a total of 300,000 are expected between

▲
Khartoum, Sudan. ©**Galyna Andrushko/Shutterstock**

BOX 2.1: **EGYPT'S SUCCESSFUL ORASCOM HOUSING COMMUNITIES PARTNERSHIP**

▲
Orascom affordable housing in Haram City, Egypt. **Photo courtesy of Orascom**

In 2006, Orascom Group, one of Egypt's largest business concerns, established **Orascom Housing Communities** (OHC). This is a joint venture with Homex, a development company focusing on affordable housing in Mexico, and two American investment companies, Blue Ridge Capital and Equity International. The rationale was to build affordable housing in Egyptian cities under a government programme that allocates subsidized raw land in new towns to developers and investors on condition that they build an agreed number of units for lower-income households on the land.

Orascom's largest project so far consists of 50,000 units to be built between 2006 and 2013 on 8.4 million m^2 in 'October 6' City. The target group is households with monthly incomes below median (EGP 2,500, or US $438.00). In the first phase, sizes varied between 38 to 63 m^2 and units were offered on a lease/purchase basis (over 10 to 15 years on affordable financial terms). Cultural preferences for the larger units have led OHC to focus on the latter in subsequent phases. To reduce construction costs, OHC uses load-bearing walls and a compact housing typology of four units per two-floor block that is well-suited to desert climate conditions. Government subsidies for lower-income families (up to 15 per cent of the cost of the house) are offered as front-end lump sums, reducing down-payments in order to facilitate access for young families. On top of this, OHC is setting up a microfinance scheme to help lower-income families make the required down-payment. A special scheme can assist any residents who run into financial difficulties and are unable to pay mortgage instalments. To pre-empt on these problems, households can first move into smaller units that are affordable to them and can change to less expensive rental units if difficulties persist.

As part of the project, OHC builds supporting community facilities, including schools, a hospital, commercial areas, a cinema complex, sporting clubs and day-care centres, which are to be managed in cooperation with the Egyptian government and/or non-governmental organizations. OHC will retain majority ownership of retail and commercial properties while leasing space to third parties.

On top of this comprehensive approach to housing development for low-income households, Orascom emphasizes sustainability, women and youth. Wastewater is collected and recycled to irrigate landscaped areas and the central open space as well as other smaller 'green' areas, sports fields and play-grounds. A local company collects and recycles solid waste. In addition, OHC has partnered with the Social Fund for Development, purchasing goods from Fund-sponsored small entrepreneurs, and has opened three youth training centres. OHC has also set up the 'El Amal' centre to provide a safe haven for street children, and a centre for women's skills development, both operated by charitable organizations.

Construction began in 2007 and the first residents moved in by late 2008. At that time, the main water line, electricity supply and sewage plants were in place and two out of the eight zones were completed. By the end of 2009, 12,000 units had been built, 3,000 more were under construction, and since then sales of completed units have picked up, reaching an average 15 per day.

Orascom now plans to develop more large-scale housing estates in Egypt and other countries facing shortages of affordable housing.[41]

BOX 2.2: **EGYPT'S INFORMAL SETTLEMENT DEVELOPMENT FACILITY**

In 2009, the Government of Egypt set up a dedicated facility to support informal settlement upgrading. The Facility is under its direct control and run by an executive director and a board chaired by the Minister of Local Development, with representatives from six government departments and three civil society organizations, together with three experts. The Facility was established and capitalized with a government seed grant of EGP 500 million (or US $87.6 million), EGP 200 million (US $35 million) in budget allocations and EGP 100 million (US $17.5 million) in grants from USAID.

The executive director of the Facility has devised a national action plan, which includes the following:

- Knowledge management, including maps of all informal settlements;
- A list of programmes and projects to be implemented;
- Identifying the technical assistance and capacity-building to be extended to those local authorities implementing projects;
- Partnerships with stakeholders, including private sector entities;
- Scheduling of projects; and
- A priority to land-based financing to generate revenue.

The Facility has requested a government allocation of land to be used as an asset in the new towns to recapitalize and speed up disbursements and avoid breakdown. In addition, the Facility has requested the following:

1. About 75,000 subsidized housing units for priority target groups requiring relocation, namely:
   - Families living in environmentally hazardous, life-threatening areas. These have been mapped across the whole country for the first time.
   - Families living in shacks, in structurally unsound buildings, and alongside health-threatening activities (dumps, noxious industries, etc.); and
2. The use of land-based financing for on-site re-housing of families living in unsanitary, dilapidated dwellings on publicly-owned land. In the first phase, the Facility has launched 25 pilot projects testing various approaches in five cities in Upper Egypt, four cities in the delta, and the three cities along the Suez Canal. The Facility is also providing technical assistance to Alexandria for its upgrading projects, which the governorate is funding from its own resources. This first phase does not include projects in the Greater Cairo region.

As it stands, Egypt's Informal Settlement Development Facility faces the following two major challenges:

1. Creating a legal framework that can accommodate the complex land transactions required for land-based financing of upgrading projects; and
2. Ensuring repayment by borrowing local authorities.[45]

2009 and 2015.[40] The Orascom Housing Communities scheme in the 'October 6' new town demonstrates the strong potential of such partnerships (see Box 2.1)

The cost to the Egyptian government of extending infrastructure to project sites in the desert has increased markedly from EGP 10.4 billion (or US $1.8 billion) in 2000/01 to 17.2 billion (US $3 billion) in 2004/05 to 36 billion (US $6.3 billion) in 2008/09 as planned urbanisation on the desert plateau gathers momentum and moves further away from the Nile valley. Land-based financing is used to defray the costs of infrastructure. Sustained demand for land and associated rapid price escalation in the new towns has enabled the government to meet the costs of infrastructure provision to new urban extensions and derive a net profit of EGP 200/m² (or US $35) on the land it sells in those areas (except for the subsidized land allocated for social housing).[42]

Still in Egypt, another determined 10-year government programme has combined regularisation, infrastructure improvements and the demolition of housing built in hazardous areas. As a result, 904 informal settlements were upgraded between 1994 and 2004. Despite the emergence of new ones, the number declined from 1,174 to 1,121 over those 10 years, while still extending over a significant 1,943 km². It should be noted that 70 per cent of slum dwellers are concentrated in the two largest cities, ***Cairo*** and ***Alexandria,*** a feature shared by other North African countries. As in other developing countries, informal settlements in Egypt are often only one step away from moving out of the 'slum' category: for 85 per cent of the 1,014 settlements in this category, this would involve better compliance with building code requirements; for the remaining 15 per cent that encroach on government-owned land, upgrading would only require legalization of tenure.[43]

Egypt has devised a national strategy to contain the spread of unplanned urbanisation around the following four principles:

- Establishing urbanisation perimeters for towns and villages and developing plans for areas within the perimeters;
- Surrounding existing, rapidly growing settlements with belts of planned projects;
- Increasing the production of housing affordable to low- and limited-income groups; and
- Steering rural migrants to the new settlements in developed areas in the desert.

Past experience demonstrates that informal developments cannot be contained by regulatory measures alone, since enforcement is at best sporadic due to corruption among local district officers in charge of authorisations and inspections.

In ***Alexandria***, the governorate has launched a demand-driven upgrading programme to improve basic infrastructure and other community services, generate economic opportunities for residents and make tenure more formal and secure through proper documentation. The first phase involved three large settlements, or about 15 per cent of the Governorate population. Four additional settlements are to be upgraded in the second phase of the project.[44]

In 2009, the Egyptian government set up the Informal Settlement Development Facility, which provides funding and technical assistance to public authority projects (see Box 2.2).

In Morocco since the 1980s, authorities have acted vigourously to eradicate *bidonvilles* (French for 'shantytowns') through upgrading, construction of apartments and provision of serviced plots. In 2003, the Moroccan government adopted a new strategy that granted the private sector a more significant role in the provision of affordable housing and credit schemes for low-income earners who had no access to mortgage finance. In 2005, the government launched the *Cities without Slums* upgrading programme in 250 neighbourhoods in 25 cities. The scheme targeted neighbourhoods with high unemployment, poor housing conditions and lack of access to basic services. An equivalent of US $900,000 was allocated to each neighbourhood. A consultative participatory process has been established to enhance social inclusion. This programme has already enabled Morocco to reduce its slum population by 65 per cent between 1990 and 2010.

Since 2004, Al Omrane, the dedicated government-owned holding company has played a major role in Morocco's *Cities without Slums* programme, funding the construction of affordable urban housing through its real estate development arm. In the process, the agency has contributed to the country's poverty reduction efforts through the creation of economic activity zones for small- and medium-sized enterprises in its urban projects. These cover a wide range of schemes: re-housing of families living in makeshift dwellings (over 75,000 in 2007 and 2008); upgrading underserviced neighbourhoods; regularising land tenure in informal settlements; and developing new towns and urban expansion zones where a share of the land is allocated to construction of affordable housing. Between 2003 and 2009, Al Omrane completed 724,000 housing units for a cumulative cost of 35.9 billion dirhams (MAD) (or US $4.6 billion).

Morocco's newly adopted capital expenditure strategy for 2008/12 focuses on greater private sector involvement through tax incentives, as well as development of mixed-income urban housing projects targeted at expatriate Moroccan workers. Al Omrane plans to build 30,000 housing units with a sales price of MAD140,000 (US $17,800); 37,200 for MAD250,000 (US $32,000) for moderate-income households; and another 37,200 at market rates to cross-subsidize the units for lower-income households. The lower-cost units are a new product that will be affordable to households with monthly earnings between MAD1,800 and 2,700 (US $229 and US $343) and will be available on a priority basis to those living in dilapidated units, as well as to public sector employees. Buyers of low-cost units will be eligible for mortgages guaranteed by *Fonds de garantie pour les revenus irréguliers et modestes* (FOGARIM), an agency created in 2004 to encourage banks to provide long-term credit to lower-income individuals and those with a less than steady source of income. The Fund guarantees monthly loan repayments of up to MAD1,500 (US $190). By mid-2009 the Fund had guaranteed 48,000 loans worth MAD7 billion (US $890 million).

In Tunisia, the government's direct involvement in the production of affordable housing has declined significantly in recent years. One of the main protagonists was the *Société nationale immobilière tunisienne* (SNIT) an independent government-owned company whose production peaked at 15,000 units a year during the Sixth Plan (1982/86). As of 2002, however, the number had fallen between 1,000 and 1,500 units a year. Given that less than one per cent of the urban population was classified as living in substandard housing in the 2004 census, current government policy has shifted to infrastructure improvements in working class neighbourhoods[46], including street lighting, water and sewer systems. The implementation of upgrading policies is the responsibility of the national *Agence de réhabilitation et de rénovation urbaine* (ARRU), which since 2002 has spent over US $72 million on urban projects that have improved living conditions for 1,140,000 people.

These policies reflect a shift away from the traditional role of Northern African governments in the 1970s and 1980s, when urban improvement schemes were the sole responsibility of specialised public agencies. Since the turn of the century, an increasingly sharp distinction has been drawn between the regularisation and servicing by local authorities of land that has already been developed, on the one hand, and, on the other, the assembly of serviced land to be developed into mixed-income housing by public and para-statal entities and private developers, with various cross-subsidisation schemes to secure private sector involvement. This approach has allowed the leveraging of public funds to deliver a range of new, improved affordable housing, in the process causing significant declines in the numbers of slum dwellers and underserviced households in informal settlements.

▲
Casablanca, Morocco ©**RJ Lerich/Shutterstock**

2.3
The Geography of Urban Land Markets

Forms of Tenure and Rights

Despite geographic and economic differences, a shared legacy of laws and institutions governing tenure, use, control and taxation of land has generated strong similarities in Northern Africa's urban land markets. Prior to Western colonization, all these countries were under Ottoman rule, where tenure systems were still solidly anchored in *sharia* law and reflected the evolution of Islamic jurisprudence over 1,500 years. Overlays of primary and derivative rights would combine to create a complex system whereby ownership of shares of a land parcel or a building could be held by different individuals. An 1897 Ottoman statute abolished government ownership of agricultural land across the empire and allowed beneficial rights holders to turn their tenure into fee-simple ownership. As a result, urban settlements were surrounded by privately-owned land.

Western colonial rule strengthened individual property rights and established the right for foreigners to own real estate. After independence, land reform combined with nationalisation of large land holdings and the repossession of property owned by foreigners who had left the country. These moves added sizeable amounts of well-located land to public land reserves. Nevertheless, public land holdings on the urban fringes fell short of accommodating the accelerated urbanisation of the 1970s and 1980s when the surface area of the main cities doubled as a result of rural-urban migration, natural demographic increases and massive inflows of private capital and remittances into urban real estate. As urban expansion was no longer constrained by government ownership of land (which, incidentally, had prevented fragmentation and conversion of agricultural land to urban use), the result was a proliferation of unplanned subdivisions of fields and rapid densification of peri-urban informal settlements.

Inheritance laws mandating division of assets among heirs have added to the fragmentation of property ownership, which turns modern-day property registration methods into a serious challenge, based as they are on recording the physical attributes of a property, as opposed to traditional systems that recorded the attributes of the parties involved.

In Egypt, the bulk of government-owned land is located in the desert. Turning privately-owned agricultural land to urban uses is prohibited, except within the designated perimeters of urban settlements. Despite government efforts to develop state-owned desert land, the formal sector has been unable to meet the demand for affordable housing. As a result, vast informal housing areas have been developed illegally on agricultural lands on urban fringes and on government-owned desert lands on the edge of the Nile valley. A 2007 World Bank study on Egyptian informal housing enumerated as many as 8.5 million informal housing units, of which:

- 4.7 million units on agricultural land within or outside municipal boundaries;
- 0.6 million on government-owned desert land within municipal boundaries; and
- 3.2 million outside administrative village boundaries.[47]

In ***Cairo***, 81 per cent of informal units sit on privately-owned agricultural land, with 10 per cent on government-owned desert land and the remainder on state-owned agricultural land.[48]

In Libya, all private property rights were abolished in March 1978, although beneficial rights to residential dwellings were maintained. The government liberalised property regulations in the early 1990s and transferred ownership of dwellings to sitting occupants who, with the exception of low-income families, made monthly mortgage payments to the government equivalent to one third of the former rent. At present, private and public land markets operate side by side, but property rights are not secure and there remains a significant degree of regulatory uncertainty.[49]

Morocco first introduced a land registration system in 1913, under colonial rule, to delineate and title all privately-owned property. In recent years, the housing shortage has driven up urban land prices.

In Tunisia, as of 2006 most land was privately held and collective land, as defined by a 1901 law, is typically tribal land. A 1964 law allowed the conversion of communal land into private holdings. In 2006, government-owned land still represented a significant portion of non-urban land, but private property was growing by an average 70,000 hectares per year.[50]

In Sudan, land law and tenure combine customary law, *sharia* and English common law and a host of tribal customs in the southern region, each of which creates distinct rules, regulations and practices. Customary law is given greater importance in the South, whereas *sharia* and common law are dominant in the North. In many instances, a combination of tradition and custom prevails, even when they are not in line with formal regulations.[51]

In addition to the private sector, charitable religious endowments, the *awqaf* (plural for *waqf*, also known as

▲
Casablanca, Morocco. ©**Giorgio Fochesato/iStockphoto**

'*habous*') are managed by a dedicated government department. To this day, they still control significant amounts of property in Northern African cities, particularly in the historic centres. They typically hold ownership rights to all or part of 20 to 40 per cent of the properties.[52] These endowments cannot dispose of such property and are not inclined to keep non-revenue earning buildings in a good state of repair, which contributes to the deterioration of historic centres. Tunisia is the notable exception since the *awqaf* were nationalised in 1956 and their properties transferred to the municipal authorities. In Egypt, a system of land swaps has been established, enabling the Ministry of *Awqaf* to exchange property in the city centre for land of equivalent value on the outskirts of the city.

Urban Land Institutions

As might be expected, land tenure systems in Northern Africa are heavily influenced by Islamic jurisprudence regarding ownership transfer and inheritance of both primary and derivative rights. In contrast, development regulations have retained little from the historic rules that governed land development and building construction. The regulations that apply today are adapted from the Western practices first introduced under colonial rule to develop European-style neighbourhoods.

Development regulations in Algeria, Morocco and Tunisia include zoning and dimensional requirements to implement locally-designed urban plans. Municipalities are also allowed to designate areas for rehabilitation or redevelopment. In Egypt, laws enacted in 1978 and 1982 introduced new regulations for the planning, subdivision and use of land, also allowing regularization of unplanned informal settlements. In 1995 and 1997, new laws authorized the sale of government-owned land to private institutions and adjusted regulations on subdivisions according to the type and proposed use of land.[53] Egypt's law N° 119 of 2008 amalgamated all current legislation and regulations governing land development and building construction, including planning design, subdivision and dimensional regulations, building codes, management of property held in co-ownership and tenancy rules. The country's urbanisation strategy unequivocally steers new developments toward desert land, with government departments and governorates facilitating implementation.[54] Despite these regulations, chaotic urbanisation has continued to spread unabated due to lack of effective control over land use, except for health and safety concerns e.g. nuisances caused by polluting activities and structurally unsound buildings.

In Libya, the government controls the planning and implementation of large projects, including new residential districts. Unplanned areas house mainly lower-income contracted migrant labour and illegal migrants. In Sudan, accelerated urbanisation in greater ***Khartoum*** has overpowered the regulatory framework, resulting in chaotic land development.

How Land Markets Operate

The main factor behind urban land development in Northern African countries is the high cost and rapid appreciation of land. No other asset has risen in value at this pace in the subregion, with average prices doubling every three years since 1970. As a result, central city densities are high and new developments have been occurring primarily on urban peripheries. Populations in historic centres have been shrinking as older residential buildings are converted to commercial uses.

Sharp discrepancies can be found between land markets in older districts, where property prices are distorted by various forms of rent control, and in urban fringes, where formal and informal settlements are under development to host urban populations that continue to grow at annual rates varying between 1.7 per cent in Tunisia to 2.5 per cent in Algeria.[55] In the face of sustained demand for land and government inability to deliver adequate amounts of serviced land, public authorities have come to tolerate informal urban sprawl as well as piecemeal enforcement of regulations and codes, as urbanised areas have doubled or even tripled in size. Underserviced areas have grown at rates two to three times faster

than urbanised areas as a whole. The percentages of the urban population living in informal settlements in Northern Africa range from 20 per cent in ***Tunis*** to upwards of 60 per cent in the ***Cairo*** Region. However, it is important to note that buildings in these settlements are of reasonably good quality, layouts are rectilinear and, except for Sudan, they rarely suffer from more than one shelter deprivation, usually lack of water-borne sewerage, or overcrowding.

In the informal sector, rising land prices have encouraged a resurgence of such traditional ownership patterns as joint ownership and various tenancy arrangements based on derivative rights. In Morocco, in particular, it is common for one party to purchase the land and for another to pay for the bulk of the building, leaving it for each party to complete the building as they see fit. In some cases, individuals sharing a common bond (professional association or kinship) have established cooperatives to acquire and subdivide land.[56] These practices enhance the affordability of urban land and housing.

In Egypt, raw land prices vary significantly, ranging from EGP 450/m^2 (or US $79) (for agricultural land that is expected to be serviced in the foreseeable future and where there is a likelihood of securing a building permit) to EGP 250/m^2 (or US $44) in more isolated locations. As might be expected, private freehold land with formal tenure status tends to command the highest prices and is often purchased as a speculative investment.[57] In informal settlements, land prices vary widely depending on location and access to services. For instance, in the north-eastern sector of the ***Cairo*** Region, the average land price increased from EGP 280/m^2 (or US $49) in 1997 to EGP 1,800/m^2 (or US $315) in 2003 as a result of proximity to the city centre and access to roads, infrastructure and public transport.[58] Serviced building plots on government-owned land are typically available at prices ranging from medium to high, but have also generated high degrees of speculation.

Still in Egypt, two main development patterns prevail. Private developers and small-scale contractors actively participate in the illegal subdivision of agricultural land for the construction of informal housing. As for developers of legal subdivisions, they have tended to rely on government-supplied land, as regulations and mandatory service standards have made it difficult to develop privately-owned agricultural land in the absence of primary infrastructure systems. The Government is a major developer in its own right, providing serviced sites in the desert for settlement by new communities, where land prices have been doubling every other year. As a result, a growing number of investment companies have become involved in financing urban development on government-provided land. In Egypt, private financing of land development has grown from about EGP 15 million (or US $2.6 million) in 2005 to EGP 3,000 million (US $526 million) in 2009; today, 16 banks and nine investment companies, with a current capitalization of EGP 1,000 million (or US $175 million) are active in the real estate market.

Land Markets, Urban Form and New Spatial Configurations

The urban form of most Northern African cities consists of a series of historic layers characterised by relatively homogeneous land markets, each with their own rules. The fabric of the historic city (*medina*) typically consists of a dense agglomeration of buildings subdivided into small dwellings, with commercial uses on the ground floor. Some of these historic centres feature on the UNESCO World Heritage List, including medieval ***Cairo***, the *medinas* of ***Tunis***, ***Fez***, ***Meknes*** and ***Marrakech*** and the *kasbah* of ***Algiers***.

Furthermore, to the exception of Tunisia, significant proportions (often up to 40 per cent) of historic district properties are owned by the *awqaf* charitable foundations. Many properties have deteriorated for lack of maintenance by absentee owners, as their rent-controlled housing attracted successive waves of rural migrants. Governments have deployed programmes to restore and preserve the historic centres as a valued cultural heritage and an architectural and urban legacy that can be attractive to domestic and foreign tourism. This effort is made more complicated by the fragmented ownership patterns and the reluctance of the *awqaf* to participate in improvement initiatives that do not generate revenue. Nevertheless, significant improvements to public spaces, streets, facades, markets and historic buildings have been made in the majority of the listed historic centres.

The next historic layer in Northern Africa's typical urban form is the *planned city* as developed during the colonial period. This consists of a Mediterranean urban pattern of multi-storey buildings, with distinct neighbourhoods reflecting the socio-economic mix of the population. In these planned cities, large proportions of the centrally located residential stock have been converted to offices as the economy began to shift to tertiary activities. Following independence, planned extensions were built through a combination of public improvements and private investment. From 1975 to 1985, land values doubled every three to four years while prices on urban fringes rose by a factor of 15 to 20.[59]

The third layer is the *peri-urban informal urbanisation* that began in the 1970s and has accommodated most of Northern Africa's sustained urban demographic growth rates of 2 to 4 per cent on an annual average basis since the 1980s. This trend was facilitated by the post-colonial resurgence of traditional tenure systems, including:

- The right of settlers to claim ownership of wasteland that they have improved;
- Acquisition of property rights through adverse possession, with a typical 10-15 years' lapse of time depending on the country; and
- Protection of inhabited dwellings from demolition regardless of regulatory status, except where the area or buildings are unsafe, or the site is needed for public use. The agency appropriating the land must provide relocation housing.[60]

These traditional rights have protected squatters on idle government-owned land and facilitated the regularisation of informal settlements. Where urbanisation of agricultural land is prohibited, land and/or property rights are transferred by notarial private contract but without the registration of the deeds or issuance of titles that are mandatory under property registration rules. In practice, this has created two parallel property transaction systems operating simultaneously in one and the same city. Unregistered titles remain commonplace and are upheld by courts, but cannot be used to challenge any owners with registered titles. Although the high cost of land is an incentive to register titles, registration is relatively expensive and therefore acts as a deterrent.

Since the 1990s, specialized public and para-statal agencies have been developing a fourth type of urban layer, namely *planned urban extensions, new towns and development corridors*. In response to high rates of urban demographic growth and associated demand for housing, these agencies began to redirect expansion beyond the urban fringe. These new districts, towns and corridors are reshaping larger centres into structured city regions. They are also effectively changing the spatial distribution of land values as these increase in and around newly developed sites. For instance in Egypt between 1995 and 2007, 110 km² of desert lands were urbanised while expansion on agricultural lands was contained to 55 km².

Across Northern Africa today and through para-statal agencies and local authorities, government plays a major role in the *formal urban land market*, opening up new areas for development with transportation and infrastructure extensions in a bid to attract private development and channel it to desired planned locations. Public authorities also redevelop dilapidated slums in city centres to take advantage of the commercial potential and release higher land values.

The Shortcomings of Conventional Urban Land Administration and Management

Over the next decade, the subregion's urban population is to grow by an estimated 27 million and both provision of serviced land and enforcement of development regulations will continue to pose significant challenges to governments. The demand for affordable housing, both rental and home-ownership, will require significant improvements in land management practices and the definition of public interventions that ensure complementary roles for local authorities and the private sector.

Across Northern Africa and since the 1980s, various decentralization laws have shifted responsibility for land planning and management to local authorities. However, political and fiscal decentralisation has lagged behind this functional devolution. Despite the growing powers of governors and the mayors of large cities, decisions regarding large projects are still made at the ministerial or cabinet level, and funding for local improvement projects must be secured from central government, too. Furthermore, provincial and municipal authorities maintain their own separate appointed executives and elected councils.

In these countries, dedicated national departments are responsible for surveying and establishing the cadastre or land register, whereas local planning departments handle land-use rules and regulations, including delineation and adjustment of building lines, height limits and land coverage ratios, as well as encroachments on public rights of way. In the larger cities, routine, day-to-day, land-related decisions are dealt with by several distinct municipal departments, such as the following:

- issuance of building permits, certificates of occupancy, orders to vacate structurally unsound buildings threatening to collapse, and demolition orders; and
- enforcing rules and regulations, including penalties for non-compliance.

Issues relating to tenure are adjudicated by the courts, which includes competing claims to ownership of land and disagreements among holders of different rights. Non-compliance with development regulations or any land uses posing health or safety threats come under administrative law and can be enforced by local authorities.

Registration of property transfers is a cumbersome and costly process in all countries in the subregion, requiring a notarial act, a formal survey of the property undertaken by

▲
Chefchaouen, Morocco. **©WitR/Shutterstock**

BOX 2.3: **LAND REGISTRATION IN EGYPT**

In Egypt, formal land registration is a lengthy and cumbersome process involving no fewer than 71 bureaucratic procedures with 31 different offices, which can take six to 14 years to complete.[63] Once equivalent to 12 per cent of property value, the registration fee has been reduced to a flat EGP 2,000 (or US $350). Nevertheless, the registration process remains both complex and costly.[64] As a result, only about eight per cent of urban properties are formally registered.[65] In Cairo, only five per cent of land parcels are registered in the paper-based deeds system.[66]

However, through a combination of the Egyptian Financial Services (EFS) programme, the Real Estate Publicity Department and the Egyptian Survey Authority, the Egyptian government is looking to encourage formal property registration. Since 2004, the Egyptian Financial Services programme, with funding from USAID, has been working with International Land Systems and the Environmental Systems Research Institute (ESRI) to implement a digitized Land Registry System. In May 2006, the government set out a more affordable, reduced-tier fee structure for registration and created the National Urban Registration Project. In July 2006, EFS envisaged converting the personal deeds system into a parcel-based index. This is going to be a very time-consuming and costly process.

As found out in the Cairo district (100,000 parcels) that had been chosen as the initial site for implementation, many of the properties have never been mapped. The Survey Authority had to dispatch field teams to survey every parcel using global positioning systems (GPS).

the specialised department, payment of a registration fee, and filing the notarial bill of sale with the land registry.[61] As a result, property owners, particularly in informal settlements, often do not bother registering their land plots.[62]

Informal Settlements as a Response to Land Market Deficiencies

When considering land and informal settlement issues in Northern Africa, it is important to draw a distinction between two different categories of unplanned urbanisation that are often lumped together and classified as *informal settlements*. The first type consists of parcels bought by limited-income households from legal owners of agricultural land on urban fringes. These land transfers are legal and can be registered. However, in some countries, the parcel cannot be used as a building plot since conversion of agricultural land to urban use is prohibited by law except within designated urban perimeters.

With this type of unplanned urbanisation, unserviced parcels cannot be legally subdivided, and buildings in these informal settlements are therefore encumbered with two instances of non-compliance: (a) illegal subdivision of land and change in use; and (b) unauthorised construction.

This category of informal settlements is currently the target of regularisation programmes. Their typical rectilinear patterns deriving from the original fields or orchards stand in sharp contrast with the organic morphology of squatter settlements, which instead tend to reflect the topography of the sites where they are located.

▲
Cairo, Egypt. ©**Andrey Starostin/Shutterstock**

Farmers intending to sell their land to an informal developer often leave the land barren. The land owner will send a request to the survey authority to declare the land as no longer arable. The land can then be sold to developers who proceed to subdivide it and sell the plots for building purposes.[67] The resulting substantial mark-up makes informal developments on agricultural land unaffordable to households with incomes below the 30th percentile and only affordable to those above, who typically fund purchases from remittances from migrant relatives. Municipalities extend services to informal settlements as a function of available financial resources. As densities increase, infrastructure becomes overloaded; lack of sewerage and accumulations of solid waste pose serious health hazards.

The second type of informal urbanisation sees a takeover of public land by unscrupulous developers in collusion with corrupt local officials. This is happening in cities combining acute housing shortages and a scarcity of developable land. Developers proceed to erect apartment buildings and sell the flats to limited- and middle-income families. Sales prices are agreed in advance and cash payments are made in three to four instalments as construction makes progress, effectively pre-financing the project. These blatant violations are concentrated on the outskirts of the larger cities in Northern Africa. Once the settlements have reached a critical mass that makes it difficult for the government to evict residents, the probability of demolition becomes quite low, the settlement is usually regularized and infrastructure is provided.

In Egypt, this phenomenon has received extensive media attention over the past two years as developers have become bolder and the buildings higher and more visible. Recently, governors have been required to take all necessary steps to stem illegal occupancy of publicly-owned land.

The persistence of these two types of informal settlements show how difficult it is for most countries in Northern Africa to provide sufficient serviced land to accommodate demand for new housing against a background of continued rapid urban expansion.

The Political Economy of Urban Land

Although any productive or beneficial uses of urban property are subject to taxation, assessment and collection of property taxes are the responsibility of government departments and only a share of the revenues is redistributed to local authorities. Owner-occupied and rental housing, commercial premises and locales used for workshops and production activities, together with the incomes they generate, are all subject to one form of taxation or another. For all its size and role, the informal economy escapes taxation, which as a result weighs as a disproportionate burden on the formal property/real estate and business sectors. Added to these distortions comes a persistent, strong reluctance

BOX 2.4: **NEW CAIRO CITY AND THE URBAN POOR**

The Greater Cairo Region (GCR) needs at least two million new housing units within the next 10 years if it is to accommodate anticipated population growth and new urban household formations across the metropolitan area. Since the government is in no position to meet this demand on its own, innovative public-private partnerships have come under experimentation. Large parcels of desert land are sold to private developers, and the proceeds enable the public sector to meet infrastructure requirements. As a result, private-sector-led new towns have been mushrooming in the desert areas surrounding the nation's hugely 'primate' capital.

One of these developments is known as 'New Cairo City'. Located just outside the metropolitan ring road and adjacent to Cairo's eastern high-income districts, the new town has evolved through five sequential master plans (1985, 1995, 1999, 2001 and 2007) which all involved radical reviews of objectives, policies, population targets and jurisdictional areas. The initial target (1985) was 750,000 residents over 1,800 ha. New Cairo now aims at 4 million over 33,620 hectares by the year 2027. The initial plan envisaged New Cairo as a satellite town hosting overflows of working-class Cairenes. However, as things now stand, the 25,000 ha of land so far allocated to private developers mainly provides accommodation for high-income and upper middle-class population segments. Small pockets of land have been allocated for relocation of low-income and poor households in self-help residential units.

It is now clear that New Cairo by and large emerges on the back of private sector development policies and decisions. Although public-private partnerships are still in fledgling stages, they seem to leave out the poor, regardless of the socio-economic balance that was the original objective. This situation has not prevented the Egyptian government from trying for more socially balanced new towns in this area, which was somewhat achieved with the relocation of low-income households. Among these were victims of a landslide in one of Cairo's poorest and most densely populated informal areas. Some of the new arrivals have found local employment in the construction industry or as domestic staff, but many complain about lack of jobs. Daily commutes to employment in Cairo are not an option as transport charges would wipe out more than half the typical daily wage. Residents of the poorer enclaves within New Cairo also become stigmatized as those better-off see them as an undesirable reminder of the steep imbalance between rich and poor prevailing in the capital proper.

The main lesson from 'New Cairo' is that for all its benefits, private sector-led real estate and housing development is unable, by itself, to deal with the complex political, social and economic aspects that are involved in any such worthy, large-scale endeavour. More specifically, it is clear that, so far, the new town initiative has done little to bring poor and low-income groups into mainstream urban life. Consequently, it is for the public sector to provide a more balanced socio-economic mix and address socio-geographic polarisation. Aggressive promotion campaigns have made new towns very popular among Cairo's well-off (including expatriate) population, who opt for gated communities with spacious gardens, swimming pools and golf courses instead of an increasingly polluted, noisy and crowded central Cairo, where they commute by private vehicle. In contrast, low-income earners are stranded in the desert, effectively jeopardising or preventing voluntary resettlement in New Cairo.

This is why public-private partnerships should not yet be considered as a new urban governance model or concept in Egypt. Decisions over policy restructuring and new housing have been taken by central government and have not yet been disseminated across local authorities. Participatory engagement of all stakeholders and institutions has so far been absent from decision-making processes.

Whereas the new town concept of privatized housing development and the sale of desert lands to fund public-sector provision of social and basic infrastructures may in principle be a sound and workable approach, and while the Government of Egypt deserves praise for its innovative approaches in the circumstances, there is still room for significant policy adjustments to address the emerging practicalities on the ground.

Sources: The Tale of the Unsettled New Cairo City-Egypt: A Review for the Implications of the Adopted Privatization and Laissez- Fair Policies on Excluding the Poor from its Housing Market, Walid N A Bayoumi, PhD thesis, Manchester University; To Catch Cairo Overflow, 2 Megacities Rise in Sand, M. El-Naggar, www.nytimes.com/2010/08/25/world/africa/25egypt.html

to tax unproductive land and vacant premises, which effectively acts as a disincentive to any kind of development.

Tax yields from the real estate sector are comparatively low relative to market values. This is primarily due to one or more of the following eight factors:

- Complex tenure systems and successive transfers of unregistered titles, resulting in unclear ownership patterns.
- Central government control of high-yield tax bases, including property taxes, which hampers updating of tax rolls.
- A perennial lag in the recording of new tax-producing assets in land registries.
- A redistribution system that is less a function of locally-raised revenues than of non-financial criteria such as population size, social fairness, geographic balance, development potential or national policies.
- Taxation schedules based on real or imputed rental values, rather than the capital value of the assets, a system that tends to understate the market value of real estate assets and their capital appreciation.
- Tenant protection regulations and rent laws that further depress property assessments based on rental valuation, thereby adding to the erosion of municipal tax bases. In Egypt, which features the most stringent rent control laws in the region, rents in the pre-1960 building stock have not increased since roll-backs to 1953 levels were enacted. Today, affluent families living in large five- or six-room apartments pay four to five time less than poor households renting two rooms in an informal settlement.
- Subsidies, tax rebates and exemptions granted to encourage specific categories of development (e.g., affordable housing).
- The exclusion from tax rolls of informal developments on urban fringes, except in Egypt.[68]

Taxation of urban property varies across countries. As of 2008, Egypt would only tax improved lands. Originally, properties in new towns were tax-exempt, but this is no longer the case.[69] Morocco levies two types of urban property tax: the *taxe urbaine* (urban tax) and the *taxe d'édilité* (council tax), both assessed on the rental value of the property. While

▲
Hammamet, Tunisia. ©**Brendan Howard/Shutterstock**

the rate of the *taxe urbaine* increases as a function of property value, residents of new units enjoy a five-year tax exemption. The *taxe d'édilité* is a flat 10 per cent levied on occupants of a dwelling to defray the cost of providing urban services. Owner-occupants benefit from a 75 per cent rebate on both taxes.[70] Unlike Morocco and Egypt, Tunisia taxes both occupied and unoccupied urban land parcels.[71] The central government collects property taxes and returns all but 10 per cent of the revenues to municipal authorities. In Sudan, urban property taxes are levied on improvements, not land, which encourages wasteful, low-density sprawl and a pattern of large parcels in affluent, centrally located neighbourhoods.[72]

This review suggests that efficient, rational property taxation systems are urgently needed in North Africa. The same holds with coordination among central and local entities responsible for land management. The multiplicity of laws and regulations governing the use, subdivision and development of land should be harmonized and streamlined. Law 119/2008 in Egypt came as a first attempt to do that. Although some clauses in the executive regulations may need revision, the law remains a significant step towards harmonised, streamlined land legislation.

New Tools for Land Administration and Management

Northern African cities are struggling to balance decentralisation as a prerequisite to participatory processes in urban management, on the one hand, and coordination of urban plans, projects, and investments among national and local authorities, on the other. An overriding concern is the economic competitiveness of cities in a changing global economy.

In this complex endeavour, policymakers are faced with the following three major challenges:

- The high costs and rapid appreciation of land, which keeps families with incomes below the 30th percentile out of formal land markets, and tends to make the informal land market less affordable. Rising land values have led to an increase in density and building heights, often in violation of land use regulations and building codes. As a result, the quality of the urban environment has suffered and both infrastructure and transport systems are overloaded. Collusion among local officials, small developers and contractors encourages weak enforcement of codes and regulations, thereby undermining efforts to manage urban land development.
- Worsening water shortages throughout the subregion, which call for conservation measures. Land development regulations should include requirements for the reuse of treated wastewater, as well as planting and landscaping that are adapted to the prevailing arid climate.
- Rising sea levels as a result of climate change, which are likely to affect settlements in coastal areas and threaten ecologically important areas and bird habitats. Urbanisation of these areas should be prohibited and every effort made to contain the spread of informal settlements on 'at risk' land.

These challenges can be met with a combination of assertive spatial planning, transparency and accountability in land management together with stringent enforcement of development controls. Even more importantly, rapid release of serviced land affordable to limited-income groups is critical to proper living standards in Northern African cities.

Some countries are experimenting with new forms of public-private partnerships to increase the supply of serviced urban land that is affordable to larger segments of the population. In Egypt, the government makes subsidized land available to developers, with off-site infrastructure to build housing that will be affordable to families with incomes below the national median. In Morocco, a share of the land developed by Al Omrane is allocated to the construction of housing for lower- and limited-income families.

2.4 The Geography of Climate Change

UN-HABITAT has identified the cities that are vulnerable to the impacts of climate change; in Northern Africa, these are almost all coastal cities including ***Alexandria***, ***Algiers***, ***Casablanca***, ***Tripoli*** and ***Tunis***. There appears to be a consensus in the international community that sea-level rise is accelerating. From 1961 to 2003, sea-level rise increased by 1.8 mm/year on average, but from 1993 to 2003 the pace accelerated to an average 3.1 mm/year.[73] Forecasts of sea-level rise in the Mediterranean range from 30 cm to over 50 cm by 2100. Although issues like solid waste management, infrastructure and environmental sanitation are among those facing any conurbation, they are particularly relevant to those coastal cities exposed to sea-level rise. These cities can respond to climate-related problems with well-adapted land management policies, preventing unauthorized settlement in high-risk areas and providing for adequate, scientifically-based treatment of structures such as seawalls, breakwaters and marinas that affect coastal currents.

Increased human-made pressure throughout most of the Maghreb has been changing the natural Northern African landscape, most likely increasing the pace of desertification. Access to fresh water (see Table 2.9), a traditionally important issue in Northern Africa, is likely to become even more difficult as agricultural and urban uses continue to compete for limited natural resources, and this situation is compounded by the increasing frequency of intermittent droughts. Demographic growth and economic development have led to overexploitation. In Algeria, Egypt, Libya, Morocco and Tunisia, water availability has already fallen below, or is approaching, 1,000 m^3 per head and per year, the standard benchmark for water scarcity.[74] Egypt and Libya are withdrawing more water annually than is renewed, and both countries are relying on desalination plants to supplement supply (see Box 2.3).

Improved water provision requires watershed management planning, adequate monitoring of groundwater levels and replenishment of aquifers for oases, as well as strict licensing of boreholes. Desalination plants have become more widespread in coastal areas on the back of advances in technologies.

One problem in North Africa is that current national and

BOX 2.5: THE CHALLENGE OF WATER SECURITY IN NORTH AFRICA

Northern Africa's water resources are limited. According to hydrologists, countries with less than 1,000m^3 in renewable water resources per head are about to face chronic shortages – and all Northern African countries already find themselves in this situation. As of 2006, Morocco had the largest resources at 886m^3 per year and per head, and Libya had the smallest at 104 m^3. Countries in the region have also experienced protracted droughts and irregular rainfalls.[75]

One of the challenges in North Africa is balancing water resources between agricultural and urban uses. For instance in Egypt, 95 per cent of water supplies are drawn from the Nile and 85 per cent of Nile waters are used for agriculture.[76] Most Northern African countries are experiencing water shortages in urban areas. With the exception of Algeria and Sudan, annual urban water consumption per head increased significantly in the 1990s, as follows:[77] Morocco, from 21.12m^3 per head in 1992 to 41.7 m^3 in 2002; Egypt: from 46.75 m^3 per head in 1997 to 72.71 m^3 in 2002; Libya: from 90.11m^3 per head in 1992 to 109.5 m^3 in 2001; Tunisia: from 30.61 m^3 per head in 1992 to 37.93 m^3 in 2002.[78]

Faced with this challenge, North African countries have deployed three main types of policies:

- *Conservation.* In Tunisia, meters, repairs and leakage reduction are part of an ongoing urban water conservation programme. In a bid to improve meter efficiency and accuracy, the Tunisian government has replaced jammed with resized meters, regulating pressure and tracking leaks, improving worn-out networks with new pipes and equipment to reduce losses.[79]
- *Reuse/recycling.* Morocco encourages wastewater reuse through technical assistance and financial incentives so long as reused water preserves resources against further pollution.[80] Egypt has been recycling wastewater for irrigation and more recently, for watering landscaped open spaces.
- *Desalination.* Tunisia has taken to desalinating brackish water through reverse osmosis in the southern part of the country. Algeria and Libya have been desalinating seawater primarily in the coastal cities. Libya has the greatest desalination capacity at about 1,200 million m^3/day, with Algeria ranking second at just under 1,000 m^3/day.[81] In Egypt , desalination provides water in resorts in the Sinai and along the Red Sea coast.[82]

TABLE 2.9: **FRESHWATER CONSUMPTION AND RENEWAL**

	Annual freshwater withdrawals (billion m³, year 2000)	Year	Renewable internal freshwater resources (m³ per head)	Renewable internal freshwater resources (billion m³)	Water Surplus/(Deficit (billion m³)
Algeria	6	2007	332	11	5
Egypt	68	2007	24	2	(66)
Libya	4	2007	97	1	(3)
Morocco	13	2007	940	29	16
Sudan	37	2006	78	64	27
Tunisia	3	2007	410	4	1
TOTAL	131		1,881	111	(20)

Source: World Development Indicators, World Bank, 2000, 2006 and 2007

sub-regional fresh water management systems overlook the cross-border nature of aquifers and rarely engage communities in conservation efforts. This is where a participatory approach emphasizing stakeholders' role, including non-governmental organisations, would greatly help. Multinational strategies coordinate the use of river basin waters, as in the case with the Nile River (see Chapter 4, Box 4.9).[83] Several initiatives are underway to address these issues, although it is too early to assess their impact. USAID and the Arab Network for Environment and Development (RAED) have formed a strategic partnership to increase regional capacity and enhance awareness in the Middle East and Northern Africa with regard to critical water issues.[84] The European Union is working with the African Union's 'Situation Room' to establish a Continental Early Warning System on climate change.[85]

World Bank initiatives in Northern Africa, both in partnership with the Arab Water Council or bilaterally with governments, focus on rationalizing water consumption. In particular, participating municipalities now take to forecasting future precipitation levels, modernizing irrigation, expanding wastewater collection and treatment, and improving groundwater management and 'water accounting'.[86] They look to curb 'non revenue' water, i.e., systemic losses due to outdated or poorly maintained distribution networks, which can account for over 30 per cent of consumption. On top of these efforts, treatment and reuse of wastewater must increase significantly (see Box 2.6).

Local Authorities and Adaptation to Climate Change

Specific geographic, cultural, economic, and political features will shape any country's adaptation efforts and the readiness, or otherwise, of local populations to change daily routines.[87] Persuading cash-strapped local authorities that they must spend resources on a problem that will only manifest itself over the longer term is just as difficult, especially in view of more pressing economic and social concerns including poverty alleviation, infrastructure deficiencies, housing shortages and inadequate public services, together

▲
Bizerte City, Tunisia. ©**Posztos (colorlab.hu)/Shutterstock**

BOX 2.6: DRINKING WATER IN EGYPT: NEED FOR A MANAGEMENT OVERHAUL

When the 50,000 residents of Al-Barada, a settlement just north of Cairo, were connected to piped water supply, the women were particularly pleased as this saved them the time and effort of queuing for daily water tanker deliveries. Before long, though, thousands became infected with typhus as the water was polluted. Water tankers are once more a daily reality in Al-Barada.

Indeed, lack of both safe water supplies and sewage treatment are among Egypt's direst problems. Every year, an estimated 17,000 children die from diarrheal dehydration due to unclean water. Although a significant 82 per cent of households in the larger cities are connected to a sewerage network, outside these major settlements the rate is only 24 per cent.

The Al-Barada incident is no exception. The problem here is that well-designed plans are often executed with poor materials by unregulated and corrupt contractors. Groundwater in Al-Barada is polluted by clogged waste water drainage channels which the local population use to dump much of their waste. The Nile itself, the source of 85 per cent of Egypt's water supplies, is seriously polluted as well. An average 550 million m^3 of industrial wastewater is dumped in the river every year, compounded by 2.5 billion m^3 of agricultural wastewater that comes polluted with pesticides and chemical fertilizers. This is not including untreated sewage that flows into the Nile, and for which no data is available. As a result, some 40 per cent of Egypt's population drink polluted water, and the number of kidney diseases in the country is one of the highest in the world.

As mentioned earlier, annual water supply per head in Egypt stands at 860m^3, well short of the 1,000m^3 international 'water scarcity' threshold. With the current 80 million population expected to grow 50 per cent to 120 million by 2050, water is going to feature as a prominent political issue throughout the Nile Basin in the years to come. Current treaties and agreements governing water use and rights across the entire Nile Basin are under review in Cairo, but Egypt also needs to amend its own national water consumption patterns. Water wastage is rife in the country, partly due to unsustainably low pricing that does not encourage water conservation. Some 85 per cent of water in Egypt is used in highly inefficient agricultural irrigation systems, and addressing water scarcity should start with the largest consumer. Unless Egypt finds better ways to manage and rationalize water demand and use, peace in North-East Africa may be at stake, as discussed in Chapter 4, Box 4.9.

Source: NRC Handelsblad, Rotterdam, 12-08-2009

with the overriding need for any city today to enhance its competitiveness as a desirable location for private productive investment and attendant job creations.

Furthermore, cities' ability to effectively respond to the anticipated impacts of climate change is constrained by three major types of factor:

1. The conflicting scenarios generated by distinct agencies and experts, which confuse city officials and compound the difficulty of deciding on mitigating action (coming on top of lack of local data regarding most of the foreseeable effects which climate change will have on any specific location).
2. Lack of the financial and technical resources needed to respond to the complex nature of the impacts.
3. Lack of control over any public or private entities that operate outside the jurisdictional boundaries of a locality but whose actions magnify the effects of climate change on that locality.[88] Nonetheless, urban authorities can put themselves in a position to mitigate the potential impacts of climate change, such as through their planning and management functions.

While ***Alexandria*** is considered one of the most vulnerable cities to sea-level rises, the city proper is built on high ground and is only threatened by storm surges. However, urban sprawl and informal urbanisation of villages in the rural hinterland are at risk of flooding if the sea level rises by more than 30 cm. An effective mitigation strategy would be to restrict development in the most flood-prone areas through stringent land management, while at the same time steering developments towards safer areas with the provision of adequate infrastructure.

As for urban sprawl, its detrimental effects are clearly evident in Northern Africa. In Tunisia, net density has decreased from 110 to 90 individuals/ha since 1975 while the population has increased by 4.5 million[89] and nearly doubled in ***Tunis*** over the same period.[90] Although some of this expansion is on safe ground, development in low-lying areas around the salt-water Lake of Tunis and along the coast is exposed to flooding as the sea level rises.

The complex nature of climate change impacts dampens the effectiveness of local responses, which would require both horizontal and vertical coordination among various entities. It is incumbent on municipalities, jointly with relevant government departments, to control urbanisation, tourism and industrial sitings while safeguarding the ecology of coastal areas.[91]

Climate Change and Cities: How Much do we Know?

Research conducted at the University of Paris highlights both a rise in minimum and maximum daily temperatures in ***Sfax***, and a significant lengthening of the hot season in this major Tunisian resort.[92] The thermal rise is attributed to phenomena known as the urban 'heat island' effect, the 'North Atlantic Oscillation' (NAO) and nebulosity increase, with annual maximum temperatures rising by over 2°C between 1970 and 2002 while minimum annual temperatures rose by no more than 1.2°C.[93] The extension of the hot season seems to have been more dramatic between 1970 and 1994, increasing in length from 25 to 35 periods[94], while the cold season shrank from 35 to 13 periods. These trends are expected to continue in the future.

Remote sensing, field observation stations and geographic information systems (GIS) are needed to collect the data required to assess and forecast climate change impacts. Egypt's Nile delta coast is already highly vulnerable to sea-level rise due to flat topology, tectonic subsidence and lack of new sediment deposits since the construction of the Aswan High Dam, with sea currents adding to vulnerability. The most affected area will be the Egyptian Mediterranean coast from ***Port Said*** to ***Rosetta***. In the two cities, the coastline at the estuary has receded by 3 to 6 kilometres due to the combined effects of beach erosion and scouring.[95]

While the extent of impacts is not precisely known, climate change is bound to throw fresh challenges at Northern African countries. Bilateral and multilateral cooperation is addressing the need for accurate information regarding local impacts. The United Nations University's Institute for Environment and Human Security (UNU-EHS) is building the capacities of central and local agencies to identify high-vulnerability flood zones around the globe as well as potential forced migration flows as a result of climate change, while establishing Early Warning Systems for natural disasters. Regarding North Africa, the World Bank has recently funded research on climate change adaptation and natural disaster preparedness in ***Alexandria***, ***Casablanca*** and ***Tunis***.

Climate Change and Urban Adaptation Strategies

In ongoing environmental research, policy debates are beginning to shift away from trend reversal to adaptation. It is generally agreed that effective action to halt environmental degradation will be slow in coming, because of political reluctance to address the economic and social root causes. Therefore, it is incumbent on all cities, and especially those more vulnerable, to develop practical strategies for adaptation. For example, in ***Algiers***, a city dominated by industrial land uses, inter-agency workshops were held in 2010 on disaster risk assessment, focusing on flash floods and mudflows, the frequent landslides of recent years and the 2003 earthquake.

Egypt is widely viewed as one of the three countries in the world that are most vulnerable to the effects of climate change. Flooding, coastal erosion and salt water intrusion in the Northern Delta will submerge lagoons and lakes and increase soil salinity, with adverse effects on agriculture. Egypt has begun upgrading its geographical information (GIS) database with high-resolution satellite images that can accurately help identify vulnerable areas along the northern coastline, positioning tide gauges to monitor changes in sea levels.[96]

Faced with these challenges, authorities in ***Alexandria*** have begun to take a number of strategic steps. The governor has established a special committee on climate change including experts in marine sciences, water resources, hydraulics, coastal zone management, remote sensing, industry and trade to advise on the impacts of climate change. The governor enjoined the committee to make the best use of available data and start developing mitigation schemes. Longer-term adaptation strategies would be based on new, more accurate data.[97]

Coastal vulnerabilities are compounded by poor land policies and uses, such as the proliferation of recreational resorts with marinas and breakwaters that affect Mediterranean coastal currents and alter natural sand deposits. Immediate concerns include significant beach erosion (up to 50m over 20 years), salt-water intrusion, and rising levels of both groundwater and Lake Mariout (to the south of ***Alexandria***) which flood streets and ground floors along the northern shore. Although climate change is not a factor behind these problems, these will all be compounded by sea-level rise. This prospect highlights the urgent need for adaptation strategies as well as reviews of land policies and uses. Based on recommendations from the climate change committee, the governor of ***Alexandria*** has already decided that submerged structures would reduce scouring and help replenish beaches, and that groundwater affecting historic monuments would be pumped out, as both problems are of some importance to domestic and foreign tourism.

It remains for the governorate to develop a strategy for managed urbanisation in the rural hinterland, where 840 hectares and expanding villages housing 400,000 are at risk of flooding by rising sea levels.[98] The need here is for a long-term plan and a land management strategy to deter further settlement expansion in high-risk areas, while consulting with the national government over any issues of more than local relevance.

▲
Alexandria harbour, Egypt. **©Javarman/Shutterstock**

2.5 Emerging Issues

Regional and International Population Mobility, Urban Economies and Livelihoods

Northern African countries are strategically located on the informal migration routes leading from sub-Saharan Africa to Europe. It is estimated that between 65,000 and 120,000 sub-Saharan Africans cross the *Maghreb* countries (Algeria, Libya, Mauritania, Morocco and Tunisia) every year, most on their way to Europe although some stay in Northern Africa. Some 100,000 sub-Saharan Africans now reside in Algeria and Mauritania, one to 1.5 million in Libya, and 2.2 to 4 million (primarily Sudanese) in Egypt. More recently, Northern Africa has also received temporary immigrants from Bangladesh, China, India, Pakistan, and the Philippines, who work in construction, trade, and services.[99]

Those immigrants who do not stay in Northern Africa move on to the northern Mediterranean shores. From the coast of Libya, many emigrants try to reach Malta, Sicily or Lampedusa. In Algeria, migrants from ***Tamanrasset*** in the Sahara travel to northern cities or through to Morocco on the border near ***Oujda***. From coastal areas like Al Hoceima, they try to reach Malaga or Almería in southern Spain. Another major migration pattern is from ***Algiers*** to Sète or Marseille, France. Emigration flows from ***Tan-Tan*** and ***Tarfaya***, Morocco, to the (Spanish) Canary island of Fuerteventura are also apparent. With increased border controls across the Strait of Gibraltar, more migrants tend to leave from Mauritania and south coastal settlements on the perilous boat trip to the Canary Islands.

▲
Marrakesh, Morocco. **©Philip Lange/Shutterstock**

MAP 2.3: **MEDITERRANEAN AND AFRICAN IRREGULAR MIGRATION ROUTES**

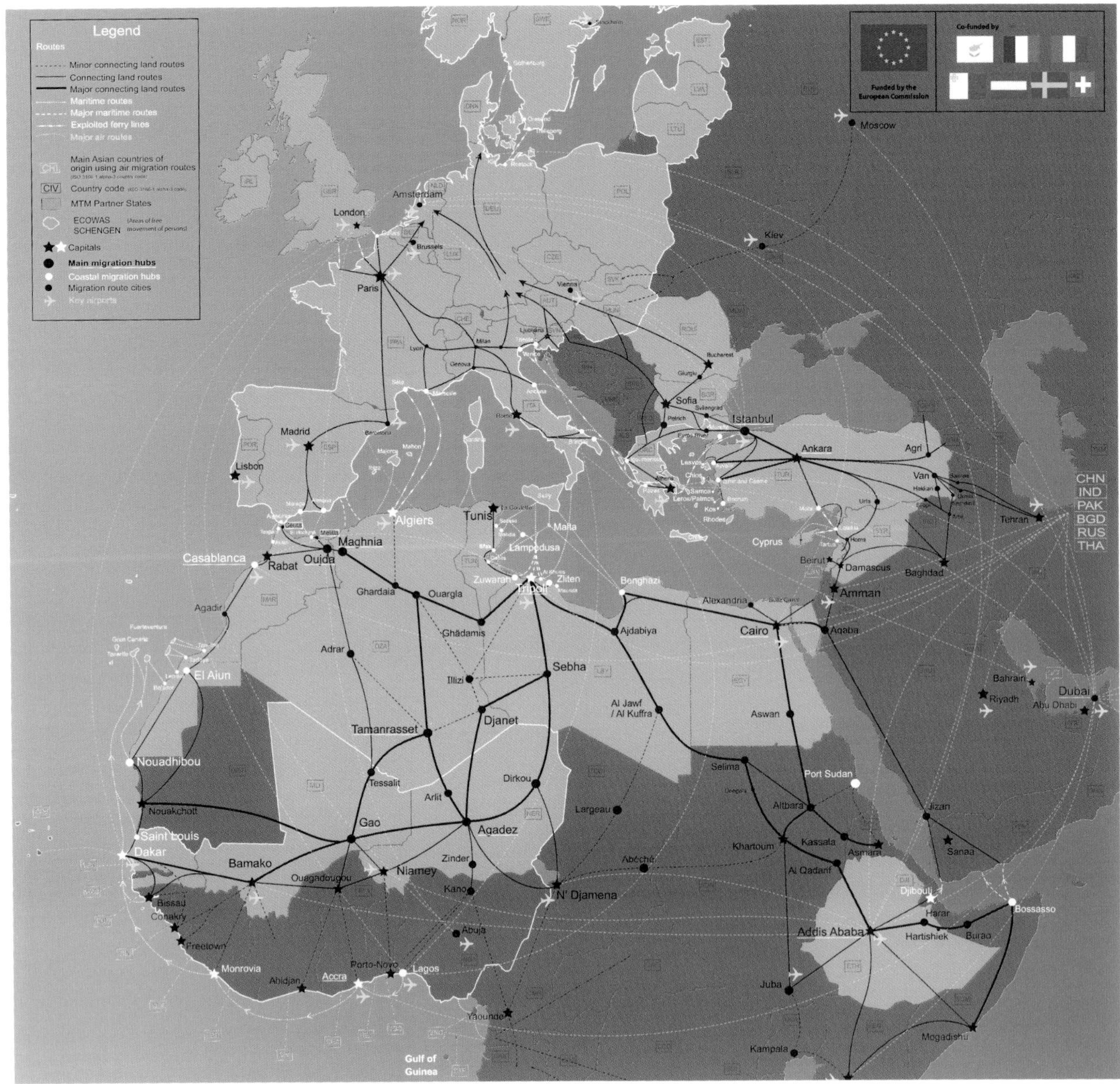

Courtesy of International Centre for Migration Policy Development, Europol and Frontex

To the exception of Libya and Sudan, Northern African countries have been experiencing sustained emigration of their working-age populations in search of jobs, primarily in Europe and the Gulf States. Between 2005 and 2010, in Algeria, Egypt, Morocco and Tunisia, the annual net numbers of emigrants ranged between 4,000 and 85,000, compared with net numbers of immigrants between 4,000 and 27,000 in Libya and Sudan.[100] As of 2008, North Africa received US $22.8 billion in remittances from expatriate workers, or about 5 per cent of the world total. However, the 2008 financial crisis has led to a decrease in emigration and a concomitant decline in remittances that has exacerbated the impact on the economy of the downturns in tourism, foreign investment and general business activity. Egypt was the largest receiver of remittances with US $8.68 billion, equivalent to 5.3 per cent of GDP in 2008. Morocco was the second largest receiver with US $6.89 billion, or 8 per cent of GDP. In Libya, recent hostile attitudes and the subsequent deportation of some 145,000 immigrants, primarily to sub-Saharan countries, have temporarily disrupted migration patterns in the region.[101]

In Morocco, many urban youths with relatively high education feel alienated and frustrated.[102] They perceive emigration to Europe as a survival strategy to escape the high rates of unemployment prevailing in urban centres at home which, at just over 35 per cent, are significantly higher than the nationwide 9.5 per cent.[103]

Inter-Regional Cooperation: The Union for the Mediterranean

Established in July 2008 to reinforce and build upon the goals of *peace, security* and *stability* set forth by the 1995 Barcelona Declaration, the Union for the Mediterranean (UfM) consists of 43 member states including all EU members and the African and Middle Eastern countries along the Mediterranean shorelines (Libya only has observer status) or the Atlantic Ocean (Mauritania).[104] The Union funds those projects best suited to advance its objectives in the following categories:

- *Renewable solar energy,* including the plans for cross-Mediterranean power lines carrying energy harvested in the Sahara.[105]
- *Transportation improvements,* with upgrading of ports and rail networks. Projects completed to date include sea freight lines between Agadir (Morocco) and Perpignan (France), and between Tunis and Genoa (Italy). The Transport Project is now considering 215 proposed improvements to coastal rail networks and seaports in the Mediterranean, the majority in Northern Africa.[106]
- *Water and sanitation.* The 'Horizon 2020' initiative aims to eradicate pollution in the Mediterranean by the year 2020. Urban areas, with discharges of industrial effluent and municipal waste water and the dumping of solid waste are the source of 80 per cent of the pollution in the Mediterranean.[107] The current objective is to provide waste water treatment for an additional two million people by 2020.[108]
- *Sustainable Urban Development.* The Union's predominantly urban orientation is based on the fact that cities are the major beneficiaries of projects. In anticipation of future cooperation and funding, Northern African cities are now looking to improved links with the European Union. In particular, coastal cities on the northern and southern Mediterranean shores are intensifying exchanges and looking to launch joint initiatives. These trends will be reinforced as UfM develops and leverages funding from the European Investment Bank and other multilateral or bilateral sources. Another Union aim is improved standards for urban housing.
- *Business Support.* The Union promotes trade between member states along the lines set out by the Euro-Med Trade

▲
Agadir, Morocco. **©Ana del Castillo/Shutterstock**

Roadmap, which the Ministers discussed in December 2009. The Roadmap emphasizes free trade and the creation of a favourable investment environment.[109]

- *Civil Protection and Disaster Management.* This includes the anticipated impacts of climate change.
- *Culture.* The Union plans to promote sustainable Mediterranean architecture and safeguard the region's architectural and urban design heritage, but has yet to highlight specific projects. Ministers were to select some early projects in 2010. In the meantime, a new Euro-Med scheme based in Marseille, known as the *Medinas 2020 Initiative,* has launched a programme for the rehabilitation and conservation of Northern Africa's historic urban centres.[110]

Ministers jointly select projects, most of which are supported by multinational rather than bilateral funding; together with Germany's KfW Bank, the European Investment Bank, the African Development Fund and the World Bank have made available over a billion Euros worth of loans for Union-approved projects.

To countries on the northern Mediterranean shores, the rationale behind the Union is to promote economic development and private investment to foster peace in the area and stem emigration to Europe. Countries along the southern Mediterranean shoreline view the scheme both as a channel for foreign direct investment and a potential stepping stone on the way to eventual EU membership.

Transnational Urban Systems

Urban corridors are typically shaped by major transportation routes and anchored by cities. Cities located along development corridors have been growing at faster rates than those in the hinterland. A major challenge is how to link hinterland cities to corridors and attract development to those urban settlements located beyond the impact areas of the corridors.

Two incipient transnational corridors are now consolidating in Northern Africa: the *Southern Mediterranean Coastal Region* and the *Nile Valley Corridor.*

The Southern Mediterranean Coastal Region

The southern Mediterranean coast was a rich agricultural area in ancient times when the climate was less arid and rainfall more substantial, as it still is in Morocco due to the proximity of the Atlantic Ocean. The rich legacy of archaeological sites such as Leptis Magna and Carthage testify to the greatness of the Hellenistic and Roman eras in the region. Whereas

▲
Leptis Magna, Libya. ©**Pascal Rateau/Shutterstock**

▲
Cairo, Egypt. ©**Joel Carillet/iStockphoto**

Egypt and Libya served as granaries to ancient Rome, the loss of perennial agriculture along the south Mediterranean coast and the shifting of trade routes led to partial decline. However, the coastal region has experienced an impressive revival in more recent times, especially since the 1960s, driven by the development of oil-related industries, manufacturing and tourism.

Tourist resorts started in Tunisia and are now expanding rapidly in Egypt, driven by private real estate development companies. As mentioned earlier, the associated breakwaters or marinas have interfered with coastal currents and marine ecology, on top of restricting public access to beaches. Industrial development has resulted in the expansion of ports and industrial zones, particularly in oil terminals, including the SUMED pipeline from ***Suez*** to ***Alexandria***, ***Al Khums***, ***Benghazi***, ***Tripoli*** and all the way to ***Algiers*** and ***Oran***.

There is little doubt that this incipient coastal corridor is to consolidate over time. The issues that have emerged so far are as follows:

- Mediating conflicts between competing land uses, since tourism and industry do not mix. Noise, fumes and pollution degrade the coastal environment prized by resort developers. In general, priority is given to ports and manufacturing, which generate exports and more jobs. In Egypt and Tunisia, tourism is a major source of foreign exchange and a crucial component of national development plans. The importance of tourism tends to ensure that it is given priority in prime coastal areas, but public access to beaches is a significant concern.
- Industry and tourism have both affected the coastal environment. The corridor badly needs a thorough assessment leading to guidelines and regulations for the protection of marine ecology, including beach flora and fauna. In this respect, national plans can be supplemented by international agreements in the future.

The Nile Valley Corridor

The Nile has traditionally acted as a link and a bond between countries in the watershed (Egypt, Sudan and Ethiopia). Trade patterns and the necessity of sharing water areas with riparian countries have reinforced contacts among cities along the river. The construction of the Aswan High Dam had temporarily interrupted traditional trade patterns as the rising waters spread over Old Nubia, forcing the resettlement of communities on either side of the border between Egypt and Sudan. Today, the level of the reservoir has stabilized and Egypt has begun rebuilding the Nubian villages on the plateau overlooking the lake, with land and housing allocated to those Nubian families displaced in 1964, or their heirs. While this 'New Nubia' stands to re-establish the physical continuity of settlements between Aswan and Khartoum, sustenance in these villages is problematic since most Nubians now work in Egyptian cities or beyond in oil-producing countries or the West.

People along the Nile valley corridor continue to interact as they have done for millennia. In many ways, the major

MAP 2.4: **EGYPT'S NATIONAL URBAN STRATEGY – 2050**

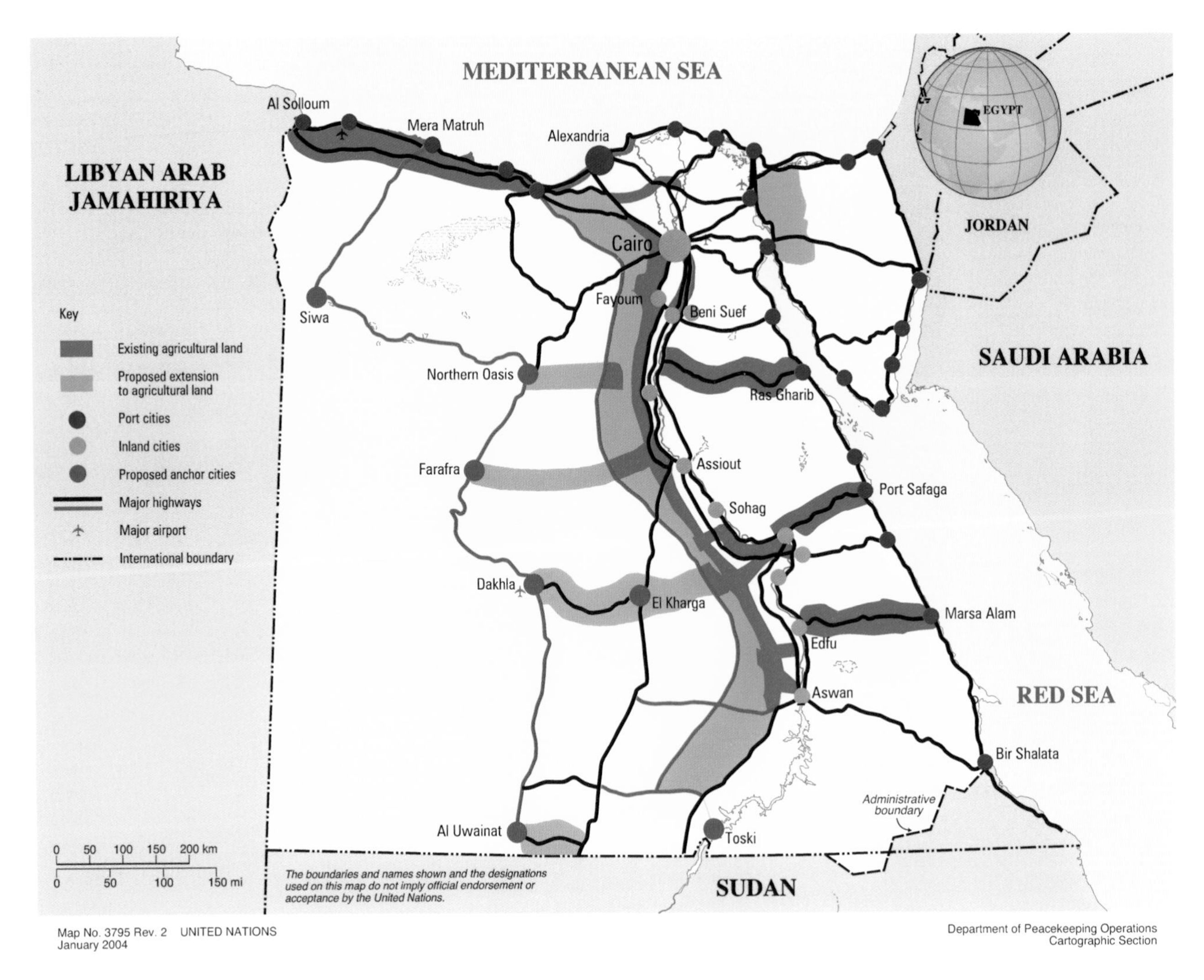

Source: GOPP, Egypt

issue today relates to use of the Nile waters by the settlements stretching along the banks. Riparian states determine their respective shares through international agreements, but the allocation of shares among cities within each country stands out as a priority, particularly in Egypt, together with the associated need for rationalised use of the water.

City Regions

Managing rapid urban growth poses a challenge to all countries in Northern Africa. In Morocco, the three national agencies involved in urban development were merged in 2004 under one holding company, the Al Omrane Group, which is now responsible for all aspects of urban and regional development. This includes the planning and implementation of extensions to existing cities and new towns with a mix of market-rate and social housing. Both projects include a wide range of economic activities and related employment, from industrial parks to handicraft.

In Egypt, the sprawl associated with rapid urban expansion is consuming already scarce agricultural land at an alarming rate, particularly in the delta region. Since 1982, Egypt's national policy has aimed to redirect urban growth onto desert land, with development corridors anchored on existing cities in the Nile Valley and new towns in the desert. Further extensions to these corridors will create new poles in natural or artificial oases. New growth nodes are also to be developed along the Mediterranean coast east and west of ***Alexandria***. In ***Cairo***, where most urban development had taken place illegally on agricultural land, the balance is beginning to shift: between 1995 and 2007 and as noted earlier, 110 km² of desert land were urbanised, while expansion on urban agricultural lands had diminished to 55 km².

Greater ***Cairo*** is the only megacity in Northern Africa and

▲
Cairo, Egypt. **©Bzzuspajk/Shutterstock**

it was also the first city region to develop in this part of the continent. The Greater Cairo Region (GCR) is home to 44 per cent of Egypt's urban population and 22 per cent of the total population. One of the densest cities in the world, Cairo faces the typical challenges of cities in the developing world: traffic congestion, pollution, overcrowded living conditions, limited green space, and high rates of unemployment. Over 40 per cent of the region's urbanised area consists of illegal settlements. The recently adopted ***Cairo 2050*** strategy proposes to enhance the competitiveness of the Egyptian capital and upgrade living conditions to international standards. The six main components of the strategy are as follows:

- De-densify the city centre and accommodate new growth with redistribution of the population to such new peripheral urban areas as the 'October 6' Governorate and the Helwan Governorate.
- Improve accessibility within the region, increasing the number of subway lines to 15 and constructing 14 new highways to link the inner and outer ring roads.
- Upgrade infrastructure and services in informal areas, resettle people living in hazardous areas and relocate polluting industries outside the conurbation.
- Improve governance with clear-cut complementary roles for governorates and district councils.
- Encourage private sector participation in development projects.
- The Greater Cairo plan also proposes to enhance the Egyptian capital's competitiveness with the following projects:
  - Establishing a world-class centre for financial services.
  - Encouraging new firms specializing in export-oriented services, including health, and the development of high-technology products.

- Preservation of historic Islamic, Coptic and Khedivial centres, with associated tourist-oriented development.

The emergence of the ***Cairo*** city region has spawned a challenge for governance. Constituent entities are typically reluctant to be amalgamated into a single metropolitan government area, which can prove unwieldy to manage and too far removed from constituents. In the case of Greater ***Cairo***, the region has been reorganised into five governorates, with two new ones in April 2008.

The Changing Role of Specialised Agencies in Local Planning and Finance

In the early 1980s Northern African countries recognized the need to redeploy their traditionally highly centralised administrative structures and enacted laws to that effect. Nevertheless, more than two decades later and as in many other regions of the world, devolution of responsibilities has not been matched by commensurate financial resources through either transfers or new sources of revenue.

As it stands in North Africa today, the decentralised framework seeks to foster participation and promote efficiency in the use of scarce resources through partnerships between central agencies (which provide finance and technical expertise), local authorities (in charge of implementing projects), and the communities that stand to benefit from the projects. The more positive examples include the following:

- In Tunisia, the government-controlled Urban Rehabilitation and Renovation Agency (ARRU) selects projects, and the National Solidarity Fund (also known as the '26/26 Fund') provides funding for those focusing on improved conditions in low-income urban districts. ARRU's current projects focus on dilapidated districts in the larger cities through partnerships among central and local authorities and the private sector. Municipalities can borrow from the Solidarity Fund to meet the costs of local infrastructure and community facilities, and transfer the borrowed funds to ARRU to undertake the projects. Project costs are split as follows: Solidarity Fund: 65 per cent; Housing Fund: 5.2 per cent; government departments: 1.4 per cent; and the private sector: 2.8 per cent.
- Morocco's Al Omrane regroups under a single holding company the country's land development and urban upgrading agencies, and secures funding for its projects.
- Egypt's General Organization of Physical Planning (GOPP) designs strategic development plans for governorates and cities, and the recently instituted Informal Settlement Development Facility provides funding and technical assistance to local authorities implementing urban improvement projects.

The strengths of specialised agencies lie in their ability to concentrate expertise and attract funding from donors as well as multilateral and bilateral development organizations. This model can be replicated in other countries. Indeed, this type of specialized agency is needed wherever a well-focused long-term intervention is in order, together with a commitment of public sector resources and resort to public powers such as eminent domain.

ENDNOTES

1. Center for International Earth Science Information Network (CIESIN), Columbia University; International Food Policy Research Institute (IPFRI), the World Bank; and Centro Internacional de Agricultura Tropical (CIAT), 2004. Global Rural-Urban Mapping Project (GRUMP): Settlement Points. Palisades, NY: CIESIN, Columbia University, 2000.
2. UN-DESA. World Urbanisation Prospects: The 2009 Revision Population Database. 2009.
3. *Ibid*.
4. Zaghloul, S.S. Meeting with the Secretary of the Cabinet, 2009.
5. The World Bank. Egypt Urban Sector Update. Washington DC: The World Bank, 2008.
6. Portail de la Région du Grand Casablanca. http://www.casablanca.ma Viewed on 9 January 2010.
7. Ali, S.A. "Greater Khartoum: The Horizontal Expansion and its Impact on the Development of Settlement" (in Arabic). Unpublished MA Thesis, Geography Department, Khartoum: University of Khartoum, 1999. Cited in Eltayeb, G. (2003). *The Case of Khartoum, Sudan*. Case study prepared for *The Challenge of Slums,* UN HABITAT Global Report on Human Settlements, 2003.
8. Royaume du Maroc, Haut Commissariat au Plan, 'Les indicateurs sociaux du Maroc en 2007.' http://www.hcp.ma/pubData/indsoc/IndicatSoc2007.pdf Viewed on 5 January 2010.
9. The World Bank. Fostering Higher Growth and Employment in the Kingdom of Morocco. Washington, DC: The World Bank, 2006.
10. Institut national de la statistique. http://www.ins.nat.tn/. Viewed on 17 December 2009.
11. Office National des Statistiques.'Enquête Emploi auprès des Ménages', 2007. http://www.ons.dz/. Viewed on 14 December 2009.
12. The World Bank. Sudan Stabilization and Reconstruction Country Economic Memorandum. Washington DC: The World Bank, 2008.
13. The World Bank. Egypt Urban Sector Update. Washington DC: The World Bank, 2008.
14. The World Bank. Morocco Basic Education Support Program. Washington DC: The World Bank, 2009.
15. The World Bank. Sudan Stabilization and Reconstruction Country Economic Memorandum. Washington DC: The World Bank, 2003.
16. The World Bank, Maghreb Department. Morocco: National Initiative for Human Development Support Project. Washington DC: The World Bank, 2006.
17. World Bank. Sudan Public Expenditure Report. Washington DC: The World Bank, 2007.
18. *Ibid*.
19. The population is 745,000 for Tunis from UNDESA (2007) and 340,000 for Sfax from the US Embassy or 265,131 for Sfax in 2004 from City Population data. UN-DESA. World Urbanisation Prospects: The 2009 Revision and City Population Tunisia. http://www.citypopulation.de/Tunisia.html. Viewed 17 January 2010.
20. CAPMAS. 2006 Census. http://www.msrintranet.capmas.gov.eg/pls/fdl/tst12e?action=1&lname=ECS.
21. 2010 estimate is 2.322 million from World Urbanisation Prospects 2007. UN-DESA. World Urbanisation Prospects: The 2007 Revision Population Database. 2007. http://esa.un.org/unup/ Viewed 4 January 2010.
22. 2010 estimate is 1.271 million from World Urbanisation Prospects 2007. UN-DESA. World Urbanisation Prospects: The 2007 Revision Population Database. 2007. http://esa.un.org/unup/ Viewed 4 January 2010.
23. UN-HABITAT. State of the World's Cities 2010/11. Nairobi: UN-HABITAT, 2010.
24. The World Bank. Morocco: National Initiative for Human Development Support Project. Washington DC, 2006.
25. UN-HABITAT. State of the World's Cities 2010/11. Nairobi: UN-HABITAT, 2010.
26. The World Bank. Egypt Urban Sector Update. Washington DC: The World Bank, 2008.
27. Faramaoui, A. Meeting with the Director General of the Facility for Upgrading Informal Settlements, 2009.

ENDNOTES

[28] *Ibid.*

[29] UN-DESA. UN Statistics Division Database. http://data.un.org/. Viewed on 7 January 2010.

[30] UN-HABITAT. State of the World's Cities 2008. Nairobi: UN-HABITAT, 2008.

[31] UN Statistics Divison Database. http://data.un.org/ Viewed on 10 January 2010.

[32] The World Bank. World Development Indicators Database, 2009 http://web.worldbank.org/WBSITE/EXTERNAL/DATASTATISTICS/0,,contentMDK:20535285~menuPK:1390200~pagePK:64133150~piPK:64133175~theSitePK:239419,00.html. Viewed on 12 February 2010.

[33] Poortman, C. J., Ahlers, T. O., Rutkowski, M., & El-Saharty, S. Republic of Tunisia Health Sector. Washington DC: The World Bank, 2006.

[34] The World Bank. Sudan Stablization and Construction Country Economic Memorandum. Washington, D.C.: The World Bank, 2003.

[35] Arab Republic of Egypt Central, Agency for Public Mobilization & Statistics. Income, Expenditure & Consumption Survey 2004/2005, 2005.

[36] The World Bank. Towards an Urban Sector Strategy. Washington DC: The World Bank, 2009.

[37] Arab Republic of Egypt Central, Agency for Public Mobilization & Statistics. Income, Expenditure & Consumption Survey 2004/2005, 2005.

[38] UN-HABITAT. State of the World's Cities 2010/11. Nairobi: UN-HABITAT, 2010.

[39] Egypt General Organization of Physical Planning.

[40] Faramaoui, A. Meeting with the Director General of the Facility for Upgrading Informal Settlements, 2009.

[41] Orascom Development Holding, 'Budget Housing Communities: Egypt' http://www.orascomdh.com/en/projects/other-projects/budget-housing-communities.html. Viewed on 15 February 2010.

[42] Zaghloul, S. S. Meeting with the Secretary of the Cabinet, 2009.

[43] Faramaoui, A. Meeting with the Director General of the Facility for Upgrading Informal Settlements, 2009.

[44] The World Bank. Egypt Urban Sector Update. Washington DC: The World Bank, 2008.

[45] Faramaoui, A. Meeting with the Director General of the Facility for Upgrading Informal Settlements, 2009.

[46] *Programme National de Réhabilitation des Quartiers Populaires.*

[47] The World Bank. Analysis of Housing Supply Mechanisms. Washington, D.C.: The World Bank, 2007.

[48] The World Bank. Towards an Urban Sector Strategy. Washington DC: The World Bank, 2009.

[49] The World Bank. Socialist People's Libyan Arab Jamahiriya Country Economic Report. Washington, D.C.: The World Bank, 2006.

[50] The World Bank. Tunisian Agricultural Policy Review. Washington DC: The World Bank, 2006.

[51] Gordon, C. "Recent Developments in the Land Law of the Sudan". *Journal of African Law*, Autumn 1986, 143-174.

[52] The *awqaf* are referred to as *habous* in Algeria and Morocco. Cf. Sait, Siraj & Hilary Lim, *Land, law and Islam – Property & Human Rights in the Muslim world*. London & New York: Zed Books, 2006; Nairobi: UN-HABITAT, 2006. About North African *medinas*, cf. Marcello Balbo ((dir.), *Médinas 2030. Scénarios et Stratégies*. Paris: L'Harmattan, 2010. For the Arabic edition: Tunis: Yamama Group, 2010.

[53] El Araby, M. (2003). The Role of the State in Managing Urban Land Supply and Prices in Egypt. *Habitat International (27)*.

[54] Law 119 of 2008.

[55] World Urbanisation Prospects: The 2007 Revision Population Database. 2007. http://esa.un.org/unup/ Viewed 14 January 2010. Sudan's urban population is still increasing at over 4.3 percent per annum.

[56] Serageldin, M. Regularizing the Informal Land Development Process. Washington, DC: USAID, 1990.

[57] El Araby, M. "The Role of the State in Managing Urban Land Supply and Prices in Egypt", *Habitat International (27)*, 2003.

[58] The World Bank. Analysis of Housing Supply Mechanisms. Washington, D.C.: The World Bank, 2007.

[59] Serageldin, M. Regularizing the Informal Land Development Process. Washington, DC: USAID, 1990.

[60] Serageldin, M. Regularizing the Informal Land Development Process. Washington, DC: USAID, 1990.

[61] The World Bank. Egypt Urban Sector Update. Washington DC: The World Bank, 2008.

[62] The World Bank. Analysis of Housing Supply Mechanisms. Washington, D.C.: The World Bank, 2007.

[63] De Soto. "Dead Capital and the Poor." *SAIS Review*, 21 (1), 2001, 13-43.

[64] USAID. EFS Tasks and Results. Washington D.C.: USAID, 2007. http://www.usaideconomic.org.eg/EFS/task_results_details.asp?tasks_id=28&no=2

[65] De Soto. "Dead Capital and the Poor." *SAIS Review*, 21 (1), 2001, 13-43.

[66] Rabley, P. Egypt Launches Parcel-Based Deeds Registry to Spur Mortgage Market. ArcNews Online, 2008. http://www.esri.com/news/arcnews/spring08articles/egypt-launches.html

[67] The World Bank. Analysis of Housing Supply Mechanisms. Washington, D.C.: The World Bank, 2007.

[68] Serageldin, M, et al. UN-HABITAT Municipal Financing and Urban Development. Nairobi : UN-HABITAT, 2008.

[69] The World Bank. Egypt Urban Sector Update. Washington DC: The World Bank, 2008.

[70] The World Bank. Economic Evaluation of Housing Subsidy Systems. Washington, D.C.: The World Bank, 2005.

[71] Deloitte. 'Tunisia Highlights: International Tax' Deloitte, http://www.deloitte.com/assets/Dcom-Global/Local%20Assets/Documents/dtt_tax_highlight_2009_tunisia%281%29.pdf. Viewed on 16 January 2010.

[72] UN-HABITAT. Urban Sector Studies and Capacity Building for Khartoum State. Nairobi: UN-HABITAT, 2009.

[73] IPCC. Fourth Assessment Report: Climate Change. Geneva, 2007. http://www.ipcc.ch/publications_and_data/ar4/wg1/en/ch5s5-5-6.html. Viewed on 7 July 2009.

[74] Karas, J. Climate Change and the Mediterranean Region. Greenpeace, 2000. http://archive.greenpeace.org/climate/science/reports/fulldesert.html. Viewed on 8 July 2009.

[75] World Bank (2009). *Water in the Arab World.*

[76] *Ibid.*

[77] 2010 FAO of the UN Statistics- Aquastat.

[78] *Ibid.*

[79] World Bank (2009). *Water in the Arab World.*

[80] *Ibid.*

[81] *Ibid.*

[82] GOPP

[83] Marquina, A. Environmental Challenges in the Mediterranean 2000-2050, Madrid: NATO Science Series, 2002.

[84] *USAID. USAID Announces Partnership with RAED on Climate Change and Water Issues USAID, 2009.* http://www.usaid.gov/press/releases/2009/pr090528_1.html *Viewed on 3 July 2009.*

[85] European Union. Climate Change and Security: Recommendations of Javier Solana. Brussels: European Union, 2008. http://europa-eu-un.org/articles/en/article_8382_en.htm Viewed on 27 June 2009.

[86] Luganda, P. 'Africa and Climate Change: Adapt, Survive, Thrive?' SciDevNet, 2007. http://www.scidev.net/en/middle-east-and-north-africa/features/africa-and-climate-change-adapt-survive-thrive.html. Viewed on 22 June 2009.

[87] Stutz, B. 'Adaptation Emerges as Key Part of Any Climate Change Plan.' Yale Environment 360, 2009 http://e360.yale.edu/content/feature.msp?id=2156. Viewed on 22 June 2009.

[88] Serageldin, M. *Climate Change in the Local Development Agenda: Promoting the Resilience through Enhanced Understanding of Early Threats*, Cambridge: Institute for International Urban Development, 2009.

[89] UN-DESA. World Urbanisation Prospects: The 2008 Revision Database. 2008. http://esa.un.org/unup/ Viewed 17 December 2009.

[90] Sustainable development and environment in Tunisia. Ministry of Environment and Sustainable Development. http://www.mdptunisie.tn/en/environnement_developpement.php?s_rub=4#1. Viewed on 14 January 2010.

[91] *Ibid.*

[92] Dahech, S, Beltrando, G, "Air Temperature Variability in Sfax between 1970 and 2002", *Geophysical Research Abstract*, 2006. http://www.cosis.net/abstracts/EGU06/04941/EGU06-J-04941.pdf. Viewed on 24 June 2009.

[93] *Ibid.*

[94] Every month is divided into 5 consecutive days periods (6 days for the last period of 31-day months and 3 days for the last period in February). Each year is then divided into 72 periods. Dahech, S, Beltrando, G, "Air Temperature Variability in Sfax between 1970 and 2002", *Geophysical Research Abstract*, 2006. http://www.cosis.net/abstracts/EGU06/04941/EGU06-J-04941.pdf. Viewed on 24 June 2009.

[95] Karas, J. 'Climate Change and the Mediterranean Region.' Greenpeace, 2000. http://archive.greenpeace.org/climate/science/reports/fulldesert.html. Viewed on 25 June 2009.

[96] van Drunen, M.A., Lasage, R. Dorland, C. *Climate Change in Developing Countries*, Wallingford, 2006.

[97] Serageldin, M. *Climate Change in the Local Development Agenda: Promoting the Resilience Through Enhanced Understanding of Early Threats*, Cambridge: Institute for International Urban Development, 2009.

[98] *Ibid.*

[99] De Haas, H. 'Trans-Saharan Migration to North Africa and the EU: Historical Roots and Current Trends' University of Oxford, 2006 http://www.migrationinformation.org/feature/display.cfm?ID=484. Viewed on 8 February 2010.

[100] UN-DESA. International Migration. New York: United Nations, 2009.

[101] De Haas, H. 'Trans-Saharan Migration to North Africa and the EU: Historical Roots and Current Trends' University of Oxford, 2006 http://www.migrationinformation.org/feature/display.cfm?ID=484. Viewed on 8 February 2010.

[102] The World Bank. Maghreb Department. Morocco: National Initiative for Human Development Support Project. Washington, D.C.: The World Bank, 2006.

[103] CIA World Factbook. Morocco, 2009. https://www.cia.gov/library/publications/the-world-factbook/geos/mo.html. Viewed on 3 January 2010.

[104] Erlanger, S. 'Union of the Mediterranean, About to Be Inaugurated, May Be Mostly Show,' *The New York Times*, July 7, 2008 http://www.nytimes.com/2008/07/07/world/europe/07sarkozy.html. Viewed on 9 July 2009.

[105] EuroMed. The First Ministerial Meeting on Sustainable Development Projects. 2009.

[106] EuroMed. Building the Motorways of the Sea. 2009.

[107] EuroMed, 'De-Polluting the Mediterranean Sea by 2020' http://ec.europa.eu/environment/enlarg/med/initiative_en.htm . Viewed on 14 January 2010.

[108] EuroMed. The First Ministerial Meeting on Sustainable Development Projects. 2009.

[109] Europa (2009). 8th Union for the Mediterranean Trade Ministerial Conference. http://europa.eu/rapid/pressReleasesAction.do?reference=MEMO/09/547&format=HTML&aged=0&language=EN&guiLanguage=en. Viewed on 14 January 2010.

[110] EuroMed. The First Ministerial Meeting on Sustainable Development Projects. 2009.

Chapter Three

03

THE STATE OF WESTERN AFRICAN CITIES

Saint-Louis, Senegal.
©Guido Potters

DIEYE
CH·A·SECK

3.1
The Social Geography of Urbanisation

For the purposes of this report, the Western African subregion includes Benin, Burkina Faso, Cape Verde, Côte d'Ivoire, Guinea, Guinea-Bissau, the Gambia, Ghana, Liberia, Mali, Mauritania, Niger, Nigeria, Saint Helena, Senegal, Sierra Leone and Togo.

Each of these countries is challenged by the need to manage the opportunities and constraints arising from an accelerating, inevitable transition to urban demographic predominance. As in many other developing regions, cities act as the engines of economic growth because they create wealth, enhance social development and provide employment. However, when not properly governed or planned, as is largely the case in Western Africa, cities can become repositories for poverty, social ills, exclusion, environmental degradation and potential hotbeds of social unrest.

MAP 3.1: WESTERN AFRICAN COUNTRIES

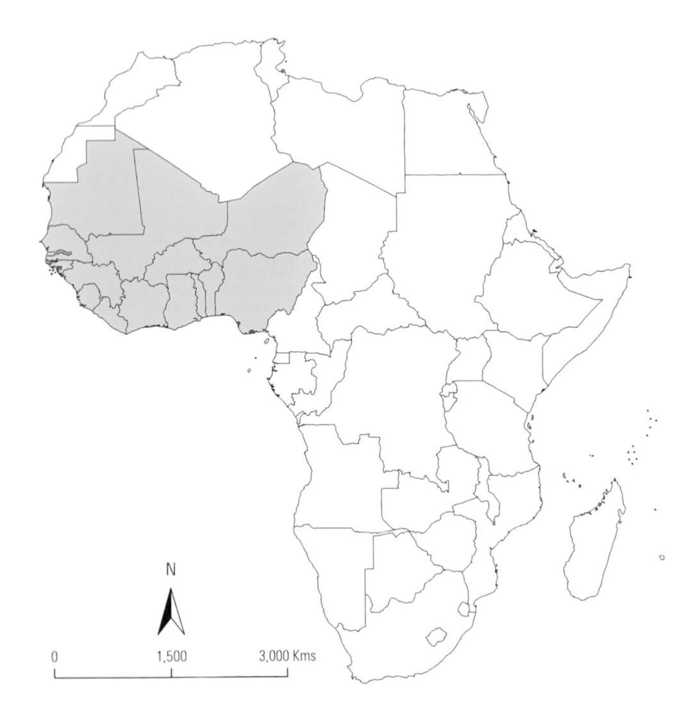

The ongoing urban transition comes under many different forms and rapidly changing conditions in Western Africa, including rapid and massive coastal urbanisation, the emergence of urban regions and domestic and cross-border development corridors. This raises many new challenges, including the rapid geographic concentration of poverty in urban areas, latitudinal and longitudinal mobility, climate change and its effects, etc. These features make urban expansion in its various guises an important common challenge for governments in the subregion, who should more than ever before see it as a priority for national policies, as well as a collective priority for the subregion as a whole, since Western Africa is an integration space where cities act as the driving force of development and modernization.

In 1950, a mere 6.6 million people lived in Western African cities. The number and the rate of urbanisation increased only slowly until 1990. Around that time, the urbanisation rate of Western Africa overtook the continental average and began to accelerate. The urban population rose to 92.1 million in the year 2000 and 137.2 million (a near 50 per cent increase) in 2010. This accelerating trend of urbanisation rates is expected to peak at an annual average rate of 6.24 per cent between 2020 and 2030, after which the trend should decelerate. Western Africa will become predominantly urban around 2020 with an estimated 195.3 million city dwellers. By 2050, that number will reach 427.7 million, or 68.36 per cent of the total population.

During the current decade up to 2020, Western Africa will become host to an additional 58 million urban dwellers, another 69 million during the 2020-30 decade and a further 79 million between 2030 and 2040. Even then, urban demographic growth will not subside in absolute terms, despite the expected onset of a declining inter-decade urbanisation trend around 2030. The 2040-50 decade is projected to add a further 84 million people to Western African cities. The message embedded in these statistics should be clear: Western African nations must give urgent attention to their rapidly growing urban populations. They must build governance and management capacities in cities of all sizes and plan for significant spending on services provision.

TABLE 3.1: **WESTERN AFRICA: URBAN POPULATION TRENDS, 1950-2050**

Population	1950	1960	1970	1980	1990	2000	2010*	2020*	2030*	2040*	2050*
Urban (000s)	6,629	12,660	22,572	37,774	60,559	92,162	137,271	195,344	264,182	343,213	427,675
Urban (%)	9.79	15.12	21.31	27.18	33.05	38.76	44.85	50.98	57.40	62.86	68.36
All Africa (%)	14.40	18.64	23.59	27.91	32.13	35.95	39.98	44.59	49.95	55.73	61.59

** Projections*
Source: WUP 2009

GRAPH 3.1: **WESTERN AFRICA: URBAN POPULATION TRENDS, 1950-2050**

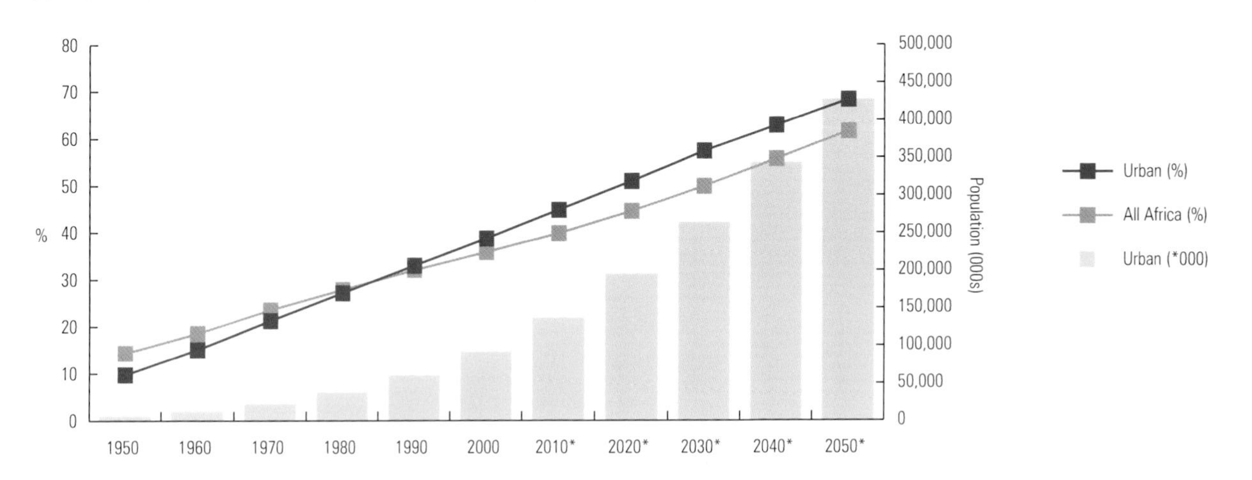

** Projections*
Source: WUP 2009

▲
Lomé, Togo. **©Peeter Viisimaa/iStockphoto**

TABLE 3.2: **WESTERN AFRICA: NATIONAL URBANISATION TRENDS, 1950-2050 (%)**

% Urban	1950	1960	1970	1980	1990	2000	2010*	2020*	2030*	2040*	2050*
Benin	4.96	9.28	16.69	27.34	34.49	38.33	42.04	47.23	53.74	60.32	66.56
Burkina Faso	3.84	4.70	5.75	8.81	13.82	17.84	25.69	34.40	42.80	50.80	58.76
Cape Verde	14.20	16.68	19.56	23.52	44.12	53.43	61.09	67.45	72.53	76.95	80.84
Côte d'Ivoire	9.86	17.68	28.16	36.93	39.74	43.54	50.56	57.78	64.13	69.65	74.64
Gambia	10.27	12.13	19.50	28.41	38.31	49.10	58.15	65.04	71.02	76.35	80.96
Ghana	15.44	23.25	28.97	31.17	36.44	43.95	51.47	58.42	64.69	70.46	75.64
Guinea	6.71	10.47	15.98	23.62	28.03	31.05	35.36	41.44	48.64	55.91	62.93
Guinea-Bissau	10.01	13.60	15.13	17.61	28.13	29.70	30.00	32.83	38.61	45.59	52.74
Liberia	12.97	18.63	26.03	35.17	40.94	44.33	47.82	52.15	57.57	63.50	69.05
Mali	8.47	11.07	14.33	18.48	23.32	28.34	35.86	43.69	51.26	58.46	65.31
Mauritania	3.10	6.88	14.56	27.37	39.67	39.99	41.43	45.45	51.71	58.18	64.38
Niger	4.86	5.79	8.79	13.44	15.37	16.19	17.11	19.25	23.47	29.70	36.81
Nigeria	10.21	16.16	22.71	28.58	35.28	42.52	49.80	56.85	63.59	69.83	75.42
Saint Helena	51.59	49.07	46.55	44.05	41.57	39.69	39.73	41.68	46.37	52.88	59.32
Senegal	17.23	23.00	30.00	35.77	38.90	40.35	42.38	46.46	52.55	58.99	65.11
Sierra Leone	12.65	17.38	23.40	29.11	32.94	35.57	38.40	42.83	49.02	55.84	62.44
Togo	4.38	10.10	21.28	24.66	30.10	36.53	43.44	50.46	57.30	63.88	69.84

** Projections*
Source: WUP 2009

GRAPH 3.2: **WESTERN AFRICA: NATIONAL URBANISATION TRENDS, 1950-2050 (%)**

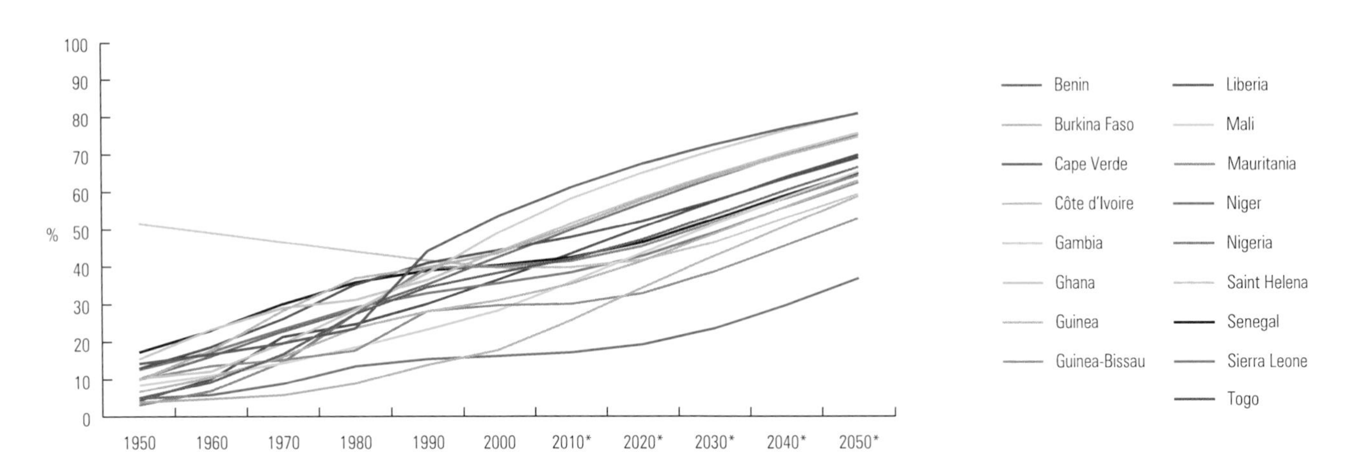

** Projections*
Source: WUP 2009

The urban geography of Western Africa varies widely across the subregion's countries. For example, in 2010, the percentage of people living in areas classified as urban was highest in Cape Verde with 61.0 per cent and lowest in Niger with 17.1 per cent and a regional urbanisation average of 42.0 per cent. Five of the subregion's 17 nations were already estimated to be predominantly urban in 2010: Cape Verde, Côte d'Ivoire, Gambia, Ghana and Liberia. The mid-range to relatively low concentrations of urban populations in some Western African countries notwithstanding, cities such as ***Porto Novo***, Benin, ***Ouagadougou***, Burkina Faso, ***Accra***, Ghana, ***Niamey***, Niger, ***Lagos***, Nigeria and ***Lomé*** in Togo, are all confronted with 'over-urbanisation'. This means that in these cities the populations are growing much faster than local economies, leading to major social and economic challenges like high unemployment rates, slum proliferation, social polarization and crime. Other commonplace urban challenges in the region include rapid changes in land use and

MAP 3.2: **DISTRIBUTION OF URBAN AREAS >10,000 INHABITANTS**

Source: Africapolis database SEDET/AFD, July 2008 ©Guèye & Thiam, Dakar, Senegal, August 2010

land cover, and deteriorating environments, not to mention the effects of climate change.

The current rapid demographic growth in cities is bound, over the next decades, to pose particularly daunting challenges in terms of poverty alleviation and environmental degradation. However, urban demographic growth cannot, on its own, account for human exposure to socio-economic and environmental risks. Rather, it is the pace of urban change that is adding to human vulnerability. This change involves rapidly proliferating, deep urban poverty that disproportionately affects women and children, which, together with ethnic and racial conflict, urban crime, homelessness and degraded urban environments all have far-reaching political and socio-economic implications. Economic prospects look bright for some Western African nations, which gives their cities the potential to improve the living conditions of countries' poorest residents. However, cities with the highest rates of population growth and urban change tend to be found in the nations with the most listless economies. For the cities, the risks of further deterioration are both obvious and there to stay.

The concentration of populations in urban areas is in principle positive, since this can generate efficiencies and economic gains through agglomeration of all kinds of resources, first and foremost human. In cities and regions with sluggish economies, however, stark spatial disparities and socio-economic polarization are becoming increasingly visible. With the demographic and spatial expansion of cities, the capacity of several Western African nations to manage and address the implications is lagging way behind. The more harmful of those implications, whether of a social, economic or environmental nature, fall especially heavily upon the poor, most of whom become excluded from the benefits of prosperity.

The problems of the urban poor cannot but affect national efforts to achieve sustainable development. In an increasingly interdependent world, high prevalence and persistence of domestic urban poverty can have implications for other nations, apart from emigration flows. Deep deprivation weakens national capacities to combat organized crime, human trafficking, armed conflict, terrorism, social unrest and the spread of diseases. These, in turn, can have severe domestic economic, environmental and security consequences, and also affect neighbouring states and the global community. In a global age, the outcomes associated with high poverty incidence can often no longer be contained within national boundaries, and can therefore also affect regional and global stability.

However, it is not just deprivation of income or consumption opportunities that forces huge numbers of urban dwellers to live in the unacceptable conditions associated with socio-economic exclusion. A broader view encompasses the non-income dimensions of poverty such as access to education and health services, gender equity and access to basic services like clean water and adequate sanitation facilities. *Inequality* is closely related to poverty and a factor in domestic wealth distribution, income and consumption. It is different from *inequity*, which refers to an ill-balanced distribution of economic, political, social and cultural opportunities.

Throughout history, one of the functions of cities has been to protect residents from the onslaughts of invaders and civil strife. Over time, the concentration of wealth, knowledge and power in cities has allowed for specialization which, in turn, has contributed to technical, cultural and social innovation and generally rising levels of economic and social prosperity. However, in Western Africa, as elsewhere in the developing world, cities have been largely unable to accommodate rapid demographic expansion and to provide new residents with jobs, land, housing as well as basic and other services (the 'urban advantage', compared with rural areas). This inability keeps millions excluded from the socio-economic benefits of urban life, and this exclusion finds its tangible expression in extensive urban slums that are hosts to millions of extremely poor households who are effectively deprived of their fair shares in national prosperity. They have little option but informal settlements and slums which, by definition, have limited if any access to urban and social infrastructures, and find themselves spatially and socially segregated from those who have the wealth or power to benefit from the urban advantage. The practical mechanisms of exclusion are complex and the segregation that began during the colonial period, and was maintained after independence by small political and economic elites, has now given way to new patterns of inequality and inequity that go beyond the distribution of urban spaces. Nevertheless, the continuing proliferation of urban slums and informal settlements remains the main manifestation of exclusion and inequality in the majority of Western African cities.

Exclusion, poverty and proliferating slums go hand in hand with poor urban governance. Breakdowns in central and local government ability to manage and steer urban growth are the inevitable consequence of geographicaly selective fiscal retrenchment by the urban public sector. In most cases, the poorer sections of the city have been all but abandoned and are essentially forced to manage by themselves. Poorly maintained drainage systems, inadequate waste collection and solid waste dumps inhabited by the underprivileged are rife in Western Africa. This spatially selective degradation of the urban environment is the result of *laisser-faire* attitudes and the consequential, uncontrolled self-help urbanisation that promotes indiscriminate urban sprawl on peri-urban space and agricultural lands; this interferes with natural drainage patterns, or adds to denuding of hillsides in pursuit of urban land.

Geographic Concentration and Clustering

With its urban population projected to double over the next 20 years, as noted earlier, a majority of Western Africans will be living in urban areas by 2020. The subregion will soon host Africa's two largest urban agglomerations, with the continued rapid growth of the already colossal demographic concentrations of ***Lagos*** and ***Kinshasa***.

While these two very large conurbations are soon to rise to the apex of Africa's urban hierarchy, they nevertheless absorb only relatively small shares of urban demographic growth: cities below one million and secondary ones (up to 500,000) are where (about three-quarters) that growth is anticipated.

Depending on respective historical, political and cultural backgrounds and development opportunities, Western African countries are urbanising in very different ways. With the exception of the desert zone comprising Mali, Mauritania and Niger, urbanisation in Western Africa over the past 30 years has been relatively dense and very rapid. From South to North and from West to East, four relatively homogeneous urbanisation strata are apparent (see Map 3.3). The area from the South Atlantic coast to 10 degrees north and from the western coast to the eastern region of Nigeria is host to the largest urban centres in the subregion. Nigeria features a particularly tight and increasingly dense network of cities

TABLE 3.3: **AFRICA'S LARGEST CONURBATIONS: CAIRO, KINSHASA AND LAGOS, 1995-2025**

	1995	2005	2010*	2015*	2025*
Cairo	9,707	10,565	11,001	11,663	13,531
Kinshasa	4,590	7,106	8,754	10,668	15,041
Lagos	5,966	8,767	10,578	12,427	15,810

* *Projections*
Source: WUP 2009

GRAPH 3.3: **AFRICA'S LARGEST CONURBATIONS: CAIRO, KINSHASA AND LAGOS, 1995-2025**

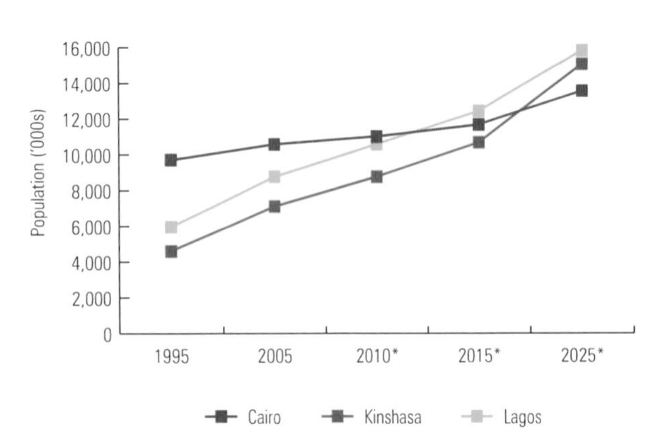

* *Projections*
Source: WUP 2009

TABLE 3.4: **NUMBER OF CITIES WITH POPULATIONS OVER 10,000, 1960-2020**

	1960	1980	2000	2020*
Benin	3	37	67	85
Burkina Faso	2	16	56	93
Cape Verde	2	2	3	8
Côte d'Ivoire	8	52	106	195
Gambia	0	1	5	8
Ghana	30	57	117	199
Guinea	4	18	26	25
Guinea-Bissau	0	1	2	9
Liberia	0	11	13	16
Mali	5	18	29	60
Mauritania	0	5	9	10
Niger	3	9	34	49
Nigeria	133	253	438	574
Senegal	8	23	42	59
Sierra Leone	2	7	11	17
Togo	4	19	38	70

** Projections*
Source: Etude Africapolis – AFD/SEDET

(zone 1). Next come the countries along the Gulf of Guinea (zone 2), where urban networks are much less dense than in Nigeria but which, nevertheless, feature dense urban pockets. The third zone is characterized by a relatively loose pattern of stagnant urban settlements and an absence of large towns. Niger is typical of this pattern, with most of its northern territories featuring a low urbanisation rate (estimated at 17 per cent in 2010) and one of the least dense urban settlement networks in Western Africa. Mauritania stands out as the exception, owing its urban vitality to the capital Nouakchott where more than 21 per cent of the nation's total population and about 75 per cent of the total urban population of the country are currently concentrated.

The fourth zone is none other than the western extension of an elongated desert strip that runs from the Red Sea to the Atlantic Ocean and separates sub-Saharan from Northern Africa. This is a particularly inhospitable area where cities are scarce. Existing settlements like ***Zouerate***, ***Chinguetti*** and ***Taoudeni*** (north-western Sahara) experience few new developments due to climatic conditions, lack of functional connections and absence of a rural demographic reservoir to feed cities. All these factors combine to restrict urban formation and growth. Insecurity and political conflict do not favour urban growth, either. However, if and when regional integration and cooperation becomes a reality and long-distance roads materialize, existing urban areas could become important new population nodes between sub-Saharan and Northern Africa. The recent opening of the trans-Saharan

MAP 3.3: **THE TYPOLOGY OF URBANISATION IN WESTERN AFRICA**

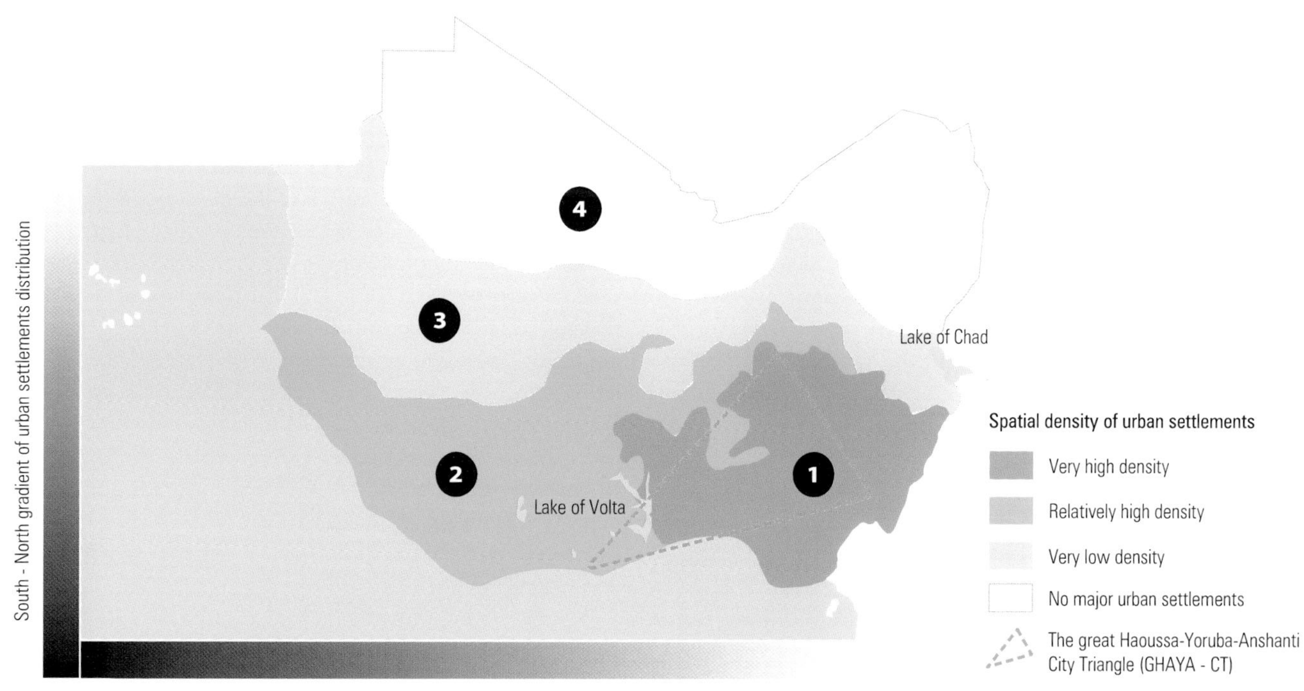

Source: Zones are digitized according to the Africapolis study conclusions. ©Guèye & Thiam, April 2010

MAP 3.4: **PROSPECTIVE URBAN POPULATION DISTRIBUTION IN WESTERN AFRICA, 2020**

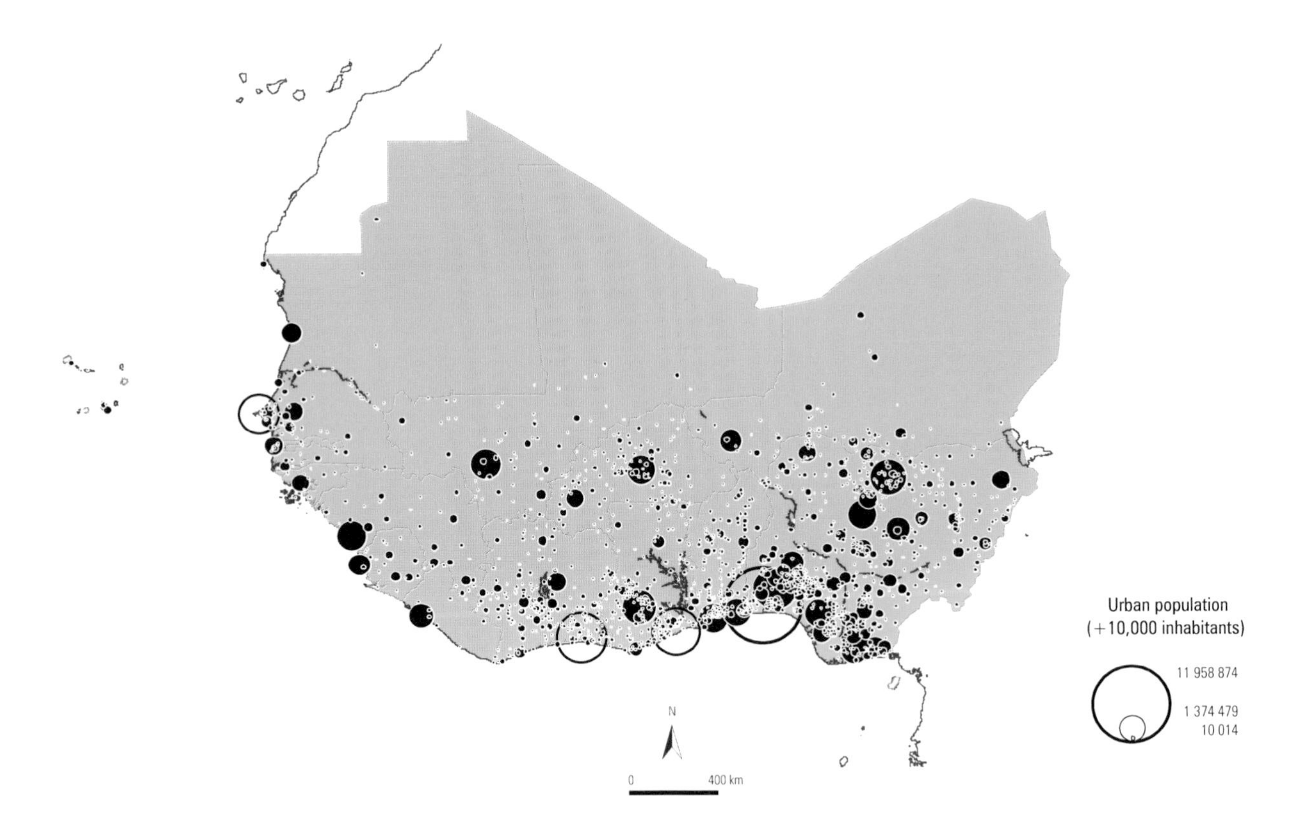

Source: Databases of Africapolis study - SEDET/AFD, July 2008. ©Guèye & Thiam, Dakar, Senegal, Sept. 09

Morocco-Mauritania highway, for instance, has shown that, with infrastructure development, settlements that have been in a state of lethargy for centuries can quickly become economically vibrant urban growth poles.

Overall, Western Africa's urban network has maintained the same configuration for decades and is not expected to change much in the near future. However, a few urban growth poles have emerged in recent years. Some of these appear as incipient regional clusters, as they connect with the dense networks in the more urbanised parts of Western Africa, particularly those in the Ashanti (Ghana), Hausa (Kano) and Yoruba (Lagos) triangle. Map 3.4 shows the population distribution projections for 2020 and the emergence of regional urban clusters in Western Africa.

The largest of these clusters is located in southern Nigeria. It extends over 160 km from ***Ondo*** to ***Illorin*** and along an east-west axis from ***Omuo*** to ***Oyo*** over a 200 km distance. This is the region with the highest urban settlements density in Western Africa, where distances between one city and the next rarely exceed 10 km. The region extends towards ***Lagos*** through a smaller cluster currently emerging north-east of the business capital and which, in time, will embrace smaller towns like ***Owode***, ***Ode Lemo*** and ***Ibefun***. In the northern Nigerian cities of ***Sokoto*** and ***Kware***, a relatively large cluster is also emerging. It is expected to absorb smaller towns like ***Guidan Madi***, ***Bunkari Silame*** and connect to border towns in Niger such as ***Birni N'Koni***, ***Malbaza Usine*** and ***Galmi***.

In southern Ghana and west of ***Accra*** in particular, a very large settlement cluster is now emerging as an extension of the Accra Extended Metropolitan Region. The cluster stretches over 200 km along an east-west axis and nearly 150 km south to north. Over the next few years, it is likely to connect to the ***Kumasi*** agglomeration, which already includes more than a dozen towns, and then turn into Ghana's first major urban corridor.

Transnational urban clusters are also beginning to emerge throughout the subregion. A large one is located between Togo and Benin and extends west to east from ***Mission-Tové*** in Togo to ***Sé*** in Benin. This cluster is part of the enormous Greater Ibadan-Lagos-Accra (GILA) corridor, and one of its more dynamic segments. The Togolese part is soon expected to connect with ***Dzodze*** and ***Penyi*** in Ghana. Other transnational clusters are to emerge over the next few years between northern Benin and southern Niger, as well as between Ghana and Côte d'Ivoire.

In view of the important role that cities play in regional development, regional urban clustering deserves special attention, especially where resulting from spontaneous spatial and geographic processes. Urban clusters are major economic activity centres. The geographic concentration of cities, and therefore of people and human activities, can be beneficial and

MAP 3.5: **PROSPECTIVE URBAN NETWORKS AND REGIONAL CLUSTERING, 2020**

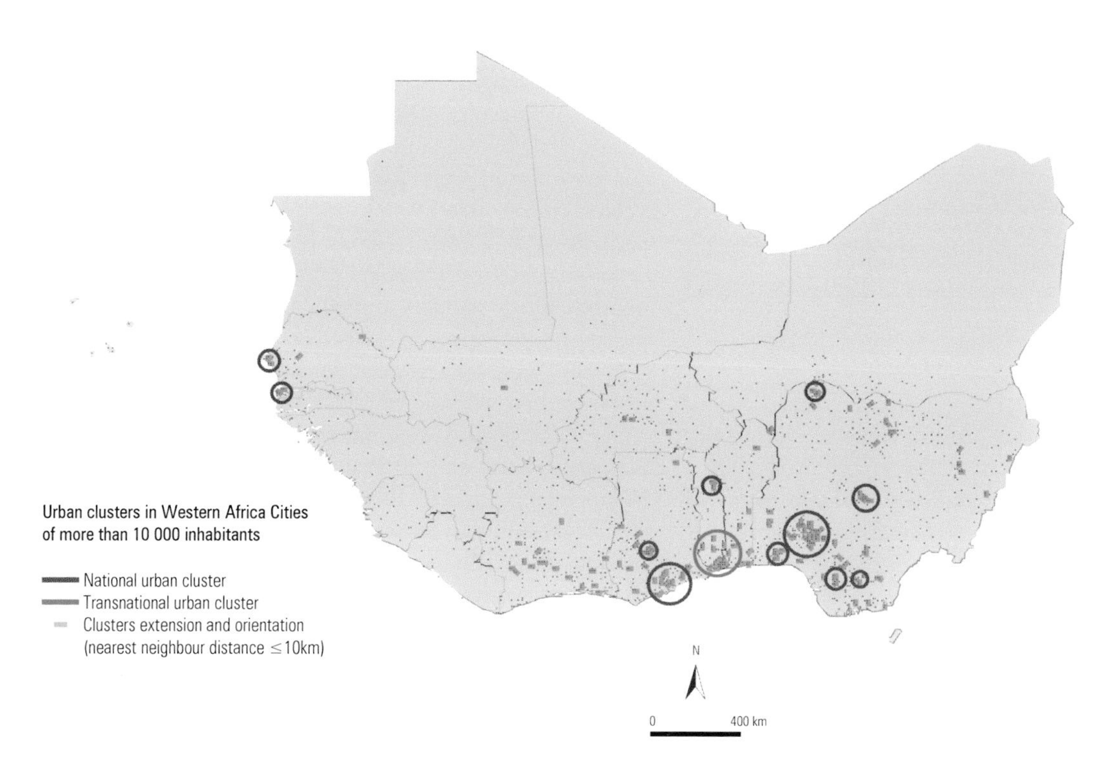

Source: Databases of Africapolis Study SEDET/AFD, July 2008. ©Guèye & Thiam, Dakar – Senegal, March 2010

should be promoted. It creates a self-reinforcing accumulation of agents of production in agglomeration economies, which will make up for logistical shortcomings and distance by linking markets and major transport infrastructure nodes such as ports, railway stations and airports. In Senegal, for example, the development of an economic and logistical hub in Diamniadio and the construction of an international airport nearby are part of a laudable effort to bring supply and demand closer together. As shown in Map 3.5, the urban cluster around ***Dakar*** is about to become one of the larger economic zones in Western Africa. This process owes as much to manufacturing and tourism as it does to the establishment of structuring facilities such as the airport and highways.

Two main factors determine the emergence of urban regions: (a) the existence of two or more metropolitan cities in relative proximity and connected by infrastructures (road, rail and/or waterways); and (b) the gradual functional integration of the metropolitan spaces with the semi-urban and rural spaces between them. In Western Africa - as is mostly the case south of the Sahara - regional urban configurations and city regions are comparatively new phenomena; the outcomes of the demographic momentum generated by large cities. The emerging urban patterns are highly conducive to domestic economic development and regional integration when and where they cross national borders and functionally link up with similar configurations in neighbouring countries. However, regional agreements on the free movement of people, goods, finance and communications are a significant pre-condition if the outcomes of regional development, integration and trade are to be maximised.

As the demographic transition accelerates larger Western African cities tend to lag behind intermediate and smaller cities. Beyond demographics, though, larger cities retain their essential roles in spatial dynamics. Their economic and political power fuels the emergence of urban regions whose catalyser and gravitational effects spur the expansion of urban peripheries, and connect with each other to form extended metropolitan urban regions, as explained below.

The emergence of urban regions in Western Africa is essentially the result of major shifts in metropolitan spatial organisation that are, in turn, one of the main outcomes of functional specialization. While central business districts and their immediate surroundings increasingly host top-level political, economic and commercial functions, the peri-urban and adjacent rural areas are mostly left to cope with rising land demands for housing and other urban functions as required by demographic growth, or as rising land prices or other factors displace residents from central to peri-urban locations. Recent high peri-urban demographic growth rates and the resulting rapid urban sprawl are mainly caused by

▲
Dakar, Senegal. ©**Brian McMorrow**

the reconfiguration of urban residential areas. This has less to do with rural migration than with the shifts of existing city dwellers to urban peripheries.

For instance, the major changes the Senegalese capital ***Dakar*** experienced during recent years have involved a revival of the city centre's administrative and commercial functions to the detriment of residential uses. The demographic ballooning of suburbs like Pikine and Guédiawaye and the large increases in urban peripheral neighbourhoods such as Rufisque, Bargny or Diamniadio, for instance, are mainly caused by land market-driven functional rearrangement. Increasing demand for central urban locations and the associated sharp rises in land values render residential functions commercially less viable and pushes them out to the urban periphery. However, the emergence of a dynamic urban region around ***Dakar*** is hampered by an obsolete and inefficient transportation network that provides poor connections between peripheral residential neighbourhoods and the city's commercial centre. Regional city configurations always demand major improvements in urban mobility, especially efficient mass transit options, to ensure that the very urban dynamism and productivity that drive city-region formation do not get stranded in congestion and associated negative environmental externalities.

The crucial role of efficient urban mobility is well understood in ***Lagos***, Nigeria's business capital and main conurbation. Huge investments are currently under way to improve urban mobility through interesting public-private partnership initiatives, as elaborated upon in Box 3.1.

Around the ***Accra*** agglomeration in Ghana, the metropolitan transportation system is relatively well developed. The urban region now extends over more than 900 km^2, more than 70 km west-east and 30 km north-south. It includes four Metropolitan Districts: ***Accra***, ***Ga West***, ***Ga East*** and ***Tema*** and is gradually encroaching on the Metropolitan District of ***Dangme West***. The spatial extension of ***Accra*** is facilitated by the good performance of its transportation system which plays a very important role in the mobility of people and production factors from the central areas toward the peripheries.

Accra clearly shows that good urban mobility through an efficient public transportation network is a major factor behind urban performance (see map 3.7). Among the Western African urban agglomerations exceeding 200 km^2, ***Accra*** is

MAP 3.6: **THE DAKAR URBAN REGION**

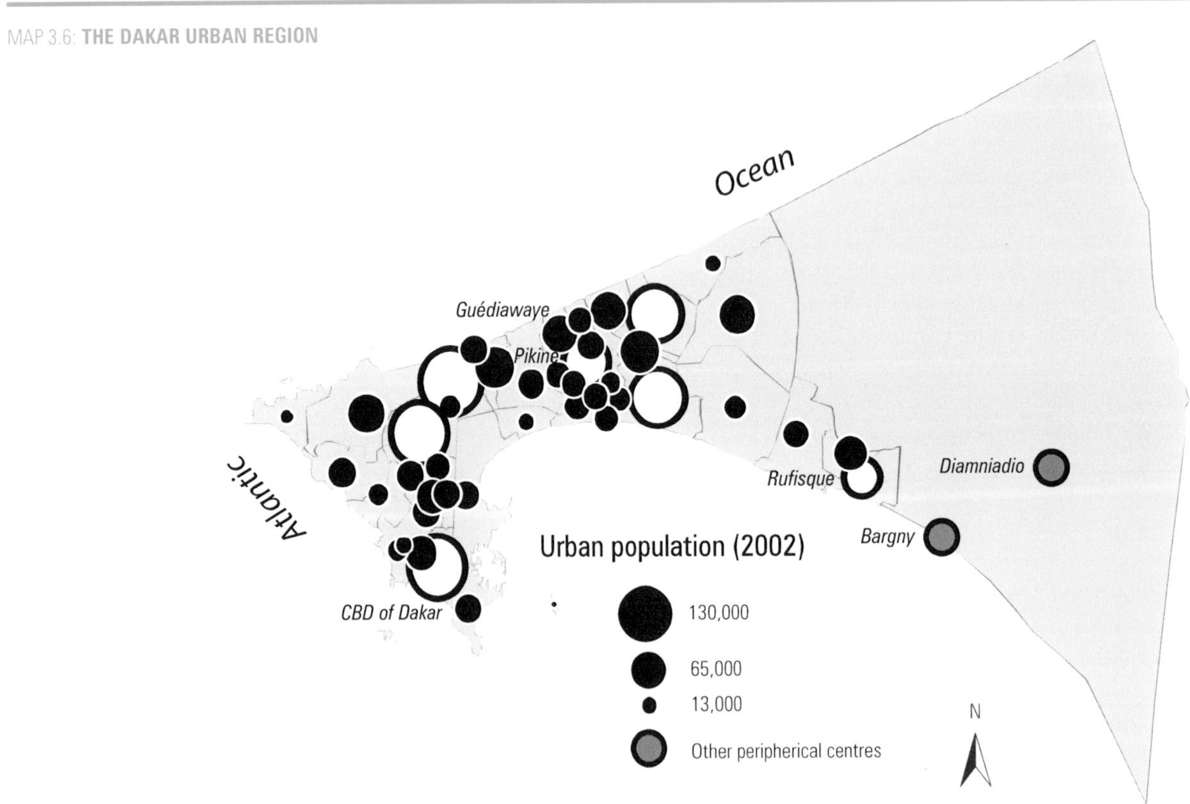

Source: DPS/DAT. ©Thiam & Guèye, April 2010

BOX 3.1: HOW GREATER LAGOS INVOLVES THE PRIVATE SECTOR IN INTEGRATED URBAN MOBILITY

▲
Traffic in downtown Lagos, Nigeria. **©George Osodi/Panos Pictures**

Whereas in 2010 the population of the City of Lagos was about 10.5 million, the Lagos City Region is host to an estimated 18 million and bound for rapid expansion in years to come. Greater Lagos now includes 16 of the 20 local authority areas in Lagos State and some 90 per cent of its population. Lagos State – the smallest for surface area – is the nation's most industrialised and employs 45 per cent of Nigeria's skilled domestic human resources. Acknowledging the urgent need to improve urban mobility, water supply and waste management, the authorities are now spending heavily on infrastructures across the metropolitan area.

Every day, some seven million Lagosians commute to work by public transport or private vehicles. It has become evident that productivity in Metro Lagos is increasingly hampered by the inadequacy of its fragmented public transportation system and heavy traffic congestion. In responce, the Lagos Metropolitan Area Transport Authority (LAMATA) has engaged in a public-private partnership to improve urban mobility through the integration of urban bus, rail and water transportation networks. An initially sceptical population is now beginning to notice the improvements. Early investments by the state have established the first Bus Rapid Transit in sub-Saharan Africa with 100 new buses and passenger capacity increased from 60,000 to 220,000. Urban mobility is further expected to improve with seven new urban rail lines totalling 246 km. Road network improvements include the upgrading of the Lekki-Epe expressway and the construction of 20 km of coastal road, funded through partnerships between private, state and federal bodies. The greatest impact, however, should be the precedent Lagos has set for improving urban mobility through public-private partnerships. For details refer to www.lamata-ng.com/.

the only one where the configuration of the transport network facilitates rapid and direct access to central areas. It takes, on the average, less than 25 minutes to commute to work, compared with 45 minutes in smaller conurbations like ***Abidjan*** or ***Conakry,*** or 60 minutes in ***Monrovia***. The ease of mobility in ***Accra*** has proven essential to good connections between the central business district and the urban region, facilitating a host of beneficial spin-offs, including ease of demographic growth absorption in peripheral towns since 1970.

Between 1970 and 2000, ***Ashiaman*** and ***Madina***, for example, have seen their populations increase from 22,000 and 7,000 to 150,000 and 76,000 respectively. These numbers are expected to reach 200,000 and 140,000 respectively by 2020, while other peripheral towns seem bound to experience even higher demographic growth rates over the next ten years. By 2020, the ***Oduponkpehe-Buduburam-Nyanyano-Bortianor*** urban agglomeration is likely to grow into a compact urban region with the potential to counterbalance Central ***Accra*** and its large north-east suburbs. This is expected to diminish the current extreme primacy of Central ***Accra*** without compromising accessibility. Further, the incipient urban zone around the peripheral town of ***Tema*** is to become more influential in the years to come and fill in any gaps in the urban fabric. Clearly, ***Accra*** and its extended metropolitan region shows how Africa's large urban agglomerations can address the debilitating urban mobility challenges they have to face.

The Links between Poverty, Inequality and Slums

Just like the cities that produce and maintain them, urban form and functions are not neutral creations. Whether classified as legal or illegal, they reflect actual organisational modes and operational systems. Over time, urban form and functions become the spatial reflexions of social change, politics and development options. In Western Africa, recent developments in urban form, particularly in the larger cities, have often occurred through crisis-like socio-economic processes. Very high urban growth rates during the past 25 years, and their consequences such as escalating urban unemployment, declining household incomes, increasingly difficult access to urban land, shelter and services, all reflect the quality of the organisation and management of cities. All-too often, though, the very social structures of urban populations have led to undesirable geographies of socio-spatial fragmentation.

The perception of the processes that underpin the spatial structuring of urban populations has changed profoundly. Contrary to earlier analyses, and partly under the influence of the urban sociology developed by the Chicago School in the 1950s, recent studies attach less importance to ethno-cultural or linguistic affinities when seeking to understand spatial and socio-economic formation and reconstitution of urban population groups, their residential choices, or the daily movements of individuals within urban spaces. For instance in ***Abidjan,*** neighbourhoods such as Petit Bouaké and Petit-Ouaga, or ***Conakry's*** Mosquée Sénégalaise indicate spatial groupings based on domestic or cross-border migratory origins, and therefore stand as remnants of an urban pattern when ethnic identity still played an essential role in residential choices. Today, ethnic identity or geographic origin no longer serve as the main factors behind the geographic structuring of groups in Western African cities. Instead, socio-economic criteria and derivative factors like poverty, social polarization and exclusion have become the main spatial determinants.

Urban poverty, social polarization and slum development have become established through a variety of social, economic and political factors that define individual or group status and, by extension, individual or collective options for political power leveraging. This has often major geographical implications for services delivery, tenure security and the soundness of government decisions. The rapid proliferation of slums is underscored by the reluctance of the urban poor to invest in permanent and safe housing due to poor security of tenure. Many urban slum communities *can* afford improvements to their living environments, but lack of political leveraging and the risk of eviction often make the expenditure too risky.

Urban poverty, social polarization and slum proliferation have distinct spatial dimensions, as people with comparable socio-economic characteristics tend to converge on the same locations. Spatial segregation is not necessarily a bad thing, though, as people have self-segregated for millennia based on language, ethnicity, profession or other social criteria. However, the spatial confinement of urban social categories

▲
Accra, Ghana. Communal toilet blocks in an informal settlement. **©Gordon Dixon/iStockphoto**

MAP 3.7: **THE SPATIAL EXTENSION OF THE ACCRA URBAN REGION**

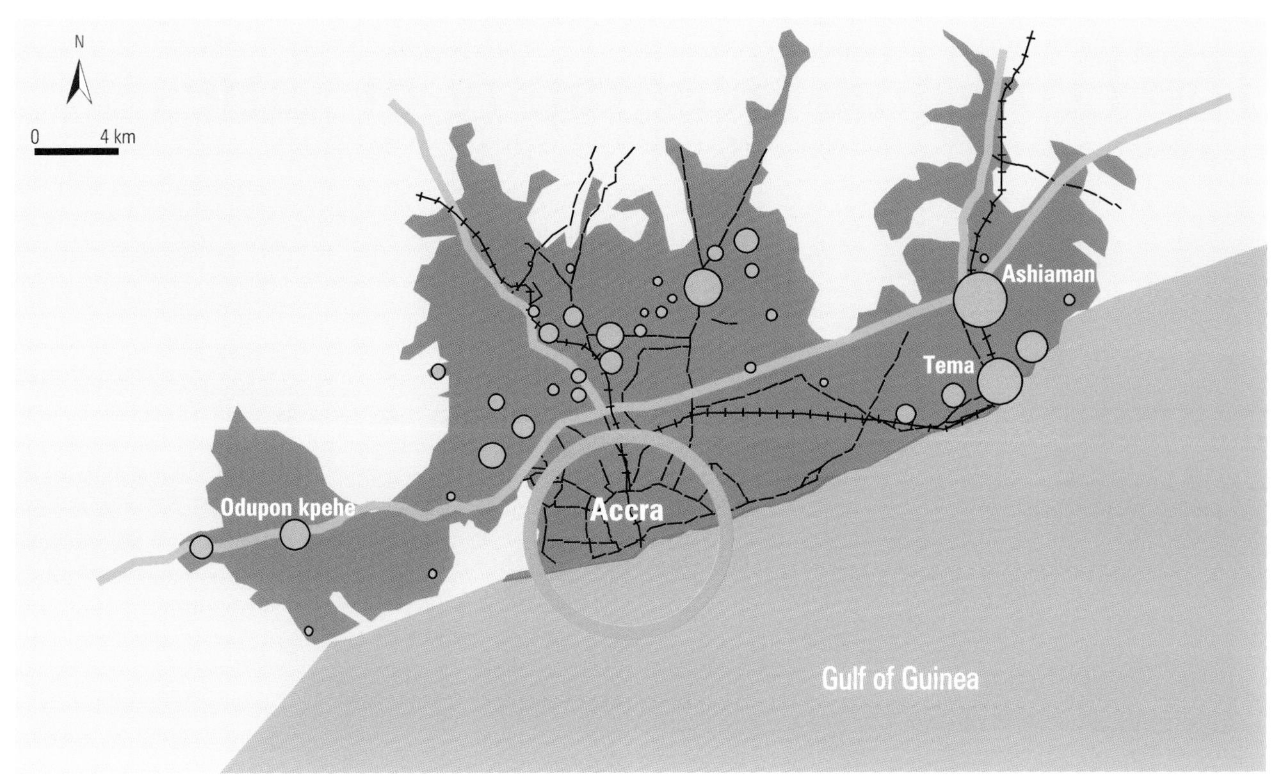

Source: Database of Africapolis report AFD/SEDET, July 2008. Digitization by Guèye and Thiam. ©Guèye & Thiam, Dakar, Senegal, Sept. 2009

- particularly the poorest - and the continuous spatial fragmentation of Western African cities are no longer entirely voluntary nowadays, which makes particular urban areas highly susceptible to political, social, economic and life-chance inequalities. These transformation processes are driven mainly by rapid and steady growth in urban populations, as well as by mismatches between supply and demand for liveable urban spaces and housing. A second factor is a direct consequence of the first and follows market-driven mechanisms. Irrespective of the resource (commodity, privilege, etc.), when demand exceeds supply, competition becomes inevitable and the poor become more vulnerable to inequalities.

Therefore, the persistence of illegal housing and the proliferation of urban slums, informal settlements and land squatting are mostly the outcome of competition for space. Formal urban land markets systematically serve the wealthy who can afford the best land and housing options, while driving out the poor. The latter are then forced into informality in the least desirable, if not uninhabitable urban areas, such as low-lying and flood-prone lands, factory fringes, garbage dumps, road reserves, etc.

Having been initially confined to larger cities, economic and residential informality is now spreading to cities of all sizes and with similar effects everywhere. In ***Lagos***, the rich and well-serviced neighbourhoods of Ikoyi, Victoria or Apapa contrast sharply with overpopulated, under-equipped and unsafe areas like Mushin, Shomolu or Iju. In ***Dakar***, one finds similar contrasts between Fann Résidence, Almadies, Corniche Ouest and central neighbourhoods like Grand-Dakar, Usines Ben Tally and Niarry Tally, or poor, dense and under-serviced peripheral areas like Pikine, Guédiawaye and Ngor. Likewise in ***Abidjan***: the rich Plateau neighbourhood has extended deeply into the popular neighbourhood of Adjamé, driving out the original, economically less affluent residents, while the middle-class neighbourhoods of Cocody and Riviera are built right up against the infamous low-income neighbourhood of Abobo. In Abidjan, spatial fragmentation is heightened by the presence of the Ebrié lagoon which, in some places, sharply demarcates urban neighbourhoods. Western Africa offers many more similar examples. In some cases, however, the emergence of urban middle classes has encouraged the materialization of distinct lower-middle income residential areas like Sacré Cœur, Libertés and Mermoz in ***Dakar***, or Ajegunleand Ilupeju in ***Lagos***.

The social geography of today's Western African cities features very clearly delineated boundaries that are determined by market forces. The gap between rich and poor is bound to deepen, not only in terms of well-being, but increasingly also as expressed in the spatial differentiation that determines access to public resources, facilities and life chances. In the current absence of effective interventions, inequalities between urban communities will inevitably increase the disparities between rich and poor urban groups, with the risk of destabilizing urban communities and the national political equilibrium alike.

3.2 The Economic Geography of Cities

Cities are humankind's most complex creations, never finished, never definitive. They are the physical manifestation of history and culture, the incubators of innovation, industry, technology, entrepreneurship and creativity. Cities around the world have moved to the forefront of global socio-economic change, with half of humankind now living in areas defined as urban and the other half increasingly dependent upon cities for their economic, social and political advancement.

As privileged spaces of accelerated social transformation, cities serve as nodes for the coordination and servicing of national economies that are increasingly becoming internationalized. This transition comes with substantial social costs, most notably a growing polarization between small, successful trans-national urban elites and increasingly impoverished majorities of city dwellers. Informal settlements keep mushrooming away from the central areas where jobs, cultural and economic opportunities are concentrated, and this phenomenon increasingly results in highly undesirable patterns of urban duality (the 'urban divide') that are not only highly discriminatory, but that also have the potential to undermine the systemic stability and dynamism of cities.

One of the most conspicuous changes over the past decades has been the growth of 'privatized' urban space, especially gated residential communities. These have emerged in part as the response to the apparent inability of public authorities to address the rise in crime and other security concerns; however, they are increasingly contributing to the fragmentation and polarization of urban space and the segregation of the poor from other segments of society. Gated communities comes in various shapes and guises, but they share the following

▲
Nouakchott, Mauritania. **©Attila Jándi/Shutterstock**

TABLE 3.5: **PEOPLE LIVING ON LESS THAN ONE DOLLAR A DAY (%), SELECTED WESTERN AFRICAN COUNTRIES**

	Population living below US $1.00 a day (%)	Share of income/consumption held by the poorest 20%	Gini coefficient
Benin (2003)	47.33	6.91	0.386
Burkina Faso (2003)	56.54	6.96	0.396
Ghana (2006)	29.99	5.20	0.428
Niger (2005)	65.88	5.85	0.439
Nigeria (2004)	64.41	5.13	0.427
Togo (2006)	38.68	7.62	0.344

Source:
1. Global Urban Observatory, UN-HABITAT
2. UN Development Report 2010 The Real Wealth of Nations: Pathways to Human Development, UNDP, NY p. 154-159

GRAPH 3.4: **PEOPLE LIVING ON LESS THAN ONE DOLLAR A DAY (%), SELECTED WESTERN AFRICAN COUNTRIES**

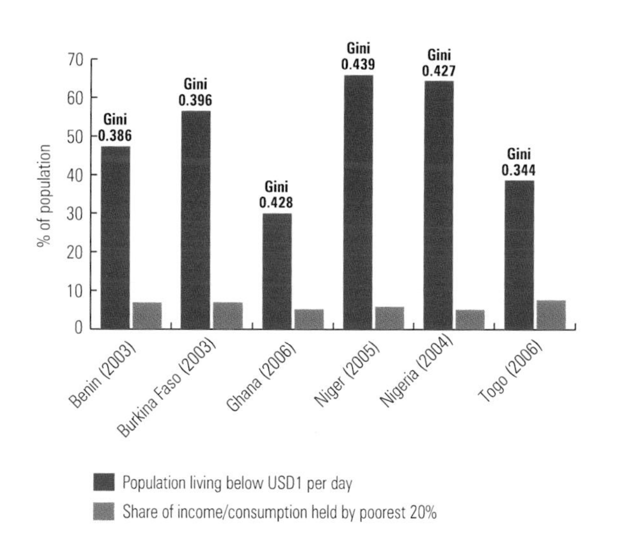

Source:
1. Global Urban Observatory, UN-HABITAT
2. UN Development Report 2010 The Real Wealth of Nations: Pathways to Human Development, UNDP, NY p. 154-159

broad functional features: (a) separation from neighbouring land by fences, walls or other constructed or natural obstructions, including symbolic barriers; (b) filtered entry through human, mechanical or electronic access control; and (c) privatized internal public areas and circulation systems. For all the generally negative nature of the opinions and practical assessments they generate, the proliferation of privately guarded urban enclaves is a fact, providing solid evidence that the ability of public authorities to maintain public security is fragile at best. However, the provision of security and protection is part and parcel of the municipal mandate. Since urban areas are mostly governed through elected and appointed local government representatives with the political and administrative mandates to provide safety and security, it can be credibly argued that the emergence of gated communities is not just an outcome of economic factors, but also political ones.

If the political system defers its own specific responsibilities to the markets, the economy becomes the political system under another name. When politics shows no empathy for the poor and the vulnerable, self-help solutions will be the inevitable outcome, as predicted by market theory. In practice, this means that anti-social and criminal solutions are at work at both ends of the income spectrum because there are no public institutions to counter or control the market. Good governance provides not just security, but also empowerment as part of a system that balances and controls the acquisition and application of individual power or opportunity. Security only for the already empowered is defeating the very notion that assisting and empowering the poor and vulnerable would result in less need for security for the wealthy.

Many Western African nations have recently experienced economic and political crises. Consequently, poverty has spread as wages have fallen while the prices of goods and services have risen. As wages slip, people buy less and falling demand puts even more people out of work. In several Western African countries, economic crises have had especially harmful effects on urban economies, because the prices of food, utilities and essential imported consumer goods have increased while currency values have fallen.

Analysts were initially optimistic that the impact of the 2008/09 global financial crisis on sub-Saharan Africa would be negligible, because African economies were among the least-exposed to the global financial system. African banks held few 'toxic assets', as they hardly ever used the high-risk financial instruments that sparked the global crisis in the first place. However, as the crisis deepened into a global recession, it became clear that many African nations would be strongly affected by the secondary effects, such as reduced demand for primary commodities and declining revenues from tourism. On current estimates, economic growth in sub-Saharan Africa slowed, from an annual average in excess of six per cent over the past five years, to a paltry 1.5 per cent in 2009. This is happening at a time when Western African countries require high rates of economic growth to outpace their population growth; to make progress in alleviating poverty; and to meet the targets of the Millennium Development Goals.

The proportion of people living in Africa on less than US $1.25 a day (the current international poverty line) has hovered around 50 per cent since 1981, but the number of poor people, in absolute terms, nearly doubled from 200 million in 1981 to 380 million in 2005, and is still increasing due to present economic constraints. Table 3.5 shows recent UN-HABITAT data for selected Western African nations on the percentage of populations living below one dollar a day (the previous international poverty line); the share of income or consumption held by the poorest 20 per cent; and the Gini coefficient measuring economic (income or consumption) equality.

The conditions reflected in Graph 3.4, give no grounds for optimism against an unfavourable global economic background. At the time of writing, the world was barely emerging from a largely unprecedented two-year economic and financial crisis. However, it is all too apparent that besides declining economic growth, the short-term effects will be further job losses and unemployment rates well above five per cent in most of the advanced economies, while in many developing countries the figure is above 20 per cent. With manufacturing, industrial output and retail sales declining, disposable incomes for households have also been reduced.

FIGURE 3.1: **THE INTERDEPENDENCE BETWEEN ACTIVITIES, INCOME AND CONSUMPTION**

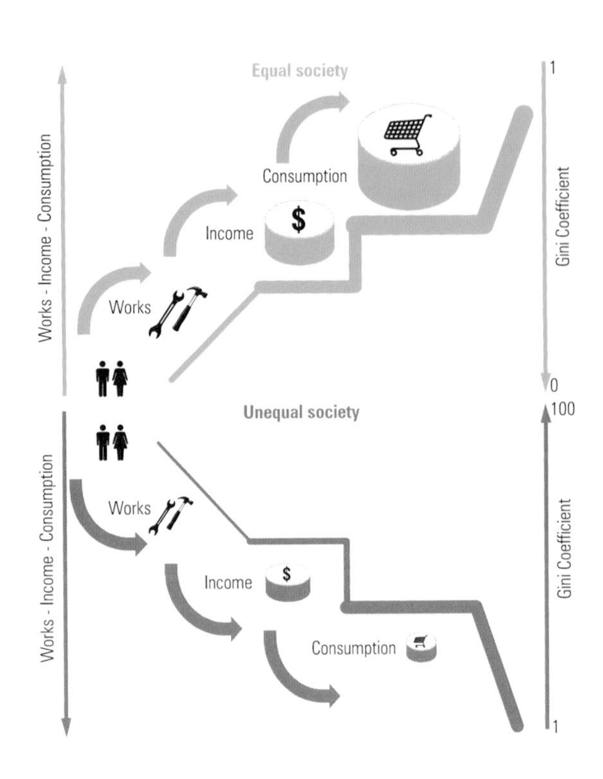

Income and Consumption

The magnitude of the socio-economic and spatial inequalities in urban societies is basically determined by two factors: (a) the permeability of the urban market (access to employment, land, housing, services and staple foods) particularly for the most underprivileged; and (b) cities' exclusionary power. The more accessible the markets, the larger the number of people who can earn an income and the higher the consumption rate will be. Conversely, the lower the number of people who have access to the labour market, the more difficult it is to earn an income and the lower the consumption rate. In the first case, the outcome is a low degree of economic inequality as reflected in a low Gini coefficient (i.e., tending towards 0) both for income and consumption (see Chapter 1, Section 1.2 for an explanation of the Gini coefficient). The situation is reversed in the second case where the bulk of income and consumption are in the hands of a minority, resulting in high Gini coefficients (i.e., tending towards 1). It is important to realize that the more a city becomes integrated in the international economy, the higher its Gini coefficient may be, because the local elites have less need to invest in local business or projects that would provide incomes to the population (similarly, local elites draw maximum benefits from the legal security generally associated with transactions with developed countries, while maintaining legal insecurity at home for their own profit and, again, to the detriment of vast population majorities). This, in a sense, is the origin of ever-growing inequality for the poor in Western African cities.

Income- and consumption-based Gini coefficients are compiled by UN-HABITAT's Global Urban Observatory (GUO) in cities in 33 African countries. A review suggests three main conclusions:

(a) significant Gini coefficient disparities can be found among African countries;

(b) the gaps between income- and consumption-based Gini coefficients can be relatively large; and

(c) large differences can be found across African cities, on the one hand, and Western African cities, on the other.

Gini coefficients denote the following degrees of inequality: below 0.299: *low inequality*; 0.3 to 0.399: *relatively low*; 0.4 to 0.449: *relatively high*; 0.45 to 0.499: *high*; 0.5 to 0.599: *very high*; and 0.6 and upwards: *extremely high*.

In Africa as a whole, urban areas in the Republic of South Africa feature the most unequal income distributions with Gini coefficients around 0.75. In Nigeria, *low* Gini coefficients are found in cities such as ***Sokoto*** (0.33) and ***Zamfara*** (0.34). In ***Kinshasa***, DRC, and in ***Pointe-Noire***, Congo, the coefficients stand at a *relatively low* 0.39. Analyses of consumption-based Gini coefficients show that in the Namibian cities of ***Hardap***, ***Omaheke*** and ***Karas*** consumption is least equal, with a Gini coefficient of almost 0.70, 0.64, and 0.61 respectively. The lowest coefficients are to be found in Tanzania and Burundi: 0.25 in ***Muleba***, Tanzania, and 0.26 in ***Kirundo***, Burundi.

▲
Agadez, Niger. ©**Tugela Ridley/IRIN**

GRAPH 3.5: **NATIONAL GINI COEFFICIENTS (INCOME OR CONSUMPTION)**

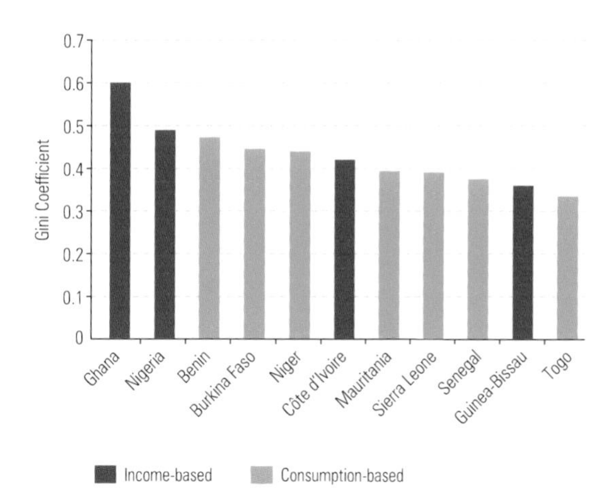

Source:
1. Global Urban Observatory, UN-HABITAT
2. UN Development Report 2010 The Real Wealth of Nations: Pathways to Human Development, UNDP, NY p. 148-151

The second conclusion is that, generally speaking, the Gini coefficient is higher for income than for consumption for two reasons: The first is the nature of wealth sharing and distribution systems in African societies. Income is generally earned individually but spent collectively. Redistribution of individual incomes by a family solidarity system makes resources available to those who have no work, increasing the numbers of those who are able to consume. One of the paradoxes of the African city is that few people have access to jobs and regular incomes, especially when compared with the vast masses of consumers. Today, this paradox appears to be all the more blatant as large amounts of undeclared incomes, including remittances from international migration, informal micro-credit, drug trafficking, money laundering, corruption etc, stimulate consumption but are not captured in statistics. Moreover, consumer markets are becoming increasingly flexible due to the dynamism of the informal sector which offers a range of goods and products at often unbeatable prices.

As far as Western Africa more specifically, UN-HABITAT research into Gini coefficients included Burkina Faso, Côte

▲
Accra, Ghana. **©Brian McMorrow**

TABLE 3.6: **MULTIPLE MODES OF LIVELIHOOD (MML) RATES: COMPARING TWO MEDIUM-SIZED TOWNS WITH THE GHANA LIVING STANDARD SURVEY (GLSS)**[a]

Category	Case study		GLSS	
	Number	Percentage	Number	Percentage
Total sample	237		4,997	
Salaried employees in total sample [b]	96	40.5	749	15.0
Salaried employees in MML	61	63.5	133	17.8
Employer [c]				
Government		67.1		21.8
Private		54.5		7.7
Other		50.0		22.2
Type of Public Institution [d]				
Ghana Education Service		88.0		
Ministry of Health		40.0		
Civil service		70.6		
Others		53.8		

a. The case study is based on a survey in Wenchi &Techiman in the Brong Ahafo region, Ghana, between 1995 and 1996. The GLSS is a national survey of 4,565 households, undertaken between 1991 and 1992 by the Ghana Statistical Service.
b. Percentages are based on total respondents.
c. Percentages are based on salaried employees in each case.
d. Data on income or type of public institution unavailable in the GLSS.
Source: Owusu (2005)

d'Ivoire, Ghana, Guinea Bissau, Mauritania, Niger, Nigeria, Senegal, Sierra Leone and Togo and found that the subregion is rich in contrasts. Ghana is where income distribution is least equal (0.60), and Guinea-Bissau where it is most equally shared, with a coefficient of 0.36 (see Graph 3.5). As for consumption, Benin is the least equal country (0.47), followed by Burkina Faso and Niger who both recorded a Gini coefficient of 0.44. For the other countries, the situation is homogeneous with Gini coefficients varying between 0.34 and 0.39.

Analysis of urban Gini coefficients based on income show that Nigeria's income distribution is least equal (0.54). In Côte d'Ivoire, the urban coefficient has improved from 0.51 in 2002 to 0.44 in 2008. In rual areas, the reduction has been dramatic (from 0.41 in 2002 to 0.22 in 2008), after increasing from 0.42 to 0.48 between 1993 and 1998. However, in ***Abidjan***, the crisis that rocked Côte d'Ivoire for more than a decade has contributed to a rising income gap with the Gini coefficient increasing from 0.41 in 2002 to 0.50 in 2008.

City-specific analysis shows that in ***Lagos*** income distribution is the least equal (0.64), while other Nigerian cities show coefficients higher than 0.40. The lowest regional income coefficient is recorded in ***Bissau*** (0.37), probably because poverty is widespread and people are equally poor. Consumption-based data for ***Freetown*** (0.32) and ***Dakar*** (between 0.37 and 0.41) suggest more equal and open consumer markets. The situation in ***Dakar*** is probably explained by the dynamism of the informal sector, which, with the advent of Chinese products, has experienced a considerable boom in the past few years.

In the final analysis, we must conclude that inequalities in income distribution and consumption in Western Africa are considerable and increasing. Côte d'Ivoire and Ghana are making efforts to better redistribute wealth, although they find it difficult to maintain their performance. Ghana's national income-based Gini coefficient changed quite erratically over time, going from 0.43 in 1988 to 0.38 in 1992 and 0.60 in 1998. This may, in part, be due to an invasion of foreign products, causing a rise in unemployment as several economic sectors stagnated or severely declined. Livestock breeding and poultry farming, for example, two of the pillars of the informal market in Ghana, were severely affected by chicken imports from South America and Europe. Benin, too, has made exceptional efforts towards increased consumption and the national Gini coefficient improved from 0.50 in 1999 to 0.47 in 2007.

How Slum Dwellers Survive

When economic conditions deteriorate, a growing percentage of urban dwellers shift from the formal to informal labour markets. Research on African urban livelihood strategies has generally followed two approaches. The first is more popular and focuses on the informal sector. The other uses the 'survival strategy' framework and analyses people's strategic responses to economic crisis, with a focus on the urban poor and other marginalized groups. Informal sector studies have played a crucial role in drawing attention to urban poverty, the potential for employment in the informal sector, and the creativity and entrepreneurial skills of informal sector participants who succeed despite non-supportive state regulation.

However, since analysis frequently tends to focus on a given economic activity rather than the people involved, many informal sector studies fail to capture the increasing numbers of urban dwellers who are deriving income from both formal and informal activities. This omission is particularly significant given the scale of this dual income pattern. Lower down the formal income ladder, any topping up of income through parallel informal activities can very well be a necessity for survival. However, sheer opportunity and frequently high returns have led many formal sector employees to join the informal sector, even though they do not necessarily need the additional income. Informal sector activities may even be monopolized locally by those who can use formal sector business as a cover, especially when it comes with inappropriate use of public office. In such cases, the formal sector has little incentive to regularize the informal one because profits can be significant and go totally unreported.

An alternative framework for the understanding of the economic strategies of the urban poor is the Multiple Modes of Livelihood (MML) approach, which focuses on the relationships between macro-level processes and domestic units. The basic argument of the MML approach to urban poverty alleviation is that macro-economic changes across Africa have

▲
Freetown, Sierra Leone. **©Tugela Ridley/IRIN**

FIGURE 3.2: **HOW SOCIO-PROFESSIONAL GROUPS PROJECT ON URBAN SPACE AND FRAGMENTATION**

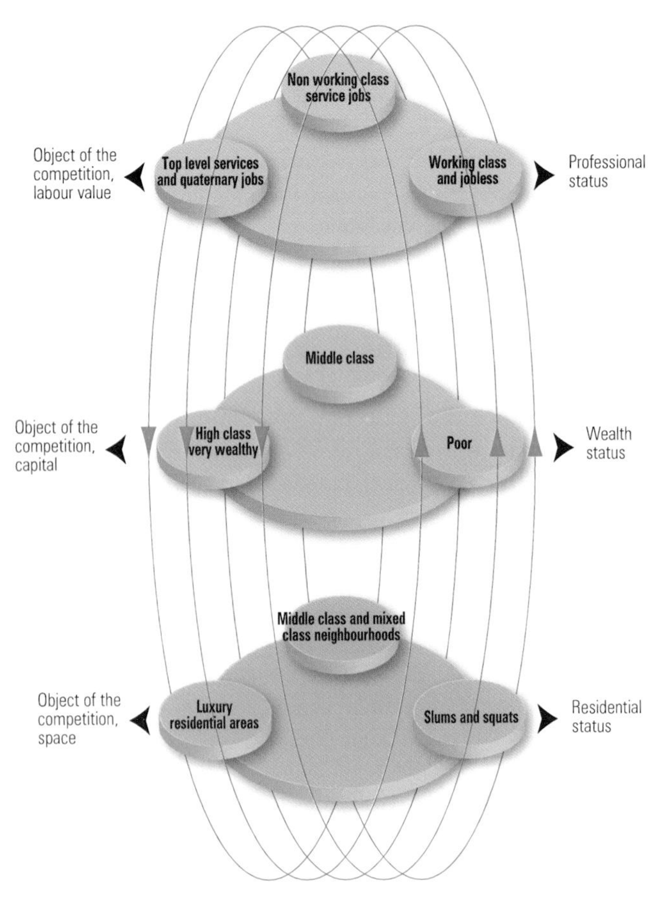

©Guéye & Thiam, Dakar 2010

created supportive environments for individuals and households from all social and economic backgrounds to diversify their sources of income. The MML approach captures the acquisition of additional jobs not only by the unemployed, but also by those primarily dependent on fixed salaries.

Mustapha (1992) has documented the livelihood strategies of the middle and the skilled classes in Nigeria to show that people of diverse socio-economic backgrounds participate in multiple economic activities. These have a long history in Nigeria, but recent economic conditions have intensified the phenomenon. Mustapha distinguishes between survival and livelihood strategies. For most (unskilled) members of the working class, engagement in multiple-mode activities is critical to individual and household survival, while, for skilled workers, multiple-mode activities are a way of containing or reversing a slide in living standards. He further argues that Nigerian working classes often confine their activities to labour-intensive, capital-scarce and low-return operations, while skilled workers draw on their superior access to financial and political resources to become involved in more effective income-generating activities. Moreover, skills often result in better business ideas or activities on better terms. For instance, skilled workers can repackage refuse collection as 'environmental sanitation' and sewing as 'fashion design' and adjust pricing accordingly. The activities of the skilled working class range from small-scale manufacturing and commercial farming to moonlighting of all types. The activities of the Nigerian unskilled working classes include commercializing private assets and skills, such as converting motorcycles into taxis, farming for those with land, petty trading for those without land, and petty abuse of office for others.

Drawing on case studies of two medium-sized towns in Ghana and a nationally representative sample (see Table 3.6), multiple livelihood strategies are clearly becoming 'the way of doing things'. The survey showed, first, that 18 to 64 per cent of salaried employees in urban Ghana were involved in multiple economic activities. Agriculture-related activities, trading and production-related activities (in that order) were the more important 'other' activities. Multiple activities frequently involve entire households. Another finding was that opportunities for multiple livelihood strategies are not equally distributed across the country. Smaller urban centres with less-diversified economies provide more opportunities for non-formal income generation than large urban centres. Finally, involvement in multiple livelihood strategies depends on gender, marital status, household size, and place of residence. Married people and those with large households are more likely to be involved in multiple activities and, in large urban centres, women are more likely involved than men.

Addressing Urban Inequality and Fragmentation

Good governance, in all its dimensions, can amplify the benefits of poverty reduction policies to a significant degree. Although various types of groupings or partnerships are emerging in response to the need for participatory governance, the status of urban citizens largely remains a solitary one. Not only have formal public institutions mostly abandoned the majority of urban residents, but any tangible collective actions that might provide some alternative sense of belonging or identity are hindered. As a result, the majority of urban citizens are trapped in vicious cycles of poverty, leaving them vulnerable to external shocks such as economic volatility and environmental disasters.

In Western African cities, as elsewhere on the African continent, urban fragmentation reflects the interdependence of income and access to land and housing. Groups occupy urban space according to income level and especially their position on the labour value scale. The correlation between income level and where people live is all the more significant, because there are hardly any mechanisms for the promotion of equality and social mixing. For the poor, in particular, any interaction is caught in a daunting vicious circle, which systematically maintains them in income and residential conditions that are often appalling. Their precarious living environments severely restrain their chances of a rewarding working life, a well-paid job or regular income, which, in turn, are two essential conditions for access to urban land and decent housing, as explained in the following section.

3.3 The Geography of Urban Land Markets

The significant diversity between Western African countries is to some extent a legacy of their colonial and post-independence backgrounds. Still, land and tenure systems and administration are where the colonial period has introduced some kind of unity within this diversity. The land governance procedures introduced by the French, the British and, to a lesser extent, the Portuguese have mostly been taken over by the newly independent States who wanted to keep tight control on land allocation and management processes.

The two prevailing legislations in the region are the French civil code and British common law. In Francophone countries, land legislation is still based on the colonial civil code which recognizes the public domain of the State that cannot be alienated; the private domain of the State that can be alienated under certain conditions; private land for which a title has been issued; customary land; and *terres vacantes et sans maître* (land with no clear status, unclaimed or vacant). Ambiguities between the concepts of 'public domain' and 'State domain' blur the boundaries between alienable and unalienable land, frequently to the benefit of those working in government bodies involved in land allocation.

▲
Danané, Ivory Coast. ©**Guido Potters**

Some Francophone countries have created another land category. Senegal, for instance, in 1964 introduced 'National Domain'[1], which includes all lands that are not part of the public or private domain of the State or local authorities, or which have not been privately appropriated and registered before the law was adopted. These lands are not State-owned but became part of the State patrimony. Likewise, in Mali[2], the National Land Domain includes all categories of land, giving the State discretionary power to add these lands to its private domain and put them on the market. In Anglophone Western African countries, land categories are more or less the same, but the concept of alienable and unalienable public land is less ambiguous.

Formal and Customary Forms of Tenure

As in other regions south of the Sahara, Western Africa is characterised by a dual system of statutory or formal tenure (as codified by law) and customary (traditional) tenure. Despite international pressure to liberalise Africa's urban land markets, government institutions retain full control over land allocation and restrict delivery of freehold titles. Vested interests and inappropriate land administration practices have colluded to produce low levels of formal title issuance. Despite enormous land reserves - as the land mainly belongs to the State - most governments are reluctant to release land on any large scale, as scarcity benefits vested interests while increasing opportunities for predatory practices. The exception is Burkina Faso, where large areas of public land have been provided for housing development, alleviating huge demand pressure and reducing land prices.

Box 3.2: Tenure Upgrading in Mali: From Administrative Allocation to Freehold

In Mali, three main types of documented residential rights are available:

1. Plot Allocation Certificates (*Décisions d'attribution*) are the most basic form of title, reflecting the right of every citizen to possess a parcel of land. These temporary user-rights are allocated by city authorities based on eligibility and priority criteria in the case of direct allocation to individuals. Upon payment of a usage tax, applicants are granted allocation certificates, which can be withdrawn if beneficiaries do not, within five years, build a housing unit that meets minimal standards.
2. Urban Occupation Permit (*Permis Urbain d'Habiter* - PUH) is a permanent user-right, although the land itself remains under state ownership. It is delivered by Land Administration services once the parcel has been developed and built (*Mise en valeur*) in compliance with government norms and building standards (floor/area ratios and building materials, in particular). These titles provide security of tenure, are transferable and can be mortgaged if registered in the Land Registry, a procedure that makes the title fully secure. Since registration is not compulsory and given the cumbersome process and costs involved, registrations are rare.
3. The freehold regime was abolished by the 1983 revolution but has been reinstated a few years ago. Ownership rights are evidenced by *Titres Fonciers* that are necessarily registered. To secure this type of title, applicants must: (a) already hold a PUH, (b) have spent at least 30 times the original usage tax on residential development, and (c) pay the government a 'price' equal to twice the original usage tax.

Formal Tenure

In the wake of rapidly emerging urbanisation, changes in the demand for secure urban land and freehold titles by investors and incipient urban middle classes in Western African cities have contributed to the development of formal private land markets. Private appropriation of land and access to freehold tenure result in land privatisation, fresh investments, market pressure on land and, to a lesser extent, tenure regularisation policies. These processes have over the past two decades been supported by new land laws and codes to either facilitate private land appropriation or to restrict its proliferation. In Nigeria, for instance, the Land Use Act of 1978 transferred ownership of all land to the government and anyone with a freehold title became a leasehold tenant with a 99-year maximum under a Statutory Certificate of Occupancy. Land tenure comes under statutory law and security of tenure is guaranteed by a Certificate of Ownership (Asiama, 2005).

In Senegal, a law allowing holders of 'Permits To Occupy' ('*Permis d'Habiter*') to convert these into freehold was to be passed in 2010. In most of Western Africa, PTOs (see Box 3.2) or equivalent titles can be converted into freehold only *after* the land has been developed. In the meantime, the government holds the prerogative to repeal ownership rights if PTO holders do not comply with the development obligations. In Western Africa, PTOs and/or housing permits (names vary depending on countries) remain the most common type of formal tenure in urban areas. As allocated to applicants by central or local administrations, PTOs are: (a) valid for a limited period of time; (b) conditional (conversion into a permanent permit or freehold requires plot development according to minimum standards or expenditure, with typical deadlines between three to six years); and (c) revocable (if not developed within the prescribed period). PTOs are recorded, though not formally registered, in the Land Book (*Livre foncier*). If the permit holder can fulfil the obligations, then the temporary permit can, in principle, be converted into a permanent permit and, in a further step, into a full, registered ownership title.

A PTO is not transferable as long as the land has not been developed. Although the security of tenure attached to PTOs is rather high, it takes the rare holder to be able to comply with the construction or investment norms and the time frame. Therefore, actual security depends heavily on government decisions. Most permits holders in government-initiated land subdivisions have not, or not yet completed the formalisation process.

Customary Tenure

Customary tenure remains, by far, the most common tenure type in the Western and Central African cities. In the strict sense of the term, customary land ownership refers to the communal possession of rights to use and allocate agricultural and grazing land by a group sharing the same cultural identity. Commoditisation of customary land delivery channels and the accelerated development of land markets have changed the nature of customary relationships, and the original form of customary tenure can no longer be found in urban and peri-urban areas, as well as in many rural areas. For this reason, it would be more appropriate to refer to 'neo-customary' land tenure and land markets (Durand-Lasserve & Mattingly, 2005).

Customary tenure covers a wide range of situations, with the degree of government recognition the main differentiation factor, as this determines both security and the potential to be integrated into formal land markets. Although customary land rights are mostly recognised by governments (by law and/or in the Constitution), this recognition is usually restricted to certain types of land or areas. This is, for instance, the case in Ghana (see Box 3.3), especially in the ***Kumasi*** region, or in ***Conakry***[3], Guinea, and more recently, with some restrictive conditions, also in Burkina Faso, Mali and Niger, where since 2000/02 the law recognises individual collective land ownership under customary rights. Still, ownership rights can be repealed if customary right holders do not comply with their obligation to develop the land within a certain period of time.

In some Western African countries - where recognition of customary systems is restricted to rural areas - customary land management is, nevertheless, often tolerated in suburban

BOX 3.3: **CUSTOMARY TENURE IN GHANA**

▲
Cape Coast township, Ghana. **©Trevor Kittelty/Shutterstock**

In Ghana, customary land rights are recognized and protected under the 1992 Constitution. Indigenous owners exercise all the powers attached to ownership: the right to own, manage, sell, receive payment, determine beneficiaries, terms and conditions of the grant, price, etc. For all these formal rights, though, customary land ownership often is considered to be informal because of the nature of the transactions in the market. About 90-95 per cent of peri-urban land in Ghana is held and managed under customary practice. Customary and statutory regulations operate side by side, making it difficult to identify who has the authority to alienate a parcel of land. (Augustinus, 2002).

About 80 per cent of the land in Ghana is held and managed under customary ownership. The remainder is held by government under various statutes and practices, which range from outright State ownership to the management of customary-owned State lands.

areas. This means that customary bodies *can* operate in urban areas, but at their own risk, given the discretionary power of central government on land.

In the former French colonies, this situation is clearly linked with the concept of freehold: (a) as defined in the Civil Code, and (b) as part of a French-inherited, centralised its political model characterised by State monopoly on land, control over land markets and its centralised land management systems. Customary tradition in suburban land subdivisions gives informal practices a degree of legitimacy and protection against eviction. Its customary land subdivisions are usually recognised in Benin, Cameroon and Namibia, although they are not legal in the strict sense of the term.

Research into the changes and dynamics observed over the last two decades in 10 Western and six Central African countries[4] shows that in Western Africa, except in the ***Kumasi*** area of Ghana[5], customary land rights have not, for long, been formally recognised by the State in urban and peri-urban areas. However, customary land rights have been tolerated, including in Senegal where these were supposed to have been eradicated. Under pressure from civil society and due to more realistic land policies, customary rights are now increasingly formally recognised (albeit conditionally) in rural and peri-urban areas in Benin 2007 and in Burkina Faso 2008. Still, government powers of eminent domain can override any legal decisions about land management, as in Mali, where collective land rights are recognised as long as the State does not need to incorporate the land in its domain. In Ghana, the State Lands Act 125, 1962, entitles the government to use eminent domain powers only with due compensation.

Although many non-formal land rights are referred to as 'customary' - including where customary practices are not effective anymore - the authorities consider many of these illegal. This is particularly the case with urban squatter settlements located on land that is unsuitable for development and does not provide occupants with any security of tenure. With the combined pressures on urban land and widespread urban poverty, squatting is, understandably rapidly increasing in Western African cities.

Urban Land Institutions

Formal Urban Land Institutions

In Western Africa, central government institutions are responsible for the initial registration of land under its own name and for allocation of land from the government's private domain through administrative permits with leasehold or freehold rights attached. In Francophone countries, registration is made in the Land Book (*Livre foncier*), under the joint responsibility of the *Direction des Domaines* (state property department) and the *Direction du Cadastre* (central land registry). In Anglophone Western Africa, the authority for registration of land rights falls under the Registrar of Titles.

Over the past two decades, land management has been gradually decentralised in Western Africa. Land allocation and some management functions regarding state property have been transferred to local entities. However, decentralisation is not uniform across countries. In Mali, for example, after having transferred land administration to municipal authorities, central government institutions are still involved in local land allocation and also retain all title registration functions. In practice, this 'decentralisation' frequently consists of little more than deconcentration to the local level branches of central government institutions, as central governments clearly remain reluctant to fully decentralize land management. Cities are supposed to benefit from land decentralisation, but this does not work as long as spatial jurisdictions are not clearly identified. Moreover, the links between land administration and land management are often not clear enough for the benefits decentralised land governance to be effective at the local level.

Customary Land Institutions

Governments in all Western African countries increasingly recognise the role of customary institutions in the allocation of land for housing. In most countries, customary land sales are now authenticated and recorded by local authorities, in what can be seen as a first step towards further tenure formalisation. In the meantime, new participants are becoming involved in customary land delivery process in a bid to keep better control over customary practices. In Ghana, for instance, chiefs and elders are still at the centre of customary land management, but Town Development Committees, made up of community members, oversee developments in the settlements. They help ensure that revenues from land transactions become available for development projects in the town. Traditional authorities continue to make land grants, but procedures are validated by Land Commissions to ensure that these grants comply with legal requirements (Asiama, 2005).

How Land Markets Operate

In Western and Central African cities, urban land can be obtained from the government, the formal private sector and customary/informal channels.

Government Allocation of Public Land

Urban land is predominantly allocated through the State, local authorities and their agencies. Burkina Faso, Côte d'Ivoire, Ghana, Nigeria, Senegal and other countries have added to supply through allocations of residential and commercial serviced plots to individuals or private developers for subdivision.

- The buyer receives full ownership of the land. The land is titled and the transfer is registered. Land is sold at or below market value. By far the most widespread government land allocation method for housing in Western and Central Africa is through administrative permits (plot allocation certificate, permit to occupy, urban occupation permit, etc.). Costs are much lower than for titled land sold outright by government. Government allocations are aimed at low-middle and middle income groups, but in practice the beneficiaries are the higher income groups.

Private Formal Land Markets

Urban and peri-urban parcels sold through formal private land markets were originally supplied through government allocation procedures. Research in Benin, Burkina Faso, Mali, Rwanda and Senegal shows that only 10 to 30 per cent of any given urban population can access land through the formal markets, through purchases of:

- Titled freehold or long-term leasehold lands put on the market by private landowners. Development rights and rural-urban conversion depend on planning, land-use and construction standards; and
- Land sold by private developers can be developed or built-up, or not. In all cases, the land rights have been or will be registered, either as freehold or long-term leasehold. Property title has been or will be issued on completion of development (i.e., provision of services, or construction in the case of private housing development). Land is sold at market prices.

Customary and Informal Land Markets

- Access to land through (neo-)customary channels provides between 60 and 80 per cent of the land for urban housing in the subregion. This format combines customary with informal and formal practice; it operates through individuals who have been granted land rights under a customary system, but who treat these rights as market goods. The format provides some form of customary legitimacy (PRUD, 2005; Durand-Lasserve, ITDG).
- Access through squatting is not predominant in Western African cities, but the numbers of squatter settlements have been on the increase for a decade or so. This form of access to land has become commoditised, as all other informal channels, and now involves payment. In many cities where customary tenure is not formally recognized, governments make no distinction between customary subdivision and squatter settlements, with both referred to as 'informal settlements'. Owners of dwelling units in customary or informal subdivisions can, in principle, apply for tenure regularisation and a more secure form of tenure, such as permits to occupy.

These predominant land delivery systems feature their own specific mechanisms for allocation and pricing, but these do no prevent strong interactions between formal and informal, public and private land markets. Taken together, land markets form a single system. Consequently, any change in one segment has repercussions on the others. For example, decreases in one type of land allocation induce increases in the others. For instance, high demand for land from private real estate developers in ***Dakar*** over the last five years has increased the pressure on informal land markets in peri-urban areas. The reverse situation can also prevail: in Burkina Faso, massive allocation of public land over the past 10 years has relieved demand pressures on informal/customary land markets.

When access to formal land markets is not possible or too expensive, urban stakeholders move to markets where security of tenure is not guaranteed, and sell the parcels back on the formal market for titled land (see Box 3.4). Some participants are in a position to buy or be allocated land in a segment of the market where it is cheap but still insecure (customary or informal land markets, or public allocation of administrative permits to occupy; they do so in a bid to secure tenure upgrading or regularisation in some form or another prior to on-selling the parcel, the rationale being to capture a significant share of the incremental value of the land. For this type of speculative transaction, access to political and administrative power is a key condition of success.

BOX 3.4: THE MARKET PRICE OF LAND DEPENDS ON THE TYPE OF TENURE

At Dialakorodji, a suburban village 15 km from the centre of Bamako, Mali, the market price of a plot of land of 400 to 900 m^2 sold by a customary owner is 150,000 to 300,000 CFA francs (XOF) (or US $320 to 640). The deed of sale is authenticated by the village head and two members of the municipal council. With the land sale thus legalised, and after payment of a development fee of XOF 50,000 (or US $160), the market value of the plot increases to reach between XOF500,000 and 1million (US $1,060 to 2,120). Where the owner can secure a freehold title, the price of the plot will be in the range of XOF2.5 to three million (US $5,300 to 6,400).

At times, the price differential is shared between the seller of the land, municipal authorities, government employees and the officials involved in the regularisation process, as well as the State Property Dept and the land registry. Part of the money goes to administrative and standard fees and taxes. The remainder is shared under informal arrangements between the land owner and those involved in the tenure regularisation process.

BOX 3.5: SENEGAL'S ATTEMPT TO REGULARIZE TENURE

Senegal, in 1991[6], decided to institutionalise the tenure regularisation process launched in 1989 and to design a national slum upgrading programme (*Programme de Restructuration de l'Habitat Spontané*). In July 1991, a decree provided the regulatory framework for settlement upgrading and tenure regularisation. In a first step, the objective was to regularise the status of some 410,000 individuals, representing 30 per cent of the total estimated population living in urban informal settlements. The programme focussed on the capital region of Dakar and Pikine, involving 41,000 plots spread over 1,400 ha (or an average 341m^2 per plot). Between 1995 and 2002, however, due to lack of human and financial resources, coming on top of obstruction from the institutions in charge of land registration and administration, the initial objective of 41,000 plots to be regularised was reduced by 90 per cent, or 4,800 plots only. The number of titles effectively delivered was even smaller: between 1991 and September 2007, fewer than 1,600 land rights titles had been delivered in the Dakar region (Dakar, Pikine and Rufisque).

The Dynamics of Western African Urban Land Markets

Over the past decade, changes in the legal and regulatory frameworks governing land management and administration have accelerated liberalisation of land markets. Reforms, new laws and codes have introduced the right to private land ownership in most Western African countries, even where land has long been considered as a matter for the government only. Still, private land ownership does not provide full protection, as governments frequently use their rights of eminent domain to appropriate land for development, including private land. However, across Western Africa, private appropriation of land and private land markets are increasingly endorsed or acknowledged by legislation or national policies, as, for instance, in Benin, Burkina Faso, Côte d'Ivoire and, more recently, in Senegal (Constitutional law N° 2001-03) or in Nigeria (through the 2002 National Housing Policy).

Another recent feature in Western Africa is that policies have come to emphasise tenure upgrading and regularisation schemes (Durand-Lasserve & Selod, 2009), despite resistance of many government institutions and agencies in charge of land administration. The current challenge is how to secure and safeguard tenure for informal settlers without losing the public sector's ability to provide improved infrastructures and services as well as redevelopment options in prime urban locations. However, regularisation of tenure has so far achieved limited results in Western African cities (see Box 3.5).

Land Markets, Urban Forms and Configurations

Land markets and land prices are the main drivers of urban spatial expansion and geographic social patterns. Demand pressures and the attendant rise in prices have gradually excluded the poor from access to urban land. At work here are four converging mechanisms that are tightly related to land markets dynamics, as follows:

- Market prices of urban land increase faster than household incomes;
- Affordable land for housing in city centres and inner fringes becomes scarce;
- Evictions of communities living in inner city slums in the name of public interest, security and public health; and
- Market-driven displacement and evictions (Durand-Lasserve in Huchzermeyer & Karam, 2007)

Uncontrolled urban sprawl is another spatial consequence of increasing land prices and expressed through informal and customary land developments. Together with steady increases in the prices of plots close to city centres, a lack of constraining regulations in areas beyond municipal administrative boundaries encourages the spatial expansion of cities in peri-urban areas, especially where statutory or customary regulation are in no position to rein in land speculation. In the longer term, the cost of urban sprawl to be borne by public authorities (provision of infrastructure and services) and by the population (higher costs for basic services and for transport) will be considerable.

The main consequence of this combination of factors is spatial social segregation, with the geography of poverty overlapping the patterns of insecure tenure and poor access to urban services and infrastructures. One of the greatest shortcomings of informal and customary land delivery systems is their inability to provide adequate services (water, sanitation, power, waste collection, roads, etc). Demand for land is such that informal and customary land developers do not see any advantage in providing basic infrastructure or even complying with minimum standards regarding layout plans. Even in areas where recognition of customary land allocation would enable control over land development, such as in the ***Kumasi*** area in Ghana, many people do not acquire planning permission before developing their land (Asiama, 2005) due to unrealistic standards, rigid and unaffordable planning norms, inefficient city planning and institutional inability to grant permits in a timely sort of way.

▲
Bamako, Mali. ©**Joseph Guiebo**

The Limitations of Conventional Urban Land Administration

Access to urban land, property registration or tenure regularization invariably involves very cumbersome administrative procedures that may take up years and involve a large number of administrations. In Nigeria, for example, anyone seeking to buy dispute-free, officially recorded property must complete 21 steps in a process that takes on average 274 days with fees amounting to 27 per cent of the property value (World Bank, 2004). In ***Dakar***, before the procedure was streamlined in 1993, delivery of property rights required 44 steps and involved 12 different central and local administrative processes. In 2005, only 25 per cent of households entitled to tenure regularisation in the informal settlement of Dalifort had been granted property rights. The city of Pikine in the Dakar Metropolitan Area has a population of 870,000, but its Land Registry can process only 3,600 registrations, transfers or land subdivision applications per year (ILD, 2009).

In Burkina Faso, conversion of a temporary administrative permit into a permanent one or into leasehold also runs against multiple bottlenecks. A distant vestige of an outdated state control approach, the conversion process can take up to one and a half year and requires many steps. It can also be seen, more bluntly, as deliberate obstruction on tenure regularisation by land administration bodies in order to facilitate corruption and other 'encouragements' from applicants. Allocation of freehold rights usually requires a case-by-case evaluation. The length and 'costs' of these procedures act as disincentives to the formalization of property rights, which in turn has repercussions on property markets. Other major obstacles hindering formal land market development include government's quasi-monopoly on land, weak and corrupt land administration, inappropriate market rules and lack of transparency.

In Nigeria, the 1978 Land Use Act vested the control and management of urban lands with state governors through a Certificate of Occupancy, while local authorities can grant customary rights of occupancy for agricultural or other purposes. In spite of these laws (or perhaps *because* of them), companies and individuals keen on acquiring urban land keep facing major hurdles, especially as 'booms' in the oil industry and urban populations have occurred in short succession. The new legislation encouraged land speculation, especially as it combined with the conventional approach to land use planning under which most Nigeria's major cities, have been developed.

In all Western African Francophone cities, planning regulations and construction norms and standards effectively hinder the development of formal land and housing markets. This is compounded by three major factors that restrict the development of formal housing finance:

- The formal land and housing development sector is almost embryonic, with limited delivery capacity;
- Private developments are priced way above what most households can afford; and
- Security of tenure is inadequate on so many plots that these cannot qualify as valid collateral to back up bank loans.

In Burkina Faso, for instance, housing loans amounted to only 0.5 per cent of GDP in 2004. Similar ratios are found in Ghana and Nigeria. Senegal and Mali do slightly better with about 20 per cent.[7] Poorly developed financial services reflect the general condition of national economies, which feature high poverty and illiteracy rates.

Until recently, most Western African governments tolerated informal land markets, as it was assumed that they would eventually give way to modern, formal land markets. It was further assumed that only secure private property could provide adequate incentives for investments in land, and that tenure security could only be achieved through land titling and registration (Durand-Lasserve *et al,* 2009). However, realities on the ground provide quite a different picture and, across Western Africa, land registration and titling have achieved very limited results and coverage.

Informal Settlements as a Response to Imperfect Land Markets

In the vast majority of Western and Central African cities, the urban poor and large shares of low- and middle-income groups cannot access public or formal private land markets. Except for Burkina Faso, public provision of urban land and housing is steadily declining throughout the subregion due to lack of resources, lack of political will, widespread corrupt practices, and administrative and technical bottlenecks. The formal private sector does not provide for low-income households, unless heavily subsidised. This situation makes informal land markets more attractive because customary and informal land delivery is more flexible, delivery time is short, transaction costs are low, and tenure is perceived as secure enough to encourage limited investment in land and housing. However, their effectiveness when it comes to reaching out to the poorest segments of the urban population, as well as their long-term sustainability and accessibility, must be questioned, especially in the absence of supportive public policies. The viability of (neo-)customary land delivery is questionable for two main reasons:

- Customary land supplies at reasonable commuting distance from cities are drying up and customary land reserves are located increasingly further from city boundaries, places of employment and public transport facilities, severely restricting the sector's ability to respond efficiently to demand for well-located urban land and housing; and
- Informality does not necessarily mean insecurity of tenure. Even when not formally recognized by government, endorsement by the community and the neighbourhood usually ensures secure tenure. However, this arrangement

West Point slum, Monrovia, Liberia. An example of an informal settlement vulnerable to surge flooding. **©Tugela Ridley/IRIN**

may deteriorate when conflicts arise among customary owners, especially between those who allocate the land and others within the group, or between customary owners and public authorities about customary claims' legitimacy.

Recent observations made in Western African cities confirm that (neo-)customary land delivery is responding increasingly to demand from middle- and lower-middle income groups' demand. Housing development projects are less and less effective in reaching people in urban areas, either in circumstances where customary practices are recognised (Ghana), or where they are tolerated and streamlined by inclusive administrative practices (Benin), or are not formally recognised (Senegal).

Drying up of customary land reserves combines with increased competition from low-middle and middle-income groups and *de facto* recognition by most states to induce accelerated commoditisation of customary land. On the other hand, government reluctance to recognise customary land delivery gives rise to urban and land policies whose unintended impacts can further hinder access of households to shelter. Legal pluralism and the diversity of land markets are not taken into account, which can only compound the effective exclusion of a majority of the African urban population.

Formalisation of land transactions under neo-customary systems is happening, if only gradually, in all urban areas, as use of witnesses in land transactions is becoming institutionalised, and transactions are frequently authenticated by local and sometimes central government administrations. Although informal land purchasers are rarely given any formal title deed, they can usually provide a paper of some sort (often a deed of sale countersigned by local government officials, or a certificate delivered by the administrative bodies in charge) that protects them against eviction attempts. Furthermore, keeping records of informal land transfers and transactions at the local level helps solve one of the main problems experienced by neo-customary land delivery, namely, the multiple allocation of the same plot of land to different buyers, a commonplace practice made possible by collusions of customary and local authorities. Keeping records also improves security of tenure; to defend their rights, people will refer to both the 'paper' and customary evidence.

The Political Economy of Urban Land

In Western African cities, the current debate on liberalisation of land markets, tenure formalisation and integration of customary land delivery into the formal land market provides an illustration of the relationship between land and political power. Under the principle of *domanialité*, government has the exclusive right to allocate and register land that has not been already privately appropriated and titled, which effectively restricts formal regularisation of informal and customary rights (Comby & Gerber, 2008). There is today in Western

▲
Freetown, Sierra Leone. **©Leonardo Viti/Shutterstock**

Africa broad consensus about the need to clarify, regulate and sometimes regularise customary tenure. Depending on those involved, the rationale for this new approach reflects various complementary and sometimes contradictory objectives:

- Protect customary ownership against market pressures, or facilitate the integration of customary within formal land markets;
- Improve security of tenure for occupants of informal and customary land developments;
- Make customary land available for agricultural and urban development;
- Increase land supply through tenure formalisation and land privatisation programmes;
- Secure investment in land and housing;
- Develop housing mortgage finance;
- Reduce the number of land conflicts; and
- Ensure social peace and stability.

The main purpose of customary tenure formalisation is to increase the supply of urban formal land markets. This is one of the conclusions of a study carried out in Mali in 2009 (ADL-GTZ, 2009). In the majority of rural areas which have attractions for investors, formalisation of customary tenure is not envisaged. However, in rural and peri-urban areas with an anticipated high economic potential and demand pressure on land, formalisation of customary tenure is considered a priority. Local and central government institutions as well as local elected bodies are usually supportive, as are society organisations who rightly see formalisation as a crucial component of security of tenure. Customary owners are usually willing to cooperate where they realise that the ongoing erosion of their customary prerogatives is irreversible under the joint pressure of the state, market forces and local authorities.

Corruption in land administration is tightly related to the principle of *domanialité*, which gives government the exclusive power to allocate land and regularise land tenure, as well as with the coexistence of formal and informal land markets that operate on different price scales. Land administrators have discretionary power whether to decide for effective tenure regularisation. As they are aware of the profits beneficiaries of land tenure regularisation are expected to yield, they will inevitably ask for a share of the anticipated profit. This situation can be observed at various degrees and , with only the odd exception, in all Western and Central African cities, fuelling corruption at all levels of land administrations and impacting on allocation of public land and tenure regularisation.

Since the market price of land depends on the degree of security of tenure attached, the typical strategy for urban land market participants will be as follows: (i) secure a non-transferable administrative 'permit to occupy' from a government institution or on the informal market; (ii) apply for tenure upgrading or regularisation and, in a later stage, for a property title, and (iii) to sell the property back on the formal market agaist the market price.

3.4

The Geography of Climate Change

Western Africa, particularly in the Sahelian confines of Burkina Faso, Mauritania, Niger and northern Nigeria, has shown recurrent weather variability since the early 1970s. The subregion experienced marked declines in rainfall and its hydrometric series around 1968-1972. With 1970 as the transitional year, average declines in rainfall before and after 1970 range from 15 to more than 30 per cent. This pattern resulted in a 200 km southward expansion of the arid Sahel region. The causes of this anomaly have yet to be clarified, but the assumption so far is that they have to do with climate change. Recorded average discharges in the largest water courses varied by 40 to 60 per cent when compared with pre-1970 levels, causing a significant shrinking of wetlands. The average surface area of the Hadejia Nguru floodplain in northern Nigeria, for instance, decreased from 2,350 km^2 in 1969 to less than 1,000 km^2 in 1995. Likewise, the inland delta of the Niger River decreased from 37,000 km^2 in the early 1950s to about 15,000 km^2 in 1990, while the surface area of Lake Chad, 20,000 km^2 during the wet years before 1970, has shrunk to less than 7,000 km^2, resulting in the splitting of the lake into two parts. Today, only the southern part contains water permanently.

The Role of Local Authorities in Adaptation to Climate Change

Both coastal and inland Western African cities suffer under the impacts of climate change. Ongoing urbanisation has densified coastal cities and, consequently, many more urban dwellers are now threatened by changing sea levels and more frequent extreme weather events. Droughts in the hinterlands stimulate eco-migration and further swell urban populations. Gone are the days when the effects of climate change were little more than vague concepts for international experts only.

▲
Flooding in Dakar, Senegal. **©Nancy Palus/IRIN**

BOX 3.6: **LAGOS: ENGAGING THE PRIVATE SECTOR IN WATER SUPPLY AND WASTE MANAGEMENT**

Whereas metropolitan Lagos generates 9,000 tonnes of waste daily, only 15 per cent of an estimated potential of 80 per cent of waste was recycled. The Lagos Waste Management Authority (LAWMA), with over 25,000 staff, aims at increasing waste recycling four-fold through improved collection. Households are encouraged to separate waste at source through discounted collection fees. A consortium including LAWMA has invested US $100 million in an integrated landfill project in Epe, while 20 waste transfer loading stations are now under construction to reduce logistical problems. Wastes are being sorted into recyclable metals, plastics, paper and organics, while the remainder is burnt to provide electricity. Composting occurs under a public-private partnership (PPP) and the output is used in the Lagos 'greening programme'. LAWMA acts both as the facilitator and PPP pioneer to attract local and international investors, and has now extended it operations to other states and even to Sierra-Leone and Ghana.

Deficient urban water supplies are one of the most urgent threats to African cities. Despite its abundance of local water resources, Lagos State faces severe challenges in water supply for industry and a rapidly growing urban population. In 2004, the Lagos State Water Corporation (LSWC) was established, a holding company under the State Government and the largest of its kind in Africa. The LSWC uses its high degree of autonomy to reduce administrative bottlenecks and increase external funding for large urban water projects. LSWC has already significantly raised the capacity of the Adiyan water works that now provides 90 per cent of all metropolitan water, while capacity expansion is in progress in Epe to serve the Lekki-Victoria Island-Ikoyi axis. The aim is to increase the current 50 per cent water coverage to between 70 and 80 per cent over the next 10 years. LSWC has also started to improve metering and is addressing systemic losses with sonic equipment to locate leakages. On top of this, efforts to raise public awareness of the need to reduce water wastage are under way (see www.lagoswater.org and www.lawma.gov.ng).

Local authorities are now directly faced with these effects on their populations, including homes and livelihoods.

More than 25 per cent of Africa's population lives within 100 km from the coast and estimates suggest that the number of people at risk from coastal flooding will increase from one million in 1990 to 70 million in 2080 (UNFCCC,2007). In Nigeria and Benin, coastal infrastructures are threatened with erosion and subsequent flooding. Mayors are expected to develop adaptation policies, but most lack the technical, human and financial resources for effective action. With their typically very narrow revenue bases, municipal authorities can rarely afford more than day-to-day operations in a hand-to-mouth manner. Already struggling as they are with essential spending on housing, services, infrastructure and development control, few local authorities can invest in disaster preparedness or adaptation interventions.

For all these shortcomings, cities in Western Africa are well aware of the potentially dramatic effects of climate change - and flooding in particular. In ***Lagos***, for instance, it is now acknowledged that flooding incidence is exacerbated by poorly engineered and waste-clogged drainage systems. As a result, Greater Lagos authorities have taken to improve services and infrastructures, in an effort that involves indigenous knowledge, livelihood support systems as well as partnerships with the private sector to fund these interventions (see Box 3.6).

Despite a number of commendable initiatives, climate change adaptation in ***Lagos*** still suffers from an exclusionary urban governance because of a reluctance to provide basic public services in informal settlements, since they are regarded as falling outside accepted urban regulation and planning systems. Lagos should develop an action plan that also addresses the plight of its citizens in informal urban areas.

Climate change is also becoming a matter of concern in other Western African coastal cities. For instance, with 50,000 individuals per square km, the ***Dakar*** coastline is one of the most densely populated in Western Africa, and a storm surge disaster could easily affect 75,000 residents whose (illegal) occupation of these coastal areas makes them particularly vulnerable. The risk of storm surge disasters is compounded by recession of the marine sands that act as an important natural barrier to sea intrusion, also adding to the risk is the lack of effective management systems to cope with any hazards once they occur. All Western African coastal cities should become more aware of the actual risks and take commensurate disaster-prevention/adaptation action, including arresting the further sprawl of settlement in vulnerable locations, and establishing post-disaster management capacities.

Climate Change: How much do we know?

The recharging of the subregion's aquifers has noticeably decreased due to declines in rainfall and surface runoff. Across the upper reaches of the Niger River in Mali, water tables have now reached the lowest-ever recorded levels, reducing the input of groundwater into major watercourses. Coastal areas too are not spared from the impacts of climate change. Beaches and dune ridges along the Western African coast show evidence of retreat, varying from between 1-2 m annually in Senegal and 20 to 30 m along the Gulf of Guinea.

Recurrent droughts create a self-reinforcing spiral of accelerated desertification and deforestation contributing to the persistence, incidence and duration of the phenomenon. Poor rainfall leads to overgrazing that strips the soil bare and increases heat reflection, exacerbating Saharan subsidence and accelerating the disappearance of vegetation and increased desert encroachment. The increase in discharge observed in the Nakambe watersheds in Burkina Faso, for instance, can be explained by run-off surfeits due to degradation of the vegetative cover and soil. Along its middle course, the Niger River has seen significantly increased solids and silting up.

Climate change has started to affect Western African national economies and those of the Sahel countries in particular for three main reasons: (a) the economic role of rain-fed agriculture; (b) inadequate water resources management; and (c) meagre replenishment of reservoirs on which some countries depend heavily for the generation of hydropower. In 1998, Ghana experienced a major energy crisis when Lake Volta dropped below the threshold required to feed the turbines of the Akosombo dam. ***Ouagadougou,*** which is supplied by natural underground reservoirs, experienced severe shortfalls in 2002 and 2003. Rainfall and river flow decreases have begun to affect urban water and energy security and, by extension, urban productivity. Drops in water availability or quality also cause heightened competition for water between agriculture, manufacturing and thirsty cities. Tensions and conflicts among countries over increasingly precious water resources are on the rise, especially along the lower half of the Niger River and in the Volta Basin.

Extreme weather events now seem to occur with rising frequency and higher environmental and socio-economic costs. In 1999, torrential rains led to the opening of the floodgates of the Kainji, Jebba and Shiroro dams in Nigeria, resulting in a heavy death toll and property losses. In the same year, an overflowing White Volta River claimed many lives and destroyed hundreds of houses in Ghana. After a devastating flood and the displacement of several hundred thousand people in 1998, the Komadugu Yobe Valley in Nigeria flooded once more in 2001. The death toll exceeded 200, with over 35,000 displaced people. Likewise in 2009, floods in Burkina Faso that followed the heaviest rainfall in 90 years, leaving seven dead and 150,000 homeless. Clearly, the need for public interventions that reduce the vulnerability of urban and rural dwellers in Western Africa is becoming more and more pressing.

▲
Drought in Ouagadougou, Burkina Faso. **©Nancy Palus/IRIN**

3.5 Emerging Issues

Migration in Western Africa

After independence, Ghana became a major regional immigration pole because the cocoa, coffee and gold producing sectors offered numerous employment opportunities. The huge immigration wave ended with the Alliance Compliance Order (1969) and the subsequent expulsion of hundreds of thousands of immigrants. Over the longer term, though, these and similar interventions do not seem to have interfered with a structural trend of regional mobility. Western Africa is a natural integration space with its cities increasingly the driving force behind development and modernization.

From the 1970s onwards, three major economic opportunity-driven systems of regional migration patterns emerged in Western Africa:

(a) the Ghana-Côte d'Ivoire axis (based on work in cocoa and coffee production);
(b) Nigeria (oil and gas); and
(c) Senegal (groundnuts production and trade).

Although these three migration patterns are still at work in Western Africa, their roles have changed. Côte d'Ivoire and Nigeria have become transit countries, a stepping stone for wealth accumulation before proceeding to other regional or foreign destinations. Economic and labour constraints guide migrations to or away from Senegal.

In Western Africa, migration occurs mainly for economic reasons and is often facilitated by identity-based networks (ethnic, family, etc). Some of the flows came in response to political or economic tensions, such as mass expulsions of foreign nationals from Côte d'Ivoire (1964), Ghana (1969), Nigeria (1983 and 1985), Mauritania and Senegal (1989), Benin (1998), or people fleeing conflict such as in Côte d'Ivoire since late 1999.

Part and parcel of the Western African mobility equation is that colonial borders cut across socio-cultural areas where mobility is so natural that it is difficult to imagine how border crossing could be prevented. For example, the Hausa cultural area has 30 million people in Southern Niger and Northern Nigeria bisected by an international border, while 15 million people belong to the Mande cultural area that extends over parts of Côte d'Ivoire, Guinea, Mali and Senegal. The same happens across the border between the Gambia and Senegal.

Given these realities, it is important to acknowledge that intra-regional migration can have beneficial aspects. For instance, the central plateau in Burkina Faso would have found it difficult to sustain rapid population growth on its steadily deteriorating lands and emigration has reduced the country's rural population to six million, instead of the estimated (and unsustainable) 15 million that would otherwise have been there. High mobility has substantially altered the demographic geography of the subregion over the past few decades. Migration and urbanisation have spawn networks of towns in previously vacant areas and these are now able to absorb excess populations from other parts of the subregion.

However, regional migration flows must be provided for in regional agreements if political and economic tensions are to be avoided. In 1979, the Economic Community of West African States (ECOWAS) agreed on a forward-looking protocol on the free movement of people and the rights of residence and establishment. Consequently, and regardless of minor discords, the ECOWAS area is becoming a sphere of free movement that is highly conducive to regional development. This is also likely to be supportive of Millennium Development Goals through dynamic regional territorial development, including development of new economic centres and increasing infrastructure financing. A truly integrated Western African subregion would outweigh most of the short-term difficulties of this dynamic process, as the political, economic and cultural realities on the ground are already solidifying the region's natural tendencies to integration, as the following section explains.

Urban Development Corridors: The New Urban Spatial Reality

In sub-Saharan Africa, as in all regions where trade between cities and their hinterlands has accelerated, urban development corridors are now emerging in the wake of rapid demographic expansion and urbanisation. An urban development corridor can emerge where two or more large urban cores are located along a single connection trunk line (road, rail, sea or river) that is organised in such a way as to attract flows of people, goods and services while large and regular trade flows pass through urban or rural transit points

▲
Dakar, Senegal. ©**DigitalGlobe**

between the larger urban cores. The part played by each of the urban nodes in the corridor is, all other things being equal, determined by respective population, physical and electronic accessibility, functional specialization and location-specific advantages, especially in economic terms. Continuous urban fabric or spatial occupation and morphological proximity are sometimes also seen as distinctive features of urban corridors, but this is not always a necessary condition. These features are more the outcomes of corridor dynamics than essential conditions for their emergence. It is the corridor's networking mechanisms that fill the spatial gaps, taking advantage of good connections among emerging conurbations.

While the concept of urban development corridors is relatively recent in Western Africa, the underlying geographical realities are not. As early as the 14th century, trade routes emerged between Northern and Western Africa that led to the rise of particularly dynamic urban centres. Examples include the ***Gao-Kano*** pre-colonial trade corridor between Mali and Nigeria, which ran through ***Sokoto*** and ***Katsina***; or the ***Timbuktu-Gao*** route starting in the Moroccan Sahara near ***Marrakech*** and extending to ***Kano*** in Nigeria[8]. British colonial rule did not attempt to change these trade and urban settlement configurations, but rather reinforced them by establishing road and rail infrastructures between these urban centres. The geographical realities underlying today's urban development corridors are, therefore, clearly not new but rather the re-establishment of age-old trade and movement patterns. What *is* new, however, is the growth of urban nodes that have so far remained unaffected by post-independence urban dynamics, as well as the nature of the forces at play and the surfacing, in some cases, of west-east corridors. A case in point is the ***Dakar-Touba*** corridor in Senegal.

The Dakar-Touba Corridor: Senegal's Urban Backbone

Near large urban areas, attention is more and more drawn to spatial transformations through which new links between towns and their surroundings are appearing. In west Senegal, these new urban dynamics are most visible along the West-East ***Dakar-Touba*** urban corridor. They have started to influence Senegal's long-term urban pattern and will especially affect the primacy of ***Dakar***. If the dynamic nature of the corridor is to be adequately apprehended, two significant aspects must come under special focus: (a) the recent, very substantial demographic expansion of Touba and (b) the presence of particularly dynamic intermediate-size urban cores along the Dakar-Touba corridor (see Map 3.8 and 3.9).

Over the past two decades, ***Touba's*** population grew at an estimated 15 per cent average annual rate. Since 1980, its population increased seven-fold to more than one million today. The resulting rapid urban sprawl has seen the surface area expand from 5.75 km^2 in 1976 to 135 km^2 today. The economy grew commensurately, despite the absence of manufacturing. Rather, Touba's boom is based on high consumption with retail outlets and service providers responding to demand with goods hauled over ever-longer distances. Touba is the end-point of large financial and commodity flows coming via Dakar, mainly from Europe and North America.

The 200 km ***Dakar-Touba*** corridor owes its dynamism to the string of towns and cities structured along the highway linking these two main urban centres. The largest, ***Thiès***, is host to more than 200,000 and stands as a major transition point along the route. A number of rural settlements that host weekly markets are found between the main corridor cities, helping maintain the commodity flows within the corridor and creating very active lateral links. Corridor dynamics are spurred on by lateral collecting points, such as the ***Touba-Toul*** market village, located about 7 km from the highway and accessible via a corridor town between ***Thiès*** and ***Diourbel***. This is also the case with ***Kayar***, a fishing town located about 15 km from the Dakar-Touba highway, accessed mainly through ***Km50***, a particularly dynamic commercial transit node. Much of the fish produced in Kayar goes to ***Touba*** and its hinterland.

▲
Thiès, Senegal. **©Ji-Elle**

MAP 3.8: **THE DAKAR-TOUBA CORRIDOR: URBAN AGGLOMERATIONS AND RURAL TRANSIT POINTS**

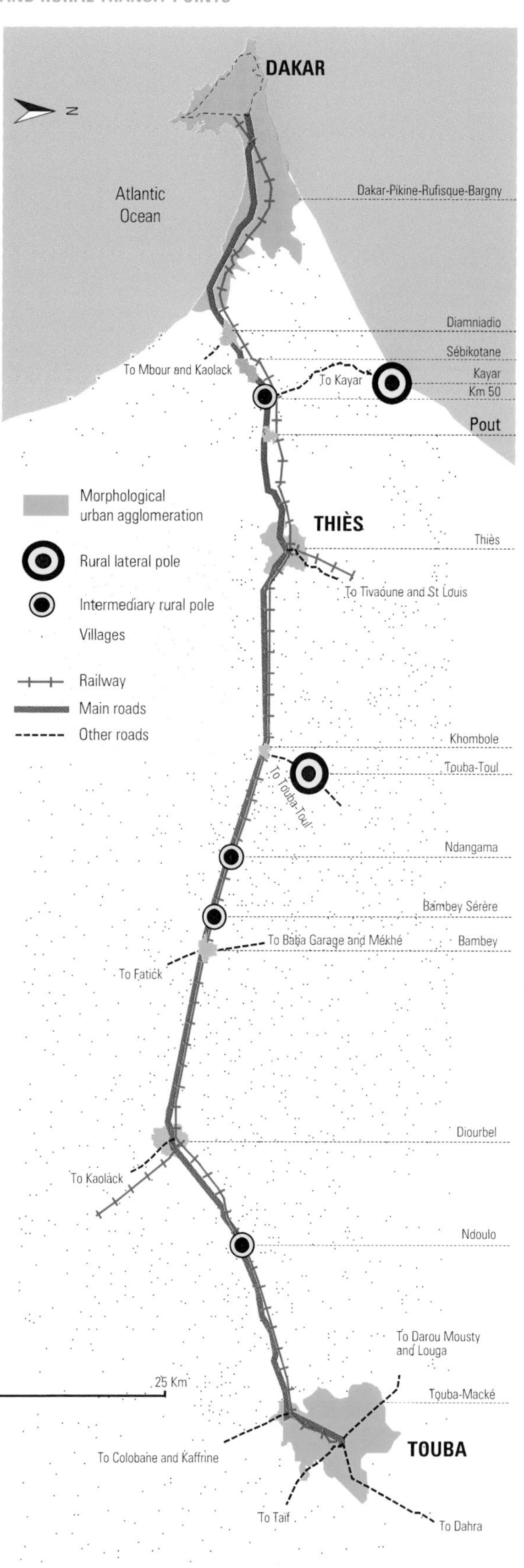

Source: Digitisation Google Earth images. ©Guèye & Thiam, Dakar, Senegal, March 2010

MAP 3.9: **URBAN POPULATION DISTRIBUTION IN THE DAKAR-TOUBA DEVELOPMENT CORRIDOR**

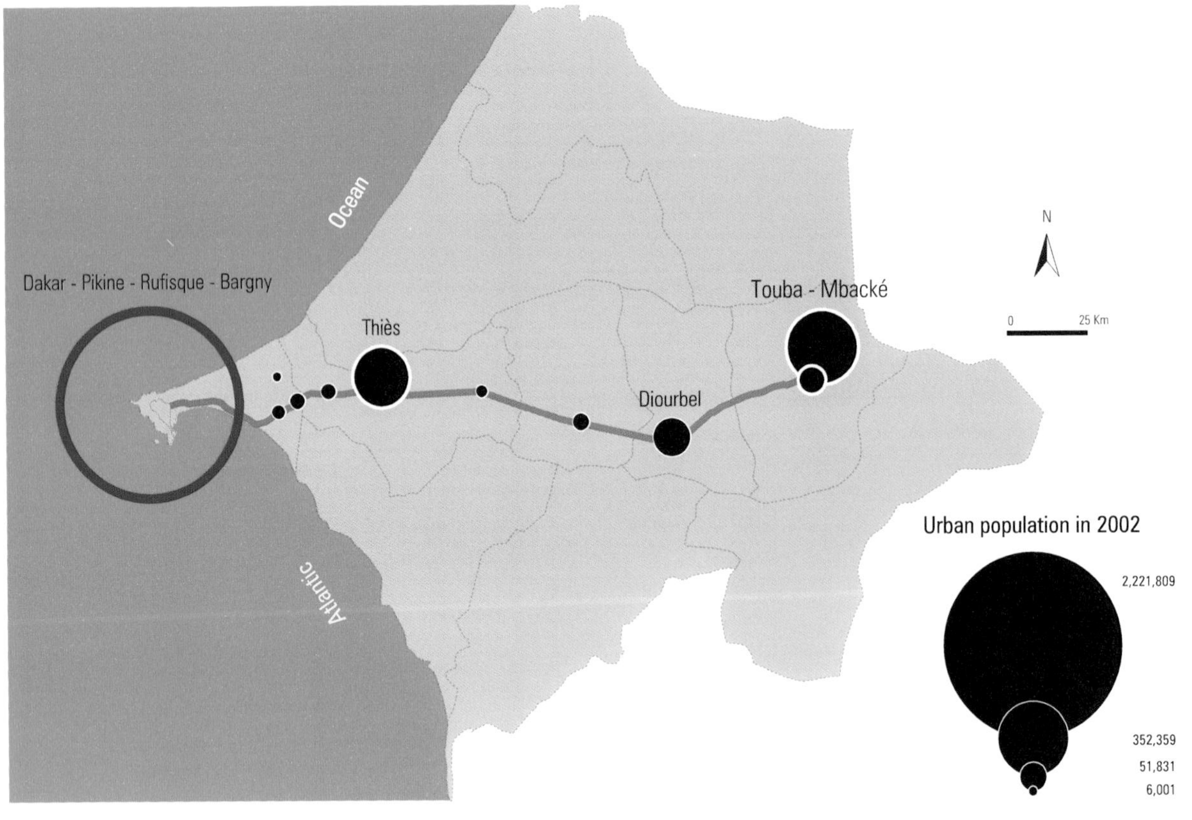

Source: ANSD – Dakar, 2002. ©Guèye & Thiam, Dakar, Senegal, March 2010

MAP 3.10: **INTERACTIONS AND POTENTIAL NETWORKS IN WESTERN AFRICA**

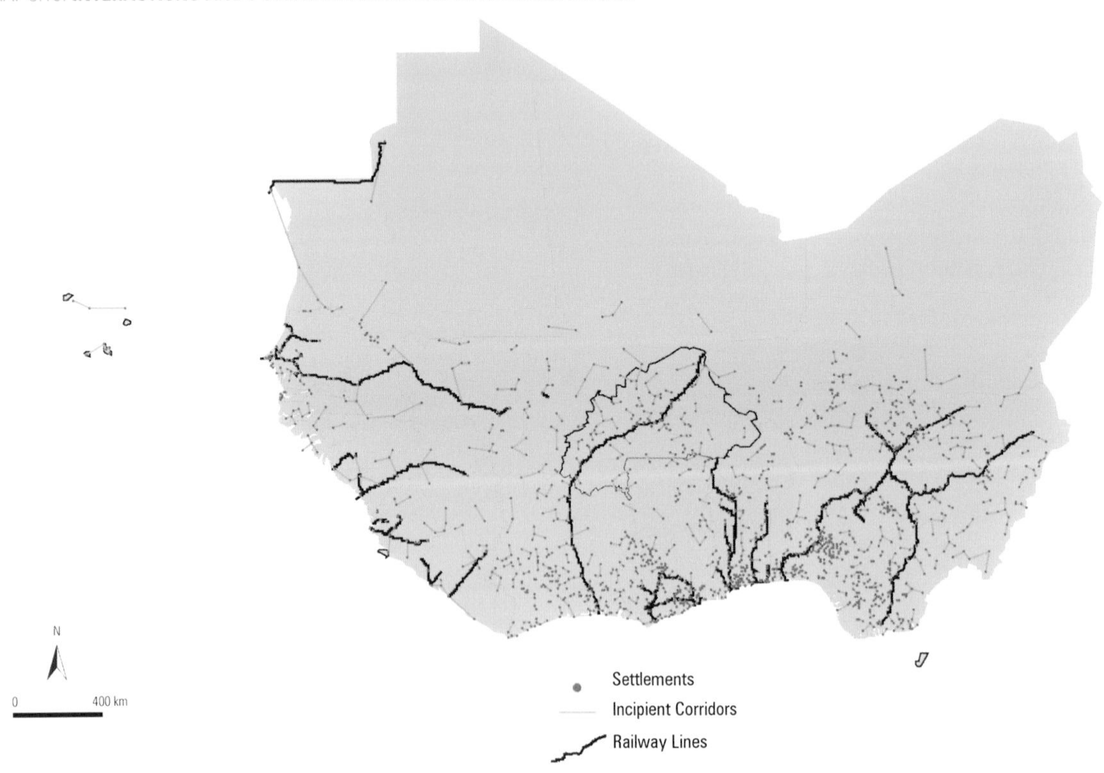

Source: Databases of Africapolis study AFD/SEDET – July 2008. ©Guèye & Thiam, Dakar, Senegal, Sept. 2009

Other Western African Development Axes and Corridors

Urban ribbon configurations are also emerging in Côte d'Ivoire, such as ***Bouaké-Abidjan***, via ***Dimbokro*** and ***Agboville***, or ***Yamoussoukro*** which emerged a few decades ago along a network of roads and railways. Another example is the ***Ouagadougou-Bobo-Dioulasso*** corridor, running along Burkina Faso's main highway that links the port of ***Abidjan*** with the Burkinabe capital.

▲
Touba, Senegal. ©**IRIN**

Some national corridors are now becoming trans-national, building linkages with cities in neighbouring countries. An example is the ***Maradi-Katsina-Kano*** corridor, connecting cities in Niger and Nigeria. ***Katsina*** plays a particularly significant transit role in movements between southern Niger and northern Nigeria. Part of this corridor follows the pre-colonial ***Gao-Kano*** trade route, showing that urbanisation is re-establishing yesterday's major trade routes. There is also the example of the emerging ***Bobo-Dioulasso-Korogho*** trans-national corridor between Burkina Faso and Côte d'Ivoire with ***Banfora*** and ***Ferkéssedougou*** as important intermediate nodes.

The urban development corridor phenomenon is expected to become more widespread on the back of expanding road networks. Map 3.10 shows a simulation of the linkages and potential development corridors in Western Africa based on the distance to the nearest neighbour. This choice of method is deliberate. In Western Africa, distance remains a key determinant factor for spatial relations, even though the policies and technologies designed to cut distances short are becoming more and more effective. In view of persistent lags in regional interconnectivity, planning the geography of future interactions and urban configurations would lose much of its significance if distance is not taken into account.

This map is interesting for at least two reasons. First, it gives notion of the potential for proactive links between cities in Western Africa; and, second, on deeper analysis, most of the arcs coincide with the patterns of logistical connections, particularly roads. For the sake of clarity, only rail networks are shown on Map 3.10.

However, while research frequently showcases urban development corridors as positive for regions, territories and socio-economic systems, the fact remains that they may come with some drawbacks. Indeed, when corridors are not well-managed, they may cause major spatial imbalances in areas outside them. This is bound to result in spatial and functional gaps, particularly in the absence of transit towns capable of diverting for their own benefit some of the opportunities attracted by the cities located along the corridor.

ENDNOTES

1. Loi N° 64-46 du 17 juin 1964, relative au Domaine national.
2. Loi N° 86-91/AN-RM du 1er août 1986, portant Code domanial et foncier, telle que modifiée par l'Ordonnance N° 92-042/P-CTSP du 3 juin 1992
3. With the new Land Code *(Code Domanial et Foncier)* adopted in 1992.
4. Rochegude, A. & Plançon, C. (2010). Décentralisation, acteurs locaux et foncier en Afrique. Mise en perspective juridique des textes sur la décentralisation et le foncier. This study covers 21 sub-Saharan countries, mostly in West and Central Africa. It provides a valuable follow-up of changes affecting the legal and regulatory frameworks governing land management and administration against a background of decentralisation over the past two decades.
5. Asiama, S. 2005.
6. Decree n° 91-748, July 29, 1991.
7. In Burkina Faso, housing prices in the formal sector and income levels are such that the newly created *Banque de l'Habitat* found in 2005 that there were about 25,000 bankable households in its potential customer base, but only about 15,000 if only salaried groups and formal entrepreneurs were included.
8. See Blin, (1990) p 27 or Toupet, (1992) p 58.

Chapter Four

04

THE STATE OF EASTERN AFRICAN CITIES

Asmara, Eritrea.
©Pietro Cenini/Panos Pictures

4.1
The Social Geography of Urbanisation

The Geographic Spread of Urban Demographic Growth

For the purposes of this report the Eastern African region includes Burundi, Comoros, Djibouti, Eritrea, Ethiopia, Kenya, Madagascar, Malawi, Mauritius, Réunion, Rwanda, Seychelles, Somalia, Tanzania and Uganda.

By 2010, about 40 per cent of all Africans resided in cities, compared with only 23.6 per cent in Eastern Africa. Urban demographic growth across the continent remained the strongest worldwide at an annual 3.3 per cent average, compared with a global 2.5 per cent rate. During the 2005-2010 period, significant discrepancies in urban demographic growth rates emerged across African sub-regions, with the strongest rate in Central Africa (4.13 per cent), followed by Western Africa (4.05 per cent), Eastern Africa (3.86 per cent) and urban growth rates below the global average in Northern and Southern Africa with 2.45 and 1.88 per cent respectively.[1]

Over the 50 years between 1960 and 2010, the urban population of Eastern Africa soared from 6.0 million to 77.1 million (see Table 4.1 for continental trends and Table 4.2 for country trends). During the incipient decade, Eastern Africa's urban population is projected to increase by another 38.9 million to 116.1 million in 2020, a 50.4 per cent growth rate. Between 2020 and 2030, the region's urban population is expected to increase by a further 56.6 million to 172.7 million; this would signal a slight slowdown compared with the previous decade, but still a significant 48.7 per cent increase over the projected 2020 urban population. By 2030, one-third of all East Africans will be living in areas classified as urban and on current projections it should take at least two decades for this proportion to reach beyond 50 per cent. By 2050, Eastern Africa's urban population is projected at 337.4 million which, with a 47.4 per cent urbanisation rate, will still leave it short of the 50 per cent 'tipping point' which the world as a whole experienced in 2008.

MAP 4.1: **EASTERN AFRICAN COUNTRIES**

In 2010, only the region's smaller states - Djibouti, Réunion and the Seychelles - had predominantly urban populations. This stage is to be reached by Somalia during the 2030-40 decade. By 2050, still only one third of all Eastern African nations are projected to be predominantly urban, leaving the region the least urbanised in Africa for many years to come.

With rural-urban migration continuing to slow down, natural growth and *in-situ* urbanisation (i.e., the absorption of smaller settlements on the growth paths of larger cities) are now the major contributors to urban demographic expansion in the region. In some countries, conflict is a significant factor in population movements, whether rural-urban, urban-rural or intra-urban migrations. The prolonged civil war in Somalia, for instance, pushes relatively large numbers of people from the main towns to areas where their clans originated. Consequently, as people flee the ongoing strife in ***Mogadishu,*** populations expand substantially in ***Lower Jubba,*** the inter-riverine areas and in previously small regional Somali towns such as ***Belet Weyne, Galkaiyo, Baidoa*** and ***Bossasso.***

Primate cities continue to contribute to urban demographic growth in Eastern Africa. However, intermediate cities (those with populations under 500 000) are now absorbing the lion's share of total urban demographic growth. The exception in Eastern Africa is ***Kigali,*** as the Rwandan capital between the year 2000 and 2005 recorded one of the world's highest growth rates - an annual 8.6 per cent average, largely due to returning refugees and people internally displaced by the 1994 conflict.

TABLE 4.1: **EASTERN AFRICA AND ALL-AFRICA URBAN POPULATION TRENDS, 1950-2050 (ABSOLUTE AND PERCENTAGE)**

Population	1950	1960	1970	1980	1990	2000	2010*	2020*	2030*	2040*	2050*
E. Africa Urban (*000)	3,434	6,047	11,211	21,38	34,660	52,641	77,194	116,130	172,766	247,674	337,493
Urban (per cent)	5.30	7.37	10.42	14.73	17.96	20.83	23.59	27.64	33.36	40.14	47.44
All Africa (per cent)	14.40	18.64	23.59	27.91	32.13	35.95	39.98	44.59	49.95	55.73	61.59

** Projections*
Source: WUP, 2009

GRAPH 4.1: **EASTERN AFRICA AND ALL-AFRICA URBAN POPULATION TRENDS, 1950-2050 (ABSOLUTE AND PERCENTAGE)**

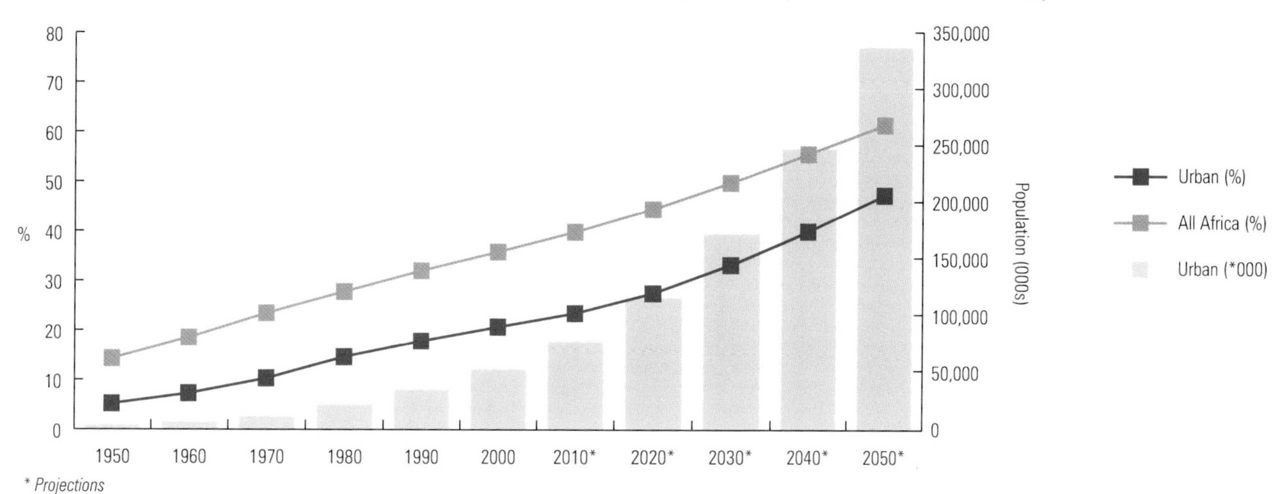

** Projections*
Source: WUP, 2009

As shown in Table 4.3, ill-balanced urban settlement hierarchies and high degrees of urban primacy among the capitals remain as defining features in a majority of countries, concentrating wealth and power in relatively narrow geographical areas, affecting the development prospects of others and, therefore, the country as a whole. This urban imbalance results in inequitable distributions of political power, unequal access to resources as well as of national wealth and the benefits of urbanisation. Therefore, Eastern Africa's ongoing urbanisation should preferably be taken as an opportunity to promote more balanced urban hierarchies and, consequently, a better geographical spread of urban populations, political power or leverage and urban livelihoods. Where urbanisation is left to itself, these aims are unlikely to be achieved. In this regard, the general trend whereby Africa's secondary cities absorb increasingly larger shares of national urban demographic growth is to be seen positively; still, governments should be far more proactive in the pursuit of a better geographic balance of urban-based economic opportunities and livelihoods. If this is to be achieved, governments must deploy concerted and prioritized interventions, investments and policy initiatives that do not only promote a more even distribution of the populations but also provide better access to national resources and urban-based economic development in particular. Over the past decades, some of the region's nations have launched commendable initiatives along these lines, but generally more proactive public interventions are required to maximize the beneficial economic and social outcomes of secondary city growth.

Faced with the negative aspects of the primacy of capital cities (traffic congestion, air pollution, land supply shortages and escalating real estate prices, among others), several Eastern African governments are considering or developing new spatial initiatives to ease the pressures on their capitals. Commendable as they are in their own right, these initiatives tend to focus on boosting the settlements on the periphery of capital cities. The problem is that this type of policy can only give medium-term relief, since all it does is merely distribute the benefits of urban concentration and agglomeration economies to the commuting distance of the primate capital. As a result, city-region development gets the benefits, when what is really needed is to stimulate economic activities in cities at a distance from the primate capital. Alongside with better-focused spatial interventions in the primate city region, additional, pro-active functional decentralisation to the benefit of secondary cities throughout a given country would have a stronger long-term effect on the geographical spread of urban opportunities.

Urban primacy remains very strong in Eastern Africa and goes back a long way. Colonial rule set the model of power centralization in the capital. However, as independence recedes ever further in the past, colonial rule can no longer serve as an excuse for Eastern Africa's imbalanced demographic con-

TABLE 4.2: **EASTERN AFRICAN NATIONS' URBANISATION TRENDS, 1950-2050 (PER CENT)**

Population	1950	1960	1970	1980	1990	2000	2010*	2020*	2030*	2040*	2050*
Burundi	1.73	2.04	2.38	4.34	6.27	8.28	11.00	14.77	19.79	26.00	33.35
Comoros	6.60	16.55	19.39	23.22	27.87	28.08	28.19	30.85	36.51	43.47	50.70
Djibouti	39.81	50.33	61.78	72.10	75.65	76.03	76.23	77.65	80.15	82.74	85.04
Eritrea	7.10	9.75	12.59	14.36	15.80	17.78	21.58	27.46	34.39	42.05	50.11
Ethiopia	4.60	6.43	8.59	10.41	12.62	14.90	16.66	19.27	23.85	30.24	37.48
Kenya	5.59	7.36	10.30	15.71	18.22	19.73	22.18	26.57	33.04	40.36	48.14
Madagascar	7.80	10.64	14.10	18.52	23.57	27.12	30.19	34.85	41.39	48.70	56.07
Malawi	3.51	4.39	6.05	9.05	11.56	15.18	19.77	25.52	32.42	40.18	48.47
Mauritius	29.33	33.18	42.03	42.35	43.90	42.67	41.84	43.36	47.98	54.33	60.55
Réunion	23.49	32.84	41.66	53.48	81.23	89.87	94.01	95.66	96.33	96.88	97.35
Rwanda	1.80	2.40	3.19	4.72	5.42	13.77	18.85	22.61	28.26	35.25	42.93
Seychelles	27.40	27.67	39.07	49.37	49.29	51.05	55.32	61.08	66.56	71.63	76.21
Somalia	12.73	17.31	22.68	26.76	29.66	33.25	37.45	43.0	49.86	56.89	63.65
Tanzania	3.49	5.25	7.85	14.56	18.88	22.31	26.38	31.79	38.66	46.25	54.01
Uganda	2.82	4.42	6.66	7.53	11.08	12.08	13.30	15.94	20.56	26.54	33.52

** Projections*
Source: WUP, 2009

GRAPH 4.2: **EASTERN AFRICAN NATIONS' URBANISATION TRENDS, 1950-2050 (PER CENT)**

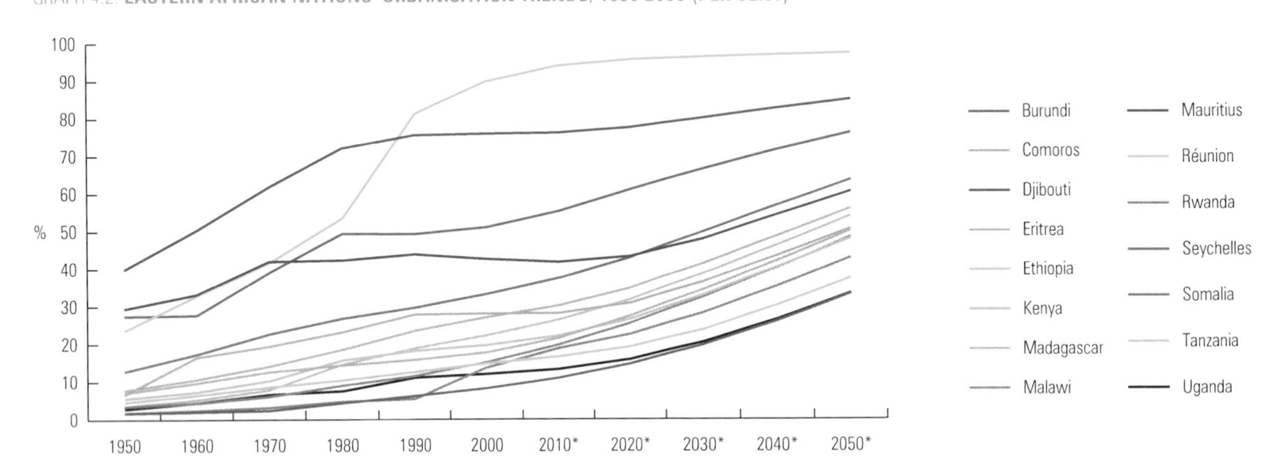

** Projections*
Source: WUP, 2009

centrations and attendant factors of political, economic and social exclusion. Today's urban challenges in Eastern Africa are increasingly the outcomes of post-independence political, economic and social policy choices (or lack thereof). Far more proactive government action is necessary given the rapid pace of urbanisation. This theme is further discussed in section 4.5 based on the example of the Greater Nairobi Metropolis.

Eastern Africa's current rapid urban demographic growth comes with a host of problems, including spiralling urban unemployment, overstretched and deteriorated infrastructure and services delivery systems, environmental degradation and acute shortages of affordable housing and residential land. These factors result in a rapid proliferation of slums, informal settlements and overcrowding. Combinations of weak urban, housing and social policies, inadequate planning and under-resourced, under-funded and therefore poorly performing government institutions, as well as many years of anti-urban policies, have made it difficult for most Eastern African municipalities to maintain a grip over ongoing urbanisation and adequately manage its spatial, economic, social and environmental effects.

The Links Between Poverty, Inequality and Slums

In Eastern African cities, the three main links between poverty, inequality and slum incidence are as follows: (a) lack of access to affordable and adequate land and housing for the predominantly poor urban populations; (b) severe inequality in domestic wealth sharing; and (c) unequal access to basic (including social) infrastructures.

Ethiopia holds the unenviable record of the highest slum

▲
Water shortages in Mathare slum, Nairobi. ©**Manoocher Deghati/IRIN**

TABLE 4.3: **THE POPULATION OF EASTERN AFRICAN CAPITALS - SHARE OF TOTAL URBAN POPULATION AND PRIMACY (2010 - PROJECTIONS)**

Country	Capital City	Population (*000)	Percentage of Total Urban Population	Second-largest City		Primacy [a]
				Name	Population	
Burundi	Bujumbura	455	11.00	Gitega	45	9.96
Comoros	Moroni	49	28.19	Mutsamudu	21	2.27
Djibouti	Djibouti	567	76.23	Ali Sabieh	87	6.51
Eritrea	Asmara	649	21.58	Keren	86	7.55
Ethiopia	Addis Ababa	2,930	16.66	Dire Dawa	330	8.87
Kenya	Nairobi	3,523	22.18	Mombasa	1,003	3.51
Madagascar	Antananarivo	1,879	30.19	Toamasina	2,856	0.65
Malawi [b]	Lilongwe	669	24.5	Blantyre	661	1.01
Mauritius	Port Louis	149	41.84	Beau Bassin	100	1.49
Réunion	Saint-Denis	141	94.01	Saint Paul	92.5	1.52
Rwanda	Kigali	909	18.85	Butare	896	1.13
Seychelles	Victoria	26	55.32	Anse Etoile	4.4	5.90
Somalia	Mogadishu	1,500	37.45	Hargeisa	650	2.30
Tanzania	Dar es Salaam [c]	3,349	26.38	Mwanza	476	7.03
Uganda	Kampala	1,598	13.30	Jinja	509	3.13

Notes: [a] *Population of the capital city divided by the population of second-largest city.*
[b] *2008 data, National Statistics Office, Malawi*
[c] *Commercial capital*
Source: WUP, 2009

BOX 4.1: **KHARTOUM SLUMS EPITOMISE EASTERN AFRICA'S TYPICAL PATTERN**

Like other large cities in the region, Khartoum features three distinct types of very low-income residential areas: (a) inner-city slum areas that over time have been absorbed in urban expansion, such as Fallata Village (Ushash Fallata); (b) *de facto* slums on the urban periphery, which had been planned as low-income residential areas and distributed to the landless; and (c) squatter settlements on and beyond the urban periphery, built on illegally occupied land by newcomers. Khartoum's slum dwellers are mostly from southern Sudan tribes such as Dinka, Nuer and Shuluk, or from the western regions of Kordofan and Darfur (Fur, Nuba, Mseiria, Zaghawa, Masalit, Borno and Rizeigat) who fled insecurity in their areas of origin during the Sudanese civil war and, more recently, the violence in Darfur.

BOX 4.2: **ENERGY IN ERITREA: ALTERNATIVE SOURCES MUST BE DEVELOPED**

Eritrea's energy supply consists mainly (70 per cent) of biomass fuels with petroleum accounting for 27 per cent. All petroleum products are imported. Electricity accounts for only three per cent of national energy supply.

Electricity is generated by thermal plants (99 per cent), with renewable sources (wind and solar) accounting for only one per cent; 78 per cent of urban residents have access to electricity, compared with only three per cent of rural residents. Nationwide, only 38 per cent of the area is connected to the grid (18 per cent of the population); the remaining 62 per cent relies on alternative energy sources. Eritrea is one of the countries with the lowest number of connections to the power grid in the world. The country has great potential for alternative energy sources including wind, solar, geothermal and hydroelectric, but these remain unexplored.

Source: Eritrean Ministry of Energy and Mines, http://www.moem.gov.er

incidence in Eastern Africa, coupled with extremely poor access to basic urban services[2]. Even those Ethiopians living in settlements that are *not* defined as slums have only limited access to infrastructure and services. In ***Djibouti City***, informal settlements continued to account for the largest share of urban expansion over the past decades. In the early 1990s, the country's total urban population of 329,300 comprised more than 240,000 slum residents (or 73 per cent). Likewise, in Eritrea, 70 per cent of the population lives in informal settlements and slums. ***Nairobi*** is host to more than 200 informal settlements, where living conditions are among the worst in Africa due to extremely high population densities: reaching 26,000 km^2 in inner-city slums like Pumwani and Maringo.

Across Eastern Africa, low-income urban residents have little if any access to formal land or housing markets. Their only access to residential land is outside the formal system or, to be more specific: informally, illegally, or through urban land invasions. These processes and their effects are described in detail in Section 4.3. As a result, and given the large numbers of low-income urban residents, the overwhelming majority of urban land and housing transactions in Eastern Africa are now informal in nature and taking place on marginal, often hazardous public or private urban land that is deprived of basic services or amenities. This exacerbates the vulnerability of the urban poor, because such informally acquired urban lands typically neither meet local authority minimum development standards nor environmental regulations. Consequently, these land plots cannot be eligible for later conversion to assets that are tradable in formal markets. Meanwhile, repeated subdivision of these marginal and under-serviced urban plots into smaller parcels continues as highly speculative informal land markets become more entrenched.

Between 40 to 60 per cent of people in unplanned settlements in Eastern Africa lack adequate water and sanitation[3]. Their access to water is only through street vendors. They pay more for poorer quality water than those residents with home connections to the municipal water network. At the moment, local authorities favour privatisation as the best remedy to this situation, as is the case in ***Nairobi***. Although private companies are quite familiar about water reticulation in formal residential areas, servicing informal settlements comes as a challenge. This is why non-governmental organisations have been trying to bridge the gaps in water supply to these urban areas. However, their success is limited as they neither have a formal mandate to provide this service nor the capacity to provide water on an adequate scale and, therefore, at affordable prices. What they manage to do, though, is to help utility companies keep any damage to water supply infrastructure and loss of water from illegal tapping at a minimum.

Access to sanitation is another major challenge for the poor in most Eastern African cities. This is notable in the slums of ***Addis Ababa***, ***Asmara***, ***Dar es Salaam***, ***Kampala***, ***Nairobi*** and many other cities. The plastic bags used to throw out toilet waste by people with no access to latrines are often called 'flying toilets' which are now heaped in large piles in the slums of ***Nairobi*** and ***Kampala***. Not surprisingly, informal and slum settlements are associated with high incidences of cholera, which is linked directly to the prevailing unsanitary conditions.

The problem of lack of sanitation is less pronounced in smaller cities like ***Bujumbura***, ***Kigali*** and the unplanned settlements on the western Indian Ocean islands of Mauritius and the Comoros. In these smaller cities, local authorities have the capacity to meet urban challenges like water and sanitation. In Mauritius, supply of services is directly linked to the fact that most residents own their properties, enjoy security of tenure and have invested in good quality conventional buildings. This is the same in the Comoros, where nearly all residents have access to clean water and modern sanitation systems. However, city size does not appear to be the critical factor in this respect as in ***Antananarivo***, about 85 per cent of the 1.9 million urban population has access to the water network and 70 per cent to some form of modern sanitation[4].

The majority of the urban poor in Eastern Africa uses either wood, charcoal, liquefied petroleum gas (LPG) or kerosene for cooking. In urban Kenya, gas and kerosene are more commonspread than wood or charcoal (47 per cent use kerosene for cooking)[5]. Research by UN-HABITAT shows that respiratory diseases are a leading cause of child mortality in urban Eastern Africa due to widespread use of wood and charcoal combined with poor residential ventilation in urban slums. Studies in Ethiopia showed a 30 per cent rise in the incidence of respiratory diseases in children below 5 years when cow dung was used, falling to 8.3 per cent with charcoal and to 4.8 per cent with kerosene.

Ethiopia, Tanzania and Uganda are now exploring the use of bio fuels. This has in turn led to conversion of food crop land into cash crop plantations. Sugar cane is the favourite alternative energy-producing crop. A variety of other crops, such as *Jatropha Curcas,* are planted on a large scale in Tanzania. However, expansion of bio fuel crop farming can in some cases involve more extensive use of fresh water for irrigation and diversion of productive agricultural land to non-food producing purposes, and this may need careful policy reconsideration.

As part of nationwide power rationing schemes, ***Addis Ababa***, ***Dar es Salaam***, ***Kampala*** and ***Nairobi***, as well as numerous smaller cities in Eastern Africa, experience recurrent electricity rationing, with adverse consequences not just for households but productivity as well. In ***Nairobi***, rationing is the result of drought-induced low water levels in dams. This has prompted the government to explore alternative sources of energy, i.e. wind, geothermal and solar, while the monopoly for production has been broken in a bid to encourage other contributions to energy security.

Regarding informal settlements, Eastern African governments take a variety of approaches. Forced eviction has long been the favourite method and in some cases continues to be viewed as acceptable. The urban poor typically hold few if any rights and are facing eviction and demolition of their homes where these are categorized as 'illegal' by uncompromising public authorities. This false solution is often stigmatised by international development agencies, civil society and local communities. Forced eviction simply destroys whatever limited assets the urban poor have managed to build up and only shifts them to other locations within or adjacent to the city.

As the shortcomings of forced eviction become more apparent, governments often turn to *in-situ* upgrading of urban slums as the only practical way forward. Examples of ongoing slum and informal settlement upgrading schemes include the Kenya National Slum Upgrading Programme (KENSUP) in various locations, and the Hanna Nassif Slum Upgrading programme in ***Dar es Salaam***. However, large-scale, city-wide slum upgrading is still missing while upgrading of social and basic infrastructures remains focused on unplanned middle-income areas where security of tenure prevails[6], rather than addressing the living conditions of the poorest segments of Eastern Africa's urban populations. Clearly, addressing the residential and services needs of urban middle and lower-middle income groups is important; especially where housing for low-income households is taken over by lower-middle income groups. However, the already deeply marginalized and disenfranchised urban poor communities need urgent attention as well.

Mauritius and the Seychelles are the only countries without slums in the whole of Eastern Africa as they feature small populations and healthy economies based on tourism, with relatively high incomes per head and, most importantly, more equitable national wealth distribution.

▲
Antananarivo, Madagascar. 85% of the 1.9 million urban population has access to the water network. **©Pierre-Yves Babelon/Shutterstock**

4.2
The Economic Geography of Cities

Economic Inequality

Although almost all Eastern African countries have experienced positive economic growth in recent years, the low-income majorities are not benefiting from the commensurate increases in wealth. Eastern Africa exhibits comparatively high socio-economic inequality with most countries exceeding Africa's *'relatively high'* average (income-based) Gini coefficient of 0.45. (For details on Gini coefficients, please refer to Section 1.2 in Chapter 1). In ***Addis Ababa,*** inequality, as reflected in a 0.61 coefficient, is *'extremely high'* and almost double the *'relatively low'* (0.38) national average. In ***Bujumbura***, *'high'* income inequality (0.47) is steeper than in urban Burundi as a whole (0.37). This clearly indicates that in urban Eastern Africa, small and privileged groups are unequally benefitting from economic growth, with very large income and consumption disparities between rich and poor.

TABLE 4.4: **GINI COEFFICIENTS - SELECTED COUNTRIES AND CITIES**

Country	City	Year	Gini coefficient [consumption]	Gini coefficient [income]
Ethiopia		1999/2000	0.28	0.38
	Addis Ababa	2003	0.56	0.61
Burundi		2006	0.3	
	Bujumbura	2006	0.47	
Kenya (national)			0.45	0.57
Kenya (all urban)				0.55
	Nairobi			0.59
Rwanda (national)		2005	0.51	
	Kigali	2005	0.47	
Tanzania (mainland)		2007	0.35	
	Dar es Salaam	2007	0.34	
Uganda (national)				0.41
Uganda (all urban)				0.43
	Kampala	2007	0.4	

Source: UN-HABITAT, State of the World Cities 2010/11.

Research by the United Nations Development Programme (UNDP) indicates that in Kenya, the wealthy earn 56 times more than the poor on average. The richest 10 per cent of the Kenyan population controls 42 per cent of the country's wealth, compared with less than one per cent for the poorest 10 per cent.[7] Trends suggest that this situation is worsening rapidly. Between the 1980s and the 1990s, the Gini coefficient for urban Kenya grew dramatically from 0.47 to 0.58,[8] signalling a significant rise in urban inequality, which is steep nationwide. Overall, Kenyan urban income inequality stands at a *'very high'* 0.55, though still lower than the national average (0.57) and in ***Nairobi*** where, with a 0.59 coefficient, it verges on the *'extremely high'* bracket. The urban poor contribute 51.5 per cent of the total poor population of Kenya and poverty, to a significant degree, is an urban issue. The country is one of the most unequal in Eastern Africa, based on both nationwide and urban Gini coefficients. ***Kisii*** and ***Migori***, for example, feature *'very high'* Gini coefficients (0.56 and 0.63 respectively) with the latter even notably higher than ***Nairobi's***.

In relative terms, ***Dire Dawa*** and ***Dar es Salaam*** stand out among the more 'equal' cities in sub-Saharan Africa, with *'relatively low'* income-based Gini coefficients of 0.39 and 0.36 respectively.[9] Tanzania as a whole shows relatively low inequality, too (0.35); most likely the outcome of many years of redistributive policies under the *ujamaa* socialist economic system, which would go to show that sustained wealth redistribution can have significant socio-economic effects. In Uganda, between 2002 and 2006, *'relatively high'* income inequality has slightly diminished (from 0.43 to 0.41) probably on the back of stronger economic growth. However, and as suggested by the case of Tanzania, reduced inequalities are not brought about by economic growth alone. Rather, low Gini coefficients are always directly linked to wealth (re)distribution (with a few African countries displaying low income inequality against a background of general poverty). The general point here is that there can be income equality at any degree of riches or poverty.

▲
Dar es Salaam, Tanzania. ©**Brian McMorrow**

How Slum Dwellers Survive

Although statistics on informal socio-economic conditions in Eastern Africa are unreliable at best, it is evident that the share of the urban population in informal employment and housing has hugely increased since the 1980s and continues to do so. Whereas a large pool of unemployed and under-employed city dwellers keeps labour costs low and therefore can make Eastern Africa increasingly competitive, the consequences of massive urban poverty almost inevitably include increased urban violence, crime, insecurity and social unrest that are in no one's interest and can scare away foreign capital.

In the years following independence, civil service jobs and housing stood many residents in Eastern African capitals in good stead. However, these top-heavy, bloated institutional arrangements soon proved too expensive for nascent post-colonial economies. Necessary but painful retrenchment followed and many lost both livelihood and shelter. This was to have a far-ranging effect on Eastern Africa's urban economies, as fewer formal employment opportunities were available to ever-larger populations. In the absence of effective social policies, informal livelihoods became the norm for most city dwellers and things have hardly changed since then, with the urban informal sector the main provider of livelihoods and housing to this day.

Addressing Urban Inequality and Fragmentation

Unequal access to social and basic infrastructures combines with highly imbalanced leveraging of political power to cause the physical and social fragmentation that is typical of Eastern African cities. Poor informal neighbourhoods with limited infrastructure and services contrast with wealthy residential areas that are serviced to much higher standards and enjoy an abundance of public goods. However, urban inequality is not only a matter of access to services and public amenities. It is also reflected in residential density differences. For many years, the urban poor in Eastern Africa have experienced the undesirable, extreme population densities that today are also and increasingly found in the large, high-rise middle-income residential developments in ***Dar es Salaam***, ***Kampala*** and ***Nairobi*** which are rapidly emerging as a new 'vertical slum' phenomenon. 'Rooming' (occupying a single-room) has become the residential norm for many city dwellers. By 1981, more than 80 per cent of the population of ***Nairobi*** lived in such rented single rooms, especially in inner-city locations, creating a remarkably contrasting pattern of residential land use with the very low-densities found in the city's leafy suburbs.

As poverty in Eastern African cities has become chronic and structural, crossing over socio-economic lines through economic advancement or via social relationships like marriage is becoming ever more a challenge. The resulting vicious circle of urban poverty is proving to be increasingly difficult to break. Evidence of additional social fragmentation along ethnic and religious lines is becoming more and more glaring, creating polarization and tensions as the driving forces of emerging 'communities of fear'. In ***Nairobi***, for instance, ethnic groups and tribally-organized gangs have taken advantage of poor law enforcement to engage in extortionist and other criminal activities.[10] This is one type of response to lack of effective urban social policies. If the needs of the poor who dominate Africa's urban populations are left unaddressed, the outcomes can only be further insecurity, social unrest and political upheaval.

A clear example of rising urban insecurity rooted in inequality and lack of effective spatial, housing, labour and social policies is the emergence of the Kikuyu 'Mungiki' and the Luo militia known as 'Taliban', again in ***Nairobi***. These politico-religious criminal organizations grew out of the former political private militias which began to feed off Nairobi's perpetual insecurity and poverty crises by means of terror, kidnapping for ransom and extortion in exchange for protection. Failure to cave in to extortion all too often leads to murder and these militias have now grown beyond any control. If the Government of Kenya is to suppress these criminal organizations, then it must address the core roots, including: (a) improved access to land and housing for the urban poor majorities, (b) redressing the massive unemployment of urban youths, and (c) meeting the basic social and physical infrastructure needs of the poorest sections of the ***Nairobi*** population.[11] In the meantime, all efforts should go to identifying the perpetrators and bringing them to court.

In October 2010, the government made a significant first step by placing 33 groupings, including *'Mungiki'* and *'Taliban'*, on a list of out-lawed organisations whose membership is now a crime purnishable with prison terms.

Currently, holistic city-wide government interventions in informal settlements remain thin on the ground in Eastern Africa. Severe lack of capital expenditure on upgraded living conditions for the urban poor is an outcome of weak political will and poor understanding of the essence of informality. Indeed, informal settlements are rarely seen for what they really are: a natural, market-led response to restricted formal access to adequate and affordable housing by low-income segments of the population. The relationships between informal housing and informal economies are still not widely understood either (see Box 4.3). So far, the most commonspread policy approach in Eastern Africa is to declare informal housing and land access illegal. With this sweeping generalization, responsibilities are unreasonably placed on the residents of informal settlements and slums, rather than on public authorities for their failure to devise urban, housing and social policies that benefit the majority of its city dwellers. As elaborated in Section 4.3, a number of feasible and productive options and directions are available to Eastern Africa.

▲
A mother and child flee a police swoop to root out 'Mungiki', Mathare slum, Nairobi.
©Julius Mwelu/IRIN

BOX 4.3: **KENYA: INFORMALITY IS THE PROBLEM, NOT POPULATION GROWTH**

▲
Selling snacks outside a mosque in Nairobi, Kenya. **©Julius Mwelu/IRIN**

The stark message from the 2009 census results, published in August 2010, is that the Kenyan population is growing very fast. Every year, one million Kenyans are added to those in need of housing, services and livelihoods, adding to already existing huge backlogs, especially in urban areas. However, rapid demographic expansion is a problem rather than an asset *only* when it outstrips economic growth, because the difference is almost always increased poverty.

Still, demographic controls should not necessarily be Kenya's first development priority as numbers are not the problem *per se*. Rather, Kenya should be worried about the pace and direction of the economy and their impacts on cities. Natural growth and continued rural-urban migration put enormous pressures to the point that one can speak of 'over-urbanisation' as urban economies lag behind and fail to generate adequate jobs. As a result of this increasing urban poverty, informality is making rapid progress in Kenyan cities. For instance, instead of a formal transportation system Nairobi relies on a chaotic, informal and dangerous minibus system (known as *'matatu')*. The city is also unable to cope with burgeoning numbers of hawkers because the authorities have only constructed one new urban market (Muthurwa Hawkers City Market) over the past 20 years. Urban slums and informal settlements are also growing much faster than formally planned neighbourhoods.

For a long time, Kenya's urbanisation policy emphasised the development of secondary towns. That was a wise approach in principle. Providing housing and roads in intermediate-sized towns such as Thika, Kitale, Homa Bay and Malindi would enable the government to divert rural migration away from the larger cities. In practice, the grand plan fell victim to a piecemeal approach. Promoting secondary cities without simultaneously and vigorously boosting their economic development and livelihood-generating capacities merely results in a transfer of poverty to smaller cities. Today, these towns are beginning to experience the same informal patterns of livelihoods and living conditions already prevailing in larger Kenyan cities: expanding slums, with mobility dependent on informal transport, increased street vending, lack of planning, and rises in violence and crime. Thika, which was constructed in the Kenyatta years as Nairobi's satellite industrial town, now is host to two slums aptly named Kiandutu (Kiswahili for 'sand fleas') and Matharau ('contempt'). The phenomenal demographic expansion of urban Kenya may be disquieting, but what is far more worrisome is the fast rate at which urban economies are going informal.

The informal sector is often hailed in Kenyan policy documents as the leading employer and therefore the saviour of the country's economy. But this ignores that economic informality is a problem, not a solution. Informal employment is nothing but a survival strategy for those excluded from the formal labour markets, in the same manner as slums are the residential survival strategy for people excluded from inefficient formal land and housing markets.

The informal sector acts not as a saviour but as a predator for the poor, often extending the most hostile and brutal labour and living conditions on disenfranchised people who are in no position to fight back. The alternative to informality is unemployment and homelessness. Energetic youths can be found loitering around Nairobi's Westlands shopping area, peddling puppies, rabbits, *mitumba* (second hand) shoes, suits or counterfeit Chinese hi-fi equipment. Informality is about maximum physical exertion, inhuman working hours and single-room occupancy in leaking slum shacks without access to water or sanitation. Informality is the main manifestation of Kenya's ineffective housing, labour and social policies and the government should therefore certainly not seek comfort in its rapid proliferation.

All of this goes to suggest that instead of a rapidly growing population, informality stands out as Kenya's biggest problem. A large, young population is a major asset for any country's economy. It should be the government's mission to make sure it is properly nurtured and taken care of in every way in order to produce maximum cumulative benefits of general well-being, prosperity and peace, instead of being stymied and marginalised by outdated, inappropriate frameworks or policies. This is why public policy should seek to eliminate informality, addressing the underlying systemic inequalities such as those enabling Kenyan political and economic elites to reap the bulk of the benefits of economic and urban growth. Kenyans should worry about the poor-quality governance provided by its leaders; its rampant corruption; its lack of housing, social and labour policies; and highly unequal access to national resources, opportunities and riches. Kenya should worry about the mushrooming urban informality and poverty that increasingly pose a threat to national political and social stability.

Source: UN-HABITAT and *High population is not the problem; high growth of the informal sector is,* by J. Kisero, Daily Nation, 7 September 2010, Nairobi

BOX 4.4: MOGADISHU: WHEN URBAN PLANNING IS LEFT TO CLAN RULE

▲
The Benadir (Mogadishu) Regional Government building. ©**Abdul Qadir Omar**

Mogadishu was established around the 10th century and kept flourishing since then as one of many East African coastal trading cities. After Italy took over Somalia in 1889, Mogadishu became the political capital and began to expand both geographically and demographically regardless of controls. This trend continued, especially after independence in 1960 when, in the absence of spatial planning, the Mogadishu urban area expanded from 1,500 ha in 1970 to 8,000 ha in 1984 and its population from 272,000 in 1970 to an estimated 1.5 million in 2010.

Lack of land-use policies, urban planning or development controls has combined with the proliferation of spontaneous settlements, with low-income newcomers driven by recurrent rural famine and strife. Already overcrowded areas have seen more makeshift shelters on any vacant land, turning into chaotic, high-density neighbourhoods in the absence of any services provision.

After the military coup of 1969, president Siad Barre sought to address the problem, including through urban spatial restructuring. However, nothing could prevail against deteriorating conditions because, from the mid-1980s, famines and insecurity in Puntland and Somaliland drove ever more people to Mogadishu. Coming from areas where violence is considered 'normal', newcomers were perceived as dangerous and undesirable. The army, para-military forces and militias often intervened violently in informal neighbourhoods. Indeed the 1980s saw many urban conflicts linked to changes in the urban fabric of Mogadishu.

The capital is where the civil war started in December 1990 which eventually led to the overthrow of Siad Barre in 1991. Disagreement over the succession plunged Somalia into yet another severe civil crisis with rampant lawlessness and clan warfare. However, Mogadishu's population seemed almost impervious as it had already been in a decidedly war-like situation for years, with associated dramatic population inflows, violence and implosion of the formal economy. Whatever urban services that were left in the capital were soon to collapse, as the para-statal bodies in charge diverted any aid flows to the security apparatus or public officials. Electricity had already become a luxury well before 1990 and economic activity in Mogadishu was at best informal.

Civil war deeply affected the urban setting and demography of Mogadishu. In 1991, most of the Daarood - a Northern Somali clan - were either killed or expelled from the city, as were many Gibil Cad of Arab descent. Simultaneously, others were arriving as they considered the capital a place where 'life and access to resources were easy and free'. Subsequent economic growth and rehabilitation in some areas in 1998 restored confidence among the population. Many middle-class newcomers invested in housing and new economic activity, even though re-armament in the capital had again reached alarming levels.

Decades of strife in Mogadishu have considerably restructured urban space and have created socio-spatial divisions which continue to prevail to this day. Perhaps the main social-spatial change was that neighbourhoods became determined by clan affiliation, with many urban districts dominated by a single clan or divided in clusters each dominated by one. Reflecting the political stalemate, the Somali capital became split into three unequal parts: (a) North Mogadishu, relatively small but with high population densities and where, due to relatively good security under the UN mission and Islamic courts, some new housing has been built; (b) South Mogadishu, effectively the rest of the city, with mixed clans in areas that mostly escaped destruction, and home to the hubs of economic activity: the international seaport and the airport; and (c) Medina, with little demographic or economic significance. For years, the division between North and South remained a painful reality, but has now begun to fade away.

With some neighbourhoods mostly resembling a nuclear blast site, lack of municipal or government apparatus for years and two decades of waste piled up in the streets, this most ravaged of cities has only managed to survive through sheer resilience and informality. Despite the odds, Mogadishu has remained connected with the rest of the world through scheduled commercial flights. Following the complete collapse of the public sector, standard services - water, electricity, telecommunications and banking - have been entirely taken over by a surprisingly vibrant private sector, which has also made inroads into health and education. Remittance-handling services provide a makeshift financial sector and, for those better-off, almost anything is available on local markets, from passports to fashionable sunglasses, as well as more lethal merchandise such as anti-aircraft artillery, ordnance and cocaine.

MAP 4.2: MOGADISHU TOWN

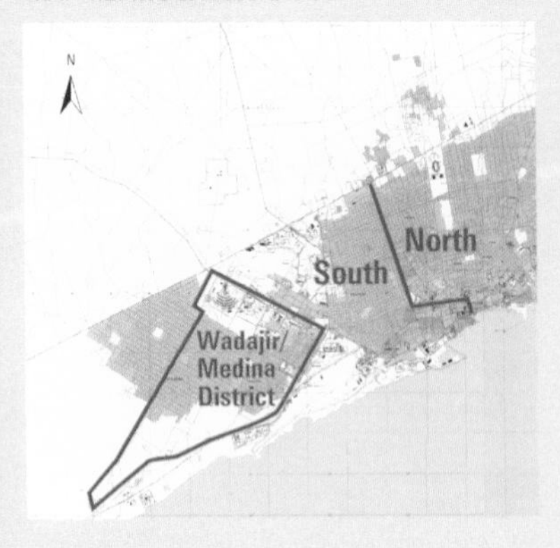

Source: Data and Information Management Unit, UNDP Somalia.

Source: Marcal R, A Survey of Mogadishu's Economy, a report commissioned by the EU, Paris, 2002.

4.3 The Geography of Urban Land Markets

Forms of Land Ownership, Tenure and Rights

All Eastern African nations feature a dual land tenure structure that combines customary (traditional) land regimes and a statutory (law-based) system operating side by side. This is a remnant of the region's colonial heritage. The British (in Kenya, Uganda and Tanzania), the Italians (in Somalia, Eritrea and Djibouti) and the French and the Belgians (in Rwanda and Burundi) introduced statutory systems of title registration in their colonial urban centres and in commercial farming areas, leaving the native urban and rural areas to continue with their customary tenure arrangements. Today's realities on the ground reflect this inherited dual system of customary and statutory systems operating in parallel. Due to frequently overlapping and hybrid arrangements, these dual tenure systems tend to create antagonisms and confusion, particularly where they interface. As a result, resolution of land disputes in Eastern Africa can at times be very complex, generating uncertainties over tenure.

The *mailo* system in Uganda (see Box 4.5), is an example of deep-seated tenure ambiguity. Whether formal or informal, the *mailo* land purchaser must pay twice, as both the title holder and the occupant of the land must be compensated. Any inconsistency between the two parties would stall the transaction. Likewise in Kenya, only title registration (freehold, leasehold, encumbrances) will confer interests on land that can be upheld in court. Moreover, any land sales agreement must be completed within six months, or documentation becomes invalid. No wonder, then, that informal transactions should frequently appear as a far more feasible option, even though they are carried out at purchaser's risk of falling prey to rogue vendors.

In post-independence Eastern Africa, it was expected that the statutory system of land tenure would ultimately prevail, being gradually introduced nationwide through successive land adjudication or registration in both urban and rural areas. Today's realities fall well short of this expectation. The fact of the matter is that in many of the region's cities, informal urban developments continue to proliferate and customary systems in urban areas have been reintroduced in the absence of effective land management and governance.

Urban Land Institutions: Land Administration and Management

Formal land administration and management in Eastern Africa is the domain of central or regional government. Even where independent land commissions have been established, as in Rwanda and Uganda, land registration remains the responsibility of the Registrar of Titles. Ethiopia is the exception, with responsibilities for land administration split between municipal authorities (for urban land) and regional government (for rural land). In Ethiopian cities land is allocated on the basis of leasehold tenure, whereas a 'permit' system extending beneficial right applies in rural areas.

Informal land markets operate similarly across Eastern Africa. Simple letters of agreement are witnessed by local administration (*kebele, wazee wa mitaa,* i.e., village elders or chiefs) together with an appropriate number of witnesses chosen by the parties to the transactions. The more affluent parties may use the services of a lawyer, land broker and/or professional surveyor, but in view of the costs this is the exception rather than the rule. In many other cases, informal land transactions take place without any documentation, relying on social recognition for ownership acknowledgment and security of tenure. The section "Informal settlements as a response to land market imperfections" on page 143 details the nature of informal land markets.

How Land Markets Operate

National and local governments in Eastern Africa influence land markets and access to land in urban areas through allocation of publicly owned parcels, provision of infrastructure and services, and through enforcement (planning controls, power of eminent domain and taxation). These policy instruments are often viewed as inequitably curtailing access to land by low-income urban groups. Whereas Eastern African constitutions and statutes often refer to social justice and the social aspects of property rights, formal urban land market operations have not been to the advantage of the urban poor who constitute the overwhelming majority of demand. The gaps between the need for urban land and its formal availability reflect those between government policies, unequal access to urban land markets and the failure of those markets to deliver. As a result, Eastern African cities are plagued by informal land transactions and the associated mushrooming of informal settlements and urban slums.

However, laws and policies regarding access to, and use of, land are, by themselves, not enough to improve urban land administration or prevent informal land acquisition. Even where restrictions on land transactions may be warranted, enforcement difficulties have more often than not generated distortions which in effect exclude those marginalised groups they were precisely intended to assist.

Formal land markets

Ethiopia and Tanzania have a history of government ownership of land due to their socialist past. In Ethiopia, all land remains government owned and in cities it is formally delivered through auction, negotiation or government adjudication. Government grants leases of up to 99 years confirmed by title deed. The formal market delivers leaseholds with a surface-based annual rent and a fixed lease period, allowing exploitation according to the land use plan. The purchaser cannot own another plot in the city and a surety deposit is required only to be released once house foundations are completed. Although the leaseholder may transfer or undertake a surety on the leasehold, the actual transfer option is weakened by Proclamation on Expropriation N° 455/2005, which disregards the market value of the land in the event of compulsory acquisition. Compensation will only be paid for improvements (buildings and structures). The problem with this formal system is that it is plagued with delays, inequity and corruption.

A parallel cash land market operates in Ethiopia where leases or beneficial interests can be exchanged through simple sales agreements. The buyer pays property transfer taxes and commissions to a middleman. Transfers become official when the real estate value has been assessed for tax purposes. However, this market largely remains beyond the means of the urban poor, and those who cannot afford the formal or parallel cash transfers can only be accommodated by informal land markets.

In Tanzania, too, land is government property and until 1995, when a new land policy recognized the value of bare land, there was no property market to speak of. Today, both customary and statutory rights are recognized and stand equal before the law. Land rights can be registered, but land under statutory occupancy cannot be disposed of within three years. However, a loophole makes it possible to sell

▲
Fianarantsoa, Madagascar. **©Muriel Lasure/Shutterstock**

only the development(s) on the land. Formal access to land can be granted in one of three ways: (a) 'right of occupancy', giving access to long- or short-term leases; (b) unallocated, abandoned or revoked land sold by land officials; or (c) under an approved land use scheme. While the allocation principle operates on a 'first come, first served' basis, the procedure is deeply flawed by slow bureaucracy and corruption. Therefore, in practice, the formal land market caters for less than 10 per cent of effective urban demand, leaving informal channels, often with semi-legal or socially regularized procedures, as the preferred option for most urban residents.

In Eastern Africa, formal urban land markets also feature elements of legislative/regulatory control through physical planning and registration of titles. Kenya is a case in point, where the government would advertise availability of public land in the *Kenya Gazette* to call for applications. Lease terms (with premiums and annual land rents calculated on the basis of cost to the government, rather than market values) are so favourable that these opportunities for cheap land have resulted in intense competition and illicit behaviour, including massive land grabbing, with a small number of well-connected people accumulating public land, in the process locking out the low-income majority of city dwellers. Once lease titles were obtained, the land was often sold at the prevailing market price, generating huge profits. Speculation and all manner of scandals in the allocation of public land became the norm. As a result, today there is virtually no vacant government-owned land left in Kenyan cities, and the formal urban land market is now almost entirely in private hands, allowing access for the wealthy only. Privately-owned property accounts for 18 per cent of total land area. Trust land (i.e., held by rural local authorities in trust for residents of the area for the purposes of customary land practices) accounts for 69 per cent. Government land (i.e., reserved for use by public bodies, or forests, national parks, game reserves, water bodies, mineral lands and any land in respect of which no individual or community ownership can be established by any legal process) comprises the remainder 13 per cent of Kenya's total land area. Urban land amounts only to 0.7 per cent of total land area and the bulk is formally titled, except for a few remaining pockets of unallocated government-owned land.

In Uganda, the land market is only beginning to develop. Since the survey and land management professions are not yet well established, the sheer lack of reliable land information makes land transactions difficult and risky. Uganda formerly featured two distinct land markets: (a) a formal market for duly registered transactions, with recorded sales and signed legal agreements; and (b) an informal market for property and land use rights that were not formally recorded. The country's 1995 Constitution abolished a previous Land Reform Decree that had converted all land to 99-year leases. The new constitution reinstated the pre-independence land tenure systems and now recognizes: (a) freehold; (b) leasehold; (c) customary tenure; and (d) *mailo* (i.e., subleases of freehold land).

Informal land markets

Eastern Africa's informal land markets also feature a rich variety of practices with various degrees of security of tenure. Probably one of the most informal land markets in the region is to be found in Somalia. After more than a decade without clear central government authority and attendant erosion of legal systems, land and property have become a major concern. Illegal occupation and land grabbing are rampant, generating fresh and continued violent conflict. Statutory law is hardly enforced and proves either inefficient or disconnected from reality. As urban land values continue to rise, speculation has become a commonplace way of adding to personal wealth. All valuable open land surrounding Somali towns has been grabbed, including by those internally displaced persons that have invaded many peri-urban areas.

Faced with a major land management problem, several Somali municipalities have taken to regularise illegal land occupation. The occupant-developer of grabbed or invaded land wishing to acquire a title deed can choose one of two options: (a) referring the case to Islamic courts for an order confirming ownership; or (b) regularizing the land claim directly with the municipal authority. If going to court, a claimant requires four witnesses who can testify by oath on the Quran to the claimant's land occupation. When a claim is referred to a municipal authority, the claimant must declare the plot location, size and duration of occupation, and pay any tax arrears. However, many claimants cannot afford the taxes, and the land then reverts to the municipality which, in turn, can evict any occupants.

Another type of government involvement in informal land markets can be seen at work in the *quartiers populaires* (low-income areas) in ***Bujumbura***. These areas have remained largely unregulated. The government is involved through issuance of mandatory provisional titles or certificates, which grant the right to occupy a parcel of land in one of these areas, in the process providing a degree of security of tenure. These titles or certificates enable the government both to regulate these transactions and to benefit from them through mandatory fees.

In neighbouring Rwanda, the formal urban land and housing markets feature a number of deficiencies, as any other in Eastern Africa. In 2002-2003, for instance, the formal land market in ***Kigali*** would meet less than 10 per cent of demand. On top of ineffective bureaucratic procedures, high land prices and transfer costs as well as unrealistically high standards (compared with average urban income) continue to push the majority of the ***Kigali*** population into illegality. Formal leasehold land rights had been granted under the *"permit to occupy"* regime, but the government retained ownership and was entitled to re-appropriate any urban or suburban land intended for housing if not developed to regulatory standards within five years. Rwanda's 2005 Organic Land Law recognized private ownership of land and opened the way for land market privatization. However, current land and housing development policies in ***Kigali*** continue to force the vast majority (90 per cent) of residents into informal markets and illegality. New formal land administration frameworks are in direct competition with the informal systems that currently prevail in over 98 per cent of the land economy of the country. Administration fees, along with the rates and methods of land taxation, are too expensive and cumbersome for any smooth adaptation of formal markets to the realities on the ground. This situation effectively deprives public authorities from the potentially vast revenues that would accrue if a majority of Rwanda's urban population found it both affordable and convenient to resort to formal instead of informal channels for access to land.

Land Markets, Urban Form and Configurations

Urbanisation inevitably results in transformations in urban morphology. Such changes in the spatial expansion of cities normally occur through planning, zoning, land-use regulations and subsequent subdivision. However, the reality on the ground is often quite different in Eastern Africa. The reasons include lack of funding and institutional capacities, which are constrained within urban administrative boundaries and outstripped by the sheer pace and magnitude of demographic expansion. Few urban managers in Eastern Africa are in a position to control urban spatial growth. Uncontrolled sprawl resulting from informal settlements in the absence of government guidelines and enforcement is a reality in many Eastern African cities. Rather than tacitly allowing uncontrolled sprawl, urban development planning should promote compact settlement patterns, in a bid to capitalise on the agglomeration economies deriving from lower per-head costs of infrastructure networks, lower demand for public transport and more efficiently planned cities. The paragraphs below explore the relationship between land markets, urban form and urban configurations in a few Eastern African cities.

Addis Ababa

Addis Ababa is a primate city, home to more than 3.5 million. It is 14 times larger than ***Dire Dawa***, Ethiopia's second largest city. ***Addis Ababa*** is sprawling on the back of limited land use planning and a strong dependency on a single mode of transport (buses). The urban surface area more than doubled from 224 km² in 1984 to about 540 km² today. However, these figures only take in the capital as delineated by administrative boundaries, and do not account for the spatial expansion that has occurred way beyond. ***Addis Ababa*** used to be known for its social and economic homogeneity, with different socio-economic groups living in close proximity. More recently, though, urban fragmentation has become obvious with the proliferation of gated communities like

▲
Asmara, Eritrea. **©Stefan Boness/Panos Pictures**

MAP 4.3: **ASMARA'S EXPANSION, 1986-2000**

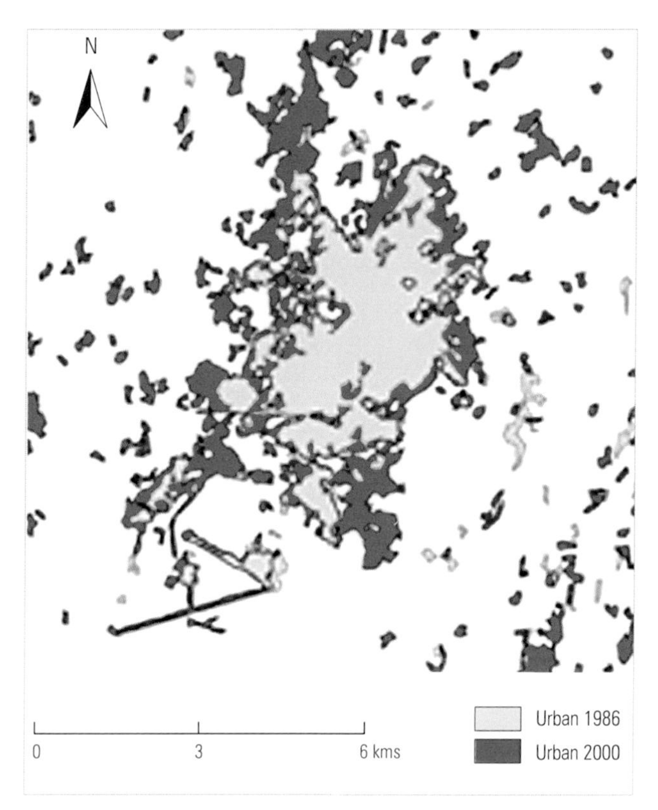

Source: Yikalo, H. Urban Land Cover Change Detection: A case study of Asmara, Eritrea, www.gisdevelopment.net

▲
Kampala, Uganda. **©Brian McMorrow**

Hayat, Sunshine, Shola, Habitat New Flower, Ropack, etc. Uncontrolled sprawl has generated further physical and social fragmentation as well as strongly delineated urban spaces.

Since land use planning is limited and urban sprawl rather significant, the morphology of Ethiopia's capital was bound to become increasingly multi-nuclear. Whereas diverse land uses should promote localised travel and transport, most of today's traffic demand is cross-sectional, forcing people to commute through several sub-centres to reach workplaces, banking or other facilities. Lack of self-sufficient sub-centres defeats the purpose of any multi-nuclear urban form. One priority for planning, therefore, would be to make sub-centres more self-contained and functional, with denser urban functions in order to reduce cross-city commutes, while at the same time re-appraising the capital's almost exclusively bus-based public transport system.

Kampala

Since independence, urbanisation and densification have continued unabated in Uganda's capital, without any control from weak urban planning. The latest Master Plan was completed in 1980 and has not been updated. Lack of an overall zoning plan has resulted in chaotic, multiple and mixed urban land uses. The city's productivity and global attractiveness are hampered by poor infrastructures and unreliable energy supplies. Urban mobility remains time-consuming and costly, especially for the poor.

The commercial and industrial spatial patterns of the city have been affected by the systems of land tenure prevailing in the whole ***Kampala*** region, as has the provision of basic residential infrastructure. Large areas of the city are placed under the *mailo* regime and remain largely unregulated, haphazardly occupied and poorly serviced if compared with the city centre and high-end residential neighbourhoods, which have long been under lease to private interests.

Asmara

Between 1986 and 2000, the surface area of Eritrea's capital expanded by more than 1,000 ha. Since independence in 1993, ***Asmara*** has experienced further changes due to demographic pressure, geographic expansion and the spatial spreading of economic activity. A time-scale series analysis shows that urban physical growth has occurred around most of Asmara, except for the north-western part. This tremendous growth in the urban built-up area and the changing spatial patterns of regional economic development has been made possible by significant improvements in infrastructure, which have driven expansion into the rural-urban fringes.

Asmara represents an urban ideal from a spatial organization point of view, one which planners all over the world should (re-)introduce in other cities. The central area features a complex mixture of uses, horizontally by plot and vertically by floor. Even in areas of one- and two-storey residential villas, small factories, workshops and retail outlets sit side by side and are all easily accessible on foot. Asmara is very much a lived-in and a liveable city, with many different layers of social and

▲
School children in Kibera slums, Nairobi. ©**Africa924/Shutterstock**

TABLE 4.5: **NAIROBI MUNICIPALITY: SLUM DWELLERS BY LOCATION AND SUB-LOCATION**

Location		Male	Female	Total	Households	Area (km²)	Density (/km²)
Kibera		206,778	177,144	383,922	121,933		
	Gatwikira	13,580	11,411	24,991	7,270	0.3	85,323
	Kibera	53,297	44,041	97,338	32,115	0.2	65,197
	Kianda	15,229	14,127	29,356	8,327	0.7	39,478
	Lindi	19,545	15,613	35,158	11,551	0.5	70,302
	Makina	12,965	12,277	25,242	7,926	0.7	38,508
	Mugumo-Ini	14,410	15,981	30,391	8,478	3.0	10,186
	Siranga	10,198	7,165	17,363	6,164	0.2	71,072
	Serangome	28,809	25,538	54,347	15,597	1.0	52,433
	Laini Saba	15,688	12,494	28,182	9,927	0.4	75,942
Embakasi		98,896	84,808	183,704	66,555		
	Mukuru Nyayo	27,277	26,026	53,303	17,357	5.9	8,983
	Mukuru kwa Njenga	71,619	58,782	130,401	49,198	12.0	16,720
Huruma		54,787	51,532	106,319	34,017		
	Huruma	37,734	34,761	72,495	23,800	0.7	103,431
	Kiamaiko	17,053	16,771	33,824	10,217	0.7	50,620
Mathare		95,866	81,450	177,316	60,798		
	Mabatini	15,286	12,974	28,260	9,809	0.4	79,740
	Mathare	11,205	9,256	20,461	6,617	0.8	25,040
	Mlango Kubwa	20,622	17,752	38,374	15,000	0.4	93,005
	Majengo	8,945	7,342	16,287	5,295	0.3	55,323
	Mathare 4A	10,211	8,565	18,776	5,627	0.2	87,209
	Mathare North	29,597	25,561	55,158	18,450	0.5	119,055
Kangemi		33,306	30,712	64,018	21,665		
	Gichagi	10,164	9,290	19,454	6,409	0.9	22,243
	Kangemi	23,142	21,422	44,564	15,256	1.6	28,298
Korogocho		21,958	19,988	41,946	12,909		
	Gitathuru	11,379	10,356	21,735	6,480	0.5	45,262
	Korogocho	5,376	5,000	10,376	3,129	0.9	46,961
	Nyayo	5,203	4,632	9,835	3,300	0.2	52,286
Viwandani		41,257	30,133	71,390	27,740		
	Landi Mawe	15,434	11,075	26,509	9,814	5.6	4,772
	Viwandani	25,823	19,058	44,881	17,926	5.7	7,859
Kahawa		7,765	8,678	16,443	5,063		
	Kongo Soweto	7,765	8,678	16,443	5,063	1.2	13,649
Total		560,613	484,445	1,045,058	350,739		

Source: 2009 Kenyan Population and Housing Census, Nairobi, August 2010.

economic interaction, most of them unplanned and informal. Streets are alive with activity. Nevertheless, incipient urban fragmentation can be sensed with the emergence of both continuous and discontinuous urban features.

Nairobi

In ***Nairobi***, urban sprawl is associated with a rapidly deteriorating quality of life that is particularly detrimental to the poorer segments' ability to meet their basic needs. Most affected are housing, water supply, sewerage and transport. Access to social services and infrastructures is dependent on income rather than population density (although there is a clear correlation between income and residential densities), with excellent standards of provision in well-off areas and next to none in high-density, low-income areas. Ethnic spatial segregation in colonial times resulted in a tri-partition of ***Nairobi***, with most Westerners residing in the north-western and western high-value areas; Asians in north-eastern areas; and Africans concentrated in densely populated areas to the east and south. Since independence, this residential segregation has been reduced in the sense that income rather than ethnicity is today's tacit criterion. Nevertheless, the ethnic partition has not been completely eradicated and these three distinct sections can still be recognized.

Nairobi requires 150,000 new housing units every year, but only 30,000 are built at best. As a result, it is mostly claimed that informal settlements and slums accommodate more than half the population in crowded, unplanned and inadequately serviced settlements. From the 2009 *Kenyan Population and Housing Census* results, however, it can be derived that the ***Nairobi*** slum population consists of a 'mere' 1,045,058 people or 33.7 per cent of a 3.1 million total population. Likewise, the census figures appear to shatter the long-standing perception that the Kibera slum neighbourhood populations add up to anything from half a million to one million people. The census data appear to set this figure at just under 400,000.

However, depending on the source, the population figures of the combined Kibera sub-locations continue to vary. The 1999 and 2009 census results suggest a 14 per cent inter-decade ***decline*** in the Kibera population from 450,000 in 1999 to 384,000 in 2009. This contrasts sharply with the area's number of registered voters for the 2005 and 2010 referendums, which recorded a half-decade (2005-2010) population ***increase*** with 23 per cent (after including those below the age of 18 years who are not eligible to vote). Moreover, it should be noted that voters' rolls do not reflect an estimated 35 percent of the total Kibera population that remains unregistered for whatever reasons.

But slum figures derived from the census should be interpreted with caution for several reasons. Firstly, the census was not an exercise in slum identification and does not enumerate incidence of insecurity of tenure. Since the internationally accepted definition of slums is based on inadequate access to safe water, sanitation and other infrastructure; poor structural quality of housing; overcrowding; and insecure residential status the census data therefore cannot give accurate figures on the number of slum dwellers. Secondly, recent claims in Kenyan papers that the total ***Nairobi*** slum population is a mere fraction of the share previously assumed appear to be based on selective interpretation of data only from major slum locations (Kibera, Embakasi, Mathare, Korogocho, Viwandani and Kahawa). Thirdly, it should also be understood that throughout Africa slum dwellers are increasingly found beyond the municipal periphery in the Greater Metropolitan Region. As ***Nairobi*** takes on a regional city scale, the wider concept of the regional city should be applied also to the count of slum inhabitants.

Indeed, formal development of residential opportunities for ***Nairobi's*** low-income populations is often proposed for the urban periphery or in areas such as ***Athi River*** and ***Mavoko,*** some 25 km away. In these locations the poor incur substantial costs, in terms of both time and money, when commuting to employment opportunities in the capital. What is often not realized is that these new outlying locations are rapidly becoming vibrant urban settlements in their own right, being spatially decentralised from the crowded metropolitan core while still within a relatively short distance from the city. Kenyan policymakers recognise that providing land to the poor is ultimately a political issue driven in many respects by concerns for distributive justice and sustainable livelihoods. However, no city was built overnight (except temporary refugee 'cities' in emergency situations). Based on relatively cheap land in the urban periphery and the expectation that ***Nairobi's*** satellite cities will, over time, provide viable and vibrant urban economies of their own, the allocation of low-income residential functions at a distance from the metropolis is preferable in the longer term, despite short-term inconveniences.

Kigali[12]

Many households were displaced across Rwanda during the 1994 conflict. Most had their assets destroyed and found themselves literally destitute after seeking a safe haven in neighbouring countries. Political stabilisation brought returnees back by the hundred thousand, causing the country's urbanisation rate to soar to 17 per cent in 2002, compared with a mere six per cent in 1991. Most returnees found themselves in direct conflict with the government and the municipality of ***Kigali*** over land tenure arrangements. In Rwanda, land is the exclusive property of the government, as individual claims to land have been erased with the loss of records during the genocide. Today, government-leased land must be developed within five years and is subject to various fees. The government is also increasingly allocating land to private companies in order to enhance revenue. Many issues arise from this approach and they have some effect on the urban system. To start with, those private companies or individuals cannot always afford the fees or build housing to agreed standards within five years, so much so that many sell off before the five years lapse and proceed to squat some other land plot. Second, the competition within the private sector has resulted to massive displacements, with evictions by both public and private institutions. Up to 96 per cent of the conflicts dealt with by Rwanda's ombudsman are land-related. The result of these tensions over the formal land market is none other than a proliferation of informal developments on under-serviced land.

The Shortcomings of Conventional Urban Land Administration and Management

In Eastern African cities, a host of legal and administrative hurdles hinder the proper operation of both formal and informal property markets. Most importantly, market information is pitifully scarce. This reflects the fact that only a fraction of land transactions are documented and registered. Moreover, lack of urban inventories makes it difficult to forecast trends in future demand for land. Another commonplace constraint is the plethora of professionals involved in land transactions (lawyers, valuers, surveyors, planners, etc.) who all add to costs and delays. One-stop shops would enable local authorities or government departments to cut procedures short and lower transfer costs.

In Kenyan cities, securing approvals for subdivisions and change of user is particularly cumbersome as it involves multiple government institutions. An application for an urban subdivision may take 29 months from formal submission with the Nairobi City Council until sub-titles are issued by the Commissioner for Lands. Similarly slow processes apply to applications for lease extensions.

The lengthy procedures and high costs associated with formal transfers are also the norm in ***Dar es Salaam***, while in Ethiopia (bureaucratic procedure and corruption aside) land transactions are severely affected by the law on power of eminent domain (Proclamation 455/2005) which only provides for compensation for improvements (buildings and structures) to land, ignoring both increased land values and length of any remaining lease period. The law also negatively affects leasehold transferability, as it only allows transfers made as surety or collateral rather than selling the leasehold interest.

In Rwanda, registration of title to land is compulsory. Nevertheless, any land rights acquired by sale, inheritance or under customary or indigenous practices (representing 98 per cent of all land holdings) remain largely undocumented- and therefore informal due to associated costs and lengthy procedures.

In Burundi, poor consultation, minimal consensus-building at the policymaking stage and limited public awareness of land policy has resulted in a confused land tenure situation. Provisions on land ownership, access and transfer as spelled out in the Land Code are barely understood and therefore hardly implemented. Less than five per cent of the land is registered and oral traditions predominate as far as ownership is concerned.

In Uganda, up to 49 procedural steps combine with the high costs of tenure regularisation for informal settlements effectively to prevent the urban poor from converting customary to formal leasehold tenure. However, few things better illustrate the impact of confused mixed forms of land tenure on urban land market transactions than the *mailo* tenure system in ***Kampala***, as discussed in Box 4.5.

▲
Kigali, Rwanda. ©**Ole Doetinchem**

BOX 4.5: **HOW KAMPALA'S *MAILO* LANDS THWART URBAN DEVELOPMENT**

In Kampala, the formal land market is constrained by structural factors like complex tenure systems, absence of a coherent policy, unrealistically high planning standards and regulations, incomplete registration systems and taxation regimes and lack of information, as well as by socioeconomic factors like speculation and corruption.

Currently, 52 per cent of Kampala is held under *mailo* tenure, 30 per cent is privately leased public land administered by the City Council (KCC), 7 per cent is owned by the government and 11 per cent by institutions. Most of the land in Kampala suburbs is also under *mailo* tenure. The dual system of ownership and the unplanned, disorganised settlement patterns on *mailo* lands have had a significant effect on the development of an efficient land market in the Kampala region.

Before an owner can sell or develop *mailo* land, tenants must be compensated or resettled (if they have occupied the plot unchallenged for more than 12 years). Tenants are recognized as 'customary owners' and have rights to sell or mortgage the land but only in consultation with the *mailo* land title deed holder. Likewise, this title deed holder cannot sell the land until the customary owners are adequately compensated. However, the tenants (customary owners) cannot sell the land as they have no clear title. With little vacant public land remaining in Kampala and much of the *mailo* land occupied by tenants, there is in effect next to no plot of substantial size available in Kampala for further residential development.

Acquiring land on leasehold terms from the City Council is equally cumbersome and may take as long as five years, largely on account of political interference, bureaucratic procedures and inevitable bribery to keep an application moving through the system.

Moreover, since urban land is scarce, the average price of a ¼ acre (1,050 m^2) in up-market Kampala is equivalent to US $120,000, compared with US $60,000 at the lower end of the market. Further out of the city (15-20km), larger tracts of unserviced *mailo* land sell for US $25,000 per acre (4,200 m^2). Therefore, construction of new urban housing estates at prices affordable to low- and middle-income groups has become virtually impossible.

Sources :Kituuka (2005); Giddings(2009)

Informal Settlements as a Response to Land Market Deficiencies

In practice, where formal land delivery systems fail or fall short, the market finds a way to meet demand. Failure of land reform to deliver affordable urban land in a timely manner and in sufficient quantities for predominantly low-income households has inevitably created informal land markets.

Eastern Africa's experience - particularly in Ethiopia, Kenya, Tanzania and Uganda, where more information is available - shows that informal land market operations fill significant governance voids. Informality helps overcome the inability of formal markets to provide for the huge demand for affordable urban plots, irrespective of the prevailing land tenure system in the country. The region's informal urban land markets operate, on the one extreme, in places where universal private tenure prevails, like in Kenya, and, at the other end of the spectrum, in cities where public authorities struggle to maintain control over subdivisions, title deed issuance and unauthorized construction in the face of increasingly prevalent illegal subdivision of privately or communally held land, as in Rwanda and Uganda. In other cases, civil servants have effectively 'privatized' formal land supply, as has happened with Tanzanian 'ten-cells' and *mitaa* land approvals.

In all cases, though, and however informal the prevailing system may appear in legal terms, land transaction processes are well-structured and governed by generally understood communal norms and procedures, and as such can play a major role in overcoming the delivery failure of formal urban land markets. Commonly endorsed and respected grassroots institutions and procedures allow for highly decentralised access to urban land, with a significant degree of security of tenure, and with prompt redress and arbitration procedures in case of disputes.

The vast potential of community regulated urban land transactions and settlement development is much underestimated and little understood by the public sector. Rather than writing off informal procedure as illegitimate, Eastern African nations should consider institutionalizing socially regulated informal land and housing markets. Unlike formal markets, they offer pragmatic, efficient and low-cost procedures that could significantly alter the slum and informal settlement situation in many of the region's cities. Recognising and institutionalising community-based land and housing management could reduce management and administration burdens on municipalities in a cost-effective manner. It would further allow for decentralised tenure and title registration as the foundations for subsequent pragmatic public sector interventions in informal settlements with regard to spatial lay-out, minimum allowable plot size and public access, as well as service provision in cooperative partnership with the grassroots institutions that micro-manage socially regulated land transactions.

Ethiopia

Under Ethiopia's informal supply system, land can be accessed without planning or documentation. Tranfer of unregistered urban land is a function of personal connections. Transactions are confirmed by simple agreements which may be endorsed by local administration (*kebele*) or by power of attorney. Although informal land allocation is widespread and the main factor behind land squatting, unplanned settlements and slums, about 90 per cent of these allocations represent informal subdivision of formal land holdings. Institutionalising these informal procedures would not just act as an incentive to land registration and facilitate municipalities' spatial and other interventions, it could also restore some of the municipal tax revenue which marginalised, ineffective formal and informal markets are unable to generate.

▲
Kampala, Uganda. ©**Duncan Purvey/iStockphoto**

Tanzania

Informal access to urban land in Tanzania can be secured through three distinct channels: (a) land invasion (quite limited in actual scale); (b) allocation by local leaders, elders or acknowledged owners, for a token fee; and, frequently (c) land is purchased in unplanned areas from an acknowledged owner and registered with a local leader or the local branch of a political party.

Informal market transactions are witnessed by relatives, friends and community leaders; legitimacy is derived from social recognition that allows redress and arbitration by community leaders in case of conflicts. Informal as these procedures may be, they help overcoming the failures of formal markets as experienced by the lower-income segments of the population. Since ward officials and dispute resolution committees are part of formal government and linked with the formal judiciary, informal land access has emerged as a recognised land regularisation sub-system with linkages to the formal land registration frameworks.

Uganda

With about 85 per cent of ***Kampala's*** 1.8 million inhabitants living in informal settlements and slums, massive failure of the formal market to deliver land for low-income residents could not appear more clearly. Many titled land subdivisions and transfers are not reflected in the land registry due to the high costs attached. Registration is a precondition for the use

MAP 4.4: **DAR ES SALAAM: FORMAL AND INFORMAL HOUSING (2002)**

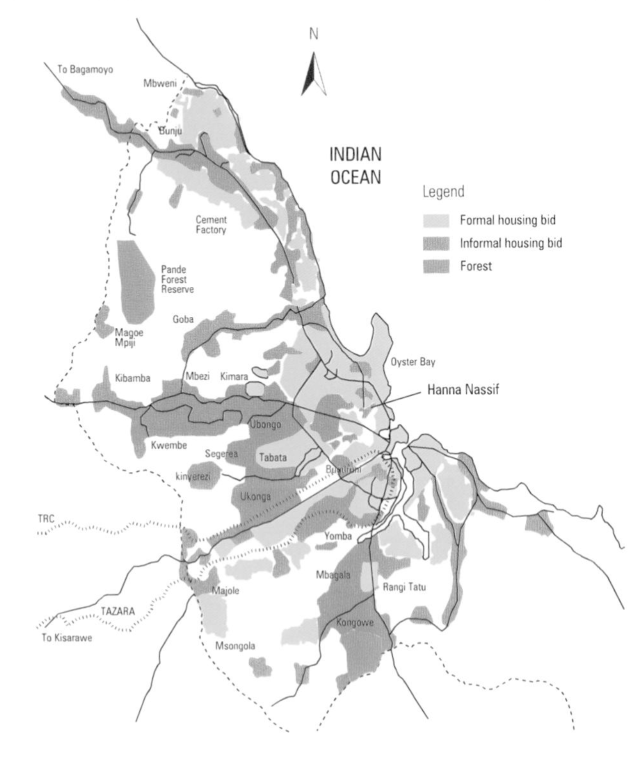

Source: Kimani. M. Investigating the Effects of Property Rights Formalisation on Property Market in Informal Settlements: The Case of Dar es Salaam City, Tanzania. MSc Thesis, IIGISEO, Enschede, 2007.

MAP 4.5: **MOMBASA INFORMAL SETLLEMENTS**

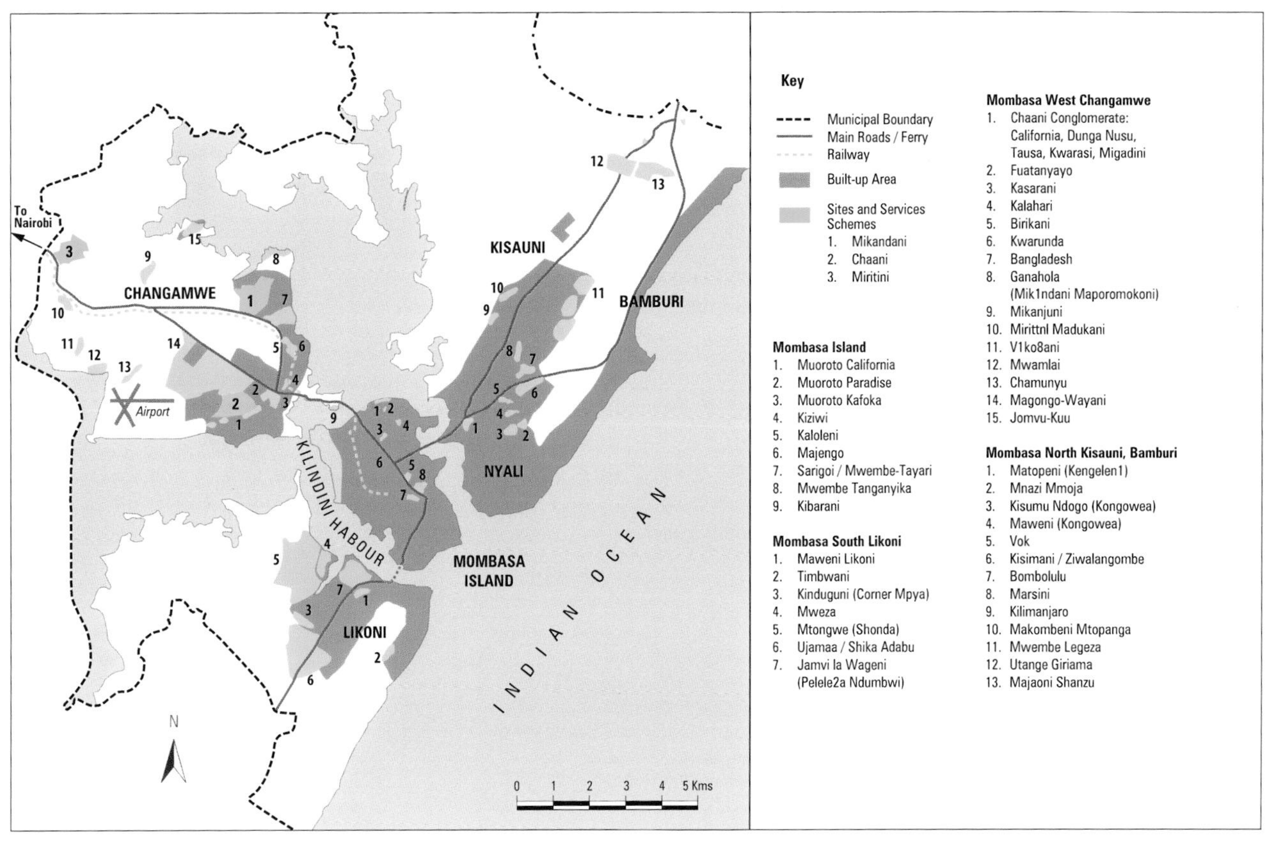

Source: Janice Edwards.

BOX 4.6: **HOW MOMBASA'S 'SWAHILI LAND MARKET' PLAYS AGAINST TENANTS**

Owners of land along the 16 km Mombasa coastline were issued with freehold titles under the Land Titles Act 1908. Any land not claimed became 'Crown land' for allocation through the formal market system. As in nearly all Kenyan cities, land in Mombasa is now mostly in private hands. Local land tenure has been influenced by the Sunni-Arab legal system, whereby third parties are allowed to own chattels (movable possessions) or crops on another person's land, sometimes in return for a rent or crop sharing. Such land users are called 'tenants-at-will' and can be evicted at short notice without compensation for improvements, although they can take the crop and chattels with them.

In the 1920s, the colonial government introduced town planning in Mombasa and in the process displaced some people who were to give way for access roads. The Municipal Council devised a 'village layout' system that allowed for large parcels to be subdivided into 120x240 ft plots for temporary accommodation for the displaced. Since the system was to ensure later re-development with higher quality housing, only temporary shelter was allowed. However, it took the authorities some time before they facilitated housing for an expanding population, and 'village layout' plots became the norm rather than the exception.

Titled land owners continued to subdivide plots for documented letting to 'tenants-at-will' who paid monthly rent. The land owner would sign documentation on behalf of the tenants for approval by the municipal council, showing the location of the plot in the overall subdivision layout. The transaction involved a simple sale agreement witnessed by the village headman (*mzee wa kijiji*) or a power of attorney witnessed by an advocate. Although tenants were given receipts for monthly land rents, they had no formal registration document. Today, more than 50 per cent of Mombasa's population lives on land accessed through what became known as the 'Swahili land market' and in accommodation referred to as 'Swahili houses' that typically provides single-room shelter.

Since much of the land in the 'Swahili land market' is available under unrecorded transactions, government agencies have no records and, consequently, act as though these markets do not exist. Should an owner decide to transfer land to a third party, the new owner can give tenants one month's notice without any compensation for improvements. With sharply rising land prices, this is not an unlikely scenario. In the Mombasa areas of Kisauni, Magongo and Likoni, for instance, a non-titled 1,000 m^2 plot was selling in 2000 for 180,000 Kenyan shillings (KES) (or US $2,200) compared with KES 300,000 (US $3,700) for titled land in the same area. These prices have since soared with titled land in Likoni going for KES 600,000 (US $7,400) and for KES 750,000 (US $9,260) and KES 1million (US $12,340), in Kisauni and Magongo respectively.

Source: Gatabaki-Kamau et al., 2000

of title deeds as loan collateral, but this is unpopular: indeed, this is perceived as a promise to forfeit the property under pressure from excessive interest rates on the loan. Moreover, successive subdivisions have shrunk many plots below legal minimum size, making formal registration more complex.

Today, informal urban land supply mechanisms are slowly gaining recognition in Uganda for their pragmatic approach. More specifically, public authorities are realising that the costs, delivery times and security of tenure associated with informal systems are suitable not just to the urban poor, but also to local authorities, which can adapt governance and regulatory modalities accordingly, in the process alleviating the burden of municipal land adjudication. The informal system is simple, well understood and adhered to and affordable; on top of this, it does not appear to be all that different from the formal urban land market as it operates in ***Kampala***, where many titled land transactions are not reflected in the land registry. All of this would suggest that, with proper steering from formal urban land authorities, the informal sector may pave the way to self-regulation of land markets in cities.

Kenya

In the wake of a near complete absence of vacant government-owned land in Kenyan cities, the following land supply sources have emerged: (a) subdivisions of titled land; (b) public development projects; and (c) transactions on untitled land. Subdivision of titled lands often renders ownership informal, as most resulting subdivision plots are not titled. Under this format, peri-urban land is bought by a group and each member is issued with a share certificate. The land is then cut up and occupied without the mandatory subdivision approval that would require proper plan layouts, cadastral surveying and provision of infrastructure and matching costly local municipal council standards. Unregistered selling of share certificates continues unabated, only witnessed by the officials of the group. Thus, like squatter settlements (illegally occupied and subdivided lands), many settlements (like the Zimmerman Estate in ***Nairobi***) cannot be titled only because they fail to meet the criteria required. As a result, formally titled land becomes classified as informal due to the physical developments thereon.

Transactions on public development projects include site-and-services or tenant-purchase schemes. Sales are carried out on the market using legal instruments such as power of attorney and may or may not be registered as *documents*, though not as land transfers. Examples in ***Nairobi*** include the National Housing Corporation 20-year tenant-purchase scheme at Nyayo High-rises, or the numerous site-and-service projects that have not been titled to date. These site-and-services plots nevertheless continue to change hands without registration.

Transactions on untitled land involve public land (way leaves, open spaces, road reserves, etc.) for which provincial authorities or council officials issue quasi-legal letters allowing 'temporary' occupation. The allottees who built structures can sell these in the informal market, witnessed by the authorities that issued the letters of allocation in the first place, or by village committees as, for instance, is the case of the Korogocho squatter settlement in ***Nairobi***.

The Political Economy of Urban Land

The relationship between land and political power is an inextricable one, as is the one between land and neo-liberal market rule. Eastern African countries are emerging from a recent past where land was either customary or owned by a colonial government. When countries became independent, these two systems of ownership continued side by side. Urban land was generally owned by government and leased to individual users to facilitate development controls, land use efficiency through planning, and collection of revenue through taxation. Public urban land allocation through the formal land markets was intended as a significant source of income for local authorities. However, things did not work that way in many of the region's countries for several reasons, including:

- Lack of capacity among local authorities with regard to participatory planning, zoning, subdivisions and development control;
- Widespread corruption among officers responsible for managing government-owned land;
- Lack of adequate, accurate and updated urban land information;
- Lack of forward planning to provide adequate supplies of land at appropriate locations and at affordable prices, a deficiency that has encouraged sharp rises in urban land prices; speculation and use of 'short-cuts' to acquire land; and
- Absence of viable legal redress options, including land restitution or compensation for undue process related to land and economic activities.

Well-connected political and economic elites have taken control of urban land, restricting equitable access for a broad array of economic uses and occupations. The non-connected majorities have systematically been excluded from formal access to urban land by cumbersome administrative processes, leaving them no option but informality with significantly different degrees of security of tenure. The resultant risky nature of informally accessed land and housing has encouraged investment in poorly-built housing in informal settlements and slums.

Informally accessed land implies loss of municipal revenue, including land transfer fees, rates or land tax. Worse still, urban land, which is a finite resource, is not always used as efficiently as it could – far from it. An effective system must be found which can deliver adequate amounts of land in a timely and cost-effective way.

Alternatives can be found in just about every Eastern African city to make better use of urban land as a municipal revenue source. For example, next to the geographical centre of ***Nairobi*** lies a former large railway yard with an eclectic selection of decommissioned rolling stock nominally serving as a railway museum. Immediately adjacent to the central business district, this functional hole in the heart of the metropolis is, perhaps, one of the worst examples of foregone spatial intervention opportunities. The value of this extremely well-located parcel of land is immense and careful redevelopment would generate much-needed revenue for the city council. Other large cities in Eastern Africa should critically review under-used urban parcels and bring to market any land which historic functional allocation can and should no longer be sustained today. Such functions include military compounds, derelict river frontages and other underused prime urban sites.

In Tanzania, the government has reformed local authority revenue collection, abolishing ineffective instruments and streamlining municipal rate systems (rate structures and collection procedures). Reforms also include central government compensation of local authorities' revenue shortfalls[13].

Urban property taxation varies significantly across Eastern African cities. For example, Tanzania will tax only buildings, and Kenya only land. Uganda makes tax assessments based on annual rental value, and Kenya on capital-based unimproved site value. Tanzania supports use of market capital value, and building valuation is based on replacement cost.

Cities in the East African Community feature similar tax collection and enforcement procedures. Penalties for late payment of rates range from 1 to 3 per cent per month in some cities.[14] To recover outstanding debt, local authorities are allowed to attach rents and go to court for charging orders on personal property to recover unpaid taxes, the alternative being to place a charge on the property. Although every Eastern African country has a variety of taxation instruments at its disposal, they are seldom used. This can have to do with ineffectual tax administration[15] and management, which make it difficult to track land owners and absentee landlords and, as a result, collection of rates is limited both in scale and scope.

New Tools for Land Administration and Management

At the moment, most Eastern African countries are modernising land administration and management systems. Kenya, for instance, has completed its land policy revision and also adopted a new constitution which allows for many types of land intervention. In Ethiopia, decentralisation of land information is under way. Generally, however, Eastern African countries feature poor land administration and information systems, although these are critical for market efficiency, and particularly to prevent unlawful public land manipulation for private gain.

High-precision tools like electronic land records based on geographic information systems (GIS) are readily available, cost-effective and especially desirable for decentralised access to land information. Many practical innovations can help improve broad-based access to land information, including:

- civil society- or community-led enumeration to collect land data on informal settlements;
- Geodetic systems using information collected by the US space agency;
- Land/geographic information systems to help create data frameworks;
- High-accuracy, off-the-shelf global positioning systems (GPS) for use by local communities; and
- One-stop shops for urban land transacations.

Moreover, land policy processes should be consultative, inclusive and participatory in order to ensure consensus and to reduce the potential for confusion or conflict due to dual tenure systems in urban areas. Recognition of the positive aspects of community-based land management - the current foundation of informal urban land markets - should be promoted to guide the transition to full residential tenure regularisation.

Rwanda and Ethiopia already recognise existing customary interests in land, provided that they convert to statutory leases whenever transactions take place. Policymakers should learn from the informal processes that handle the bulk of Eastern Africa's urban land transactions as a starting point for reform. Learning from informal market operations is the only feasible way forward if land management and administration processes and procedures in East African cities are to be adjusted to the realities on the ground.

▲
Dar es Salaam, Tanzania. **©Lance Bellers/iStockphoto**

4.4
The Geography of Climate Change

Local Authorities and Adaptation to Climate Change

Local authorities in Eastern Africa are lagging when it comes to addressing the challenges of climate change, and hardly any have policies or programmes in place. This contrasts with national governments, many of whom now are involved through the United Nations Framework Convention on Climate Change (UNFCCC). The governments of Burundi, Ethiopia, Rwanda, the Seychelles, Tanzania and Uganda have developed National Adaptation Plans of Action with support from Framework Convention services. Kenya has developed a National Climate Change Strategy of its own. Ethiopia and Tanzania have also developed various adaptation programmes.

There is, however, not much present in terms of *urban* adaptation strategies. Oxfam, the World Bank, and UN-HABITAT have all commissioned studies in order better to understand the effects of climate change on cities. UN-HABITAT is now exploring urban climate change-related mitigation and adaptation. In Eastern Africa, a pilot study has been undertaken in ***Kampala***, but the recommendations have not yet been implemented. While awareness has been enhanced in a number of other Ugandan cities, many are yet to develop their own adaptation and mitigation strategies.

Current measures to deal with extreme weather events in Eastern African cities are basic at best. These piecemeal though positive initiatives cannot deal with climate disasters like extreme flooding, drought, fires, strong winds, etc. The effects of climate change appear to be increasingly destructive for urban infrastructures and systems in Eastern Africa. In 2009, 31 mayors from various African countries endorsed the 'Nairobi Declaration' in a bid to enhance integration of climate change interventions into their urban development plans. But here too, the recommendations have yet to result in policies and practical programmes. With a proper framework,

▲
Flood waters near Jamame, Southern Somalia. **©Manoocher Deghati/IRIN**

ongoing initiatives should be integrated into cohesive urban climate change adaptation programmes; they include clearing of urban drains; providing flood controls before the onset of seasonal rains; improved water and sanitation in urban informal settlements; and the development and maintenance of urban open spaces.

Climate Change and Cities: How much do we know?

Meteorological stations in several Eastern African countries provide basic weather information and climatic data. However, this information in not used optimally, partly because it has been specifically designed for the aviation and agricultural sectors, rather than for urban managers.

National meteorological institutions are linked with regional and international organizations that work on various aspects of local and regional climate. In Eastern Africa, one such institution is the Climate Prediction and Application Centre (ICPAC) which operates in ***Nairobi*** under the aegis of the subregional Intergovernmental Authority on Development (IGAD). The facility focuses mainly on drought monitoring, although its mandate includes provision of information on climate change disaster management for Burundi, Djibouti, Eritrea, Ethiopia, Kenya, Rwanda, Somalia, Sudan, Tanzania and Uganda[16]. The information, though available, is seldom used to manage or mitigate the effects of climate change on Eastern African cities.

The Intergovernmental Panel on Climate Change (IPCC) Fourth Assessment Report (the 'Physical Science Basis'), is a major resource for climate change information on Eastern African cities[17]. The report includes regional climate change projections and reviews anticipated effects, vulnerabilities and suggestions for adaptation. The report also provides information on regional and sector-specific effects. It includes systemic information on climatic phenomena, as well as their effects on agriculture, food security, biodiversity, safe water and health. The report finds that Africa's low capacity for adaptation is worsened by the high incidence of poverty. Authors further state that:

'...it is very likely that climate change will make sustainable development more difficult [for African countries], particularly as measured by their progress toward achieving Millennium Development Goals for the middle of the century. Climate change will erode nations' capacities to achieve Goals calibrated in terms of reducing poverty and otherwise improving equity by 2050, particularly in Africa...' [18]

Sustainable development would reduce the vulnerability of many African countries. The Organization for Economic Cooperation and Development (OECD) has reviewed the climate change vulnerability of low-elevation cities in Africa[19]. Of the capital cities in Eastern Africa, ***Dar es Salaam***, ***Djibouti*** and ***Victoria City*** stand to be the most severely affected by rises in sea level, although the capital of the Seychelles would be less vulnerable due to its proactive policies.

National adaptation strategies to climate change are quite similar across Eastern Africa. Most are drawn from the National Adaptation Plans of Action (NAPAs) sponsored by UNFCCC. The strategies in the region aim mainly at developing economic resilience. Infrastructure is one of the

▲
Lamu Island, Kenya. ©**William Davies/iStockphoto**

▲
Low cost housing in Victoria, Mahé, Seychelles. ©**Sapsiwai/Shutterstock**

sectors that are short-listed for interventions through climate change adaptation. Capital expenditure on improved physical infrastructure in critical areas such as water resources would reduce economic and social pressures on city residents. However, most of the current initiatives are in the agricultural and forestry sectors, focusing on land use changes rather than urban areas.

The Seychelles

In the Seychelles, the main strategy for climate change adaptation pursues the right balance between development and environmental protection. A growing population and increasing demands by the tourism industry are putting under strain an environment that is home to scores of birds, reptiles and plants native only to the Seychelles. In 1990, ***Victoria City*** became the first African city to draw up a 10-year environmental management plan. The archipelago features the highest proportion of environmentally protected land in the world, i.e., more than 50 per cent of its total surface area. However, achieving the right balance between development and the environment presents small island states with tough challenges.[20] ***Victoria City*** is low-lying and vulnerable to the effects of climate change, especially storm surge flooding and sea-level rise. However, the Seychelles authorities have developed dedicated policies for protection against sea-level rise and adaptation for the poorer segments of the population. An example of an adaptation initiative is the land reclamation project on Mahé, the largest island, to provide additional space for housing. Mahé is home to 90 per cent of the islands' population of 85,000.[21] One of the Seychelles' strategies is to encourage property developers to set up independent trust funds to finance environmental projects in local communities.

Eritrea

Climate change also poses serious challenges to Eritrea. The country's development priorities include agriculture, livestock keeping, forest conservation, water resource management, coastal and marine environmental protection and safeguarding public health. Eritrea has developed a National Adaptation Plan of Action (NAPA) consistent with ongoing national strategies, plans and frameworks for sustainable development. The resulting adaptation projects are closely linked with national plans regarding poverty reduction, improved food security, disaster preparedness and prevention strategies, as well as promotion of sustainable development. In terms of policies and as part of NAPA, Eritrea looks to mainstream adaptation to climate change into national development, including through sector-specific policies.

Burundi

Burundi's strategies for climate change adaptation focus mostly on current disruptions in rainfall and hydrometric series in most parts of the country. Rainfall deficits have compounded aridity, significantly drying up wetlands, rivers

BOX 4.7: **KAMPALA LEADS THE CLIMATE CHANGE INITIATIVE IN EASTERN AFRICA**

As the recognised engines of national economic development, cities today are also major contributors to local environmental deterioration and pollution as well as to the attendant worldwide climate change and its challenging effects. Being part of the problem, cities are also part of the solution, and this is the rationale behind the *Cities and Climate Change Initiative* which UN-HABITAT launched in early 2009 at the request of its Governing Council.

The Initiative provides city authorities with the expertise, policy advice, methodologies and information they need to meet the daunting challenges. The newly-created Sustainable Urban Development Network (SUD-Net) complements these efforts, including with exchange of best practice. The project operates in partnership with the UN Development (UNDP) and Environment (UNEP) Programmes and a wide range of other relevant organisations.

No region in the world is more exposed to the effects of climate change than Africa. Therefore, it was natural for two African cities – Maputo, the capital of Mozambique, and Kampala, the capital of Uganda – to feature among the four 'pilot' conurbations that have been selected to launch the initiative in the developing world. Indeed, both cities provide an apt illustration of the typical threats climate change is posing for conurbations in the developing world.

Kampala is home to 1.2 million along the shores of Lake Victoria. The city is already experiencing increased rainfall. Surface run-off and fragile drainage systems have increased the vulnerability of infrastructure, housing, social services and livelihoods. Since these effects are not felt with the same intensity across the conurbation, area-specific vulnerability analysis provides better clues on mitigation and adaptation measures. Pollution from domestic biomass fuels and increased motorised transportation add to pollution, and therefore energy efficiency is a significant concern. Low-income settlements are located in high-risk areas with poor sanitation and prone to flooding, with inadequate waste management contaminating water resources and run-off weakening hill slopes. Encroachment on fragile ecosystems and blockage of the drainage systems has increased the occurrence of flash floods, with serious health consequences.

Against this challenging background, the initial assessment carried out under the Initiative has made the following three main recommendations: (i) establishing a national/city climate change network comprised of various stakeholders addressing climate change; (ii) enhancing the awareness and capacities of the Kampala City Council with regard to climate change mitigation and adaptation; and (iii) increasing the synergies and links between national and local climate change policies and programmes through consultations and policy dialogue.

Various demonstration projects including city 'greening', alternative energy, clean wood use, climate-proofing of infrastructure and energy-efficient urban transport systems are now under way in Kampala.

Source: UN-HABITAT, Cities and Climate Change – Initial lessons from UN-HABITAT. Nairobi: UN-HABITAT 2009.

and lakes. Torrential rains and extreme temperatures also go to highlight the country's ever-growing vulnerability to climate change. Declining agricultural production, associated loss of human lives, repetitive floods, landslides, increased risks of diseases and loss of biodiversity, etc., are among the consequences of climate change in Burundi. The government's commitment to addressing the issue is evidenced in the 2007 National Adaptation Plan for Action, which rationale is to identify immediate and urgent steps toward adaptation and mainstreaming them in the country's development strategies. Human and institutional capacity building is also included in the Plan.

Tanzania

In ***Dar es Salaam*** adaptation strategies to climate change are designed at different levels, depending on the groups involved. They are largely in line with the National Adaptation Plan of Action. A dedicated implementing authority has been established and budgets allocated for some adaptation schemes. A major shortcoming is that adaptation efforts are not yet integrated into other national development programmes. In the energy sector, Tanzanian parliamentarians have recommended that the government look for alternative sources of energy and reduce dependence on climate-sensitive hydro-electric power. However, most of the poor in ***Dar es Salaam*** still rely on charcoal for primary energy needs.

Water stress (i.e., excessive demand) and flooding worsen sanitation conditions in low-income areas. The ***Dar es Salaam*** Municipal Council has privatized water supply and waste management to improve service delivery, which, has indeed largely happened. However, challenges remain as better access to adequate water and sanitation services largely keeps eluding the poorer segments of the population.

Somalia

Climate change information on ***Mogadishu*** is scarce. However, in a 2005 report, on the '*State of the Environment in Somalia*' [22], the United Nations Environment Programme (UNEP) highlighted some of the country's climate-change related problems. ***Mogadishu*** is vulnerable to recurrent droughts, which come as symptoms of complex inter-linkages between five distinct factors: population growth, dwindling resilience of the fragile eco-system, environmental degradation, weather cycles, and the absence of agricultural or other type of rural development.

Across Eastern Africa, some opportunities to combine mitigation of the effects of climate change with local environmental improvements can already be found. A 2003 survey showed that 25 per cent of Kenyan children in areas without waste collection suffered from diarrhoea, compared with 10 per cent in areas where waste was collected[23]. In Ethiopia, incidences of respiratory diseases are six times higher in areas where waste remains uncollected[24]. Box 4.8 outlines urban waste management problems on the East African island of Madagascar.

BOX 4.8: **HOLISTIC URBAN INTERVENTIONS IN ANTANANARIVO**

▲
Antananarivo, Madagascar. **©Mogens Trolle/Shutterstock**

Together with growing numbers of visitors and changing consumption patterns, demographic expansion results in greater volumes of solid waste in Madagascar's capital Antananarivo. Services are not up to the challenge as only 25 per cent of Antananarivo's solid waste is collected with only a fraction recycled. Substandard waste collection encourages illegal dumping along the roadside and on beaches, while lack of suitable landfill sites is a challenge to waste processing. Open waste burning is commonplace, with the attendant threats to air quality and public health.

Water quality comes under threat when solid waste is dumped in or near surface or groundwater resources (UNEP, 1998). Intensive animal rearing, especially goats around urban areas, is a further issue for the environment and human health. Contamination and eutrophication (over-fertilization causing a surfeit of algae) of water courses lower the ability of the natural systems to provide vital functions such as water quality regulation and nutrient cycling, while at the same time affecting biodiversity and providing breeding sites for parasites and bacteria.

However, the Municipality of Antananarivo has decided to meet the challenge under a holistic approach, with help from Cities Alliance and UN-HABITAT. The *City Development Strategy for Antananarivo, Infrastructure Development, Urban Services Improvement and City Poverty Strategy* sets out four major objectives: (i) infrastructure improvement; (ii) urban poverty reduction; (iii) crime prevention for urban safety and; and (iv) formulation of a metropolitan-wide institutional and fiscal framework. The strategy provides decision-makers and financial institutions with a medium- and long-term vision of metropolitan development and a framework for short- and medium-term water drainage, waste water and solid waste management interventions. Neighbourhood-scale strategic plans focus on basic services and improved infrastructure as well as the socio-economic integration of underprivileged and vulnerable groups. The objective of Component (iii) is to coordinate and develop schemes under the existing strategic and action plan for urban safety. All these are envisaged as components in a new institutional and fiscal framework to be developed for the Antananarivo metropolitan area.

The strategy and action plan have been adopted and institutional arrangements for implementation are now under review. Simultaneously, a metropolitan transportation strategy is under development as part of a separately funded programme by another donor. So far, 16 neighbourhoods have developed strategic plans, and the Municipality has adopted a methodology and a framework for replication. A new municipal department for support to local and partner initiatives has been created. Recommendations for a municipal strategy for housing and land tenure regularization are forthcoming. However, legislative reform has not yet been completed.

This example from Madagascar shows how sector-specific problems can give rise to mutually supportive city or metropolitan-wide interventions with multiple objectives through holistic approaches.

Sources: UN-HABITAT, City Development Strategy for Antananarivo, Infrastructure Development, Urban Services Improvement and City Poverty Strategy.

BOX 4.9: **EASTERN AFRICA AND THE NILE WATER DILEMMA**

▲
The River Nile, Egypt. **©Doctor Jools/Shutterstock**

Egypt was granted near total control over the use of all Nile waters under a 1929 agreement signed by the United Kingdom on behalf of its Eastern African colonies. The agreement was reaffirmed in a 1959 treaty that guaranteed access for Egypt and Sudan to 55.5 and 14.5 billon m^3 respectively, out of a total annual volume of 84bn m^3. The 6,695 km-long River Nile, together with its upstream tributaries, wetlands and lakes, currently sustains life for at least 300 million people in an area sprawling over 3.1 million km^2 in 10 riparian nations (Burundi, DR Congo, Egypt, Eritrea, Ethiopia, Kenya, Rwanda, Sudan, Tanzania and Uganda). All these nations have fast-growing populations and face increasing competition for water between cities, manufacturing, agriculture and energy generation. Most Nile basin countries have not yet taken advantage of the potential the river holds in terms of urban water supplies, hydropower generation, and irrigation; but with climate change further contributing to regional water scarcity, access to the waters of the Nile and its tributaries has now become a factor of significant regional tension.

The 1929 treaty prohibits any activities that could threaten the volume of water reaching Egypt, giving the country's government the right to inspect and veto water extractions along the entire length of the Nile and its tributaries. From independence onwards, Eastern African nations have expressed their discontent with the treaty and have lobbied for a review. On the one hand, Egypt and Sudan are largely deserts and oppose any new treaty that would reduce their historic powers of control and water shares. On the other hand, several Eastern African riparian countries argue that they were not parties to the 1929 and 1959 arrangements and consider them as outdated vestiges of a long-bygone colonial era.

A significant share of the 900 million people worldwide without access to adequate supplies of safe drinking water can be found in Africa, and particularly in water-stressed Northern and Eastern Africa. Fresh-water shortages are already worsening under pressure from rapid demographic growth and competition among thirsty cities, manufacturing and agriculture; they will be further exacerbated by changing rainfall patterns and climate variability. Moreover, with the forthcoming 2011 referendum on the status of Southern Sudan, an 11th riparian nation may have to be taken into account in any redistribution of rights to the Nile. The world's longest river holds great potential for social-economic development, but the bulk of the populations living in the basin are still waiting for energy generation and irrigation schemes that would boost modern farming. Short of a new protocol on Nile waters, extreme poverty is bound to continue in the basin.

For more than a decade, Nile Basin countries have tried for a new framework agreement to manage the waters and, in 1999, they agreed on the Nile Basin Initiative, a transitional arrangement on negotiated, equitable use of water resources. The shares of Egypt and Sudan will almost inevitably be reduced if all riparian nations must have equal or proportional access. However, even after 10 years of intense negotiations and promises to agree on a deal no later than 2010, Egypt and Sudan are still reluctant to relinquish their preferential rights; these amount to a combined 94 per cent leaving only six per cent of Nile waters for the eight other countries. Under the current treaties, these eight countries cannot embark on any Nile-based, large-scale hydropower generation or irrigation projects unless Egypt consents.

In June 2010, Ethiopia, Kenya, Rwanda, Tanzania and Uganda agreed on a new pact for fairer sharing of the Nile waters and the removal of Egypt's right of veto, with Burundi, the Democratic Republic of Congo and Eritrea considering following suit. But Egypt's President Hosni Mubarak – who has threatened in the past to go to war with any country interfering with the Nile – has so far refused to join the pact, claiming that protecting the Nile water supplies is an issue of national security for his country. Egypt described as 'provocative' the Ethiopian inauguration of a hydroelectric dam on Tana River, a tributary, in May 2010 and tension over access to the Nile is becoming one of the most prominent diplomatic and security issues in the region. However, in July 2010, Egypt made undisclosed offers of financial support to upstream countries as part of its diplomatic and political efforts to ease the by-then raging controversy.

It is becoming increasingly clear that if water is left out of the equation, there can be no long-term way of meeting the combined effects of rapid demographic growth, the need to provide domestic food and water security for Nile Basin nations, competing claims over access to water, and climate change. On 28 July 2010, the United Nations General Assembly – recognising the world's increasingly scare water resources as an important issue – declared that access to safe and clean drinking water is a human right, and one that is essential to the full enjoyment of life and the realisation of all other human rights. With any consensus on a new Nile treaty still elusive, alternative directions must be explored alongside international negotiations, including changes to household water consumption patterns, water recycling and conservation, rationalising current irrigation and agricultural practice, reducing corporate water consumption, reducing water pollution, appropriate water pricing, and even possibly exploring the viability of bulk imports from non-water-stressed regions.

While the world population grew three-fold over the course of the 20th century, water consumption grew six-fold. Given the regional scarcity of this critical resource, fresh water consumption patterns clearly *must* be rationalised if this liquid element is not to turn into a prominent new source of international violence.

4.5
Emerging Issues

Domestic Urban Development Corridors and Transnational Urban Systems[25]

Uganda: The Kampala-Entebbe Corridor

Kampala is the largest city on the Lake Victoria shores, at the end of the railway linking Uganda's capital with the Kenyan port of ***Mombasa*** on the Indian Ocean. This turns ***Kampala*** into a major logistic hub in the region, with onward freight links to Burundi, Rwanda, the eastern regions of the DRC and to Southern Sudan.

The 40 km Kampala-Entebbe highway is rapidly emerging as the core of a ribbon-shaped urban development corridor, connecting Entebbe International Airport - another major regional logistics hub - with the capital and the whole area.

Demographic expansion within the Kampala-Entebbe corridor now results in planning, traffic, infrastructure, housing and social challenges that require holistic, integrated, area-wide decision making among the public authorities in ***Kampala***, Wakiso District and ***Entebbe***. The agenda should include transportation networks, waste management, infrastructure and the development of light industrial, commercial and residential functions within the corridor. Continued demographic and economic growth of the ***Kampala*** and ***Entebbe*** Municipalities and rapid development of the area between them can result in greater economic efficiency and productivity if spatial, economic and social interventions are planned, coordinated and implemented as an area-wide initiative.

Holistic sustainable development (including social) of this incipient corridor calls for prompt administrative and legal reforms to ensure continued close cooperation between the

▲
Kampala, Uganda. **©Frank van den Bergh/iStockphoto**

MAP 4.6: **THE KAMPALA-ENTEBBE URBAN CORRIDOR**

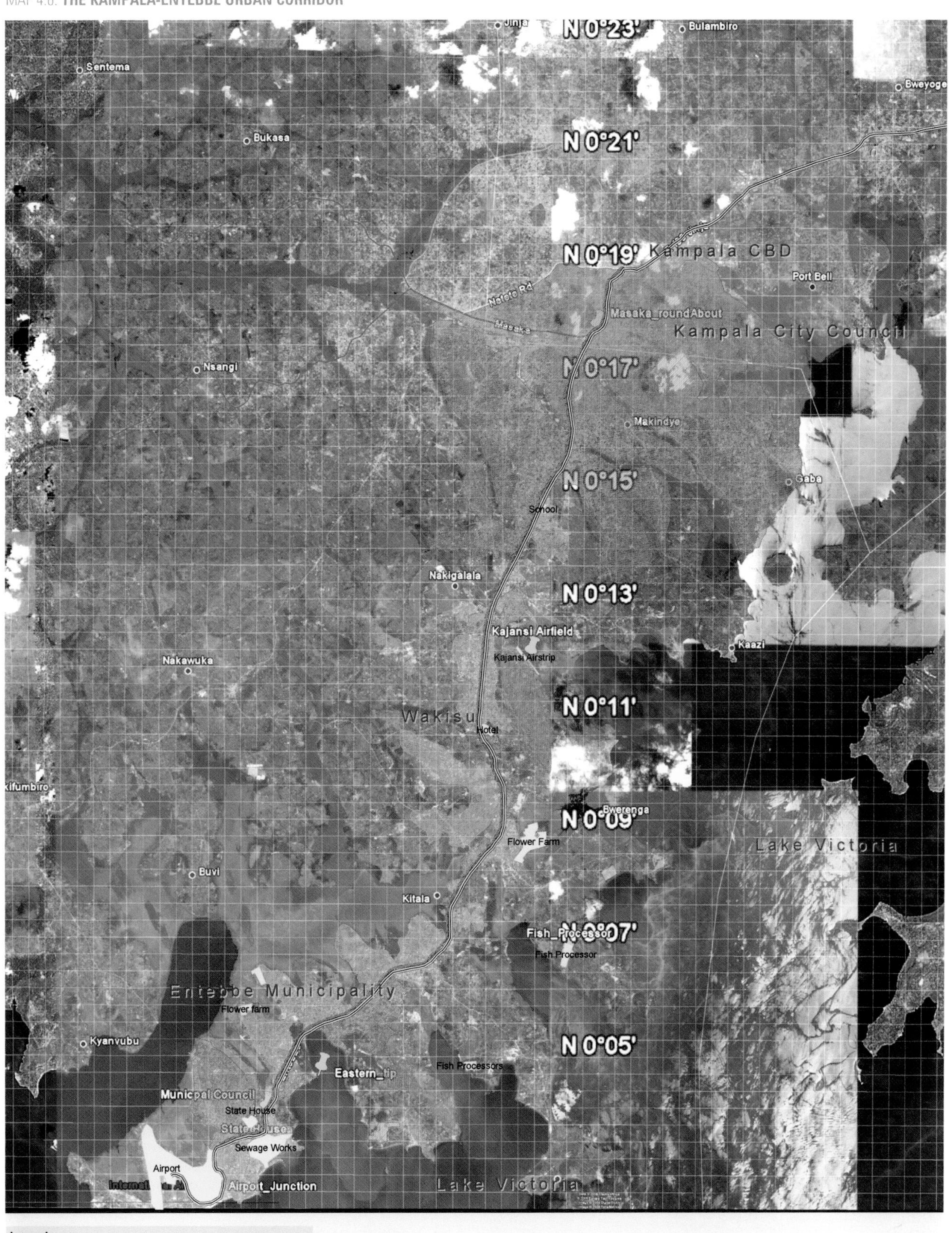

Legend

 Existing Road Corridor

Notable Structures

Built-Up Residential and Commercial Areas

Commercial Development - Kampala CBD, Entebbe and Growth Points

Mixed Developments - Mainly Residential

Mixed Developments - Mainly Agricultural

1:112,493

0 0.5 1 2 3 4 Kilometers

Data Sources: Google Earth Pro
Analysis & Layout: Joshua Mulandi
Date:14/07/2008
Disclaimer: Map prepared for illustration only

MAP 4.7: **NAIROBI METROPOLITAN REGION**

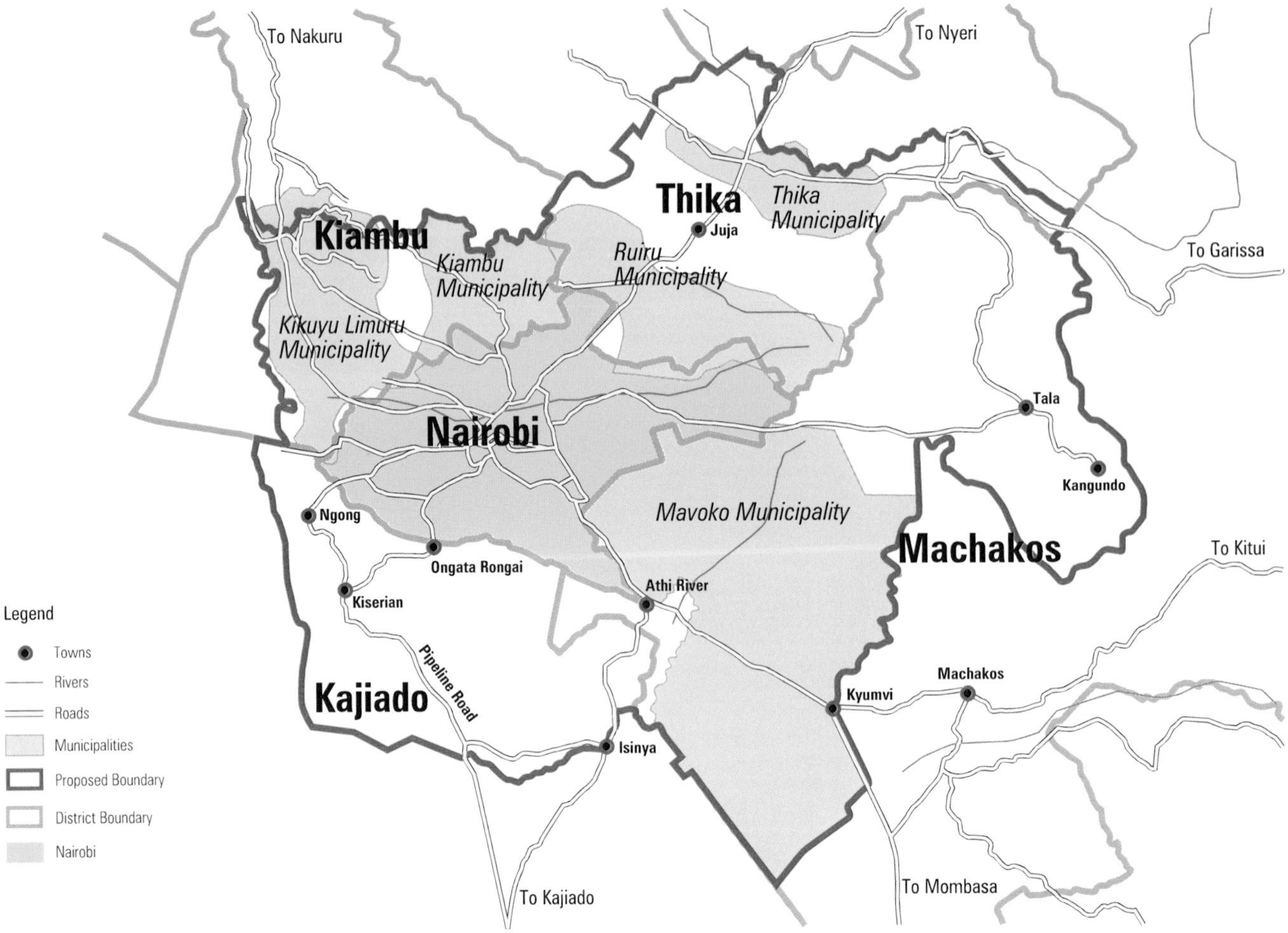

local authorities involved. On top of this, perhaps the most important immediate objective would be the development of a prospective medium-term vision (including the economy and transportation) through broad participatory processes, to be complemented by a strategy for resource mobilisation involving not just government but also financial and other partnerships.

Kenya: The Greater Nairobi Metropolitan Area

A number of factors influence the geographic sprawl of Greater Nairobi, and a number of others should be put to good use. On the southern side, urban developments are restricted by the topography of the Great Rift Valley and the Nairobi National Park, a wildlife sanctuary. The western and north-western outskirts threaten to encroach onto the very agricultural lands that feed the metropolitan area. Small rural settlements in the agricultural hinterlands of ***Kikuyu***, ***Kiambu***, ***Ruiru***, ***Tigoni*** and parts of ***Limuru*** are turning into fast-growing informal settlements with a mixture of residential and commercial functions.

Nairobi's spatial growth towards and beyond ***Thika*** to the north also encroaches on agricultural lands that are essential for the productivity and sustenance of the capital. Significant room is available in the southeast direction along the Nairobi-Mombasa highway towards the towns of ***Mavoko*** and ***Machakos***. The surface area of Mavoko Municipality is almost equal to that of the entire ***Nairobi*** Municipality, and largely empty due to semi-arid conditions. Currently, much of the urban growth of ***Nairobi*** is being directed there, although weak planning and enforcement of development controls is replicating the inefficiencies that are endemic to unplanned towns. An additional problem may be future water insecurity for this semi-arid region, as the ice cap of Mount Kilimanjaro, a major source of fresh water for the area, is rapidly disappearing.

Instead of adding to ***Nairobi's*** already significant primacy through unrestricted growth in its peri-urban areas and along its infrastructural life lines, holistic *regional* planning as well as economic and functional decentralisation away from the

Greater Nairobi peri-urban areas would be advisable. The spontaneously occurring linear growth along the logistical lines of Greater Nairobi is creating urban corridors that geographically spread the capital's economic, spatial and infrastructural synergies over an area vastly exceeding the current municipal boundaries. Establishing settlements at distances exceeding 100 km from the city centre is a more desirable approach, as current developments are simply allowing Greater Nairobi to grow further and ever more primate.

The desirability of the current spatial growth of the Greater Nairobi Metropolitan Area in a holistic context of forward-looking economic, social, industrial, and spatial policy must come under critical review. Indeed, in 2008, the Government of Kenya took the first step toward an area-wide approach with the introduction of a Ministry of Nairobi Metropolitan Development, and issued the ambitious *Nairobi Metro 2030 Vision*, a medium-term development proposal for the Greater Nairobi Metropolitan Area. The Vision has come under criticism for largely being a window-dressing proposal that fails to view Greater Nairobi in its national context and which is inward, rather than outward looking. Nevertheless, the proposed creation of a Nairobi Metropolitan Region (NMR) offers a prime opportunity for well-designed interventions that can help preserve open lands (including the Nairobi National Park) around the sprawling city where any further developments should be subject to strict controls.

The proposed Metropolitan Region could also offer prospects for directing economic activity to a ring of satellite settlements between 60 and 100 km away, but linked to the core through high-speed infrastructure connections such as intra-urban highways. However, to start addressing increasingly debilitating traffic congestion, it is recommended that light rail connections be built between the ***Nairobi*** central business district, on the one hand, and rapidly expanding satellite and future metropolitan dormitory settlements like ***Machakos***, ***Thika*** and ***Limuru***, on the other. Diverting population away from the metropolitan region over significant distances would not add to ***Nairobi's*** primacy while reducing vulnerability to natural disasters. With its location at the edge of the Rift Valley, the Kenyan capital is exposed to seismic and volcanic risks that are still calling for some serious assessment.

An almost inevitable, though so far largely dismissed step, in the process of diverting population away from the metropolitan region would be the relocation of a number of governmental departments. Various government departments have no overwhelming need to be physically located in the capital. With recent developments in communication technologies, there is little justification to stick with the physical centralization of government functions in the capital, other than possibly the Ministries of the Interior and Foreign Affairs, as well as the Office of the President. Nearly all other line ministries could be located in intermediate cites or new towns, including coastal cities like ***Mombasa***, ***Kilifi*** and ***Malindi*** or westwards to ***Nakuru***, ***Kisumu*** and other outlying secondary cities.

Not only would such an approach alleviate current traffic congestion in the capital through reductions in daily commutes, but relocation of large numbers of civil servants would relieve pressures on the ***Nairobi*** land and housing markets while stimulating the economies of the secondary cities. This, in turn, may have positive effects on the current unsustainably rapid proliferation of slums and informal settlements in ***Nairobi***, as relocated civil servants would create large numbers of livelihood opportunities for maids, gardeners, drivers, *askaris* (security guards) and other low-wage earners that today are mostly accommodated in Nairobi slums.

Taking a wider regional and national approach to decentralised economic activity and urban demographic growth is the sole credible and sustainable way forward for ***Nairobi*** and, indeed, the primate cities of Eastern Africa as a whole. The secondary cities in Eastern Africa, currently absorbing some three-quarters of the region's significant urban population growth, would also greatly benefit from a better spread of economic opportunities through decentralization.

ENDNOTES

1. All statistical data derived from World Urbanisation Prospects: The 2009 Revision, Department of Social and Economic Affairs, Population Division, United Nations, New York, 2010.
2. See also UN-HABITAT, State of the World Cities Report: Harmonious Cities (2008-9)
3. Joint EC/UN habitat workshop, Urbanisation Challenges in Africa,2005.
4. See www.unep.org/dewa/Africa/publications/AEO
5. UN-HABITAT, State of the World Cities Report: Harmonious Cities (2008-9)
6. UN-HABITAT, State of the World Cities Report, 2007
7. UNDP figures on Millennium Development Goals
8. UN-HABITAT, State of the World Cities Report: Harmonious Cities (2008-9)
9. Ali-Dinar, B., (2009). Urban Inequality in Global Perspective. African Studies Center - University of Pennsylvania, Africa.
10. Anderson, David (2002) Vigilantes, violence and the politics of public order in Kenya. African Affairs 101:531-555 (2002)
11. Citynoise.org/article/8094 Accessed 16 April 2010.
12. Durand-Lasserve, Alain (2007) Market-Driven Eviction Processes In Developing Country Cities: the Cases of Kigali in Rwanda and Phnom Penh in Cambodia. Global Urban Development Magazine 3(1)
13. Fjeldstad, Odd-Helge (2006) Chapter in Karin Millett, Dele Olowu & Robert Cameron, (eds) Local governance and poverty reduction in Africa. Joint Africa Institute (www.afdb.org/jai).
14. Kelly, Roy (2000) Property Taxation in East Africa: The Tale of Three Reforms.
15. *Ibid.*
16. See www.icpac.net.
17. UNFCC (2007) IPCCC Fourth Assessment Report.
18. *Ibid*
19. UN-HABITAT, State of the World Cities Report: Harmonious Cities (2008-9)
20. Allianz Knowledge. Protecting Seychelles, a tough challenge 2009
21. *Ibid.*
22. UNEP, State of the Environment in Somalia - A Desk Study (2005)
23. UN-HABITAT, State of the World Cities Report: Harmonious Cities (2008-9)
24. *Ibid.*
25. This section is an update of a similar section in the State of African Cities report 2008. Nairobi: UN-HABITAT.

Chapter Five

05

THE STATE OF CENTRAL AFRICAN CITIES

Kinshasa, Democratic Republic of the Congo.
©Irene 2005. Licenced under the Creative Commons Attribution 2.0 Generic Licence

5.1
The Social Geography of Urbanisation

Geographic Concentration and Clustering

For the purposes of this report, the Central African subregion comprises Angola, Cameroon, the Central African Republic (CAR), Chad, Congo, the Democratic Republic of Congo (DRC), Equatorial Guinea, Gabon and São Tomé e Príncipe. The total land area of the subregion is 5,366 million km^2, or 17.7 per cent of the land area of Africa as a whole.

In 2010, the Central African subregion had a total (estimated) population of 128,909,000, with 55,592,000 (or 43.1 per cent) living in areas classified as urban. The region remains the continent's least urbanised region after Eastern Africa (23.6 per cent). However, Central Africa is rapidly catching up with the continent's more urbanised subregions. Since the 1980/90 decade, when urban populations grew by a 3.65 per cent annual average, steady decade-interval urbanisation rate increases have been observed: 4.6 per cent in 1990-2000; 5.91 percent over the 2000/10 decade; 6.48 per cent projected for 2010/20; and 6.63 per cent for 2020/30. From 2030 onwards, these decade-interval urbanisation rate increases will begin to decline: to 6.23 per cent in 2030/40 and 5.98 per cent in 2040/50. This downward trend is to set in sometime around 2022 and after the subregion's population has become predominantly urban.

MAP 5.1: **CENTRAL AFRICA COUNTRIES**

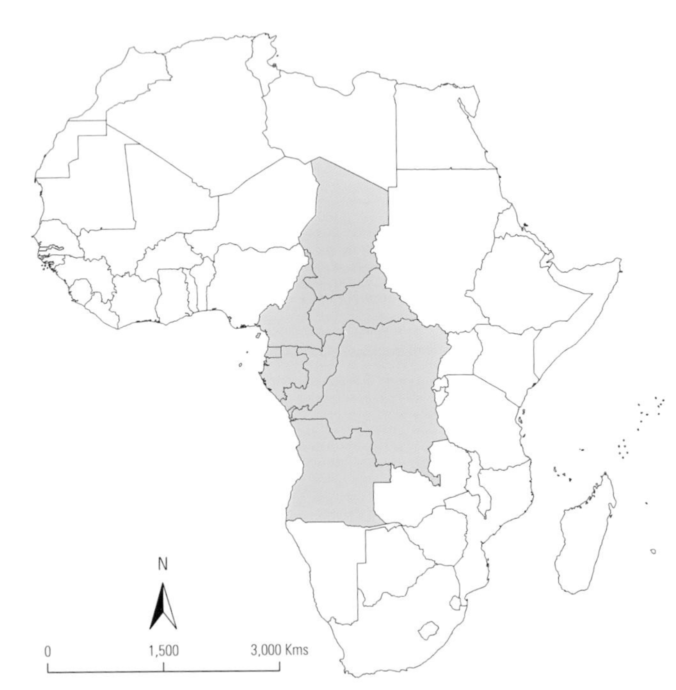

With these high urbanisation rates, Central Africa's urban population has more than doubled from 23,741,000 in 1990 to 55,593,000 in 2010. It is projected that the urban population will reach the 100 million mark sometime around 2022, reaching 112.7 million by 2030 and 185.9 million by 2050. Urban demographic growth rates are set to continue, although at a slower pace, until 2030 or (most likely) even beyond (see Table 5.1). After a 19.1 million increase in the 2000/2010 decade, these slower growth rates in a still-expanding urban population are to add 25.9 million urban dwellers during 2010/20 and 31.2 million during 2020/30.

In 2010, Gabon, with 86 per cent of its population living in cities, was the region's most urbanised nation by far, followed by São Tomé e Príncipe (62.2 per cent) and Congo (62.1 per cent). Least urbanised were Chad (27.63 per cent), the DRC (35.22 per cent) and Equatorial Guinea (39.7 per cent) who all remained below the Africa-wide urbanisation average of 39.9 percent. During the 2000/2010 decade, Angola and Cameroon were the most rapidly urbanising Central African countries with respective rate increases of 9.5 and 8.5 per cent, with both having become predominantly urban just before 2005; by 2010, their respective urbanisation rates had risen to 58.5 and 58.4 per cent respectively (estimates). These are expected to reach just under two-thirds by 2020 and more than 75 per cent by 2040.

At the lower end of urbanisation trends, Equatorial Guinea, the DRC and CAR are not projected to become predominantly urban until after 2030 and Chad only around 2042. Only by then will all Central African populations be more urban than rural. During 2010/20, though, the decade-interval growth rate of Central Africa's urban populations is likely to be highest in Chad (22.8 per cent), compared with 12.8 per cent in Angola, 12.1 per cent in Cameroon and as low as 3.1 per cent in Gabon, which suggests a converging trend among urbanisation rates over time.

▲
Libreville, Gabon. **Photogragh courtesy of IISD/Earth Negotiations Bulletin**

TABLE 5.1: **CENTRAL AFRICA: TREND IN URBAN POPULATION, 1950-2030**

Population	1950	1960	1970	1980	1990	2000	2010*	2020*	2030*
Urban (000s)	3,657	5,687	10,161	15,578	23,741	36,486	55,592	81,493	112,727
Urban (%)	14.00	17.72	24.82	28.96	32.61	37.21	43.12	49.60	55.92
All Africa (%)	14.40	18.64	23.59	27.91	32.13	35.95	39.98	44.59	49.95

** Projections*
Source: WUP 2009

GRAPH 5.1: **CENTRAL AFRICA: TREND IN URBAN POPULATION, 1950-2030**

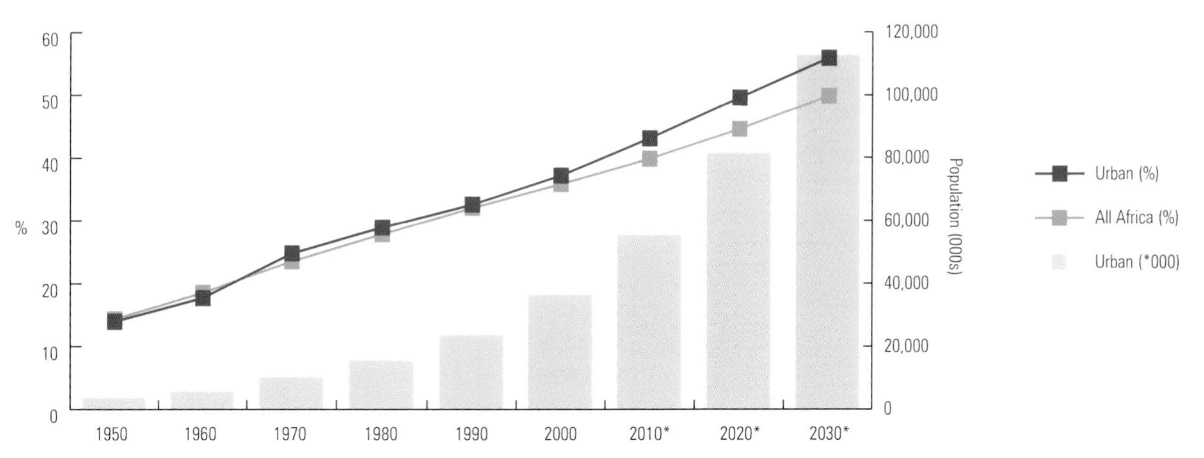

** Projections*
Source: WUP 2009

TABLE 5.2: **CENTRAL AFRICA: NATIONAL URBANISATION TRENDS, 1950-2030**

Population	1950	1960	1970	1980	1990	2000	2010*	2020*	2030*
Angola	7.58	10.44	14.96	24.30	37.14	48.99	58.50	66.04	71.62
Cameroon	9.33	13.94	20.30	31.92	40.72	49.86	58.40	65.47	70.99
Central African Republic	14.42	20.10	27.33	33.87	36.83	37.64	38.94	42.47	48.43
Chad	4.50	6.70	11.57	18.79	20.81	23.38	27.63	33.93	41.24
Congo	24.93	31.60	39.13	47.86	54.32	58.32	62.12	66.34	70.87
DR Congo	19.10	22.30	30.30	28.72	27.82	29.84	35.22	42.03	49.16
Equatorial Guinea	15.46	25.54	26.95	27.87	34.75	38.81	39.70	43.28	49.43
Gabon	11.40	17.40	32.00	54.68	69.14	80.15	86.03	88.77	90.62
São Tomé e Príncipe	13.49	16.07	29.52	33.48	43.65	53.42	62.23	69.02	74.05

** Projections*
Source: WUP 2009

GRAPH 5.2: **CENTRAL AFRICA: NATIONAL URBANISATION TRENDS, 1950-2030**

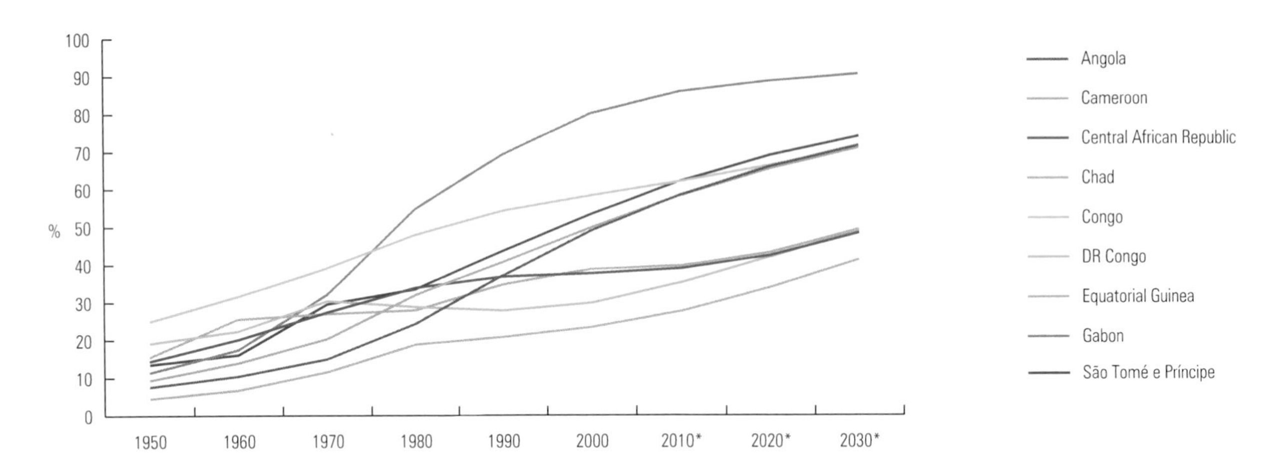

** Projections*
Source: WUP 2009

Geographic Concentration and Clustering

Urban populations in Central African countries are overwhelmingly concentrated in a few major cities, mostly the national capitals. As shown in Table 5.3, all Central African capitals are primate cities, except ***Yaoundé*** in Cameroon. ***Luanda***, the capital of Angola, for instance, is more than four times larger than the second-largest city ***Huambo***, while ***Kinshasa*** is 5.6 times the size of the DRC's second largest city, ***Lubumbashi*** and 5.8 times the size of the third-largest, ***Mbuji-Mayi***. The highest degree of urban primacy is found in Congo, where the capital ***Brazzaville*** is 16.3 times larger than the second largest city ***Pointe-Noire***.

Political power, manufacturing, employment, basic infrastructure and social services are all concentrated in and around Central Africa's major urban centres, in complete disregard of geographical balance. Rural areas are mostly neglected and little, where any, public spending, makes living conditions particularly difficult for the rural poor.

In Congo, the primacy of ***Brazzaville*** can be explained by the fact that its population increased sharply between 1997 and 2000, when civil war devastated the country and people fled the countryside and the smaller cities to seek refuge in the capital. Brazzaville's population continues to grow rapidly compared with the second-largest city in the country, ***Pointe-Noire***, due to continued rural-urban migration away from ravaged rural economies, rising unemployment, lack of basic goods in the countryside, as well as emigration from ***Kinshasa***, which sits opposite ***Brazzaville*** right across the Congo River.

Douala, rather than the capital city ***Yaoundé***, is Cameroon's largest conurbation. The country's main business centre accommodates almost 11 per cent of the national population and 18.8 per cent of Cameroon's urban dwellers. ***Luanda*** and ***Brazzaville*** account for about a quarter of their respective countries' total populations, while ***Kinshasa***, one of the fastest growing conurbations in sub-Saharan Africa, accommodates more than 13 per cent of the DRC's total 2010 population of 66 million.

With large cities concentrating economic opportunity, it should not come as a surprise that urban areas have attracted large-scale rural (and in times of conflict also cross-border) migrant flows. Comparatively high birth rates and better health services in cities have also contributed to the rapid growth of urban populations (see Tables 5.4 and 5.5).

However, the subregion's constant and rapidly changing demographic fluidity makes urban statistics somewhat unreliable in the absence of recent census data. Obtaining accurate population data is a challenge in many Central African cities, because in some countries, census surveys have not occurred for decades and many municipalities do not collect demographic data on their own. Moreover, such data is often contradictory and significantly different across sources, with figures provided by public administrations often particularly inaccurate and incomplete. In the DRC, for instance, no census has taken place for more than 25 years and data for large urban centres like ***Kinshasa***, ***Mbuji-Mayi*** and ***Kananga*** are often little more than educated guesses. For ***Kinshasa***, the Population Division of the United Nations Department of Economic and Social Affairs (UNDESA) arrives at a figure of 8.754 million, while the African Development Bank's estimate is more than 10 million. Apart from different numbers, the definition of what constitutes an urban area also varies from country to country, making it difficult to compare urban populations in the subregion. In this report, UNDESA data have consistently been used, if and where available.

▲
Yaoundé, Cameroon. ©**David Hecht /IRIN**

TABLE 5.3: **CENTRAL AFRICAN CITIES >750,000 INHABITANTS, 2010 (PROJECTIONS)**

Country	City	Population	Primacy
Angola	Luanda	4,772,000	4.62
Angola	Huambo	1,034,000	---
Cameroon	Douala	2,125,000	1.17
Cameroon	Yaoundé	1,801,000	---
Chad	N'Djamena	829,000	---
Democratic Republic of Congo	Kinshasa	8,754,000	5.6
Democratic Republic of Congo	Mbuji-Mayi	1,488,000	---
Democratic Republic of Congo	Lubumbashi	1,543,000	---
Democratic Republic of Congo	Kananga	878,000	---
Democratic Republic of Congo	Kisangani	812,000	---
Republic of Congo	Brazzaville	1,292,000	16.37

Source: WUP 2009

TABLE 5.4: **COMPARATIVE TRENDS IN FERTILITY RATES, CENTRAL AND SUB-SAHARAN AFRICA**

Period	Total fertility rate (children per woman)	
	Central Africa	Sub-Saharan Africa
2000-2005	6.22	5.41
2005-2010*	5.67	5.08
2010-2015*	5.18	4.66
2015-2020*	4.66	4.20
2020-2025*	4.15	3.77
2025-2030*	3.68	3.40

**Projections*
Source: WUP 2009

Over the past five years, demographic growth has been significantly faster in urban areas than in whole individual countries. In those countries where populations were estimated to be more urban than rural in 2010, the excess factor was 1.6 or more, while in predominantly rural countries that factor was smaller: 1.1 in Equatorial Guinea, 1.2 in CAR and 1.3 in Congo.

Inter-decade urban demographic growth rates between 2010 and 2050 are projected to remain high, though on a decelerating trend, reflecting the ongoing urban transition in Central Africa. In those countries where the population is already predominantly urban, demographic growth is decelerating (either because rural or other migration has slowed down or stopped, or because birth and death rates are lower, or both – see below), whereas in the other countries growth is found to be fluctuating, though still overall declining as well. However, urban populations continue to grow in absolute terms, although at a decelerating pace, particularly in cities in the more populated Central African

TABLE 5.5: **SELECTED POPULATION DATA, 2010 (PROJECTIONS)**

Countries	2010* Total Population (000s)	2005-2010* (%)		Crude Birth Rate/1,000	Crude Death Rate/1,000
		Population Growth Rate	Urban Growth Rate		
Angola	18,498	2.67	4.49	40.4	15.2
Cameroon	19,552	2.26	3.73	34.2	13.2
Central African Republic	4,422	1.88	2.33	33.2	15.7
Chad	11,206	2.77	4.56	43.7	15.5
Congo	3,683	1.91	2.54	31.9	12.3
DR Congo	66,020	2.76	4.61	42.5	15.8
Equatorial Guinea	676	2.60	2.99	37.4	13.8
Gabon	1,475	1.84	2.41	25.7	8.9
São Tomé e Príncipe	163	1.61	2.99	29.4	6.8

**Projections*
Source: UNDESA, WUP 2009 and World Population Prospects 2008

TABLE 5.6: **INTER-DECADE ABSOLUTE AND RELATIVE INCREASES IN URBAN POPULATIONS, 2005-2050**

Country	2000-10*		2010-20*		2020-30*		2030-40*		2040-50*	
	000s	%	Abs.	%	000s	%	000s	%	000s	%
Angola	4,117	58.9	5,072	45.6	5,600	34.6	6,000	27.5	6,258	22.5
Cameroon	3,745	47.3	4,829	36.8	4,363	27.4	4,555	22.4	4,484	18.0
Central African Republic	345	24.5	513	29.2	710	31.3	830	27.9	875	23.0
Chad	1,215	61.9	1,875	59.0	2,789	55.2	3,601	45.9	4,317	37.7
Congo	565	31.9	783	33.5	765	24.5	786	20.2	753	16.1
DR Congo	8,719	57.5	12,947	54.2	16,548	44.9	19,220	36.0	20,669	28.5
Equatorial Guinea	70	34.1	104	37.8	148	39.1	177	33.6	197	28.0
Gabon	303	30.6	287	22.2	274	17.4	245	13.2	213	10.2
São Tomé e Príncipe	28	37.3	33	32.0	37	27.2	37	21.4	33	15.7
Total	19,107	52.4	26,443	47.6	31,234	38.3	35,451	31.4	37,799	25.5

**Projections*
Source: WUP 2009

countries, as shown in Table 5.6. This would suggest that the demographic clustering in Central African cities will further increase as urbanisation makes progress - a worrisome prospect, as explained below.

In parallel with rapid urban demographic growth, living conditions in Central African cities have undergone dramatic changes. Significant shortfalls in access to urban livelihoods, adequate shelter, and urban land have remained unresolved. Large numbers of low-income and poor households have been forced to move between and within cities - especially to the urban peripheries - as they could no longer bear the costs of living in formally planned urban areas. Whether they come from outside the city or have been evicted from inner-city areas, the peri-urban areas where they now live effectively confine them to the margins of urban life both literally and figuratively. On top of the geographical isolation from the city's economic resources, livelihood opportunities and social infrastructures, these poor populations are also increasingly becoming excluded from participation in mostly urban-based political life. This creates and reinforces highly undesirable patterns of geographical, social and economic exclusion - the root causes of the 'urban divide' - and dysfunctionality that can threaten the social, economic and political viability of these urban systems, if left unaddressed.

Current rapid demographic growth in Central African cities is the combined result of five factors, as follows: (a) high national fertility rates; (b) rural-urban migration; (c) declining urban mortality rates; (d) displacement through conflict; and (e) economic growth in some of the region's countries, which attracts cross-border migrations. These factors contribute to peri-urban sprawl, spatial segregation and concentration of the urban poor in non-serviced areas on or beyond the urban

GRAPH 5.3: **URBAN, RURAL AND TOTAL POPULATIONS IN CENTRAL AFRICA, 2000-2050**

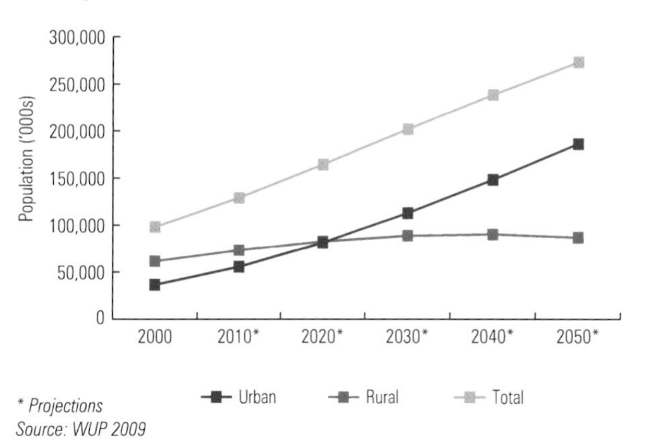

* *Projections*
Source: WUP 2009

fringes, as those populations simply cannot afford shelter in formally planned urban areas.

In the subregion's capitals and other large cities, until fairly recently, the poor were typically concentrated in the 'indigenous' urban neighbourhoods left over from the colonial era. Today, they are increasingly found in unplanned suburbs on or beyond the urban periphery. In ***Kinshasa***, for example, most of the poor are now concentrated in peripheral districts such as Kimbanseke, Masina, Kingasani, Kindele, Malueka, Mpasa and Mikonga. Likewise, in ***Brazzaville***, the majority of poor people live in Mikalu, Mfilou and Talangayi. In ***Luanda***, most poor people live in Petrangol, Palanca and Mabore. In recent years, the built-up areas of these cities have expanded dramatically; mostly without any formal spatial planning or infrastructures due to lack of urban management

BOX 5.1: ENERGISING URBAN GOVERNANCE IN AN OIL-DOMINATED ECONOMY: THE CASE OF ANGOLA

African governments' revenues from oil and gas are set to rise from US $80 billion in 2006 to approximately US $250 billion in 2030, giving the continent's hydrocarbon-exporting countries the means to speed up economic and social development and alleviate poverty. However, history has shown that oil- or, more generally, commodity-based riches will only lead to economic and social development if governments manage the revenues that accrue in a wise and honest way.

Oil became Angola's top revenue-earner in 1973 and Sonangol, the state-owned company managing the hydrocarbon reserves, has controlled all oil revenues since 1976. Angola is currently experiencing a construction boom and its gross domestic product (GDP) grew an average 16 per cent per year between 2006 and 2008. Nevertheless, a wide gap remains between national revenue and the living conditions of the majority of Angolans. GDP per head is approximately US $4,400, but some 70 per cent of the population lives on less than one dollar a day. This is not surprising since, between 1985 and 2004, capital flight out of the country amounted to an estimated totaled 216 per cent of official GDP.

Poverty is rampant in the vast informal settlements and slums of the capital Luanda. Although the government is building one million houses over four years, it is estimated that, just in the Greater Luanda Region, some three million people lack decent housing. Housing projects like *Copacabana Residencial*, a 720-apartment complex valued at US $100 million, contrast sharply with urban slums and forced evictions of those living there, with 15,000 people displaced in July 2009 alone.

Currently, less than 30 per cent of Angola's population has access to electricity or clean fuels for cooking like liquefied petroleum gas (LPG), kerosene or biogas. About 150,000 people, mainly women and children, die prematurely every year because of indoor air pollution from wood and charcoal burning. An estimated 70 percent of Angolan businesses rely on backup diesel generators to compensate for chronic power outages.

An abundant, clean and affordable energy source is crucial to public health, social welfare and economic productivity. Improving access to energy will entail fundamental political and legislative reform, as well as strengthened institutional and financial capabilities to implement such programmes. Universal access to electric or LPG cooking throughout the Western and Central Africa regions would cost an estimated US $18 billion - a mere 0.4 per cent of the regions' projected 2007-2030 cumulative oil revenues. Establishing universal access to electricity in Angola would require a mere 0.1 per cent of the country's projected revenues.

Civil society struggles to hold the Angolan government to account on the use of its oil revenues, because public information on actual revenue flows remains very scarce. The transition to, and consolidation of, a democratic Angolan State is still ongoing, as the country is trying to recover from a devastating civil war that lasted nearly 30 years. Likewise, civil society is yet fully to develop its capacities for engaging the government in dialogue to pave the way for democratic, equitable and sustainable development. However, when civic relationships are individualized rather than institutionalised, civil society often has difficulties engaging the government. It might nevertheless be possible for Angolan civil society to create political space if the unspoken, yet implicit lines that may not be crossed are used to pave the way for dialogue and negotiation in areas that *are* open to debate. The short-term objective is, therefore, to promote a culture of engagement and collaboration that can yield results in the longer term.

The problem is that Angola may not have much time to negotiate a new social contract with civil society, because its proven oil and gas reserves are modest, and very much so if compared with those, for instance, of Equatorial Guinea or Nigeria. Angolan oil output was projected to peak by 2010 and its petrodollar-based national budget could go into deficit between 2015 and 2018, if no alternative sources of government revenue are found.

If Angola persists in its current patterns of elite-centred consumption and near-exclusive reliance on oil and gas revenues, it will probably face an economic downturn around 2020. The revenue shock of 2008 triggered by declines in oil and diamond prices came as a foretaste of what may lie ahead. Unless current oil-based wealth is wisely invested in economic diversification, urban productivity, universal access to clean and cheap energy and urban social and basic infrastructures, the next decade could see an abrupt end to rising expectations among the millions of urban Angolans who legitimately aspire to stable, middle-class lifestyles.

Sources: World Energy Outlook 2008; Angola: Failed yet Successful, AfricaFocus Bulletin, 10 August 2009; Oil and Governance Report, March 2008, www.ethicsworld.org/publicsectorgovernance/; Electricity Distribution Modernization in Luanda, Angola, United States Trade and Development Agency, www.devex.com.

▲
A new formal housing development in Luanda, Angola. ©**Pedro Alphonso Kingungu**

capacities and development control. As they find themselves overwhelmed by demographic momentum, cities have tacitly allowed poor and low-income people to build structures in the least-desirable areas. Consequently, urban poverty has gradually become geographically determined and spatially segregated from the planned city. Although there is officially no ethnic segregation, *de facto* market-driven segregation between rich and poor now determines who resides where in the city. The wealthier urban population, including foreigners, live in the well-serviced, formally planned sections of the city, i.e. high-income neighbourhoods mainly built during the colonial period or immediately after independence. Rapidly rising costs of centrally located land increasingly drives out the poor to unplanned and under- or non-serviced areas.

The Links between Poverty, Inequality and Slums

The affordability criteria that enforce urban spatial segregation by distinct income groups are not necessarily an undesirable phenomenon. For thousands of years, cities around the world have voluntarily segregated population groups on the basis of shared affinities, such as ethnicity, religion or cultural identity. Urban segregation is undesirable, however, the moment it becomes an involuntary process, because under such conditions spatial distance results in often insurmountable social, political and economic distance. Involuntary geographical segregation creates inequity, poorer and fewer life chances, or hampered social mobility. This, in turn, leads to undesirable degrees of urban fragmentation and dysfunctionality that affect all, rich and poor.

In the subregion's oil-producing nations, market forces now increasingly keep the poor away from the city proper, as rapidly rising costs of urban housing and land push the planned city beyond affordability. However, oil-producing nations are not the only ones facing this problem. In other Central African cities, too, the costs of land and housing have also risen sharply. High-income residential units in the downtown area of Gombe, ***Kinshasa***, for instance, can cost in excess of one million US dollars. Housing in less-privileged areas, such as Masina and Kingasani, although less than US$ 30,000, are still way beyond what the bulk of the local populations can afford[1]. Due to rapidly rising urban property prices, accommodating limited- and low-income households is often no longer considered as financially viable in up-and-coming residential areas. These categories fall victim to neighbourhood gentrification and are evicted by 'market forces' to make room for high-income residential and commercial developments in privileged areas of the planned city. Not only does their relocation to outer city fringes imply significantly increased transportation costs to city-based livelihoods and economic opportunities, but in many cases it also reduces interactions with different social groupings, because socio-economic contacts at the periphery mostly remain restricted to other poor urban dwellers. In this way, relocation of the urban poor further reinforces inequality.

The extent of the deterioration in living standards in Central African cities has become an acute problem, as have the large numbers of people affected. Economic growth in many of the subregion's economies has gone hand in hand with a proliferation of extreme urban poverty, including sharp declines in real incomes and the concomitant inequality among the populations. In ***Bangui***, CAR, ***Brazzaville***, Congo, ***Kinshasa***, DRC, ***Luanda***, Angola, and ***N'Djamena***, Chad, as well as in many smaller cities in the subregion, social infrastructures (health and education) have deteriorated to appalling levels. With the major economic sectors facing difficulties, the informal economy has become the main livelihood provider in many cities, pushing millions into daily battles for survival.

Table 5.7 shows that large shares of the population in Central Africa have no access to clean water. Since access to health care is mostly limited to rich people, it is not surprising that, in six of the 10 Central African countries, more than a third of the population is not expected to live beyond the age of 40, while the reduction in infant mortality remains slower than expected. It is deplorable that Africa still has by far the lowest life expectancy and highest infant mortality rates of any major region of the world. Clearly, Central African countries have failed to invest sufficiently in the well-being of their people and, as is always the case, the poor are the most affected.

The urbanisation of poverty is a dramatic development on the African continent, generating sharp contrasts between the affluence of business districts or high-income residential areas on the one hand, and massive human suffering in sprawling informal settlements and slums, on the other.[2] These trends are the entirely unnecessary and unacceptable result of lack of inequitable shared resources and opportunities in an environment where corruption and wealth hoarding are endemic. The politico-commercial bourgeoisie in the region leverages its control or influence over government and state-owned companies to plunder their countries, squandering national resources in flagrant and unscrupulous pursuit of personal riches[3], at the expense of desperately needed spending on basic infrastructure and social services such as public transport, clean water, electricity, education and health.

In ***Brazzaville***, ***Kinshasa***, ***Libreville***, ***Luanda***, ***Malabo*** and ***Yaoundé***, for instance, political and economic elites are becoming richer at the expense of the vast majorities or urban poor. In some of these cities, 10 per cent of the population reaps more than 60 per cent of the total income, all too often causing life-threatening situations. In Cameroon, for example, a child born into the poorest 20 per cent of households is more than twice as likely to die before the age of five as one born in the richest 20 per cent. Likewise in oil-rich Angola, despite an annual economic growth of 16.6 per cent (2006/07), slum households constitute more than 80 per cent of the urban population. Poor living environments, inadequate sanitation and water supply all add to the health challenges of slum dwellers, leading not only to more illnesses and deaths, but also to higher health care costs, lower school enrolment and retention rates, and lower labour productivity.

The failure of Central African nations to address urban poverty and inequality has led to the emergence and rapid proliferation of slums in all cities in the subregion, depriving large shares of the urban populations of opportunities to meet their basic needs. Besides severe inequality and socio-economic exclusion, urban slum dwellers frequently also experience malnutrition. Today's widespread incidence of hunger is deplorable and entirely unnecessary, but many poor families in Central Africa and a large share of its urban population are chronically malnourished.

In many of the subregion's urban slums, women play an essential role in household survival, but female slum dwellers carry most of the burden of social inequality and exclusion. Nearly 95 per cent of female slum dwellers acknowledge that they need support systems, including short- and medium-term credit, to allow them to improve the quality of their work and the running of their households. To face the continuous financial and employment crises, slum dwellers have been promoting gender equality, advocating for women to take more control over household management and decision-making. As a result, gender relations within urban and slum households have somewhat improved[4] in recent years, but much still needs to be done to improve female slum dwellers' living conditions.

TABLE 5.7: **HUMAN POVERTY INDICATORS IN CENTRAL AFRICAN COUNTRIES (2007)**

	Population without access to clean water (%)	Population not expected to reach age 40 (%)	Life expectancy at birth (years)	Children <5 underweight (%)	Literacy 15 years and older (%)
Angola	49	38.5	46.5	31	67.4
Cameroon	30	34.2	50.9	15	67.9
Central African Republic	34	39.6	46.7	29	48.6
Chad	52	35.7	48.6	34	31.8
DR Congo	54	37.3	47.6	31	67.2
Congo	29	29.7	53.5	14	81.1
Equatorial Guinea	57	34.5	49.9	19	87.0
Gabon	13	22.6	60.1	12	86.2
São Tomé e Príncipe	14	13.9	65.4	9	87.9

Source: UNDP, Human Development Report, 2009

5.2
The Economic Geography of Cities

Income and Consumption: Gini coefficients

Balanced income distribution is important for sustainable development, because it turns less wealthy households into effective consumers and influences social cohesion; it has the potential to reduce the extent of poverty and affects people's health[5]. Although information on incomes in Central African cities is scarce, available data suggests that income distribution is uneven both across the subregion and across countries. Urban income inequality is increasing and the gap between rich and poor widening. Whereas research on income and consumption inequality is mostly carried out and measured on a national basis, this section analyses urban income and consumption inequalities in selected (mainly capital) cities of Central Africa based on the data compiled by UN-HABITAT's Global Urban Observatory (GUO). Data for cities such as ***Luanda, Malabo, N'Djamena*** and ***São Tomé*** are not available. In the case of ***Luanda*** and ***N'Djamena***, national data has been used instead.

Some Central African nations feature high income-based Gini coefficients (see Table 5.8), implying that national income and wealth is poorly shared, with large sections of the population living on low incomes and consumption. Cities cannot develop and perform optimally if a small group dominates most of the resources and opportunities, while the majority remains impoverished and marginalized.

Angola is where the nationwide income-based Gini coefficient is the highest, and indeed the country is the most unequal in the region in almost every sphere of life. These disparities are reflected in distribution of income and access to education, clean water, sanitation, healthcare, electricity, adequate housing and urban land. Given Angola's vast oil wealth, its fair distribution appears to be a major problem. Income-based coefficients are also high in ***Brazzaville, Libreville*** and ***Yaoundé***.

Equitable distribution of wealth and achievement of social goals are essential components of development and good governance, over and above economic growth *per se*[10]. Urban inequality in Cameroon, Congo, the DRC and Gabon is steep, while the economic and financial problems Chad, CAR, the DRC, Congo and São Tomé e Príncipe are facing, coupled with various civil wars during the last two decades, have all had huge though unequal effects on the consumption patterns of various segments of the population. In the subregion, the income gap between rich and poor has widened since the mid-1980s because of: (a) public sector retrenchment, (b) lay-offs in the private sector due to declining foreign investment, (c) the collapse of agricultural and industrial sectors, and (d) reduced export incomes.[11]

▲
Luanda, Angola. **©Nathan Holland/Shutterstock**

TABLE 5.8: **GINI COEFFICIENTS FOR SELECTED CENTRAL AFRICAN COUNTRIES AND CITIES**

Country	Gini Coefficient
Angola	0.586
Chad	0.397
Bangui	0.420[7]
Brazzaville	0.450[9]
Kinshasa	0.390[8]
Libreville	0.414
Yaoundé	0.410[6]

Source: African Statistical Yearbook 2009

GRAPH 5.4: **GINI COEFFICIENTS FOR SELECTED CENTRAL AFRICAN COUNTRIES AND CITIES**

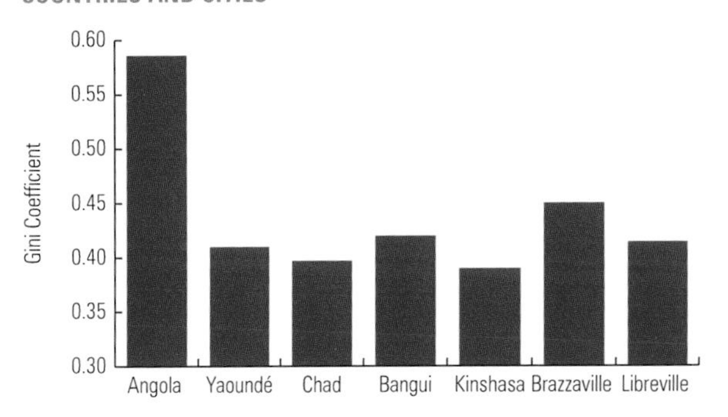

Source: African Statistical Yearbook 2009

Income inequality has forced many households to make drastic cuts in consumption, foregoing non-essential expenditures such as clothing, shoes, and home furnishings, and incidentally causing dramatic price declines in many Central African cities. In ***Kinshasa***, for example, the average amount spent on food represented 74 per cent of the total household expenditure in 2008[12], up from an already high 70 per cent in 2002[13]. The concomitant fall in the consumption of non-essential items had repercussions on the incomes of those producing or selling those goods. However, there is more to steep income and consumption inequalities than just the urban economic aspects. Data has shown that political tensions and social disturbances are rife in cities where income and consumption inequalities are high, as in ***Bangui***, ***Brazzaville***, ***Kinshasa***, ***Luanda*** and ***Yaoundé*** (whose coefficients range between 0.43 and 0.58). Highly unequal income distribution is clearly among the lead causes of underdevelopment and conflict in Central Africa.

With oil-based economic booms, the capitals of Angola, Chad, Congo, Equatorial Guinea and Gabon have seen increases in the numbers of well-paid highly-skilled workers. But oil wealth tends to fuel price inflation, while poor wealth distribution reinforces existing income and consumption inequalities and widens the gap in basic needs satisfaction. Social scientists researching the effects of different income patterns have shown that wealth distribution inequalities are not only detrimental to development, but that high urban income inequality affects urban social stability and cohesion.

How Slum Dwellers Survive

Despite economic progress realised in many Central African countries, endemic corruption, looting of state funds and lack of business ethics and ethos impede income distribution and national wealth sharing. This created havoc in the urban labour markets, in particular between 1980 and 2000, and impoverished urban populations are often experiencing multiple deprivations[14]. Drastic reductions in real urban wages, significant urban income disparities and high levels of urban unemployment and the resultant urban poverty have all forced slum dwellers in the subregion to supplement their incomes, using combinations of appropriate and/or inappropriate measures.[15]

To make ends meet, numerous low or unpaid civil servants in the subregion's cities (many of whom are slum dwellers) have little option but to combine their formal job with informal activities. In many Central African cities, economic and political crises have led to the decline, absence and sometimes hijacking of municipal services by unpaid civil servants or traditional chiefs. In ***Kinshasa,*** residents are now reinventing public order, through new forms of social organisation, to compensate for the overwhelming failures of the nation state.[16] Civil servants in ***Kinshasa*** often remain unpaid for months on end and, by necessity, have developed parallel offices to allow them to derive income outside official structures. Fake receipts, fraudulent use of official stationery and forged signatures enable them to top up wages, instead of putting the collected revenue in the public treasury.[17] This has created a vicious circle of 'privatised' municipal income, depriving municipalities of much-needed revenues.

In order to survive in an expensive city where cash is king and to relieve their often severe state of poverty, civil servants make it impossible to get public services without additional 'facilitation' charges. After months without pay, civil servants demand fees from the public or companies in need of their services. In almost all government offices, civil servants can either issue official or look-alike private receipts, with any monies charged ending up in the public coffers or private pockets, depending on the type of receipt. Another common feature is the looting of office stationery, computers, furniture, air conditioning equipment, fax machines, photocopiers, cars, etc. by civil servants at all levels after every cabinet reshuffle.[18]

The supply of urban jobs and regular wages has decreased dramatically in Central Africa while the labour force has grown rapidly. In response, urban slum dwellers have developed their own local survival initiatives through self-employment within the informal sector. Evidence shows that, in all Central African cities, the informal economy keeps growing, even as (or because) the formal sector remains stagnant.

The range of activities subsumed under the informal sector umbrella in Central Africa is extremely diverse, including production, distribution and service enterprises, as well as outright illegal operations. These change from one city to another, but mostly involve low-skilled or manual production and services provision, or small-scale retail trade. Informal

TABLE 5.9: **ANNUAL URBAN AND GDP GROWTH RATES IN CENTRAL AFRICAN COUNTRIES**

Country	Average annual urban growth rate 2000-2010* (%)	2010* Urban Population (%)	GDP growth 2007 (%)	GDP/head Growth 2007 (%)
Angola	4.40	58.50	23.4	20.1
Cameroon	3.73	58.40	3.8	1.3
Chad	4.92	27.60	0.6	-2.1
Central African Republic	2.07	38.90	4.2	2.3
DR Congo	5.07	35.20	6.5	3.5
Congo	2.88	62.10	-1.6	-3.6
Equatorial Guinea	2.59	39.70	-	-
Gabon	2.32	86.00	5.6	4.0
São Tomé e Príncipe	3.19	62.20	3.8	-
Average	**3.46**	**52.06**	**5.1**	**3.6**

* *Projections*
Source: World Bank, World Development Indicators 2009; UN DESA, 2008

▲
Informality in Kinshasa. **©Benjamin Makutu**

businesses in ***Bangui*** employ more than 70 per cent of the population, while in ***Brazzaville, Kinshasa, Luanda, Malabo, N'Djamena*** and ***Yaoundé*** it accounts for more than 50 per cent of all jobs created. ***Kinshasa*** provides examples of the important role played by the urban informal sector. It provides almost 95 per cent of all public transport services, nearly 98 per cent of household waste collection, 95 per cent of construction workers, plumbing or mechanical repairs, and it has a nearly 90 per cent share in local trade[19]. In their daily quest for survival and well-being, the *kinois* (inhabitants of Kinshasa) have invented a set of codes, discourses, systems and practices that enable the community as a whole to ward off the long-predicted apocalypse.

Many slums in Central Africa are home to hardworking communities, whose human aspirations are modest - improved living conditions in the absence of government assistance. However, incomes for many urban dwellers in the subregion have, over the past years, deteriorated to almost meaningless levels and, consequently, many household survival strategies are now based on non-income sources.

Addressing Urban Inequality and Fragmentation

The rapid and sustained demographic growth of Central African cities has outpaced municipal authorities' capacities to provide jobs, services and infrastructures, as well as proper management and financing. Many municipal structures are ill-prepared to play the role that should be theirs in the face of rapid demographic expansion, growing informality and economic inequality, with the attendant urban fragmentation and dysfunctionality.

One of the most important Central African demographic characteristics, as shown in Table 5.10 and Graph 5.4, is the massive 'youth bulge', i.e. a median 42.1 per cent of the population below 15 years (or slightly less than the all-Africa 44 per cent median). The percentage of those aged 65 or more is low in all Central African countries, reflecting the very poor life expectancies associated with poverty, exclusion and inequality.

TABLE 5.10: **POPULATION BY AGE GROUP IN 2008**

	0-14		15-64		65+	
	000s	%	000s	%	000s	%
Angola	4,049.2	43.5	5,007.0	53.8	253.2	2.7
Cameroon	7,718.6	40.8	10,531.9	55.7	669.8	3.5
Central African Republic	1,857.4	42.0	2,397.4	54.2	169.5	3.8
Chad	5,114.3	46.1	5,653.0	51.0	320.4	2.9
DR Congo	30,692.1	47.5	32,342.6	50.1	1,566.8	2.4
Congo	1,605.3	41.7	2,118.1	55.1	123.8	3.2
Equatorial Guinea	219.1	42.2	279.5	53.8	21.1	4.1
Gabon	464.0	34.4	823.8	61.0	62.4	4.6
São Tomé e Príncipe	65.6	40.9	88.0	54.9	6.6	4.1

Source: African Statistical Yearbook 2009

GRAPH 5.5: **POPULATION BY AGE GROUP IN CENTRAL AFRICA, 2008**

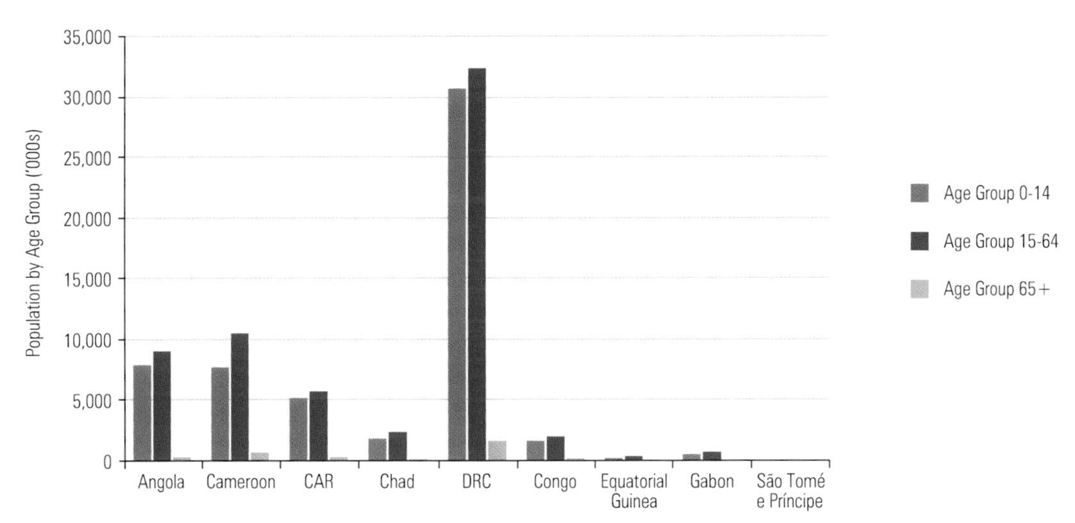

Source: African Statistical Yearbook 2009

Research shows that governments and municipalities have started to put in place a number of strategies to tackle inequality and fragmentation of society. Municipalities are working with local groups to launch integrated urban development initiatives, with the aim of enhancing the quality of life of the more underprivileged urbanites. They look to improve public infrastructure and facilities, health services and housing in some low-income areas through support to local self-help development projects, providing employment to local people and sponsoring local cultural events. In some cities, assistance is also extended to the periphery and suburbs through improvement of agricultural production and the protection of natural resources.

Gender relations within Central African cities are another area where central governments and municipalities are working to reduce inequality and exclusion. Faced with low female literacy rates, governments and municipalities have secured UNICEF to promote schooling and improve enrolment rates for girls. Urban authorities are also promoting increased employment of women in the urban public sector and their better inclusion in public and political life. As Pacione has argued:

'In an inclusive city, urban residents feel they are important contributors to decision-making, from political aspects to more simple daily life questions. This level of participation guarantees them to have a stake in the benefits of development of the city. The concepts of human relationships, citizenship and citizen rights are all integral parts of an inclusive city[20].

Some progress has been achieved in the fight against urban inequality and fragmentation in Central African cities, but many urban dwellers remain frustrated with the persistent injustice they face in the housing market, schooling, multiple discrimination in workplaces, gender exclusion in the labour market, and glaring inequality between the rich and the poor within the same city.

5.3 The Geography of Urban Land Markets

Reliable data on Central African land markets is scarce, except, perhaps, for Cameroon, where recent research provides some insights. If anything, this 'knowledge gap' across the subregion underlines the limited attention paid, until recently, to urban land governance.

Central African urban land markets operate in legal frameworks similar to those observed in Western Africa. However, tensions, confrontation and negotiation between public institutions and emerging social forces appear to be more acute in Central than in Western Africa. In addition, Angola, the DRC, Congo and Guinea-Bissau have experienced protracted periods of instability, conflict and subsequent reconstruction that have all had negative effects on urban governance, institutional reform efforts and land governance. Against this unsettled background and with the effects of rapid urbanisation, Central Africa is now going through radical breaks with its rural roots and identities, and these require pragmatic governance reforms, especially with regard to urban land.

The Forms of Urban Land Tenure

Urban land tenure problems in Central Africa are similar to those already described in Section 3.3 of this report on the urban geography of land markets in Western Africa. The main difference between Western and Central Africa, though, has to do with urbanisation, since the two subregions do not share the same urban traditions. The colonial and post-independence backgrounds are different, although both subregions share the French and Portuguese heritage of land legislation, management and administration based on a colonial civil code tradition (Rochegude & Plançon, 2010). Another difference is the wider gap between institutional, legal and regulatory frameworks of land governance in Central than in Western African cities.

Colonial rule introduced formal urban land administration in Central Africa, as codified in statutory law, with ownership details documented in central land registries and associated land rights enforceable in court. However, customary land

▲
Kinshasa, Democratic Republic of the Congo. **©Dieter Telemans/Panos Pictures**

management in Central Africa's rural and peri-urban areas remains largely unaffected by these institutional and legal frameworks. Not surprisingly, confrontations between customary practices and public land management are a rapidly growing source of political, economic and social friction that remains unresolved to this day and which is exacerbated by rapid urbanisation, economic change and market pressures on urban and peri-urban lands.

The three defining features of the formal land governance system prevailing in Central Africa are as follows: (a) registration is the criterion for the creation of rights, rather than any contractual documentation; (b) at the core of land administration is the properties registry, where transactions and rights are recorded; and (c) the registrar, which is always a government body, guarantees the validity of entries in the registry, providing a high degree of tenure security.

In practice, however, despite the legal obligation to register property rights, only a fraction has gone through the procedure. The reasons include central government monopoly on land allocation, lack of allocation transparency, cumbersome registration procedures and requirements, lack of broad access to land and housing finance and, consequently, the continuing predominance of customary forms of tenure. Therefore, and contrary to Western Africa, formal private ownership of urban land remains limited in Central Africa.

Land allocation by central or local government remains the most important land delivery channel across Central Africa. Residential land is accessed mainly through a 'Permit to Occupy' (PTO) for a specific duration during which the recipient *must* develop the plot and build a dwelling unit. Only then can this temporary permit be converted into a permanent one and, in principle, into a title granting either long-term leasehold or freehold rights. Although these permits are not transferable, public allocation of urban plots with PTOs has created an active informal urban land market in the development(s) on the land, rather than the land itself. Although this process includes a degree of informality, tenure is quite secure.

Throughout the subregion, public allocation of land is determined by social factors (and preventing land speculation is one) and planning objectives (orderly occupation and development of urban and peri-urban areas). For all these commendable conditions, though, public land allocation is a source of governmental power that is open to abuse. In practice, complex allocation procedures and lack of transparency encourage land allocation in dubious, corrupt conditions by land administration services who argue that their processing capacities are inadequate.

In the DRC, the State Domain is the most important land category, as Law 73-020 of 1973 established the State, in principle, as the owner of all land. The Domain is, therefore the source of all land rights, whether user rights or long-term and permanent leaseholds (*concession perpétuelle*). The State can delegate its land management prerogatives to statutory entities, especially for development purposes.

In Angola, land and tenure legislation is rooted in the Civil Code which provides the sole relevant framework. Under the post-independence (1975) constitution, the State is sole owner of all land. Only land usufruct (beneficial rights) can be transferred to legal entities or individuals for a (renewable) minimum 25 and a maximum 60 years. This form of usufruct can be transferred. In 1992, Decree 46A gave provincial governments the right to grant land concessions, including in urban areas where the land is also under state control. However, the law is ambiguous, unclear and leaves many areas undefined, and enforcement is a challenge in peri-urban areas (Cain, 2003).

In Gabon, the law identifies four categories of urban land, depending on the nationality of the occupant, the type of construction and the location of the land (urban or peri-urban), each of which comes with different degrees of security of tenure (leasehold for the first three categories, occupation permits for the fourth one).

Customary Tenure

Across Central Africa, customary tenure prevails under various forms, with sharp intra-regional legal contrasts. Some nations formally recognize customary tenure. In Cameroon, for instance, customary rights have been formally recognized since 1974. They can, in principle, be converted into formal titles, although, in practice this is a rare occurrence due to the rather ambiguous relationship between government land administration services and customary communities (Rochegude & Plançon, 2010).

Others countries, such as the DRC and Gabon, do not formally recognize customary land rights. In the DRC, only user rights (*droits de jouissance*) are recognized, not property rights, and only on condition that the property has been developed (*mise en valeur*). User rights are secure and can be mortgaged to access credit. Nevertheless, the customary system remains the main provider of land in rural and peri-urban areas. One of the questions currently under debate is whether customary communities can be allocated permanent leaseholds. In principle, that would be possible but, again, this is a rare occurrence as it requires intensive negotiations between government institutions and customary authorities. This awkward legal situation continues to generate land-related conflicts.

In Gabon, under Decree N° 77 (1977), Art. 2, land ownership through adverse possession by Gabonese citizens is recognized by law after five years' public, continued and peaceful occupation of urban plots not exceeding 2,000 m^2 (or a maximum of 10 ha in rural areas). This could, theoretically, also apply to customary land tenure, but the decree is, in practice, not enforced on customary land. However, whether recognized or not, customary tenure generally comes with some rights to allocate and transfer land, and usually also provides a fairly high degree of security. Recognition or otherwise of customary rights does not appear to have any effect on formal land markets, the simple reason being that formal land delivery caters to only a fraction of the demand for land.

To some extent, the various tenure arrangements described

above seemed to be supportive of land governance in Central Africa, until rapid urbanisation began to set in. Against a background of relentless demand for urban land, pressures on formal and customary markets and associated price rises, squatter settlements and social instability began to mushroom in many Central African cities. This fairly recent phenomenon can, among many others, be observed particularly in ***Kinshasa***, DRC, and in ***Luanda***, Angola: in these two cities, slums and informal settlements are proliferating in areas that are not claimed by customary or other owners and are, mostly, unsuitable for urbanisation. Although these illegal settlements come, at least in part, as the outcome of rapid, conflict-driven rural-urban migration, the shares of urban populations living in informal settlements are also increasing in the Central African Republic and Cameroon; two countries that have not experienced any periods of protracted conflict (Bopda, 2005).

Urban Land Institutions

Institutional frameworks are very similar in Central and Francophone Western African countries. In all Central African countries, land administration and management fall under the responsibility of multiple administrative entities with weak inter-institutional coordination. In Gabon, for example, land administration is shared between the Department of Domains, the Land Registry (which falls under the direct responsibility of the country's president) and the Department of Cadastre and Topography (which is under the Ministry of Housing and Urban Planning). This creates major obstacles to development, approval, implementation and enforcement of land governance reforms. Nevertheless, during the past two decades, all Central African countries have attempted to decentralise land administration and management. However, with institutional hindrances, and the subregion's strong centralist traditions, decentralisation has achieved limited results.

A top-down national process imported from more advanced countries, decentralisation has been embraced by many African governments. In practice, decentralisation frequently amounts to little more than de-concentration of functions to *local* branches of *central* government institutions, because governments remain reluctant to transfer land management decisions and processes to local authorities. Moreover, in most Central African countries, the links between the legal frameworks of land administration (the status of the land) and land management (who can use the land for what) are not sufficiently developed or clear to enable local operators to benefit from decentralised land governance. Such limitations can, for instance, be observed in Gabon, where land is allocated at the *Département* and *District* levels, but nevertheless remains under the authority of central government representatives (*Préfets*). Likewise in Cameroon, where the land registry was decentralised in 2005 to the level of "*Départements*", but the decentralisation of land administration responsibilities to *Communes* and *Communautés urbaines* remains restricted as central government still plays a key role in decision-making at the local level.

In institutional terms, Central African countries are all responding differently to customary practices. While Cameroon recognises customary institutions, public authorities frequently deny them the right to allocate land, especially in urban and peri-urban areas.

Traditional chiefdoms today stand as the legacies of ancestral structures and norms and continue to play a fundamental role in land management. Being linguistic, cultural and political entities, they are recognised by government authorities as yet another component of spatial administration. Their role was formalised by decree in 1977 (decree N° 77/245 restructuring traditional chiefdoms) and in 1982 (decree N° 241/82). Traditional chiefs and auxiliary notabilities sit, by right, on consultative committees and advise on land registration and concessionary allocation, although any final decision remains with government officials. Chiefs also play a role in land dispute settlement.

In the DRC, where customary approaches to land management are *not* formally recognised, traditional leaders nevertheless play a significant role, as few decisions affecting customary land are made without prior consultation and negotiation with the communities involved, in part because these communities help ensure local peace and social stability.

How Land Markets Operate

In Central Africa, urban land initially gets onto the markets in one of four different ways:

1. *Land allocation through public agencies* (municipal, federal or state) is the formal urban land supply channel. The procedure comprises registration of tenure arrangements, title deeds, lease agreements, etc. Security of tenure is high, with rights to the land enforceable in court, while the title can serve as collateral for formal housing loans. However, in Central Africa, formal urban land markets remain embryonic, except in city centres, and over the past decades all efforts to provide land to the urban majorities through formal allocations have failed;
2. *Allocation of public land through illegal transfer* by government employees is usually supported by a registered land title, lease agreement or other formal documentation; these rights are bankable;
3. *Allocation of customary urban land* can take different forms, but under severe urban land demand, customarily allocated plots have become subject to commoditisation. Private rights on customary land can increasingly be bought as in formal land markets. Tenure rights are not registered, albeit they are often recorded in local registers. Consequently, security of tenure is fragile; and
4. *Land squatting* is rapidly on the rise across Central African cities, as a response to rising land price trends and migration of very poor rural populations who simply cannot afford any of the previous land access options. Security of tenure for this category is basically non-existent.

Structural weaknesses in formal land allocation and the attendant inability to cater for low-income urban populations

BOX 5.2: **CAMEROON: ANTAGONISMS IN CUSTOMARY LAND MARKETS**

Traditional community chiefs are the main providers of land for housing in Douala and Yaoundé. They do this in cooperation with informal intermediaries and brokers, as well as formal and informal land and housing developers. Government and municipal employees in land administration services act as facilitators, while lawyers and magistrates ensure continuity between formal and informal land delivery processes.

Customary practice is now gradually adapting to higher demand for urban land. After negotiation with other community members, customary land right holders sign away their customary rights *(Attestation d'abandon de droits coutumiers)* and transfer them to the buyer. This document is countersigned by witnesses and local authorities. This procedure is becoming ever more commonplace in cities, stimulating customary urban land markets. Still, government services are not officially involved in these customary land markets and look to enforce laws. For example, these services do not recognise customary deeds of sale even where authenticated by witnesses or civil servants. They will also routinely deny applications for registration or land title on customary land, but with many exceptions depending on applicants' social status and networks.

Source: Bopda, 2005

BOX 5.3: **TRANSACTION DOCUMENTATION IN INFORMAL REAL ESTATE MARKETS, LUANDA**

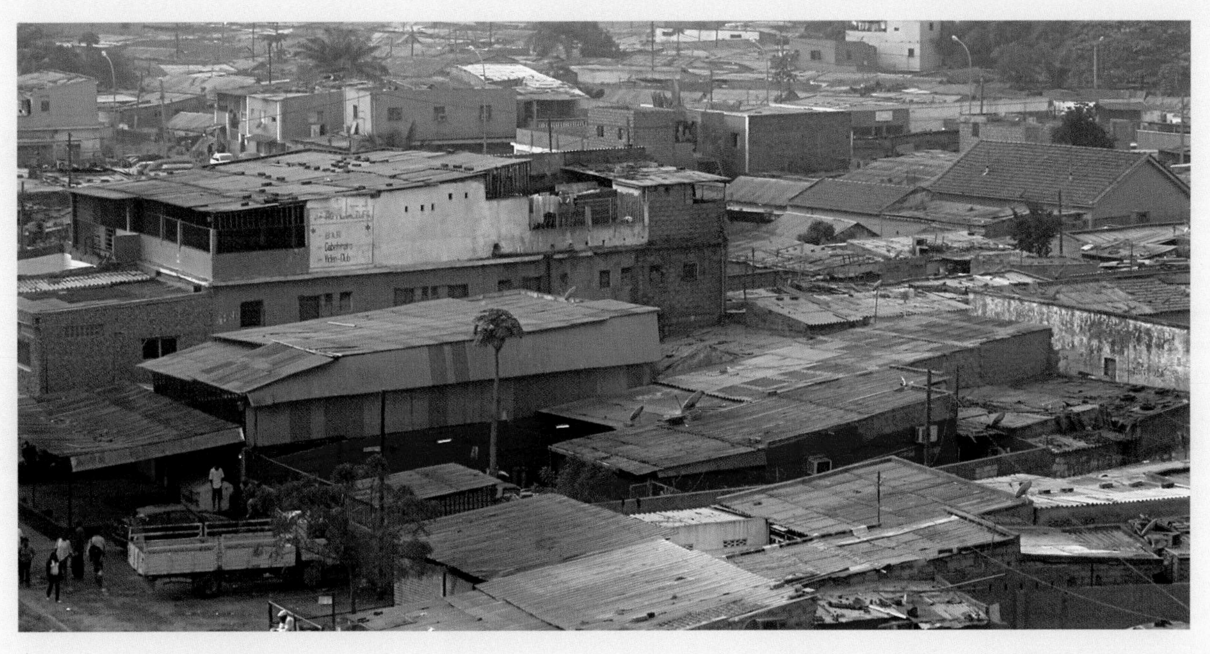

▲
Luanda, Angola. **©Jaspreet Kindra/IRIN**

Most of the land surrounding Luanda has been allocated through customary or informal delivery. These lively, albeit unregulated and 'illegal' urban real estate markets present opportunities for the government to fund infrastructure upgrading from rates, fees and eventually taxation through land titling and regularisation.

Although formal registration of property transactions is typically sidestepped, 80 per cent of the residents interviewed across peri-urban Luanda claimed to posses some form of documentation proving their land purchase, land occupation rights or land rental. Only 16 per cent had no supporting document. 'Purchase and Sale' contracts made up 20 to 30 per cent of these documents, with 10 to 25 per cent of these signed by a local administration. Some documents are just receipts of fines paid to the local administration for unauthorised occupation.

However, the majority of the reported documents do not confer any legal occupancy rights whatsoever, although most residents mistakenly believe they do. Fewer than 20 per cent of those interviewed had some form of legal ownership title or formal rental contract with an owner holding legal title to the land. About 43 per cent of the respondents had no knowledge of the legal concept of land rights, and only 13 per cent had a reasonable awareness of land rights.

Since a new land law proposes stripping informal occupants of any tenure rights, the majority of those living in Luanda's peri-urban areas and *musseques* (urban slum settlements) are at risk of becoming illegal and can portend subsequent eviction.

Source: Cain, 2003

have boosted the emergence of alternative urban land markets. Given the scale of the demand, it should perhaps not be surprising that informal and (neo-)customary markets are now meeting up to 90 per cent of Central Africa's urban residential land demand - the highest rate in all of sub-Saharan Africa.

Most transactions on these markets are not formally recognized and therefore risky. But since these alternative markets offer the sole option for poor urban households, the risks simply have to be borne, although - and this is a crucial point - they discourage spending on decent housing. Worldwide experience has shown that, if given security of tenure, slum dwellers, despite their poverty, are willing and capable to build fairly adequate housing through self-help. The risk of eviction, rather than poverty *per se*, accounts for the appalling housing standards prevailing in urban slums.

During the past decades, most of the cities in the subregion displayed a surprising capacity to adapt to economic change and rapid urban expansion. In all Central African cities, customary and informal land delivery systems are adapting and now treat land rights as freely exchangeable market commodities. In ***Kinshasa*** and ***Brazzaville***, for instance, customary and informal operators are now the main providers of urban land. However, public authorities do not formally recognize customary or informal land transactions, as in Cameroon. Rather, they try to enforce repressive laws, regardless of the fact that public servants in land administration (Cadastral and Land Affairs Departments), public representatives at neighbourhood level (*chefs de quartier*) and mayors are all actively involved in customary and informal land transactions (Flouriot, 2010, personal communication) (see also Box 5.2).

Land Markets, Urban Form and Configurations

Over time, formal urban land markets substitute income- or social class-based segregation for the colonial legacy of ethnic urban segregation, often with largely similar outcomes, namely clear, systematic segregation between rich and poor urban neighbourhoods. The real problem came when cities began to 'over-urbanise' that is, when demographic growth significantly outpaced the capacity of urban economies to cater to their various economic needs and requirements.

▲
Yaoundé, Cameroon. **©Pozzo di Borgo Thomas/Shutterstock**

BOX 5.4: CAMEROON: UNCONTROLLED EXPANSION OF INFORMAL SETTLEMENTS AT THE PERIPHERY OF CITIES

In Cameroon, 'urban' refers to any land located within the boundaries of those agglomerations categorised as 'urban centres' which poses the problem of the delineation of rural peripheries and, more particularly, peri-urban areas. Anarchic extensions take the form of illicit occupation of state property; this can sometimes involve a degree of formalisation (for lack of full legalisation) which consists of 'selling' parcels that have been more or less subdivided by customary holders. For lack of control or proper information, this process can even end up with transfers of plots from the state public or private domain. This more or less *bona fide* land anarchy effectively adds to the already severe problem of large city management, and to this day government services seem to be totally powerless, regardless of their powers under law.

Source: Rochegude & Plançon, 2010

With rapid increases in urban populations, the land values in former indigenous neighbourhoods tend to rise sharply, especially near city centres, which adds to demand pressures and the associated risks of market-driven displacement to insecure tenures. In areas where demand is high, economically weaker households are exposed to the market pressures and are forced out of the area, because tenure status as provided under dual formal and informal/customary rules can become 'reinterpreted'. Such market-driven eviction can also happen where multiple forms of overlapping tenure status sit side by side. Formal markets, as rigidly backed by the law and market forces, cannot provide land at scale to house the poor. Informality is pushed to marginal lands within the city and the more affordable peri-urban areas and urban fringes. The political, social and spatial outcomes of these processes are quite predictable and almost uniform across urban Africa.

Given the generally limited capacities of local government institutions to enforce urban development control, the markets fill the governance void, either formally or informally, and settlement on any 'vacant' urban land by poorer people becomes widespread. Eviction will push settlers to some other vacant tract. When no more vacant urban lands are available, the poor move to affordable rural land on the urban fringes where eviction is less likely, especially if the land lies beyond municipal boundaries.

That is how the urban poor become increasingly concentrated on under-serviced, marginal and hazardous lands within the city or on sprawling peri-urban fringe areas, which, again, leaves them spatially segregated from economic opportunity and much more exposed to unhealthy living environments and worsening spirals of extreme poverty.

Even more clearly than in Western African cities, the patterns of physical urban expansion in Central Africa are characterised by lack of planning and uncontrolled urban sprawl. This is the consequence of a combination of four factors: (i) rapid urban demographic growth, (ii) the share of customary and informal land delivery processes in the supply of land, (iii) rigid and unenforceable legal frameworks with regard to planning and land administration, and (iv) widespread corruption and illicit practices.

In 2005, the urbanised area of ***Kinshasa*** extended over more than 500 km^2, expanding by 8 km^2 every year and almost exclusively by dint of illicit, informal, 'self-help' urbanisation. Far from being 'anarchic', as often claimed, occupation follows an orthogonal urban pattern inherited from the colonial period. Plots are relatively large, at 300 to 500 m^2, while the built-up area - often with fairly good quality construction - does not exceed 100 m^2. This results in urban sprawling, with low densities (between one and five individuals per 100 m^2) (Flouriot. 2005).[21] In 2005, no affordable plots (i.e., between US $300 and 500) were available within a radius of 40 to 50 km from central Kinshasa. Subserviced plots of 750 m^2 located 20 km away from the city centre would still cost about US $1,000 (Flouriot, 2010).

In all Central African capital cities, stringent construction standards combine with insecure land tenure to fuel the proliferation and spatial expansion of slums. Administrative boundaries turn planning regulation enforcement into a challenge: dual urban land management and administration systems can operate and even co-exist fairly smoothly, but only when the territories under their respective control are clearly demarcated and separated. The problem in the post-independence period, however, has been that these dualistic urban land markets and their respective regulatory frameworks have triggered more and more urban land conflicts when they began to intrude on each other's physical territory.

Bopda (2005) once watched a rush of 'landless' people in ***Yaoundé*** and ***Douala*** (in fact, households without any land or shelter) to customary lands in the far-out periphery. The rush came in response to persistent lack of government policies in favour of access to land or housing for low-income categories. The pressure on land is exacerbated by private-sector developers. Since available land prevents them from operating at scale, they must go into business with (neo-) customary land market participants. For the sake of efficiency, informal developers will typically turn to customary property owners (when they are not one of them) in order to purchase parcels, which adds to land scarcity and urban sprawl.

The Limitations of Conventional Land Administration

A series of obstacles undermine the efficiency of formal urban land and housing markets in Central Africa; they include the following: (a) time-consuming and cumbersome land allocation procedures, (b) costly transactions, (c) slow tenure regularisation, (d) inappropriate land policies given the scarce financial resources of the urban poor; (e) fragmented, outdated or partially enforceable legislation; (f) inefficient dispute settlement institutions and procedures; and (g)

▲
Roof construction, Central African Republic. ©**Anthony Morland/IRIN**

general failure of land administration to register land rights.

Security of tenure for the poor is a major urban problem in the subregion. Even when informal land is titled, non-compliance with municipal regulatory requirements, such as minimum plot size, space standards and infrastructural criteria, can render illegal any developments on the land. Attempts have been made in most countries of the subregion to streamline public land allocation and tenure regularization procedures, but with limited results because the main obstacles to reform are to be found within land governance institutions.

In all Central and Western African nations, access to land allocated by the State requires an extensive series of steps: 137 in Gabon, for instance, involving seven administrative bodies. Procedures are not transparent either, since documents in the Department of Domains, the Department of the Cadastre and in the Land Register (*Livre foncier*) are not freely accessible to the public, a major factor behind the general reluctance to register land. In 1995, ***Libreville*** consisted of an estimated 150,000 built-up plots, of which only a paltry 6,000 were titled, and another 6,000 temporary titles (*titres provisoires*) had been issued (Comby, 1995).[22] Recent observations confirm that the situation has not significantly improved since then. As the result of this debilitating lack of administrative expediency, 90 per cent of residents in Libreville have little alternative but to rely on informal land delivery and occupancy. In all countries of the subregion, the predominance of unregistered ownership further makes the tracing of title chains over time almost impossible, and fraud all the easier. This overwhelming degree of informality has tangible effects on formal land and housing markets: the potential for collateralized lending (backed by the relevant, securely held plot) is drastically reduced, which in turn makes the achievement of the construction requirements attached to PTOs a self-defeating condition, since compliance with those requirements is a prerequisite for permanent property rights.

In Angola, a 1992 law placed the responsibility for land access on the state. The problem is that the public institutions regulating land access lacked the capacity for transparent, accountable implementation. State management of land was disorganized, with fragmented institutional responsibilities

> **BOX 5.5: CAMEROON'S CUSTOMARY LAND HOLDERS CANNOT AFFORD DEVELOPMENT COSTS**
>
> In Cameroon, customary stakeholders are not in a position to make proper land subdivisions. Since they have no formal land titles, they are not authorised to subdivide parcels or sell land plots.
>
> The alternative for them is to subdivide plots regardless of planning standards, since these are not enforceable on customary land. They hardly ever call in surveyors from the Land Registry to help with subdivision and demarcation, for fear of being deprived of part of the plot and becoming aware of it only once the process is completed. In case they wished to comply with planning standards when making subdivisions, they could not afford the costs and would not have the necessary political connections, even where they hold a title. Therefore, customary operators act in a piecemeal sort of way, subdividing parcels and selling individual plots as required by demand or their own financial needs.
>
> There can be no doubting that if customary channels for land delivery were to be recognised by public authorities, this would remove the attractions they hold for low-income people as land values would rise. Therefore, operating on the margins of formal legality serves the poor well.
>
> *Source: Bopda, 2005*

▲
Goma, DRC. ©**Laudes Martial Mbon/IRIN**

and a lack of clear records that made land administration open to gross abuse. The system gave advantage to those who understood the system and knew the people in charge. In 2004, under pressure from civil society organizations, changes were introduced that allow informal occupiers to legalize their tenure status within a three-year period, but since the state administration still lacks the capacity to process the resultant tens of thousands of requests, the backlogs are enormous.

Across Central Africa, allocation of public land by local and municipal authorities is undermined by corruption, especially where institutions are heavily under-resourced, as in Chad, the Central African Republic and the DRC. This situation has nothing to do with land market shortcomings, but rather a deeply rooted pattern of behaviour. In these nations' post-independence administrative tradition, land allocation prerogatives shifted to the newly independents states but without the procedures, institutions or independent bodies to monitor operations. ***Brazzaville***, ***Kinshasa***, ***Libreville***, ***Luanda*** and ***Malabo***, to mention a few, lack the procedures for legal and administrative scrutiny which could stop illegal sales of public land. Corruption is difficult to address where urban land administration and registration is poor, land records are incomplete, access to land ownership information is lacking and whatever available information is held by a variety of government bodies. Deep grassroots mistrust of court decisions on land disputes is not helpful either.

Informal Settlements as a Response to Land Market Imperfections

In Central African countries, and without any exception, formal urban land markets force out the urban poor, strengthening new alternative land delivery systems in peri-urban areas because they can deliver at scale, they are cheap, and they provide a 'fast-track' access to plots. However, informal land delivery fails to provide secure tenure, even though residents of informal and customary settlements do enjoy *de facto* security. The numbers of land-related conflicts are rapidly spiralling out of hand, representing 80 per cent of all court cases in ***Kinshasa***, for example, (Flouriot, 2005) and a majority of the cases in ***Brazzaville***, ***Douala***, ***Luanda*** and ***Yaoundé***.

Whereas in Western African cities the dynamics between government land institutions, on the one hand, and customary and informal/customary developers, on the other, are converging when it comes to land delivery, the situation in Central Africa is a problematic one. For Central African government institutions (Departments of State Domain and the Cadastre), the integration of customary land developments is made difficult by inappropriate land management and planning models, poor model implementation and centralised administrative traditions; at the same time, widespread corruption hinders streamlining and integration of informal land delivery methods. Community-level organization is usually weak; it can also be beset by political problems, with customary leaders and democratically elected representatives vying for legitimacy, as in Cameroon, Congo or the DRC.

Simultaneously, customary systems are eroded by market pressures as customary land reserves dry up along city fringes. Access to customary land is now possible only in those areas far from city centres. Customary land delivery is further marginalized by the proliferation of intermediaries and brokers, including land surveyors as increasingly important mediators between buyers, customary land holders and government services. Lack of resources, technical culture, skills and know-how on the part of customary developers creates further planning and environmental problems.

The Political Economy of Urban Land Markets

Land tenure is a social relation of appropriation and exclusion. Land represents power in political, social and economic terms. In all countries of the subregion, land legislation is based upon the principle of *domanialité*, which grants the state an exclusive monopoly on any land that has not been appropriated and titled. This principle was inherited from the French and Portuguese colonial tradition and today is upheld in the name of national unity and economic development. It provides a framework for the allocation of public land and access to ownership. In practice, implementation of the principle of *domanialité* varies across countries. For example, it may or may not recognize customary rights - but the basic principle remains the same: it places all land not held under a title in the state domain.

This gives public administrations discretionary powers to allocate land, recognise customary rights or formalize informal land occupations under the terms and conditions defined by law. The state prerogative with regard to *domanialité* puts government officials in a powerful position, as they can arbitrarily allocate (for a fee) land rights that can subsequently be transferred at market prices. In many Central African nations where democratic practices and transparent land management procedures do not prevail, this practice is deeply rooted in land administration services, to the benefit of government clienteles. This is not only fuelling corruption, it also generates rivalries between government institutions in charge of land management and administration. This situation stands as a major obstacle to decentralized land governance, as transfer of land prerogatives to local authorities deprives central government land administration of resources and power (UNCHS, 1999).

'Legality *v.* customary legitimacy' is another conflict area between statutory and non-statutory institutions. That is why, in Central Africa, governments are so reluctant formally to recognize customary land rights. When these rights are recognized, as in Cameroon, customary land transfers are not permitted or strictly limited. In Angola, only customary user rights are recognized; this is the one and only exception in the subregion, as though the emergence of customary land markets would deprive government land institutions of their *de facto* monopoly on land. Still, paradoxically, the legitimacy of customary institutions is not questioned. Their role with regard to social control is acknowledged, as well as their critical contribution to the provision of affordable land for housing. They are simply not considered as legal entities, implying that they cannot yield the full benefits of the land transactions they control, since land delivery remains a government prerogative.

No country in the Central Africa has launched any tenure formalization or regularization programme, even where the necessary legal instruments are available, as in Cameroon and Angola. Lack of tenure regularization is usually justified by technical reasons, such as lack of administrative capacity or the illegal status of settlements, a situation that is also symptomatic of attempts by interest groups within the state apparatus to maintain scarcity on land markets, as long as illegal but tolerated informal and customary land delivery acts as a 'safety valve' to relieve the shortage of affordable urban housing.

Land as a Municipal Revenue Source

In ***Libreville***, ***Luanda*** and ***Malabo,*** public authorities have in the past resorted to a variety of instruments (including leases and outright sales) to capture rapidly rising land values and use the proceeds to spend on infrastructure. Capturing land values indeed is a one of the main avenues for recouping many urban infrastructure costs. But at a time that Central African cities are facing a rapidly escalating scramble for urban land, sales of public land by local and municipal authorities are increasingly tainted with lack of transparency, secretive decision-making and corruption. Where governance is weak and highly corrupt, public urban land is often captured by politicians or high-ranking officers in the armed forces and sold to local businesses, or illegally transferred to foreign buyers.

Across the subregion, local protests against public land purchases by businesses from the Far East, the Gulf States or Western multinationals are on the rise. Unless illegal sales on this non-renewable municipal resource are curbed, the outcome can only be increased evictions of poor and lower-middle income urban dwellers, along with significant foregone municipal own-source funding. The reality, however, is that many countries or cities in Central Africa have no adequate legal or administrative mechanisms to protect public land. Revenue collection services are often understaffed and inefficient, while large amounts of collected revenues never reach local authority accounts.

This is the background against which urban land has ceased to serve as a major source of municipal revenue in many Central African cities. In ***Bangui***, ***Brazzaville***, ***Kinshasa*** and ***Yaoundé***, land sales have all but ceased to fund urban infrastructure or even to increase government revenues. Corruption has become so commonplace that it now interferes with urban development processes. A rigorous debate on the use of land revenues, land administration and land management is urgently needed to explore workable alternatives, and to enable urban land to once more play its crucial role in the funding of municipalities.

5.4
The Geography of Climate Change

Much of Central Africa has a humid tropical climate with dense rain forest cover. The subregion also features extensive savannas north and south of the Congo Basin. The Atlantic coast is humid and warm, while a dry desert climate prevails in the north of the subregion, especially in north Cameroon and Chad. Many countries experience a dry and a rainy season, and monthly temperatures average between 21° and 34°C.

In Angola, forests sprawl over about 30 per cent of the territory, while the DRC's more than 100 million ha of rain forest covers nearly 50 per cent of the country. Much of Congo and Gabon is covered by forests, too, as are southern Cameroon and the South of the Central African Republic. These rainforests hold vast biodiversity and timber reserves, and coastal countries are rich in fish resources.

However, recent trends of environmental losses in coastal regions and rain forests are worrisome. Central Africa is expected to become predominantly urban around 2022, but current rapid increases in urban populations already alter the regional environment, in general, and urban areas in particular. Urban areas of all sizes face increased risks from water scarcity and flooding. Coastal areas are threatened by sea level rise at a time when urban demographic pressures keep mounting.

▲
Brazzaville, Congo. **©Laudes Martial Mbon/IRIN**

The Role of Local Authorities in Adaptation to Climate Change

Recurrent flooding in cities across Central Africa is the result of multiple factors, but mostly the outcome of human behaviour, including sustained demographic growth and associated settlement in flood-prone areas, lack of storm water drains or poor maintenance of infrastructures in many urban neighbourhoods, inadequate urban management and extreme poverty. As more people move to cities, unplanned and uncontrolled developments cover large tracts of land with houses, roads and other infrastructure, which compound flooding, as soils can no longer absorb runoff water.

As serviced urban land is unaffordable to them, poor city dwellers frequently build their homes in unsuitable or hazardous locations, such as near waterways which make them vulnerable to flooding. Lack of drainage systems and uncollected garbage blocking storm water drains slow down runoff water flows and cause flooding. With extreme weather events associated with climate change becoming more frequent, the urban poor are increasingly at risk.

One of the main contributors to climate change in Central Africa is the use of wood and charcoal for cooking, as this contributes significantly to deforestation and land degradation, besides indoor air pollution. Repeated economic and other crises and general deterioration of urban electricity infrastructures have forced many urban households to use charcoal or fuel wood, on top of those that already do because they cannot afford electricity. Extensive fuel wood use is therefore not just a result of poverty but also a matter of widespread failure to give cities energy security.

Since the beginning of the year 2000, many municipalities have issued rules and regulations to address the effects of climate change. In ***Bangui, Brazzaville, Kinshasa, Libreville, Luanda*** and ***Yaoundé,*** policy documents such as Environmental Management Programmes and other instruments have provided the legal frameworks needed to address climate change. Significant improvements have already been felt, including thanks to the involvement of private companies operating under scrutiny or supervision of public agencies and international non-governmental organisations.

Most local authorities in Central Africa have devised emergency policies to deal with climate change, especially in urban areas. The rationale is mostly to stop the continuous destruction of the environment and to save urban dwellers' lives and livelihoods. Many local authorities, especially in cities on the Atlantic coast, are currently working with non-governmental organisations and local communities to reduce vulnerability to the social and economic effects of climate change. However, although many municipalities have some climate-change-related arrangements in place, most are not working well and implementation is hindered by lack of urban planning and local financial resources.

Climate Change: How much do we know?

Although climate change in cities is a major threat to living conditions, poverty reduction initiatives and development in general, the majority of Central African city dwellers are not familiar with the notion or its implications. These are mainly debated in political and scientific arenas by the media and non-governmental organisations. The majority of urban dwellers only speak their local dialects and translation of climate change notions does not always clearly convey their meaning. Public awareness-building gatherings, like town hall or community meetings, could help overcome these knowledge-sharing difficulties. Whereas many urban dwellers are aware of deforestation around their cities and have noticed changes in weather patterns, few realize the relationships between these events and the way each and everyone's behaviour can help mitigate the effects of climate change.

Currently, the debate on climate change is taking place mainly among a small number of intellectuals, politicians, scientists and, to a lesser extent, urban managers. As non-governmental organisations and the media increasingly share their knowledge, resources and ideas, more people are becoming aware of climate change and its effects, but much more needs to be done. Since agricultural production in the region relies mainly on rainfall, rural populations, too, must be informed if they are to contribute to any adaptation or mitigation efforts.

In order to address local knowledge gaps, authorities at municipal, city and national levels should invest in awareness-raising through the media, scientists, schools, religious and community leaders at all levels to build awareness of the problem and understanding of the necessary responses.

Urban Strategies for Adaptation to Climate Change

Urban energy security is critical for economic growth and poverty alleviation in the region. In Africa, where wood, charcoal, and other biomass meet about 80 per cent of the domestic primary energy needs, over 550 million people lack access to modern energy supply.[23] But this can change.

The DRC has one of the largest hydro-electric power plants in Africa with a 150,000 MW capacity, or three times Africa's current power consumption. The Inga Dam on the Congo River, has, on its own, the potential to generate 40,000 to 45,000 MW, which could meet the needs of the entire Southern African subregion. The Congo River, more than 4,500 km long, is second only to the Amazon for discharge and features the most important water falls in Africa, with the potential to supply 'clean' and renewable electricity to vast areas of Africa, generating huge incomes in the process. The DRC currently exports electricity to Angola, Burundi, Congo, Rwanda, Zambia and Zimbabwe.

BOX 5.6: INNOVATIVE *BRIQUETTES BIOMASSES* ARE POPULAR IN DRC

Poor and low-income households in Bukavu, Goma and other towns in the DRC are experimenting with a new source of energy called *briquettes biomasses*. This alternative to charcoal and firewood is made from leaves, tree bark and agricultural wastes. The briquettes reduce pollution, wastes and deforestation. *Briquettes biomasses* have been developed by scientists at the National Park of Virunga, the Congolese Institute for the Conservation of Nature and a non-governmental organisation known as 'Environment, Natural Resources and Development'. The environment-friendly *briquettes* are available at about half the cost of the charcoal or firewood equivalent and are 70 per cent more energy-efficient.

These economic and environmental benefits make *briquettes biomasses* increasingly popular in the eastern regions of the DRC. The raw material is widely available in cities across the region, making production easy. This in turn can bring environmental and socio-economic benefits to municipalities and local communities as jobs are created, forests, savannas and woods are saved, and the cost of solid urban waste management is reduced. Adequate financial, technical and management support would help promote local manufacturing.

In sharp contrast, only eight per cent of the DRC population has access to electric power because of poor (where any) grid maintenance. Current electricity export income flows should be deployed to supply cheap energy to the DRC, including its cities. The highly competitive costs of this clean and renewable energy source can give manufacturing and living conditions a massive boost, putting an end to the current biomass-related deforestation and air pollution. All that is required is the political will to divert electricity export incomes to the upgrading and extension of domestic electricity infrastructures and facilities. In a country the size of the DRC, this is no small feat, but the DRC has a moral duty to do so, creating hundreds of thousands of jobs as the grid is extended and better maintained.

Environmental degradation in Central African cities and their environmental footprints are closely associated with poverty incidence. The high cost of electricity and lack of livelihood opportunities have accelerated environmental degradation, as has the need for poor urban dwellers to use the land for food and biomass production purposes. Many municipalities in the region are looking to promote alternative, cheap and relatively 'clean' new energy sources such as the *briquettes biomasses* produced in the eastern part of the DRC (see Box 5.6).

Although their financial resources are often limited, African governments are working to cut carbon emissions, protect carbon sinks and put in place strategies to tackle a phenomenon - climate change - for which they hardly have any responsibility in the first place. Adaptation and climate risk management are more and more becoming core development objectives in Africa. In 2007, for example, the DRC moved to preserve the largest tropical rainforests in the world after the Amazon.[24] The strategies now under development by Central African governments take into account the impact of cities on the environment, given their concentrated demand for energy, water, infrastructure and services.

While climate variability is not a new factor in Africa's history, the incidence and severity of extreme weather events, including floods and droughts, has increased sharply in recent years and projections indicate that this trend may intensify, further increasing the region's natural vulnerability.[25] Faced with these prospects, local authorities in ***Libreville*** and ***Yaoundé*** have substantially increased budget allocations for improved urban environment. Putting a halt to deforestation in and around cities located in vulnerable coastal regions has become a priority. Together with the United Nations Development Programme (UNDP), ***Libreville*** and Gabon's Ministry of Public Health and Hygiene have arranged for the collection of waste in residential areas and the city centre. Nearly 200 young people from Libreville work in 11 selected areas, clearing up waste for 300,000 urban residents and otherwise cleaning up the city. Households pay XAF5,000 (about US $10) per month for the service and household waste clearing has become a source of employment for otherwise jobless urban youngsters.

Cities like ***Kinshasa, Luanda, Malabo, N'Djamena, São Tomé*** and ***Yaoundé*** are implementing projects to preserve the local environment and tackle eco-system degradation. Around the hinterlands of ***Luanda*** and ***Kinshasa***, trees have been planted to help re-forestation and in other cities, efforts are underway to stop deforestation, too. Furthermore, many countries in the region are members of the Congo Basin Forest Fund, which supports projects, including safeguard of the rainforest with assistance from the United Kingdom and Norway. Central and local governments in the region have recognized that curbing deforestation around their cities (and in the Congo Basin region in general) would provide a cost-effective way of fighting climate change on a regional scale.

▲
Stagnated water in the outskirts of a Chad town. **©UN-HABITAT**

5.5
Emerging Issues

Population Mobility, Urban Economies and Livelihoods

Migration has been a social process for millennia and a human response to patterns of uneven development. Apart from involuntary movements resulting from human-made or natural disasters, most people migrate for economic reasons.[26] Typically, they seek employment, a permanent residence or a social safety net as they have fallen into poverty.[27]

Despite the fact that migration is encouraged by the Economic Community of Central African Countries (ECCAC), countries like Angola, Equatorial Guinea, Gabon and São Tomé e Príncipe continue to see migration as undesirable, the cause of law-and-order problems, environmental disasters, economic exploitation, or political tensions and violence. However, other ECCAC member states have realised the importance and benefits of free migration, including an ability to bring positive economic and other changes to their countries.

Cameroon, Chad, Congo and the DRC have come to understand that migrants are agents of economic, technologic and cultural change and that they often represent extensive networks of exchange between countries and people. Urban authorities in these countries are well aware that cities are nodes of economic power, both within their individual countries and within the global economy and that cross-border flows of people, goods and finance can be beneficial. Cities' influence results not only from population concentration but also from their location-specific and economic advantages, including agglomeration economies and the associated economies of scale. Urban population growth generally goes hand in hand with increased production/income per head and declines in overall poverty. Cities can generate and sustain the economic growth of an entire country and are hosts to agents of change and development while acting as vibrant places for the creation and transfer of knowledge and wealth.

Any politician and urban manager in Central Africa who remain hostile to free movement of people, goods and finance must better understand the critical role that cities can play in poverty alleviation. Together with cross-border movements of people, migration combines with domestic and inter-city mobility to bring different benefits that can enhance people's welfare in urban areas on both sides of national borders. Especially in countries where migration is still seen as the cause of tension and instability, authorities at local, city and national levels should more objectively analyze the effects of cross-border migration. Most migrants are highly motivated people in search of employment or other economic opportunities, and they can also be vectors of economical, technological and cultural change who need to be supported and integrated within the city and the economy. They should be viewed for what they really are: human resources with different types of knowledge and cultures that can complement those prevailing in the host location. Well-administered and well-governed cities that are open to new ideas, cultures and technologies can be a country's best catalysts of economic growth and human development.

Trans-national Urban Systems

The Kinshasa-Brazzaville Mega Urban Region

Separated only by the Congo River, ***Brazzaville*** and ***Kinshasa*** are the geographically closest capital cities in the world after Vatican City and Rome, Italy. With a combined 2010 population exceeding 10 million people, the Kinshasa-Brazzaville conglomeration is the world's most populous trans-border metropolitan area.

Brazzaville is the capital of the Republic of Congo. The city is currently the largest, most populous and prosperous city in the country. ***Brazzaville*** was founded in 1880 on one of the northern banks of the Congo River near a Bateke village. It was named after its founder, French explorer Pierre Savorgnan de Brazza.

Before Belgian colonisation, ***Kinshasa*** was a conglomerate of several Bateke and Humbu villages and an important local trade centre. In 1880, ***Kinshasa*** was a village with 30,000 inhabitants where indigenous people traded bush meat, pottery, raffia, tobacco, boats, crafts and tools, clothes, alcohol, food and ivory.[28] In 1842, when the British explorer Henry Morton Stanley arrived there, ***Kinshasa*** was already an important commercial centre with various economic activities and connections with other parts of the region. Therefore, the urban system was not brought in from outside.[29]

Despite their common languages, French and Lingala,

MAP 5.2: **BRAZZAVILLE- KINSHASA CONGLOMERATION**

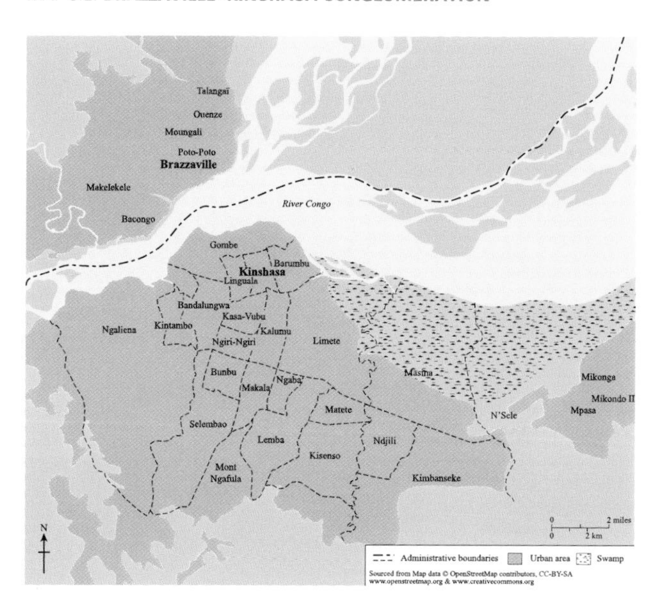

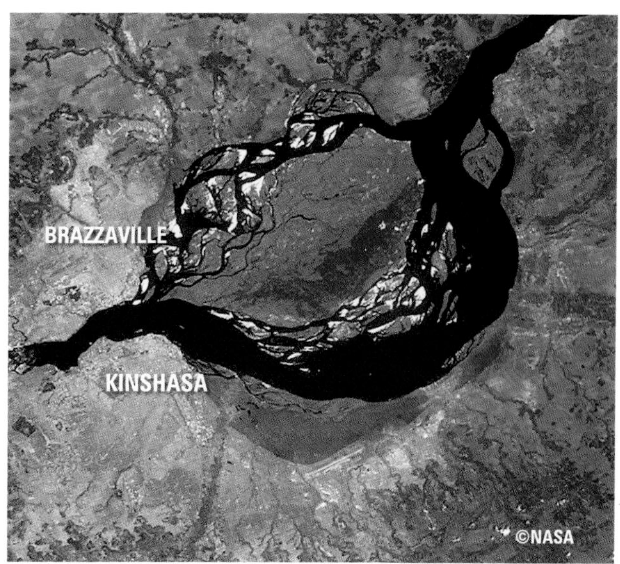

there has always been a degree of benign competition between ***Brazzaville*** and ***Kinshasa***. The two cities have grown together and influenced each other through commercial and cultural exchange. In recent years, cooperation between ***Kinshasa*** and ***Brazzaville*** has increased in several ways and people's lives now are influenced to a large degree by cross-border contacts. An estimated three million people cross the river every year to trade in informal markets on ferries, islands in the river and around the ports. Young people cross from ***Brazzaville*** to ***Kinshasa*** for educational purposes and to enjoy the nightlife. National and local radio stations and TV channels serve both sides of the border. However, the international border along the river remains ill-determined, leaving the status of some of the islands in the Malebo Pool of the Congo River somewhat vague. Being free of any jurisdiction, they are an attractive location for illicit trade. Economic and cultural links affect both cities in many ways and some businesses in Kinshasa would be wiped out if the border were to close, and *vice-versa*. ***Kinshasa*** and ***Brazzaville*** have become interdependent in the supply of food, clothing, pharmaceuticals and manufactured goods. In the 1980s, the cities were officially twinned and, in 1991, the construction of road and rail bridges between them was first explored, before running into political and financial difficulties.

The ***Kinshasa-Brazzaville*** urban region is one of the fastest growing cross-border urban conglomerations in sub-Saharan Africa and is currently experiencing various types of change. The mega urban region is host to high concentrations of the economic, industrial, social, health and political activities of both countries and employment opportunities for large numbers of people on both sides of the river. If political, economic and spatial cooperation can be sustained and improved, the Kinshasa-Brazzaville urban conglomeration could very well become one of the most important urban regions in Africa in economic and political terms.

However, as in many other large urban conglomerations around the world, the Kinshasa-Brazzaville mega urban region is facing numerous problems. Both cities are seriously affected by their rapid demographic growth against a background of substandard urban governance and management. Infrastructures are poorly maintained and in need of serious upgrading. Underdeveloped urban road networks, poorly maintained roads and rapidly increasing numbers of vehicles cause serious traffic congestion and road accidents. Other problems include poor energy supply and management of wastes. Both cities consume enormous amounts of energy and produce very large amounts of waste that is incinerated, buried or simply discharged into the Congo River. Many other urban problems also remain unresolved or unaddressed and both cities urgently need to clean up their acts.

Although some political differences remain over the protection of national interests, the Kinshasa-Brazzaville cross-border flows of people, labour, goods, services and cultures is indicative of the regional potential that could be opened up with an effective regional road network.

The Luanda-N'Djamena Development Corridor

Like any other region of the world, Central Africa, is experiencing ever-more intense migration and other cross-border movements of people, goods, services and finance as the outcome of globalization, rapid demographic growth, increasing mobility and geographically uneven development. Over the past decades, these forces have stimulated the emergence of new urban spatial configurations. These include mega urban regions like the cross-border ***Kinshasa-Brazzaville*** urban conglomeration discussed above, as well as a host of spontaneously emerging and/or deliberately promoted urban development corridors along major infrastructure lines connecting the economic nodes of the African continent. In Central Africa, an emerging huge regional corridor between ***Luanda***, Angola, and ***N'Djamena***, Chad, is one of the most important developments in this regard.

▲
Luanda, Angola. ©**Hansjoerg Richter/iStockphoto**

MAP 5.3: **THE EMERGING LUANDA-N'DJAMENA CORRIDOR**

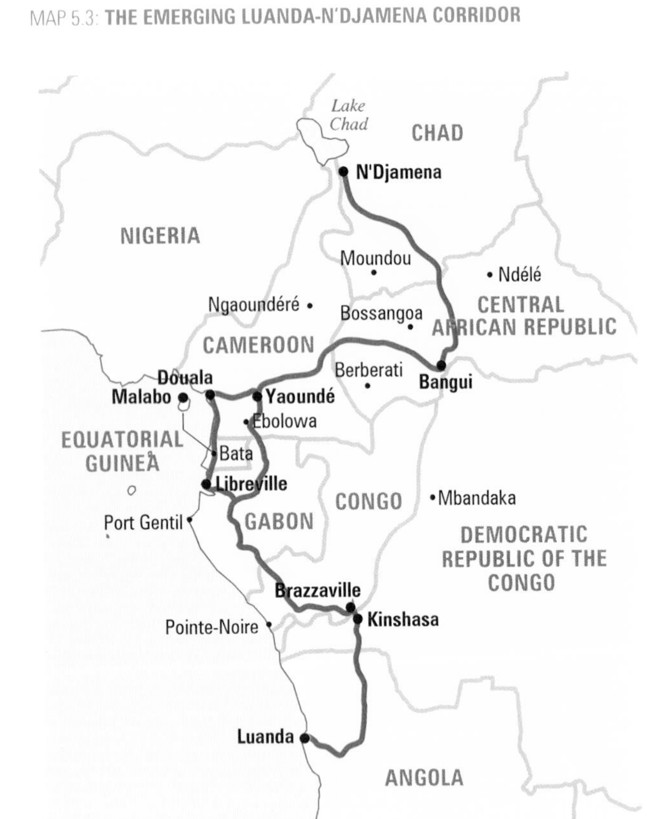

Source: Geographic Guide http://www.geographicguide.com/africa-map.htm

Central Africa as a whole is still deeply underdeveloped in terms of road, rail and water-borne transportation connections. In fact, most Central African capitals are still better linked to European cities by air and by sea than among themselves. Poorly developed cross-border infrastructures severely hamper the mobility of people, goods and services between the larger Central African cities and stand as significant obstacles to regional economic cooperation and integration.

The member states of the Economic Community of Central African States (CEEAC) met in 2004 in ***Brazzaville*** and adopted a plan to develop a reliable and competitive regional transportation network with a view to facilitating effective and affordable regional movements and integration. Complementing the initiative were plans to reduce transport costs, boost economic development and create additional jobs to tackle widespread poverty. Since 80 per cent of goods and 90 per cent of people movements in the region occur by road, priority went to their development, supported by a pledge of US$6.41 billion to develop or improve the trunk roads linking the region's capital cities by 2010. However, implementation is slow and it is clear that that objective will not be met by 2010, since currently only the capital cities ***Libreville*** and ***Yaoundé*** have been linked.[30]

Early construction of the ***Luanda-Brazzaville*** section of this regional road network should be a matter of high regional priority. A functional, efficient Luanda-Brazzaville road corridor would connect the more than 14 million inhabitants of the larger cities along the way. Early construction of the ***Brazzaville-Libreville*** section is equally important, as this would create a link all the way to ***Yaoundé***. Completion of this road network would connect an estimated 20 million people in the larger cities and conurbations, while also unlocking many secondary towns, villages and rural areas along its path, serving an estimated additional five million people.

Many of the cities along this proposed Central African road network are located on the Atlantic coast with port facilities, while the ***Brazzaville-Kinshasa*** mega urban region features ports along the Congo River. Most of these cities are hosts to the largest ports in their respective countries and, consequently, they play significant roles in domestic economic development. Interconnections among these major economic hubs would greatly enhance the potential for regional integration through cost reductions in logistics and enhanced trade and labour flows, including the prospect of elevating some of the domestic ports to regional prominence.

In order to reduce greenhouse gasses from road transportation, while facilitating cross-border trade and the movements of people between the Central African Republic, Congo and the DRC, cities in the subregion should also develop bulk transportation along cross-border waterways, such as the Congo and Ubangi Rivers: this could include links between ***Brazzaville-Kinshasa*** and ***Mbandaka***, ***Lisala*** and ***Kisangani*** in the DRC, making them far more intense than is currently the case. The same applies to ***Brazzaville-Kinshasa***, ***Bangui*** and ***Bangassou*** (CAR) on the Ubangi River.

However, if trans-national and regional cooperation between cities along these emerging logistic corridors is to be strengthened, the construction of major roads will not be enough. ECCAC governments must be more proactive and use regional cooperation to stimulate economic and social development in their cities, turning them into engines of national *and* regional growth. Smooth cross-border flows will also require a significant degree of regulation, if only to address current, non-negligible illegal or fraudulent cross-border operations.

Financing from the African Development Bank has enabled the governments of Congo and the DRC to start addressing cross-border issues, like improved trade and other links between ***Kinshasa*** and ***Brazzaville***. Similar initiatives are urgently required along other sections of the proposed regional road network. The example of the Kinshasa-Brazzaville mega urban region highlights the potential of regional cooperation for mutual benefit and for improved economic, financial, trade and migration relations. Significantly enhanced regional cooperation among ECCAC member states would also be an important step forward in improved economic and social development for the benefit of an estimated 25 million people along this proposed major regional transportation route.

City Regions

City regions are large urbanised territories consisting of one or more metropolitan areas and their surrounding towns, villages and rural areas featuring high and intense degrees of daily interaction. In city regions, economic and other activities extend beyond the confines of the leading metropolitan city and involve multiple surrounding smaller municipalities, to the extent that in economic, infrastructural and other terms the urban region could be considered as one single, if complex, urban structure.

As happens elsewhere in the world when urbanisation runs apace, many cities in Central Africa are now experiencing significant urban sprawl. Most of this expansion happens spontaneously, beyond any form of control by public authorities, as cities overtake their own administrative limits and encroach on rural hinterlands, in the process absorbing villages, towns and inter-mediate cities lying in their growth path. In these spatial urban growth processes, settlements merge physically and economically, creating large conurbations and new spatial configurations.

Most cities in the Central Africa, especially national capitals, were established or significantly developed during the colonial era as administrative and trading centres. At that time, they were significantly smaller, as reflected in original designs. If Central African governments and local authorities continue largely to sit on their hands in the face of sustained expansion of capital and other cities, the spatial, social and mobility outcomes will ultimately become highly undesirable. Funding priorities must be re-assessed. Urgently needed urban interventions and institutional reforms in favour of holistic, region-wide urban governance will only become increasingly unaffordable the longer they are postponed. New urban configurations require novel urban management and

TABLE 5.11: **THE PROSPECTIVE FASTEST GROWING CITIES IN CENTRAL AFRICA, 2010-2020**

Country	City	2010*	2020*	2010-20*
		Population (conurbation) (000s)		Change (%)
Angola	Luanda	4,772	7,080	48.4
Cameroon	Douala	2,125	2,815	32.5
Cameroon	Yaoundé	1,801	2,392	32.8
DR Congo	Kinshasa	8,754	12,788	46.1
DR Congo	Mbuji-Mayi	1,488	2,232	50.0
DR Congo	Lubumbashi	1,543	2,304	49.3
Congo	Brazzaville	1,292	1,703	31.8

*Projections
Source: WUP 2009

institutions that are adapted to the multi-nuclear nature of city regions. Short of these reforms, large cities will become fragmented, dysfunctional and increasingly difficult to live in, and may turn into significant hotbeds of environmental, social and political risk.

On current trends, all larger Central African cities are to experience significant demographic growth and expand way beyond their administrative municipal limits between 2010 and 2020. ***Luanda***, for example, has absorbed in its spatial growth the nearby towns of ***Benfica*** and ***Viana***, while ***Kinshasa*** has engulfed ***Kinkole*** to the the east, ***Kimwenza*** to the north and ***Matadi-Mayo*** to the west. To put the scale of this spatial expansion in proper perspective, the distance between ***Kinkole*** and ***Matadi-Mayo*** is more than 100 km, and Greater Kinshasa keeps expanding.

Current urban expansion in the DRC is due to the fact that after independence in 1960, the capital gained prominence over all other cities in this vast country. ***Kinshasa***'s population was only one million in 1970, growing to 3.5 million in 1990, 5.6 million in the year 2000 and an estimated 8.7 million in 2010. Projections are that that, by 2020, ***Kinshasa*** will be host to 12.78 million, becoming the largest and most populous conurbation in Africa after ***Lagos***. With a prospective demographic growth rate of 71.8 per cent between 2010 and 2025, ***Kinshasa*** is expanding significantly faster than any other capital city in Central Africa.

Among the large non-capital cities in Central Africa, the populations of ***Mbuji-Mayi*** and ***Lubumbashi*** are expected to grow by 50.0 and 49.3 per cent respectively between 2010 and 2020. The momentum started between 1992 and 1994 when, under instructions from the Mobutu regime, Kasai Congolese were expelled from the Katanga Province. Nearly two million people left Katanga and most moved to Western Kasai and its capital ***Mbuji-Mayi***, whose population has since

▲
Kinshasa, DRC. **©Eddy Isango/IRIN**

then increased rapidly. In ***Lubumbashi,*** demographic growth results from an economic boom in the mining industry over the past 10 years, with attendant developments like the establishment of foreign mineral companies in the city and the revival of various types of business linked to the sector. These have spurred immigration of job-seeking people from inside and outside the Kasai province.

Despite rapid urban growth and the emergence of city regions (and in the case of ***Kinshasa-Brazzaville*** a cross-border mega urban region), many central governments and local authorities appear to have only limited awareness of the potentially harmful consequences of unbridled and unguided urban spatial growth. City regions, like urban development corridors, need careful consideration, focusing not only on the way emerging spatial configurations will affect current and future urban management needs, but also the huge concentrations of people and economic activity which can carry serious risks for urban dynamism and stability. These risks may take many different forms and often appear simultaneously, from debilitating traffic deadlocks that undermine productivity, to severe environmental degradation and societal frictions. Unequal access to services, employment and an often concomitant, emerging urban fragmentation, are the main catalysts for escalating insecurity and crime, grassroots discontent and social unrest. Unless well-managed, very large population concentrations can easily become unstable, threatening urban systemic continuity, and ultimately become a risk factor to the political, economic and social sustainability of a whole nation.

Cities are national economic powerhouses and the generators of the lion's share of national production of goods and services. ***Kinshasa,*** for example, hosts 52 percent of all trade in the DRC 19 per cent of manufacturing, 21 per cent of services, 25 per cent of all construction companies, 33 per cent of transport and communications, 21 per cent of banking, 18 per cent of general services, 33 per cent of higher education institutions and the largest medical infrastructure in the country.

It is unlikely that Central African cities can sustain their significant political and economic roles if urban management practice and institutions do not evolve and grow commensurate to rapid physical and demographic expansion. Ignoring massive urban poverty and the needs of under-served urban population majorities is no longer a viable option, nor is the perpetuation of steep inequalities in access to the benefits of urban life. Sustained urban growth is a reality that will not go away for decades to come. The need for holistic interventions and effective reforms is more urgent than it has ever been. Spatial planning and development control, urban employment, transportation, urban mobility and housing all call for radical overhauls. Perhaps the most important task is social policy reform in order to address urban poverty promptly and effectively. Reform may be difficult, unsettling and costly, but the consequences of inaction may be far worse.

ENDNOTES

1. République Démocratique du Congo, Ministère de l'Urbanisme et de l'Habitat, Rapport Annuel, 2008, unpublished.
2. Fjeldstad, O-H. "Local Revenue Mobilization in Urban Settings in Africa", Workshop on Local Governance and Poverty Alleviation in Africa, African Development Bank, Tunis, 21-25 June 2005, p. 1
3. For more details about the way corruption operates in Central African countries, read Iyenda, G., *Op. Cit*, Gender Relations, Bread Winning and Family life in Kinshasa. pp. 200-203.
4. For more details about the involvement of women in survival strategies in Central Africa, see Iyenda, G. & Simon, D., Gender Relations, Bread Winning and Family life in Kinshasa (With), in *Cities in Contemporary Africa,* Palgrave Macmillan, New York, 2007, pp. 221- 240.
5. Stewart, F. "Income Distribution and Development", Working Paper N° 37, QEH Working Paper Series, Oxford: University of Oxford, March 2000, p. 1.
6. Poverty Reduction Strategy Paper (IMF – August 2003)
7. SFFPT Technical Committee, World bank, CAR Poverty Reduction Strategy Paper 2008-2010
8. IMF, Poverty Reduction Strategy Paper, 07/330, September 2007
9. Congolese Households Survey Strategy Paper (RBCSP 2008-2010)
10. Stewart, F., "Income Distribution and Development", Working Paper No 37, QEH Working Paper Series, Oxford: University of Oxford, March 2000, p.3
11. For more details about SAP in Africa, see Simon, D. (ed.), Structurally adjusted Africa. Poverty, debt and Basic Needs, Pluto Press, 1988; and Potter, D. & Mutambirwa, C. "Basics are now a luxury": Perceptions of Structural Adjustment's Impact on Rural and Urban Areas in Zimbabwe, Environment and Urbanisation, Vol.10, No1; 1998, pp.55-77
12. Data collected in Kinshasa, July 2009
13. Iyenda, G. Households' Livelihoods and Survival Strategies Among Congolese Urban Poor. Alternative to Western Approaches to Development, New York and Ontario: The Edwen Mellen Press, 2007, p.123.
14. UN. The Millennium Development Goals Report 2009, New York: UN, 2009, p.47
15. *Ibid.*
16. Trefon, T. (ed.). *Reinventing Order in the Congo: How People respond to State failure in Kinshasa*, London: Zed Books, 2004, p.2.
17. Iyenda, G. Livelihoods and Survival Strategies Among Congolese Urban Poor. Alternative to Western Approaches to Development, New York and Ontario: The Edwen Mellen Press, 2007, pp202-210.
18. *Ibid*, p. 202
19. Iyenda, G. , *op. cit.*
20. *Ibid.*
21. Flouriot. J. (2005) Kinshasa 2005. Trente ans après la publication de l'Atlas de Kinshasa
22. Comby, J. 2005. Le cadastre dans l'économie du Gabon. Mission d'évaluation. Rapport pour le Ministère de la Coopération, Paris, 1995).
23. Africa's development in a changing climate. Key policy advice from World Development Report 2010 and making climate resilient: a World bank Strategy for sub-Saharan Africa, Washington DC: World Bank, 2009
24. UN. The Millennium Development Goals Report 2009, New York: UN, 2009, p.43
25. World Bank. Africa's development in a changing climate. Key policy advice from World Development Report 2010 and making climate resilient: a World bank Strategy for sub-Saharan Africa, Washington DC:World Bank, 2009
26. Pacione, M., *Urban Geography*, Oxon and New York, Routledge, p. 484
27. UN. The Millennium Development Goals Report 2009, New York: UN, 2009, p.8
28. De St Moulin, L., Contribution à l'Histoire de Kinshasa (I), *Zaïre Afrique*, No 108, Kinshasa, 1976, P. 463.
29. For more details, see Iyenda, G., Livelihoods and Survival Strategies Among Congolese Urban Poor. Alternative to Western Approaches to Development, New York and Ontario:, The Edwen Mellen Press, 2007, p.68
30. For more information about this project, refer to http://www.investiraucameroun.com/immobilier-et-btp-actu/ceeac-8000-milliards-de-fcfa-pour-les-routes/pdf

Chapter Six

06

THE STATE OF SOUTHERN AFRICAN CITIES

Cape Town, South Africa.
©Wiw/Shutterstock

6.1
The Social Geography of Urbanisation

The Southern Africa region as defined[1] by UN-HABITAT (2008), brings together cities in a set of countries with close physical, linguistic, cultural, political economy and developmental features. The people in this set of countries generally describe themselves as belonging to Southern Africa, a description that may not coincide with non-African denominations or boundaries as determined by colonisers or empires, many of which are endorsed wholesale in global reports by international organisations.

Southern Africa includes nine countries: Angola, Botswana, Lesotho, Mozambique, Namibia, the Republic of South Africa, Swaziland, Zambia and Zimbabwe.

While it may be true that rapid urbanisation in Africa has not been associated with corresponding economic growth, in Southern African cities (to the exception of Zimbabwe) urbanisation has gone hand in hand with growth in real gross domestic product over the past decade although both urbanisation and economic growth have been highly uneven over time and unequal across this region.

MAP 6.1: **SOUTHERN AFRICAN COUNTRIES**

Urban geography recognises the importance of spatial unevenness in development outcomes. It further acknowledges the changes in spatial thinking and capital outlays needed for sustainable development, like targeted infrastructure and investment incentives to promote growth, on one hand, and to reduce inequalities on the other. A geographical perspective can add to our understanding of uneven urban development in Southern Africa in several respects. The main point is an appreciation that prevailing inequalities are a product of the history of political power relationships, institutions and international factors that continue to reproduce social differentiations at various scales. Consequently, this chapter highlights that addressing inequalities in urban welfare is unlikely to emerge without struggles over power. This chapter also shows that policy-making is a process whereby socio-economic and political interests are defended by those with power, and that technocratic interventions alone may not necessarily be enough.

Looking at geography beyond mere physical space in a bid to understand uneven development links, one must keep in mind the importance of the notion of deregulated governance in Southern Africa. In this perspective, governance is viewed as the manner or the processes through which power is mobilised, leveraged and used, not only between the state and society but also within state institutions and within and among civil society institutions - both individually and collectively[2]. Despite a dominant view that governance processes occur in the framework of regulations and formal rules, much of the governance engagement in Southern Africa is played out in deregulated spheres or within systems where 'withdrawal of regulatory power creates a different logic of resource allocation, accumulation and authority'.[3]

Following two decades of various degrees of neoliberal reform in the subregion, deregulation and informality have become *de facto* modes of planning and a defining feature of state and society governance. As will be shown with ***Maputo, Harare, Luanda, Lusaka*** and to a lesser extent ***Cape Town, Durban*** and ***Johannesburg***, the capacity to provide services and infrastructure as well as to plan and invest for economic growth and job creation is uneven and continues to diminish. Nevertheless, government in Southern Africa remains powerful and in a position to influence society through a variety of deregulated modes of action, actors and relations. Government retains the monopoly to declare some urban activities legal and legitimate, while condemning others as illegal, illegitimate and targets for demolition. But most crucially, it is within the state's discretion to place itself outside the law to practice development or urban governance and to manage competing urban interests that are major sources of economic, political and social difference in urban Southern Africa.

It is in this capacity to 'informalise' itself that the typical Southern African state apparatus has engaged in administrative manipulations of race, ethnicity, class and gender as well as repeated forced evictions that have shaped city forms in the region. Zimbabwe's 2005 'Operation *Murambatsvina*' is an example of resort to state informality in a bid to assert control over a political economy which normal bureaucratic systems could no longer contain[4].

Informality from above enables the state to criminalize some activities while promoting others. It is a calculated and purposive mode of governance and resource allocation. Governance in Southern Africa is thus a complex, ubiquitous and multi-actor game of power structures that are integral to regulated and deregulated formal structures. These structures' interactions at different moments give rise to urban wealth enclaves sitting next to slums. While corruption is the term ordinarily used to describe some of these activities, this does neither capture the deregulated governance detailed here nor does the term expose state manipulation and violence to control and reproduce itself, especially in times of crisis.

▲
Harare, Zimbabwe. **©Lakis Fourouklas/Shutterstock**

This section focuses on Southern Africa's large capital cities, those with populations over 750,000 or smaller other towns of national and subregional significance. Except for the Republic of South Africa, primacy is a defining characteristic of these large cities, with a major one at the apex of the urban hierarchy accommodating between 18 and 30 per cent of the total national urban population. The Republic of South Africa features a triple apex (***Johannesburg, Durban*** and ***Cape Town***) unless the ***Gauteng*** city region (inclusive of ***Pretoria*** and ***Johannesburg***) is considered as a single urban entity, in which case a primacy pattern emerges here as well.

Over the 2000-2010 decade, the Southern Africa subregion retained its position as the most urbanised on the continent, with the rate increasing from 53.8 to 58.7 percent. The subregion is projected to reach a two-thirds urban majority some time around 2025. Decade-interval urbanisation growth rates peaked during 1990-2000 at 7.0 per cent when the subregion also passed the 50 per cent urbanisation mark. Southern Africa has now entered a period where decade-interval urbanisation growth rates are expected to slow down, to 4.9 per cent for 2000-2010 and a continuing steady slowdown to 2.1 per cent in the 2040-2050 decade.

As projected for 2010, the urbanisation rates of individual countries in the subregion varied significantly. The Republic of South Africa, 61.7 per cent urbanised, is way ahead of the least-urbanised nations of the subregion, Swaziland and Lesotho, with 2010 urbanisation rates of 21.3 and 26.8 respectively. The latter two are starting to catch up, particularly from 2020 onwards, with projected high inter-decade urbanisation growth during the 2020-2030 decade of 17.7 and 29.0 per cent respectively. By 2040, Swaziland will be the only Southern African nation without an urban majority. However, the increase in urbanisation rates during the 2010-2020 decade will be most rapid in Lesotho (6.5 per cent), Botswana (7.7 per cent) and Namibia (6.4 per cent) compared to 0.9 per cent for Swaziland.

▲
Johannesburg, South Africa. **©Cliff Parnell/iStockphoto**

TABLE 6.1: **SOUTHERN AFRICAN URBAN POPULATION, 1950-2050 (ABSOLUTE AND PERCENTAGE)**

Population	1950	1960	1970	1980	1990	2000	2010*	2020*	2030*	2040*	2050*
Urban (*000)	5,869	8,277	11,118	14,752	20,502	27,657	34,021	38,809	43,741	48,119	51,917
Urban (%)	37.7	42.0	43.7	44.7	48.8	53.8	58.7	63.5	68.3	72.9	75.0
All Africa (%)	14.4	18.6	23.6	27.9	32.1	35.9	39.9	44.6	49.9	55.7	61.6

•Projections
Source: WUP 2009

GRAPH 6.1: **SOUTHERN AFRICAN URBAN POPULATION, 1950-2050 (ABSOLUTE AND PERCENTAGE)**

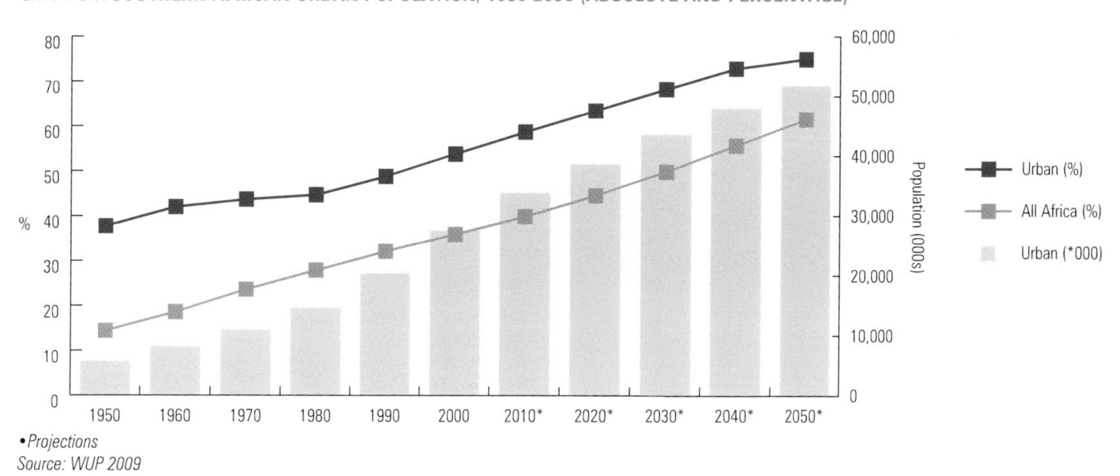

•Projections
Source: WUP 2009

TABLE 6.2: **SOUTHERN AFRICAN NATIONS' URBANISATION 1950-2050 (%)**

Country	1950	1960	1970	1980	1990	2000	2010*	2020*	2030*	2040*	2050*
Angola	7.58	10.44	14.96	24.30	37.14	48.99	58.50	66.04	71.62	76.37	80.54
Botswana	2.72	3.06	7.83	16.48	41.93	53.22	61.13	67.59	72.69	77.14	81.66
Lesotho	1.35	3.42	8.61	11.45	13.97	19.97	26.88	34.55	42.35	50.21	58.06
Mozambique	2.38	3.67	5.78	13.11	21.10	30.69	38.43	46.27	53.70	60.75	67.39
Namibia	13.41	17.91	22.29	25.07	27.66	32.37	37.98	44.41	51.49	58.59	65.34
Republic of South Africa	42.23	46.62	47.81	48.43	52.04	56.89	61.70	66.56	71.32	75.68	79.57
Swaziland	1.75	3.91	9.71	17.85	22.91	22.64	21.37	22.29	26.24	32.52	39.50
Zambia	11.50	18.15	30.35	39.82	39.41	34.80	35.70	38.92	44.71	51.56	53.36
Zimbabwe	10.64	12.61	17.36	22.37	28.99	33.76	38.25	43.92	50.71	57.67	64.35

•Projections
Source: WUP 2009

GRAPH 6.2: **SOUTHERN AFRICAN NATIONS' URBANISATION 1950-2050 (%)**

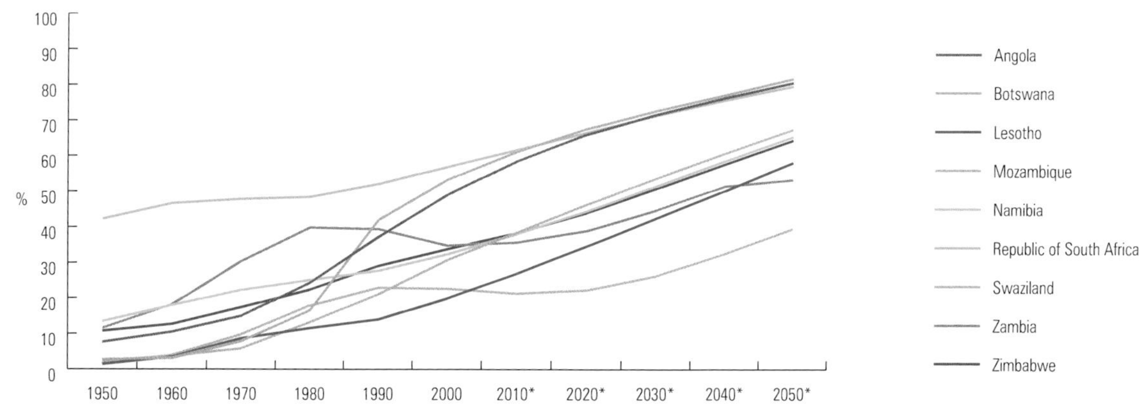

•Projections
Source: WUP 2009

▲
Lusaka, Zambia. ©**Cordelia Persen. Licenced under the Creative Commons Attribution - NoDerivs 2.0 Generic Licence**

The Future is Young: Patterns in Urban Demography

Southern African cities effectively highlight the enduring socio-political and economic effects of decades-long apartheid and its entrenched inequalities, which subsequent neoliberal economic policies have only exacerbated. However, major urban requirements like employment, infrastructure, services and good governance are made more glaring if one reflects on the structure and composition of the urban populations. Consider ***Johannesburg***, ***Harare*** and ***Lusaka***. Those under 20 contribute 57 per cent of the total population in ***Lusaka***, 44 per cent in ***Harare*** and 33 per cent in ***Johannesburg*** (see Table 6.3 and Graphs 6.3 and 6.4). This young population demands urban services, housing, serious planning for employment, education, infrastructure, and participatory governance.

Although rural-urban migration continues, it is no longer the major source of urban demographic growth in ***Lusaka*** and ***Harare***. The main growth factors are now natural increase and inter-urban migration. This partly explains the bulge in the pyramids with ***Harare*** a major recipient of domestic (male and female) immigrants aged 14 to 40.

As urban poverty increased due to loss of employment following economic adjustments in the 1990s, parents sent children to rural communal areas where education costs were lower and where government and non-governmental organisations helped with food handouts. Urban health infrastructure also deteriorated in ***Harare***, especially in the years just prior to the 2002 census, often forcing relocation of the terminally ill and vulnerable groups to rural areas. The cumulative impact of these phenomena partly explains the proportionately lower presence of children of school age (6-19 years) in ***Harare***. After the year 2000, the economically active (especially women) were moving to urban areas in the wake of agricultural decline. Research revealed that more females than males departed Zimbabwe's rural resettlement areas with ***Harare*** and other urban areas as the destinations[9].

TABLE 6.3: **AGE STRUCTURES OF SELECTED CITIES IN SOUTHERN AFRICA**

Age Group	Johannesburg[a] (%)	Harare[b] (%)	Lusaka[c] (%)
0 - 4	10	13.7	18.5
5 -19	23	31.2	38.1
20 – 25	10	14.7	10.0
25 – 65	53	38.5	32.8
≥65	5	2.0	0.9

(a) For Johannesburg: projected 2010 population: 3.8 million[8] with a sex ratio of 102 men for every 100 women
(b) Harare: projected 2010 population: two million with a sex ratio of 99.9 men for every 100 women.
(c) Lusaka: projected 2010 population: 1.3 million with a sex ratio of about 100.4 men to every 100 women.

A significant proportion of the region's urban children and youths are orphans, or street children, or live in vulnerable conditions. Whereas governments have made efforts to invest in education, for which they should be commended, the rate of employment creation does not match demand. Education does not create sufficient job-generating entrepreneurs, and standards are unequal across social groups.

Based on figures for formal employment, unemployment rates range from 22 per cent in ***Tshwane***, 23 per cent in ***Cape Town***, 26.3 per cent in ***Johannesburg***, 30 per cent in ***eThekwini*** to as high as 80 per cent in ***Harare***[10]. In the

GRAPH 6.3: **LUSAKA POPULATION - AGE-SEX STRUCTURE, YEAR 2000**

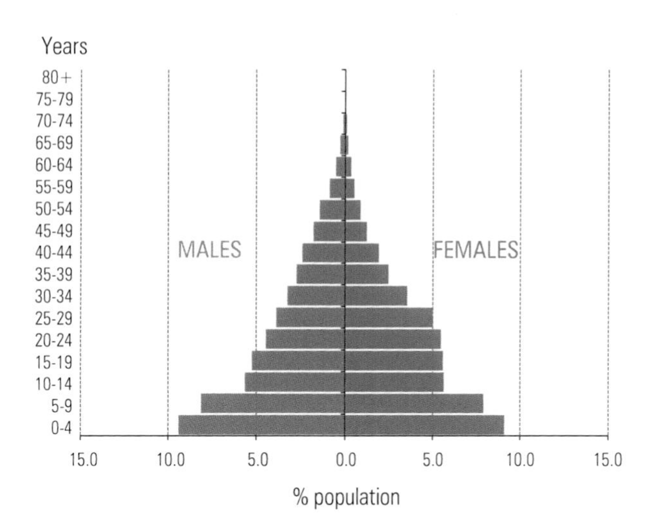

Source: Data from Lusaka Integrated Development Plan, June 2000

GRAPH 6.4: **HARARE POPULATION - AGE-SEX STRUCTURE**

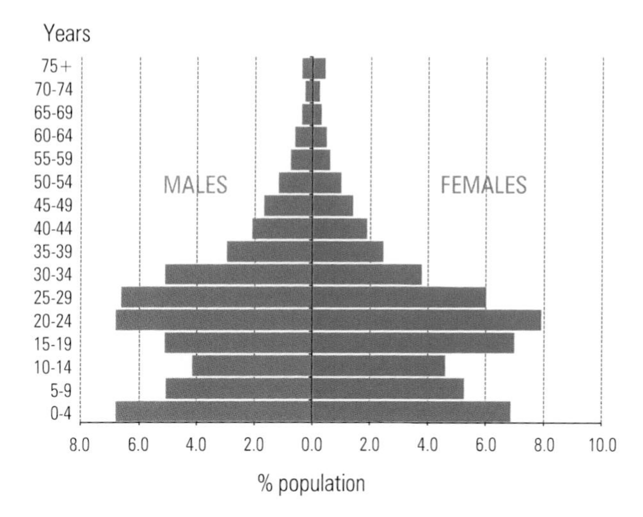

Source: Data from National Census 2002

Republic of South Africa, despite huge expenditures on education since 1994, *The Economist* reported 80 per cent of the schools as dysfunctional, with only 39 per cent of the black children passing matrix maths exams in 2008 (despite a low pass threshold of 30 percent) compared with 98 per cent of the whites. Moreover, 28 per cent of whites achieved a score of at least 80 per cent, compared with just 2 per cent among blacks.[11]

Multiple deprivations can be found in low-income urban areas, especially in informal settlements. Some of these discrepancies have to do with history, including resource allocations and adopted cultures. However, the future lies clearly in how well countries improve the conditions and opportunities for the urban majority who happen to be children, youth and young people.

The Links between Poverty, Inequality and Slums

A legacy of uneven urban development on the basis of race or class continues to prevail in urban Southern Africa. In many instances, the racial dimension (black *vs.* white) is, perhaps, becoming less visible as socio-economic class is gaining prominence, although the various socio-economic strata retain clear ethnic-based associations. On the one hand, one can find the 'world city'-inspired and aspirant cultures with market-driven investments, as physically expressed in urban 'glamour' zones, gilded entertainment sites in middle- and upper-class suburbs and for tourists, gated shopping malls and residential communities[12]. On the other hand, overcrowded, resources- and services-deprived townships and informal settlements proliferate and are hosts to a majority of the population, including black Africans from rural areas and migrants from other Southern African countries and beyond. Although rural-urban migration remains significant, nowadays it does not exceed 8 per cent as a proportion of the total population. Migration to cities has many dimensions, such as circular migration to and from rural areas and countries in the subregion and stepwise migration whereby migrants settle in lower-order cities before moving on to larger ones. Stepwise migration means that smaller urban settlements experience higher rates of immigration relative to large conurbations.[13]

Deprived urban communities are largely neglected or overlooked by formal governance systems, or viewed as pathological. As was the case in the colonial and apartheid eras, development plans continue to target squatter settlements for demolition, with residents relocated to urban ghettos on the city periphery, far away from jobs, social networks and services. In ***Durban***, ***Cape Town*** and ***Johannesburg***, recurring social catastrophes (especially fires and floods devastating entire communities) are viewed by officials as 'natural disasters' or faults caused by their low-income victims[14]. Yet, they are clearly a product of asymmetric public policy choices that favour the wealthy at the expense of the poor.

The poor are most exposed and vulnerable to disasters and disease. Graph 6.5 highlights the prevalence of HIV/AIDS

GRAPH 6.5: **HIV PREVALENCE, 15-49 AGE GROUP, REPUBLIC OF SOUTH AFRICA, 2002**

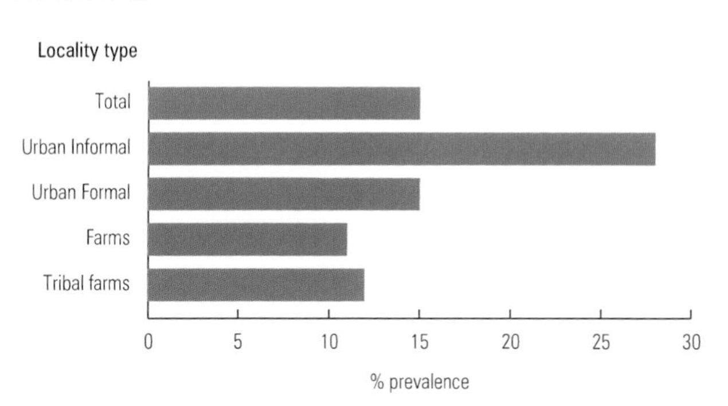

Source: Data from SACN (2004).

▲
Street children in the CBD, Harare, Zimbabwe. **©Annie Mpalume/IRIN**

among the more vulnerable age groups (15-49 years) in the Republic of South Africa. HIV/AIDS prevalence is highly correlated to poverty as well as to overcrowded, poorly services urban slums and informal settlements. These are areas with substantial inward and outward migration flows and multiple deprivations, a combination of factors conducive to the spread of diseases such as cholera, HIV/AIDS and tuberculosis.

Horrific fires in Alexandra, ***Johannesburg***, are a product of informal settlement layout, overcrowding, highly combustible building materials and inadequate strategies for fire prevention compared with upper-class areas like neighbouring Sandton.[15] As argued and illustrated by fledging grassroots squatter settlement activism in ***Durban***, the most effective prevention of such fires would be provision of affordable electric power to replace the fire hazard of paraffin lamps and candles.[16]

The Geography of Disease and Urban Water and Sanitation Infrastructure

The improvement of water and sanitation is at the core of the United Nations Millennium Development Goal to reduce urban slum incidence. Consequently, water and sanitation conditions act as major indicators of urban inequalities. In ***Harare*** and other cities in Zimbabwe, for instance, the geography of a major cholera outbreak in 2008-2009 shows that a majority of both cholera cases and fatal impacts were concentrated in deprived high-density suburbs. Although the whole of metropolitan ***Harare*** went without water for many months, cholera patterns followed income, plot density, and infrastructure patterns. In the wealthy suburbs, the impact was marginal as these households could afford to drill boreholes and access solar power, while the poor had to make do with contaminated surface water or shallow wells. Whereas the city's waterborne sewage system collapsed due to lack of water, the wealthier residents could flush toilets with borehole water. In contrast, the poor had access only to low quality water and sanitation alternatives, particularly the so-called Blair Toilets (ventilated improved pit latrines). Given the small plot sizes and overcrowding in these areas, prolonged use of pit latrines contaminated the shallow wells. Map 6.2 depicts the cholera patters for the peak period October 2008 to May 2009 in ***Harare***. Other than for Hatcliffe to the north, Mabvuku and Epworth to the east, Harare's low-income and high-density neighbourhoods are located to the west of a diagonal southeast to northwest line. The map is evidence of the extent to which reductions or collapse of public outlays on infrastructure (water, sewerage, electricity, health) had different welfare effects across the richer or poorer segments of the Harare population.

These gross geographic inequalities have been compounded by the collapse in urban livelihood opportunities, and it may not come as a surprise that the affected poor have developed a historical consciousness that exposes continuities between present day conditions and those prevailing under colonial rule and apartheid. If these obstacles remain unaddressed, the main culprit is none other than denial among intransigent ruling elites, neoliberals, development agencies and policymakers. While neoliberal thinkers point to corrupt local officials, opportunism and implementation problems as the major obstacles, the urban crisis in Southern Africa is rooted in cost recovery-driven and commodified cities that deliver residential and services patterns the poor majorities cannot afford.

Misplaced priorities and inadequate funding for public infrastructure in neoliberal-oriented national budgets further expose the poor to worldwide economic downturns.[17] Misplaced policy priorities are illustrated in the Republic of South Africa where, in 2002, the government was purchasing sophisticated weaponry worth US $5 billion on top of further millions to recapitalise the World Bank's subsidiary the International Development Association, while millions of poor urban residents saw their water and electricity disconnected or were evicted from their land and homes for their inability to make payments. As many as 20,000 households per month were disconnected from water and power distribution networks.[18] The legacy of such priority decisions is still felt by the affected communities and has contributed to the rise of protests against once popular leaders.

To address the legacy of unequal, poorly resourced and inefficient urban service delivery, the past decade witnessed the adoption of full cost-recovery of basic services such as water, electricity, waste removal and health care. Water, for instance, is considered a commercial or economic good rather than a critical social or welfare item. Delivery of services has shifted from the public authorities to private firms and 'arms-length companies' like the Johannesburg Water Pvt. Ltd. Furthermore, in the name of decentralisation and good governance, central governments have off-loaded complex delivery challenges to poorly-resourced local authorities, many of which retained anti-poor bureaucrats.

For water services in ***Durban***, ***Cape Town*** and ***Johannesburg*** (from 2002 to 2004), privatisation and cost recovery entailed installation of prepaid, self-disconnecting water meters in Soweto and other poor community suburbs. The poor get a Free Basic Water (FBW) allocation of 6,000 litres/month per standpipe. This commendable free water provision, however, on the average lasts only twelve days because the number of people served by the standpipe is at times double that of the allocation calculation. Water allocation per standpipe instead of per person is biased towards wealthier households with fewer children. Once the free-of-charge amount expires, the supply disconnects automatically. Poor households frequently go without clean water and their dignity, health and security become severely compromised. Not surprisingly, the frustration arising from such conditions has contributed

MAP 6.2: **THE GEOGRAPHY OF CHOLERA IN HARARE, 2008-2009**

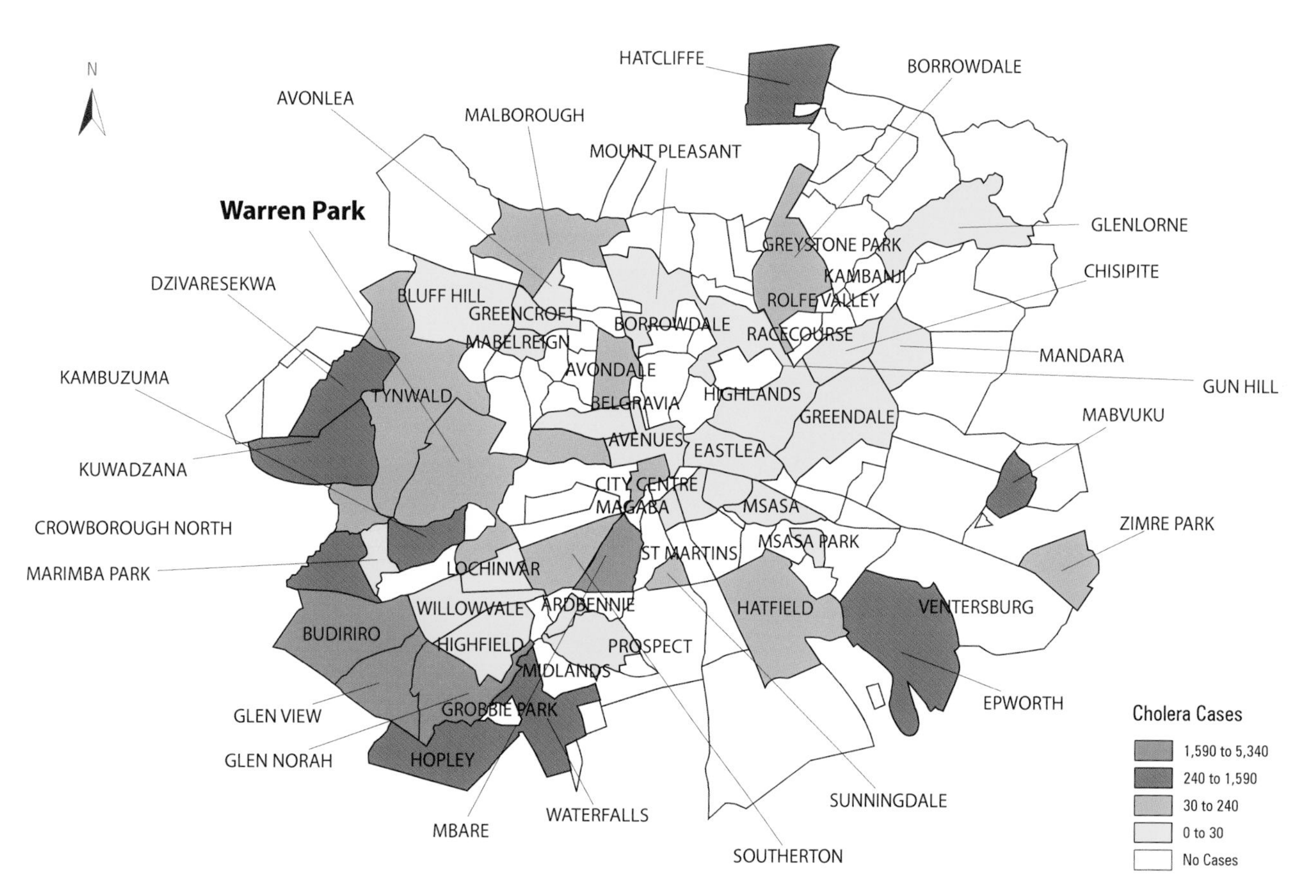

Source: Data from SACN (2004)

to community protests – 6,000 annually from 2004 to 2005 and up to 10,000 per year from 2005 to 2007[19] (see Box 6.1).

Bond & Dugard argue that prepaid water as part of cost-recovery measures costs lives, operates at the expense of basic needs, and violates constitutionally guaranteed rights. While poor areas are installed with automatically disconnecting meters, conventional meters prevail in the rest of the city. Rich households can purchase and use water on credit and accumulate arrears, get notices before water is disconnected and take corrective measures, whereas the poor cannot. High-income households have access to highly inequitable, unlimited amounts of water for their gardens, car washing, swimming pools and baths. The ideology of water commodification is starkly at odds with the emerging ideology of conservation, like it has always been at odds with the values associated with human rights and social justice.

With the above examples, the irrelevance of ideology to today's development challenges becomes clear. As in many other countries, an ideology of public service and social responsibility has been bullied out the door by one that appeals more to economic security of the individual through personal accumulation of wealth and isolation from others. In this perspective, commodification of public services is little else than an ideological strategy to steal from the middle class and keep the poor in their place. The rationale behind prepaid metres in poor urban neighbourhoods of Namibia and the Republic of South Africa came partly in response to a culture and history of non-payment associated with the fight against apartheid that was now leading to bankruptcy among local authorities. Nevertheless, it should be realised that the resulting inequalities and resentment foster xenophobia, violence and racism that undermine the long-term investment and social harmony the subregion badly needs.

▲ Khayelitsha, Cape Town, South Africa. **©Don Bayley/iStockphoto**

BOX 6.1: **WATER COST RECOVERY: SELF-DISCONNECTING PRE-PAID WATER SUPPLY IN URBAN SOUTH AFRICA**

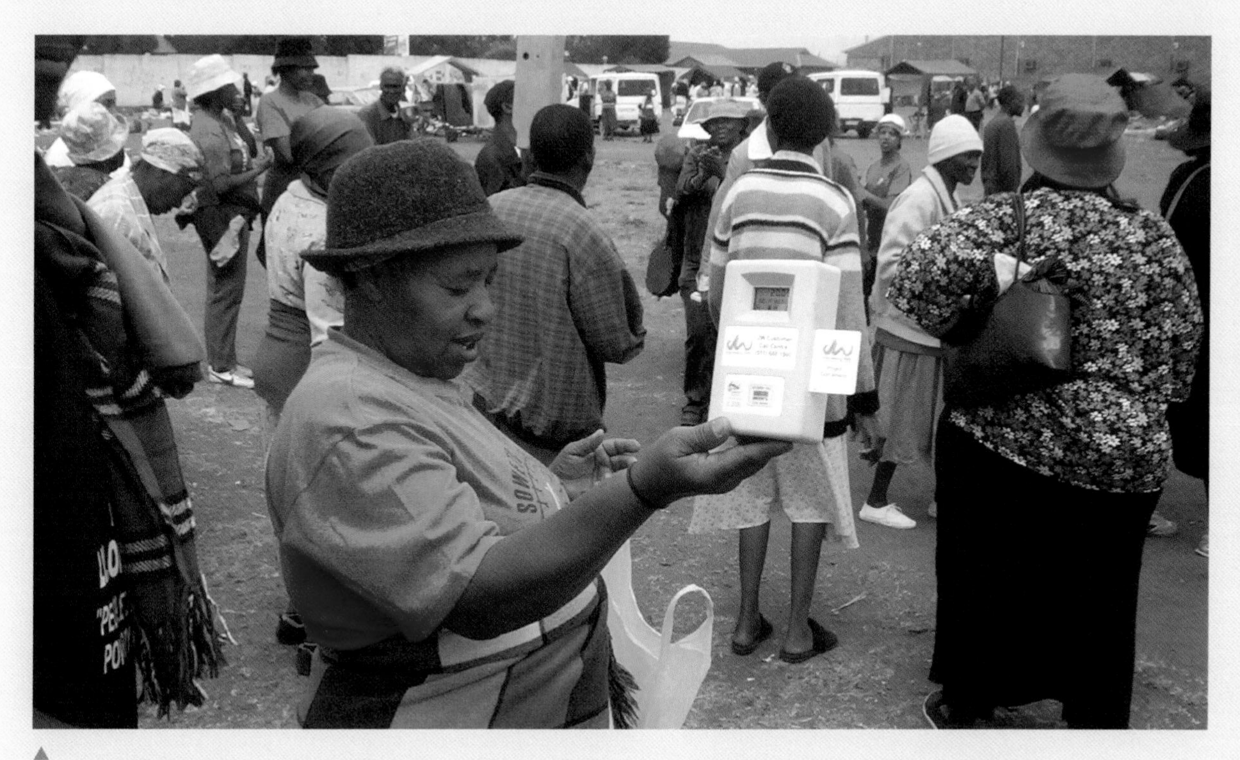

▲
A march in Johannesburg, South Africa, to protest against pre-paid water meters, corruption, harrasment and evictions. **©Indymedia South Africa**

Since 2006, civic groups, progressive lawyers and residents from Phiri, an area of Soweto just outside Johannesburg, jointly brought an action before the High Court to challenge the constitutionality of the prepaid water meters and the adequacy of the Free Basic Water (FBW) allocation. They demanded the same rights as rich households and a free allocation of 50 litres per person per day as stipulated in the 1994 ANC Reconstruction and Development Programme. The now famous *Mazibuko* case has significance beyond the Republic of South Africa in a number of respects. First, in a groundbreaking judgement in 2008, the High Court ruled the pre-payment system unlawful and unconstitutional and said the free allocation must be raised to 50 litres per person per day. When the respondents appealed to the Supreme Court, this ruling was reaffirmed, but the free allocation was reduced to 42 litres per person per day, still way above the current 25 litres. The ruling did not oblige the local authority to actually supply this amount of water even though it had the resources to do so. It also failed to tackle the systemic problem of automatic disconnection and further failed to provide residents with the choice of conventional water meters as provided in Johannesburg's richer suburbs.

Second, although the case shows the power of organisation and the importance of addressing the issue at multiple fronts – streets protests, negotiations and courts – it highlights that, without free legal service, access to justice remains remote, complex and drawn out for the majority of the poor. The High Court application comprised 6,000 pages of record, filled some 20 arch lever files and captured technical inputs from global water experts on the amount of water that meets basic rights.

Thirdly, whereas poorly-resourced local authorities and officials are blamed for failing to deliver services, the case highlights that the strategies for urban service delivery need resolution at the national level. Although it can only be implemented at the local level, the provision of water and other urban services ultimately remains the responsibility of national governments by ensuring adequate funding and policy strategies that promote efficiency while upholding the rights of all, including the poorest.

A fundamental fourth point is that, while overt racial discrimination in Southern African economies disappeared on the advent of majority rule, '... attempts to implement neoliberal development policies in many ways result in reinforcing and reproducing the after-effects of the legacy of racial discrimination'.[20]

Fifthly, trends of cost recovery and commodification of basic services simply have to be reined in. Practitioners should think more comprehensively about rights-based approaches to urban management and essential basic service delivery. Yet, this is still contested terrain and only politics will be able to dismantle the 'services apartheid' prevailing in Southern Africa.

The hopes raised for an emerging rights-based urban management and service delivery in Southern Africa were crushed when the case eventually went before the Constitutional Court in 2009. In a unanimous decision, the Court ruled that Johannesburg City had not violated any constitutional rights of the Phiri residents and that the prepaid meters were an acceptable water management instrument.

Sources: Mazibuko and Others v. the City of Johannesburg and Others (Case number 06/13865 in the Johannesburg High Court) and Supreme Court of Appeal Case No. 489/2008; Bond, P. & Dugard, J. The case of Johannesburg water; What really happened at the pre-paid Parish –pump, in Law Democracy and Development,2008, 1-28, http://www.ukzn.ac.za/ccs/

6.2
The Economic Geography of Cities

▲
Durban Market, South Africa. **©Cliff Parnell/iStockphoto**

GRAPH 6.6: **REAL ECONOMIC GROWTH IN SOUTHERN AFRICA, 2006-2011**

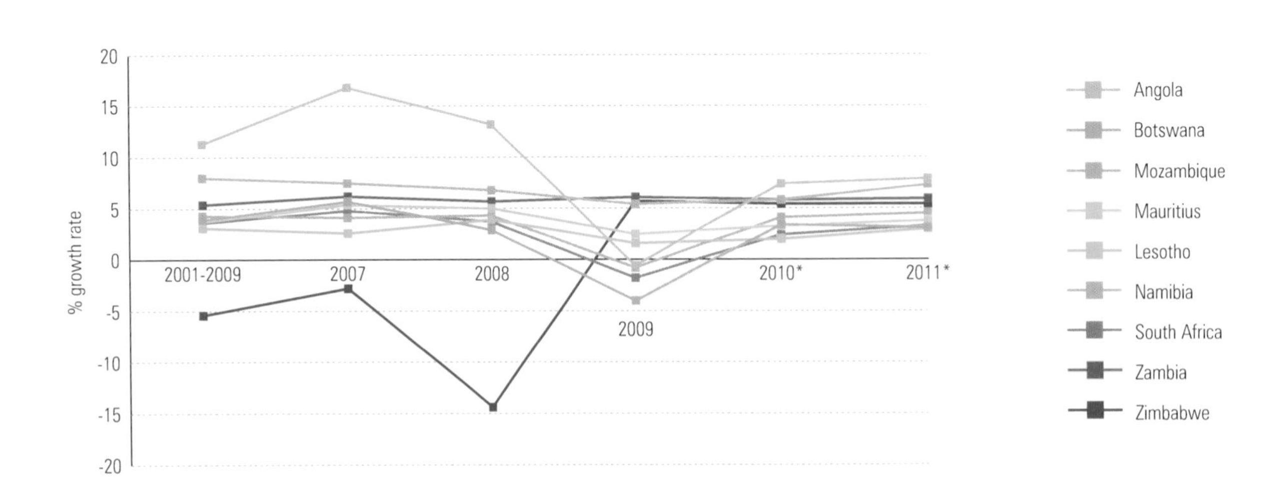

Source: Data from Africa Economic Outlook, Africa Development Bank and Economist Intelligence Unit. (Figures for 2010 and 2011 are estimates)

TABLE 6.4: **URBAN WATER CONSUMPTION PER HEAD IN SELECTED SOUTHERN AFRICAN CITIES**

	Typical High-Income Areas	Typical Deprived Low-Income Areas
Cape Town	60m^3/household/month	6m^3/household/month
eTekwini	60m^3/household/month	6m^3/household/month
Harare	250 litres/person /day	80 litres/person/day
Johannesburg	60m^3/household/month	6m^3/household/month
Maputo	16m^3/household/month	5m^3/household/month
Tshwane	60m^3/household/month	6m^3/household/month

Sources: Compiled from multiple municipal and other sources

The Impact of the Global Economic Recession on Southern Africa

Over the past decade, Southern Africa experienced positive real economic growth averaging 4.8 per cent (or 5.3 per cent if Zimbabwe is excluded), but in 2009 this was slashed to a paltry 1.4 per cent (excluding Zimbabwe) due to the worldwide recession[21] (see Graph 6.6). With a mix of economies dependent on commodity exports (diamonds, chrome, platinum and heavy metals) and global trade of goods and services, Southern Africa was hit harder by the recession than the other regions on the continent. Export commodity prices declined heavily between 2008 and 2009, while 2010 has not seen much improvement[22] and the region's recovery will be slow especially when compared to that of East Africa.

The effects of the recession in terms of job losses and infrastructure decay were only mitigated by government action, particularly those associated with large-scale sporting events. Since the locations were agreed years before these events took place, rather on a spur of a moment, this was a timely coincidence for Africa. As will be elaborated later in this report, in 2010 Southern Africa hosted the Africa Cup of Nations Games in ***Luanda***, Angola, followed by the football/soccer World Cup Games in the Republic of South Africa, and the All Africa Games in ***Maputo***, Mozambique. These public sector-driven initiatives stimulated private sector capital outlays in new infrastructure and business. They also in effect paved the way for a speedy economic recovery in the subregion. Beyond the host countries, tourism received a significant boost from these events, especially in Botswana, Malawi, Zambia and Zimbabwe.

Another factor that dampened the impact of the recession was a favourable amount of rainfall, which lowered prices of agricultural produce in urban areas. The urban poor purchase unprocessed fresh agricultural products from rural hinterlands and also grow food in urban and peri-urban spaces to supplement the little they can afford in stores. In cities like ***eThekwini***, ***Gaborone***, ***Harare***, ***Lusaka***, ***Maputo*** and ***Maseru***, urban agriculture has developed significantly in the last decade. However, arable peri-urban land has increasingly come under threat from urban expansion while authorities remain ambivalent and/or hostile to urban agriculture. Against this background, the *2003 Harare Declaration on Urban Agriculture*[23], in which African ministers committed to promote this type of activity, is a commendable initiative that will hopefully encourage further expansion, especially in efficient, intensive food production in peri-urban areas, and preserve some prime agricultural lands from built development.

Income and Consumption Inequality

Southern Africa suffers from extreme poverty and inequality that run along class and racial lines, and stands out as the 'most unequal' subregion on the continent. In the Republic of South Africa, for instance, the proportion of those living in poverty is dramatically on the rise. Between 1992 and 2001, poverty among black South Africans rose from 50 to 60 per

TABLE 6.5: **URBAN INEQUALITIES IN SOUTHERN AFRICA – TRENDS IN GINI COEFFICIENTS**

		Gini Coefficient Year One		Gini Coefficient Year Two		
City	**Country**	**Year**	**Coef.**	**Year**	**Coef.**	**% Change**
Lusaka	Zambia	2003	0.61	2006	0.66	8
Cape Town	Republic of South Africa	2001	0.69	2005	0.67	-3
eThekwini	Republic of South Africa	2001	0.75	2005	0.72	-4
Tshwane	Republic of South Africa	2001	0.75	2005	0.72	-4
Johannesburg	Republic of South Africa	2001	0.78	2005	0.75	-4
Windhoek*	Namibia	1993	0.63	2003	0.58	-8
Maputo*	Mozambique	1996	0.44	2003	0.52	18
Gaborone	Botswana	1993	0.54	2003	0.50	-7

Source: Global Urban Observatory, UN-HABITAT 2009
** All Gini coefficients are income-based, except for Maputo and Windhoek (based on consumption).*

▲
Boa Vista informal settlement in Luanda, Angola. ©**Jaspreet Kindra/IRIN**

cent compared with 26 to 29 per cent for the 'Coloured' group, 8 to 11 per cent for the Asian group and from 3 to 4 per cent for Whites. The 1993 breadline or basic income for subsistence was defined as SAR755/month (US $251) and SAR1,270/month (US $129) in 2001 to account for inflation. (In 1993 the average exchange rate was US $1 = three South African Rand (SAR) and in 2001 US $1 = SAR9.8.)

Consumption of urban services is highly correlated with the segregated nature of cities, with higher-income areas consuming disproportionately more than the poorer neighbourhoods. Implicitly, this also shows the different relations groups maintain with the environment. Table 6.4 shows water consumption per head in selected cities and intra-urban consumption differences by income group. Very poor households in urban South Africa consume 6 m^3 of water per month compared to 60 m^3 for high income households. Considering that low-income households can comprise 10 to 15 people compared with as few as three in high-income ones, the disparities are glaring. Consumption volumes are also dependent on the quality of infrastructure, as illustrated by the case of ***Maputo***. For high-income areas with indoor water connections, consumption ranges between 100 and 130 litres per person per day, or about double the 73-80 litres consumed in areas with yard connections where access to water is shared with neighbours. At the lower end of the poor communities, water is collected from public standpipes outside the yard. For these groups, collecting water is a daily chore and water consumption is as low as 30 litres per person per day.[24] This compromises health and quality of life while compounding the effects of diseases like HIV/AIDS which require regular flushing of toilets and cleaning of patients, utensils and living areas.

The distribution of water in terms of gender, racial and socio-economic groups is more unequal than the distribution of income. In the Republic of South Africa, more than 50 per cent of raw water goes to commercial (largely White-owned) farms, of which half goes wasted in poor irrigation techniques and inappropriate crop choices. Another 25 per cent goes to

▲
Windhoek, Namibia. **©Attila Jándi/Shutterstock**

mining and 12 per cent is consumed by households ,with half of that going to White households' gardens and swimming pools. All in all, less than 10 per cent of available water is consumed by the majority, i.e., of Black households.[25] Inequalities are replicated in other areas of basic needs such as electricity. In ***Luanda***, a mere 25 per cent of the city's five million people with access to electricity supply accounts for 75 per cent of national electricity consumption.[26]

Income and consumption inequalities are probably best captured by the urban Gini coefficients displayed in Table 6.5. Other than ***Windhoek*** and ***Maputo***, where the indicator is based on consumption, the coefficient is based on income data (see Chapter 1 for a description of the Gini coefficient). The major message is the steep inequality prevailing in cities, and generally much more so than in rural areas. To the exception of Maputo's *'relatively low'* coefficient in 1996, all the other ratios range between *'high'* and *'extremely high'* on the Gini scale. The coefficients in ***Lusaka*** (0.61 in 2003 and 0.66 in 2006) are much higher than those for rural areas (0.42 and 0.54, respectively).[27] Meanwhile, income inequalities are growing in both rural and urban areas. However, inaccuracies may arise when comparing consumption- and income-based Gini coefficients (UN-HABITAT 2010: 60-62). No figures are available for Luanda (let alone Angola), one of the major cities in the region. As far as Namibia is concerned, both the United Nations and the US Central Intelligence Agency estimate the nationwide Gini coefficient above 7.00 (or more than *'extremely high'*), but ***Windhoek*** is well below that, indicating that the country's rural areas are more unequal than cities.

A second major feature is the general rise in urban inequalities in Southern Africa. The only exception is the Republic of South Africa, where marginal declines were observed between 2001 and 2005 thanks to the redistributive policies of the first decade of majority rule, but only future can tell whether these declines can be sustained. On the other hand, in ***Maputo*** inequalities have turned from *'relatively low'* to *'high'* in recent years, clearly suggesting that since the late 1990s the benefits of Mozambique's economic growth have not been well shared.

6.3
The Geography of Urban Land Markets

Land dispossession of indigenous Africans was at the core of settler colonialism and apartheid, and has shaped the political economy and identities of the region ever since. This includes violent struggles for independence and majority rule, and the subsequent widespread culture of impunity that prevails as far down as the household level. However, the transfer of political power from colonial and apartheid authorities to indigenous elites since the 1970s has not led to fundamental restructuring of the land legacy. What is prevailing instead is continuity and re-entrenchment of colonial land laws, policies, administrative procedures and infrastructures. The 'willing buyer, willing seller' approach adopted to redistribute land in Namibia, the Republic of South Africa and Zimbabwe has been slow to meet the needs of marginalised poor households. Even in Zimbabwe, where fast-track land reforms have been deployed since the year 2000, colonial administrative structures remained intact generally, and in urban areas in particular.

Political change and land policies in Southern Africa have been adaptive and co-optive rather than radical, only giving African elites more power to access or consolidate control over local and national economies.[28] One of the ideals sustaining the struggle for independence, i.e., turning land into a resource to be liberated to the equitable benefit of all, remains unrealised. Consequently, land continues to be a central bone of contention in politics, identity, culture and the economies of the region. Land markets in today's Southern Africa are defined by the following features:

- Inequitable access and distribution, with the majority of the population marginalised in both rural and urban areas.
- Duality in legal, administrative and economic systems and tenures - one set for rural and another for urban; one set for indigenous African spaces and another for the former European spaces now appropriated by local elites, tourism, expatriates and the descendents of settler colonials.
- Highly bureaucratic and slow land delivery systems for urban development, encouraging unproductive land hoarding, speculation and banking, with maximum rewards to the propertied class.
- An 'export enclave' economy controlled by new elites and their global alliances, as opposed to a subsistence, peripheral, rural and urban informal economy where the majority hardly eke out a living.
- Untrammelled reconduction of colonial policy orientations, administrative infrastructures and the inherent violation of the majority's rights.
- Landlessness, uncontrolled urban development, squatter settlements, urban squalor and overcrowding, environmental pollution, degradation and unhealthy low-income areas in cities.

The colonial and apartheid era in Southern Africa instrumentalised land laws to dispossess indigenous African economies and control their livelihoods while supporting the European and global economies. Not much has changed since in Namibia, the Republic of South Africa or Zimbabwe, much-heralded fast-track land reforms not withstanding. Consequently, short of radical change to the fundamentals, applying new policies and techniques can amount to little more than exercises in futility.

The Forms of Urban Land Tenure

Land tenure refers to the terms and conditions under which rights to land resources (including water, timber, soil, etc.) are acquired, retained , used, transmitted, shared, inherited or disposed of. In line with inherited colonial practice, existing policies and laws have promoted freehold tenure in urban areas. However, in ***Maseru***, Lesotho, and ***Gaborone***, Botswana, customary land tenure is significant in both urban and peri-urban areas. Elsewhere in Southern Africa, urban freehold tenure sits side by side with leasehold tenure, especially in ***Lusaka*** and ***Maputo,*** where land nationalisation has been reversed only recently. In these cities, governments retain ownership of land while investors and households can acquire 50 to 99-year leaseholds. Thus, urban land in Southern Africa falls into several categories: private freehold, customary or communal land (leasehold where traditional authorities are effectively in charge of allocation and dispute resolution) and public land owned by government and leased to individuals for private use over a specified period of time.

Under customary tenure, ownership is communal rather than individual. Individuals do not pay for the land allocated to them, or then only a token fee, but they retain right of use for as long as they effectively occupy the land. This leaves them holders not owners. Upon vacating the land, they can claim compensation only for any developments on the land, not for the land itself. These aspects of customary tenure are dominant in rural areas and are similar to leasehold tenure in urban areas. In ***Gaborone*** and ***Maseru***, significant areas that were originally rural customary lands are now part of the municipal area and remain under the administration of tribal land boards rather than the municipality. Conversion of these peri-urban customary agricultural lands to urban use, while often essential, does not provide sufficient incentives for customary land holders to release the land.[29] When this land is eventually released, compensation is generally an inadequate of true market value.

Land Boards are a culturally specific feature of communities that were not fully incorporated into the direct control and management of colonial systems. Their brand of decentralised governance is unique to such areas. However, with rapid economic growth and urbanisation, traditional systems have come under pressure. Inadequate funding and lack of personnel has dented their ability to provide effective administration. In the 1990s, The Government of Botswana introduced market value, enabling customary land to be transferred at market prices and without the need for approval from the land boards. However, without guaranteed access to alternative livelihoods, land holders are unwilling to sell their plots even at the market price. This suggests that land reforms without significant alternative sources of income for land holders will not alter their perception of, or relations to, land.

Land Institutions and Administration

It is important to explain the difference between urban land *administration* and urban land *management.* Land administration is the process of determining and registering land ownership, value and use, and sets out the procedures and registration rules of land right transfers. Land registration, although time-consuming and often costly, is a necessary condition for the proper operation of formal land markets, because these are mainly about transactions and the associated documentation. Land management, in contrast, refers to the processes of directing use and development of land resources. This will often entail setting restrictions and/or standards of land development, which both influence land values. Land administration and management are complementary and determine the efficiency of formal and informal land markets. Outside the customary systems unique to ***Maseru*** and ***Gaborone***, Southern Africa has established consolidated institutions for land management and administration.

However, formal land processes are bureaucratic, hardly accessible and expensive. Recent research[30] views Southern Africa as a subregion with high availability of land information. On an index with 100 as the maximum score for information *availability*, Southern Africa scored 75.5 compared with a worldwide average of 70.6. However,

▲
The outskirts of Maputo, Mozambique. **©AmigoDia. Licenced under the GNU Free Documentation Licence.**

GRAPH 6.7: **TIME REQUIRED TO PROCESS A LEASE FOR ACCESS TO URBAN INDUSTRIAL LAND - VARIOUS REGIONS/COUNTRIES, (DAYS)**

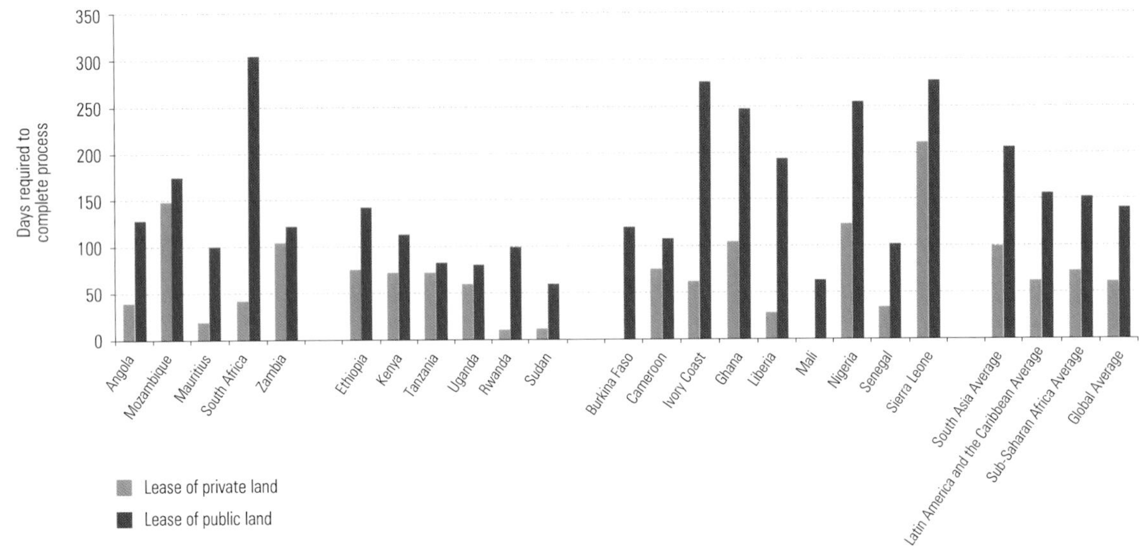

Source: Data from IAB 2010, World Bank, Washington

TABLE 6.6: **AVAILABILITY AND ACCESSIBILITY OF LAND INFORMATION IN SOUTHERN AFRICA (BASED ON MAIN CITIES) (100 = FULLY AVAILABLE OR FULLY ACCESSIBLE)**

	Country	Availability of Land Information Index	Accessibility of Land Information Index
Southern Africa	Angola	60.0	36.8
	Mozambique	62.5	33.3
	South Africa	85.0	47.4
	Zambia	75.0	37.5
	Regional Average	**75.5**	**37.26**
Eastern Africa	Ethiopia	2.5	0.0
	Kenya	85.0	22.2
	Tanzania	62.5	36.8
	Uganda	77.5	25.0
	Rwanda	50.0	38.5
	Sudan	30.0	30.8
	Regional Average	**51.25** (or 61.0 without Ethiopia)	**26.88** (32.26)
Western Africa	Burkina Faso	50.0	31.6
	Cameroon	55.0	52.6
	Ivory Coast	75.0	47.4
	Ghana	85.0	30.0
	Liberia	15.0	28.6
	Mali	5.0	28.6
	Nigeria	67.5	50.0
	Senegal	75.0	50.0
	Sierra Leone	30.0	26.3
	Regional Average	50.8	38.3
Sub-Sahara Average		**58.5**	**41.3**
Global Average		**70.6**	**33.9**

Source: Compiled and calculated from Investing Across Borders 2010: 82-168, World Bank, Washington DC

accessing land information, is difficult in Southern Africa, although the regional index (37.26) is an improvement over the continental average (33.9), while ranking below the world average (41.3) and West Africa (where the accessibility index stands at 38.3, but a lower information availability index (50.8) than Southern Africa.

In general, access to land information worldwide is difficult even in regions where such information is available, like Southern Africa (see Table 6.6). Access to this information can be improved with geographic information systems (GIS), sharing data across government departments and posting basic land information on government websites.

Availability of and access to land information is critical for urban development, particularly for investment, as well as for residential developments by the poor. At a time of global recession, attracting both foreign and local investment is important. For Southern Africa, while foreign investment can be of non-regional origin, in some cities such as ***Gaborone, Lusaka, Maputo*** and ***Maseru***, regional investors, and particularly from the Republic of South Africa, play an increasingly significant role. In Mozambique, a significant number of South African investors are active in real estate, tourism, infrastructure, peri-urban horticulture and mining. Ease of access to land is a critical factor that affects the location, sectors, as well as breadth and depth of investment. In other words, reducing the barriers to land access is important for economic growth, employment creation and poverty alleviation. These barriers and burdens include the following:

- Lack of land information, leading to costly and time-consuming research in distinct agencies;
- Unhelpful land regulations and procedures for land purchase and leasing;
- Weak land laws, land rights and security of tenure (whether freehold or leasehold); and
- Non-existent or weak land arbitration systems.

Rules regarding land access to foreign investors and the time to process land leases vary across the region. For instance, Angola and the Republic of South Africa allow purchase of public and private land for foreign direct investment purposes, while Mozambique does not allow any type of land purchase. In Zambia foreign investors can purchase private though not public land.

According to *Investments Across Borders 2010*, where land is leased the process can take as little as 19 days for private land in Mauritius, but as much as 10 months for public land in the Republic of South Africa.[31]

Land- and Property-Based Local Authority Revenues

The question of improved municipal finance features high in the *Habitat Agenda* as a major issue for public services delivery. In Southern Africa, the problem of municipal government finance has often been perceived as the gap between financial resources or revenues on the one hand, and expenditure needs on the other.[32] This fiscal gap arises from lack of elasticity of municipal income; in other words, revenues do not grow in tandem with urban populations and economic needs.

With the current global economic slowdown, the importance local government finance has become more evident. Most analyses of the recession have focused on regional and global economies, but it is at the level of local basic services (waste removal, water and sanitation, street lighting, road upgrading, electricity, ambulance services, etc.) that people experience the effects of the global slowdown.[33] In Namibia and the Republic of South Africa, municipalities make bulk purchases of water and electricity from public utilities for distribution to households, whereas in Angola, Botswana, Lesotho, Mozambique, Swaziland, Zambia and Zimbabwe some of these services are provided directly to consumers by the relevant public authorities. Some large municipalities also run their own police service independently from national forces. As in many regions of the world, most local authorities derive the bulk of their income from central government transfers or grants. However, with the global recession, between 2008 and 2009 (and possibly into 2011) central governments have accumulated huge budget deficits (see Graph 6.8), which may result in reduced disbursements to local authorities as a result.

Consequently, local authorities are left to their own devices when it comes to finance. They should see this as an opportunity to develop innovative ways of expanding their own revenue sources. They should opt not just short-term for deficit reduction measures, but also take current economic conditions as an opportunity to renegotiate their mandates with central government. This opportunity is more appropriate in countries experiencing constitutional changes, such as Zimbabwe (or recently Kenya in Eastern Africa). Respective roles, mandates and functions could be set out or clarified, as for instance in Botswana's constitution.[34] Improved governance would provide for any increases in rates or user fees in a transparent and participatory manner that ties them to better service delivery. Some would object that this would make property owners pay for urban expenditures; but it should be understood that the most valuable properties have all been serviced through previous municipal budgets, and it would only be fair if services were extended to new urban areas. Where public-private partnerships or debt funds infrastructures, more transparency and stakeholder participation are in order.

Local authorities derive their own revenue from service fees, user charges, land rents, urban land and property taxes (rates), income from local authority investments or businesses. Land rents, rates and taxes can provide significant revenue and, for instance, contribute as much as 25 per cent of income for ***Gaborone,***[35] up to 50 per cent for ***Lusaka***[36] and between 20 and 30 per cent for cities in the Republic of South Africa.[37] However, the full potential of this financial resource is rarely realised due to poor collection methods, weak billing systems, incomplete valuation rolls (the basis for rates),

GRAPH 6.8: **PUBLIC FINANCES IN SOUTHERN AFRICA, 2008 AND 2009 COMPARED.**

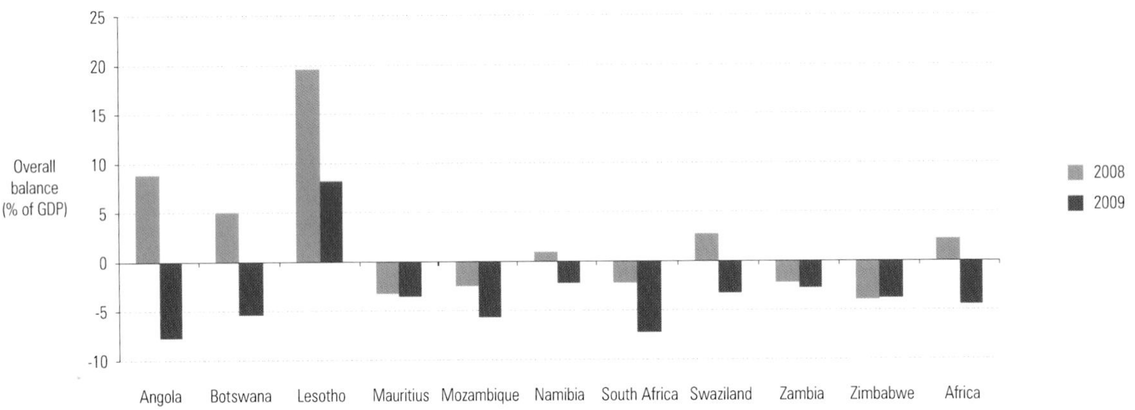

Source: Data from 'Data and Statistics', Africa Economic Outlook. www.africaeconomicoutlook.org/en/

political interference, as well as high numbers of defaulters and debtors (including government departments). Given the importance of land- and property-based sources, current practice needs greater scrutiny if revenues are to be improved. Between 2003 and 2006, rates collection increased across the board in the cities of the Republic of South Africa; between 2003 to 2005 the actual revenue collected as a percentage of budgeted revenue increased from 14 to 83 per cent in ***Lusaka*** due to computerisation and capacity-building in the finance department. Updated valuation rolls would further increase rate collection ratios.[38]

All countries in the region levy taxes from which local authorities derive incomes, including value added tax (VAT), property transfer and capital gains tax, estate duty and donations tax, as well as urban property taxes also known as property rates. Except for Mozambique, all other countries in the subregion levy rates, including Angola where even 26 years of civil war saw no disruption of property tax collection. However, value added, transfer (stamp duty), estate and capital gains taxes are all levied at the national rather than the local level. This leaves local authorities with just rates (land and property tax) as the main immediate source of land-based incomes.

▲ SADC headquarters, Gaborone, Botswana. **©Gerald Mashonga/iStockphoto**

Local authorities utilise various methods to compute rates, which they base on land or site value, improved site value, site and improvements, or improvements only. A few municipalities use more than one of these tax bases to any significant degree.[39] Botswana and Zambia only use improved value as a basis for rates, which seems to penalise those property owners that develop their properties relative to those that hold large tracts of land for speculative purposes. All countries in the subregion use valuation rolls to compute rates. The problem is that due to lack of expertise or capacity (or political interference), valuation rolls are often not up to date. Countries also apply different taxation rates for different types of property: for instance residential rates may be lower than those on commercial or industrial land or property.

In Botswana, Namibia and the Republic of South Africa, rates are set every year. The critical difference is that when rates remain static for years, even if conditions on the land or property have changed and warrant rate changes, either the local authority loses revenue, or some residents end up relatively overcharged and others undercharged.

The problem of valuation rolls is important in property taxes. Countries in the subregion use rolls based on valuation of each and every property. The preference for this method is of a political and institutional nature even in the face of capacity constraints. Apart from the Republic of South Africa, the number of valuers should be increased, or alternative valuation and rating systems applied. If they want to enhance

BOX 6.2: **DISCRIMINATORY FORMAL LAND ALLOCATION RULES – MASERU, LESOTHO**

▲
Maseru, Lesotho. **©Netroamer. Licensed under the Creative Commons Attribution 3.0 Unported License**

A survey of 390 households in Maseru (90 in up-market neighbourhoods and 300 in informal settlements) used three proxy indicators to determine the socio-economic status of household heads: (a) educational qualification; (b) employment status; and (c) household possessions. The survey found a positive correlation between educational achievement and formal access to land in up-market urban neighbourhoods. Household heads with university, secondary or vocational education were the major (87 per cent) beneficiaries. Over four-fifths of households had obtained plots under 'free state grants'. Some had purchased land from 'free state grant' beneficiaries, in violation of the law, since land in Lesotho can neither be bought nor sold. State-granted plots were sold by those who had obtained more than one housing plot, taking advantage of their superior knowledge of the formal rules. Employment status and household possessions were found to be positively correlated with education levels.

The Lesotho Land Act 1979 provides for advertisement of available plots in local newspapers and government gazettes. Individual requests for land grants are declared after application with urban land committees, which make decisions after interviewing applicants. The survey showed that socio-economic status influenced plot allocation through patronage, elite networks and corruption. The survey also exposed an absence of formal selection criteria, and the fact that plot allocation had degenerated into personalised relations of reciprocity.

A similar analysis of the socio-economic status of households in informal settlements was made to establish which types of households benefited from formal rules and procedures. Of the 300 household heads interviewed, 48 per cent had either not attended school at all or had only primary education; 36 per cent had low secondary or vocational training and 16 per cent had a university education. The survey concluded that access to residential land in informal settlements was open to a wide range of households, including the poorest. However, since plot acquisitions in informal settlements became highly commercialised after 1980, land became less accessible to the very poorest households.

Source: Leduka, R. C. Informal Land Delivery Processes and Access to Land for the Poor in Maseru, Lesotho., in Informal Land Delivery Processes in African Cities: Working paper 5, Birmingham: University of Birmingham, 2004

the contribution of land-based revenue but do not have the institutional capacity, local authorities should consider a flat tax for all properties in any area not yet listed on the valuation roll, and add such properties to the rating system. This mechanism would stand until the rolls have been updated by valuers.

To explain their weak financial positions, local authorities often point to government centralising of resources. However, before seeking to broaden their revenue bases, local authorities must fully exploit the provisions in their current legal mandates, especially improvements in effective fee collection as witnessed in ***Lusaka***. Short of full prior exploitation of existing mandates, a call for constitutional change and broadening of mandates will be difficult to sustain.

How Urban Land Markets Operate

A variety of land transaction instruments are in use in Southern Africa. In formal urban land markets, statutory registered titles are the norm, with much of the transfer procedure undertaken by registered real estate agents. For informal urban land markets, administrative instruments range from verbal promises to witnessed written agreements. In cities like ***Maseru*** and ***Gaborone***, informal urban land transactions can entail an exchange of certificates formally provided by government bodies.

Rules, procedures and processes relating to urban land transactions can generally be divided into formal and informal, as elsewhere in sub-Saharan Africa, with enforcement contingent on market type. Formal market agreements are enforceable through the courts of law. Enforcement of informal agreements varies, but usually involves mediation, local courts and ultimately statutory/common law courts. Formal rules of land access are derived from state law or legislative frameworks that specify taxation and other public sector requirements for land acquisition, tenure, transactions, registration and land use. Access to land through formal channels is notoriously lengthy and cumbersome, especially where the state or government is the only source of land. Applicable rules and regulations are usually neither widely known nor understood by ordinary urban residents. The resultant bureaucratic delays lead to increased transaction costs and foster 'palm greasing' to speed up transactions. Box 6.2 shows how formal rules and procedures, as described in recent research on ***Maseru***, tend to discriminate on the basis of wealth, educational or economic status.

Formal housing finance also discriminates against lower-income households in Botswana and the Republic of South Africa where both middle-income and poor households are not catered for in the formal systems. In Botswana, as of 2004, households earning less than an annual 4,400 pulas (BWP) (or US $630) do not qualify for state land because they cannot afford housing that meets minimum formal planning standards and regulations. Those earning less than an annual BWP24,000 (US $3,439) do not qualify for building material loans offered under government self-help housing schemes, which effectively sidelines them, too. Likewise, in the Republic of South Africa the lending practices of the banks as well as government subsidy programmes have created a large gap in the formal property markets, excluding those households too poor for standard bank loans though not enough for subsided housing schemes.

Wherever formal markets cannot deliver, for whatever reasons, informal markets will fill the gap with hybrid alternatives that combine formal rules with customary and social practices. Although these informal market procedures are not necessarily recognised by public authorities and may at times even be plain illegal, they are regarded as socially legitimate by those who use them. With this divergence between the formal rules based on law, and procedures based on 'everyday-life practice', alternative land supply systems evolved side by side. They cater to a range of residential options, from squatting to customary allocation for illegal subdivision of private or public lands.

Under pressure from ongoing rapid urbanisation, the spatial expansion of cities in Southern Africa has increasingly led to commercialisation of informal access to land with payment in cash or in kind, including distress land sales. Therefore, informal transactions are now more often committed to writing, as this confers at least a perception of *de facto* security. This has triggered changed attitudes among some of the region's authorities. For instance, in ***Maseru*** where over 80 per cent of urban land demand is met informally, customary allocations are now routinely recognised by formal law. Informally acquired lands now can even be registered as formal leaseholds. However, informal procedures, even when recognised, remain fraught with pitfalls because the land rights are often ill-defined, or there may be unresolved plot

▲
Maputo, Mozambique. **©Cordelia Persen. Licensed under the Creative Commons Attribution-NoDerivs 2.0 Generic Licence**

BOX 6.3: HOW MOZAMBIQUE CAN REGAIN CONTROL OF 'SPONTANEOUS' URBANISATION

In 2003, the Ministry of Agriculture of Mozambique commissioned a study to assess the efficiency of rural land allocation across the nation. The report was published in 2006 and highlighted significant differences in social justice between the various forms of allocation of rural land. In 2006, and with UN-HABITAT support, the Ministry for Coordination of Environmental Affairs, which is in charge of land use management and spatial planning, commissioned a similar study on urban land markets based on the cities of Manica and Nacala. The aim was to identify the dynamics of urban land markets, assess existing defenses against social inequity, reverse unsustainable urban growth trends, and maximise the socio-economic uses of urban land. The rationale also included identifying the factors behind medium- to long-term sustainable urban growth, the best ways of achieving secure tenure, and the promotion of pro-poor housing alternatives under the 'slum target' set by Millennium Development Goals.

The research in Manica and Nacala identified four existing channels for access to urban land: customary systems (19 per cent), State allocation (13 per cent), simple occupation in good faith (6 per cent) and indirect access (62 per cent). Indirect access is the major form of urban land access because, by law, land cannot be sold in Mozambique. However, Land Law 14/97 allows ownership transfer of urban buildings and then automatically grants land use rights for the entire plot. Together, these four categories effectively (though not efficiently) allocate land as, bar the odd exception, anyone has access to land, so much so that Mozambican cities are not plagued by the homelessness that is a defining feature of so many other African cities. The implication is that any attempts at interfering with the four above-mentioned channels of access to urban land are not desirable.

The 2010 study further established that 63 per cent of the demand seeks land in peri-urban areas, 17 per cent in urbanised areas (*'Zona de Cimento'* – Cement City) and 20 per cent in the urban green belts. Three types of markets are found operating in Mozambican cities; theoretically distinct they may be, but intertwined in practice: urban land, housing, and the rental housing markets. Three broad land market forces are at work: the government, formally allocating urban land; the private sector, allocating land through the formal markets; and civil society, which deals with informal markets (subdivision, sub-renting or simple occupation) without prior formal authorization.

Neither the government nor the formal markets on their own feature the capacity for efficient allocation required to match the scale of demand for urban land, or to smooth out the interactions of this demand within the surrounding rural areas. The government is now gradually being replaced by the market as the main adjudicator of land (especially in peri-urban areas where the demand is highest). As a result, urban land becomes commodified and land values rise, to the detriment of social justice as the urban poor find are left out.

In Mozambique, urban expansion is a spontaneous phenomenon. The government claims it is in no position to control this, while the private is keen to stress that this is none of its business apart from any opportunities for profitable investment. Individual initiatives determine investment behaviour: the poor spend on land in a bid to secure more effective tenure; the rich will only do so when and where tenure is guaranteed.

Some of the main recommendations in the 2010 report can be summarized as follows:

1. The prevailing mechanisms of urban land allocation should be maintained, but a progressive registration procedure must be rapidly established.
2. New land management and administration models must be introduced in order to facilitate regularisation of all informal land rights transactions and to bring transparency, clarity and efficient sustainable use of urban land.
3. Existing housing loan schemes should be reviewed to include the poor and promote self-help home improvements.
5. A participatory system for land use planning and management devolved to the neighbourhood level would ensure more inclusive approaches to the challenges of rapid urbanisation.
6. A new concept of 'buffer zones' between formal and informal urban areas must be introduced in order to safeguard urban agriculture while extending adequate service provision to informal urban areas.

The 2010 report further highlights government and municipal inability to urbanise new land, deliver new infrastructure or provide urban services at a pace that can match growing demand. This inability must be overcome because it promotes exclusion of the poor, uncontrolled urban growth, the emergence of new, larger slums, and increased urban poverty. Against this background, the research called for the introduction of new tools for city managers and local governments in neighbouring districts that put local authorities in a better position to forecast urban growth within their respective boundaries, and help them to undertake preventive measures to reverse undesirable trends, including the proliferation of urban poverty.

Source: Negrão, J. Urban Land Markets in Mozambique, Cruzeiro do Sul - Research Institute for Development, Maputo, forthcoming. www.iid.org.mz

boundary overlaps, while contracts are not always enforceable under formal law. Moreover, transaction costs remain disproportionally high, which often deters land investment.

In ***Maputo***, urban informal land markets mostly involve purchase of rural lands that are newly incorporated in the city, subdivision of existing urban plots, and occupation of urban lands that are inappropriate for housing development. The informal urban markets involve exchange of unregistered land and cater principally to the urban poor and those excluded from access to land under state allocation processes.

The formal markets are confined to the consolidated areas of ***Maputo*** (the 'Cement City') and involve exchange of registered rights to land and property. They cater mainly to the urban rich through sale of improvements on the land and horizontal co-properties (what would normally be considered 'sectional titles' in the Republic of South Africa).

Most documented land disputes in Southern Africa bear on disagreements among individuals and between individuals and central or local government. The Republic of South Africa features the most organised grassroots movements in the

▲ Johannesburg, South Africa. Satellite image of Soccer City stadium. Shaped roughly like a rectangle with rounded corners, the stadium sports high walls that cast long shadows toward the south-west. Capable of seating 94,700 spectators, Soccer City is nevertheless dwarfed by nearby slag piles left over from decades-long mining operations. On the opposite side of the slag piles from Soccer City is Diepkloof, one of several settlements comprising Soweto. The roughly circular-shaped settlement shows a street grid typical of residential areas, with small, closely packed houses. **©NASA Earth Observatory**

subregion, including the *Abahlali base Mjondolo* (Abahladi) and the Landless People's Movement. Ironically, government and landowners perceive these social movements in criminal terms rather than as the voice of genuine citizen concerns.

Other disputes between individual land owners and public authorities involve appropriation of land from customary owners without compensation, or with compensation equivalent only to the value of unexhausted improvements on the land. Faced with the predominant power and influence of government, individual land owners or loosely organised groups of individual owners rarely win these disputes. Instead, many resort to less confrontational options such as false compliance or benign neglect of formal government rules and regulations.

Many land disputes occur among individuals, especially in informal settlements. However, too many significant differences between countries and cities stand in the way of any meaningful generalisations. Disputes, especially in informal markets, often arise from issues like dual or multiple land sales, extra-legal land allocation by public authorities, contentious land/property ownership, extension of plot boundaries, unauthorised occupation of land and land inheritance. Such disputes are mostly resolved through informal mechanisms involving customary or community leaders. However, despite the often uncertain nature of rights to land in informal or other irregular urban settlements, disputes that defy local remedies often end up in the formal law courts where, quite surprisingly, the legality of rights over disputed, informally acquired land parcels rarely becomes an issue in its own right.

Informal Settlements as a Response to Land Market Deficiencies

Informal markets are plagued by several serious inherent problems, which include conflicting and unrecorded ownership claims, simultaneous multiple sale of property, high transaction costs and defective property rights. The dual system of land ownership and administration in the region acts as a major constraint on the operation of land and housing markets. In most Southern African cities, no information is available on the numerical size or volume of transactions that take place, whether in formal or informal markets, the sums of money involved, the amount of land transacted, or the general pattern of land prices/values. And this is happening while in some cities in the region, over 70 per cent of the population are thought to access land through informal channels.

In the Republic of South Africa, the poor access land through occupation, spill-over and encroachment, unofficial subdivision, allocation by local figures of authority or committees and a variety of rental practices. Accessing urban land outside the formal market grew by 26 per cent (informal settlements and backyards) between 1996 and 2006. Several studies have revealed that 63 per cent of households in informal settlements had participated in secondary markets through purchasing a house from someone else. Over the same period, an estimated 14 per cent of households in site-and-services and 12 per cent in Reconstruction and Development Programme (RDP) settlements had transacted informally.

6.4
The Geography of Climate Change

The Role of Local Authorities in Adaptation to Climate Change

Cities have a unique position in the climate change debate. On one hand, through their prolific use of fossil fuels for transport, manufacturing and electricity generation they are significant generators of carbon emissions while, on the other, they are generators of added value to the economy. Taking the Republic of South Africa as an example, national energy consumption by sector is as follows: industry: 40 per cent; transport: 24 per cent; residential: 18 per cent; mining: 7 per cent , commerce: 6 per cent; and agriculture 3 per cent.[40] In urban areas, this energy comes from electricity and liquid fuels (petrol, diesel, paraffin).

Energy-related carbon emissions in urban areas follow a broadly similar pattern, with industry producing 50 per cent followed by transport (25 per cent) and residential (19 per cent), commerce (4 per cent) and mining (1 per cent). In terms of greenhouse gas emissions by source of energy or fuel type, electricity contributes 66 per cent of carbon dioxide (CO_2) emissions compared with 23 per cent from liquid fuels.[41]

Cities also occupy a unique position in that they are crucibles of political and governance innovations. They should therefore play major roles in climate change interventions. At the local level, this role can be appreciated by what can be described as the 'urban local authority dividend'[42]: the multiple role of local authorities as regulators, administrators, taxing and licensing authorities, strategic land use planners/ developers and consumers, as well as providers of a vast array of goods and services. This 'local authority dividend' enable urban managers to support and stimulate behaviour change among stakeholders - business and citizens alike. Local authorities are in a position to support and stimulate energy-efficient and 'green' industries. They have the closest continuous link with the population, enabling them to foster local participatory and pro-poor climate response strategies, and global environmental change in general.

> *Southern African cities have traditionally prioritized the private car and there is still a strong roads lobby that influences the transport agenda in its largest economy, the Republic of South Africa. Although there is agreement that the focus needs to shift towards non-motorised transport, designs for such alternatives are poorly supported and there is no clear indication of the direction cities should adopt for the future.*
>
> Source: SACN, 2009: 9

GRAPH 6.9: **METROPOLITAN ENERGY CONSUMPTION BY FUEL TYPE IN SOUTH AFRICA**

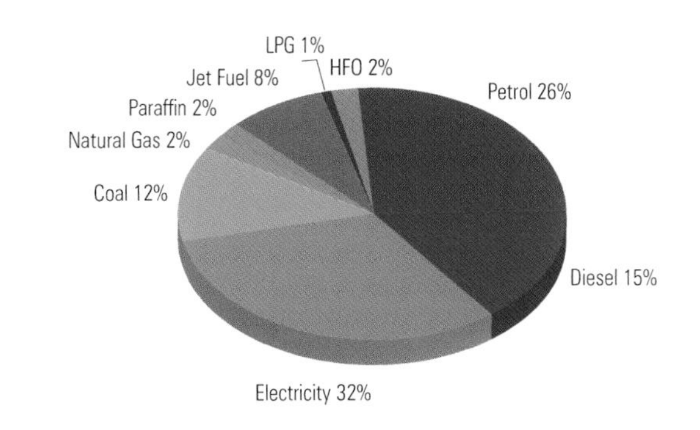

Source: State of the Energy Report for the City of Cape Town 2007, p.25

Spatial planning is one of the major mandates vested in local authorities. However, past and current planning has promoted highly dispersed cities with long commuting distances, with housing for low-income households located on the urban peripheries or beyond. Poor public transport, a bias towards private cars and poorly maintained vehicles are features of all the cities in the region.

It is recognized that Africa has contributed very little to the problems associated with climate change but it may be a major recipient of its negative effects. This global inequality is replicated at the city level in Southern Africa, where the poor majority commute by public transport with low carbon emissions per head, while the middle class and the rich, who are significantly fewer in numbers, commute by private car and produce more carbon emissions. Suburbs combine high rates of car ownership and access to subsidised bus routes. In contrast, the low-income groups in peri-urban townships benefit from poor bus services and have consequently shifted their patronage to more reliable informal 'taxis'. The rail system, which would have been more effective in reducing carbon emissions, has seen a decline in passenger numbers, largely due to poor service, poor safety on carriages and a lack of integration with other transport modes (buses and informal taxis)(DBSA, 2006: 41). Though more reliable, informal taxis are characterised by poor customer care, dangerous driving, overcrowding and poorly maintained vehicles.

Inequality also prevails regarding electricity, the production of which is a major source of CO_2. Poor households in ***Cape Town*** spend10 to15 per cent of incomes on energy, compared with 3 to 5 per cent for high-income households. Households without access to electricity (the poorest of the poor) contribute 6kg of CO_2 per month, compared with 240kg for the low-income group and as many as 750kg per household per month for middle- and upper-income groups.[43]

Local authorities can reduce urban dependence on oil and carbon footprints in a number of ways, including:

- City, neighbourhood and building designs that prioritise energy efficiency, shorter commutes, cycling and public transport options over private transport;
- Environmental-economic legislation and actions, including renewable energy technologies in industry, public and residential buildings and generally integrating 'green' policies in municipal by-laws;
- The 'local authority dividend' puts city managers in a position to take the lead 'green' procurement strategies that give priority to climate change adaptation/mitigation;
- Pooling municipalities' purchasing power to procure services, goods and 'green' technologies would generate cost savings while creating a critical mass for climate change-compliant decision-making, with the attendant demand for novel products and services; and
- Creating incentive programmes to develop 'green' enterprises.

What Urban Climate Change Knowledge is Available?

Over the past decade, governments in Southern Africa have developed national climate change frameworks that seek to balance mitigation and adaptation policies, while fostering climate change-resilient, low-carbon economies and societies. These moves seek to integrate national with global initiatives, but largely take place outside urban local government.

In its Fourth Assessment, the International Panel on Climate Change indicates that in Africa, a 2°C rise in temperature would lead to a 50 per cent decrease in crop yields by 2020. Therefore, it is not surprising that emerging national climate

▲
A flood simulation exercise in Mozambique. **©David Gough/IRIN**

change policies in Southern Africa (e.g., in Botswana and Zambia) focus strongly on agriculture. National ministries of agriculture, environmental and water affairs feature as leaders in the climate change policy responses, with the urban sector remaining largely 'invisible' as an explicit policy domain. As a result, urban authorities and local stakeholders are lagging latecomers and marginal to the key debates. Most are at the early, learning stages and reactive rather than pro-active agenda-setters. Only in Mozambique (see Box 6.4) and the Republic of South Africa, where climate change-induced sea-level rise threatens the economies of cities like ***Maputo, eTekwini*** and ***Cape Town***, has there been an urban dimension to national climate change strategies. However, the responses from inland cities (***Johannesburg, Harare, Tshwane, Lusaka,*** and ***Gaborone***) regarding water scarcity, energy and food are not well incorporated in these policies.

In order to strengthen their awareness and knowledge and be in a position better to influence truly national responses to climate change, local authorities have seen the need to reinforce city-to-city networks and partnerships, especially within the framework of the International Council for Local Environmental Initiatives (ICLEI) and United Cities and Local Governments (UCLG) as illustrated by the July 2009 Tshwane Climate Change Roadmap Summit for local governments and partners. These networks enable urban authorities to share knowledge on climate change, and to lobby national governments and international partners regarding issues of capacity building and financing of carbon emission reduction strategies in cities. The Republic of South Africa has benefited from its partnership with the Government of Denmark through the Urban Environment Management Programme (UEMP). The South African Cities Network has been able to develop new city climate mitigation programmes that can be funded through the national public infrastructure facility. The scheme brings together a number of municipalities and therefore can achieve widespread benefits in a short time. At the local level, partnerships with professional bodies and research centres are also pivotal, such as one with the Green Building Council of the Republic of South Africa to develop a Green Star Rating Tool, and the National Biodiversity Institute on urban biodiversity and reforestation strategies. In 2009, ***Cape Town*** established a climate change knowledge think-tank regrouping academics and scientists to undertake reviews and assessments of the effects of climate change on the city. This research will enable the city to be more proactive in its response to climate change.[44]

BOX 6.4: MAPUTO LEADS THE 'CLIMATE CHANGE INITIATIVE' IN SOUTHERN AFRICA

The *Cities and Climate Change Initiative was* launched by UN-HABITAT in early 2009 at the request of its Governing Council to assist in the major, worldwide re-alignment of public policies towards adaptation and mitigation. The Initiative provides city authorities with the expertise, policy advice, methodologies and information they need to meet this daunting challenge. The newly-created Sustainable Urban Development Network (SUD-Net) complements these efforts (see Box 6.4). The whole project operates in partnership with the UN Development (UNDP) and Environment (UNEP) Programmes and a wide range of other relevant organisations.

No other region in the world is more exposed to the effects of climate change than Africa. Therefore, it was natural for two African cities – Maputo, the capital of Mozambique, and Kampala, the capital of Uganda – to feature among the four 'pilot' conurbations that have been selected to launch the initiative in the developing world. Indeed, both cities provide an apt illustration of the typical threats climate change is posing for conurbations in the developing world.

Sitting on the Indian Ocean coast, Maputo (population 1.1 million, and close to 3 million for the metropolitan area) is highly vulnerable to the effects of climate change. Rapid demographic growth increases the demand for housing and infrastructure, with the poorer residents relegated to risk-prone urban areas.

A preliminary assessment of potential climate change effects was carried out under the Initiative and identified five vulnerable areas: (i) coastal zones and ecosystems; (ii) human settlements and infrastructure; (iii) health, food security and waste management; (iv) the transportation system; and (v) wetlands and urban agriculture. In Maputo, the main climate-related hazards with destructive consequences are floods, droughts, rising sea level and storms (cyclones). These pose serious risks of flooding of the lowest areas, which are the most populated and where slum dwellers are concentrated.

The assessment also identified the six main steps to be taken to design a well-adapted climate change adaptation strategy for Maputo, namely: (i) actively involving major stakeholders from the public, business and academic sectors, civil society and development partners in the process of raising awareness about the impacts of climate change at all levels; (ii) establishing an appropriate institutional arrangement between the city and the central government; (iii) creation of a municipal 'Natural Disasters Risk Reduction' unit; (iv) preparing a more in-depth assessment of the effects of climate change in Maputo, in order to determine the required adaptation and/or mitigation measures to be implemented; (vi) developing methods and tools for the analysis of climate change effects, in order to facilitate the financial planning and decision-making and preparation of a Climate Change Adaptation and Mitigation Plan, which identifies priority interventions to be implemented in the short, medium and long term; and (vii) creating coordination mechanisms with new initiatives or ongoing projects, in order jointly to identify potential sources of funding to ensure continuity of operations.

One immediate outcome of the assessment was a mangrove preservation project in the Maputo area, which serves to demonstrate the methods and results of adaptation/mitigation.

Source: UN-HABITAT, Cities and Climate Change – Initial lessons from UN-HABITAT. Nairobi: UN-HABITAT 2009

BOX 6.5: AN INNOVATIVE NETWORK FOR SUSTAINABLE URBAN GOVERNMENT

Climate change is a vast and complex phenomenon and if cities are to become more sustainable all tiers of government must benefit from a wide range of knowledge and experience. This is the rationale behind the Sustainable Urban Development Network ('SUD-Net'), a worldwide interdisciplinary link supported by UN-HABITAT.

SUD-Net assists cities in a variety of ways: mobilizing partners and networks, building partnerships, implementing innovative, pro-poor projects, stimulating the acquisition and sharing of knowledge, and disseminating good practice. The network provides access to up-to-date information (tools and guidelines, resource packages, documents) as well as feedback on ongoing debates, initiatives and activities at the global, regional, national and local levels. SUD-Net also supports institutional capacity-building through improved governance and leadership against a background of decentralized public authorities. Over the past year or so, links have been established with local urban knowledge networks, city councils and universities, as well as the World Bank.

Urban Climate Change Adaptation Strategies and the Energy Sector

Southern Africa faces an energy crisis, as became evident between 2005 and 2007 when severe power shortages hit industry, business and more generally the quality of life. The region relies on hydro-electric and coal-based thermal power and is supplied by national utility companies such as ESKOM (Republic of South Africa), NamPower (Namibia), ZESCO (Zambia), Empresa Nacionale d'Electricidade (Angola) and Electricidade de Moçambique (Mozambique).[45] Since the region is prone to droughts, though, hydro-electric power generation is exposed to significant risk, which recent climatic variability can only compound. Although the Republic of South Africa produces nuclear electric power, this contributes less than 5 per cent of national grid volume and future capacity expansions are controversial. Meanwhile, a massive 74 per cent of the country's electricity supply comes from coal-fired power stations.

The region produces and uses over 80 per cent of all the electricity generated in sub-Saharan Africa. However, supply from existing energy infrastructure has fallen well below demand and the region has only managed to cope because of energy imports from the Democratic Republic of Congo, whose economy uses relatively little of its significant production. Most of the Republic of South Africa's energy is consumed by industry, mining and cities. The 10 largest cities consume 50 per cent of the available electricity. Ninety-six per cent of this electricity is generated by ESKOM with at least 70 per cent generated from highly-polluting low-grade coal (similar patterns are found in Zimbabwe and Namibia).[46] Taking ***Cape Town*** as an example, coal-fired electricity accounts for 28 per cent of its energy consumptions but results in 66 per cent of total carbon emissions of the conurbation.[47] Emissions in dense manufacturing provinces like ***Gauteng*** are even higher. As shown in Graph 6.10, the major end-users of electricity are manufacturing industries, with mining operations and domestic consumption coming second and third.

Consequently, if any significant reduction of coal-related carbon emissions is to be achieved, it will require major changes in power-generation for manufacturing and mining, as reductions in the commercial and domestic sectors would have a limited effect.

In the household sector, energy use inequalities persist. The high cost of providing electricity infrastructure to the urban periphery and beyond means that many poorer urban communities go without power at all. The implications are evident in ***eTekwini*** and ***Luanda,*** lack of electricity in low-income areas leads to widespread use of candles, paraffin and charcoal. These are a major cause of fires while charcoal is associated with environmental degradation in peri-urban areas, greenhouse gas emissions, domestic pollution and severe lung conditions. The upfront costs of universal provision of electricity may look hefty, but this is the least costly solution in the long run. It might be worth remembering here that in colonial days, one of the reasons for extending electricity to ***Harare*** and ***Bulawayo*** was to preserve the environment from the damages caused by firewood exploitation in peri-urban areas.

One aspect of Southern Africa's more or less open energy crisis is the ageing of power plants and infrastructure. This is especially the case with Zimbabwe's coal-fed thermal power stations. Although the country's industries are operating at a mere 10 per cent capacity, energy demand is not met and the situation can only worsen if and when operational capacity improves to even 50 per cent in the near future, as is expected. However, as Zimbabwe's economy recovers and the Republic of South Africa emerges from the global economic slowdown, a more serious power crisis can be anticipated from as early

GRAPH 6.10: **ELECTRICITY END-USER DISTRIBUTION IN THE REPUBLIC OF SOUTH AFRICA**

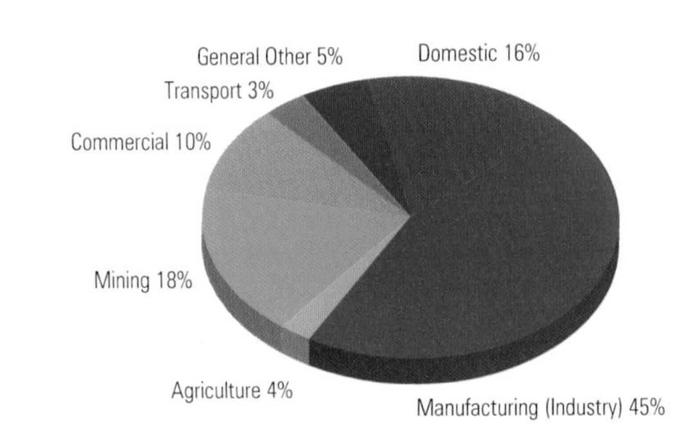

Source: Compiled from DBSA (2006: 74)

▲
A coal-fired power station in Cape Town, South Africa. **©Simisa. Licenced under the Creative Commons Attribution-Share Alike 3.0 Unported Licence**

as 2010, with load shedding likely to resume.[48] The crisis was evident during the 2010 football World Cup when electricity demand was already at its peak due to the winter season: poorer communities were the first targets for load shedding to avoid disruptions in the areas associated with the event.

A major aspect of the crisis has to do with the structure of the sector: national utilities are in charge of all power generation, transmission and distribution, and local authorities have no say over production volumes or energy use. Legislative and institutional arrangements do neither give city authorities any power over energy, nor do they encourage power utilities to invest in alternative sources. Against this background, the energy crisis in Southern Africa offers opportunities to rethink and encourage decentralised investment in renewable energy sources, especially the abundant wind and solar power potential for residential water heating and lighting. Ocean wave power for coastal cities like ***Maputo***, ***Durban*** and ***Cape Town*** could be explored. Alternatives that have not been fully developed include bio-fuels and electricity from wastes and sugar cane. As for energy conservation, it is neither encouraged nor rewarded by current governance structures. A combination of user information campaigns and appropriate technologies could bring significant savings. Mass solar water heaters alone could save 20-30 per cent of household energy.

Solar power is viewed largely as adequate for rural electrification rather than for urban consumers. Despite the associated environmental damage, the region still largely relies on coal-based thermal power stations. The availability of huge coal reserves seems to drive the decision making and investment policies of major power utilities rather than climate change-related considerations. For instance, ESKOM's new programme commits the Republic of South Africa on a carbon intensive path even as the government shifts focus to a low-carbon economy.[49] However, isolated initiatives point in the right direction, i.e., a diversity of alternative sources of urban energy, as exemplified by ***eTekwini*** Municipality's gas to electricity project in three municipal landfill sites. Capturing landfill gasses reduces greenhouse gas emissions and can yield 10 megawatts every year.

6.5
Emerging Issues

The Development Role of Mega-Sporting Events

The year 2010 witnessed a bonanza of sporting events for Southern Africa. The Confederation of African Football organised the African Cup of Nations, staged during January 2010 across four cities in Angola where the Chinese constructed four new stadiums, rebuilt roads and upgraded airports. Then came the football World Cup Finals in the Republic of South Africa in June-July 2010, in nine cities with the opening and final games in ***Johannesburg***. While this section will focus on the soccer World Cup, it should be noted that the development rationales and effects of these major events can also be found in the All-Africa Games that were staged in ***Maputo*** in the second half of 2010.

Mega sporting events continue to be viewed as catalysts for economic development in the hosting nation. The opportunity to showcase the host nation improves the country's image, attracting investment and job creation, boosting tourism and leaving behind a legacy of urban development legacy (infrastructures and housing).[50] In Southern Africa, investment in infrastructure (stadiums, media, entertainment and leisure, transportation, hotels, security) was the main expected benefit associated with these events.[51] At the planning stage in 2004, the estimated budget was in the region of SAR15 billion (US $1.9 billion) with SAR8.4 billion (US $1.08 billion) and SAR6.7 billion (US$865 million) for stadiums and infrastructure, respectively,[52] funded through partnerships among government, local authorities and private investors.[53] The objective was not only to deliver a successful sporting event but to integrate the related capital expenditure into broader plans that would leave a legacy of improved cities in the Republic of South Africa.

▲
Bafana Bafana supporters at the World Cup 2010. **©Jonathan Larsen/Shutterstock**

This legacy was the major benefit the Republic of South Africa expected to reap from the World Cup 2010.[54] Legacy embodies inheritance and transformation; not just the transfer from one generation to another but also the transformation of a society from one state to another. Beyond economic gains in terms of employment, it was about promoting inclusive urban space and moving away from the apartheid-era political economy of marginality for the majority. The event elicited reflections upon identity and affirmed social standing and belonging on a national, regional (SADC) and worldwide scale. In contrast to the 1995 World Rugby Cup, for instance, the 2010 FIFA World Cup highlighted the inclusion of the majority black South Africans, and Africa in general, as citizens in the global society, who were able not just to participate in the consumption of global culture but also to produce it.

Neighbouring countries including Angola, Botswana, Lesotho, Mozambique, Namibia, Swaziland, Zambia and Zimbabwe collectively used the football World Cup to develop and market their own tourism industry. In this respect, the seven-country Trans-Frontier Conservation Area (TFCA) provided tourists with varied options. Infrastructures included rehabilitation of the Maputo-South Africa railway line (US $57 million) and hotels, casinos and leisure facilities (US $500 million).[55] The positive effects were clearly well beyond the sporting events, strengthening the flows of goods and people in the ***Maputo-Johannesburg*** development corridor. Political integration within the SADC was also enhanced and a sense of success and global belonging was felt by Africans throughout the continent and the diaspora (see Box 6.6).

Soccer is favourite sport of the majority poor black populations of Southern Africa. Consequently, staging the event in the Republic of South Africa and locating some of the major venues in poor or low-income townships brought more than a 'feel good' effect – a sense of triumph and equality that was shared in the whole of Southern Africa as well. 'Soccer City', the venue for the opening ceremony and six subsequent games, is a stone's throw away from Soweto, the largest low-income township in the region. Similarly, for the 2010 African Cup of Nations in Angola, the stadiums were located in or close to poor neighbourhoods, sending a strong political message of inclusive development and global citizenship.

Although new stadiums were built for the games in each of the host cities, the Moses Mabhida stadium in ***Durban*** probably best illustrates how the World Cup infrastructure and investments have been used for urban development and local economic strategies. Post-2010 ***Durban*** hopes to be a successful (s)port city able to host future Olympic, Commonwealth and continental games. The 70,000 stadium was designed as an iconic and unmistakeable silhouette on the ***Durban*** skyline and, more functionally, to spur the urban economy.[56] The design has political symbolism in that its Y-shaped arch which ascends from one end of the stadium in two prongs to join in the middle and descend in one prong at the other end – a reflection of the country's flag – symbolises political unity. In a country and a region where interracial and inter-ethnic tensions lie only just below the surface, such physical symbolism helps project the nation's long-term desires for social unity.

▲
Supporters at the World Cup 2010. **©NewZimbabwe.com**

Whereas some analysts query the economic and employment-creation effects of major global sport events in general, these elicit more immediate and tangible concerns for urban development.[57] The Government of the Republic of South Africa used the event as an opportunity to redistribute development and justify projects that would otherwise never have happened. The N2 Gateway Housing Development in ***Cape Town***, for instance, was fast-tracked for completion to beautify the area before the 2010 Cup, rather than as the planned housing project it had been for several decades.[58] Massive forced removal of the area's residents and the stiff resistance from so-called squatters highlighted the unequal legacies experienced by different groups of society. Similar displacements of the poor, alleged violations of rights and corruption were recorded for Mbombela stadium in Mpumalanga province. These forced removals have been compared to those of the apartheid years. However, the World Cup rhetoric and the overwhelming support for this event, both within the city and nationwide, enabled the authorities to proceed and ride the storm of resistance.

The above example indicates that the positive effects of mega sporting events at the local level are not uniform and can be challenged by those excluded and evicted. Despite general enthusiastic support for the games in the Republic of

BOX 6.6: **AFFIRMATION AND BELONGING TO GLOBAL SOCIETY**

The lasting legacy of the 2010 football World Cup was also shared by Zimbabwe, a country whose economy and society are emerging from a decade of social upheaval and economic depression. A visit by the Brazilian national football team to Zimbabwe to play the country's own national team in June 2010 did Zimbabweans proud and instilled a sense of belonging to the global community. The game was watched by 60,000 including the president and the prime minister, not including millions through TV and radio, while others simply enjoyed the idea that during their lifetime, Brazil – the five-time World Cup winners – visited Zimbabwe, the first foreign football team to do so since independence. The event brought desperately needed positive coverage in global media. It left a legacy of hope and confidence while reiterating a message that, despite the troubles of the past decade, Zimbabweans were united, dignified and a determined people whose warmth makes the country a place for good global business.

Source: New Zimbabwe.com , 3rd June 2010

▲ The Moses Mabhida Stadium, Durban, South Africa. ©**Jbor/Shutterstock**

South Africa and the continent at large, those living close to the venues were disturbed. In Soweto, ***Johannesburg***, female food traders were removed from their usual selling points outside the Soccer City stadium for the duration of the World Cup. The policy of keeping the poor out of sight denied these women good business over the period[59] and stood in stark contrast to the reported record US $3 billion tax-free profits made by FIFA.[60] Likewise, in ***Luanda***, where electricity supply is low at best, the poor were not able to watch the Africa Cup of Nations games on television as electrical power was diverted. Clearly, poverty and polarization are very real conditions with differential gains from mega sporting events and related urban development.

But all in all, the 2010 World Cup surpassed expectations and silenced 'Afro-pessimists'. The event gave the world a well-organised tournament with great hospitality that had a galvanising effect on sports in Africa. On top of the *vuvuzela*, it also helped market the region's potential in various areas, highlighted the ongoing transition in Southern Africa and reminded the world of the gross poverty and inequality that undermines the region's dream of a post-apartheid inclusive society. With this window of global awareness and empathy, Southern Africa should deploy the radical equity-focused programmes and structural economic changes that are required to tackle poverty. The enthusiasm, unity of purpose and efficiency with which leaders delivered the World Cup should now be replicated in the areas of housing, water, electricity, health and education. According to Ellen Chauke, a 56-year old unemployed who demonstrated at the start of the tournament, poor Africans were not against the World Cup, but:

We are against a government that does not treat people right. We are still living in shacks. We don't have electricity. We don't have running water and we have 100 people to a toilet. We want the world to see South Africa is not working for [all] its people.[61]

Trans-Boundary Development: Insights from the Maputo development corridor

Since the 1990s, formal transnational development corridors and spatial-economic development initiatives have been promoted to unleash the growth potential in transport corridor areas and Southern Africa in general.[62] However, the subregion also features many informal or spontaneous transnational development corridors that take advantage of highly permeable borders allowing for social, cultural, human and economic interaction in much of the subregion for centuries. In colonial times, these informal corridors contributed to the integration of local economies into global trade flows. They became channels or spaces for migrant labour to and from mining and agricultural regions of the Republic of South Africa and Rhodesia (Zimbabwe). The Tete Corridor (Zimbabwe, Mozambique and Malawi), the Beira Corridor (Zimbabwe and Mozambique), the Limpopo-Gauteng corridor (Zimbabwe and the Republic of South Africa) and the Maputo Development Corridor (Mozambique and the Republic of South Africa) are examples of such informal corridors, some of which were formally recognised during and after colonial rule.

The Maputo-Gauteng Development Corridor

In the early 1900s, agreements between the Republic of South Africa and Mozambique gave rights to the Witwatersrand Native Labour Association (WENELA), representing the group of major South African mining firms, to recruit black African labourers from Mozambique for South African mines on condition that 47.5 per cent of export traffic from ***Witwatersrand*** (Gauteng Region) would go through ***Maputo***.[63] As the result, an economic transport and population corridor formally linked ***Maputo*** to ***Gauteng*** (see Map 6.3). Forty-per cent of exports from ***Gauteng*** went though ***Maputo*** in the 1970s, but this figure declined during the Mozambican civil war in the 1980s and much of the infrastructure became derelict.[64]

Mozambique developed similar corridors to the then-Rhodesia – the Beira Corridor – and Malawi – the Tete Corridor. Functionally, these corridors extend well beyond the narrow geographical confines of roads and railways to include permanent trade spaces on the sides, in the process creating fresh opportunities for hawking, smuggling, etc. Flows of people on a subregional scale, mostly women buying and selling goods, took to operating in tandem with male labour migration. However, these *de facto* cross-border economies remain largely outside the intellectual debates that inform integrated regional development policy. When discussing formal regions like the ***Maputo-Gauteng*** Development Corridor, the origins, purpose, governance and impacts of the historical and social undertones must be borne in mind.

MAP 6.3: **THE MAPUTO-GAUTENG DEVELOPMENT CORRIDOR**

Source: SADC (2007) Report of study on the corridor/Spatial Development Initiative. Gaborone: SADC Secretariat

MAP 6.4: **TRANSNATIONAL DEVELOPMENT CORRIDORS IN SOUTHERN AFRICA**

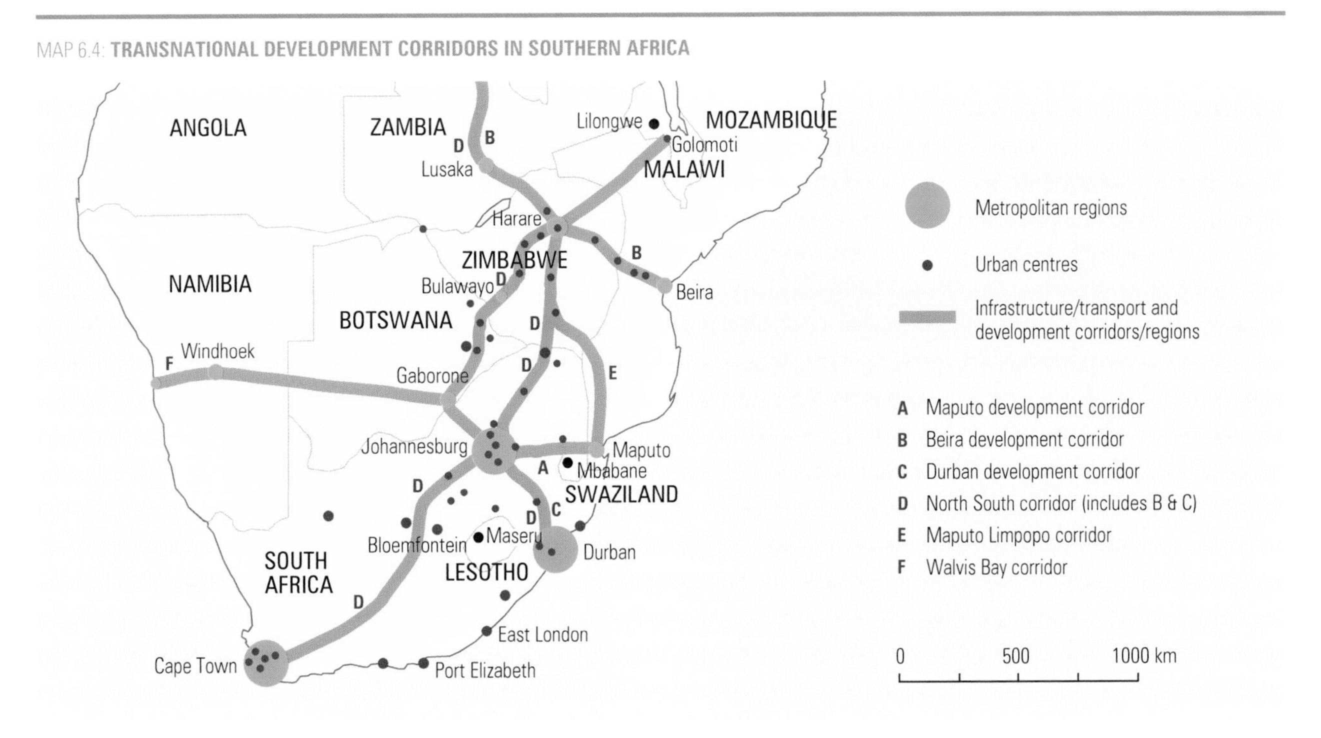

After the advent of majority rule in the Republic of South Africa and the end to civil war in Mozambique a few years earlier, the two countries revised the formal operations of the ***Maputo-Gauteng*** Development Corridor as a spatial and economic development initiative. As with the Beira Corridor in the 1980s, rehabilitation and upgrading of transport infrastructures (the N4 toll road, railway lines and port facilities) was at the core of this initiative, to facilitate freight movement between Gauteng and the port of Maputo. However, unlike the Beira Corridor, its Maputo-Gauteng equivalent also contributes to the development of both Maputo Province – home to about 40 per cent of Mozambique's population – and the Mpumalanga Province of the Republic of South Africa through which most of the corridor runs. Industrial, agricultural and tourism investments feature high on the agenda and the benefits are supposed to trickle down over the whole area.

Other Major Trans-national Development Corridors in Southern Africa

Table 6.7 illustrates the diversity of development corridors in the subregion. The ***Maputo-Gauteng*** Development Corridor benefits from more private sector participation than any other, while in the Beira Corridor the public sector has crowded out the private one. However, the more generally favoured option today is a policy shift from government-based infrastructure development to market-led and export-oriented growth based on competitive positioning in the international economy.

The institutional structure of each development corridor is largely a by-product of history and opportunities in the partner countries. The ***Maputo-Gauteng*** corridor shows that its market-led rejuvenation leaves little room for the government

TABLE 6.7: **THE DIVERSITY OF TRANS-NATIONAL DEVELOPMENT CORRIDORS IN SOUTHERN AFRICA**

Name of Corridors and Institutional Leaders	Geographic Focus and Key Objectives	Anchor Projects
Maputo Development Corridor Leaders: • Maputo Corridor Logistics Initiative • Republic of South African Ministry of Transport • Mozambique Ministry of Transport	An economic corridor linking Gauteng province (Johannesburg, Pretoria, etc.) to the closest port – Maputo in Mozambique. • rehabilitate core infrastructure along the corridor • maximise the investment potential of the corridor area • ensure that development impact is maximised for disadvantaged communities • Ensure sustainable, participatory and integrated approach to development.	• Reconstruction of Witbank-Maputo road • Rehabilitation and management of Maputo port • Rehabilitation and upgrading of railway network in southern Mozambique • Development of electricity infrastructure from Republic of South Africa into Southern Mozambique • Development of Mozambique Aluminium Smelter (MOZAL) • Development of the Belluluane Industrial Park (BIP) • Development of natural gas resources.
Beira (Zambezi) Development Corridor Leaders • Departments of Transport and Communications - Mozambique and Zimbabwe.	An economic development corridor linking Zimbabwe, Zambia, DR Congo and Malawi to the port of Beira, Mozambique. The Zambezi River basin is a resource-rich hinterland that can act as a platform for future development. Prior to 1994, the Beira corridor was developed to guarantee economic survival of the land-locked states during the war in Mozambique and destabilisation from the Republic of South Africa.	• The Moatize power station • Expansion of Cabora Basa hydropower dam and development of new downstream dam at Mpande Uncua. • Upgrading Sena railway line to facilitate the transfer of coking coal to Beira. • Upgrading of Beira Port • Development of the Inchoper-Gorongosa-Caia Highway.
North-South Corridor Leaders • Federation of East and Southern African Transporters Associations • Sub-Sahara Africa Transport Program	This corridor extends from the industrial centre of Gauteng Region (Republic of South Africa) to Zimbabwe, Zambia, DR Congo and Malawi to the north & to Durban on the Indian Ocean • The busiest corridor in southern Africa, yet has many bottlenecks (crossing points at Beitbridge, Chirundu and Victoria Falls) and security issues • Development and management systems delayed by the crisis in Zimbabwe over the last decade as international partners shunned the country. • Plan is to upgrade infrastructure, remove bottlenecks, standardise operational systems.	• Construction of a new bridge at Chirundu (2002) • Reconstruction of highway between Lusaka and Chirundu • New border post facilities at Chirundu to accommodate One Stop Border operations. • Improve border crossing facilities at Musian/Beitbridge • Manage migration and health issues along the corridor
Limpopo Development Corridor Leaders • Departments of Transport and Communications - Mozambique and Zimbabwe	An initiative between Zimbabwe, the Republic of South Africa, Mozambique and eventually Botswana and Zambia, focused on the Limpopo River Basin • Foster increased economic activity through investment in processing of minerals, agricultural production, rehabilitation of key infrastructure and tourism (the Gaza-Kruger-Gonarezhou Trans Frontier Park).	• Concessioning of Limpopo railway line • Rehabilitation of road network and further road linkage between Maputo Development Corridor and the Xai Xai Pafuri Route • Development/Upgrading of new RSA/Mozambique border facilities in the Greater Limpopo TFP • Bridge over Limpopo River at Mapai and upgrading of roads to the coast • Mining of minerals, development of electricity • Rehabilitation and development of Chokwe Irrigation Scheme

Source: Modified from SADC (2007) Report of study on the corridor/Spatial Development Initiative. Gaborone: SADC Secretariat.

to promote people-centred development. The large investment projects that have emerged in the region have visibly contributed to growth of national income in participating countries, but more broad-based positive effects on livelihoods remain uncertain in the short term. This hark s back to the informal, policy-invisible dynamics of these corridors, which act as channels for phenomena like migration and trade that have direct effects on many people's livelihoods.

Through their own Development Community (SADC) and the New Partnership for Africa's Development (NEPAD), Southern African countries have promoted corridors or spatial development to foster economic growth and (sub)regional integration.[65] However, more harmonization is needed between these corridor initiatives, on the one hand, and the development planning of metropolitan/city regions, on the other. Anchors in these corridors, such as infrastructure projects in the Maputo, Beira and North-South Corridors, create greater (sub)regional inter-city mobility. HIV/AIDS support institutions have begun to use these corridors as a framework for the planning and delivery of health services and information, an approach that should also be considered by regional and metropolitan authorities. This is just one example in a multiplicity of opportunities created by domestic and trans-national development corridors. This relatively new spatial, political, economic and social phenomenon can benefit the subregion in many ways which it is for further research to explore.

ENDNOTES

1. *The State of African Cities 2008: A framework for addressing urban challenges in Africa*. Nairobi: UN-HABITAT/ECA
2. Lindell, I. *The multiple sites of urban governance: insights from an African City*, in *Urban Studies*, 45 (9) 2008 1879-1901.
3. Ananya R., *Why India cannot plan its cities; informality, insurgence and the idiom of urbanization*, in *Planning Theory*, 8 (1) 2009 76-87, page 83
4. Tibaijuka, A. (2005) *'Report of the Fact Finding Mission to Zimbabwe to Assess the Scope and Impact of Operation Murambatsvina by the UN Special Envoy on Human Settlement Issues*, Nairobi: UN-HABITAT.
5. Data compiled from City of Johannesburg Integrated Transport Plan 2003 – 2008.
6. Computed from census data, *Census 2002 National Report*, Central Statistical Office, Causeway, Harare.
7. Data compiled from the Lusaka Integrated Development Plan, 2001
8. Projected from pp2-8 in State of Cities Report 2006, South African Cities Network, Braamfontein, Johannesburg.
9. Kinsey, B. H. (2010) Who went where and why: patterns and consequences of displacement in rural Zimbabwe after February 2000. Journal of Southern African Studies, 36 (2): 339 – 360.
10. South African Cities Network (2004) South African Cities HIV/AIDS: Challenges and Responses. P. 36, SACN: Braamfontein, Johannesburg.
11. The Economist, 14th January, 2010, Johannesburg.
12. Murray, M. *Fire and Ice: Unnatural disasters and the disposable urban poor in post-apartheid Johannesburg*, in *International Journal of Urban and Regional Research*, 33.1 2009 165-192 (p. 172-173).
13. SACN (2006: 2-18).
14. Bond, P. & Dugard, J. *The case of Johannesburg water; What really happened at the pre-paid Parish –pump* in *Law Democracy and Development,2008, 1-28*, http://www.ukzn.ac.za/ccs/]
15. Murray, page 170, *ibid*.
16. http://www.abahlali.org/
17. Bond, P. *When Social Protest is the Logical Reaction to Economic Violence*. Eye on Civil Society Column, (The Mercury)
18. Bond, P., *Unsustainable South Africa*
19. Bond P. & Dugard, J. 2008, p. 3 *ibid*
20. Mhone, G. *Labour market discrimination and its aftermath in Southern Africa* in Bond, P. (ed.) *Beyond enclavity in African economies: the enduring work of Guy Mhone*. Centre for Civil society, University of Kwa-Zulu Natal , 2007.
21. Africa Economic Outlook, "African economies will gain strength in 2010 and 2011", African Development Bank.
22. *Ibid*.
23. see Municipal Development Partnerships, Harare, On-Line: http://www.mdpafrica.org.zw/
24. Data from AdeM, the water provider for Maputo, electronic communications, 12th March 2010.
25. Bond 2002,
26. pp 30. *'Angola Country Report'* , Economist Intelligence Unit, London, December 2006
27. Extracted from the UN-HABITAT Global Urban Observatory, 2009.
28. Paper No3. 2009, National Land Policy 2009, , Ministry of Lands, Nairobi, Government of Kenya.
29. Nkambwe, M. (2003) Contrasting land tenures; subsistence agriculture versus urban expansion in the rural-urban fringe of Gaborone, Botswana. . . *International Development Planning Review, 25 (4); 291 – 405.*
30. Investing Across Borders 2010, The World Bank, Washington DC.
31. *Ibid*, page 52.
32. UN-HABITAT (2009) *Challenges of Municipal Finance in Africa: with special reference to Gaborone City, Botswana.* Nairobi, United Nations Habitat, p. 3.
33. Ingram, G. K and Hong, Y. H. (2010) (eds.) *Municipal Revenues and Land Policies. Proceedings of the 2009 land policy conference*. Cambridge, Massachusetts: Lincoln Institute of Land Policy.
34. UN-HABITAT (2009)
35. UN-HABITAT (2009: 20)
36. UN-HABITAT (2007) *Zambia: Lusaka Urban Profile. . .* Nairobi: UN-HABITAT. see pp. 15.
37. South African Cities Network (2007) *State of City Finances Report 2007*, Johannesburg: South African Cities Network pp. 52 – 65.
38. *Ibid*.
39. Franzsen, R.C. D & McCluskey, W. J. (2005) An exploratory overview of property taxation in the Commonwealth of Nations. Working Paper. Cambridge, Massachusetts: Lincoln Institute of Land Policy.
40. City of Cape Town (2007) The State of Energy Report for the City of Cape Town 2007. Cape Town, p. 23.
41. *Ibid*, pp26-27)
42. Mbiba, B. & Ndubiwa, M. (2009) Bulawayo: The role of local authorities in promoting decent work. Chapter 4 in Lawrence R. & Werma, E. (eds.) *Labour Conditions for Construction: Building cities, decent work and the role of local authorities*. Oxford: Blackwell Publishing Ltd.
43. City of Cape Town (2005: 30) Cape Town energy and Climate Change Strategy. Cape Town.
44. Cape Town Climate Change Think Tank, On-Line: www.capetown.gov.za
45. EIA, "The Southern African Community Analysis Brief" 2005, On-line: http://www.eia.doe.gov/emeu/cabs/sadc.html
46. DBSA (2006: 74)
47. City of Cape Town (2007: 7) State of Energy Report for the City of Cape Town 2007. Cape Town.
48. Darren Parker "Load shedding may resume early next year" Engineering News, South Africa, 2009.
49. P. 2, South African Cities Network (2009) *Sustainable Cities 2009*. Johannesburg: South African Cities Network
50. Preuss, H. *Economics of the Olympic Games-Hosting the games 1972-2000*. Sydney: Walla Press in conjunction with the Centre for Olympics Studies., 2002.
51. Bob, U. & Swart, K. "Resident perceptions of the 2010 FIFA Soccer World Cup stadia development in Cape Town" Urban Forum, 20: 47-59, 2009.
52. FIFA "Inspection Group Report for the 201 FIFA World Cup". Geneva, FIFA, 2004.
53. "With a wave and a smile, Mandela gives the dream finale" *The Guardian, Monday 12th July 2010, pp. 2-3.*
54. Gold, J. & Gold, M. (2009) *Future Indefinite? London 2010, the spectre of retrenchment and the challenge of Olympic sports legacy*. In *The London Journal 34 (2): 179 – 197*.
55. http://www.sa201.gov.za/ last visited 18th September 2010.
56. "An Icon for the people" About the Stadium, Durban-FIFA 2010 World Cup, Host City. http://fifaworldcup.durban.gov.za
57. "World Cup legacy is troubling issue for South Africans" *The Times, Friday 26th March 201*, pp. 108 -109.
58. Newton, C. "*The reverse side of the medal*, in *Urban Forum*, 20: 93-108, 2009.
59. 'The world Cup won't help us' pp. 5 – 9 , *The Guardian – G2, 3rd June 2010*.
60. "Sceptics drowned out by another rainbow miracle: South Africa has risen above all pessimism" World Cup 2010, *The Observer, Sunday, 11th July 2010*, pp. 5. London.
61. "Money, jobs and prestige, but will the legacy last?" *The Guardian, Tuesday 1st June 2010*. pp. 4 -5, London.
62. DBSA (2006) *The DBSA Infrastructure Barometer 2006: Economic and Municipal Infrastructure in South Africa*. Midrand: Development Bank of Southern Africa
63. pp. 4 in Soderbaum, R. & Taylor, I. (eds.) *Regionalism and uneven development in Southern Africa: the case of Maputo Development Corridor*. Ashgate Publishing Limited, Aldershot, England, 2003.
64. *Ibid*
65. see Southern Africa Development Community (SADC) (2007) "Study on the Corridor/Spatial Development Initiative" prepared by Corridor Development Consultants (Pvt) Ltd.. Gaborone, Botswana, SADC Secretariat; Japan International Cooperation Agency (JICA) (n.d.) *A Passage Across Borders: Towards Growth and Development Transcending Borders in Africa*. Tokyo: Japan International Cooperation Agency; SADC (2008) "Regional Trade for Aid Donor Conference: North – South Corridor Pilot Project". SADC/COMESA Advance Conference Paper, March 2008, Gaborone, Botswana, SADC Secretariat.

Statistical Annex

TABLE 1: **TOTAL POPULATION AND URBAN POPULATION BY MAJOR AREA, REGION AND COUNTRY, 1990-2025**

		Total Population (thousands)							
Area	**Note**	**1990**	**1995**	**2000**	**2005**	**2010***	**2015***	**2020***	**2025***
Sub-Saharan Africa	**e**	**518,053**	**593,183**	**674,842**	**764,328**	**863,314**	**970,173**	**1,081,114**	**1,193,752**
Africa		**638,729**	**726,285**	**819,462**	**921,073**	**1,033,043**	**1,153,038**	**1,276,369**	**1,400,184**
Eastern Africa		**192,959**	**219,874**	**252,710**	**287,413**	**327,186**	**372,455**	**420,200**	**468,766**
Burundi		5,681	6,167	6,473	7,378	8,519	9,413	10,318	11,161
Comoros		438	493	552	616	691	767	838	907
Djibouti		560	624	730	805	879	953	1,027	1,111
Eritrea		3,158	3,206	3,657	4,473	5,224	6,009	6,719	7,404
Ethiopia		48,292	56,983	65,515	74,661	84,976	96,237	107,964	119,822
Kenya		23,433	27,492	31,441	35,817	40,863	46,433	52,034	57,573
Madagascar		11,273	13,121	15,275	17,614	20,146	22,853	25,687	28,595
Malawi		9,451	10,144	11,831	13,654	15,692	17,998	20,537	23,194
Mauritius	1	1,056	1,129	1,195	1,252	1,297	1,337	1,372	1,400
Mayotte		92	122	149	174	199	224	250	277
Mozambique		13,543	15,945	18,249	20,834	23,406	25,957	28,545	31,190
Réunion		604	664	724	784	837	886	931	973
Rwanda		7,150	5,440	7,958	8,992	10,277	11,743	13,233	14,676
Seychelles		72	76	81	83	85	86	89	91
Somalia		6,596	6,521	7,394	8,354	9,359	10,731	12,246	13,922
Uganda		17,731	20,954	24,433	28,699	33,796	39,710	46,319	53,406
United Republic of Tanzania		25,455	29,972	34,131	39,007	45,040	52,109	59,603	67,394
Zambia		7,910	9,108	10,467	11,738	13,257	14,980	16,916	18,890
Zimbabwe		10,461	11,713	12,455	12,475	12,644	14,029	15,571	16,780
Middle Africa		**72,813**	**86,424**	**98,060**	**113,185**	**128,909**	**146,148**	**164,284**	**182,891**
Angola		10,661	12,539	14,280	16,618	18,993	21,690	24,507	27,441
Cameroon		12,233	14,054	15,865	17,823	19,958	22,169	24,349	26,478
Central African Republic		2,928	3,335	3,746	4,101	4,506	4,927	5,340	5,747
Chad		6,105	7,128	8,402	10,019	11,506	13,120	14,897	16,906
Congo		2,446	2,782	3,036	3,417	3,759	4,225	4,699	5,094
Democratic Republic of the Congo		37,016	44,921	50,829	59,077	67,827	77,419	87,640	98,123
Equatorial Guinea		379	452	529	609	693	781	875	971
Gabon		926	1,084	1,233	1,369	1,501	1,639	1,779	1,915
Sao Tomé e Príncipe		116	128	140	153	165	180	197	216

Urban Population (thousands)							
1990	**1995**	**2000**	**2005**	**2010***	**2015***	**2020***	**2025***
146,673	**181,582**	**220,606**	**266,935**	**321,400**	**384,696**	**456,580**	**537,128**
205,225	**248,074**	**294,602**	**349,145**	**412,990**	**486,525**	**569,117**	**660,589**
34,660	**42,983**	**52,641**	**63,778**	**77,194**	**94,663**	**116,130**	**141,973**
356	445	536	703	937	1,199	1,524	1,912
122	140	155	172	195	224	259	302
424	475	555	612	670	732	798	875
499	532	650	868	1,127	1,463	1,845	2,282
6,095	7,921	9,762	11,892	14,158	17,084	20,800	25,487
4,271	5,214	6,204	7,429	9,064	11,190	13,826	17,070
2,657	3,385	4,143	5,020	6,082	7,381	8,953	10,836
1,093	1,345	1,796	2,367	3,102	4,048	5,240	6,689
464	488	510	528	542	565	595	634
33	51	71	88	100	113	129	148
2,857	4,181	5,601	7,188	8,996	11,000	13,208	15,612
491	572	650	724	787	842	891	934
387	451	1,096	1,577	1,938	2,411	2,993	3,694
35	38	41	44	47	50	54	58
1,956	2,049	2,458	2,939	3,505	4,299	5,268	6,451
1,964	2,444	2,952	3,601	4,493	5,719	7,381	9,604
4,807	6,157	7,614	9,441	11,883	15,060	18,945	23,625
3,117	3,379	3,643	4,108	4,733	5,543	6,584	7,837
3,033	3,717	4,205	4,475	4,837	5,743	6,839	7,921
23,741	**30,088**	**36,486**	**45,225**	**55,592**	**67,781**	**81,493**	**96,522**
3,960	5,516	6,995	8,966	11,112	13,564	16,184	18,942
4,981	6,371	7,910	9,672	11,655	13,775	15,941	18,112
1,078	1,241	1,410	1,561	1,755	1,991	2,268	2,596
1,271	1,563	1,964	2,531	3,179	4,005	5,054	6,342
1,329	1,570	1,770	2,056	2,335	2,712	3,118	3,494
10,299	12,773	15,168	18,967	23,887	29,858	36,834	44,715
132	176	205	237	275	321	379	448
641	817	989	1,145	1,292	1,437	1,579	1,719
51	62	75	89	103	118	136	155

		Total Population (thousands)							
Area	**Note**	**1990**	**1995**	**2000**	**2005**	**2010***	**2015***	**2020***	**2025***
Northern Africa		**147,767**	**163,943**	**179,525**	**195,444**	**212,921**	**230,595**	**247,564**	**263,120**
Algeria		25,283	28,265	30,506	32,855	35,423	38,088	40,630	42,882
Egypt		57,785	63,858	70,174	77,154	84,474	91,778	98,638	104,970
Libyan Arab Jamahiriya		4,365	4,834	5,346	5,923	6,546	7,158	7,699	8,144
Morocco		24,808	26,951	28,827	30,495	32,381	34,330	36,200	37,865
Sudan		27,091	30,841	34,904	38,698	43,192	47,730	52,309	56,688
Tunisia		8,215	8,935	9,452	9,878	10,374	10,884	11,366	11,797
Western Sahara		221	259	315	440	530	625	723	775
Southern Africa		**41,980**	**47,240**	**51,387**	**55,041**	**57,968**	**59,658**	**61,134**	**62,674**
Botswana		1,352	1,550	1,723	1,839	1,978	2,106	2,227	2,337
Lesotho		1,602	1,726	1,889	1,995	2,084	2,168	2,244	2,306
Namibia		1,417	1,620	1,824	2,009	2,212	2,412	2,614	2,810
Republic of South Africa		36,745	41,375	44,872	48,073	50,492	51,684	52,671	53,766
Swaziland		864	969	1,080	1,124	1,202	1,287	1,376	1,455
Western Africa		**183,210**	**208,805**	**237,781**	**269,990**	**306,058**	**344,182**	**383,187**	**422,733**
Benin		4,795	5,723	6,659	7,868	9,212	10,647	12,177	13,767
Burkina Faso		8,814	10,127	11,676	13,747	16,287	19,013	21,871	24,837
Cape Verde		354	398	439	477	513	548	584	616
Côte d'Ivoire		12,610	14,981	17,281	19,245	21,571	24,210	26,954	29,738
Gambia		896	1,085	1,302	1,526	1,751	1,985	2,227	2,478
Ghana		14,968	17,245	19,529	21,915	24,333	26,925	29,567	32,233
Guinea		6,147	7,478	8,384	9,221	10,324	11,844	13,467	15,158
Guinea-Bissau		1,022	1,166	1,304	1,473	1,647	1,848	2,065	2,296
Liberia		2,167	1,945	2,824	3,334	4,102	4,665	5,253	5,858
Mali		8,655	9,549	10,523	11,833	13,323	14,993	16,767	18,603
Mauritania		1,988	2,270	2,604	2,985	3,366	3,732	4,091	4,443
Niger		7,904	9,302	11,031	13,102	15,891	19,150	22,947	27,388
Nigeria		97,338	110,449	124,842	140,879	158,259	175,928	193,252	210,057
Saint Helena	2	6	5	5	5	4	4	4	5
Senegal		7,538	8,660	9,902	11,281	12,861	14,526	16,197	17,861
Sierra Leone		4,084	3,989	4,228	5,107	5,836	6,557	7,318	8,112
Togo		3,926	4,432	5,247	5,992	6,780	7,607	8,445	9,282

**Projections*
Source: United Nations, Department of Economic and Social Affairs, Population Division (2010). World Urbanization Prospects: The 2009 Revision. CD-ROM Edition - Data in digital form (POP/ DB/WUP/Rev.2009).

Notes:
(e) Sub-Saharan Africa refers to all of Africa except Northern Africa, with the Sudan included in sub-Saharan Africa.
(1) Including Agalega, Rodrigues, and Saint Brandon.
(2) Including Ascension, and Tristan da Cunha.

0 and/or 0.0 indicates that the magnitude is zero or less than half of the unit employed.
Years given refer to 1 July.

Urban Population (thousands)							
1990	1995	2000	2005	2010*	2015*	2020*	2025*
65,763	**75,884**	**85,656**	**96,338**	**108,912**	**122,718**	**137,341**	**152,385**
13,168	15,828	18,246	20,804	23,555	26,409	29,194	31,779
25,124	27,340	30,032	33,197	36,664	40,712	45,301	50,506
3,305	3,674	4,083	4,561	5,098	5,654	6,181	6,647
12,005	13,931	15,375	16,835	18,859	20,999	23,158	25,235
7,211	9,393	11,661	14,128	17,322	20,889	24,804	28,924
4,760	5,493	5,996	6,455	6,980	7,537	8,096	8,636
190	226	264	356	434	518	606	658
20,502	**24,302**	**27,657**	**30,969**	**34,021**	**36,439**	**38,809**	**41,307**
567	759	917	1,055	1,209	1,359	1,506	1,642
224	293	377	464	560	665	775	887
392	483	590	705	840	991	1,161	1,346
19,121	22,543	25,528	28,499	31,155	33,147	35,060	37,084
198	223	244	246	257	276	307	347
60,559	**74,817**	**92,162**	**112,835**	**137,271**	**164,924**	**195,344**	**228,403**
1,654	2,104	2,553	3,148	3,873	4,733	5,751	6,936
1,218	1,532	2,083	2,961	4,184	5,708	7,523	9,610
156	194	235	274	313	353	394	432
5,011	6,198	7,524	9,014	10,906	13,138	15,574	18,161
343	476	639	823	1,018	1,228	1,449	1,688
5,454	6,922	8,584	10,467	12,524	14,818	17,274	19,861
1,723	2,204	2,603	3,042	3,651	4,520	5,580	6,823
288	348	387	436	494	574	678	812
887	829	1,252	1,535	1,961	2,325	2,739	3,206
2,018	2,437	2,982	3,786	4,777	5,964	7,325	8,842
789	904	1,041	1,206	1,395	1,609	1,859	2,152
1,215	1,467	1,785	2,177	2,719	3,439	4,417	5,767
34,343	42,931	53,078	65,050	78,818	93,881	109,859	126,591
2	2	2	2	2	2	2	2
2,932	3,431	3,995	4,641	5,450	6,413	7,524	8,806
1,345	1,364	1,501	1,880	2,241	2,649	3,134	3,708
1,182	1,473	1,917	2,394	2,945	3,572	4,261	5,005

TABLE 2: **PERCENTAGE OF POPULATION RESIDING IN URBAN AREAS AND AVERAGE ANNUAL RATE OF CHANGE OF THE URBAN POPULATION BY MAJOR AREA, REGION AND COUNTRY, 1990-2025 REGION**

		Percentage of Population Residing in Urban Areas (per cent)								Average Annual Rate of Change of the Urban Population (per cent)						
Area	**Note**	**1990**	**1995**	**2000**	**2005**	**2010***	**2015***	**2020***	**2025***	**1990-1995**	**1995-2000**	**2000-2005**	**2005-2010***	**2010-2015***	**2015-2020***	**2020-2025***
Sub-Saharan Africa	**e**	**28.31**	**30.61**	**32.69**	**34.92**	**37.23**	**39.65**	**42.23**	**44.99**	**4.27**	**3.89**	**3.81**	**3.71**	**3.60**	**3.43**	**3.25**
Africa		**32.13**	**34.16**	**35.95**	**37.91**	**39.98**	**42.20**	**44.59**	**47.18**	**3.79**	**3.44**	**3.40**	**3.36**	**3.28**	**3.14**	**2.98**
Eastern Africa		**17.96**	**19.55**	**20.83**	**22.19**	**23.59**	**25.42**	**27.64**	**30.29**	**4.30**	**4.05**	**3.84**	**3.82**	**4.08**	**4.09**	**4.02**
Burundi		6.27	7.21	8.28	9.53	11.00	12.73	14.77	17.13	4.43	3.72	5.43	5.75	4.93	4.80	4.54
Comoros		27.87	28.30	28.08	27.89	28.19	29.17	30.85	33.30	2.70	2.08	2.07	2.51	2.75	2.90	3.10
Djibouti		75.65	76.07	76.03	76.01	76.23	76.79	77.65	78.80	2.26	3.12	1.96	1.82	1.76	1.73	1.86
Eritrea		15.80	16.59	17.78	19.41	21.58	24.35	27.46	30.82	1.28	4.01	5.79	5.22	5.21	4.64	4.25
Ethiopia		12.62	13.90	14.90	15.93	16.66	17.75	19.27	21.27	5.24	4.18	3.95	3.49	3.76	3.94	4.06
Kenya		18.22	18.97	19.73	20.74	22.18	24.10	26.57	29.65	3.99	3.48	3.61	3.98	4.22	4.23	4.22
Madagascar		23.57	25.80	27.12	28.50	30.19	32.30	34.85	37.89	4.85	4.04	3.84	3.84	3.87	3.86	3.82
Malawi		11.56	13.26	15.18	17.34	19.77	22.49	25.52	28.84	4.16	5.77	5.53	5.41	5.32	5.16	4.88
Mauritius	1	43.90	43.28	42.67	42.18	41.84	42.22	43.36	45.28	1.04	0.86	0.71	0.53	0.80	1.05	1.27
Mayotte		36.06	41.46	47.73	50.23	50.08	50.50	51.59	53.33	8.34	6.79	4.23	2.58	2.54	2.63	2.68
Mozambique		21.10	26.22	30.69	34.50	38.43	42.38	46.27	50.06	7.61	5.85	4.99	4.49	4.02	3.66	3.35
Réunion		81.23	86.12	89.87	92.40	94.01	95.04	95.66	96.02	3.06	2.58	2.16	1.65	1.35	1.13	0.94
Rwanda		5.42	8.29	13.77	17.54	18.85	20.53	22.61	25.17	3.06	17.75	7.28	4.12	4.37	4.32	4.21
Seychelles		49.29	49.85	51.05	52.88	55.32	58.22	61.08	63.86	1.22	1.86	1.07	1.38	1.32	1.60	1.44
Somalia		29.66	31.43	33.25	35.19	37.45	40.06	43.02	46.33	0.93	3.64	3.57	3.52	4.08	4.07	4.05
Uganda		11.08	11.66	12.08	12.55	13.30	14.40	15.94	17.98	4.37	3.78	3.98	4.43	4.82	5.10	5.27
United Republic of Tanzania		18.88	20.54	22.31	24.20	26.38	28.90	31.79	35.06	4.95	4.25	4.30	4.60	4.74	4.59	4.42
Zambia		39.41	37.10	34.80	35.00	35.70	37.00	38.92	41.49	1.62	1.50	2.41	2.83	3.16	3.44	3.49
Zimbabwe		28.99	31.73	33.76	35.87	38.25	40.94	43.92	47.21	4.07	2.47	1.25	1.55	3.43	3.49	2.94
Middle Africa		**32.61**	**34.81**	**37.21**	**39.96**	**43.12**	**46.38**	**49.60**	**52.78**	**4.74**	**3.86**	**4.29**	**4.13**	**3.96**	**3.68**	**3.39**
Angola		37.14	43.99	48.99	53.96	58.50	62.54	66.04	69.03	6.63	4.75	4.97	4.29	3.99	3.53	3.15
Cameroon		40.72	45.33	49.86	54.27	58.40	62.14	65.47	68.40	4.92	4.33	4.02	3.73	3.34	2.92	2.55
Central African Republic		36.83	37.23	37.64	38.07	38.94	40.40	42.47	45.17	2.82	2.54	2.04	2.33	2.52	2.61	2.70
Chad		20.81	21.92	23.38	25.26	27.63	30.53	33.93	37.51	4.14	4.57	5.07	4.56	4.62	4.65	4.54
Congo		54.32	56.41	58.32	60.17	62.12	64.18	66.34	68.59	3.33	2.41	2.99	2.54	2.99	2.79	2.28
Democratic Republic of the Congo		27.82	28.43	29.84	32.11	35.22	38.57	42.03	45.57	4.31	3.44	4.47	4.61	4.46	4.20	3.88
Equatorial Guinea		34.75	38.83	38.81	38.94	39.70	41.14	43.28	46.13	5.73	3.13	2.88	2.99	3.08	3.30	3.36
Gabon		69.14	75.36	80.15	83.60	86.03	87.68	88.77	89.74	4.87	3.81	2.93	2.41	2.13	1.89	1.69
Sao Tomé e Príncipe		43.65	48.63	53.42	58.06	62.23	65.87	69.02	71.69	4.10	3.70	3.37	2.99	2.82	2.80	2.51
Northern Africa		**44.50**	**46.29**	**47.71**	**49.29**	**51.15**	**53.22**	**55.48**	**57.91**	**2.86**	**2.42**	**2.35**	**2.45**	**2.39**	**2.25**	**2.08**
Algeria		52.09	56.00	59.81	63.32	66.50	69.34	71.85	74.11	3.68	2.84	2.62	2.48	2.29	2.01	1.70
Egypt		43.48	42.81	42.80	43.03	43.40	44.36	45.93	48.12	1.69	1.88	2.00	1.99	2.09	2.14	2.18
Libyan Arab Jamahiriya		75.72	75.99	76.37	77.01	77.89	78.99	80.29	81.62	2.12	2.11	2.21	2.23	2.07	1.78	1.45
Morocco		48.39	51.69	53.34	55.21	58.24	61.17	63.97	66.65	2.98	1.97	1.81	2.27	2.15	1.96	1.72
Sudan		26.62	30.46	33.41	36.51	40.10	43.77	47.42	51.02	5.29	4.32	3.84	4.08	3.74	3.44	3.07
Tunisia		57.95	61.47	63.43	65.35	67.28	69.25	71.23	73.21	2.86	1.75	1.48	1.56	1.54	1.43	1.29
Western Sahara		86.16	87.15	83.86	80.79	81.83	82.87	83.90	84.92	3.43	3.16	5.94	3.97	3.55	3.14	1.63

Area	Note	Percentage of Population Residing in Urban Areas (per cent) 1990	1995	2000	2005	2010*	2015*	2020*	2025*	Average Annual Rate of Change of the Urban Population (per cent) 1990-1995	1995-2000	2000-2005	2005-2010*	2010-2015*	2015-2020*	2020-2025*
Southern Africa		**48.84**	**51.44**	**53.82**	**56.27**	**58.69**	**61.08**	**63.48**	**65.91**	**3.40**	**2.59**	**2.26**	**1.88**	**1.37**	**1.26**	**1.25**
Botswana		41.93	48.98	53.22	57.35	61.13	64.55	67.59	70.27	5.84	3.77	2.80	2.73	2.34	2.04	1.74
Lesotho		13.97	16.96	19.97	23.28	26.88	30.66	34.55	38.47	5.36	5.08	4.16	3.76	3.42	3.08	2.69
Namibia		27.66	29.81	32.37	35.07	37.98	41.10	44.41	47.91	4.18	4.02	3.53	3.52	3.31	3.16	2.96
Republic of South Africa		52.04	54.49	56.89	59.28	61.70	64.13	66.56	68.97	3.29	2.49	2.20	1.78	1.24	1.12	1.12
Swaziland		22.91	23.05	22.64	21.92	21.37	21.49	22.29	23.84	2.41	1.80	0.16	0.83	1.47	2.08	2.46
Western Africa		**33.05**	**35.83**	**38.76**	**41.79**	**44.85**	**47.92**	**50.98**	**54.03**	**4.23**	**4.17**	**4.05**	**3.92**	**3.67**	**3.39**	**3.13**
Benin		34.49	36.76	38.33	40.01	42.04	44.45	47.23	50.38	4.82	3.87	4.19	4.15	4.01	3.90	3.75
Burkina Faso		13.82	15.13	17.84	21.54	25.69	30.02	34.40	38.69	4.60	6.14	7.03	6.92	6.21	5.52	4.90
Cape Verde		44.12	48.77	53.43	57.41	61.09	64.44	67.45	70.12	4.34	3.78	3.11	2.66	2.41	2.17	1.88
Côte d'Ivoire		39.74	41.37	43.54	46.84	50.56	54.27	57.78	61.07	4.25	3.88	3.61	3.81	3.72	3.40	3.07
Gambia		38.31	43.84	49.10	53.90	58.15	61.83	65.04	68.10	6.53	5.91	5.04	4.27	3.74	3.31	3.06
Ghana		36.44	40.14	43.95	47.76	51.47	55.04	58.42	61.62	4.77	4.30	3.97	3.59	3.36	3.07	2.79
Guinea		28.03	29.48	31.05	33.00	35.36	38.17	41.44	45.01	4.93	3.32	3.12	3.64	4.27	4.21	4.02
Guinea-Bissau		28.13	29.81	29.70	29.60	30.00	31.07	32.83	35.36	3.79	2.15	2.37	2.51	3.00	3.32	3.60
Liberia		40.94	42.62	44.33	46.05	47.82	49.84	52.15	54.73	-1.35	8.25	4.08	4.90	3.40	3.28	3.15
Mali		23.32	25.52	28.34	31.99	35.86	39.78	43.69	47.53	3.77	4.04	4.77	4.65	4.44	4.11	3.76
Mauritania		39.67	39.83	39.99	40.40	41.43	43.11	45.45	48.45	2.73	2.83	2.94	2.91	2.86	2.89	2.93
Niger		15.37	15.77	16.19	16.62	17.11	17.96	19.25	21.06	3.78	3.93	3.97	4.44	4.70	5.01	5.33
Nigeria		35.28	38.87	42.52	46.17	49.80	53.36	56.85	60.27	4.46	4.24	4.07	3.84	3.50	3.14	2.84
Saint Helena	2	41.57	40.35	39.69	39.67	39.73	40.37	41.68	43.67	-1.63	-1.10	-1.45	-1.33	-0.32	1.29	1.46
Senegal		38.90	39.62	40.35	41.14	42.38	44.15	46.46	49.30	3.14	3.04	3.00	3.22	3.25	3.20	3.15
Sierra Leone		32.94	34.21	35.51	36.82	38.40	40.39	42.83	45.71	0.29	1.91	4.51	3.50	3.35	3.37	3.36
Togo		30.10	33.24	36.53	39.95	43.44	46.96	50.46	53.92	4.41	5.27	4.44	4.15	3.86	3.53	3.22

Projections
ource: United Nations, Department of Economic and Social Affairs, Population Division (2010). World Urbanization Prospects : The 2009 Revision.
D-ROM Edition - Data in digital form (POP/DB/WUP/Rev.2009).

otes:
a) Sub-Saharan Africa refers to all of Africa except Northern Africa, with the Sudan included in sub-Saharan Africa.
1) Including Agalega, Rodrigues, and Saint Brandon.
2) Including Ascension, and Tristan da Cunha.

and/or 0.0 indicates that the magnitude is zero or less than half of the unit employed.
minus sign (-) before a figure indicates a decrease.
ears given refer to 1 July.

TABLE 3: **POPULATION OF URBAN AGGLOMERATIONS AND AVERAGE ANNUAL RATE OF CHANGE OF URBAN AGGLOMERATIONS WITH 750,000 INHABITANTS OR MORE IN 2009, BY COUNTRY, 1990-2025**

		Population of Urban Agglomerations (thousands)							
Country	**Urban Agglomeration**	**1990**	**1995**	**2000**	**2005**	**2010***	**2015***	**2020***	**2025***
Algeria	El Djazaïr (Algiers)	1,815	2,023	2,254	2,512	2,800	3,099	3,371	3,595
Algeria	Wahran (Oran)	647	675	705	736	770	827	902	970
Angola	Huambo	326	444	578	775	1,034	1,305	1,551	1,789
Angola	Luanda	1,568	1,953	2,591	3,533	4,772	6,013	7,080	8,077
Benin	Cotonou	504	577	642	720	844	1,016	1,217	1,445
Burkina Faso	Ouagadougou	537	667	921	1,328	1,908	2,643	3,457	4,332
Cameroon	Douala	931	1,155	1,432	1,767	2,125	2,478	2,815	3,131
Cameroon	Yaoundé	754	948	1,192	1,489	1,801	2,103	2,392	2,664
Chad	N'Djaména	477	565	647	732	829	960	1,170	1,445
Congo	Brazzaville	704	830	986	1,172	1,323	1,504	1,703	1,878
Côte d'Ivoire	Abidjan	2,102	2,535	3,032	3,564	4,125	4,788	5,550	6,321
Côte d'Ivoire	Yamoussoukro	136	218	348	556	885	1,273	1,559	1,797
Democratic Republic of the Congo	Kananga	353	451	552	705	878	1,087	1,324	1,583
Democratic Republic of the Congo	Kinshasa	3,564	4,590	5,611	7,106	8,754	10,668	12,788	15,041
Democratic Republic of the Congo	Kisangani	362	450	535	664	812	1,002	1,221	1,461
Democratic Republic of the Congo	Lubumbashi	655	826	995	1,252	1,543	1,899	2,304	2,744
Democratic Republic of the Congo	Mbuji-Mayi	580	749	924	1,190	1,488	1,838	2,232	2,658
Egypt	Al-Iskandariyah (Alexandria)	3,063	3,277	3,592	3,973	4,387	4,791	5,201	5,648
Egypt	Al-Qahirah (Cairo)	9,061	9,707	10,170	10,565	11,001	11,663	12,540	13,531
Ethiopia	Addis Ababa	1,791	2,144	2,376	2,633	2,930	3,365	3,981	4,757
Ghana	Accra	1,197	1,415	1,674	1,985	2,342	2,722	3,110	3,497
Ghana	Kumasi	696	909	1,187	1,519	1,834	2,139	2,448	2,757
Guinea	Conakry	895	1,045	1,219	1,411	1,653	2,004	2,427	2,906
Kenya	Mombasa	476	572	687	830	1,003	1,216	1,479	1,795
Kenya	Nairobi	1,380	1,755	2,230	2,814	3,523	4,303	5,192	6,246
Liberia	Monrovia	1,042	464	836	1,202	827	728	807	932
Libyan Arab Jamahiriya	Tarabulus (Tripoli)	862	984	1,022	1,059	1,108	1,192	1,286	1,364
Madagascar	Antananarivo	948	1,169	1,361	1,590	1,879	2,235	2,658	3,148
Malawi	Blantyre-Limbe	370	446	538	667	856	1,103	1,407	1,766
Malawi	Lilongwe	266	362	493	662	865	1,115	1,422	1,784
Mali	Bamako	746	910	1,110	1,368	1,699	2,086	2,514	2,971
Morocco	Agadir	403	536	609	693	783	869	948	1,020
Morocco	Dar-el-Beida (Casablanca)	2,682	2,951	3,043	3,138	3,284	3,537	3,816	4,065
Morocco	Fes	685	785	870	963	1,065	1,173	1,277	1,371
Morocco	Marrakech	578	681	755	837	928	1,023	1,114	1,198
Morocco	Rabat	1,174	1,379	1,507	1,647	1,802	1,973	2,139	2,288
Morocco	Tangier	423	510	591	686	788	877	958	1,030
Mozambique	Maputo	776	921	1,096	1,341	1,655	1,994	2,350	2,722
Mozambique	Matola	319	401	504	636	793	961	1,139	1,326

Average Annual Rate of Change (per cent)						
1990-1995	1995-2000	2000-2005	2005-2010*	2010-2015*	2015-2020*	2020-2025*
2.17	2.17	2.17	2.17	2.03	1.68	1.29
0.86	0.86	0.86	0.90	1.43	1.73	1.47
6.17	5.25	5.87	5.78	4.64	3.46	2.85
4.39	5.66	6.20	6.01	4.62	3.27	2.63
2.73	2.13	2.28	3.19	3.69	3.62	3.44
4.32	6.45	7.32	7.25	6.52	5.37	4.51
4.30	4.30	4.20	3.69	3.07	2.55	2.13
4.59	4.59	4.45	3.80	3.11	2.57	2.15
3.38	2.72	2.48	2.48	2.93	3.96	4.23
3.31	3.44	3.46	2.42	2.55	2.49	1.95
3.74	3.58	3.24	2.92	2.98	2.95	2.60
9.36	9.37	9.36	9.32	7.27	4.06	2.83
4.92	4.03	4.89	4.40	4.26	3.95	3.57
5.06	4.02	4.72	4.17	3.96	3.62	3.25
4.34	3.45	4.32	4.03	4.19	3.96	3.58
4.62	3.73	4.60	4.17	4.15	3.87	3.49
5.09	4.20	5.06	4.48	4.22	3.88	3.50
1.35	1.83	2.02	1.98	1.76	1.64	1.65
1.38	0.93	0.76	0.81	1.17	1.45	1.52
3.60	2.05	2.05	2.13	2.77	3.36	3.56
3.35	3.35	3.41	3.30	3.01	2.66	2.35
5.34	5.34	4.94	3.76	3.08	2.70	2.38
3.11	3.08	2.92	3.17	3.84	3.83	3.61
3.65	3.67	3.79	3.78	3.86	3.91	3.87
4.81	4.79	4.65	4.50	4.00	3.76	3.69
-16.18	11.76	7.27	-7.47	-2.56	2.06	2.88
2.64	0.77	0.71	0.89	1.48	1.51	1.17
4.20	3.04	3.10	3.34	3.47	3.46	3.39
3.73	3.74	4.30	4.99	5.06	4.87	4.55
6.17	6.17	5.89	5.35	5.08	4.87	4.54
3.96	3.97	4.19	4.32	4.11	3.73	3.35
5.70	2.58	2.57	2.44	2.07	1.75	1.46
1.91	0.62	0.62	0.91	1.49	1.52	1.26
2.72	2.04	2.04	2.02	1.92	1.70	1.42
3.26	2.07	2.07	2.06	1.95	1.72	1.44
3.22	1.77	1.77	1.80	1.81	1.62	1.35
3.73	2.98	2.98	2.75	2.16	1.75	1.46
3.43	3.47	4.03	4.21	3.73	3.29	2.94
4.55	4.56	4.68	4.41	3.84	3.39	3.04

Country	Urban Agglomeration	Population of Urban Agglomerations (thousands)							
		1990	1995	2000	2005	2010*	2015*	2020*	2025*
Niger	Niamey	432	542	680	848	1,048	1,302	1,643	2,105
Nigeria	Aba	484	545	614	691	785	914	1,058	1,203
Nigeria	Abuja	330	526	832	1,315	1,995	2,563	2,977	3,361
Nigeria	Benin City	689	845	975	1,124	1,302	1,523	1,758	1,992
Nigeria	Ibadan	1,739	1,993	2,236	2,509	2,837	3,276	3,760	4,237
Nigeria	Ilorin	515	580	653	735	835	972	1,125	1,279
Nigeria	Jos	493	556	627	706	802	934	1,081	1,229
Nigeria	Kaduna	961	1,083	1,220	1,375	1,561	1,811	2,087	2,362
Nigeria	Kano	2,095	2,360	2,658	2,993	3,395	3,922	4,495	5,060
Nigeria	Lagos	4,764	5,966	7,233	8,767	10,578	12,427	14,162	15,810
Nigeria	Maiduguri	598	673	758	854	970	1,127	1,303	1,480
Nigeria	Ogbomosho	622	704	798	904	1,032	1,201	1,389	1,576
Nigeria	Port Harcourt	680	766	863	972	1,104	1,283	1,482	1,681
Nigeria	Zaria	592	667	752	847	963	1,120	1,295	1,471
Rwanda	Kigali	219	278	497	775	939	1,138	1,392	1,690
Senegal	Dakar	1,405	1,688	2,029	2,434	2,863	3,308	3,796	4,338
Sierra Leone	Freetown	529	603	688	785	901	1,046	1,219	1,420
Somalia	Muqdisho (Mogadishu)	1,035	1,147	1,201	1,415	1,500	1,795	2,156	2,588
Republic of South Africa	Cape Town	2,155	2,394	2,715	3,091	3,405	3,579	3,701	3,824
Republic of South Africa	Durban	1,723	2,081	2,370	2,638	2,879	3,026	3,133	3,241
Republic of South Africa	Ekurhuleni (East Rand)	1,531	1,894	2,326	2,824	3,202	3,380	3,497	3,614
Republic of South Africa	Johannesburg	1,898	2,265	2,732	3,263	3,670	3,867	3,996	4,127
Republic of South Africa	Port Elizabeth	828	911	958	1,002	1,068	1,126	1,173	1,222
Republic of South Africa	Pretoria	911	951	1,084	1,274	1,429	1,514	1,575	1,637
Republic of South Africa	Vereeniging	743	800	897	1,029	1,143	1,211	1,262	1,313
Sudan	Al-Khartum (Khartoum)	2,360	3,242	3,949	4,518	5,172	6,046	7,005	7,953
Togo	Lomé	619	795	1,020	1,310	1,667	2,036	2,398	2,763
Uganda	Kampala	755	912	1,097	1,318	1,598	1,982	2,504	3,189
United Republic of Tanzania	Dar es Salaam	1,316	1,668	2,116	2,680	3,349	4,153	5,103	6,202
Zambia	Lusaka	757	902	1,073	1,265	1,451	1,666	1,941	2,267
Zimbabwe	Harare	1,047	1,255	1,379	1,513	1,632	1,856	2,170	2,467

**Projections*
Source: United Nations, Department of Economic and Social Affairs, Population Division (2010). World Urbanization Prospects : The 2009 Revision. CD-ROM Edition - Data in digital form (POP/ DB/WUP/Rev.2009).

Average Annual Rate of Change (per cent)						
1990-1995	1995-2000	2000-2005	2005-2010	2010-2015*	2015-2020*	2020-2025*
4.54	4.55	4.42	4.22	4.35	4.65	4.96
2.38	2.38	2.38	2.55	3.04	2.93	2.57
9.31	9.16	9.16	8.33	5.01	3.00	2.43
4.08	2.85	2.85	2.95	3.13	2.88	2.50
2.73	2.30	2.30	2.46	2.88	2.75	2.39
2.38	2.38	2.38	2.55	3.03	2.92	2.56
2.39	2.39	2.39	2.56	3.04	2.93	2.57
2.39	2.39	2.39	2.55	2.97	2.84	2.48
2.38	2.38	2.38	2.52	2.89	2.73	2.37
4.50	3.85	3.85	3.76	3.22	2.61	2.20
2.37	2.37	2.37	2.54	3.01	2.90	2.54
2.49	2.49	2.49	2.65	3.04	2.90	2.53
2.38	2.38	2.38	2.55	3.00	2.88	2.52
2.39	2.39	2.39	2.56	3.02	2.90	2.54
4.77	11.63	8.86	3.85	3.84	4.02	3.88
3.67	3.68	3.64	3.25	2.89	2.75	2.67
2.62	2.63	2.62	2.76	2.99	3.06	3.05
2.04	0.92	3.28	1.17	3.59	3.67	3.66
2.10	2.52	2.59	1.93	1.00	0.67	0.65
3.77	2.60	2.15	1.75	1.00	0.69	0.68
4.26	4.11	3.88	2.51	1.08	0.68	0.66
3.53	3.75	3.55	2.35	1.05	0.66	0.64
1.93	1.00	0.90	1.27	1.06	0.83	0.82
0.85	2.61	3.24	2.29	1.16	0.79	0.77
1.48	2.30	2.75	2.09	1.16	0.82	0.81
6.35	3.95	2.69	2.70	3.12	2.95	2.54
5.00	5.00	5.00	4.82	4.00	3.27	2.84
3.79	3.68	3.68	3.85	4.31	4.67	4.83
4.75	4.75	4.73	4.46	4.30	4.12	3.90
3.49	3.49	3.29	2.74	2.77	3.05	3.10
3.62	1.89	1.85	1.51	2.57	3.13	2.57

TABLE 4: **URBAN POPULATION, PROPORTION OF URBAN POPULATION LIVING IN SLUM AREA AND URBAN SLUM POPULATION AT MID-YEAR BY COUNTRY**

Estimates 1990-2007

	Urban Population (thousands) [a]					Proprotion of urban population living in slum area (per cent) [b]					Urban Slum Population (thousands)				
Country	**1990**	**1995**	**2000**	**2005**	**2007**	**1990**	**1995**	**2000**	**2005**	**2007**	**1990**	**1995**	**2000**	**2005**	**2007**
Angola	3913	5418	6824	8684	9505				86.5					7512	
Benin	1786	2282	2770	3397	3684	79.3	76.8	74.3	71.8	70.8	1416	1753	2058	2439	2608
Burkina Faso	1226	1554	1971	2555	2827	78.8	72.4	65.9	59.5	59.5	966	1125	1300	1520	1682
Burundi	357	450	552	749	858				64.3					481	
Cameroon	4983	6372	7908	9657	10381	50.8	49.6	48.4	47.4	46.6	2534	3161	3825	4578	4841
Central African Republic	1108	1284	1454	1596	1665	87.5	89.7	91.9	94.1	95.0	969	1152	1337	1502	1582
Chad	1272	1568	1979	2563	2819	98.9	96.4	93.9	91.3	90.3	1259	1512	1858	2341	2546
Comoros	147	172	196	223	234	65.4	65.4	65.4	68.9	68.9	96	112	128	153	162
Congo	1316	1576	1868	2172	2296				53.4					1160	
Côte d'Ivoire	5079	6200	7423	8704	9277	53.4	54.3	55.3	56.2	56.6	2710	3367	4102	4892	5249
Democratic Republic of the Congo	10556	12892	15126	18860	20841				76.4					14409	
Egypt	23972	25966	28364	31062	32193	50.2	39.2	28.1	17.1	17.1	12029	10166	7978	5312	5505
Equatorial Guinea	118	148	167	188	199				66.3					125	
Ethiopia	6455	8381	10339	12687	13813	95.5	95.5	88.6	81.8	79.1	6163	8001	9164	10380	10923
Gabon	635	796	948	1079	1127				38.7					418	
Gambia	369	508	680	872	951				45.4					396	
Ghana	5677	7180	8856	10763	11566	65.5	58.8	52.1	45.4	42.8	3717	4221	4615	4890	4945
Guinea	1691	2159	2547	2970	3176	80.4	68.8	57.3	45.7	45.7	1359	1485	1458	1358	1451
Guinea-Bissau	286	355	407	473	503				83.1					393	
Kenya	4273	5193	6167	7384	7982	54.9	54.8	54.8	54.8	54.8	2345	2848	3379	4044	4370
Lesotho	224	292	377	461	496				35.1					162	
Madagascar	2836	3598	4390	5313	5733	93.0	88.6	84.1	80.6	78.0	2636	3186	3694	4283	4470
Malawi	1092	1338	1764	2293	2545	66.4	66.4	66.4	66.4	67.7	725	889	1171	1522	1722
Mali	1789	2229	2787	3537	3896	94.2	84.8	75.4	65.9	65.9	1685	1890	2101	2332	2569
Morocco	12005	13931	15375	16763	17377	37.4	35.2	24.2	13.1	13.1	4490	4904	3713	2196	2276
Mozambique	2857	4180	5584	7084	7718	75.6	76.9	78.2	79.5	80.0	2161	3216	4368	5632	6175
Namibia	392	494	608	708	751	34.4	34.1	33.9	33.9	33.6	135	169	206	240	252
Niger	1202	1465	1801	2161	2331	83.6	83.1	82.6	82.1	81.9	1005	1217	1487	1774	1909
Nigeria	33325	42372	53048	65270	70539	77.3	73.5	69.6	65.8	64.2	25763	31127	36930	42928	45309
Rwanda	395	468	1126	1619	1753	96.0	87.9	79.7	71.6	68.3	379	411	898	1160	1198
Senegal	3075	3603	4200	4891	5203	70.6	59.8	48.9	38.1	38.1	2172	2154	2055	1863	1982
Sierra Leone	1346	1417	1605	2057	2194				97.0					1995	
Somalia	1992	1962	2346	2884	3136				73.5					2120	
Republic of South Africa	19034	22614	25827	28419	29266	46.2	39.7	33.2	28.7	28.7	8794	8978	8575	8156	8399
Sudan	6903	9233	12034	15043	16420				94.2					14170	
Togo	1192	1501	1974	2492	2722				62.1					1548	
Uganda	1976	2477	2983	3632	3955	75.0	75.0	75.0	66.7	63.4	1482	1858	2238	2423	2507
United Republic of Tanzania	4814	6143	7551	9313	10128	77.4	73.7	70.1	66.4	65.0	3725	4528	5291	6186	6580
Zambia	3201	3436	3637	4017	4198	57.0	57.1	57.2	57.2	57.3	1826	1962	2080	2298	2404
Zimbabwe	3040	3742	4273	4706	4911	4.0	3.7	3.3	17.9	17.9	122	138	142	842	879

Source: Global Urban Indicators Database 2010

a: United Nations Department of Economic and Social Affairs Population Division - World Urbanization Prospects: The 2009 Revision

b: Computed from country household data using the four components of slum (improved water, improved sanitation, durable housing and sufficient living area)

TABLE 5: **PROPORTION OF URBAN HOUSEHOLDS WITH ACCESS TO IMPROVED WATER SOURCE, IMPROVED SANITATION, FINISHED MAIN FLOOR MATERIALS, SUFFICIENT LIVING AREA AND CONNECTED TO TELEPHONE AND ELECTRICITY BY CITY**

Country	City	Year	Access to improved water	Access to improved sanitation	Finished main floor materials	Access to sufficient living area	Access to telephone	Access to electricity
Angola	Luanda	2006	51.4	92.4	97.4			75.5
Angola	Other cities/towns	2006	70.6	61.6	68.9			50.6
Benin	Cotonou	1996	99.0	71.2	98.1	77.7		56.6
Benin	Cotonou	2001	100.0	80.9	97.5		12.7	73.7
Benin	Djougou	1996	84.3	45.1	71.2	79.7		23.5
Benin	Djougou	2001	82.9	29.0	79.3		3.6	40.9
Benin	Djougou	2006	90.6	51.9	76.5	75.8	3.9	47.4
Benin	Other cities/towns	1996	58.4	34.9	66.7	83.4		21.2
Benin	Other cities/towns	2001	59.5	22.9	62.9		3.8	25.3
Benin	Other cities/towns	2006	82.5	47.3	79.0	78.6	5.7	55.6
Benin	Porto Novo	1996	57.7	50.8	79.4	78.6		29.4
Benin	Porto Novo	2001	72.5	50.3	86.7		13.6	58.1
Benin	Porto Novo	2006	77.0	68.4	94.3	73.0	8.1	66.9
Burkina Faso	Other cities/towns	1992	53.4	39.6	78.0	78.3		26.1
Burkina Faso	Other cities/towns	1999	73.6	44.6	89.8	82.8	5.4	38.2
Burkina Faso	Other cities/towns	2003	89.1	46.5	90.6		9.6	47.8
Burkina Faso	Ouagadougou	1992	74.8	49.5	91.1	82.9		31.5
Burkina Faso	Ouagadougou	1999	88.5	51.5	95.0	83.9	13.7	41.3
Burkina Faso	Ouagadougou	2003	98.3	67.3	96.5		25.1	56.7
Burundi	Bujumbura	2005	81.4	47.1	58.3	66.1		
Burundi	Gitega	2005	64.1	34.5	61.3	80.4		
Burundi	Ngozi	2005	87.2	34.8	28.7	75.2		
Burundi	Other cities	2005	30.0	10.0	39.5	68.4		
Cameroon	Douala	1991	80.5	27.7	93.2	84.2		82.4
Cameroon	Douala	1998	77.2	80.8	92.7	91.2	7.6	93.8
Cameroon	Douala	2004	86.9	76.0	88.1	90.4	5.6	95.9
Cameroon	Douala	2006	99.2	79.9	90.9	89.7		
Cameroon	Other cities/towns	1991	72.5	23.6	65.2	84.3		50.3
Cameroon	Other cities/towns	1998	72.0	79.9	74.1	88.2	2.7	70.1
Cameroon	Other cities/towns	2004	82.5	76.5	70.3	86.9	2.3	66.1
Cameroon	Other cities/towns	2006	83.6	71.2	70.5	87.5		
Cameroon	Yaoundé	1991	86.3	29.4	91.3	82.8		87.4
Cameroon	Yaoundé	1998	93.7	81.9	92.4	85.4	11.5	96.3
Cameroon	Yaoundé	2004	97.9	79.8	93.2	87.6	5.6	96.2
Cameroon	Yaoundé	2006	99.5	79.9	95.6	87.3		
Central African Republic	Bangui	1994	74.9	49.5	45.0	83.4	5.8	15.3
Central African Republic	Other cities/towns	1994	33.4	46.9	12.6	86.2	0.1	2.3
Chad	N'Djaména	1997	30.6	69.9	20.9	69.0	2.8	17.2
Chad	N'Djaména	2004	87.8	65.4	25.5	71.9	6.5	29.2
Chad	Other cities/towns	1997	30.5	40.4	9.9	66.1	0.3	3.5
Chad	Other cities/towns	2004	63.9	39.5	14.1	69.9	0.8	7.8
Comoros	Moroni	1996	95.7	67.6	72.4	88.1	13.0	55.1
Comoros	Other cities/towns	1996	94.2	69.9	63.2	66.5	7.4	50.4
Congo	Brazzaville	2005	96.8	70.3	94.4	76.8	2.6	59.2

Country	City	Year	Access to improved water	Access to improved sanitation	Finished main floor materials	Access to sufficient living area	Access to telephone	Access to electricity
Congo	Other cities/towns	2005	91.8	59.5	84.5	77.5	1.4	38.4
Côte d'Ivoire	Abidjan	1994	98.7	84.2	99.3	67.5		73.5
Côte d'Ivoire	Abidjan	1998	56.8	66.3	98.5	77.4	6.5	80.2
Côte d'Ivoire	Abidjan	2005	98.6	79.3	97.9		49.5	95.0
Côte d'Ivoire	Abidjan	2006	98.3		99.8	56.8		
Côte d'Ivoire	Other cities/towns	1994	55.1	70.6	97.2	72.8		65.4
Côte d'Ivoire	Other cities/towns	1998	97.9	76.8	98.9	72.7	13.2	90.6
Côte d'Ivoire	Other cities/towns	2005	71.9	57.0	95.3		32.9	78.0
Côte d'Ivoire	Other cities/towns	2006	84.9		97.2	63.0		
Democratic Republic of the Congo	Bandundu	2007	92.4	48.2	12.7		0.2	0.7
Democratic Republic of the Congo	Bas-Congo	2007	94.5	65.7	76.2		2.1	49.9
Democratic Republic of the Congo	Equator	2007	17.0	71.4	10.6		0.7	0.8
Democratic Republic of the Congo	Kasai Occidental	2007	44.7	56.3	18.9			2.3
Democratic Republic of the Congo	Kasai Oriental	2007	95.8	84.6	29.3		1.1	3.7
Democratic Republic of the Congo	Katanga	2007	79.4	77.2	46.1		3.3	44.0
Democratic Republic of the Congo	Kinshasa	2007	92.3	80.8	89.8		0.6	82.0
Democratic Republic of the Congo	Maniema	2007	83.2	73.1	9.0			26.4
Democratic Republic of the Congo	Orientale	2007	76.7	72.0	15.5			26.8
Democratic Republic of the Congo	Other cities/towns	2007	93.7	69.4	36.6		2.7	22.6
Egypt	Fayoum	1992	87.5	54.5	62.5	54.5		97.7
Egypt	Fayoum	1995	92.7	50.4	78.1	53.3		97.8
Egypt	Fayoum	2000	100.0	79.9	82.6	98.0	28.2	100.0
Egypt	Fayoum	2003	100.0	75.3	89.4		50.6	97.6
Egypt	Fayoum	2005	100.0	70.0	91.7	98.0	61.7	100.0
Egypt	Alexandria	1992	99.5	85.4	99.0	76.3		98.4
Egypt	Alexandria	1995	99.7	79.4	95.7	80.5		99.8
Egypt	Alexandria	2000	99.7	89.0	98.6	95.2	44.0	99.4
Egypt	Alexandria	2003	99.8	92.9	98.5	98.1	65.7	99.8
Egypt	Alexandria	2005	99.9	94.1	100.0	98.0	71.5	99.9
Egypt	Asyut	1992	92.6	63.2	82.4	64.7		96.3
Egypt	Asyut	1995	94.7	61.8	71.2	77.0		96.1
Egypt	Asyut	2000	100.0	59.0	87.6	94.0	19.5	98.5
Egypt	Asyut	2003	100.0	66.4	94.2	95.6	44.5	99.3
Egypt	Asyut	2005	100.0	74.0	93.9	96.9	63.3	99.5
Egypt	Aswan	1992	96.7	66.5	77.8	60.4		97.2
Egypt	Aswan	1995	95.5	56.8	68.6	71.4		98.2
Egypt	Aswan	2000	100.0	71.4	85.0	93.0	45.5	99.1
Egypt	Aswan	2003	100.0	64.6	83.1	96.2	56.9	100.0
Egypt	Aswan	2005	99.9	72.0	90.6	95.8	63.7	100.0
Egypt	Beni Suef	1992	88.1	51.9	56.9	69.4		94.4
Egypt	Beni Suef	1995	88.9	57.6	77.8	68.7		96.0
Egypt	Beni Suef	2000	99.1	74.4	90.6	94.9	41.9	98.3
Egypt	Beni Suef	2003	100.0	83.3	80.6	97.2	56.9	100.0
Egypt	Beni Suef	2005	100.0	71.3	90.2	95.1	62.3	99.3
Egypt	Cairo	1992	99.5	79.1	99.1	75.1		99.1

Country	City	Year	Access to improved water	Access to improved sanitation	Finished main floor materials	Access to sufficient living area	Access to telephone	Access to electricity
Egypt	Cairo	1995	98.6	76.2	98.2	82.9		99.0
Egypt	Cairo	2000	100.0	84.7	98.7	94.3	54.1	99.9
Egypt	Cairo	2003	99.9	89.4	98.9	96.0	73.4	99.9
Egypt	Cairo	2005	99.6	89.2	99.6	96.8	82.4	99.7
Egypt	Damanhur	1992	97.0	70.5	97.0	80.3		98.5
Egypt	Damanhur	1995	99.3	77.6	99.3	90.8		100.0
Egypt	Damanhur	2000	91.5	61.9	95.8	94.7	27.0	98.9
Egypt	Damanhur	2003	100.0	79.2	100.0	94.8	44.8	100.0
Egypt	Damanhur	2005	100.0	96.7	100.0	99.3	85.3	100.0
Egypt	Damietta	1992	100.0	85.8	100.0	90.8		99.2
Egypt	Damietta	1995	96.7	73.6	91.2	84.1		97.8
Egypt	Damietta	2000	100.0	84.0	100.0		43.8	100.0
Egypt	Damietta	2003	100.0	82.7	98.8		61.7	100.0
Egypt	Damietta	2005	100.0	88.3	97.7	97.7	51.6	100.0
Egypt	Ghurdqah	1995	54.8	76.8	97.2	87.6		98.9
Egypt	Ghurdqah	2000	100.0	73.7	96.7	98.7	55.9	99.3
Egypt	Ghurdqah	2005	91.8	79.1	100.0	99.4	77.8	100.0
Egypt	Giza	1992	91.4	71.7	95.4	78.5		97.2
Egypt	Giza	1995	89.1	72.8	94.0	79.3		98.4
Egypt	Giza	2000	100.0	84.0	99.7	97.0	51.4	99.4
Egypt	Giza	2003	99.7	86.2	98.5	97.9	78.7	99.7
Egypt	Giza	2005	98.0	84.7	99.1	96.6	72.0	99.8
Egypt	Ismailia	1992	96.3	78.9	97.2	83.2		98.2
Egypt	Ismailia	1995	94.2	85.1	97.6	82.1		99.1
Egypt	Ismailia	2000	100.0	80.7	99.6	99.2	55.4	100.0
Egypt	Ismailia	2003	100.0	85.7	99.4	98.7	53.2	100.0
Egypt	Ismailia	2005	100.0	86.7	99.3	97.3	71.0	100.0
Egypt	Kafr El-Sheikh	1992	100.0	67.9	97.4	80.8		100.0
Egypt	Kafr El-Sheikh	1995	100.0	70.2	89.4	77.9		99.0
Egypt	Kafr El-Sheikh	2000	98.8	79.2	97.7	97.1	47.4	100.0
Egypt	Kafr El-Sheikh	2003	100.0	69.8	96.9	99.0	61.5	97.9
Egypt	Kafr El-Sheikh	2005	100.0	88.1	98.8	98.8	78.6	100.0
Egypt	Kharijah	1995	93.5	69.9	84.6	74.0		99.2
Egypt	Kharijah	2000	100.0	70.0	82.2		36.7	97.8
Egypt	Kharijah	2005	100.0	75.0	92.2		56.3	100.0
Egypt	Mansurah	1992	99.5	80.6	94.1	86.0		98.9
Egypt	Mansurah	1995	96.5	82.5	98.8	80.5		99.6
Egypt	Mansurah	2000	99.7	80.3	98.0	98.4	42.8	99.3
Egypt	Mansurah	2003	100.0	86.8	100.0	99.3	61.2	100.0
Egypt	Mansurah	2005	100.0	86.1	99.3	99.0	54.6	100.0
Egypt	Other cities/towns	1992	96.6	67.0	91.2	73.7		98.1
Egypt	Other cities/towns	1995	96.5	69.4	95.6	81.1		99.6
Egypt	Other cities/towns	2000	99.5	76.8	93.3	96.4	39.6	99.3
Egypt	Other cities/towns	2003	99.9	81.5	96.1	98.6	50.2	99.6

Country	City	Year	Access to improved water	Access to improved sanitation	Finished main floor materials	Access to sufficient living area	Access to telephone	Access to electricity
Egypt	Other cities/towns	2005	98.1	81.9	98.2	97.0	67.9	99.6
Egypt	Port Said	1992	96.5	90.1	97.3	80.9		96.7
Egypt	Port Said	1995	98.7	90.1	99.6	83.2		99.3
Egypt	Port Said	2000	96.5	95.8	98.1	97.4	63.6	99.8
Egypt	Port Said	2003	100.0	94.6	99.3	98.9	78.3	100.0
Egypt	Port Said	2005	97.6	95.7	97.0	98.8	77.0	99.9
Egypt	Qena	1992	98.8	74.4	84.9	62.8		100.0
Egypt	Qena	1995	89.9	68.2	69.8	76.7		96.1
Egypt	Qena	2000	98.9	61.0	72.2	92.0	22.5	99.5
Egypt	Qena	2003	100.0	62.9	74.3	96.2	44.8	100.0
Egypt	Qena	2005	99.6	74.4	89.4	95.2	78.9	99.8
Egypt	Sawhaj	1992	90.6	67.7	74.0	71.7		96.9
Egypt	Sawhaj	1995	89.8	65.4	71.7	73.9		96.0
Egypt	Sawhaj	2000	100.0	58.6	70.3	85.2	28.9	98.4
Egypt	Sawhaj	2003	100.0	66.7	95.1	92.6	58.0	100.0
Egypt	Sawhaj	2005	100.0	62.2	88.8	94.4	49.0	100.0
Egypt	Suez	1992	99.5	84.3	99.1	79.8		99.5
Egypt	Suez	1995	99.1	82.2	98.7	80.4		99.3
Egypt	Suez	2000	99.7	89.1	97.8	98.6	46.1	99.5
Egypt	Suez	2003	100.0	90.7	99.7	99.7	66.6	99.7
Egypt	Suez	2005	100.0	89.9	99.9	99.5	79.0	100.0
Egypt	Tahta	1992	96.6	59.1	89.4	78.7		99.6
Egypt	Tahta	1995	99.2	75.6	87.4	82.8		98.3
Egypt	Tahta	2000	100.0	82.0	97.3	97.6	33.5	99.7
Egypt	Tahta	2003	100.0	83.1	98.8	98.8	54.2	100.0
Egypt	Tahta	2005	100.0	97.0	100.0	99.7	80.8	100.0
Ethiopia	Addis Ababa	2000	98.4	47.4	66.7	64.1	20.6	97.1
Ethiopia	Addis Ababa	2005	99.9	71.8	83.4	65.0	46.1	96.9
Ethiopia	Nazret	2000	81.9	53.5	29.8	64.6	13.8	92.4
Ethiopia	Nazret	2005	99.1	51.1	52.4	67.5	33.8	95.5
Ethiopia	Other cities/towns	2000	83.1	34.6	22.7	60.3	3.8	68.8
Ethiopia	Other cities/towns	2005	89.7	41.6	36.9	62.6	19.0	78.5
Gabon	Libreville	2000	99.7	83.4	97.0	85.7	20.4	95.5
Gabon	Other cities/towns	2000	86.9	72.0	81.1	87.7	12.7	82.4
Gambia	Banjul	2005	82.7	97.7	98.5	74.8		
Gambia	Other cities/towns	2005	92.1	93.4	93.8	79.9		
Ghana	Accra	1993	99.8	66.2	99.5	77.6	0.0	90.1
Ghana	Accra	1998	97.7	69.5	99.7	80.3	12.3	92.0
Ghana	Accra	2003	88.5	81.4	98.8		31.9	84.3
Ghana	Accra	2006	60.8	87.7	97.3	73.0		
Ghana	Other cities/towns	1993	72.2	54.4	98.2	74.9	0.0	68.2
Ghana	Other cities/towns	1998	82.1	75.4	98.2	77.8	1.6	77.2
Ghana	Other cities/towns	2003	81.0	73.2	95.6		7.6	74.1
Ghana	Other cities/towns	2006	87.3	81.4	93.4	74.1		

Country	City	Year	Access to improved water	Access to improved sanitation	Finished main floor materials	Access to sufficient living area	Access to telephone	Access to electricity
Guinea	Conakry	1999	82.7	84.8	98.7	70.7	7.2	71.4
Guinea	Conakry	2005	96.4	80.3	98.7		28.9	94.5
Guinea	Other cities/towns	1999	43.3	62.7	82.2	77.3	3.7	33.4
Guinea	Other cities/towns	2005	80.0	57.7	82.6		11.8	32.6
Guinea-Bissau	Bissau	2006	93.4	35.1	88.7	55.4		
Guinea-Bissau	Other cities/towns	2006	61.0	10.4	48.9	74.9		
Kenya	Mombasa	1993	83.0	68.9	76.0	82.1		37.2
Kenya	Mombasa	1998	73.9	61.3	79.8	79.6	7.4	47.5
Kenya	Mombasa	2003	89.1	68.0	83.3	81.7	29.6	43.5
Kenya	Nairobi	1993	92.2	73.4	75.2	77.9		50.8
Kenya	Nairobi	1998	92.1	84.3	82.9	78.0	11.2	60.1
Kenya	Nairobi	2003	93.3	82.9	87.4	81.7	44.4	71.4
Kenya	Other cities/towns	1993	87.3	74.7	83.8	77.6		36.2
Kenya	Other cities/towns	1998	80.1	71.0	75.7	77.6	7.6	35.7
Kenya	Other cities/towns	2003	64.6	67.3	74.1	76.4	24.3	35.0
Lesotho	Maseru	2004	98.3	74.7	94.8		50.2	33.1
Lesotho	Other cities/towns	2004	90.7	68.4	90.3		34.4	15.6
Liberia	Monrovia	2007	81.6	51.9	92.8			8.1
Liberia	Other cities/towns	2007	82.8	28.7	57.3			3.2
Madagascar	Antananarivo	1997	80.1	52.9	53.5	57.7	3.6	55.7
Madagascar	Antananarivo	2003	85.7	56.4	69.7		21.4	67.8
Madagascar	Other cities/towns	1997	48.0	33.0	34.2	53.7	0.8	25.5
Madagascar	Other cities/towns	2003	66.5	39.6	52.3		6.3	43.1
Malawi	Blantyre	2006	97.4	48.5	79.9			
Malawi	Lilongwe	1992	86.3	54.5	54.5	78.0		18.5
Malawi	Lilongwe	2000	92.1	59.4	63.9			29.9
Malawi	Lilongwe	2004	92.9	58.7	65.1	83.1	26.1	32.5
Malawi	Lilongwe	2006	91.9	44.1	59.6			
Malawi	Mzuzu	2006	94.0	42.1	62.9			
Malawi	Other cities/towns	1992	92.6	55.1	56.9	73.4		20.3
Malawi	Other cities/towns	2000	96.0	58.0	70.4			28.1
Malawi	Other cities/towns	2004	90.0	54.5	63.0	82.8	19.2	28.8
Malawi	Other cities/towns	2006	95.1	32.9	47.3	99.9		
Mali	Bamako	1996	70.5	51.6	89.0	75.5	3.7	33.7
Mali	Bamako	2001	89.4	72.5	74.1		15.7	55.8
Mali	Bamako	2006	95.6	81.1	81.9	71.5	19.6	72.1
Mali	Other cities/towns	1996	45.7	46.2	44.4	77.6	1.6	13.4
Mali	Other cities/towns	2001	54.4	57.7	42.5		3.9	21.0
Mali	Other cities/towns	2006	68.9	63.2	44.0	76.7	7.1	32.1
Mauritania	Nouakchott	2001	94.4	58.2	62.9	49.2	7.2	47.2
Mauritania	Nouakchott	2007	31.2	77.5	0.7	59.8		
Mauritania	Other cities/towns	2001	68.4	63.7	49.0	49.4	6.0	53.9
Mauritania	Other cities/towns	2007	73.1	53.1	0.5	63.5		
Morocco	Casablanca	1992	99.1	92.9	98.8	72.6		78.7

Country	City	Year	Access to improved water	Access to improved sanitation	Finished main floor materials	Access to sufficient living area	Access to telephone	Access to electricity
Morocco	Casablanca	2004	100.0	98.9	100.0	84.9	77.0	99.2
Morocco	Fes	1992	100.0	100.0	98.3	67.2		100.0
Morocco	Fes	2004	99.6	99.6	99.6	73.8	57.9	97.7
Morocco	Meknes	1992	99.2	99.2	93.9	61.4		84.1
Morocco	Meknes	2004	99.2	97.0	95.4	74.2	68.4	97.3
Morocco	Marrakech	1992	100.0	94.7	97.3	71.8		90.4
Morocco	Marrakech	2004	99.7	99.7	99.5	79.2	17.7	98.3
Morocco	Other cities/towns	1992	88.9	92.3	95.1	72.7		86.1
Morocco	Other cities/towns	2004	95.3	96.7	97.5	85.0	64.0	91.4
Morocco	Rabat	1992	96.5	92.5	95.2	79.6		83.9
Morocco	Rabat	2004	99.9	99.7	97.9	88.2	69.7	99.0
Morocco	Tangier	1992	95.9	99.6	97.1	64.9		87.6
Morocco	Tangier	2004	95.5	100.0	99.8	84.3	77.4	89.4
Mozambique	Maputo	1997	87.4	49.9	83.2	77.3	6.9	39.2
Mozambique	Maputo	2003	82.8	48.8	88.6	84.6	5.2	28.8
Mozambique	Other cities/towns	1997	67.3	38.3	55.3	73.0	5.1	23.1
Mozambique	Other cities/towns	2003	66.5	39.3	51.3	80.9	5.5	24.4
Namibia	Other cities/towns	1992	93.4	71.0	77.0	77.4		58.7
Namibia	Other cities/towns	2000	99.1	85.2	83.6	85.6	42.3	74.5
Namibia	Other cities/towns	2007	97.4	76.6	80.9	86.4	30.5	73.2
Namibia	Windhoek	1992	98.0	92.7	94.9	79.9		70.0
Namibia	Windhoek	2000	97.0	79.0	86.6	83.3	40.5	71.9
Namibia	Windhoek	2007	98.6	87.1	90.3	88.1	37.1	83.4
Niger	Niamey	1992	52.8	78.5	82.1	71.0		37.2
Niger	Niamey	1998	63.5	47.7	86.8	72.8	4.1	51.0
Niger	Niamey	2006	94.7	65.7	72.4	66.2	6.5	61.1
Niger	Other cities/towns	1992	66.6	59.2	54.3	65.7		20.6
Niger	Other cities/towns	1998	70.9	37.7	57.7	65.0	2.8	26.8
Niger	Other cities/towns	2006	92.1	51.2	51.0	63.2	2.2	37.8
Nigeria	Akure	1999	94.1	58.8	94.1	88.2		76.5
Nigeria	Akure	2003	63.5	61.4	100.0	72.7	9.1	95.0
Nigeria	Damaturu	1999	61.5	71.8	76.9	61.5	2.6	64.1
Nigeria	Damaturu	2003	49.9	52.6	42.0	64.5	2.0	59.8
Nigeria	Effon Alaiye	1999	32.8	48.9	82.3	91.3	2.2	93.3
Nigeria	Effon Alaiye	2003	18.6	49.5	96.9	70.0		93.7
Nigeria	Ibadan	1999	93.3	13.3	66.7	80.0		33.3
Nigeria	Ibadan	2003	27.6	64.2	96.9	69.9	14.8	98.9
Nigeria	Kano	1999	54.8	58.8	76.4	69.7	4.5	82.2
Nigeria	Kano	2003	65.7	58.8	93.5	80.0	9.8	92.6
Nigeria	Lagos	1999	88.6	84.7	96.2	60.5	8.2	98.9
Nigeria	Lagos	2003	88.2	72.8	99.8	60.8	31.8	99.8
Nigeria	Ogbomosho	1999	62.3	46.1	95.9	79.3	12.6	95.9
Nigeria	Ogbomosho	2003	68.1	38.0	94.4	84.9	7.7	94.4
Nigeria	Other cities/towns	1999	61.2	58.5	87.0	74.4	5.0	79.9

Country	City	Year	Access to improved water	Access to improved sanitation	Finished main floor materials	Access to sufficient living area	Access to telephone	Access to electricity
Nigeria	Other cities/towns	2003	66.3	64.0	86.1	79.7	9.1	78.6
Nigeria	Owo	1999	34.4	68.8	100.0	83.2	9.9	95.3
Nigeria	Oyo	1999	35.0	65.8	95.8	84.4	3.6	92.1
Nigeria	Zaria	1999	74.4	55.8	98.8	59.3	4.6	94.2
Nigeria	Zaria	2003	78.0	67.7	98.7	66.3	12.4	100.0
Rwanda	Kigali	1992	52.0	50.2	64.6	86.0		36.0
Rwanda	Kigali	2000	81.8	72.3	71.8		8.6	44.4
Rwanda	Kigali	2005	68.9	80.6	67.6		8.3	40.8
Rwanda	Other cities/towns	1992	47.3	54.1	45.1	84.6		21.8
Rwanda	Other cities/towns	2000	78.5	66.8	57.8		7.5	36.7
Rwanda	Other cities/towns	2005	54.4	68.3	32.2		2.1	12.8
Senegal	Dakar	1993	95.8	64.2	98.7	65.6		70.0
Senegal	Dakar	1997	95.5	70.8	99.8	65.8	20.4	80.2
Senegal	Dakar	2005	98.3	91.1	95.7			
Senegal	Other cities/towns	1993	70.8	57.3	83.1	71.0		44.1
Senegal	Other cities/towns	1997	72.7	57.6	86.0	70.4	9.7	55.0
Senegal	Other cities/towns	2005	82.2	77.2	83.6			
Sierra Leone	Freetown	2005	89.4	72.8	95.8	72.2		
Sierra Leone	Other cities	2005	78.2	57.3	63.9	66.4		
Republic of South Africa	Cape Town	1998	95.8	83.4	93.7	90.9	49.6	88.0
Republic of South Africa	Durban	1998	98.4	90.1	97.1	90.0	46.3	84.3
Republic of South Africa	Other cities/towns	1998	98.8	81.7	93.0	86.0	40.9	85.6
Republic of South Africa	Port Elizabeth	1998	97.2	68.5	83.4	79.2	27.0	63.3
Republic of South Africa	Pretoria	1998	100.0	62.5	87.5	75.0	18.8	56.3
Republic of South Africa	West Rand	1998	99.4	84.8	83.4	86.9	47.6	75.0
Swaziland	Manzini	2006	92.8	79.9	99.4	87.1	17.7	60.5
Swaziland	Mbabane	2006	88.6	76.9	96.4	89.3	29.1	59.9
Swaziland	Other cities/towns	2006	94.6	86.7	97.5	92.1	15.9	70.3
Togo	Kara	2006	92.4	24.7	96.2	86.9		
Togo	Lomé	1998	88.6	81.7	98.0	77.0		51.2
Togo	Lomé	2006	92.9	78.2	99.0	74.8		
Togo	Other cities/towns	1998	80.0	49.1	92.4	82.2		31.4
Togo	Other cities/towns	2006	87.2	45.1	92.6	84.0		
Togo	Sokode	2006	69.4	49.6	95.8	86.8		
Uganda	Kampala	1995	60.4	58.9	77.2	62.0	3.0	49.4
Uganda	Kampala	2001	94.2	63.2	86.3		20.3	55.2
Uganda	Kampala	2006	92.6	100.0	87.7	71.6	5.4	59.0
Uganda	Other cities/towns	1995	57.0	53.5	58.1	67.0	1.8	32.0
Uganda	Other cities/towns	2001	84.8	54.5	61.8		9.0	33.5
Uganda	Other cities/towns	2006	86.5	88.8	59.2	70.0	1.1	26.0
United Republic of Tanzania	Arusha	1992	92.9	58.0	54.1	66.5		21.1
United Republic of Tanzania	Arusha	1996	96.1	50.4	61.2	77.5		32.6
United Republic of Tanzania	Arusha	1999	97.8	39.6	51.5			5.9
United Republic of Tanzania	Arusha	2004	94.6	62.5	62.2	77.7	35.0	35.0

Country	City	Year	Access to improved water	Access to improved sanitation	Finished main floor materials	Access to sufficient living area	Access to telephone	Access to electricity
United Republic of Tanzania	Dar es Salaam	1992	90.5	54.1	80.0	77.1		31.7
United Republic of Tanzania	Dar es Salaam	1996	85.4	51.4	87.9	83.4		45.2
United Republic of Tanzania	Dar es Salaam	1999	90.1	51.9	86.5			46.9
United Republic of Tanzania	Dar es Salaam	2004	81.1	55.6	93.8	84.1	43.4	59.8
United Republic of Tanzania	Other cities/towns	1992	71.3	50.0	43.1	79.2		21.5
United Republic of Tanzania	Other cities/towns	1996	71.9	55.2	54.9	82.7		31.6
United Republic of Tanzania	Other cities/towns	1999	90.9	53.0	56.1			27.5
United Republic of Tanzania	Other cities/towns	2004	76.4	57.7	61.6	85.1	19.8	29.1
Zambia	Chingola	1992	93.7	93.3	98.0	63.5		71.5
Zambia	Chingola	1996	76.6	85.9	98.4	76.6		78.1
Zambia	Chingola	2002	89.1	93.5	92.6		3.0	75.7
Zambia	Chingola	2007	90.4	86.7	90.4	75.9	9.6	76.5
Zambia	Lusaka	1992	97.1	67.5	92.2	69.2		34.5
Zambia	Lusaka	1996	93.9	70.3	96.8	75.1		50.7
Zambia	Lusaka	2002	97.2	67.6	97.5		13.0	44.2
Zambia	Lusaka	2007	92.4	83.5	95.1	69.3	4.9	57.0
Zambia	Ndola	1992	90.0	74.6	88.2	68.9		35.4
Zambia	Ndola	1996	92.3	85.1	92.5	72.6		52.0
Zambia	Ndola	2002	88.0	82.0	83.5		16.8	52.8
Zambia	Ndola	2007	74.1	64.5	81.6	78.3	8.1	38.9
Zambia	Other cities/towns	1992	75.9	61.1	65.9	76.0		26.7
Zambia	Other cities/towns	1996	69.2	56.3	60.7	71.8		24.8
Zambia	Other cities/towns	2002	83.0	55.2	57.1		6.2	24.2
Zambia	Other cities/towns	2007	75.2	53.1	68.5	72.9	3.9	34.3
Zimbabwe	Harare	1994	98.7	98.1	94.9	83.8		74.5
Zimbabwe	Harare	1999	99.6	97.2	96.5		19.9	84.7
Zimbabwe	Harare	2005	99.2	98.4	99.2	82.5	17.5	86.3
Zimbabwe	Other cities/towns	1994	99.4	97.0	94.8	82.4		86.9
Zimbabwe	Other cities/towns	1999	99.6	98.4	97.8		13.2	90.2
Zimbabwe	Other cities/towns	2005	99.5	97.0	99.6	86.7	25.2	94.6

Source: Global Urban Indicators Database 2010

TABLE 6: **PROPORTION OF URBAN HOUSEHOLDS WITH ACCESS TO AN IMPROVED WATER SOURCE AND IMPROVED SANITATION FACILITY BY COUNTRY**

		Improved water source								Improved sanitation facility				
Country	**Year**	**Total Improved water**	**Piped water**	**Public tap**	**Pump/ borehole**	**Protected well**	**Improved spring/ surface water**	**Rainwater**	**Bottle water**	**Total Improved sanitation**	**Flush toilet [a]**	**Ventilated improved pit latrine**	**Pit latrine with slab or covered latrine**	**Composting toilet**
Angola	2006	58.6	31.3	11.6	1.2	10.6	3.8	0.1		80.8	48.1	1.8	29.6	1.4
Benin	1996	74.1	56.4	2.3	4.8	7.5		3.0		50.6			44.6	
Benin	2001	78.2	62.6	4.9	4.9	5.0		0.8	0.1	48.3	6.3	30.2		
Benin	2006	82.4	61.2	5.2	7.1	6.5	0.4	1.9		50.7	8.1	27.3		
Burkina Faso	1992	66.3	26.0	40.2						45.6	4.7	1.4		
Burkina Faso	1999	80.9	25.0	47.7	8.2				0.1	48.0	3.9	0.8		
Burkina Faso	2003	93.9	32.6	56.0		5.4				57.2	8.9	14.6		
Burundi	2005	77.5	43.2	24.6	0.0	0.1	9.5		0.2	43.3	26.1	4.8	12.3	
Cameroon	1991	76.5	33.9	34.8	2.3			0.1	5.5	25.5	14.0			
Cameroon	1998	76.5	37.1	37.5	1.9					80.4	18.1	42.3		
Cameroon	2004	86.0	34.7	34.6	6.0	4.1	6.7			77.0	14.1	42.1		
Cameroon	2006	90.2	41.2	29.0	10.6	4.1	4.7		0.7	74.9	18.7	3.6	28.9	
Central African Republic	1994	51.6	4.9	38.2	8.5					48.0	2.4	7.7		
Chad	1997	30.5	11.6	11.7		7.2				53.0	1.0	27.3		
Chad	2004	73.5	18.6	23.4		30.0	1.5	0.1		49.9	5.8	11.4		
Comoros	1996	94.6	38.8	34.9				20.9		69.2	7.6	32.1		
Congo	2005	94.8	86.8		3.2	1.1	3.2		0.4	65.9	9.1	25.6		
Côte d'Ivoire	1994	78.3	50.8	27.3					0.1	77.8	29.3	34.7		
Côte d'Ivoire	1998	79.3	59.2	19.9				0.2		72.0	24.7	23.9		
Côte d'Ivoire	2005	85.2	66.6	10.6		7.7	0.1		0.2	68.1	29.2	9.2		
Côte d'Ivoire	2006	90.5	66.9	6.9	0.9	15.7			0.1		39.6	2.2		
Democratic Republic of the Congo	2007	79.6	21.9	36.9		6.0	14.7		0.1	73.7	13.2	5.7	33.2	
Egypt	1992	97.2	91.4	5.9						75.1	50.1			
Egypt	1995	96.6	92.4	4.1						74.8	52.4			
Egypt	2000	99.5	97.0	2.0		0.3			0.2	81.1	62.6			
Egypt	2003	99.9	98.6	1.2		0.2				84.8	68.9			
Egypt	2005	99.2	98.0	0.9	0.1	0.1			0.2	86.5	72.6			
Ethiopia	2000	86.1	28.8	52.0		2.1	3.2			38.6	1.9	1.9		
Ethiopia	2005	93.7	47.5	42.6		1.2	2.3			50.8	6.9	3.7	37.6	2.6
Gabon	2000	94.4	52.2	40.8		0.8			0.1	78.7	30.2	27.2		
Gambia	2005	91.1	53.4	34.8	1.2	1.4			0.4	93.8	38.4	0.7	54.7	
Ghana	1993	80.2	37.2	38.6	3.7			0.7		57.8	15.6	27.8		
Ghana	1998	87.6	41.4	42.6	3.2			0.5		73.3	18.4	36.9		
Ghana	2003	83.1	33.4	39.1		10.1		0.5		75.5	21.2	40.8		
Ghana	2006	78.7	25.9	39.1	7.2	5.8		0.3	0.4	83.5	23.6	47.1	12.7	
Guinea	1999	64.5	29.7	34.0			0.8			75.6	7.7	47.6		
Guinea	2005	88.3	27.4	40.6		19.2	1.1			69.1	7.0	3.1	49.8	
Guinea-Bissau	2006	83.7	30.1	17.1	7.0	28.2	1.2		0.1	27.6	27.5	0.1		
Kenya	1993	88.8	55.8	31.4	0.9			0.6		73.3	44.8	6.9		
Kenya	1998	84.5	58.2	25.9				0.4		75.7	43.1	10.7		

Country	Year	Total Improved water	Piped water	Public tap	Pump/ borehole	Protected well	Improved spring/ surface water	Rainwater	Bottle water	Total Improved sanitation	Flush toilet [a]	Ventilated improved pit latrine	Pit latrine with slab or covered latrine	Composting toilet
		Improved water source								Improved sanitation facility				
Kenya	2003	78.5	49.4	21.8		6.0		0.7	0.7	73.5	39.0	11.7		
Lesotho	2004	95.3	68.4	22.0		4.9				72.2	7.7	40.7		
Liberia	2007	81.9	7.1	11.0	3.7	59.6	0.1		0.4	46.3	29.7	7.2	8.7	0.7
Madagascar	1997	61.4	17.7	38.3	5.4					41.3	7.4	8.9		
Madagascar	2003	73.9	17.8	46.7		9.4				46.1	7.4	3.0		
Malawi	1992	90.9	33.6	48.5		8.8				54.9	13.9	1.2		
Malawi	2000	94.8	41.7	41.8	8.3	3.0				58.5	16.4	1.0		
Malawi	2004	91.1	29.3	45.2		16.7				56.1	16.2	2.3		
Malawi	2006	94.6	27.6	49.3	15.4	2.3				42.3	9.7	1.0	31.7	
Mali	1996	55.6	15.7	33.5	6.4					48.4	2.9			
Mali	2001	70.5	27.0	32.0		11.5				64.5	13.9	19.0		
Mali	2006	79.2	32.7	36.3		9.8			0.3	70.1	6.1	41.8		
Mauritania	2001	84.6	28.1	49.7		6.8				60.3	4.1	8.1	30.9	
Mauritania	2007	49.7	32.1	15.5	0.4	1.6	0.1		0.1	66.7	34.9	10.3	21.5	
Morocco	1992	94.4	76.4	17.7					0.3	93.7	90.3	1.8		
Morocco	2004	97.4	85.2	10.8		0.8			0.6	98.1	97.8			
Mozambique	1997	70.7	46.8	23.7				0.2		40.3	12.2			
Mozambique	2003	68.9	39.6	19.4		9.4		0.3		40.6	7.5			
Namibia	1992	96.4	81.8	14.6						84.9	82.8	0.6		
Namibia	2000	98.1	77.0	20.9						82.0	77.5	2.1		
Namibia	2007	97.9	79.5	17.3					0.9	81.1	76.3	4.0	0.5	0.3
Niger	1992	61.5	22.7	38.6				0.2	0.1	66.4	5.9	55.8		
Niger	1998	68.0	26.6	37.4	3.8	0.3				41.7	4.2			
Niger	2006	93.2	35.2	55.6		2.3			0.2	57.0	6.1	32.3		
Nigeria	1999	62.9	24.0	25.8	12.4			0.3	0.4	62.8	30.6	8.8		
Nigeria	2003	67.0	14.4	18.5		31.1		0.5	2.4	63.1	28.7	5.5		
Rwanda	1992	50.4	7.0	43.4						51.6	10.6			
Rwanda	2000	79.5	33.5	42.5		3.5				68.3	6.9	30.8		
Rwanda	2005	60.8	14.1	41.3		5.3		0.1	0.1	73.7	5.4	47.1		
Senegal	1993	84.8	54.1	30.0	0.7					61.1	25.4	11.1		
Senegal	1997	85.2	64.2	20.2	0.1			0.1	0.6	64.9	26.7	11.1		
Senegal	2005	91.5	75.7	13.5		1.9			0.4	85.2	65.5	9.3		
Sierra Leone	2005	84.1	23.8	30.4	2.1	26.2	1.5	0.1	0.1	65.4	10.5	0.4	54.5	
Somalia	2006	56.4	36.1	14.6	1.8	3.7			0.3	77.0	63.1	1.8	12.2	
Republic of South Africa	1998	98.3	86.6	11.3	0.2				0.1	84.0	79.6			
Swaziland	2006	92.3	72.6	15.2	2.5	1.2	0.5	0.1	0.1	81.2	49.7	11.3		
Togo	1998	84.2	51.3	23.6	1.6	7.6		0.1		65.3	21.5		43.9	
Togo	2006	90.5	11.6	64.8	7.4	4.9	0.2	0.8	1.1	66.1	32.3	14.2	19.7	0.3
Uganda	1995	58.6	12.7	31.9	13.5			0.4	0.2	56.1	9.2	6.2		
Uganda	2001	89.3	12.1	51.2	13.9	11.1		0.4	0.7	58.7	9.1	7.9		
Uganda	2006	89.4	20.2	39.3	12.6	15.3		0.5	1.6	94.1	8.6	13.6	43.7	
United Republic of Tanzania	1992	77.8	39.6	38.2						51.7	4.5	3.1		

						Improved water source						Improved sanitation facility		
Country	**Year**	**Total Improved water**	**Piped water**	**Public tap**	**Pump/ borehole**	**Protected well**	**Improved spring/ surface water**	**Rainwater**	**Bottle water**	**Total Improved sanitation**	**Flush toilet [a]**	**Ventilated improved pit latrine**	**Pit latrine with slab or covered latrine**	**Composting toilet**
United Republic of Tanzania	1996	77.8	31.5	46.3						53.7	5.0	3.3		
United Republic of Tanzania	1999	92.3	48.2	31.9	6.0	5.2	0.8		0.2	49.5	4.1	3.2		
United Republic of Tanzania	2004	78.9	52.0	15.7	3.2	6.6		0.1	1.3	57.4	9.1	12.0		
Zambia	1992	89.2	55.5	33.6						72.0	47.9	1.0		
Zambia	1996	85.4	46.7	33.9	4.7					71.2	45.6	0.3		
Zambia	2002	89.8	43.5	38.2		8.1			0.1	71.1	42.3	2.5		
Zambia	2007	82.5	39.7	36.9		5.6			0.3	69.8	33.8	7.1	28.7	0.1
Zimbabwe	1994	99.0	92.6	4.8	0.7	0.9				97.6	94.6	1.4		
Zimbabwe	1999	99.6	90.9	7.5	0.5	0.7				97.8	93.7	2.9		
Zimbabwe	2005	99.4	92.7	4.5	0.9	1.3				97.5	92.7	3.4	1.4	

Source: Global Urban Indicators Database 2010

Notes:

a. Flush toilet includes the categories: flush/pour flush to piped sewer system, flush/pour flush to septic tank, and flush to pit latrine.

TABLE 7: **GINI COEFFICIENTS FOR URBAN AT NATIONAL LEVEL, SELECTED COUNTRIES**

Country	Year	Gini coefficent
Algeria	1995[i]	0.35
Benin	2007[c]	0.47
Botswana	2001-02[i]	0.50
Burkina Faso	2003c	0.48
Burundi	2006c	0.49
Cameroon	2001[i]	0.41
Central African Republic	2003[c]	0.42
Côte d'Ivoire	2008[i]	0.44
Democratic Republic of the Congo	2004-05[c]	0.40
Egypt	1997[c]	0.39
Ethiopia	2004-05[c]	0.44
Ethiopia	1999-00[i]	0.57
Kenya	1999[i]	0.55
Kenya	2006[c]	0.45
Malawi	1998[c]	0.52
Mauritania	2004[c]	0.39
Morocco	1998[c]	0.38
Mozambique	2002-03[c]	0.48
Namibia	1993[i]	0.63
Namibia	2003[c]	0.58
Nigeria	2006[i]	0.54
Republic of South Africa	2005[i]	0.76
Togo	2006[c]	0.31
Uganda	2005-06[i]	0.43
Zambia	2006[i]	0.66
Zimbabwe	1998[i]	0.60

Source: Global Urban Indicators Database 2010

Notes:
i. Refers to Gini coefficients based on Income
c. Refers to Gini Coefficients based on Consumption

TABLE 8: **GINI COEFFICIENTS FOR SELECTED CITIES AND PROVINCES**

Country	City	Year	Gini
Burundi	Bujumbura	2006[c]	0.47
Cameroon	Yaoundé	1996[i]	0.44
Cameroon	Douala	1996[i]	0.46
Central African Republic	Bangui	2003[c]	0.42
Congo	Brazzaville	2005[i]	0.45
Congo	Pointe-Noire	2005[i]	0.39
Côte d'Ivoire	Abidjan	2008[i]	0.50
Democratic Republic of Congo	Kinshasa	2004-05[c]	0.39
Ethiopia	Addis Ababa	2003[i]	0.61
Ethiopia	Addis Ababa	2003[c]	0.56
Ethiopia	Bahir Dar	2000[c]	0.36
Ethiopia	Jimma	2000[c]	0.36
Ethiopia	Dire Dawa	2000[c]	0.39
Ethiopia	Mekelle	2000[c]	0.39
Ethiopia	Awassa	2000[c]	0.41
Ethiopia	Dessie	2000[c]	0.49
Gabon	Libreville and Port Genti	1996[i]	0.45
Ghana	Accra	1992[i]	0.50
Guinea- Bissau	Bissau	2006[i]	0.37
Kenya	Nairobi	2006[i]	0.59
Lesotho	Maseru	1993[i]	0.58
Morocco	Casablanca	2006[i]	0.52
Mozambique	Maputo	2002-03[c]	0.52
Nigeria	Lagos	2006	0.64
Rwanda	Kigali	2005[i]	0.47
Senegal	Dakar	2001-02[c]	0.37
Sierra Leone	Freetown	2002[c]	0.32
Republic of South Africa	Buffalo City (East London)	2005[i]	0.75
Republic of South Africa	Cape Town	2005[i]	0.67
Republic of South Africa	Ekurhuleni (East Rand)	2005[i]	0.74
Republic of South Africa	eThekwini (Durban)	2005[i]	0.72
Republic of South Africa	Johannesburg	2005[i]	0.75
Republic of South Africa	Mangaug (Bloemfontein)	2005[i]	0.74
Republic of South Africa	Msunduzi (Pietermaritzburg)	2005[i]	0.73
Republic of South Africa	Nelson Mandela Bay (Port Elizabeth)	2005[i]	0.72
Republic of South Africa	Tshwane (Pretoria)	2005[i]	0.72
Togo	Lomé	2006[c]	0.30
Uganda	Kampala	2002[c]	0.47
United Republic of Tanzania	Dar es Salaam	2007[c]	0.34

Source: Global Urban Indicators Database 2010

Notes:
i. Refers to Gini coefficients based on Income
c. Refers to Gini Coefficients based on Consumption

TABLE 9: **PERCENTAGE OF FEMALE AND MALE AGED 15-24 YEARS IN INFORMAL EMPLOYMENT BY SHELTER DEPRIVATION**

		Female							Male						
	Year	Urban	Rural	Non-Slum	All Slum	One Shelter deprivation	Two Shelter deprivations	Three Shelter deprivations	Urban	Rural	Non-Slum	All Slum	One Shelter deprivations	Two Shelter deprivations	Three Shelter deprivations
Benin	1996	92.9	97.0	89.4	94.9	91.2	98.2		71.4	66.7					
Benin	2001	91.0	97.6	84.2	94.3	93.3	94.8		68.2	84.3	58.1	81.1	77.0	85.2	100.0
Benin	2006	79.8	91.7	87.6	79.3	87.2	78.3	88.8	69.8	82.3	28.3	76.5	64.5	79.8	
Burkina Faso	1992	87.5	97.6	76.9	88.1	88.5	87.7	88.2							
Burkina Faso	1999	84.0	99.1	42.9	85.2	85.7	81.8		55.7	85.7	40.0	68.4	58.3	71.7	81.1
Burkina Faso	2003	82.8	95.6	83.0	82.3	77.8	91.3		20.7	31.0					
Cameroon	1991	78.8	93.8	69.6	82.0	80.0	80.6	90.0							
Cameroon	1998	69.9	84.4	65.4	75.0	74.4	74.5	85.7	62.0	60.2					
Central African Republic	1994	96.8	98.0	88.9	97.2	96.8	97.0	98.0	75.2	81.1	100.0	77.0	86.2	82.9	70.0
Chad	1996	99.3	99.2	90.9	99.2	96.2	100.0	99.3	71.3	74.2					
Chad	2004	83.6	84.1	83.2	83.7	85.5	85.3	80.9	60.2	68.9	73.4	58.6	50.4	63.6	73.6
Comoros	1996	93.4	95.6	88.2	90.4	94.1	100.0	93.4	54.5	78.8	81.8	65.9	62.5	61.9	80.0
Congo	2005	92.5	97.5	90.3	93.7	94.8	90.9	97.7	52.0	66.3	50.6	52.7	52.3	51.3	67.0
Côte d'Ivoire	1994	88.0	95.0	84.8	93.6	94.1	92.0								
Côte d'Ivoire	1998	77.6	81.7	68.4	88.9	88.8	92.6		35.3	42.4	37.9	36.6	26.8	52.0	40.0
Egypt	1992	4.7	18.1	0.0	12.8	14.3									
Egypt	1995	15.5	40.4	14.3	12.5	16.7									
Egypt	2000	13.7	17.5	12.5	20.0	28.6									
Egypt	2003	19.6	17.1	23.7											
Egypt	2005	22.4	27.1	17.6	29.3	40.6	19.9								
Ethiopia	2000	86.2	98.5	90.9	86.1	80.8	87.6	93.8							
Ethiopia	2005	69.9	93.4	55.7	73.0	65.2	73.3	90.4	16.8	30.6	11.5	17.7	21.7	18.5	9.7
Gabon	2000	75.6	83.0	74.1	77.2	79.3	73.1	70.0	71.0	62.1	68.8	70.9	73.8	66.7	62.5
Ghana	1993	80.8	94.0	82.1	79.9	80.0	81.5	50.0							
Ghana	1999	79.7	92.4	77.6	82.4	82.8	83.3	100.0	43.1	44.6	46.9	42.3	40.7	41.7	55.6
Ghana	2003	85.2	95.2	81.3	89.5	88.9	94.1		30.1	29.4	28.6	30.8	31.9	25.4	71.4
Guinea	1998	82.1	89.2	69.0	83.0	81.6	85.1	84.2	64.7	83.1	33.3	72.6	68.3	69.6	79.2
Guinea	2005	98.6	96.9	99.0	97.8	96.9	100.0	100.0							
Kenya	1993	45.4	64.2	35.3	58.2	53.7	60.0								
Kenya	1998	54.4	74.5	52.9	56.7	58.4	56.5	46.7	50.0	55.6	41.4	55.8	50.0	42.2	64.0
Kenya	2003	63.8	73.1	57.6	70.4	67.5	72.5	86.7	5.3	11.7	8.3	9.0	5.9	11.3	10.8
Madagascar	1997	77.7	90.5	78.3	77.3	78.1	69.7	94.7							
Malawi	2000	72.6	92.7	52.8	80.2	78.2	85.7	66.7							
Mali	1996	93.7	98.2	72.7	94.2	92.5	94.1	97.3	62.6	89.8					
Mali	2001	91.2	96.1	89.6	92.1	92.1	91.4		53.3	56.0					
Morocco	1992	23.4	62.5	22.1	25.1	21.8	50.0	66.7							
Morocco	2004	50.2	71.5	49.8	52.9	35.0	66.7								
Mozambique	1997	63.9	83.3	24.0	71.8	68.7	72.7	86.7	46.8	63.9	0.0	56.7	46.7	48.1	62.5
Mozambique	2003	70.9	88.6	65.6	71.7	68.9	72.8	88.2	8.5	12.9	7.1	9.8	7.9	5.0	18.5
Namibia	2000	38.0	46.5	33.6	53.1	65.4	43.2	100.0							

	Year	Female							Male						
		Urban	Rural	Non-Slum	All Slum	One Shelter deprivation	Two Shelter deprivations	Three Shelter deprivations	Urban	Rural	Non-Slum	All Slum	One Shelter deprivations	Two Shelter deprivations	Three Shelter deprivations
Niger	1998	92.1	98.7	87.5	92.7	92.2	93.5	86.4	57.2	84.0					
Nigeria	1990	68.6	87.7	58.0	71.6	69.4	75.5	66.7							
Nigeria	1999	77.2	89.7	67.6	81.1	71.4	90.9	100.0	59.2	67.3	58.3	65.2	60.5	67.9	68.6
Nigeria	2003	59.0	78.6	59.0	78.6	73.5	82.6	95.0	16.8	26.0	5.9	23.8	9.0	31.0	33.3
Rwanda	1992	22.2	51.9		29.3	19.0	42.9	40.0							
Rwanda	2000	65.2	61.3	60.9	67.9	62.5	71.4	87.5	47.5	60.5	10.0	55.2	50.8	55.3	60.0
Rwanda	2005	60.0	80.8	50.9	69.8	67.7	68.7	92.0	23.2	39.8	17.1	29.9	23.9	32.5	52.1
Senegal	2005	84.0	85.0	81.2	91.0	91.4	90.2	92.8	23.9	24.8	23.8	24.0	29.6	22.1	23.8
Republic of South Africa	1998	39.3	50.7	38.1	46.9	46.2	45.5								
Togo	1998	94.3	96.6	95.8	93.3	93.1	93.3	100.0	60.1	52.6					
Uganda	1995	58.8	83.7	38.5	62.9	56.3	65.4	87.5							
Uganda	2001	74.4	81.7	76.9	74.1	68.9	83.1		14.9	22.2	25.0	19.6	14.9	24.1	19.3
United Republic of Tanzania	1992	65.7	86.9	58.1	66.8	64.7	69.0	77.8							
United Republic of Tanzania	1996	100.0	100.0	100.0	100.0	100.0	100.0	100.0							
United Republic of Tanzania	1999	69.3	94.8	66.7	69.7	70.3	62.8		59.3	80.3	50.0	68.5	61.1	68.4	87.5
United Republic of Tanzania	2004	70.6	91.0	69.2	71.4	70.4	70.7	78.6	4.7	24.8	8.3	2.4	3.3		8.3
Zambia	1996	72.3	94.2	57.7	82.4	81.9	77.9	96.8	51.1	74.5	46.7	60.4	47.5	61.9	82.8
Zambia	2002	68.7	92.6	59.6	73.9	74.5	72.8	66.7	11.4	47.1	17.7	23.1	9.8	21.4	48.1
Zimbabwe	1994	55.2	60.8	53.9	67.9	65.2	80.0		38.7	40.3	37.7	41.6	40.7	40.0	46.2
Zimbabwe	1999	53.6	62.8	52.0	67.4	69.6	65.0								

Source: Global Urban Indicators Database 2010

TABLE 10: **NET ENROLMENT RATE IN PRIMARY EDUCATION BY CITY (FEMALE AND MALE)**

Country	City	Year	Male	Female
Benin	Cotonou	1996	88.6	58.5
Benin	Cotonou	2001	90.8	68.6
Benin	Djouguo	1996	80.3	61.3
Benin	Djougou	2001	78.3	69.0
Benin	Porto-Novo	1996	64.8	58.4
Benin	Porto-Novo	2001	72.5	55.6
Burkina Faso	Ouagadougou	1992	76.1	72.9
Burkina Faso	Ouagadougou	1999	77.5	69.4
Burkina Faso	Ouagadougou	2003	86.7	82.3
Cameroon	Yaoundé	1991	94.3	91.4
Cameroon	Yaoundé	1998	95.6	93.0
Cameroon	Yaoundé	2004	90.6	90.6
Central African Republic	Bangui	1994	76.5	72.9
Chad	N'Djaména	1996	61.8	50.1
Chad	N'Djaména	2004	70.3	59.9
Congo	Brazzaville	2005	88.4	89.2
Côte d'Ivoire	Abidjan	1994	73.9	61.0
Côte d'Ivoire	Abidjan	1996	58.4	46.0
Côte d'Ivoire	Abidjan	2005	87.0	66.6
Egypt	Alexandria	2003	79.5	85.2
Egypt	Alexandria	2005	84.2	83.9
Egypt	Al-Qahirah (Cairo)	2005	87.2	87.6
Egypt	Assiut	2003	82.9	82.6
Egypt	Assiut	2005	86.7	79.5
Egypt	Aswan	2003	83.9	78.9
Egypt	Aswan	2005	85.6	90.8
Egypt	Beni Suef	2003	100.0	82.4
Egypt	Beni Suef	2005	86.1	89.1
Egypt	Port Said	2003	93.1	82.2
Egypt	Port Said	2005	86.7	84.9
Egypt	Suez	2003	88.7	80.0
Egypt	Suez	2005	85.2	81.2
Ethiopia	Addis Ababa	2000	81.0	72.6
Ethiopia	Nazret	2000	95.2	93.4
Ethiopia	Nazret	2005	75.3	74.2
Gabon	Libreville	2000	93.4	92.6
Ghana	Accra	1993	85.9	87.9
Ghana	Accra	1999	91.4	84.9
Ghana	Accra	2003	78.2	73.1
Guinea	Conakry	1999	53.1	50.9
Guinea	Conakry	2005	77.6	70.8
Kenya	Nairobi	1993	69.4	70.1
Kenya	Nairobi	1998	88.4	80.9
Kenya	Nairobi	2003	85.8	84.0
Lesotho	Maseru	2004	75.2	83.6
Madagascar	Antananarivo	1997	82.4	84.5
Madagascar	Antananarivo	2003	89.0	90.6
Malawi	Lilongwe	1992	72.2	72.1
Malawi	Lilongwe	2000	87.8	84.7
Malawi	Lilongwe	2004	87.5	88.3
Mali	Bamako	1996	76.3	63.3
Mali	Bamako	2001	82.1	72.9
Morocco	Casablanca	2004	96.7	93.3
Morocco	Fès	2004	92.3	93.8
Morocco	Maknes	2004	97.2	98.2
Morocco	Marrakech	2004	98.4	95.5
Morocco	Rabat	2004	94.9	94.4
Morocco	Tangier	2004	91.4	94.1
Mozambique	Maputo	1997	82.3	83.4
Mozambique	Maputo	2003	89.7	90.8
Niger	Niamey	1992	65.2	58.9
Niger	Niamey	1998	76.2	69.7
Nigeria	Akure	1999	100.0	100.0
Nigeria	Akure	2003	93.4	90.6
Nigeria	Damaturu	1999	23.5	23.3
Nigeria	Damaturu	2003	45.9	54.9
Nigeria	Effon Alaiye	1999	85.8	100.0
Nigeria	Effon Alaiye	2003	93.3	100.0
Nigeria	Ibadan	1999	77.8	88.9
Nigeria	Ibadan	2003	55.9	64.7
Nigeria	Lagos	1999	81.4	74.9
Nigeria	Lagos	2003	80.0	83.5
Nigeria	Ogbomosho	1999	55.7	40.0
Nigeria	Ogbomosho	2003	75.4	89.4
Nigeria	Owo	1999	70.1	74.0
Nigeria	Oyo	1999	75.9	73.5
Nigeria	Oyo	2003	60.0	40.0
Nigeria	Zaria	1999	45.8	48.1
Nigeria	Zaria	2003	56.1	64.4
Rwanda	Kigali	1992	75.8	81.9
Rwanda	Kigali	2000	74.7	73.4
Rwanda	Kigali	2005	89.7	92.0
Senegal	Dakar	1993	57.9	48.7
Senegal	Dakar	2005	74.0	74.0
Republic of South Africa	CapeTown	1998	87.8	85.3
Republic of South Africa	Durban	1998	77.1	81.7
Republic of South Africa	Port Elizabeth	1998	80.8	77.2
Republic of South Africa	Pretoria	1998	60.0	100.0
Republic of South Africa	West Rand	1998	78.3	85.7
Togo	Lomé	1998	89.3	82.7
Uganda	Kampala	1995	78.9	82.7
Uganda	Kampala	2001	90.8	86.2
United Republic of Tanzania	Arusha	1992	42.1	51.0
United Republic of Tanzania	Arusha	1996	69.0	62.9
United Republic of Tanzania	Arusha	1999	83.4	60.4
United Republic of Tanzania	Arusha	2004	84.1	91.6
United Republic of Tanzania	Dar es Salaam	1992	62.0	58.0
United Republic of Tanzania	Dar es Salaam	1996	63.2	64.0
United Republic of Tanzania	Dar es Salaam	1999	62.4	83.9
United Republic of Tanzania	Dar es Salaam	2004	89.0	87.0
Zambia	Chingola	1996	87.2	93.9
Zambia	Chingola	2002	84.7	82.8
Zambia	Ndola	1996	81.4	79.6
Zambia	Ndola	2002	76.0	76.5
Zimbabwe	Harare	1994	94.2	90.6
Zimbabwe	Harare	1999	90.1	90.2
Zimbabwe	Harare	1999	12.2	14.3

Source: Global Urban Indicators Database 2010

TABLE 11: **INTERNATIONAL MIGRANTS AND INTERNALLY DISPLACED PERSONS**

		By Country of Asylum				By Country of Origin			Internally displaced persons		International migrants		
		Refugees	Asylum seekers	Returned refugees	Stateless persons	Refugees	Asylum seekers	Returned refugees	Displaced	Returned	Percentage		
	Note	2005	2005	2005	2005	2005	2005	2005	2005	2005	1995	2000	2005
World		**8,394,373**	**773,492**	**1,105,544**	**2,381,886**	**8,394,373**	**773,492**	**1,105,544**	**6,616,791**	**519,430**	**2.9**	**2.9**	**3.0**
Africa											**2.5**	**2.0**	**1.9**
Algeria	1	94,101	306	1	-	12,006	1,391	1	-	-	1.1	0.8	0.7
Angola		13,984	885	53,771	-	215,777	8,352	53,771	-	-	0.3	0.3	0.4
Benin		30,294	1,695	-	-	411	272	-	-	-	2.4	1.9	2.1
Botswana		3,109	47	-	-	4	11	-	-	-	2.4	3.2	4.5
Burkina Faso		511	784	-	-	607	211	-	-	-	4.7	5.1	5.8
Burundi		20,681	19,900	68,248	-	438,663	8,268	68,248	11,500	-	4.8	1.2	1.3
Cameroon		52,042	6,766	-	-	9,016	4,860	-	-	-	1.2	1.0	0.8
Cape Verde		-	-	-	-	5	14	-	-	-	2.4	2.3	2.2
Central African Republic		24,569	1,960	74	-	42,890	1,843	74	-	-	2.0	1.9	1.9
Chad		275,412	68	1,447	-	48,400	3,113	1,447	-	-	1.1	1.3	4.5
Comoros		1	-	-	-	61	516	-	-	-	8.6	8.7	8.4
Congo		66,075	3,486	346	-	24,413	8,174	346	-	-	5.8	6.4	7.2
Côte d'Ivoire		41,627	2,443	2	-	18,303	6,356	2	38,039	-	15.7	14.0	13.1
Dem. Republic of the Congo		204,341	138	39,050	-	430,625	55,962	39,050	-	-	4.6	1.4	0.9
Djibouti		10,456	19	-	-	503	218	-	-	-	5.8	4.0	2.6
Egypt		88,946	11,005	-	96	6,291	2,329	-	-	-	0.3	0.3	0.2
Equatorial Guinea		-	-	-	-	477	59	-	-	-	0.9	1.0	1.2
Eritrea		4,418	1,591	1	-	143,594	4,034	1	-	-	0.4	0.4	0.3
Ethiopia		100,817	209	147	-	65,293	16,235	147	-	-	1.3	1.0	0.7
Gabon		8,545	4,843	-	-	81	57	-	-	-	14.7	16.5	17.7
Gambia		7,330	602	-	-	1,678	662	-	-	-	13.3	14.1	15.3
Ghana		53,537	5,496	1	-	18,432	2,351	1	-	-	5.9	7.6	7.5
Guinea		63,525	3,808	3	-	5,820	3,277	3	-	-	11.6	8.7	4.3
Guinea-Bissau		7,616	166	-	-	1,050	250	-	-	-	2.7	1.4	1.2
Kenya		251,271	16,460	-	-	4,620	11,444	-	-	-	1.3	1.1	1.0
Lesotho		-	-	-	-	6	7	-	-	-	0.3	0.3	0.3
Liberia		10,168	29	70,288	-	231,114	6,000	70,288	237,822	260,744	9.3	5.2	1.5
Libyan Arab Jamahiriya	2	12,166	200	-	-	1,535	769	-	-	-	10.5	10.5	10.6
Madagascar		4,240	5,331	-	-	203	19	-	-	-	0.4	0.4	0.3
Malawi		-	-	-	-	101	3,849	-	-	-	3.2	2.4	2.2
Mali		11,233	1,833	-	-	520	353	-	-	-	0.6	0.4	0.3
Mauritania		632	92	-	-	31,651	2,304	-	-	-	5.1	2.4	2.1
Mauritius		-	-	-	-	27	18	-	-	-	1.0	1.3	1.7
Morocco		219	1,843	-	4	2,920	463	-	-	-	0.4	0.4	0.4
Mozambique		1,954	4,015	-	-	104	371	-	-	-	1.6	2.0	2.1
Namibia		5,307	1,073	53	-	1,226	41	53	-	-	7.5	7.5	7.1
Niger		301	48	-	-	655	591	-	-	-	1.4	1.0	0.9
Nigeria		9,019	420	7,401	-	22,098	14,039	7,401	-	-	0.6	0.6	0.7

	By Country of Asylum				By Country of Origin			Internally displaced persons		International migrants		
	Refugees	Asylum seekers	Returned refugees	Stateless persons	Refugees	Asylum seekers	Returned refugees	Displaced	Returned	Percentage		
Note	2005	2005	2005	2005	2005	2005	2005	2005	2005	1995	2000	2005
Réunion										11.9	14.6	18.1
Rwanda	45,206	4,301	9,854	-	100,244	15,880	9,854	-	-	1.1	1.1	1.3
Saint Helena										14.4	19.4	24.8
São Tomé and Príncipe	-	-	-	-	24	-	-	-	-	5.6	5.2	4.8
Senegal	20,712	2,629	-	-	8,671	1,850	-	-	-	3.5	2.9	2.8
Seychelles	-	-	-	-	40	10	-	-	-	5.5	5.9	6.1
Sierra Leone	59,965	177	210	-	40,447	5,950	210	-	-	1.3	1.0	2.2
Somalia	493	98	11,952	-	394,760	30,467	11,952	400,000	-	0.3	0.3	3.4
Republic of South Africa	29,714	140,095	-	-	268	165	-	-	-	2.6	2.2	2.3
Sudan	147,256	4,425	18,525	-	693,267	13,476	18,525	841,946	-	3.8	2.6	1.8
Swaziland	760	256	-	-	13	5	-	-	-	4.0	4.1	4.4
Togo	9,287	420	3	-	51,107	7,479	3	3,000	6,000	3.8	3.3	3.0
Tunisia	87	26	-	-	3,129	365	-	-	-	0.4	0.4	0.4
Uganda	257,256	1,809	24	-	34,170	4,313	24	-	-	2.9	2.2	1.8
United Republic of Tanzania	548,824	307	-	-	1,544	5,250	-	-	-	3.7	2.6	2.1
Western Sahara	-	-	-	-	90,652	24	-	-	-	1.1	1.1	1.0
Zambia	155,718	146	-	-	151	481	-	-	-	2.8	3.3	2.4
Zimbabwe	13,850	118	-	-	10,793	17,326	-	-	-	5.4	5.2	3.9

Source: UNHCR, 2006; United Nations, 2006.

Notes:

1. According to the Government of Algeria, there are an estimated 165,000 Sahrawi refugees in Tindouf camps.

2. 2004 data for the Libyan Arab Jamahiriya (refugees and asylum-seekers).

TABLE 12: **TRANSPORT SAFETY AND TRANSPORT INFRASTRUCTURE**

	Road safety					Roads		
	Injury rate per 10,000 vehicles	**Fatality rate** per 10,000 vehicles	**Injury rate** per 100,000 population	**Fatality rate** per 100,000 population	**Fatality rate** per 100,000 population	**Total Km**	**Passengers** m-p-km	**Goods hauled** m-t-km
	1996	**1996**	**1996**	**1996**	**2004**	**1999-2003**	**1999-2003**	**1999-2003**
Algeria	237	24	124	13	...	104,000	...	...
Angola	...	...	...	...	...	51,429	166,045	4,709
Benin	100	14	53	7	...	6,787	...	...
Botswana	791	62	355	28	...	25,233	...	...
Burkina Faso	...	...	...	...	...	12,506	...	...
Burundi	...	...	...	...	...	14,480	...	...
Cameroon	329	52	39	6	...	80,932	...	...
Cape Verde	1,640	112	172	12	...	...	...	...
Central African Republic	3,104	339	16	2	...	23,810	...	...
Chad	144	7	6	0	...	33,400	...	...
Comoros	...	8	...	2	...	...	...	...
Congo	170	23	33	5	...	12,800	...	...
Côte d'Ivoire	...	...	...	...	...	50,400	...	...
Dem. Republic of the Congo	...	...	...	...	...	157,000	...	...
Egypt	100	20	37	7	...	64,000	...	...
Eritrea	...	...	...	...	...	4,010	...	...
Ethiopia	853	195	13	3	...	33,856	219,113	2,456
Gabon	235	28	86	10	...	32,333	...	...
Gambia	...	...	...	...	...	3,742	16	...
Ghana	621	73	48	6	...	47,787	...	...
Guinea	1,111	121	58	6	...	44,348	...	...
Guinea-Bissau	...	...	...	...	...	4,400	...	...
Kenya	558	64	80	9	...	63,942	...	22
Lesotho	439	87	82	16	...	5,940	...	...
Liberia	...	...	...	...	...	10,600	...	...
Libyan Arab Jamahiriya	...	...	150	21	...	83,200	...	...
Madagascar	105	3	6	0	...	49,827	...	...
Malawi	700	193	39	11	...	28,400	...	...
Mali	177	16	8	1	...	15,100	...	...
Mauritania	...	...	...	...	...	7,660	...	...
Mauritius	375	15	318	13	...	2,015	...	...
Morocco	...	...	212	10	...	57,694	...	18
Mozambique	...	...	...	...	...	30,400	...	...
Namibia		9	38	8	...	42,237	47	591
Niger	...	...	...	...	...	10,100	...	...
Nigeria	166	65	20	8	...	194,394	...	...
Rwanda	...	...	...	...	...	12,000	...	...
Senegal	710	64	103	9	...	13,576	...	...
Sierra Leone	199	21	16	2	...	11,300	...	...
Somalia	...	...	...	...	...	22,100	...	...
Republic of South Africa	217	17	341	27	25	362,099	...	434
Sudan	...	...	...	...	...	11,900	...	...
Swaziland	251	44	179	31	...	3,594	...	...
Togo	...	...	...	...	...	7,520	...	...
Tunisia	...	...	...	...	...	18,997	...	16,611
Uganda	497	122	33	8	...	70,746	...	...
United Republic of Tanzania	879	111	40	5	...	78,891	...	...
Zambia	235	39	60	10	...	91,440	...	...
Zimbabwe	252	17	161	11	...	97,267	...	...

Sources: World Bank, 2006: Road Federation, 2004.

Notes:
TEU - Container capacity is measured in twenty-foot equivalent units
m-p-k million passenger- km
m-t-k million ton-km
... data not available

Motor vehicles		Railways			Port traffic	Air	
Number per 1000		Route km	Passengers m-p-km	Goods hauled m-t-km	TEU (000)	Passengers (000)	Freight m-t-km
1990	2003	1999-2004	1999-2004	1999-2004	2004	2004	2004
55	...	3,572	950	1,945	311	3,236	21
19	...	2,761	...	...	...	223	64
3	...	438	66	86	...	46	7
18	92	888	171	842	...	214	0
4	...	622	...	...	...	62	0
...	...	...	...	...	...	...	...
10	...	974	308	1,115	...	358	23
...	...	...	...	...	...	...	...
1	...	...	...	...	...	46	7
2	...	...	...	...	...	46	7
...	...	...	...	...	...	...	...
18	...	1,026	76	307	...	52	0
24	...	639	148	129	670	46	7
...	...	4,499	140	491	...	95	7
29	...	5,150	40,837	4,188	1,422	4,584	248
1	...	306	...	...	...	...	...
1	2	...	...	...	...	1,403	117
32	...	650	92	1,949	...	433	62
13	8	...	...	...	...	...	...
8	...	977	85	242	...	96	7
4	...	837	...	...	...	...	...
7	...	...	...	...	...	...	...
12	11	1,917	226	1,399	...	2,005	193
11	...	...	...	...	...	...	...
14	...	490	...	...	...	...	...
165	...	2,757	...	...	...	850	0
6	...	883	10	12	...	514	13
4	...	710	25	88	...	114	1
3	...	733	196	189	...	46	7
10	...	717	...	...	...	128	0
59	119	...	...	...	382	1,089	220
37	45	1,907	2,614	5,535	561	3,004	62
4	...	2,072	137	808	...	299	5
71	82	...	...	...	...	281	56
6	...	...	...	...	...	46	7
30	...	3,505	973	39	513	682	10
2	...	...	...	...	...	...	...
11	14	906	138	371	...	421	0
10	4	...	...	...	...	16	8
2	...	...	...	...	...	...	...
139	144	20,047	10,001	106,549	2,675	9,876	930
9	...	5,478	32	889	...	476	41
66	83	301	...	...	...	90	0
24	...	568	...	...	...	46	7
48	88	1,909	1,242	2,173	...	1,940	20
2	5	259	...	218	...	46	27
5	...	2,600	471	1,351	...	248	2
14	...	1,273	186	554	...	49	0
32	50	...	...	...	...	238	17

TABLE 13: **MAJOR DISASTER INCIDENTS, 1980-2000**

	Cyclones			Droughts			Earthquakes			Floods			Population affected by conflicts
	Number of events	Loss of lives		Number of events	Loss of lives		Number of events	Loss of lives		Number of events	Loss of lives		
	Annual average	Annual average	Per million	Annual average	Annual average	Per million	Annual average	Annual average	Per million	Annual average	Annual average	Per million	Annual average
Algeria	...	...	...	...	...	...	0.38	137.19	5.79	0.71	13.33	0.50	37.0
Angola	...	...	...	...	...	...	...	...	...	0.24	1.38	0.11	79.0
Benin	...	...	...	...	...	...	...	...	...	0.48	4.67	0.91	-
Botswana	...	...	...	...	...	...	...	...	...	0.14	1.48	1.07	-
Burkina Faso	...	...	...	...	...	...	...	...	...	0.24	2.10	0.23	-
Burundi	...	...	...	0.1	0.29	0.05	...	...	...	0.10	0.57	0.10	16.0
Cameroon	...	...	...	...	...	...	...	...	...	0.24	1.76	0.13	-
Cape Verde	0.1	1.52	5.07	...	...	...	...	...	...	...	...	...	-
Central African Republic	...	...	...	...	...	...	...	...	...	0.24	0.33	0.09	3.6
Chad	...	...	...	0.33	142.86	27.87	...	...	...	0.29	4.00	0.63	43.0
Comoros	0.19	2.81	5.97	...	...	...	...	...	...	...	...	...	-
Congo	...	...	...	...	...	...	...	...	...	0.14	0.10	0.03	6.0
Côte d'Ivoire	...	...	...	...	...	...	...	...	...	0.10	1.33	0.10	-
Democratic Republic of the Congo	...	...	...	...	...	...	...	...	...	0.19	3.05	0.07	18.0
Djibouti	...	...	...	...	...	...	...	...	...	0.19	8.57	18.26	23.4
Egypt	...	...	...	...	...	...	0.1	27.19	0.45	0.14	28.95	0.48	-
Eritrea													70.0
Ethiopia	...	...	...	0.57	14,303.19	286.24	...	...	...	1.00	27.14	0.50	24.0
Gambia	...	...	...	...	...	...	...	...	...	0.10	2.52	2.09	-
Ghana	...	...	...	...	...	...	...	...	...	0.19	9.95	0.60	-
Guinea	...	...	...	0.14	0.57	0.1	...	...	...	...	...	...	-
Kenya	...	...	...	0.29	4.05	0.16	...	...	...	0.24	12.86	0.50	-
Lesotho	...	...	...	...	...	...	...	...	...	0.14	1.90	1.19	-
Liberia	...	...	...	...	...	...	...	...	...	0.05	0.48	0.19	28.0
Madagascar	0.71	48.81	3.87	0.24	9.52	0.78	...	...	...	...	...	...	-
Malawi	...	...	...	...	...	...	0.05	0.43	0.05	0.43	23.33	2.36	-
Mali	...	...	...	...	...	...	...	...	...	0.29	1.81	0.18	-
Mauritania	...	...	...	0.33	106.81	57.86	...	...	...	...	...	...	-
Morocco	...	...	...	...	...	...	...	...	...	0.33	39.62	1.40	-
Mozambique	0.33	22.1	1.41	0.43	4,764.29	357.06	...	...	...	0.33	41.33	2.66	46.0
Namibia	...	...	...	...	...	...	...	...	...	0.29	4.57	0.47	40.0
Niger	...	...	...	...	...	...	...	...	...	0.62	12.67	0.12	-
Rwanda	...	...	...	...	...	...	...	...	...	0.05	2.29	0.34	23.0
Senegal													6.0
Sierra Leone	...	...	...	...	...	...	...	...	...	0.05	0.57	0.14	24.0
Somalia	...	...	...	0.24	29.57	4.14	...	...	...	0.52	117.62	15.38	3.0
Republic of South Africa	...	...	...	...	...	...	0.14	1.62	0.05	0.67	54.71	1.38	22.0
Sudan	...	...	...	0.48	7,142.86	294.05	...	...	...	0.57	15.52	0.57	65.0
Swaziland	0.05	2.52	4.04	...	...	...	...	...	...	...	...	...	-
Togo	...	...	...	...	...	...	...	...	...	0.19	0.14	0.04	-
Tunisia	...	...	...	...	...	...	...	...	...	0.14	8.43	1.13	-
Uganda	...	...	...	0.29	5.48	0.29	0.14	0.33	0.02	0.14	7.05	0.36	45.0
United Republic of Tanzania	...	...	...	...	...	...	0.05	0.05	0	0.71	22.00	0.77	-
Zimbabwe	...	...	...	...	...	...	...	...	...	0.10	5.05	0.41	-

Source: United Nations Development Programme, 2005.

Notes:

Number of earthquakes - These include events equal or greater than a magnitude of 5.5 on the Richter scale.

... *data not available*

– *magnitude zero*